There is more
to biking, than only
the woods. Enjoy it
Christmas

Seattle Outdoors

HIKING & CYCLING: PUGET SOUND & CASCADES

BOB DREISBACH

Dedication

My son Carl and I offer a reason for the attraction of summits. At the beginning of the cross country part of most summit hikes, a range of possible routes offers. This range is narrowed (organized) on the ascent, just as living things organize a part of their environment as they grow. Finally, near the summit, the options shrink to a single possibility. The beginning of the return trip again presents many choices. In order to arrive back at the starting point, almost every step requires a decision, just as life makes us select from potential pathways. With the hope that the contents will expand the possibilities, this book is dedicated to all summit baggers, and especially including Phil Dickert, my companion on many summits.

Photo credits: Dorothy Cook: back cover top.
Cover design: Lynne Faulk, Hingepin Publishing.

Library of Congress Catalog Card Number 00-130197

ISBN 0-942153-13-8

Printed in United States of America

Published by:

ENTROPY CONSERVATIONISTS
20123–60th Ave. NE
Kenmore WA 98028-1933

TABLE OF CONTENTS

(**B** = Bicycle or Hike, **T** = Transit accessible.)

North Cascades Region

Introduction and Notes.

This book could have been subtitled: **Confessions of a Summit Bagger**, but it has a more serious purpose. If we wish to save more of the forests for recreation, we need to put an alternative in place of the logging industry. One possibility: spread and expand recreation uses in the forest as widely as possible, using these areas as a resource that does not get depleted. The few accessible hiking areas that are near Seattle are obviously heavily used: count the vehicles at High Point (Exit-20 from I-90) at any time during daylight hours. Any mountain area in Europe comparable to the I-90 corridor will have several times as many trails.

With adequate accomodations, our mountain recreation areas could draw thousands of users from all over the world. Consider the number of users that the Wonderland Trail around Mt. Rainier would have with lodges every five to ten miles. All the Wilderness Area could have similar heavy use. Trails would need to be upgraded to stand the load. Compare trails in Europe that have been in use since Roman times that are not as degraded as many trails in the Cascades. Loss of a wilderness experience from crowding is not the problem that some people think. Visit Tiger Mountain on a weekend in summer when more than 100 vehicles will be parked at the trailheads, but see few or no people on many of the trails. The scenery and the experience is not spoiled by the presence of people. Perhaps it is time to examine the reasons why people go to mountains.

To expand trail opportunities near Seattle, several unused areas could be developed for intense recreational use: the lakes and summits immediately north of Mt. Si, the area south of US-2 and east of Sultan that includes Mt. Index and Mt. Persis, and the Ragged Ridge area northeast of Goldbar. Ragged Ridge is an untouched 50^+-square mile area that contains dozens of lakes and summits, including Lake Isabel (cover). At one time this lake had a road and a resort. Now, only the most adventurous get to Lake Isabel.

Building and maintaining trails and back-country lodges could replace at least some of the logging industry.

The hiking trails in this book are divided into five difficulty classifications: **Walks** through **Hike-4**†.

Walk. Mostly on paved surfaces, little gain, no possibility of getting lost. Any walking shoe is satisfactory.

Hike-1. Well-defined trail, few or no junctions, little possibility of getting lost. Lug-soled shoes helpful for rocky and muddy places. Many people do this level of trip without a trail map or compass.

Hike-2. Trail less defined, confusing junctions, possibility of going the wrong way. GT or USGS map and compass useful. Some of the trails at this level have steeper and more exposed places than **Hike-1**.

Hike-3. Off trail hiking. USGS map and compass necessary, altimeter useful. Lug-soled boots important. Some of these trips are especially rewarding when done on spring snow–April through June–when an ice ax is necessary (see below–Snow). **CMA**: orienteering challenges that require compass, USGS map, and altimeter.

Hike-4†. These routes are distinctly not for everyone. USGS map and compass necessary, altimeter recommended. Technical difficulty and exposure can approach that of the easiest route on the final summit rocks of Mt. Si or McClellan Butte. Sturdy lug-soled boots essential. New snow may upgrade these trips to technical difficulty greater than **Hike-4†**. Carry a line for a safe descent.

Snow. For snow trips, carry an ice ax and know how to use this tool safely. An ice ax is also useful in steep meadows.

Bicycle trips. Bicycle tours in this book were surveyed from 1995-1999. Expect changes, since many of these routes are still under revision. Please walk bicycles on urban trails unless bicycling is permitted.

Maps. All users should have a highway map and the local forest or street map. For trail hiking, maps supplied by the National Forests or Green Trails (GT) are ordinarily sufficient. For hikes beyond **Hike-1**, the USGS 7-1/2' maps (listed) are most often best. Some of the USGS maps do not show trails as well as the Green Trails maps. The USGS maps (public libraries) are not copyright protected and can be copied. For travel on Weyerhaeuser property, use Weyerhaeuser maps.

Free maps and information. Washington State Highways, Bellevue Parks, Kirkland Parks, Kirkland Downtown, King County Public Art, Seattle Convention Center, Olympia Information, Chambers of Commerce, Cougar Mtn. (at trailheads), King County Bicycling Guidemap, Seattle Bicycling Guidemap, Mt. Rainier, Transit. Web sites: www.fs.fed.us/R6/mbs (and links).

Permits and Trail Fees. Most Wilderness Areas and National Parks require permits for back country travel. These are available at Ranger Stations. The National Forests now require fees for parking at trailheads. Inquire at Ranger Stations and the Outdoor Recreation Information Center, in REI, Eastlake Ave. and John St., Seattle.

Seattle–Olympia Region

Central Seattle Area. From the Lake Washington Ship Canal to the south city limit and east of the Duwamish River.

SEATTLE DOWNTOWN, high point 250', 6 miles, minimum gain (Maps: Seattle Tourmap, USGS Seattle South). **Walk**. Ride Metro transit to Convention Place Station.

From Convention Place Station, walk south on 9th Ave. to the Washington State Convention and Trade Center. Enter the Convention Center and find Visitor Information (Seattle Tourmap, other maps and information). Exit south from the building to **Freeway Park**. Wander the park, then exit north on the east side of the Convention Center to Pike St. at Terry Ave. Turn right (southwest) into Hubbell Place. Where Hubbell Place narrows to go under Freeway Park, turn left (south) and ascend steps and a paved path to emerge on Terry Ave. Turn south, then go right (west) on University St. At 9th Ave., descend steps to return into Freeway Park. Go southwest in the park, taking time to explore **The Canyon** near the southwest corner where, in summer, 27,000 gallons of water per minute pour over ledges. Exit to 6th Ave. at Seneca St. Go south on the east side of 6th Ave. to pass **Floyd Naramore Fountain** south of Seneca St. At the last pocket of green in Freeway Park before crossing Spring St., look down to frantic I-5 below.

Cross 6th Ave. and continue south. At Marion St., look east to the twin towers of St. James Cathedral. At Jefferson St., descend west to 5th Ave., then turn south to the intersection of Terrace St. Turn east and ascend steps and a ramp to emerge on Yesler Way. Cross south and ascend on Yesler Way to enter **Kobe Terrace Park** immediately west of the I-5 Freeway. Walk southeast in the park, passing the **Kobe Lantern** and miniature gardens maintained by local residents. Exit to Main St., then descend south on 7th Ave. S across S Jackson St. to the **International Children's Park** (playground)at Lane St. Now return north to King St. Turn west to Maynard Ave. Enter **Hing Hay Park** with Oriental style shelter. Continue west on S King St. to the International District Metro Station, styled Oriental and Futuristic. The **Waterfront Streetcar** station is north across Jackson St. Turn south to Airport Way S. Cross and go west across 4th Ave. S. Walk south along 4th Ave. S. At the first freeway ramp, bend southwest to follow a paved path. Watch for a lone horse chestnut tree that might have predated the freeway. Emerge to S Royal Brougham St.

Turn west to Alaskan Way to find a paved path (flowers) that goes north on the east side of Alaskan Way. At S Main St., go right (east). Pass the **Klondike Gold Rush National Historic Park** east of First Ave. S, then enter **Waterfall Garden Park** at the corner of 2nd Ave. S (tables). Return west into **Occidental Park** to find Totem Poles and wood statues. The park is partially paved with **Wilkeson sandstone.** Exit north from the park, return west to First Ave., then go north to **Pioneer Square** at Yesler Way to find another totem pole and more Wilkeson sandstone paving. Metsker Maps is one block north.

Now proceed west on Yesler Ave. to the waterfront. Find the passenger ferries to Bremerton and Vashon Island immediately west at the south end of the Washington Ferry docks. Tour the ferry complex, then go north to **Waterfront Park** (fishing access). After visiting the raised viewpoints and water sculptures, return south to University Street. Turn east and ascend steps to First Ave. **Hammering Man** is across the way at the Seattle Art Museum. Turn left (north) for one block, then descend west at Union St., passing Hostelling International. At the waterfront, go north on the east side of Alaskan Way to the Pike Place Hill Climb. Ascend steps east into Pike Place Market. Emerge from the market at Pine St., then go east to **Westlake Center Park** at 4th Ave. to admire the water curtain and flower displays. An entrance to the Metro bus tunnel is nearby or find many surface buses.

WEST POINT BEACH, high point 100', 6 miles, minimum gain (Maps: USGS Seattle North, Shilshole Bay). **Hike-2**. This beach walk from Elliott Bay to the Ballard Locks is recommended only at the lowest tides, zero or below (see US West Seattle Yellow Pages for tide tables). Take a Metro bus to the last stop on Elliott Ave. W before Elliott Ave. W turns into 15th Ave. W (Burger King). If driving, park east of the railroad tracks on W Galer St.

From the bus stop, walk west on Elliott Ave., then enter the ramp to the Magnolia Bridge at 14th Ave. W. Continue north on the ramp at W Galer St. to view the landslide that closed the ramp in 1999. Return to Galer St. Walk west on W Galer St. across the railroad tracks. Turn northwest on a pedestrian-bikeway that begins at the Pier 91 entrance. Follow the railroad tracks past the Port of Seattle storage yards. At the north boundary of the storage yards, turn left (west) and follow the fence around the west side of the storage yards to pass south on 23rd Ave. W under the Magnolia Bridge to **Smith Cove Park** (toilet) at the intersection of 23rd Ave. W and Marina Park Drive. Turn right (west) to the end of Marina Park Drive where a path descends to the beach. Note the sand cliffs above that have been stabilized by the application of pink concrete.

Continue west on the tide flats, passing below the unstable sand cliffs of the Magnolia District. Along the way are remnants of decaying past constructions that have succumbed to landslides and tides. At one point, find a number of rusty automobile engines that had been used in a construction. Pass stone walls that were built in an attempt to slow recession of the cliff to protect the houses above. After passing the last houses at the south edge of **Discovery Park**, the tide flats consist of a soft clay stratum that extends east under the park. This clay was deposited in a meltwater lake as the Puget Glacier receded. Notice that the shoreline trees are leaning at many angles, indicating that the surface above this clay layer is constantly moving, making it unsuitable for construction. This active **landslide zone** is south of the sandy cliffs of Discovery Park.

Pass the West Point Lighthouse and continue on or near the beach along the north edge of the Metro Treatment Plant to the **glacial erratics** sitting on the tide flats below the steep slopes north of the Metro Treatment Plant. These rocks were brought here from Canada during the last glacial age. At the lowest tides, continue northeast on the tide flats.

To leave the route at the northeast end of the Metro Treatment Plant, ascend on the North Beach Trail, which begins at the northeast corner of the Metro Treatment Plant. On reaching the first paved road, go east to the North Parking Area and a Metro 33 bus stop. Those who continue northeast on the tide flats will cross more of the clay stratum (see above) to end at **Commodore Park** on the south side of the Ballard Locks. To reach a vehicle parked on Elliott Ave., ascend south on W Harley St., which is south across Commodore Way from the entrance to Ballard Locks, to cross a bridge over the Burlington Northern railroad tracks and reach Government Way and Metro 24 or 33 bus stops. For other Metro buses, cross the locks to the north side.

DISCOVERY PARK LOOP, high point 325', 21 miles, 500' gain (Maps: USGS Seattle South, Seattle North, Shilshole Bay). **Bicycle**. This trip begins at the International District Station of Metro. If driving, find on-street parking south of Jackson St. On Sunday, park free under the Alaska Way Viaduct. Find parking also at the Ballard Locks. Join the route on W Commodore Way,

Take any Metro tunnel bus to the starting point at the Metro International District Station. Ride west on S Jackson St. to the Puget Sound waterfront. Visit the viewpoint that looks south toward the container loading docks from the south side of Pier 48. Now walk north on the west side of Alaskan Way. Next is **Alaska Square**, a public boat landing and fishing access. Pass the Winslow and Bremerton Ferry docks, the Harbor Patrol Station, the Fireboat Station, **Waterfront Park**, and the Aquarium with viewing platforms. From the north end of Alaskan Way, proceed into **Myrtle Edwards Park** and **Elliott Bay Park** on the shore. Pass the controversial three-dimensional forms **Adjacent, Against, Upon** before reaching the concrete silos of the grain-loading terminal at mile 3.5 where ships from exotic places are loaded.

At the west end of the waterfront park (fishing pier, restrooms), exit north toward Elliott Ave. W to a junction with W Galer St. Turn north on a bikeway on the west side of the railroad tracks, passing Pier 91 of the Port of Seattle. At the north boundary of the Pier 91 storage area, turn left (west) and follow the bikeway around Pier 91 and go south, passing **Smith Cove Park** (mile 6, picnicking, water in season, toilet) at the south end of 23rd Ave. W. Turn right (west) on Marina Park Drive to the end of the road (beach access). Return on Marina Park Drive and 23rd Ave. W to the Magnolia Bridge. Turn right (east) on a ramp and ascend to the bridge. Go left (west) into Magnolia Blvd. W, passing **Magnolia Park** (restrooms in summer). Continue northwest to a viewpoint at mile 9. West of the viewpoint, descend steps to Perkins Lane W. Ride and walk northwest on Perkins Lane W, taking time to observe the terrain features. The **cliffs** above and below are sand deposits left from past glaciers. These cliffs occasionally collapse. Continue northwest on Perkins Lane W past W Bertona St., a public shoreline access. Reach W Emerson St. at the south boundary of **Discovery Park**.

Turn east to the Discovery Park entrance gate opposite 43rd Ave. W. Go north in Discovery Park, riding only on the paved paths and roads. One-half mile into the park, a road goes west to West Point and another road goes north to the **Daybreak Star Indian Cultural Center**. After exploring Discovery Park, exit east on W Government Way at 36th Ave. W, mile 12. Continue northeast on Government Way to 32nd Ave. W. Turn left (north) on 32nd Ave. W into a pathway to cross the Burlington Northern railroad tracks and reach W Commodore Way at W Harley St. and the south entrance to the Ballard Locks, mile 13.

From Ballard Locks Parking. Walk bicycle across locks to join the route on W Commodore Way.

Go east on W Commodore Way, passing a Public Waterfront Access 0.2 mile east of Ballard Locks. Where W Commodore Way turns south, continue east into Fisherman's Terminal and follow the edge of the docks south and east. Turn south on 16th Ave. W to an underpass at the southeast boundary of Fisherman's Terminal. Go east under the bridge ramp on the north side of the street, turning right to the on-ramp. Go left (east) on the Ballard Bridge on-ramp sidewalk. Where the sidewalk bends north, find a stairway. Descend west to a paved path and continue east under the Ballard Bridge ramp. Ascend stairs to the sidewalk along W Nickerson St. Cross W Nickerson and continue east on the sidewalk.

At 13th Ave. W, descend north 100' to the level of the railroad track. Turn east on the south side of the railroad track, passing an active waterfront, including a Foss tugboat dock. At 6th Ave. W, jog left (north) to W Ewing St. and continue east. Find waterfront access at 3rd Ave. W. Continue east on a gravel track, now on the north side of the railroad tracks, passing under the Fremont Bridge.

East of the Fremont Bridge, ride east and south in parking lots near busy Westlake Ave. N, passing many water related activities. Take time to visit the 1505 Westlake North Center with its greenery-filled atrium. Where Westlake Ave. N bends southeast (mile 18), cross Westlake Ave. N into Eighth Ave. N and continue south, bending southwest on Roy St. to Dexter Ave. N. Go south on Dexter Ave. N, crossing over Broad St. At Denny St., bend left (southeast) into 7th Ave., then turn right (southwest) on Bell St. at the first intersection. Go three blocks and turn left (southeast) on 4th Ave. (sidewalk). Look for public art in the forecourt of the Sedgwick James Building at the west corner of Lenora St. Return northeast to 5th Ave. Turn southeast on 5th Ave., walking on the sidewalk as necessary to avoid stalled or heavy traffic. Pass the **Seattle Public Library** between Spring St. and Madison St. After 5th Ave. bends south at Yesler St., reach the Metro International District Station south of Jackson St., mile 21. To reach parking under the Alaskan Way viaduct, ride west on Jackson St.

ARBORETUM–CAPITOL HILL, high point 500', 8 miles, 500' gain (Maps: USGS Seattle South, Seattle North). **Hike-1**. The trip begins at the Montlake Bridge over the ship canal, reached by Metro 25, 43, 44, or 48 or take any of the Metro buses that stop on SR-520 at Montlake Blvd. E and walk north on Montlake Blvd. to E Shelby St., one block south of the Montlake Bridge.

If driving, leave SR-520 at the Montlake Exit and drive east and south on Lake Washington Blvd. E, which begins at Montlake Blvd. Park at **Washington Park Arboretum**. Join the route at the **Graham Visitor Center**. On Sunday, park free in the University of Washington Stadium Parking Lot (south of the stadium) and walk to the Montlake Bridge.

From the southwest corner of the Montlake Bridge, walk south to E Shelby St., then go west to the waterfront. Find a path that follows the south shore of the ship canal east to pass under the Montlake Bridge. Continue east, ascending stairs as necessary to reach a viewpoint where the ship canal expands into Union Bay. Go right (southeast) into a path that continues east into the **Foster Island Nature Trail**. The following stops have been established on this trail:

(1) Entrance sign. The leaning tree to the right behind the sign is Pacific willow and the tall trees directly behind the sign are black

cottonwood. Look for clematis on the trees southeast of the path. (2) The trail crosses a bridge. The edges of the water are covered by water lilies. In the summer, look down into the water to see milfoil reaching from the bottom almost to the surface. This exotic plant has invaded many of the shallow parts of Lake Washington. (3) Step onto Marsh Island. What appears to be land is a mat of vegetation that will eventually become peat. Look closely at the water edge to see the fibers and roots. (4) Water lilies cover the water at the edge of the land. The showy blooms form in early summer. (5) The edge of the land is a dense growth of cattails and European iris. South of the path is a forest of willow trees.

(6) The woody plants are willow. (7) Walk south on a branch to a dock viewpoint. Look for details of the structure of the island at the water edge. (8) A common herbaceous plant is **purple loosestrife**, another invader that suppresses the native plants. Come in the fall to see the seed head containing hundreds of seeds. (9) A large colony of cattails. (10) North and south of the trail, European white birch stands above the lower vegetation. Dead snags of this species are common since the tree is less tolerant of water than willow.

(11) Note a clump of white birch to the north, standing on higher land. (12) A colony of reed canary grass, a common marsh plant, is south of the path. (13) Willow surrounds a clump of black cottonwood trees. Find a single hawthorn and a single ninebark in the group of shrubs on the west side of the path. (15) Blackberry, another exotic, invades this area.

(16) Turn left (north) to a viewpoint over Union Bay. The stranded logs are left from the time when this shoreline was used as a booming ground to make up rafts of logs to take through the ship canal. (17) A colony of spirea (hardhack) is north of the path. (18) Take the branch to the right to reach a float with bench. (19) Return to the main path and go east to another bridge. Look north to see the edge of the tangle of logs and old iron that make up part of the island. (20) In the fall, if the wind is blowing from the north, rafts of milfoil pile up against the bridge.

(21) Another colony of reed canary grass. (22) The path enters a floating walkway to waterbird and lake viewpoints. Note the remains of older trail segments now below the water surface. Since these islands consist of vegetation that is on the way to becoming **peat**, the surface sinks if excessive pressure is applied. Even walking on the path will eventually press the surface below the water level. Running and bicycling speed the sinking process. (23) Another viewpoint. The pilings remain from former use of the area to make up log booms. (24) The edge of the marsh is important in providing food for fish and birds. (25)

Salmonberry grows profusely in a slightly drier location.

(26) Purple loosestrife replaces a cattail marsh. Look for 6" runways through the vegetation. Muskrats and rats make homes here. (27) Turn left (north) on a branch path to a raised viewpoint that looks down on a former location of the path, now below water level. Late in the fall and winter, look for **islands** that appear in Union Bay. These islands consist of vegetation that had accumulated on the shallow bottom, floated to the surface by methane released during decomposition.

The trail continues east to Foster Island, where the character of the vegetation changes completely. Large trees–alder, maple, and even madrone–grow here. Bend south to go under SR-520 and continue near the water to reach the beginning of the **Washington Park Arboretum**.

Pick up a map of the arboretum at the **Graham Visitor Center**. Explore paths along Azalea Way to the south end of the arboretum near the New Zealand exhibit. Return north near Lake Washington Blvd. E, crossing to the west side to tour the Japanese Garden. From the Japanese Garden, go north on the west side of Lake Washington Blvd. E to E Interlaken Blvd. Ascend along the northeast side of E Interlaken Blvd. or continue on the path east of E Interlaken Blvd. to 26th Ave. E and follow the street southwest to the bridge. Ascend a ramp to E Interlaken Blvd. and continue northwest on E Interlaken Blvd. across 24th Ave. E. At a junction with 23th Ave. E, stay on E Interlaken Blvd., blocked to motor vehicles. Where the paved road bends sharply across a deep ravine, turn southwest on a trail and ascend on the west side of a ravine to emerge at the intersection of E Galer St. and 19th Ave. E. Go south on 19th Ave. E for one block to E Highland St. Turn west across 15th Ave. E into **Volunteer Park**.

Bend south in Volunteer Park to the **Water Tower** at the south boundary. Ascend in the water tower for the 360° panoramic view from the platform at the top. Look for the following summits: Whitehorse (36°), Three-Fingers (38°), Glacier Peak (60°), Stickney (62°), Index (74°), Phelps (83°), Lennox (86°), Bessemer (98°), and Si (106°). From the Water Tower, go north to pass the **Seattle Asian Art Museum** (free first Tuesday of the month) and the **Volunteer Park Conservatory** (free). From the conservatory, descend west along the street for two blocks. Turn right and follow a path west of the tennis courts to exit into E Galer St. Continue west to 10th Ave. E. Bend north two blocks to E Blaine St. Turn west and descend steps, crossing Broadway Ave. E and reaching Lakeview Blvd. E at the foot of the steps. Cross Lakeview Blvd. E and find a steep trail and road descending under I-5, rejoining E Blaine St. at Franklin Ave. E. Go west, crossing Eastlake Ave. E (Metro stop) to reach Fairview Ave. E near the shore of Lake Union.

Turn north and walk various alleys, walkways, and short sections of Fairview Ave. E to the University Bridge. Cross to the north side of the ship canal, descend west and south to the Burke–Gilman Trail and walk east to the University of Washington campus. Find a Metro bus stop one block north on Campus Parkway at Brooklyn Ave. NE, or descend south under the University Bridge to NE Boat St. and go east along the shore of Portage Bay and the ship canal to the Montlake Bridge for parking by the stadium or cross the bridge and follow the route from the beginning to reach parking in the Arboretum.

INTERLAKES, high point 200', 11 miles, 200' gain (Maps: USGS Seattle North). **Walk**. The trip begins at the Montlake Bridge over the ship canal, reached by Metro 25, 43, 44, 48 or take a Metro bus on SR-520 to Montlake Blvd. E. Walk north on Montlake Blvd. to E Hamlin St., one block south of the Montlake Bridge. If driving, on Sunday, park free at the parking lot south of the University of Washington stadium. On other days, park at the Graham Visitor Center in the **Washington Park Arboretum**.

From the Montlake Bridge, go south on the east side of Montlake Blvd. (Lake Washington Loop). Turn left (east) on E Hamlin St., then go right (south) on 24th Ave. E across E Lake Washington Blvd. to a 'T' junction in an alley. Turn left (east) to the first corner, then go right to E Roanoke St. and left to 25th Ave. E. Turn right (south) on 25th Ave. E to E Lynn St. Turn left (east) on E Lynn St. and proceed into a path in the **Washington Park Arboretum** that crosses Lake Washington Blvd. E on a narrow bridge. Continue east to the Graham Visitor Center at the north end of Arboretum Drive E. Go south on Arboretum Drive E or on a path, taking time to appreciate the blossoms when in season.

On reaching Lake Washington Blvd. E at the junction with Arboretum Drive E (mile 2), cross the street into the parking area on the west side of the street and turn north parallel to Lake Washington Blvd. E to pass the Japanese Garden. At the next street, E Interlaken Blvd., turn left (west) and ascend to the crossing of 24th Ave. E. Continue northwest on E Interlaken Blvd. Explorable paths turn south at several places along the boulevard. Look for clematis growing on the trees. Exit from E Interlaken Blvd. (mile 4) to Delmar Drive E and continue northwest. At the junction with Roanoke St., stop at a viewpoint over SR-520 and look east to the Cascade Mountains. Go west on Roanoke St. to **Roanoke Park** at 10th Ave. E (water, picnicking, playground with equipment, no restrooms).

Return east on Roanoke St. into Delmar Drive E and descend southeast to Boyer Ave. E, mile five. Turn north on 16th Ave. E to **Montlake Park** at E Calhoun St. (restrooms and 0.1 mile trail). A path at the south boundary goes north under SR-520 to the Montlake Bridge. After visiting the wetlands, return south on 16th Ave. E to E McGraw St., turning west to Boyer Ave. E. The street bends north as 12th Ave. E, then northwest into Fuhrman Ave. E. At E Martin St., descend steps north to Portage Bay Place at the **floating home** moorage. Walk to the east end of the street for a view of floating and shoreside homes. Return west on Portage Bay Place under the University Bridge to the intersection of Fuhrman Ave. E and Eastlake Ave. E. Cross the University Bridge, then descend south to NE Northlake Way, mile seven.

Turn west on NE Northlake Way near the shore of Lake Union. A paved path begins west of Latona Ave. NE. On approaching the towering metal structures at **Gas Works Park**, reach a junction with the Burke–Gilman Trail near Meridian Ave. N. Cross south over N Northlake Way to find a trail that follows the shoreline southwest into Gas Works Park. Tour Gas Works Park (restrooms), including a viewpoint on the shore of Lake Union. Also visit the high point of the park with its display of public art. Return to N Northlake Way at Meridian Ave. N and go east, taking the left fork to stay on the Burke–Gilman Trail along N Pacific St.

At Brooklyn Ave. N, go north one block to find Metro buses on NE Campus Parkway or continue west on the Burke–Gilman Trail past the buildings of the University of Washington Medical Center. Where the Burke–Gilman Trail turns north, cross east over Montlake Blvd. N to parking by the University Stadium.

LAKE UNION–PUGET SOUND, high point 450', 7 or 9 miles, 500' gain (Maps: USGS Seattle South, Seattle North). **Hike-1**. Begin at the south end of the University Bridge (Metro 70). Walk west on Fuhrman Ave. and south on Fairview Ave. E near the shore of Lake Union, passing floating homes and many boating related activities. Street end parks at the west end of E Hamlin St. and E Newton St. have picnic tables and access to Lake Union. Find a public boat landing near the refurbished City Light Power Plant. Follow the shoreline around the south end of Lake Union (restrooms off Chandlers Cove).

Visit the **Center for Wooden Boats**, with displays of various wooden craft. Continue west and north to Galer St., passing **South Lake Union Park** at Waterways 3 and 4 (benches and gardens). Turn left (west) and ascend the Galer ramp and steps on the south side of the West Lake Union Center (impressive atrium) to cross Dexter Ave. N. Continue up steps to Aurora Ave. N. Turn north along Aurora Ave. N to Lynn St. Cross under Aurora Ave. N and return south to the Galer steps.

Ascend west toward the summit of Queen Anne Hill. At 5th Ave. N, turn south through a parking area to pass a barrier and descend. Find **'Bhy' Kracke Park** on the north side of the street. Facilities: pergola, playground, rhododendrons in spring and massed cotoneaster in fall. Find a zig-zag path and ascend west, exiting to Comstock Place at Bigelow Ave. N. Cross and ascend steps to Lee St. Continue west, crossing 3rd Ave. N into a driveway. Turn left (south), then go west around the south end of a building to 2nd Ave. N. Now go west on Lee St., passing a Fire Station. Turn left (south) on 1st Ave. N to the end of the street and descend steps west to Queen Anne Ave. at W Comstock St. Turn south on Queen Anne Ave. to W Highland Drive. Turn right (west) to pass **Kerry Park** with public art and view. Continue west to **Parsons Garden Park** at W Highland Drive and 7th Ave. W. Facilities: shelter, pergola, flagstone and paved paths. The park can be reserved for events. Turn north on 8th Place W to the end of the guard wall for views.

Return south to W Highland Drive and descend west to the next street. Turn south and descend to the beginning of **Kinnear Park** at the corner of Olympic Way W. Enter Kinnear Park and descend to the west edge of the park. Turn east and follow the south boundary of the park to a narrow path with guard rail descending the slope. At tennis courts, go west on a path to Elliott Ave. W at W Roy St. (mile 7). Find a Metro stop, or turn northwest around Pier 86 to reach **Elliott Bay Park**. Go southeast along the shoreline to reach downtown Seattle and Metro stops (mile 9).

DISCOVERY PARK, high point 325', 8 miles, 450' gain (Maps: USGS Seattle North, Shilshole Bay). **Hike-1**. Take Metro 17, 44, or 46 to the north entrance into Chittenden Locks at 30th Ave. NW and NW 54th St. in Ballard or take Metro 33 to the North Parking Area in **Discovery Park**. If driving, drive west from Ballard on NW Market St. into NW 54th St. and park at the locks. To drive to Discovery Park, from the south end of the Ballard Bridge on 15th Ave. NW go west on W Emerson Place, W Gilman St., and W Government Way. After entering the park, follow signs to the North Parking Area and follow the route as described below, beginning at the Wolf Tree Nature Trail. Guide at park office.

From the Metro stop at the north entrance to the Chittenden Locks, cross the locks south and pass the fish ladder. Turn west and follow the shoreline until the shoreline path ends. Ascend to W Commodore Way and continue west to 40th Ave. W. Turn left (south) and ascend. Turn right (west) along the north edge of the North Parking Area to find the **Wolf Tree Nature Trail** descending north near the west boundary of the parking area. As the Nature Trail begins, note three young Douglas fir trees on the east side of the trail and a bigleaf maple tree with multiple trunks on the west side. Read the informative sign at a 'Y', then go right (east) to the first stop.

(1) These deciduous trees are red alders, used in furniture and valuable in the forest ecosystem as nitrogen fixers, like peas and beans. Near an alder tree with a double trunk 25' east of sign (1), find a young western hemlock, a shade tolerant conifer, and a Douglas fir, not ordinarily shade tolerant. Compare the sparse foliage on this tree with the three Douglas fir trees near the entrance that get more sunlight. (2) Observe the dense understory of salmonberry and sword fern, both shade tolerant. (3) The tall stump on the north side of the trail is a broken bigleaf maple that is sprouting many branches. Brittleness is a characteristic of these trees and they are not safe trees to climb.The loss of this tree has opened the forest canopy and benefitted the plants of the understory. The decaying trunk will provide nutrients to many plants in the area. (4) Scheuerman Creek. Look for animal trails and tracks near the stream. This stream is surface runoff and is large after a winter storm. (5) Fifteen feet north of the sign find a 3' diameter red cedar. Note the scars on the trunk that resulted from a falling bigleaf maple. Sword fern is common near the sign. North of the red cedar tree, note a decayed stump of a Douglas fir that was logged more than one hundred years ago.

(6) A huckleberry plant is growing on the top of a Douglas fir stump. The stump provides a germinating place above the dense vegetation at ground level. Lower down the slope to the northwest, note a bigleaf maple with a crown of multiple branches, having lost its top many years ago. The bigleaf maple at (3) may look like this in several decades. (7) Many specimens of Oregon grape surround an old bigleaf maple. The swellings on the trunk of this tree are burls, a random growth of woody material that is sometimes used for art objects. Look north to a western hemlock. Elderberry is common on both sides of the trail. (8) Red cedar trees grow in a field of sword fern and elderberry. (9) A 4' diameter Douglas fir stands next to the trail. Look for the cones on the ground. These have the characteristic three-pronged feathery bract between the scales. The thick bark of this tree protects it from fire damage and insect attack. North of the Douglas fir, find a clump of young red cedar trees. (10) Cross a small stream with a maidenhair fern growing on the bank. Look for animal tracks near the stream.

(11) Note holes in the exposed wood of a red cedar tree. These were made by insects. (12) The Wolf Tree, named because it claims a large territory, is south of the trail. This red alder started to grow after the area was logged in the 1870's. After the trunk was broken sometime in the past, it grew the large side branch that the tree supports without breaking. Go 35' west on the trail from sign (12) to a decaying Douglas

fir next to a still living Douglas fir. Examine the many holes in this decaying tree, made by birds and insects. These holes allow fungi and bacteria to invade the dead wood and speed the decay process, returning the nutrients slowly for reuse by the remaining vegetation. (13) A fallen tree reveals a shallow root system in an area where groundwater is almost at the surface during much of the year. (14) Wooden walkways cross a wetland. Note many skunk cabbage plants but fewer salmonberry. The odor of the skunk cabbage attracts insects which are trapped by the plant and become part of its nutrient supply. The skunk cabbages blossom in May and June. (15) A wooden walkway crosses Scheuerman Creek. Compare the appearance of the creek here with that found at (4) where the slope of the ground is steeper. Climb steps to a higher level where the trees are mostly bigleaf maple. A trail branch goes west to the **Daybreak Star Indian Cultural Center**.

(16) Find a clump of western yew west of the path. A chemical in the bark is being studied for use in the treatment of cancer. This plant is in the same family as english yew, used for making archery bows. (17) Nettles are common in this dense red alder stand. The trees have lost the lower branches as a result of crowding. (18) The dense canopy provided by red alders and bigleaf maples keeps ground plants to a minimum, allowing visual corridors through the forest. (19) Find a vine maple on the east side of the path, and on the west side, a mountain ash.

From the entrance to the **Wolf Tree Nature Trail** go west 200'. Turn right (north) on a path to ponds and the **Daybreak Star Indian Cultural Center** where artifacts are on display both in and outside the building. Find an **ethnobotanical garden** on the west side. A description of the species of plants in the garden is available. Descend north from the Cultural Center building to the **North Vista** for a view of Mt. Baker and other Cascade Mountains. Turn southwest and ascend on a paved road that is gradually being removed by **landslides**. After passing the landslide area, cross a meadow to the beginning of the North Beach Trail, which descends to the beach north of the Metro Treatment Plant. After reaching the beach, look north 500 feet to boulders sitting in the water near the shoreline. These **erratic boulders** were brought here by glaciers during the last ice age. They can be approached during the lowest tides.

Turn southwest and walk a path along the shoreline at the edge of the Metro Treatment Plant to the West Point Coast Guard Light Station. During fog, do not go west of the light station. The fog horn will damage hearing. Continue southeast along the shoreline or on the path nearby. At the lowest tides, the shoreline is accessible south to Marina Park Drive, but during most of the year, visitors must ascend along the paved road to the first trail crossing. Turn right (south) and ascend to the top of the bluff and continue along the bluff to the south entrance (restrooms). The bluffs, which consist of poorly consolidated sand, are receding rapidly, possibly as the result of deforestation, which has allowed excessive water intrusion. The seepage of this water at the base above a stratum of clay undermines the cliffs.

From the south entrance (Metro 19 stop), walk north to the first building, a church, one of the remnants of the military presence when this area was part of Fort Lawton. Continue northeast on roads and paths to the Park Headquarters (information and exhibits). Cross W Government Way to a military cemetery. Find a Metro 33 bus stop at W Government Way and 36th Ave. W. To return to the North Parking Area, go north on paths past the cemetery. If returning to the locks from the Park Headquarters, go northeast on W Government Way until W Government Way turns east at 32nd Ave. W. Go left (north) on W Gay St. over railroad tracks on a walkway to W Commodore Way and the Chittenden Locks.

LAKE WASHINGTON SOUTH, high point 175', 41 miles, 800' gain (Maps: USGS Seattle South, Mercer Island, Renton). **Bicycle**. This trip circles counterclockwise around the south end of Lake Washington and can be started at any place on the route. The suggested starting point has parking (weekends only) and access by Metro (226, 240, 340).

Begin at the South Bellevue Park & Ride. From the Metro Stop at the Park & Ride, go south to the signal. Stay on the east side of Bellevue Way S for two blocks. Turn left (east) into an access road and immediately go left into a path on the east side of the street that continues south. Cross a parking area, mile 0.3, and enter a paved path. Pass a junction on the left with a paved connector to the eastbound I-90 bikeway. Now turn southwest on the paved bikeway, emerging to street and going west to **Enatai Park** at mile 1.0 (restrooms. swimming beach, viewpoint). From Enatai Park, go north under I-90, then turn right (east) on SE 34th St. to enter the I-90 bikeway at mile 1.2. Ride west on the I-90 bikeway. Cross a street at mile 1.8, N Mercer Way at mile 2.1 and Shorewood Drive at mile 2.5. Where the bikeway crosses Island Crest Way, mile 3.1, **Luther Burbank Park** is 0.5 mile east on SE 26th St. After crossing Island Crest Way, the bikeway follows N Mercer Way past the Mercer Island Park & Ride. Cross N Mercer Way at 76th Ave. SE, mile 3.7, and ascend to the top of the I-90 tunnel (restrooms, water, view). The bikeway now descends past playgrounds, playfields, and a viewing area with seats. At the west end of the I-90 bridge, ascend on a ramp and S Irving St. to reach Lake Washington Blvd. S (mile 6.5). Turn south to a viewpoint east. Follow Lake Washington Blvd. S, then descend in curves through **Coleman Park** to reach the shoreline at **Mt. Baker Park** (restrooms, guarded swimming area).

Continue south on the bikeway to **Gennessee Park** (playfields) and **Stanley Sayers Park**, with its many piers for hydroplanes. Pass Lakewood Moorage at mile 9.7 (no public access) near a wetland. Leave Lake Washington Blvd. S at mile 10.8 to take the loop clockwise around **Seward Park**, finding restrooms at mile 12.1 and 13.2 and passing fish rearing ponds (now closed) at the east end of the peninsula. Ride bicycles only on the road at the lake shore. The three miles of trail in the interior are reserved for pedestrians.

Return west to Seward Park Ave. S and turn south. Take Lakeshore Drive S, go west on S Eddy St., and south on 57th Ave. S to **Martha Washington Park** (beach access). Ascend west on S Holly St. to reach Seward Park Ave. S. Continue south on Seward Park Ave. S to pass **Beersheva Park** (swimming beach, restrooms, picnicking, playground) and **Atlantic City Boat Ramp** at mile 16.3. Cross Rainier Ave. S (SR-167) at mile 16.8 and continue south on 56th Ave. S. Turn west on Roxbury St. and south on 54th Ave. S. Cross Renton Ave. S to **Kubota Gardens** at 55th Ave. S, mile 17.4. Park bicycle and wander a mile of trails in the garden. From Kubota Garden (mile 17.7) ride southeast on Renton Ave. S. After passing 68th Ave. S, enter a district of stores. Opposite 72nd Ave. S, mile 19.2, turn right (south) into **Skyway Park** (playgrounds, playfields, restrooms, water). Tour the paved paths of Skyway Park before returning to Renton Ave. S, mile 20.2.

Cross Renton Ave. S into 72nd Ave. S. Go north one block, then turn east on S 116th Place before continuing north on 72nd Place S. Jog east on S 116th St., north on 74th Ave., west on S 115th St., and north on Crestwood Drive S. Turn left on Lakeridge Drive S, and again left into Rustic Road at S 108th St. Descend on Rustic Road and Cornell Ave. S to reach Rainier Ave. S at **Lakeridge Park**, mile 21.6 (restrooms and playgrounds). Now go southeast on Rainier Ave. S, which has a wide parking lane that can be used as a bikeway. At mile 23.7, turn left (east) into the frontage road around Renton Municipal Airport and continue south and east, meeting the Cedar River at mile 25.1. Go north to a bridge (mile 25.5) over the Cedar River, cross the bridge, then continue north on a path to a view of Lake Washington, passing restrooms, picnic areas, and playgrounds.

The Cedar River lies between Renton Airport (west) and Boeing Company (east). Return south along the Cedar River, passing under streets to the **Renton Senior Center** at mile 27.5 and the **Renton Public Library** at mile 28. This library is built over the Cedar River and the bridge often provides a view of fish in the river. Continue south to tour around the Renton Community Center and Carco Theater. A paved bikeway on the south side of the Cedar River follows the river east to Maple Valley.

Return north past the **Renton Public Library**. After passing Renton Stadium, turn east through the Boeing Plant on N 6th St. to Park Ave. N. Go north on Park Ave. N into Lake Washington Blvd. N, entering **Gene Coulon Beach Park** (swimming beach, picnicking, restrooms, shelter, food, beach access). Exit north from the park.

Continue north on Lake Washington Blvd. N within sight of Lake Washington. At mile 34.1, turn right into a paved bikeway along the west side of I-405. Emerge on Hazelwood Lane (becomes SE 106th Ave. NE). Cross the railroad tracks into **Newcastle Beach Park** (enclosed swimming area, tables, playfields, restrooms). Return east across the railroad tracks to the bikeway continuing north on the west side of I-405 (mile 37). The bikeway ends at Coal Creek Parkway (mile 37.5) just west of I-405. Find Metro 240, 340 stops near I-405 at Coal Creek Parkway. Turn left on Coal Creek Parkway, which becomes 118th Ave. SE, and continue west and north. At first the street has no shoulder, then a narrow to wide gravel shoulder on the west side of the street. Pass the entrance to the **SE 40th St. Boat Launch and Marina** at mile 38. Join an east-west bikeway before reaching an underpass under I-90. Factoria Shopping Mall is 0.6 mile to the right (east) on this I-90 bikeway.

After passing under I-90, turn left (west) into the Mercer Slough Bikeway, crossing a bridge to Bellevue Way SE. Turn north on a bikeway, passing parking and blueberry fields, to the South Bellevue Park & Ride, mile 39.4.

For an alternate return to the South Bellevue Park & Ride from the I-90 underpass at 118th Ave. SE, continue north on the East Mercer Slough Bikeway along 118th Ave. SE for one mile, until the Bikeway ends at a junction with 118th Ave. SE. Turn left (west) into **Bellefields Trails** (walk bicycle), to a junction in a remnant of ancient forest at former Lake Washington shoreline. The Bellefields trail system has interpretive signs. Turn left at the junction and walk bicycle along the path in the wetland, turning left at the next junction. The path to the right goes to the **Bellefields Educational Center** on 118th Ave. SE. Cross the bridge over Mercer Slough to another junction. The right branch goes past Overlake Farm to the **Winters House**, north of the South Bellevue Park & Ride. The left branch returns to Bellevue Way SE and the South Bellevue Park & Ride.

LAKE WASHINGTON NORTH, high point 400', 44 miles, 800' gain (Maps: USGS Seattle North, Seattle South, Kirkland, Mercer Island, Edmonds East, Bothell). **Bicycle.** This trip circles clockwise around the north end of Lake Washington and can be started at any place on the route. The suggested starting point has parking and access by Metro 307, 340, and 372 buses.Begin near the north end of Lake Washington at **Tracy Owens Station** (restrooms). Leave Metro bus at 61st Ave. NE. If driving, take SR-522 (Bothell Way NE) to 61st Ave. NE. Turn south from SR-522 then go west to the parking area.

Ride east near Bothell Way NE on the Burke–Gilman Trail. At the underpass under 68th Ave. NE, turn south on 68th Ave. NE, passing **Kenmore Park** at 1.0 mile. The street becomes Juanita Drive NE before reaching NE 153rd Place at the corner of **St. Edward Park** (mile 2). Continue south on Juanita Drive NE, passing the entrance to St. Edward State Park. At mile 2.8, turn west on Holmes Point Drive and descend to Lake Washington. Pass a street end access to Lake Washington (mile 4.3) and **O. O. Denny Park** (restrooms). After passing Denny Park, ascend southeast and northeast to return to Juanita Drive NE.

Turn south to **Juanita Beach Park** (restrooms). At mile 8, pass Juanita junction and turn south on the causeway across the Juanita Bay wetlands (informative signs). After crossing the causeway, turn right on paved pathways into **Juanita Bay Park** (restrooms, picnicking, water). Paths give access to viewpoints along the lakeshore. Continue west in the park to exit to 10th St. Ride south into 14th Ave. W.Turn southwest on 6th St. W to pass near **Waverly Park** (beach access) on Waverly Way. Go south on Waverly Way, into **Waverly Site**, once the location of a Junior High School. Follow a trail to exit at the intersection of Central Way, Market St. and Lake Ave. W. Turn north to view the Peter Kirk Building (1889) at 620 Market St., built by the founder of Kirkland. Return south and continue along the waterfront in **Kirkland Marine Park**. At mile 10, pass the end of Kirkland Ave. The **Kirkland Public Library** is two blocks east on Kirkland Ave. and the Kirkland Senior Center in **Peter Kirk Park** next east has public art.

Go south on the waterfront, using walkways along the shore where possible (walk bicycle), passing **Marsh Park** (restrooms and public art), **Houghton Beach Park** (lakeshore access), and **Carillon Point** (restrooms, view). Carillon Point is built on the site of a former shipbuilding operation (1901-1946). The walkway ends at the **Yarrow Bay Wetlands** (no access), which close the south end of Yarrow Bay. Return to Lake Washington Blvd. and continue south, passing NE 38th Place. Go right (west) on NE Points Drive on the north side of SR-520 (mile 14), passing a motor vehicle barrier to reach 92nd Ave. NE. Ride south on 92nd Ave. NE to NE 24th St. Continue west on the north side of I-90 into a bikeway that passes the **Wetherill Nature Preserve**. Park bicycle and tour the trails of the park to the shore of Lake Washington. Look for the following native plants: black cottonwood, Oregon ash, red alder, birch, bitter cherry, willow, hazel, cascara, indian plum, elderberry, and spirea. Along the path near the Nature Preserve, find huckleberry and Oregon grape.

Continue on the bikeway past the Hunts Point City Hall to 84th Ave. NE. Turn south one block on 84th Ave. NE to resume the westbound bikeway immediately north of SR-520. Traverse through Evergreen Point transit station to emerge at Evergreen Point Road (76th Ave. NE). Park bicycle and walk northeast to tour paths in **Fairweather Nature Preserve**. Look for the following native plants: big leaf maple, madrone, hazel, red cedar, salal, Oregon grape, elderberry, ocean spray, thimbleberry, salmonberry, and indian plum.

To visit **Wetherill Nature Preserve** and **Fairweather Nature Preserve** as a separate trip, take any Metro bus that stops at the Evergreen Point Transit Stop. These nature preserves provide no parking for motor vehicles. From the transit stop, walk west to Evergreen Point Road and an entrance to the Fairweather Nature Preserve. Tour the nature preserve, then from the southeast corner of the preserve, walk east on the walkway north of SR-522, jogging one block north at 84th Ave. NE (Hunts Point Road) then continue east past Hunts Point City Hall to Wetherill Nature Preserve.

From Fairweather Nature Preserve, turn south, crossing SR-520 and continuing south on 76th Ave. NE to Medina City Hall on the shore of Lake Washington (lakeshore access, restrooms). The building (1913) was the waiting room for a ferry to Seattle. From Medina City Hall, go east on Overlake Drive NE, rounding Groat Point to join Lake Washington Blvd. NE (mile 19). Turn southeast, passing **Clyde Beach Park** (restrooms) and **Meydenbauer Park**, mile 19.5 (restrooms). Before reaching Main Street in Bellevue, find **Whaler's Cove Park** (beach access) on the shore of Lake Washington. Go east on Main Street, then turn south on Bellevue Way, a busy street with a sidewalk. After one mile on Bellevue Way, turn right on 107th Ave. SE and go south into 108th Ave. SE. Reach I-90 at mile 23. **Enatai Park** (restrooms in summer, guarded swimming beach, viewpoint) is south under I-90.

From the intersection of 108th Ave. SE and I-90, go east 300' on the north side of I-90 to enter the I-90 bikeway. Ride west on the bikeway to Mercer Island. After a short descent, **Luther Burbank Park** (restrooms) is off to the right on 84th Ave. SE. Continue west on the bikeway, reaching the North Mercer Island Park & Ride at mile 25. Go west on the bikeway, ascending to a park above the I-90 tunnel (restrooms, water). Go southwest, passing along the south edge of playfields to rejoin the I-90 bikeway on the north side of the bridge. At the west end of the bridge, ascend to Lakeside Ave. S. Turn north, going through **Frink Park** to Lake Washington Blvd. at the North Leschi Marina (mile 29). Continue north along the shore of Lake Washington, passing **Madrona**

Park (restrooms). One mile after leaving Madrona Park, at the corner of McGilvra Blvd., ascend left (northwest) on Lake Washington Blvd. E. Cross E Madison St. and descend into **Washington Park Arboretum**. At the corner of 26th Ave. E, leave Lake Washington Blvd. E to go west on E Calhoun St. Turn north on 25th Ave. E past E Roanoke St. into a narrow alley. Turn left (west) in this alley for two blocks, then go north on 23rd Ave. E across Lake Washington Blvd. and SR-520 to E Shelby St. Turn west to Montlake Blvd. E, then go north across the ship canal bridge. At NE Pacific St., cross to the Burke–Gilman Trail. Ride north to Tracy Owens Station.

DUWAMISH INDUSTRIAL LOOP, high point 100', 25 miles RT, minimum gain (Maps: USGS Seattle South). **Bicycle.** Begin at the Metro International District Station on Jackson St. If driving, park at the Jack Perry Memorial Viewpoint off southbound Alaskan Way south of the intersection with Royal Brougham Way and join the route as described below.

From the Metro International District Station, ride west on Jackson St. to Alaskan Way, then turn south on the bikeway on the east side of Alaskan Way. Where the bikeway ends at Royal Brougham Way (mile 0.8), cross Alaskan Way and continue south on the sidewalk or wide shoulder on the west side of the street. Visit the **Jack Perry Memorial Viewpoint**, which has picnic tables, benches, and access to the Duwamish Waterway, at mile 1.3. From the viewpoint, continue south on a wide sidewalk on the west side of Alaskan Way and E Marginal Way S, then turn west at Spokane St., mile 2.6, passing the **Spokane Street Fishing Access** on the north side of the street. Stay west on a bikeway, which crosses to the south side of Spokane St. at 11th Ave. SW, mile 3.0, before going west over the low-level Duwamish Bridge. After descending from the bridge, reach a junction in the bikeway, mile 3.5, signed: Alki Point via Harbor Ave. SW. At this junction, leave the bikeway, turning left (south) on Marginal Place SW to meet W Marginal Way SW at 17th Ave. SW. Stay on the sidewalk on the west side of the street and ride south on W Marginal Way SW for two blocks. Cross east over W Marginal Way SW to a **Duwamish Waterway Public Access** and the beginning of the Duwamish Bikeway, mile 3.8. Visit the public access, then continue south on the bikeway along W Marginal Way SW, reaching another public access at mile 4.7 (signs) where Kellogg Island, a nature preserve, is offshore in the Duwamish Waterway (no access).

Continue south on the Duwamish Bikeway to SW Michigan St., mile 6.3. Turn left (east), crossing 2nd Ave. SW and, after going under SR-509, bend right (southeast) along Marginal Way S into the sidewalk along the east side of SR-99. Turn left (east) on S Holden St. at 2nd

Ave. S, mile 7.3, and continue to the bank of the Duwamish River for the view of the waterway. Return on S Holden St. to Riverside Drive and turn right (north), going west on S Webster St. and north on 2nd Ave. S travelling through an area of small industries to another viewpoint over the Duwamish River at a street end. Return south and east on different streets to S Holden St. at Riverside Drive. Go south on 7th Ave. S, then turn left (east) on S Kenyon St. to 10th Ave. S, bending south to **Duwamish Waterway Park**, mile 9.4, which has tables and water access. From the park, go east on S Elmgrove St., south on 12th Ave. S, and east on S Center St. to a waterway overlook. Return to 12th Ave. S and proceed south. At S Orr St., go southeast to a fragment of red brick paving, an extension of 14th Ave. S. Cross the brick road, go east under the 14th Ave. bridge ramp, and curve southeast into Dallas Ave. S. Pause frequently for views of the Duwamish Waterway. Pass South Park Marina, which has boat repair and storage facilities. At the end of the street, bend right into S Donovan St., then go west to 14th Ave. S, mile 10.3. Turn south on the sidewalk on the east side of 14th Ave. S, and, at S Director St., proceed south on a walkway.

The walkway emerges into Marginal Place S. Continue south on this street that parallels SR-99, but has almost no southbound traffic. The street at one place passes close to the Duwamish Waterway. After crossing S 102nd St., continue south on the bikeway into **North Weir Park** (restrooms, fruit trees, river view). Bend east to a pedestrian bridge over the Duwamish River at mile 12.8. At low tide, 0.0' or below, pause on the bridge to view the river as it drops over a stony ledge (North Weir) into the pool at the end of the dredged channel. Find a viewpoint with benches on the east side of the river. After visiting the viewpoint, return to the pedestrian bridge and go east on S 112th St., crossing Pacific Highway South. Go north on E Marginal Way S to mile 14. Turn east on Boeing Access Road, bending southeast before turning back north under a westbound lane into Airport Way S. Turn left into King County International Airport. Go north on the airport Perimeter Road, passing the main building of the airport at mile 16.6 and leaving the north end of the airport at mile 17.5. Turn left (west) on S Hardy St., crossing 13th Ave. S to S Ellis Ave. Go south to S Warsaw St. Turn right into a motor pool area to view the Georgetown steam plant, built in 1906 and inside the Boeing Field perimeter fence. Nearby is the site of the first settlement in the Seattle area. Go north on Ellis Ave. At S Myrtle St., turn left (west) to cross Marginal Way S. Immediately west of Marginal Way S, go south on 8th Ave. S to find a shoreline park on the Duwamish River and a view of the river. Return to Ellis Ave. S and go north and northeast to 13th Ave. S. Turn left to the intersection of 13th Ave. S and S Bailey St. for a view of **Georgetown City Hall** with its memorial clock tower. Now go north on Airport Way S to cross a bridge over multiple railroad tracks. At mile 21.5, Industrial Way S, continue north to pass the buildings that were the Rainier Brewery. At the north end of the buildings, diverge right (northeast) to ascend on a gravel road. Explore this road as it travels north under the western edge of I-5. Return to the Rainier Brewery and continue north on Airport Way S. Turn west at S Lander St. to the Metro Busway and Metro buses north and south. To return to a vehicle parked at Jack Perry Memorial Viewpoint, go north on any street west of the busway and left (west) over multiple railroad tracks on Royal Brougham Way.

BEACON HILL TO RENTON, high point 350', 13 miles, 550' gain (Maps: USGS Seattle South, Des Moines). **Bicycle or Walk parts.** Ride Metro 36 to the **Beacon Hill Playground** (restrooms, tables, benches) at S Holgate St. and 14th Ave. S.

Ride south on 14th Ave. S. At mile 0.3, turn southeast into Beacon Ave. S. Diverge north at 16th Ave. S, east on S Bayview St. and north on 17th Ave. S to circle and admire the **Beacon Hill School**. Return to Beacon Ave. S and continue southeast. At Spokane St., pass a playground, the Jefferson Park Golf Course, and the Jefferson Community Center, mile 1.6. Diverge right (west) at the Community Center to a viewpoint west and the Jefferson Park Lawn Bowling Club. Return to Beacon Ave. S at the Veteran Administration Medical Center on a paved road through the golf course. Cross S Columbian Way at mile 2.4 and begin a paved path in the Beacon Ave. S median. At S Myrtle St., turn right (east) to the east boundary of **Van Anselt Park** (playground) to view public art.

Cross S Holden St. at mile 5.0. The median path ends at S Barton St. where Beacon Ave. S bends into 39th Ave. S. Continue south, passing **Benefit Park** (playground, tables, shelter) into Carkeek Drive S, which winds east down the hill to Martin Luther King Jr. Way. Cross into S Henderson St. and go east to Renton Ave. S (mile 7.1), then turn right (southeast). At 51st Ave. S, go south past S Hazel St., then turn left (southeast) on Beacon Ave. S along the upper edge of a steep slope with views to the south. Turn south on 64th Ave. S (mile 9.8). At S 129th St., diverge right (west) to M. L. King Jr. Way (SR-900) to go southeast on this busy street to the next street, 68th Ave. S (mile 10.6). This street descends quickly to cross the Black River (now brown) near railroad tracks and the Renton Waste Water Treatment facility (upstream). At the intersection of Monster Road SW and Oakesdale Ave. SW, ascend southwest on Monster Road to **Waterworks Garden Park** on the east side of the street where monumental columns of **basalt** line the entrance. Compliments to the artist on this impressive use of one of natures wonders. Park bicycle to explore the Knoll, Funnel, Grotto,

Passage, and Release areas of the park. Return to bicycle and ascend southwest on Monster Road to an outlook at a water tower. Return (north) to the junction with Oakesdale Ave. SW. Go left (northwest) for one block to find an entrance to a path along the Black River at a grass opening on north side of the street. Walk the path east to a heronry viewpoint on the bank of the Black River. Continue south on the path to rejoin the bikeway near Oaksdale Ave. SW. Follow the paved path south under Oakesdale Ave. SW, emerging at the corner of SW Grady Way and Oakesdale Ave. SW (Metro 340).

Cross at the intersection and continue south on a paved path on the west side of the Black River, going under I-405 to reach SW 16th St. Cross the street and begin **Springbrook Creek Trail**, a paved path in restored wetlands east of a Boeing facility. The paved path ends at mile 12.8. Leave bicycle and explore the wetlands and edges of ponds in **Springbrook Creek Park**. Return north to SW Grady Way to find a Metro 340 stop at the intersection with Oakesdale Ave. SW, mile 14.

West Seattle Area. West of the Duwamish River and south to the Seattle city limit.

ALKI BEACH, high point 150', 14 miles one-way bicycling, 9 miles one-way walking, 150' gain (Maps: USGS Seattle South, Duwamish Head). **Bicycle or Walk**. If bicycling, begin at the Metro International District Station on Jackson St. If walking, take Metro 37 to the first stop on Harbor Ave. SW, or take Metro 21, 22 to the last stop on SW Spokane St. under the West Seattle Freeway.

From the Spokane St. bus stop, walk west on a pathway on the north side of Spokane St. to Harbor Ave. SW. Turn north to reach the beach walkway. If driving, park off Harbor Ave. SW in Seacrest Park and walk or ride north. Metro 37 follows most of this route and can be used to reach any part.

From the Metro International District Station, ride west on Jackson St. to Alaskan Way, then turn south on the bikeway on the east side of Alaskan Way. Where the bikeway ends at Royal Brougham Way (mile 0.7), cross Alaskan Way and continue south on the sidewalk or wide shoulder on the west side of the street. Visit the Jack Perry Memorial Viewpoint, which has picnic tables, benches, and water access, at mile 1.2. From the viewpoint, continue south on a wide sidewalk on the west side of Alaskan Way, then turn west at Spokane St., passing a fishing access on the north side of the street. Stay west on a bikeway, which crosses to the south side of Spokane St. at 11th Ave. SW before going west over the low-level Duwamish Bridge. After descending from the bridge, reach a 'Y' in the bikeway. Take the left (west) branch, signed: Alki Point via Harbor Ave. SW. Keep left at the next 'Y' to exit from the bikeway into 22nd Ave. SW. Go right (west) at the first street (SW Andover St.) and continue west across Delridge Way SW to the end of the street. Jog south on 28th Ave. SW one block , then continue west on Yancy St. to SW Avalon Way, mile 4.2. Turn right (north), passing under the West Seattle Freeway into Harbor Ave. SW. Begin a paved bikeway on the east side of Harbor Ave. SW at mile 5.3, part of **Port of Seattle Waterfront Park**. Turn into the access road to explore the facilities: viewing platforms and tower, 1.5 miles of paved walkways and steps, marine oriented decorations and playground, barge terminal, and beach overlook. Return to Harbor Ave.

Pass **Seacrest Park** (mile 7.5), a marine park with fishing pier and restrooms where scuba divers congregate on weekends. At mile 8.1, the path rounds Duwamish Head southwest and passes picnic tables, viewpoints with benches, and access steps to beach level. Near **Alki Point**, mile 10.1, pass the **Alki Art Studio**, restrooms, replica of the Statue of Liberty, and a Memorial to the first pioneer landing. The paved promenade along the waterfront ends here. Ascend to Alki Ave. SW and continue southwest to reach the Alki Point Light Station (call 206-217-6123 for tours) after turning south at Point Place SW. Continue into Beach Drive SW to pass a street end park with beach access and an information display. Find **Mee-Quah-Mooks Park** (toilets, water access, and view promenade) at mile 11.6. Reach **Loman Beach Park** at mile 13.6 (shoreline access and a tennis court) at the intersection of Lincoln Park Way SW, 48th Ave. SW, and Beach Drive SW. Continue south on Beach Drive SW along the east side of waterfront houses to enter **Lincoln Park** (picnicking, trails, shelters, restrooms). Pass **Coleman Pool** (salt water) at mile 14.5 before reaching Fauntleroy Way SW and Metro 54 bus stops at mile 15.1. If walking, return to a vehicle parked at Seacrest Park by following the outgoing route back to Loman Beach Park at 48th Ave. SW and a Metro 37 stop.

SCHMITZ PARK, high point 300', 2 miles of trails, 200' gain (Maps: USGS Duwamish Head). **Walk**. The chief attraction of this park is its many ancient trees, both standing and fallen. Take Metro 56 to SW Admiral Way and SW Stevens St. or, if driving, enter parking off SW Admiral Way at SW Stevens St.

Walk south into the park. For a sampler, continue south, keeping to the right at trail junctions to exit the park on 53rd Ave. SW near SW Manning St. Go south on 53rd Ave. SW, turn left (east) on SW Charleston St, and left on 51st Ave. SW to pass Schmitz Park Elementary School. Turn north in the alley on the east side of the fence enclosing the elementary school, then go west on SW Hines St. to reenter park. Descend on trails to return to the starting point. Look for the following native plants: western hemlock, red cedar, Douglas fir, indian plum, salmonberry, elderberry, hazel, and salal.

CAMP LONG, 340', 2 miles of trails, 200' gain (Maps: USGS Seattle South). **Walk.** Ride Metro 21 to Camp Long off 35th Ave. SW near SW Dawson St., or park at Camp Long (telephone 206-684-7434).

Facilities: displays, cabins, climbing rock, ponds, alder forest, restrooms, water. Find the following native plants, some with numbered markers: madrone (1), hawthorn (4), larch (5), birch (6), bitter cherry (10), Oregon ash (11), yellow cedar (12), hazel (13), Douglas fir (14), snowberry (15), cascara (9), willow (19), yew (20), ocean spray (21, 23), huckleberry (24), rose (25), alder, hemlock, elderberry, bigleaf maple, dogwood, indian plum, salal, currant, vine maple, red cedar, Oregon grape, ponderosa pine, red-osier dogwood, white pine, mountain ash, rhododendron, thimbleberry, salmonberry, and juniper.

WESTCREST TO DUWAMISH RIVER, high point 450', 15 miles one-way, 300' gain (Maps: USGS Duwamish Head, Seattle South). **Mtn. Bicycle.** Ride Metro 21 to Camp Long at SW Dawson St. and 35th Ave. SW.

Enter **Camp Long** and park bicycle. Walk around the park, visiting the various facilities (see above). Return to bicycle and ride south on 35th Ave. SW to SW Morgan St., mile 0.7. Turn east and descend on curving SW Sylvan Way to Delridge Way SW, mile 1.7. Turn south on Delridge Way SW to SW Henderson St., mile 2.7. Turn east on SW Henderson St. to **Westcrest Park** at 8th Ave. SW, mile 3.4. Ride east into the park, making a loop south past restrooms and parking, then stop on the south side of the reservoir for a view of the Cascade Mountains. Mt. Si is directly east.

Ride east and north around the reservoir to a trail junction south of the intersection of SW Cloverdale St. and 5th Ave. SW. Turn right and ride a path southeast and south, taking a left fork (south) into a narrower path in the forest where the wider path curves around and ascends west. Exit from the forest into 4th Ave. SW, mile 4.4, and go right (south). Turn left (east) on SW Cambridge Place to Olson Place SW, a busy street. Descend northeast on Olson Place SW to the intersection with Myers Way (stoplight). Go north on Myers Way until Myers Way turns right (east) to cross SR-509. Make a left turn off Myers Way under the southbound on-ramp into First Ave. S. Go north on First Ave. S past an SR-509 on-ramp (stoplight). At the next stoplight, go left (northwest) on a bikeway on the north side of SW Michigan St. (mile 6.6). Turn right (north) on West Marginal Way SW on the Duwamish Bikeway following a railroad track. Cross the railroad track at mile 7.7 to find an interpretive sign and a viewpoint east toward Kellogg Island.

Continue north, passing a shoreline access at mile 8.0 (toilets), and the **Duwamish Public Access** at mile 8.6 (viewpoint, shelter, fishing pier, picnic tables, toilets). The paved bikeway ends here. Cross W Marginal Way SW and proceed north on the sidewalk into 17th Ave. SW and Marginal Place SW, which ends at an entrance to a bikeway. This bikeway joins the W Spokane St. Bikeway. Now turn right (east) on the bikeway under the West Seattle bridge, mile 8.9. Ascend east on the bikeway, crossing the low-level bridge over the Duwamish Waterway to reach 11th Ave. S at mile 9.5. Turn right and circle west under the bridge to Klickitat Ave. SW on the west side of Harbor Island. Go north, now on 16th Ave. S, passing structures of Lockheed Shipbuilding on the left. Turn east on S Florida St. and again north on 13th Ave. SW to a viewpoint north near a railroad car loading dock. Go east to the west side of the container loading terminal, mile 10.9, then turn south along the west boundary of the container loading terminal. Watch containers being loaded on ships. Turn east on the north side of Spokane Street on a bikeway to reach E Marginal Way SW, mile 12.3. From here, a Metro busway east of 4th Ave. S and north of Spokane St. provides bus access north or south.

If not leaving the route here, go north on the sidewalk on the west side of E Marginal Way SW. The street becomes Alaska Way before passing the **Jack Perry Memorial Viewpoint** at mile 13.5 and the **Coast Guard Museum** at mile 13.8 (open 9am-3pm weekdays). A bikeway on the east side of Alaska Way begins north of Royal Brougham Way. Turn east on S Jackson St. to the International District Metro Station, mile 15.

South King County Area.
From the south Seattle city limit to the south border of King County.

FAUNTLEROY PARK TO FORT DENT PARK, high point 400', 22 miles one-way, 200' gain (Maps: USGS Seattle South). **Mtn. Bicycle or Hike-1 parts.** Ride Metro 54 to the bus stop on SW Barton St. near SW Director St.

Walk bicycle south through **Fauntleroy Park**, crossing a creek and taking branches to several viewpoints into the wetlands. Common native plants in the park include: huckleberry, salmonberry, bigleaf maple, red cedar, alder, western hemlock, salal, hazel, bitter cherry, and madrone.

After emerging to SW Roxbury St., which is not a through street to the east, return into the park and continue east on trails and streets to 35th Ave. SW. Turn south to SW Roxbury St., then go east to **Roxhill Park** at 28th Ave. SW., mile 2.1. Facilities in the park include: tables, restrooms, playfields, and playgrounds with equipment. Return to the entrance on SW Roxbury St. and proceed south on 28th Ave. SW to SW 104th St. Go east to 24th Ave. SW, then turn north to **North Shorewood Park** (restrooms, playgrounds and play equipment), north of SW 102nd St. Go east on trails through the park. With luck, emerge from the east side of the park and proceed to the intersection of 21st Ave. SW and SW 100th St. Ride east on SW 100th St., then turn south on 14th Ave. SW to **White Center Park** (picnic area, restrooms, indoor facilities). After leaving the park at the south boundary, return west to 16th Ave. SW. Turn south to SW 112th St., mile 5.

Ride east on SW 112th St. across 10th Ave. SW to **Lake Garrett** in **Lakewood Park** (shelter, restrooms, picnic tables, beach, fishing piers, and paved paths). Wander the paths in the park, then exit from the northeast corner to 5th Ave. SW at SW 108th St. Go right (east) on SW 108th St. to 1st Ave. S and turn right (south) to S 112th St. Turn left (east) on S 112th St. to 4th Ave. S. Bend right (southeast) on 4th Place S into 5th Ave. S to go under SR-509. Continue east across 8th Ave. S to S 112th St., which becomes Glendale Way S, bending toward the south. At S 118th St., bend left (east) into Des Moines Memorial Drive, mile 8.2. Cross S 96th St. at mile 9.9 (signal), then go northeast over SR-99 into 14th Ave. S to enter the South Park shopping area. To leave the route here, find a Metro 130 stop at the corner of Cloverdale St. and 14th Ave. S, mile 10.7.

To continue the route, proceed northeast over the Duwamish River on the 14th Ave. S bridge. The street becomes 16th Ave. S before reaching E Marginal Way S. Turn south on E Marginal Way S, crossing to a wide shoulder or side walk along this busy street. At mile 12.7, pass the **Museum of Flight**, which overshadows one of the early buildings of the Boeing Airplane Company. Turn west on S 112th St. to a pedestrian bridge over the Duwamish River (benches). During minus tides, look north from the bridge to North Weir, a cascade in the river. Return on S 112th St. to Pacific Highway S. Cross east over the street and south over the bridge to find the bikeway on the south side of the river. Pass under the Allentown Bridge, mile 16.2, then, after going under I-5, return west to Interurban Ave. S to continue S along the west edge of the Foster Golf Links. Turn left (east) into the bikeway along the shore of the river at S 141st Place and, at mile 19, cross a bridge over the Green River into **Fort Dent Park**. The **Black River**, which formerly carried the flow from Lake Washington to Puget Sound, joins the Green River east of this bridge. Facilities in the park include: playgrounds, playfields, restrooms, picnic tables, shelters, and ponds.

Leave the park south on the sidewalk on the east side of the Southcenter Blvd. bridge, mile 20, turning left into a bikeway to follow the west bank of the Green River under Interurban Ave. and I-405 (picnic tables and benches). After passing I-405, exit to 68th Ave. S briefly, then reenter the bikeway along the west bank of the Green River to reach **Bicentennial Park** (restrooms, water) at Strander Blvd. Go west on Strander Blvd. to the Southcenter Transit Center (Metro 150, 340, etc.) on Andover Park W, mile 22.

SEAHURST–SALTWATER PARKS, high point 400', 9 miles hiking or 24 miles bicycling, 700' gain hiking, 1600' gain bicycling (Maps: USGS Des Moines, Poverty Bay). **Mt. Bicycle or Hike-1 part**. For a great winter or early spring hike, ride Metro 136 to SE 128th St. and Ambaum Blvd. SW. If bicycling, ride Metro 135 or Metro 136 to SW 116th St. at 16th Ave. SW.

Hikers go south on Ambaum Blvd. SW and west on SW 130th St., curving into 16th Ave. SW, then, where the main street bends to become SW 131st St., continue south on 16th Ave. SW, to **Seahurst Park**, mile 0.4. Bicyclists ride west on SW 116th St., then descend south on 21st Ave. SW, bending southwest into SW 122nd St. Turn right on Marine View Drive SW, then go left at the next intersection to descend to Shorewood Drive SW. Turn left (southeast) and follow Shorewood Drive SW as it winds over Salmon Creek. After ascending sharply, the street becomes Shorecrest Drive SW. Turn left (east) on SW 131st St. to 16th Ave. SW, then go right (south) into Seahurst Park, mile 2.0.

A trail and road begin here (no bicycles on trails). Both descend west and south into Seahurst Park. If on the road, descend in switchbacks, at first on the north side of a deep canyon, reaching the beach level at a building of the Marine Technology Laboratories, a training facility, mile 3.0. Descend a ramp near the building to the beach and go north to the park boundary then return south along the beach promenade or on the road to the parking area, mile 3.4 (restrooms).

Continue on a road to the south edge of the park, mile 3.8. Return north to beach parking (mile 4.1) and ascend east on Seahurst Park Road, which bends south and becomes 13th Ave. SW before meeting SW 144th St. Turn right (west) on SW 144th Place. Where this street becomes SW 146th St., go left (south) on 20th Ave. SW. Turn right (west) on SW 152nd St. at mile 5.8. West of 22nd Ave. SW, turn left (south) into Maplewild Ave. The **Indian Trail** begins at mile 6.8 on the right side of Maplewild Ave. where SW 160th St. would be (no parking, no sign, house number 16002 is 100' north on the east side of street).

Walk bicycle south along this narrow trail, taking time to appreciate the gardens and houses. Pass a street end beach access at mile 7.1 (no parking). Reach the end of the trail at SW 170th St. near SW Three Tree Point Lane, mile 7.6 (parking for residents only). Leave bicycle and walk beach south to Three Tree Point (Point Pully) and return. The beach is public access during daylight hours but the grounds at the Point are not open to the public. For hikers, to end the trip here and find a Metro stop, go east on SW 170th St. to Maplewild Ave. SW. Turn northeast on Maplewild Ave. SW to 33rd Ave. SW. Go right (south) on 33rd Ave. SW, ascending into SW 170th St. Turn left (north) on 31st Ave. SW to the Metro 136 stop at the corner of SW 169th St., 0.7 mile from SW 170th St. at SW Three Tree Point Lane.

To continue on the bicycle route, ride south on SW Three Tree Point Lane to SW 171st St. Turn west to the end of the street at a gate for a view of Three Tree Point, now private property. Return east on SW 171st St. to exit on Maplewild Ave. SW, then turn south. Find a public beach access at mile 8.0 (no parking) where Maplewild Ave. SW turns into SW 172nd St., a street with the flavor of Mediterranean Europe: the houses close together and the front wall of houses almost on the edge of the street. Vashon Island is west. Continue east on SW 172nd St., starting uphill at mile 8.4. On the hill north madrone trees flourish, blossoming profusely in May. The street becomes SW Sylvester Road at mile 9.0. Turn right into SW 172nd St., which becomes 13th Ave. SW, descending to cross Miller Creek. The street name changes to 12th Ave. SW before exiting to SW Shorebrook Drive. Go left and ascend east to Marineview Drive SW. Proceed south on a quiet street (sidewalk). Reach **Nature Trails Park** at mile 10.9. Tour the park, with its prolific growth of skunk cabbage.

Exit from the park (mile 11.3) and continue south, ascending to an intersection with Normandy Park Drive. Go south on Marineview Drive SW (sidewalk). In May, the flowers along the street are magnificent. Reach **Marine View Park** (toilet) at mile 13.0. The path to the beach is 0.5 miles RT and 275' of elevation gain. Join SR-509 at mile 13.4 and go right (south) to enter the town of Des Moines (stores). Turn right (west) on S 227th St. to the shoreline. Ride north along the waterfront, viewing many boating related activities. At the end of parking, jog east and continue north into **Des Moines Beach Park**. Follow the paved road northeast, passing the Des Moines Senior Center and several other buildings. Continue up Des Moines Creek, passing a gate, to the end of an abandoned road for a bit of quiet (except for aircraft). Return west, staying on the north side of the creek, passing picnic areas, shelter, restrooms, and beach access, mile 16.2. Turn left (south) across the creek. Reenter marina parking and go west to the fishing pier. Leave bicycle and walk to the end of the fishing pier to see what fish are being caught. Vashon Island is west.

Return to bicycle and ride south along the waterfront. Exit east on S 227th St. to Marine View Drive, mile 16.9. Turn south, going straight ahead (south) where Kent-Des Moines Road (SR-516) turns left (southeast). Pass the decorative Masonic Home at mile 17.7 and continue on Marine View Drive. At S 255th St., turn right (west), then go south on 8th Place S into **Saltwater State Park**, reaching the beach at mile 18.9. Ride or walk north along the beach to the end, then return to the parking area (restrooms, water, shelter, picnic tables, trails). Take time to view the camping area. Leave the beach at mile 20, ascending northeast. Find an exit to Marine View Drive behind the trailer dump station and continue south across a high bridge (narrow walkway). Turn left (east) into Woodmont Drive S, mile 21.2, ascending to 16th Ave. S. Turn right (south) to S 272nd St. Go left (east) across SR-99 and I-5 to a Metro 194 stop on the I-5 northbound on-ramp at mile 23.5.

SEATAC–SOUTHCENTER, high point 450', 15 miles, 700' gain (Maps: USGS Des Moines). **Bicycle or Walk parts**. Take Metro 174, 194, 340 to SeaTac Airport, 375'. For Metro access to individual parks, see below.

Ride southeast on the airport sidewalk to Pacific Highway S (SR-99). Go south on SR-99 to S 188th St. Turn left (east) to **Valley Ridge Park** east of 46th Ave. S, mile 1.6. Facilities: playground, playfields, public art. Return on S 188th St. to 37th Ave. S. Turn left (south) to S 192nd St., right (west) on S 192nd St., left (south) on 36th Ave. S, and right (west) on S 194th St. to **Angle Lake Park**, mile 3.1 (Metro 174). Facilities and activities: swimming beach, tables, viewpoint, restrooms, dock. Exit west to SR-99 and go south to S 200th St. Turn right (west) and descend to a crossing of Des Moines Creek under the SeaTac Airport landing pattern. Turn left (south) into **Des Moines Creek Park**. Park bicycle and explore downstream in the park.

Return to bicycle and continue west on S 200th St. to 18th Ave. S. Turn north along the west edge of Tyee Golf Course, pausing to watch aircraft landing or departing. The street bends into S 196th St. before emerging on Des Moines Memorial Drive, mile 5.1. Turn right (north), then go right (east) on S 192nd St., which rounds north into 16th Ave. S along the edge of the airport. At busy S 188th Way turn right (east) briefly to watch aircraft, then proceed northwest on S 188th Way, passing under SR-509 at mile 6.3. Pass 8th Ave. S, then turn north on Des Moines Drive, mile 6.9, going right (east) on S 176th St. to pass **Airport Park** (wetland, no facilities) north of S 176th St. Cross SR-509 before bending left (north) into 12th Ave. S along the airport fence. At S 170th St., turn right (east) into **Viewpoint Park**, mile 7.9, for a view of the airport.

Return to 12th Ave. S and go right (north) to S 156th Way. Turn right (northeast) across the north end of the airport. The street becomes 154th St. At 24th Ave. S, go right (south) on Airport Service Road to S 160th St., mile 10.7. Turn left (east) and proceed across SR-99. Where the street bends right (southeast) and becomes Military Road S, stay on S 160th St. to reach **McMicken Heights Park**. Reach the park also by taking Metro 340 to 51st Ave. S at S 160th St. or, from the Southcenter Transit Center, go west on Strander Blvd., north to Klickitat Drive, and west into a walkway that ascends on the south side of Klickitat Drive. Leave the walkway part way up the hill and ascend steps to a pipeline right-of-way that exits to 53rd Ave. S. Go right (north), then continue up on S 159th St. to the park. Find shelters, tables, charcoal grills, restrooms, playground, **Crystal Spring**, a viewpoint east, and many native plants: red cedar, alder, vine and bigleaf maple, Douglas fir, hemlock, Oregon grape, salal, Indian plum, and elderberry. Descend steps and a path to the lower level at the intersection of 51st Ave. S and S 159th St.

To leave the park, descend on S 159th St. to 53rd Ave. S. Either go right (south) briefly on 53rd Ave. S before descending on a pipeline right-of-way and steps to a walkway, or go left (north) on 53rd Ave. S to Klickitat Drive. Find a walkway on the south side of Klickitat Drive and descend southeast under I-5. At Southcenter Parkway, go right (south) to Strander Blvd. Turn left (east) to find a Metro Transit Center (Metro 150, 340, etc.) on Andover Park W, mile 14.

FEDERAL WAY–AUBURN, high point 498', 18 miles one-way, 100' gain (Maps: USGS Poverty Bay, Auburn). **Bicycle**. Ride Metro 194, etc., to Federal Way Transit Center, 420'.

Ride west in the parking area to the first cross way. Turn north on the sidewalk along a busway that becomes 25th Ave. S. Cross S 320th St. into Gateway Center, continuing north and northeast around the east end of the buildings (REI). Exit into 28th Ave. S. At S 312th St. (mile 0.9), turn west, then enter north into **Steel Lake Park** (restrooms, shelter, swimming beach, tables, fishing pier, playground). After circling the park, return to the entrance and cross S 312th St. to explore the south section of Steel Lake Park (playfields). Return to S 312th St. and go east to 28th Ave. S. Turn right (south), taking the first left into Gateway Center to return to S 320th St., mile 2.8.

Turn left (east) on S 320th St., crossing I-5. At mile 3.5, turn right (south) on Weyerhaeuser Way S, then go left at the first branch road to a fishing access on **North Lake**. Return to Weyerhaeuser Way S (mile

4.4) and continue south, passing entrances to Weyerhaeuser Technology Center on the right. Reach a complex interchange with S 336th St., exiting to Weyerhaeuser Way S to enter right (west) into the grounds of Weyerhaeuser Corporate Headquarters. Either take the first road to the left around the headquarters building to the **Bonsai Gardens** and **Rhododendron Gardens** or go right to a trail north into forested grounds. Park bicycle at the path entrance (foot travel only) and walk paths around the north and west sides of **Weyerhaeuser Lake**. On nearing the headquarters building, exit to the street, cross, and find a path on the west side of the street that goes south to the Bonsai Gardens (free) and Weyerhaeuser Rhododendron Gardens (fee). The exhibits in the Bonsai Gardens change.

To reach the gardens by bus, take Metro 174 or 194 to S 336th St. at Pacific Highway S. Walk east on S 336th St. under I-5 to an entrance into Weyerhaeuser Corporate Headquarters east of I-5. Go right (south) on this entrance road to the gardens. If driving, take Exit-142 from I-5 into eastbound SR-18. Exit to 32nd Ave. S (Weyerhaeuser Way S) and go north to the entrance to Weyerhaeuser Corporate Headquarters. Keep left around the south side of the main building to parking.

Return to Weyerhaeuser Way S and go south, crossing SR-18 (bicycle mile 6.0). At mile 6.2, turn east on S 344th St., then jog north into S 342nd St., to cross a wetland at the north end of Lake Geneva. At 46th Ave. S, go right (south) to a broad path on the west side of 46th Ave. S into **Lake Geneva Park**. Proceed south to a paved path at a playground. Turn right (west) and follow the path past a shelter to a fishing pier. Return to the shelter, then take a path to the right (east) to 46th Ave. S. Turn right (south), crossing S 349th St., mile 7.8. Continue to S 352nd St., then go left (east) to Military Way S. Turn south to **Five Mile Lake Park** at mile 9.2. Facilities: swimming beach, tables, shelters, restrooms, playground, dressing rooms with showers.

Exit east from Five Mile Lake Park (mile 9.7), turning left (north) on Military Way S to S 364th St. Go right (east), crossing 55th Ave. S to enter 55th Place S, a one-way street. Descend steeply southeast, crossing a junction with 58th Place S into 56th Place S to the West Valley Highway, a busy two-lane street with no bike lane, mile 11.2. Turn left (north) to Ellingson Road, mile 11.6, then go right (east) under SR-167. Continue east on Ellingson Road, which also doesn't have a bike lane but has some sidewalk. Pass the Interurban Bikeway at mile 11.8, the Algona-Pacific Library at mile 11.9, and the Union Pacific Railroad tracks at mile 12.3. Go under the Burlington Northern Railroad tracks at mile 13 to A St. SE. Make a choice here. Either go north on the sidewalk along A St. SE, turning east on 6th St. SE just south of SR-18 to find the Metro 150 stop, or, for a tour of south

Auburn, continue east from A St. on 41st St. SE to D St. SE. Turn north to 37th St. SE, then go east to M St. Go north to 29th St. SE and return left (west) to F St. SE. Now go north to Auburn Way S and continue northwest on the sidewalk on the west side of Auburn Way S to 6th St. SE. Turn west to the Metro 150 stop where the bus waits before beginning the run to Seattle, bicycle mile 17.

TUKWILA–GREEN RIVER LOOP, high point 200', 43 to 63 miles, 150' gain (Maps: USGS Auburn, Black Diamond, Renton, Des Moines, Poverty Bay). **Bicycle**. Ride Metro 150, 340, etc., to the Southcenter Transit Center. If driving, find on-street parking. For a shorter ride, see **Short Version** below.

From the Southcenter Transit Center, ride south to Strander Blvd., the first cross street. Turn left and ride east. **Bicentennial Park** on the west side of the river has water and restrooms (mile 0.5). Continue east on Strander Blvd., crossing the Green River and the West Valley Highway. Go east one block past the West Valley Highway on a dead end street to the **Interurban Bikeway**. Turn right (south) and ride on a converted rail route under a power line. At mile 1.9 jog right (west) on S 180th St. to cross this busy street at a signal. Cross S 212nd St. at mile 4.3, S 228th St. at mile 5.3, and pass under I-405 at mile 6. At mile 6.1, pass the Kent Park & Ride on the south side of James St.

At mile 6.5, pass a playfield with water and toilets. Cross the Green River and the Green River Bikeway at mile 7.6. Shortly after crossing the Green River the Interurban Bikeway crosses one set of railroad tracks and continues south for one mile with tracks of the Union Pacific Railroad on both sides of the Bikeway. Several spur track crossings require care. Cross Main St. (Auburn access) at mile 12.2, then pass under SR-18 at mile 12.5. To visit **Blue Heron Marsh**, turn right (west) on 15th St. SW (mile 13) for one mile to West Valley Highway, then go north 0.4 mile. Look for nests in alder trees southwest of the pond. Best time: February through April. The Supermall of the Northwest is north of 15th St. SW.

Find picnic tables, shelter, stores, and food at mile 14.3 (1st Ave. N). The **Algona-Pacific Library** is east 0.1 mile on Ellingson Road (mile 15, food, stores). Where the Interurban Bikeway ends (mile 15.5) turn left (east) on 3rd Ave. SW into the town of Pacific, passing the **Algona Senior Center** at mile 16 and **Algona Park** with water, restrooms, playfields, picnic tables, and access to the White (Stuck) River at mile 16.6. Continue east on the street, now 3rd Ave. SE, to the end at the railroad track and another access to the White River. Turn left (north) on Skinner St. to the first stoplight, Ellingson Road. Turn right (east) under the railroad track to the next stoplight at A St. SE (mile 17.6). Turn left and ride north to 29th St. SE. Turn right (east) on 29th St. SE to F St. SE, a quiet street. Turn left (north) on F St. SE to 17th St. SE, then go right (east) to M St. SE at the Goodwill Store (mile 20) and an intersection with Auburn Way S. To leave the route here, find a Metro 150 stop on 6th St. SE west of Auburn Way S. To continue the route, skip the next paragraph below.

Short Version. To bypass the ride on the Interurban Bikeway and shorten the ride by 20 miles, take Metro 150 to the last stop in Auburn on 6th St. SE. Ride east on 6th St. SE to Auburn Way S. Turn north under SR-18, then go east on 4th St. SE. Jog north at M St. into 3rd St. SE and continue as described below.

Turn north on M St. SE across Auburn Way S (SR-164) at a stoplight. Continue north on M St. SE, passing under SR-18. Turn right (east) on E 3rd St. and again right (south) on R St. (mile 21), which becomes Auburn–Black Diamond Road, and ride south and east. Beyond mile 22, before reaching the SR-18 underpass, find an access road into **Green River Park**, an undeveloped King County Park. After going under SR-18, turn right (east) on SE Green Valley Road, staying on this road as it follows the Green River, crossing the river to the north bank at mile 24. At mile 28, pass **Metzler Park**, a segment of East Green River Park. Cross the junction of 218 Ave. SE and 212 Way SE at mile 30. Turn right (east) into **Flaming Geyser State Park** at mile 31 and ride one mile east in the park to the end of the road (restrooms).

Return into Auburn on SE Green Valley Road and Auburn-Black Diamond Road. On reaching R St. SE (mile 43), continue north to a 'T' intersection with 8th Ave. NE. Turn right (east) on 8th Ave. NE which becomes SE 320th St. on the east side of the river. Turn left (north) on Riverside Ave (104th Ave. SE), going left on SE 307th Place into Green River Road, reaching **Isaac Evans Park** (picnicking and restrooms) at mile 45. A foot bridge in the park allows access to the west bank of the river where a track on the dike goes north for 1.5 miles, ending in a thicket by the river. Continue north on the east side of the Green River, passing the Auburn Golf Course. At mile 48, turn left (northwest) on 94th Place S and after 0.1 mile go left into the Green River Bikeway provided by the city of Kent. Pass under S Central Ave. at mile 50 and continue on the bikeway along the Green River. The bikeway exits to S 266th St. 0.3 miles after passing under S Central Ave. Go west to 79th Ave. S. Turn north to reach the intersection of 80th Ave. S and S 259th St. on the west side of a railroad track. Turn west on S 259th St., crossing 78th Ave. S. After going under another railroad track, cross the Interurban Bikeway (mile 51) near the Green River. Turn south toward the river then west to stay on the east bank of the river. Pass a pedestrian bridge across the river at mile 53 near the south end of a golf course. The bikeway continues along the border of the golf course for 1.5 miles, passing another pedestrian bridge across the river. Continue north, alternating between Russell Road and the bikeway on the river bank. Reach **Van Doren's Landing Park** (playfields) at mile 56 and **Anderson Park** (picnic tables), before reaching an intersection with S 212th St. at mile 57. A campground is east on S 212th St.

Pass under S 212th St. and continue north on Russell Road for one mile before turning left to continue north on the bikeway along the Green River. Pass **Briscoe Park** with shelter, tables, and toilets at mile 59. At mile 60, near S 180th St., cross a bridge to the west side of the Green River. Follow the river north into Tukwila, reaching **Bicentennial Park** (restrooms, water, shelter, and picnic tables) at Strander Blvd. (mile 62). Ride west on Strander Blvd. to Andover Park W to the Transit Center.

LAKE YOUNGS AND SOOS CREEK TO KENT, high point 600', 10 to 21 miles, 600' gain (Maps: USGS Auburn, Renton, Maple Valley). **Mtn. Bicycle or Hike-1 parts.** The route passes through miles of wetland in **Big Soos Creek Park** where walks with a naturalist occur from June to September (call 206-286-4171 for information). Ride Metro 155 to the intersection of SE Petrovitsky Road and 151st Ave. SE. For access **Big Soos Creek Park**, drive north on 148th Ave. SE from Kent-Kangley Road to parking (toilets) on the east side of 148th Ave. SE. For access to the **Lake Youngs Perimeter Trail**, drive Old Petrovitsky Road off SE Petrovitsky Road to parking (restrooms). Take connector trail south to the Lake Youngs Perimeter Trail.

From the Metro 155 stop, cross Petrovitsky Road south into 151st Ave. SE and ride southeast into SE 183rd Drive, heading toward a forested hill that is inside the Lake Youngs Reservation, a reservoir for the Seattle Water Department. Turn southwest on 153rd Place SE at mile 0.3 to the Lake Youngs Perimeter Trail at a pipeline (mile 0.5). Turn east on the Perimeter Trail along the fence. Watch for deer inside the reservation. At mile 1.1, the perimeter trail runs parallel to Old Petrovitsky Road and at mile 1.4, find an access path from Old Petrovitsky Road. Go left (north) mile on this path to restrooms.

Continuing east, the Perimeter Trail touches or parallels Petrovitsky Road in places before turning southeast along Lake Youngs Road. At mile 4, turn south on 184th Ave. SE, crossing the inlet pipeline coming from the Cedar River Watershed. Leave 184th Ave. SE at mile 4.1 to follow the trail along the boundary fence, making jogs to the south before emerging on SE 224th St. to go west (mile 5.9). Turn north at mile 6.4 to follow the trail along the west boundary of the reservation, emerging near 148th Ave. SE at SE 216th St. Continue north on the perimeter trail to SE 208th St. at mile 8.1. Make a choice here. Either return to parking off Petrovitsky Road or continue to Soos Creek.

If returning to parking off Petrovitsky Road, continue north on the Lake Youngs Perimeter trail, passing SE 200th St. at mile 8.6, and **Lake Youngs Park** on the west side of 148th Ave. SE at mile 8.9. Turn east at SE 183rd St. along the north boundary to reach the path that goes north to parking at mile 10. Total distance around the lake is 9.5 miles.

To go west to Big Soos Creek, at mile 8.1 turn left (west) on SE 208th St. At Soos Creek, mile 8.8, **Gary Grant Park** is north (restrooms, shelter, playground, nature trail). From Gary Grant Park, go south on the paved trail on the west side of Soos Creek, passing a pond in wetland and crossing to the east side of Soos Creek at mile 9.2. At mile 10.5, SE 224th St., jog right (west) on the street across Big Soos Creek to find a continuation of the trail. At mile 11.9, find a signalized crossing of SE 244th St. At mile 12.3, a branch path goes left (west) to a parking area (toilets). Continuing south, reach the end of the trail in **Big Soos Creek Park** at mile 13.8 (toilets). Ride south on 148th Ave. SE to **Lake Meridian Park** on the west side of the street. Go south through the park (shelters, tables, restrooms, boat ramp, swimming area, life guard).

From Lake Meridian Park (mile 14), ride west on Kent-Kangley Road. At mile 18, at a street-side parking area on the south side of Kent-Kangley Road, descend steps into **Mill Creek Park** (shelter, restrooms, ponds, creek, and gardens). A rough path ascends the creek for 0.5 mile. Continue west in the park and in parking lots to pass the **Kent Senior Center** and join Smith St. At Central Ave., turn north to James St., then go west to the Kent Park & Ride and Transit Center (mile 21, Metro 150, etc.). The Interurban Bikeway runs north and south along the east side of the Park & Ride.

LAKE YOUNGS TO WHITE RIVER, high point 621', 30 miles one-way, 800' gain (Maps: USGS Auburn, Renton, Maple Valley). **Mtn. Bicycle or Hike-1 parts.** Tour Lake Youngs, Big Soos Creek, Green River Community College, Auburn, Auburn Game Farm Park, and Roegner Park on the White River. Ride Metro 155 to the intersection of SE Petrovitsky Road and 151st Ave. SE.

Cross Petrovitsky Road south into 151st Ave. SE and ride or walk southeast into SE 183rd Drive. At mile 0.3, turn southwest on 153rd Place SE to a pipeline (mile 0.4). Turn left (south), then go right (west and south) on the gravel trail along the edge of the jungle of vegetation inside the Lake Youngs Reservation. Native plants in view include: Douglas fir, western hemlock, red cedar, salal, huckleberry, bigleaf maple, and red alder. Watch for deer.

At mile 2.1, leave the Lake Youngs Reservation and turn right (west) on SE 208th St., descending to Big Soos Creek at **Gary Grant Park**, mile 2.9 (picnic tables, shelter, playground, restrooms, wetland overlook). After circling north on a paved path, ride south on the paved **Big Soos Creek Trail** on the west side of the creek, passing a pond and crossing a bridge to the east side of the creek at mile 3.3. At mile 4.0, SE 224th St., jog right (west) over the creek on the road to find the trail continuing south near a cattail marsh. Look up the hill west to a decaying barn, evidence of the dairy industry that once occupied this valley. At mile 5.8, find a signalized crossing of SE 244th St., and at mile 6.2, a trail goes right (west) to parking (toilets). Continue south to the end of the trail (parking, toilet), mile 7.3. Ride south on 148th Ave. SE on a wide shoulder, passing a fishing access and boat launch ramp on Lake Meridian at mile 7.5. Turn right (west) into **Lake Meridian Park** at mile 7.6. Go south through the park (shelters, tables, restrooms, boat ramp, swimming area, life guard in summer). If walking, find a Metro 168 stop on Kent-Kangley Road at the south boundary of the park, mile 7.6.

If riding, go west on Kent-Kangley Road, then turn left (south) on 132nd Ave. SE (mile 8.9). At the intersection of SE 288th St., look east to MacDonald Point Lookout (90°), and northeast (38° – 44°), to the summits of Tiger Mountain. At mile 11.4, round west into SE 312nd St. for 0.4 miles before turning south on 124th Ave. SE to enter **Green River Community College** at SE 320th St., mile 12.3. Reach the Community College also by Metro 181 bus. From the Metro bus stop, to find the Student Center (food, restrooms), walk west on Mathews Way.

Explore the campus. At the southeast boundary of the parking lot that encloses the campus on the south side, find a paved accessible trail (no bicycles) that goes south to a viewpoint overlooking the Green River valley and the ridges east. Look for the communication towers on Grass Mountain (114°). At the south end of the paved trail, a wide dirt trail makes a 1.5 mile loop through the forest. Farther west, another trail, possibly unmarked, begins at the south edge of the southernmost parking lot and descends to the Green River (one mile). At 0.4 mile, this trail connects with a trail that goes east and north, following the boundary fence above SR-18 for part of the way, to join the paved trail near the viewpoint at the southeast corner of the campus plateau. A third trail goes west from the west edge of the south parking lot to SE 326th Place and 116th Ave. SE. From this intersection, a trail winds south and east for 0.5 mile to return to the south parking lot.

After wandering the campus, return to SE 320th St. (mile 16) and ride west, descending on 107th Place SE and 105th Place SE to an intersection with Lea Hill Road. Go south to a bridge over the Green River. Proceed west on 8th St., turning south on R St. NE to 3rd St. SE, then go west on 3rd St. SE to M St. SE. Now turn south on M St. SE to Auburn Way S, mile 20. A Metro 150 stop is northwest off Auburn Way S on 6th St. SE. Cross Auburn Way S, then turn east on 17th St. SE and stay on the sidewalk along Auburn Way S. Exit into Howard Road and continue to R St. SE. Turn right (south). At 30th St. SE, turn left (east) into **Auburn Game Farm Park**, mile 21. Facilities: restrooms, ball fields, shelters, playgrounds with equipment, tennis courts, paved paths to the White River and gravel and dirt paths along the river. After exploring the park, return west to R St. SE, mile 22.5, and go south, passing **Ballard Park** on the north bank of the White River (shelter, tables). Cross the White (Stuck) River into Kersey Way. Turn left (east) at mile 22.9 on Stuck River Drive to another part of the Auburn Game Farm Park, entering the park on a paved path on the left (north) side of the road at mile 23.3. Find shelters, restrooms, paved paths, gravel path north to the river bank, and campground with partial hookups.

After circling the park, return west to Kersey Way, then go south to Dravetz Road SE, mile 24.9. Turn right (west) to **Roegner Park**, which begins at mile 25.4. Turn east on a path on the river bank to the end of the pavement (mile 25.6), then return west on the path. Facilities: shelters, restrooms, river access, picnic tables, playground with equipment. On leaving the park, mile 27.0, go southwest on Dravetz Road past Auburn Riverside High School, then west on Dravetz Place and a connecting paved path to East Valley Highway. Turn north across the White River into A St. SE. Proceed north to 6th St. SE. Find the Metro bus stop east on 6th St. SE.

SPRING LAKE–WILDERNESS LAKE, high point 896', 41 miles RT, up to 1400' gain (Maps: USGS Maple Valley, Hobart, Black Diamond, Renton). **Mtn. Bicycle**. From Renton, ride Metro 149 on the Maple Valley Highway (SR-169) to the intersection with 194th Ave. SE (Jones Road), elevation 200'. For additional destinations in Spring Lake Park, see **Spring Lake–Lake Desire–Echo Mountain** below.

Ride west and south on 194th Ave. SE, which becomes 196th Ave. SE at the first intersection. Turn right (west) on SE 162nd St., which becomes successively 194th Ave. SE, SE 160th St., and 193rd Ave. SE. Continue south on 193rd Ave. SE, passing SE 161st St. before turning right (west) on SE 163rd St. Turn left (south) at the stop sign on 190th Ave. SE, mile 0.6. Pass under power lines at mile 0.8 with a view of Tiger Mtn. (east). Stay left on 190th Ave. SE at SE 174th Way and SE 176th St. Where 190th Ave. SE ends (mile 1.5), continue south on a trail that follows an easement, emerging on W Spring Lake Drive SE at mile 1.7. Turn right (west) to **Spring Lake Park**, mile 2.1. A public fishing access descends south to Spring Lake (boat ramp, toilets, Otter Lake on USGS map). From the gate, ride southwest into **Spring Lake Park** on a gravel road, then turn left (south) on a branch road at mile 2.3.

Pass a trail to **Spring Lake Fen** (possibly unsigned) in 0.1 mile then meet the outlet stream from Lake Desire at mile 2.8. Return north to the entrance to Spring Lake Fen. Leave bicycle and explore this marshy area as far as the shore of Spring Lake. Return to bicycle and go right (northeast) to the park entrance. Turn right to the Spring Lake fishing access for another view of the lake. Leave Spring Lake Park (mile 4.8), going east into W Spring Drive SE. Pass a junction with E Spring Lake Drive SE and join SE 183rd St. before reaching 196th Ave. SE at mile 5.8. Turn south on 196th Ave. SE to SE Petrovitsky Road, mile 6.9. Ride southeast, joining Sweeney Road SE briefly before turning left on SE 232nd St., which crosses over SR-18 and becomes SE 231st St. before reaching the Maple Valley Highway (SR-169), mile 10.

Turn south on the west side of SR-169 to the next street, Wax Road (McDonalds), then go southeast. South of the Maple Valley Postoffice, find a wide gravel track and continue south. A path on the left (east) connects with the **Maple Valley–Black Diamond Rail Trail**, reaching the trail near the south end of a tunnel under SR-169. Turn left (north) and ride the rail trail under SR-169 and SE 231st St., descending to meet the **Cedar River Rail Trail** at the bottom of the hill, mile 11.1. Ride east, crossing the Cedar River on erector set railroad bridges at mile 11.9, mile 12.6, and mile 14.7, to the end of the trail at the Landsburg Road, mile 16. The railroad grade beyond enters the Cedar River watershed (closed).

Return west on the Cedar River Trail to the Maple Valley junction, mile 20.9. Turn south on the trail past the Wilderness Shopping Center, riding under 232nd St. SE at the first underpass, and under SR-169 at the second underpass. Continue south on the trail toward Black Diamond. Enter the **South King County Arboretum** at mile 22.4 (fence). Several trails give access to the arboretum and a sign (subject to vandalism) sometimes provides a map. Near the fence marking the south boundary of the arboretum, trails go west to **Lake Wilderness Park** (picnicking, shelters, restrooms open April to October). Pass the south end of Lake Wilderness at mile 23.2. Reach the Kent-Kangley Road at mile 24.3. Turn left (east) to SR-169 and go north to return to the Wilderness Shopping Center at Maple Valley, mile 27.4. The Metro 149 stop is north of SE 231st St. on the east side of SR-169.

The **Cedar River Rail Trail** north from Maple Valley to Renton (13 miles) is gravel for the first 5 miles and paved for the last eight miles (Jones Road) into Renton. Gain access to the rail trail one mile north on SR-169 from the Wilderness Shopping Center . A park two miles east of Renton has restrooms (open April-October), shelter, and picnic tables. If entering Renton from the Cedar Valley Rail Trail on the south side of the Cedar River, find a pedestrian bridge under I-405 at the east edge of Renton that crosses to the north side of the Cedar River. After crossing the river, turn left (northwest) across Houser Way, then go southwest to the northeast bank of the Cedar River. Now follow the walkway northwest near the Cedar River to pass the Renton Library, which spans the Cedar River (look for fish). Emerge on Bronson St. near Metro stops.

SPRING LAKE–LAKE DESIRE–ECHO MOUNTAIN, high point 896', 4 miles of trails, 500' gain (Maps: USGS Maple Valley). **Hike-2**. Drive west from the Maple Valley Highway (SR-169) at 194th Ave. SE, which becomes 196th Ave. SE at the first intersection. Continue south on 196th Ave. SE to SE 183rd St. Turn right into SE 183rd St. and again right into E Spring Lake Drive SE. Follow this street as it becomes W Spring Lake Drive SE to **Spring Lake Park** (may not be signed), one mile from 196th Ave. SE, elevation 500' (toilets).

Walk southwest from the entrance on a gravel road, then turn left (south) on a branch road 0.2 miles from the park entrance. Find a minimum trail 200' south of the junction that goes east into the Spring Lake Fen, an open boggy flat west of the lake. Find the following plants along the trail: western hemlock, red cedar, lichen, huckleberry on nurse stumps, vine maple, and salal. Near the lake the ground is carpeted with deep moss and patches of light gray lichen. One or more paths reach the lake near the south end.

To reach the summit of **Echo Mountain**, 896', go right (north) at the first junction 0.2 mile from the entrance, then, at subsequent junctions, take the uphill fork, topping out on the road 0.7 mile from the park entrance, east of a water tank. Leave the road and ascend north on a steep, narrow, eroded, branch trail, the last bit over bedrock ground smooth by the **Puget Glacier**. The summit (896') is covered by clumps of service berry. Other plants: orange honeysuckle, kinnikinick, willow, ocean spray, and indian plum. Look for Mt. Rainier (south) and Tiger Mtn. (east).

To visit **Lake Desire**, walk the road and trail west from the park entrance. Where the trail joins a wider road, continue west. Pass the first branch trail left, which goes to a street and more trails, then take the next branch left to a lake access.

FLAMING GEYSER STATE PARK, high point 400', 5 miles of trails, 200' gain (Maps: USGS Auburn, Black Diamond). **Bicycle and/or Hike**. Ride Metro 150 to the last stop in Auburn. Ride east on 6th St.

SE to Auburn Way S. Turn north under SR-18, then go east on 4th St. SE. Jog north at M St. into 3rd St. SE. Turn right into R St. and continue on Auburn–Black Diamond Road and SE Green Valley Road. Reach the park 11 miles from the bus stop. If driving, two miles east of Auburn on SR-18, take exit to Auburn-Black Diamond Road. Drive east on SE Green Valley Road to the State Park, 8 miles east of SR-18. Park in the picnic area at the end of the road (restrooms).

The flaming geyser is east of the end of the road. A 1400' deep test hole made in 1911 penetrates several coal seams and allows methane associated with the coal to escape. Now the bore hole has been plugged and only a few bubbles of methane rise in the water at the bottom of the pit. Methane still escapes from a pipe in the center of the plug. If not burning, relight with spark or match.

Trails: The river trail ascends east along the river for one mile and ends at steeply dipping sedimentary beds that descend into the water. A hill trail (landslides) begins in the picnic area at the east end of the paved road and ascends south past the flaming geyser test hole. A spring farther along emits toxic hydrogen sulfide, which arises from sulfur in the coal. This trail ascends west, with a branch north to the park entrance. Various trails return east, passing picnic areas, play areas, and restrooms.

MACDONALD POINT LOOKOUT, high point 3280', 8 miles RT, 2500' gain (Maps: USGS Cumberland, Eagle Gorge). **Hike-1 or Mt. Bicycle**. From the Maple Valley Highway, SR-169, at the junction with SR-516, Drive east on the Kent-Kangley Road for 3.6 miles. Turn southeast on Retreat-Kanaskat Road SE for 3.2 miles to the junction with the Cumberland-Kanaskat Road SE. Continue east on the Kanaskat-Kangley Road SE for 0.7 miles. Where Kanaskat-Kangley Road bends north, park 7.5 miles from the Maple Valley Highway at the junction with SE Courtney Road, elevation 874'.

Ride or hike east across two nearly imperceptible abandoned railroad grades then immediately turn left after the second railroad grade on a gated forest road (0.1 mile, W-5000) and ascend north. At mile 0.4, 1050', road W-5002 turns right. Pass a viewpoint west at mile 0.6. At mile 1.0, 1340', road W-5005 goes left. Cross a stream at mile 1.3, 1540', then pass road W-5009 on the left. After road W-5010 goes right at mile 1.5, the clearcuts above and below the road are colorful with foxglove and fireweed in July. At mile 2.3, 2160', stop at a gated branch road that descends north for a partial view toward Tiger Mountain and a better view west and south. Find more roads at mile 2.6. At mile 3.4, 2820', reach a quarry and a fork in the road.

Take the right, uphill, fork on road W-5012, going right (uphill) at the first junction and left (uphill) at the second junction to reach the crest of the ridge. Take the right fork to the lookout site, now a communication point that uses a cylindrical metal tower. The view south includes Grass Mtn. (163°) and Mt. Rainier. The road along the crest of the ridge goes east another 0.5 mile and ends at 3200' at the edge of dense older forest on the west slope of a 3301' point.

GREEN RIVER GORGE, high point 844', 14 mile loop, 800' gain (Maps: USGS Cumberland). **Bicycle**. Ride Metro 149 to Black Diamond. If driving, park at the Park & Ride in Black Diamond, elevation 640'.

Ride south on SR-169, passing Jones Lake at mile 0.4 (no access). Pass SE Green Valley Road (mile 1.6), then pause on the bridge over the Green River Gorge to admire waterfalls and sandstone cliffs. At mile 4.1, turn northeast on the Enumclaw–Franklin Road, entering the valley of the Green River at mile 7. Go left on Green River Gorge Road (mile 8.1) to a high bridge over the Green River with views of cliffs, waterfalls, and water-carved bedrock in the canyon (no parking and no off-road access).

From the bridge, proceed north on Green River Gorge Road, pausing for views of snow-covered (in winter) hills: McDonald Point ($68^{c}irc$). At mile 11, turn north into a fishing access on Lake Number 12. Beginning at mile 12, a board fence on the right (north) side of the highway partially obscures the view of an open pit coal mine. The strata containing the coal dip steeply into a lake at the bottom of the pit. West of the pit, the rounded hills are old mine dumps.

Continue west into Black Diamond, then go west on Baker St. to the Black Diamond Museum (open Thursday, Saturday and Sunday). From the museum, the Black Diamond Bakery is south on Railroad Ave.

Parks:

WEST HYLEBOS STATE PARK, high point 240', 1 mile of trails and board walks, minimum gain (Maps: USGS Poverty Bay). **Walk**. Take Metro 174, 194, etc., to the South Federal Way Park & Ride and walk west, or if driving, leave I-5 at Exit-142 and go west on S 348th St. to the park, 0.3 miles past the South Federal Way Park & Ride.

Facilities: wetland, ponds, peat bog, nature trail. The water gaps in the bog can be more than 10' deep. Find the following native plants, many with explanatory signs: bitter cherry, indian plum, blackberry, salmonberry, alder, red cedar, bigleaf maple, currant, vine maple, Pacific crabapple, rose, western hemlock, Sitka spruce, salal, cascara, labrador tea, black twinberry,, elderberry, red huckleberry, red osier dogwood, spirea, mountain ash, and false azalea.

The Denny Cabin, built by David Denny in 1889, has been moved here and is being restored.

KANASKAT–PALMER STATE PARK, high point 880'(Maps: USGS Cumberland). **Hike-1**. The park is located south of the Green River and eight miles north of Enumclaw on the Enumclaw-Kanaskat Road, which begins from SR-410 as 284th Ave. SE one mile east of SR-169. To reach the park from the north, drive east from the Maple Valley Highway (SR-169) at the junction with SR-516. At 3.6 miles from SR-169, turn southeast on Retreat-Kanaskat Road SE for 3.2 miles. Turn south on Cumberland-Kanaskat Road SE for 3.6 miles to the park entrance. Facilities: camping, hiking trails, boating access to the Green River. Visit at both high and low water.

Loop, 4 miles, 200' gain. **Hike-1**. At the entrance to the park, where the road is divided around a grass and tree island, look for a gated grass path into the forest west of the entrance. Hike north to a junction in a grove of 3'-diameter cedar trees near the Green River. Turn right 450' to a sandstone ledge beside a deep pool at a sharp bend in the Green River. Return to the junction in the cedar trees after exploring one or more paths to the river. Continue north on the path, passing picnic tables, a shelter, and a group camp area. Next pass a boater parking area on the left with restrooms and, on the right, trail access to the river and a boater put-in by a quiet pool. Now the Perimeter Trail continues north with occasional views of the river and trail access, then bends west, leaving the river before making a zig-zag up the hill to pass on the north side of the main camping area (restrooms). Turn right (northwest) at the next trail junction to return to the river, passing a day-use parking area: restrooms, shelter, paved paths, picnic tables. Take the right fork at trail branches to reach a viewpoint where the river, at a sharp bend to the south, drops over a sandstone ledge. Sandstone cliffs enclose the river on the north side.

Return from the river on the path to the parking and day use area, then turn south on a path near the river. Return to the river on several different paths for views of pools and rapids. Reach another day use picnic area near the river at the lower boater take-out where the river turns west and sandstone cliffs bar the way on the south bank. At the river edge a sandstone ledge is exposed at low water. Now leave the river, turning east to a paved road. Walk north on the road to a road junction. From this junction, follow a grass path south in the forest, bending east to the park entrance. To reach the Perimeter Trail from the main camping area, walk northwest from the north side of the restrooms, then follow the trail as described above.

NOLTE STATE PARK, 780' (Maps: USGS Cumberland). **Walk.** Find the park four miles south of Kanaskat-Palmer State Park (see above) or four miles north of SR-410 at Enumclaw on the Enumclaw-Kanaskat Road (284th Ave. NE). Facilities: picnicking and swimming, no camping, no power boats.

North Seattle Area.

From the ship canal into south Snohomish County.

UNIVERSITY OF WASHINGTON, high point 220', 3 miles RT, 200' gain (Maps: University of Washington, USGS Seattle North). **Walk.** This tour of the campus supplements the description given in *A Campus Walk*, available free along with a map of the campus from the Visitors Information Center, 4014 University Way NE. Begin at the north end of the Montlake Bridge, reached by Metro 25, 43, 44, 48, or park in the stadium parking lot free on most Saturday afternoons and Sundays.

If starting from the east side of Montlake Blvd., go east on a path, then return west at a branch to a stairway. Descend south and go west along the Montlake Cut under the Montlake Bridge. If starting from the west side of Montlake Blvd., go west to descend a stairway south to the water level, then turn west. At the west end of the paved path, ascend steps to the grounds of the Center for Human Development and Disabilities and continue west near the waterfront. Pass a pond where salmon return that were raised in the Department of Fisheries Hatchery. In the summer and fall this pond is sometimes teeming with fish. Continue west to pass a viewpoint with tables, benches, and interpretive sign, then bend south around the Marine Sciences building where much equipment used in research is stored. At the west end of the building, turn right (north) to 15th Ave. NE and pass west of the Health Sciences group of buildings. At NE Pacific Ave., bend right (northeast) to a pedestrian overpass and cross NE Pacific Ave. Turn left (west) on the Burke-Gilman Trail past the Physics Building with state-of-the-art **sundial**. Turn right (north) on the west side of the Physics Building and ascend steps. Look in the windows of the Physics Building to see the **Foucault Pendulum**.

Exit northeast to Stevens Way and go north to the next street. Turn west on Asotin Place and follow the street around to the north. Ascend steps on the right to examine an architects model for a pedestrian overpass. Continue north over Stevens Way, passing between a parking garage and Meany Hall (brick). Find a statue of George Washington looking east near the Henry Art Gallery. Stay north on paved paths to the grounds south of the Burke Museum at the northwest corner of the campus where several examples of petrified wood, fossilized palm leaves, and other rocks are displayed. Turn east over Memorial Drive to the Observatory, then go south to pass west of **Denny Hall** with bell tower (1895), the oldest building on campus. Bend around the south side of Denny Hall, then go northeast to pass between Raitt Hall and the Art Building. Enter the Social Sciences quadrangle, lined with Japanese cherry trees that blossom in April. Circle the quadrangle, then exit from the east side to the Edvard Grieg Garden, noted for rhododendrons. Northwest of the Grieg Garden, find a specimen of *Sequoia gigantea*.

Exit south from the Grieg Garden and turn west along the joined Allen and Suzzalo Libraries (note remarkably different architectural styles) into Red Square with **Broken Obelisk**. Cross Red Square to the west side, then descend steps south into a sunken garden with metal sculpture and bamboo plants. Go east and south through the underground parking garage to Grant Lane. Bend left across the street to six examples of granitic rock spaced in the lawn. Go south on the next walkway to the east into the courtyard of Johnson Hall where rock specimens are on display.

Continue south into the Atmospheric Sciences building for a look at the current weather displays in the southwest corridor on the second floor: air temperature, barometric pressure, wind speed, and wind direction. Exit south from Atmospheric Sciences, turning left (east) to the **Rose Garden** and Drumheller Fountain. Return west to Okanogan Lane, go south briefly, then turn west across the south side of Benson Hall. Descend steps east into the Medicinal Plant Garden to find plants with identifying markers. Continue east in the botanical displays, then cross south over Stevens Way to the east side of Anderson Hall, which houses the College of Forest Resources. Go south between Anderson Hall and Winkenwerder Hall to find a display slice of a 7' diameter red cedar tree under Winkenwerder Hall. Return north to Stevens Way and go east and north past More Hall (bust of James J. Hill). Turn right (east) to find, on the north side of More Hall, a small concrete building that houses a subcritical nuclear reactor.

Now go east to the Burke-Gilman Trail. Turn south and east to cross 25th Ave. NE. Turn north along 25th Ave. NE to pass public art (UW mascot). Bend east around Hec Edmundson pavilion, then follow the waterfront north. Cross east over the first bridge into a parking lot and nature study area. Find a gravel path and walk east and south to the shore of Union Bay. In winter, ponds fill subsidence depressions in the underlying landfill. Look for plantings of red-osier dogwood, Oregon ash, red alder, snowberry, oceanspray, bulrush and sedges. Older cottonwood trees predate the landfill. Follow the trail to a viewpoint. The relief is the result of subsidence as the garbage sinks into 150 feet of underlying peat. Follow the trail northeast to the Center for Urban Horticulture and explore the gardens.

Return west across parking lots and a bridge. Turn south and follow roads along the waterfront east of the stadium. The grass playing fields along the way feed hundreds of Canada geese in winter. At the ship canal, turn west past the Canoe House and a climbing rock to return to the starting point at the Montlake Bridge.

BALLARD LOCKS–LAKE WASHINGTON LOOP, high point 360', 26 miles, 550' gain (Maps: USGS Shilshole Bay, Seattle North). **Mt. Bicycle**. Take Metro 17, 44, or 46 to Ballard Locks or park at Ballard Locks.

Ride northwest on NW 54th St. and Seaview Ave. NW to the beginning of Shilshole Marina at mile 1.0. Explore north along the waterfront of Shilshole Bay beginning at Pier A. The Port-of-Seattle Administration Building, in the center of the marina at mile 1.4, has restrooms and a restaurant. Continue north to the end of **Golden Gardens Park** (mile 2.8). Return south to the bathhouse in Golden Gardens Park, then go east through a railroad underpass into a parking area. Go north to a trail that ascends diagonally up the steep slope to a meadow (restrooms, picnic tables, and playground). Ride and walk north until the trail ends in a thicket. This level area is the top of **landslides**, and the leaning trees indicate continuing movement. Note recent landslides. The cliffs are poorly consolidated deposits left by the Puget Glacier. These deposits are still actively eroding and receding, possibly more rapidly now as a result of human intervention. Return to the meadow, and ascend on the road to the corner of NW 85th At. and 32nd Ave. NW (mile 4.5).

Ride east on NW 85th St. to 8th Ave. NW. Turn south to NW 83th St. and continue east on a quiet street. At Aurora Ave. N, go north to NW 85th St. and cross. At Midvale Ave. N, turn north to N 90th St. Go east one block to Stone Ave. N. Turn north to the Indian Heritage School. Go north on the west side of the buildings. After passing the last of the school buildings, ride diagonally northeast across a parking area to the next building. Descend a short flight of steps and continue northeast to Ashworth Ave. N at N 92nd St. Go north to **Licton Springs Park**. Licton Springs, a warm spring once used by the Indians and later as a spa and source of mineral water, now barely flows. Pavement and buildings have reduced the underground water source. Several ponds (winter) remain from ancient wetlands. Signs tell the history of the park. Facilities: picnicking, restrooms.

From Licton Springs Park, go east on N 95th St. to the **North Seattle Community College** for a tour of the campus. From the campus, return west to Wallingford Ave. N or to less travelled Densmore Ave. N. Turn south to **Green Lake Park** at the corner of East Green Lake Drive N and Wallingford Ave. N (mile 10). Ride southwest on the shoreline path around Greenlake, going counterclockwise past the Bathhouse Theater. At the water sports viewing stand, leave the lake to a path into **Woodland Park** along the north edge of tennis courts. Go west into forest, then turn south and follow trails until near the south boundary. Return north on a paved path to cross a foot bridge west over Aurora Ave. N. Pass the **Rose Garden** and circle clockwise around the Zoological Gardens to Phinney Ave. N. At N 57th St., turn east through playfields and along the boundary of the Zoological Gardens. At Aurora Ave. N, turn south on a path to the first foot bridge. Cross Aurora Ave. N into Woodland Park and continue east, passing picnic tables and parking areas to return to Green Lake. Go east on the lakeshore path. Before reaching the building that houses the swimming pool, bend east to reach E Greenlake Way N at the north end of Ravenna Blvd. (mile 15). Ride southeast on the bikeway on Ravenna Blvd. to Brooklyn Ave. N. Turn north on Brooklyn Ave. N to a path into **Ravenna Park** (ride bicycles only on paths at least 5' wide). Descend along the creek in Ravenna Park, finding a sulfur spring near the creek east of the 20th Ave. NE bridge, and exiting the park at a playfield to NE 55th St. Cross and ride southeast on Ravenna Place NE to NE Blakeley St.

Cross to the east side of 25th Ave. NE and go south, turning east into University Village Shopping Center (stores, restaurants) at the first street. Turn to the south in the shopping center. At the south perimeter road, turn left (east) and exit on a walkway under NE 45th St. Cross Montlake Blvd. NE. Circle west and south around the golf driving range, turning east at the first street across parking lots to a stream channel. Turn south on roads to Lake Washington. Go south and west along the shoreline at the east edge of the University of Washington to the Montlake Bridge (mile 19) and Metro stops. To return to the Ballard Locks, find the Burke–Gilman Trail across NE Pacific St. Go west for 6 miles on the Burke–Gilman Trail and the Ship Canal Bikeway .

GOLDEN GARDENS TO RICHMOND BEACH, high point 300', 6 miles one-way, 300' gain (Maps: USGS Seattle North, Shilshole Bay, Edmonds West). **Hike-2**. This hike is recommended only at the lowest tides, preferably zero or less (see tide tables in US West Seattle Yellow Pages). Take Metro 46 to the end of the line at **Shilshole Marina** and walk north along the shoreline or ride Metro 48 to the end of the line at the west end of NW 85th St., elevation 300'.

From Metro 48, descend steps across 32nd Ave. NW from NW 85th St. into **Golden Gardens Park** and turn north. From Metro 46, walk the beach north. The first exit from the beach after leaving Golden Gardens occurs at **Carkeek Park** (pedestrian railroad overpass, restrooms, picnicking) two miles after leaving Golden Gardens. Walk stony beach for one-half mile after leaving Carkeek Park, then continue on sandy beach with wide tide flats for most of the rest of the way to Richmond Beach. North of Carkeek Park, rocks tumbled from the railroad embankment block the route require minor scrambling except at tides of -1.5 feet. Watch for the geysers of clams along the route (not safe to eat). At **Richmond Beach Park** (restrooms, picnicking), ascend paths and stairways to the park entrance. Walk north on 20th Ave. NW to NW 195th St. to the Metro 315 stop.

SHILSHOLE TO MARYMOOR PARK, high point 150', 33 miles one-way, minimum gain (Maps: USGS Shilshole Bay, Seattle North, Edmonds East, Bothell, Kirkland, Redmond). **Bicycle**. Take Metro 46 to Shilshole Marina in Ballard at NW 71st St. and Seaview Ave. NW or take Metro 44 or 17 to Ballard Locks and ride west on NW 54th St. and Seaview Ave. NW. Road log miles begin at the Metro 46 stop north of the Administration Building (restaurant, restrooms) at Shilshole.

For the view north and west, loop north one mile along the waterfront through **Golden Gardens Park** to the end of the path before riding south along the edge of the marina. Detour west to the end of the **fishing pier** at Pier A. Continue south on Seaview Ave. NW, then go east into NW 54th St. Stop at the **Hiram Chittenden Locks** (mile 3, restrooms) for a tour of the locks, gardens, and the fish ladder on the south side of the locks.

From the Locks, continue east on NW 54th St. into NW Market St. Bend right into Shilshole Ave. NW at 24th Ave. NW (mile 3.5). Where the arterial angles left, continue under the Ballard Bridge ramp into NW 45th St. Turn right on Leary Way NW, and again right (south) at 8th Ave. NW to the west end of the ship canal bikeway. Where the bikeway ends at an industrial area, follow markings under the Fremont Bridge. Rejoin the bikeway and continue east. Under the Aurora Bridge, ascend north to view the **Fremont Troll** at 34th St. Return to bikeway at the waterfront and continue east past marinas, ship chandlers, and a ship repair drydock. At the west edge of **Gas Works Park** (mile 7), turn right to tour around the remaining gas works equipment and to the beach for the view across Lake Union toward downtown Seattle (restrooms).

From Gas Works Park, cross N Northlake Way to a choice of bikeways. The high route goes east on the **Burke–Gilman Trail**, a converted railroad grade along N Pacific St., and the low route follows a bikeway along N Northlake Way to pass marinas, restaurants, and taverns. The two routes rejoin at Brooklyn Ave. N after crossing under I-5 and the University Bridge. Continue east on the Burke–Gilman Trail to the **University of Washington Campus** (mile 9). In addition to many interesting buildings, blossoming cherry trees and rhododendrons (March to May) make a detour into the campus worthwhile. To reach the cherry trees, turn north on 15th Ave. NE to NE 42nd St., then go east past Denny Hall (1895). The cherry trees are east of the next row of buildings. To return to the Burke–Gilman Trail, continue east and descend Pend Oreille Road to the trail on the west side of 25th Ave. NE.

The Burke–Gilman Trail bends north along the east edge of the campus, going past a shopping center after crossing 25th Ave. NE (mile 10). At mile 13, turn right (east) on NE 65th St. to cross Sand Point Way NE into **Magnuson Park** on the shore of Lake Washington. On nearing the lake, go right (south) to the shoreline at the park boundary. Now proceed north near the shore where board sailors congregate on windy days. Pass **Sound Garden** (a wind organ of tuned vertical pipes) that is worth a special visit during high wind. The wind organ is best during gusty conditions. Continue north and west past the NOAA facility (cafeteria) at the north end of Magnuson Park. Exit west at the north end of Magnuson Park to Sand Point Way NE and ride north to NE 90th Place. Turn right (northeast), then bend north to cross a foot bridge into **Matthews Beach** (playground, picnicking, swimming, restrooms in summer). At the north edge of the park, rejoin the Burke–Gilman Trail (mile 15). Reach Lake Forest Park Shopping Center (bakeries, restaurants) at NE 170th St. (mile 19). After another mile, pause at **Tracy Owen Station**, which has restrooms, playground, picnic tables, beach, and a fishing pier.

From Tracy Owen Station, go east on the Burke–Gilman Trail to the underpass at 68th Ave. NE (mile 21). **Kenmore Park**, 0.4 mile south on 68th Ave. NE at NE 170th St., has picnic facilities, playground, restrooms in summer, and a brilliant display of rhododendrons in spring. At 73rd Ave. NE, view a **heronry** (February to April), by crossing Bothell Way NE to the Kenmore Park & Ride (one block east on Bothell Way). The heronry is beyond the north end of the Park & Ride in the tops of trees growing in a wetland. The herons return about the first of February and nest activity is visible until the trees leaf. The heronry is also visible from the **Kenmore Library**, three blocks north from the Burke–Gilman Trail on 73rd Ave. NE.

At Wayne Golf Course (mile 22), visit a segment of the **Yellowstone Road**, which was opened in 1914 as the first paved link between Bothell and Seattle, by going north 50' across a parking area to the brick paving (informative sign). More bricks are exposed east of Bothell Way at the intersection of Waynita Drive NE. Until the first floating bridge across Lake Washington was opened in 1939, this was the main road east from Seattle.

At mile 23, two bridges cross the Sammamish River. From the east end of the bridges, paved trails go southeast to **Blyth Park** (restrooms, trails, picnicking, playground, access to the Sammamish River). **Bothell Landing Park** is next on the Burke–Gilman Trail. A footbridge crosses the Sammamish River to a nature trail, restrooms, playground, museum, the Beckstrom Log Cabin (1883), a Bothell Schoolhouse (1885), the Lytle House (1898), and the Northshore Senior Day Center. At 102nd Ave. NE (underpass), the **Northshore Senior Center** is 0.25 mile south on 102nd Ave. NE. An exercise course begins here. The trail crosses to the north side of the river (mile 24) before passing under I-405. After going under railroad and street bridges (mile 26), find **Wilmot Gateway Park** (restrooms, playground, shelter, tables, ampitheater, river access) and a ramp that joins NE 175th St. in Woodinville (Metro 307 stop). The Trail continues south on the east side of the Sammamish River, passing more exercise course, **Woodin Creek Park** (courts, horseshoe pits, shelter), restrooms, picnic areas, an espresso stand, shelters, and a parking area before going under NE 145th St. (mile 28). Two wineries and a brewery are west on NE 145th St. (tours). At mile 32, pass Redmond City Hall, the **Redmond Library**, and the **Redmond Senior Center**. Next are exits to Redmond Way, a picnic area and shelter, and a ramp to the river. Cross the river to the west side at Leary Way. Reach the bridge into **Marymoor Park** at the end of the Burke–Gilman Trail, mile 33. Facilities: trails, shelters, restrooms, velodrome, playgrounds, model airplane field, picnicking areas, and access to Lake Sammamish. The Clise Mansion (1904), originally a hunting lodge, houses the Marymoor Museum. Look for the sign describing archeological research at nearby Native American campsites.

Find Metro 249 and 251 stops on W Lake Sammamish Parkway NE at the entrance to Marymoor Park or return to Seattle on the Sammamish River trail and the Burke–Gilman Trail. For other Metro stops, go north on the Sammamish River Trail, crossing the river at Leary Way NE. Go east to 161st Ave. NE and north to the Redmond Park & Ride. To reach a Metro 307 stop, return north eight miles on the Sammamish River trail and take the NE 175th St. exit east into Woodinville.

SAMMAMISH RIVER TO BOTHELL, high point 480', 5 miles one-way, 700' gain (Maps: USGS Bothell, Kirkland). **Mtn. Bicycle**. This route makes an alternate return from the Sammamish River Trail at NE 145th St. to the Burke–Gilman Trail between Kenmore and Bothell. For Metro access, ride Metro 307 to Woodinville. Ride west to the Burke–

Gilman Trail and south to NE 145th St.

Where the **Sammamish River Trail** crosses NE 145th St., ride west and northwest on Woodinville–Redmond Road (SR-202), passing two wineries and a brewery. Find the **Tolt River Pipeline** (gate) 0.2 mile northwest from NE 145th St. Ascend west, crossing 132nd Ave. NE and 124th Ave. NE before reaching **East Norway Hill Park** (picnic table, no other facilities). Continue west along the pipeline to the frontage road on the east side of I-405. Go right to NE 160th St., cross I-405 west and ride southwest on the Juanita–Woodinville Road to 112th Ave. NE. Turn right (north) to return to the pipeline. Go west on the pipeline and ascend to Norway Hill, elevation 480'. On reaching 104th Ave. NE, leave bicycle and walk west past a gate to a view of the Olympic Mountains. Return to bicycle and ride south on 104th Ave. NE and 105th Ave. NE to NE 145th St. Go west to Waynita Way. Turn right (north) to the Burke–Gilman Trail at Wayne Golf Course. Go left (west) to Seattle or Metro stops at 80th St. NE.

SNO–KING LOOP, high point 540', 20 miles, 2300' gain (Maps: USGS Edmonds East, Bothell, Kirkland). **Bicycle.** This trip makes a loop with significant elevation gain in King and Snohomish Counties. Take Metro bus to the Lake Forest Park Shopping Center at NE 170th St. (307) or Ballinger Way NE (340). If driving, park at Tracy Owen Station off Bothell Way at 61st Ave. NE and ride west one mile on the Burke–Gilman Trail to Forest Park Shopping Center.

Mileage log begins at the corner of NE 170th St. and Bothell Way NE. Ride north through Forest Park Shopping Center (bakeries, restrooms) and ascend the ramp between Rite-Aid and Washington Mutual. Cross Ballinger Way at the signal into NE 175th St. Tun left on 47th Ave. NE to NE 178th St. Turn right and ride northeast on NE 178th St., which becomes NE 182nd St. Turn left on 58th Ave. NE (mile 1.0) to NE 187th St. Turn left again, staying on NE 187th St., ascending steeply to 53rd Ave. NE. Stop to look back (east) at the Cascade Mountains. NE 187th St. points just to the left of Mount Index. After a jog to the south on 53rd Ave. NE (mile 1.5), continue west on NE 187th St. NE 187th St. rounds to the north and descends to a stop sign. Go left and follow NE 187th Place, 47th Ave. NE, and 47th Place NE to emerge on Horizon Crest at the junction of 47th Ave. NE and NE 195th St. (mile 2.4). Bend left (west) on NE 195th St., passing south of a reservoir to an outlook. NE 195th St. points west at Mt. Constance (270°). Mount Jupiter (262°) and The Brothers (258°) are south of Mt. Constance. Go north on 45th Ave. NE into a trail that passes west and north of the reservoir into **Horizon View Park**, rejoining 47th Ave. NE. At the north end of the playground, find a concrete platform (now used for basketball practice) remaining from a Nike missile battery that was located here during the 1940's . The street (47th Ave. NE) points north at Mt. Baker with Mt. Shuksan the sharp point barely visible to the right.

Continue north to the next street corner, NE 201st Place (mile 3.0). Go right (east) on NE 201st Place one block for a view east to the Cascades, including Whitehorse (44°), Three Fingers (46°), Glacier Peak (65°), Phelps (100°), and Mt. Si (125°). Return west on NE 201st Place across 47th Ave. NE and continue into NE 197th St. Go right (northeast) on NE 203rd St. into 45th Ave. NE, rounding left (west) into NE 205th St. Turn right on 42nd Ave. NE, entering Snohomish County. The street becomes Alaska Way when it curves east. At the first intersection beyond a cemetery, turn left (west) on 35th Ave. W and proceed to 236th St. SW. Turn right (north) to cross Brier Road. The summit directly east from 236th St. SW is Mount Persis. Mount Index is the next summit right. Stay on 236th St. SW as the street curves north down the hill, then turn right (east) on Castle Way to 234th Place SW. Now go left to Locust Way (mile 5.5). Turn left (north), crossing Swamp Creek, to 228th St. SW. Ascend steeply east on a busy street with a walkable shoulder. At the crest of the ridge, pass the Federal Emergency Management Agency on the right (south) with its deep bomb resistant bunkers built on a former Nike site. Turn right (south) on Meridian (Pontius) to 240th St. SE (mile 7.5). Go left (east) on 240th St. SE to Bothell Way NE (mile 8.2). Descend right (south) into Bothell. At NE 183rd St., **Bothell Library** is two blocks west on 98th Ave. NE. Turn east to 102nd Ave. NE, then go right (south) to Main St. Turn left (east) to 104th Ave. NE. Jog right (southeast) on Kaysner Way briefly, then go left (east) on Valley View Road to 108th Ave. NE and the Bothell Pioneer Cemetery where many of the city's founders are buried. Return to 102nd Ave. NE and go south over SR-522 and the Sammamish River. Reach the junction of Riverside Drive (mile 11.4) at the entrance to the **Northshore Senior Center**.

Choose from two routes here. One route turns east on Riverside Drive for 0.4 mile, then goes south on 112th Place NE, and west on NE 164th Place into NE 168th St. to reach 104th Ave. NE at the crest of the ridge (adds one mile). The other route continues south from the junction of 102nd Ave. NE and Riverside Drive NE on an easement, turning right (west) at a junction half way up to round past an old reservoir into 105th Ave. NE. Continue southeast up the paved street, going right (west) after joining NE 168th St. to reach 104th Ave. NE. On the way up the hill, look north for a view of Mt. Baker (20°) and northeast to Glacier Peak (64°) and Mt. Stickney (70°). Go south along the crest of Norway Hill on 104th NE with views of the Cascade Mountains. At the Norway

Hill sign on 104th Ave. NE, look for distinctive Mt. Phelps (96°) and Mt. Si (126°).

Coast south on 104th Ave. NE to reach NE 145th St. Turn right (west) on NE 145th St., then go left (south) on 100th Ave. NE to NE 132nd St. (mile 15). Go right (west) on NE 132nd St. into 90th Ave. NE. At NE 134th St., turn left (west), south on 87th Ave. NE, and west on NE 132nd St. to reach Juanita Drive, passing Finn Hill Junior High School at 84th Ave. NE. Turn right (north) on Juanita Drive. The entrance to **Big Finn Hill Park** is 0.2 mile east on NE 138th St. (toilets). Continue north on Juanita Drive to NE 147th St. at a shopping center. Turn left (west) and descend into **St. Edward State Park**. Keep right to a parking area (restrooms). Leave bicycle and walk down to the lakeshore for a view toward the towers of Seattle and the Olympic Mountains. Return to Juanita Drive. Turn left (north) to Bothell Way NE (mile 20) and the Metro 307, 340 stops. To reach parking at Tracy Owen Station, turn left (west) on the Burke–Gilman Trail on the south side of Bothell Way.

NORTH LAKE SUMMITS, high point 540', 8 miles, 1200' gain (Maps: USGS Edmonds East, Bothell). **Hike-1**. This route goes generally east near or on the Seattle Water Department Tolt River pipeline. Take Metro 307 to NE 170th St. or Metro 340 to Ballinger Way NE off Bothell Way NE at the Lake Forest Park Shopping Center (bakeries). If driving, park at Tracy Owen Station off Bothell Way at 61st Ave. NE and go west one mile on the Burke–Gilman Trail to Forest Park Shopping Center.

Walk east and north across the shopping center and continue northwest on Ballinger Way. Where Ballinger Way bends left, continue northwest on 40th Place NE to 45th Place NE. Go right (southeast) into 46th Ave. NE and ascend to Horizon View. At NE 195th St., look west at the Olympic Mountains. Go north on 45th Ave. NE into a trail and path in **Horizon View Park** around a reservoir. Continue circling east and south to return to NE 195th St. Go right (west) on NE 195th St. for 50' to find a pipeline swath descending south. Follow this grass slope as it curves around to the east and descends across 47th Place NE to NE 193rd St.

Cross NE 193rd St. and ascend southeast on the pipeline across NE 190th St. Follow the pipeline east over 53rd Ave. NE and 58th Ave. NE, descending. At 61st Ave. NE, turn left (north) to NE 190th St. Go right (east) and after one block, bend right (southeast) into 61st Place NE. Turn left (east) on NE 187th St., which becomes NE 187th Place. Go left (north) again on 62nd Ave. NE into Kenlake Place NE. At sign, 'Lakemore Estates', ascend right (east) on steps and path to emerge on

62nd Ave. NE. Go left (north) into a sloping playfield (no facilities). At the north end of the playfield, find a path ascending right (northeast) in alder trees to 63rd Ave. NE. Cross and continue east on NE 194th St., bending south into 64th Place NE. At NE 192nd Place, descend east to 65th Place NE. Go north, bending west into 65th Ave. NE, then continuing north. Follow NE 196th St., 66th Place NE, and NE 195th St. down to 68th Ave. NE. Cross into **Swamp Creek Park** (picnic tables). Exit east to 73rd Ave. NE. Go right (south) to NE 192nd St., left to 80th Ave. NE, and right (south) to Bothell Way NE.

Cross Bothell Way NE at a signal. Go left (east) on the Burke–Gilman Trail, passing through a tunnel. At the Sammamish River, cross a bridge and follow a path into **Blyth Park** (restrooms). Cross the playfield southeast (boggy in winter) to find a trail that switchbacks east up the slope. At the south end of the third switchback, continue on a track (steep) that ascends southeast or contour south. Follow one of these tracks until it intersects a pipeline and power line right-of-way at the south boundary of the park. Turn left (east) and ascend steeply to the high point of Norway Hill (480') at a survey monument (view of the Olympic Mountains). Turn left (north) on 104th Ave. NE, then bend right (east) into NE 168th St. At the first intersection, turn left (north) on 105th Ave. NE and descend, bending northwest to the end of the street, now 102nd Ave. NE. Leave the pavement, continuing into a track that curves east, then descends north to 102nd Ave. NE. Go north on 102nd Ave. NE across the Burke–Gilman Trail, the Sammamish River, and SR-522. Turn right (east) to find the Metro 307 and 340 bus stops at the Bothell Park & Ride on the north side of SR-522. Take west bound Metro 307, 340, or 372 to 61st Ave. NE to return to a car parked at Tracy Owen Station or walk the Burke–Gilman Trail west (4 miles).

KENMORE TO RICHMOND BEACH, high point 540', 9 miles one-way, 900' gain (Maps: USGS Edmonds East, Edmonds West). **Hike-2**. This route follows near or on the Seattle Water Department pipeline to its end at water towers, then follows streets. Take Metro 307 or 340 to 61st Ave. NE in Kenmore at the north end of Lake Washington or park at Tracy Owen Station by turning south off Bothell Way (SR-522) at 61st Ave. NE and going left (west) into the parking area (restrooms).

Walk north on 61st Ave. NE for 0.3 mile to the Seattle Water Department Pipeline on the left (west) side of the street. Ascend on the pipeline, crossing 58th Ave. NE and 53rd Ave. NE. Continue northwest near or on the pipeline over NE 187th St. before descending to cross NE 190th St. Stay on the pipeline swath as it ascends to Horizon View, crossing 47th Place NE before reaching the top of the hill south of a reservoir. Turn right on NE 195th St. and left on 47th Ave. NE to circle counterclockwise around the reservoir, getting views of Mt. Baker from 47th Ave. NE before turning left to go west on the north side of the reservoir and south on the west side of the reservoir to return to NE 195th St. Descend south on 46th Ave. NE and west on 45th Place NE to 40th Place NE. Bend north to NE 195th St., then go west to Ballinger Way NE. Cross southwest into 25th Ave. NE. Turn northwest on Forest Park Drive NE to the pipeline right-of-way.

Turn west on the overgrown path along the pipeline to cross Lago Creek (no bridge), or, if the blackberry vines on the pipeline right-of-way are too intimidating, go left (southwest) on NE 196th St. and 15th Ave. NE. Turn north on 14th Ave. NE for one block to NE 195th St. Turn west to ascend over a ridge and I-5 footbridge. Stay on NE 195th St. to 1st Ave. NE. Brave the blackberry vines on a powerline easement to continue west or detour one block south. Go west on N 194th St. to Meridian Ave. N. Continuing west on N 195th St. At Ashworth Ave. N, go left to N 192nd St., bending right into Firlands Way N. At Linden Ave. N, go north to N 195th St. Continue west on N 195th St., then turn left (south) on 8th Ave. NW, going right on NW 190th St. to Richmond Beach Drive. Descend west to a cluster of stores. Turn left (south) on 20th Ave. NW to **Richmond Beach Park** (restrooms, bridge to beach).

Find the Metro 315 on Richmond Beach Drive NW between NW 195th St. and NW 196th St. by going west on NW 190th St., north on 22nd Ave. NW, and left on NW 190th Place.

KENMORE–EDMONDS LOOP, high point 475', 29 miles, 1200' gain (Maps: USGS Edmonds West, Edmonds East). **Mt. Bicycle**. Take Metro 307 or 340 to 61st Ave. NE in Kenmore or park at Tracy Owen Station, south off Bothell Way (SR-522) at 61st Ave. NE (restrooms).

Ride north on 61st Ave. NE, which becomes 61st Place NE after passing 60th Ave. NE. Turn left (west) on NE 200th St., rounding north into 61st Ave. NE, which becomes 23rd Ave. W (Dunlap) on entering Snohomish County. Turn left (west) on 236th St. SW (mile 2), passing Brier Road and descending through a large apartment complex to cross a branch of Lyon Creek. Pass Cedar Way (44th Ave. W) to 48th Ave. W. Turn right (north) on 48th Ave. W to **Terrace Creek Park**. In the park, ascend along Terrace Creek, exiting to 221st St. SW one block west of 48th Ave. W. Go left to 52nd Ave. W. Turn right (north), then left (west) on 220th St. SW. Mountlake Terrace City Hall and Library are located in **Veterans Park** one mile south on 58th Ave. W.

Cross I-5, then turn right (north) on 66th Ave. W (mile 6), passing Manna Milling, a bulk foods distributor, north of 218th St. SW. Turn left (west) on 212th St. SE, which becomes 212th St. SW after crossing US-99 into Edmonds. Go right (north) on 76th Ave. W, left (west) on

206th St. SW, and right (north) on 82nd Ave. W. At 204th St. SW, go northwest into **Pine Ridge Park**. If driving, find parking off 204th St. SW at 83rd Ave. W. Walk or ride the trails of the park (0.5 mile total), passing **Goodhope Pond** and exiting west to the intersection of 208th St. SW and 86th Place W.

Ride east on 208th St. SW, crossing 76th Ave. W. After passing College Place Middle School, turn north on a path along the west boundary of the Lynnwood Golf Course. Follow the path as it bends around the north boundary of the golf course. Enter the grounds of the **Edmonds Community College**. Tour the campus to observe the buildings, plantings, and public art, then return to the north entrance and proceed north to 196th St. SW. Go west, turning north on 74th Ave. W to 191st St. SW. Bend west into 75th Ave. W, then go west at 190th St. SW to 76th Ave. W. Turn left (south) one block to 191st St. SW. Now go west to 80th Ave. W. Turn right (north) one block and enter **Sierra Park**. Facilities: nature trail for the blind with descriptive signs in Braille. Look for the following native plants: yew, red cedar, red alder, salal, Douglas fir, blackberry, salmonberry, thimbleberry, elderberry. If driving, find parking off 190th St. SW west of 80th Ave. W. Return south on 80th Ave. W, east on 191st St. SW, north on 76th Ave. W, and east on 190th St. SW to 75th Ave. W. Turn north to an entrance into **Lynndale Park**. Wander through the park (two miles of trails), eventually exiting north on a paved path to Olympic View Drive at 186th St. SW.

Proceed west on Olympic View Drive through the shopping center of Perrinville, crossing 76th Ave. SW and continuing on Olympic View Drive to pass along a forested ravine in **Southwest Park**. Park bicycle and hike one or more of the trails. At 180th St. SW, one trail goes southwest up a minor rise to a plateau with multiple loops of gravel and dirt (open to bicycles), another trail descends north to a stream, and a third trail descends north into the west end of the park. After continuing on Olympic View Drive, pause at a view toward the Olympic Mountains and Mt. Baker. Continue on Olympic View Drive across Puget Drive W (SR-524) into Olympia Ave. Go south on Olympia Ave. to Main St. and the entrance to **Yost Park**. Park bicycle and walk the well-kept trails of the park (2 miles total). Return to the entrance and go west on Main St. Turn right (north) on 7th Ave. to Casper St. (SR-524), then go left (west), leaving SR-524 where SR-524 bends south into 3rd Ave. N. Continue southwest at sign 'No Outlet' to reach Sunset St. N on the bluff above the beach. Pause for impressive views west and north. Reach Main Street in Edmonds at mile 18.

Turn right across the railroad tracks to **Bracketts Landing**, a marine park with geological and marine exhibits (restrooms, changing rooms, showers). Scuba divers congregate here on weekends. From Bracketts

Landing, go south on Railroad Ave., passing the **Edmonds Senior Center**. At Dayton St., bend right (west) into Admiral Way and continue south to **Marina Beach Park**, which has tables, play equipment, beach access, and paved and gravel paths. Return north on Admiral Way to Dayton St., cross the railroad tracks, then go south on the first street into a commercial area. Keep right to **Edmonds Marsh**: bird watching decks, walkway (no bicycles on paths), and interpretive signs.

Return to Dayton St., then go east to Sunset Ave. (SR-104). Turn south on SR-104 to Pine St. Go right (west) to **Deer Creek Fish Hatchery** where an organization raises salmon. Return east on Pine St. across SR-104, passing **City Park** (restrooms in summer) to 3rd Ave. S. Turn right (south) to cross under SR-104 into Woodway Park Road. Pass **Deer Park Reserve** (no trails) in the ravine of Deer Creek, continuing on 114th St. W, 116th St. W, 23rd Ave. NW, and NW 201st St. to Richmond Beach Road at NW 196th St. and 24th Ave. NW (Metro 315 stop on east side of 24th Ave. NW, mile 23). Turn left (east) to 20th Ave. NW and go south on 20th Ave. NW to **Richmond Beach Park** (restrooms).

After visiting the beach in Richmond Beach Park, return on 20th Ave. NW and ascend east on Richmond Beach Road to the 'Y' where Dayton Ave. N turns south (mile 25). Take the left fork to continue east into NE 185th St., crossing Aurora Ave. N (Fred Meyer). After crossing I-5, **Shoreline Library** is 0.5 mile to the right (south) on 5th Ave. NE at NE 175th St. From NE 185th St., turn left (north) on 10th Ave. NE, bending right into Perkins Way NE at NE 190th St. Round to the east on Perkins Way NE, crossing 15th Ave. NE at a stop light. Stay on Perkins Way NE as it descends along forested McAleer Creek. Cross NE 178th St. into Brookside Blvd. to Bothell Way at the Forest Park Shopping Center (mile 28). Find the Metro 307 stop on Bothell Way or a Metro 340 stop on Ballinger Way at the northeast edge of the shopping center. To return to Tracy Owen Station, cross Bothell Way to the Burke–Gilman Trail and ride east one mile.

PIPELINE: BOTHELL–SAMMAMISH RIVER, high point 480', 8 miles RT, 1500' gain (Maps: USGS Bothell, Kirkland). **Hike-2**. Take Metro 307 or 340 to the Bothell Park & Ride. From the Park & Ride, go west to 102nd Ave. NE. Turn south and cross bridges over SR-520 and the Sammamish River. After crossing the river, go west through the parking area to the Burke–Gilman Trail. If driving, park off 102nd Ave. NE south of the bridge over the Sammamish River. Reach 102nd Ave. NE by driving into Main Street in Bothell from SR-522.

Walk the Burke–Gilman Trail west down the river to a bridge. At the east end of the bridge, leave the Burke–Gilman Trail and follow the path southeast into **Blyth Park** (restrooms). Cross the meadow southeast to a trail ascending the slope on switchbacks. At the third switchback, ascend a track southeast or contour south to the Seattle Water Department pipeline. Ascend steeply under powerlines to the crest of Norway Hill at a survey monument. Look west to the Olympic Mountains.

Follow the pipeline east across 104th Ave. NE, then descend to cross 112th Ave. NE. Continue on the pipeline swath to 115th Ave. NE by ascending a ramp left (north). Go south on 115th Ave. NE and east on NE 160th St. across I-405. Turn south on 116th Ave. NE. South of Kingswood Townhomes, turn left (east) on the pipeline swath, crossing 119th Ave. NE before reaching **Norway Hill Park** (tables). The pipeline crosses 124th Ave. NE, 132nd Ave. NE, and 134th Ave. NE, before descending steeply to the Woodinville–Redmond Road. Turn right. At NE 145th St., find a cluster of wineries and breweries: Ste. Michelle, Columbia, and Redhook (tours, restrooms, gardens, ponds, shelter). Ste. Michelle winery is built on Hollywood Farm, the country estate (1913) of Frederick Stimson. Look for fish ponds and peafowl.

Return along the Tolt Pipeline on the outgoing route to 104th Ave. NE, the street at the top of the hill after crossing I-405. Turn right (north) on 104th Ave. NE and round into NE 168th St. Go left (north) on 105th Ave. NE and descend, curving west to the end of the pavement, now 102nd Ave. NE. Continue into an easement which curves east to meet an extension of 102nd Ave. NE. Go north to reach the starting point at the Sammamish River or the Bothell Park & Ride.

NORTHWEST KING COUNTY PARKS, high point 520', 21 miles one-way, 900' gain (Maps: USGS Seattle North, Edmonds East, Edmonds West, Bothell). **Bicycle or Walk parts**. Ride Metro 314 to 15th Ave. NE and NE 155th St., or ride Metro 377 to 15th Ave. NE and NE 160th St. If driving, park at Tracy Owen Station off Bothell Way at 61st Ave. NE and walk or ride southwest to the Metro 314 bus stop on the northwest side of Bothell Way at Ballinger Way NE.

From the bus stop on 15th Ave. NE at NE 155th St. (mile 0.0), go north to NE 160th St. Enter **Hamlin Park** on a paved path. Where the path ends at a street, continue east on pavement to a junction of paths at the edge of dense forest. Leave bicycle and explore a fringe of forest near a school. Return to bicycle and go west along the south side of a playfield, then turn right (north) to picnic tables, shelter, and restrooms (open summer). Explore the forest north, staying on trails and avoiding steep slopes to cross the high point in the park, 430'. Exit from the park at NE 165th St. and 22nd Ave. NE. Go west on NE 165th St. to 18th Ave. NE, then turn south to reenter Hamlin Park, descending into a valley. At a junction before reaching the parking area, turn northwest on a trail to the park boundary at NE 168th St. and 16th Ave. NE.

Go west on NE 168th St. to 15th Ave. NE, south to NE 165th St., and west to 9th Ave. NE. Leave bicycle and enter **Northcrest Park**, going north on paths in this bit of wildland to NE 170th St. Look for the following native plants: salal, huckleberry, red cedar, white pine, Douglas fir, western hemlock, spirea, mountain ash, bitter cherry, rose, madrone, dogwood, red alder, willow, birch, and hawthorne.

On leaving the park, mile 1.8, go east to 10th Ave. NE, then turn south. At NE 155th St., continue south on the east side of the playfields of **Paramount Park** past a street end barrier. Where 10th Ave. NE bends west into NE 151st St., mile 2.7, descend southeast into **Paramount Park** on the Fallen Tree Trail (posts 4-4) to Dragonfly Meadow. Hidden Hemlock Trail (5-5) goes north to NE 152nd St. Fern Trail (10-10) begins north of an isolated red alder (6) in the north end of Dragonfly Meadow and goes north to the Hidden Hemlock Trail. A planted area (14) is south from the main trail on the east side of Little's Creek.

Look for the following native plants near numbered posts: alder (6), big leaf maple (3), bitter cherry (1), black cottonwood (12), blackberry (4-4), cascara (north of 7), dogwood (southeast of 14), Douglas fir (10-10), hazel (4-4), huckleberry (4-4), larch (14, not a native but similar), lodgepole pine, madrone, mountain ash (5-5), ponderosa pine (4-4), red cedar (2), red currant (14), red elderberry (8), rose (14), salmonberry (7), snow berry (14), spirea (1), vine maple (4-4), and westerm hemlock (9, 10-10).

From the meadow area at the center of the park, go north on Hidden Hemlock Trail (5-5) to exit on 11th Ave. NE at NE 152nd St. Go east to 12th Ave. NE, then turn north to NE 155th St. Turn left (west) and cross under I-5 to **Twin Ponds Park**, mile 4.5. Tour the park (restrooms, picnic tables, viewpoint over a pond, wetlands). Return to NE 155th St. (mile 5.1) and continue west. Turn north on Meridian Ave. N, then go west on N 160th St. to Densmore Ave. N. Jog right (north), then west. Go north on Ashworth Ave. N and west on N 165th St. across Aurora Ave. N. Richmond Highlands Community Center is north of N 165th St. on Fremont Ave. N. Continue west on N 165th St. to Carlyle Hall Road. Go northwest to Greenwood Ave. N (mile 7), then turn into **Shoreline Community College** (Metro buses). Find a bicycle rack and leave bicycle.

Hike-2, 2 miles. Walk to a parking area at the northeast corner of the Community College grounds. Proceed north to the end of parking. Descend northwest in the dense forest of **Shoreview Park** on steep and narrow user-made trails (some fallen trees) on the south side of Boeing Creek. At a junction with a built trail, turn right (north) and descend on steps to cross Boeing Creek. Continue north on trails to NW 175th St. The flood damage erosion scar in the canyon dates from 1996. Go south and west on a trail, descending to the west boundary of the park. A footlog crosses Boeing Creek to a trail that ascends west but this trail may be blocked by fallen trees. If this trail is not passable, return to the previous crossing of Boeing Creek and proceed west and south to an area of playfields and tennis courts near Innis Arden Way. **Hidden Lake** at the southwest corner of the park is not accessible. Return east past tennis courts into trails that ascend to emerge at a playfield north of the buildings of the Community College. Explore the Community College, then return to bicycle and exit south from the campus to Innis Arden Way, mile 8.

Go southeast to Greenwood Ave. N at N 160th St. Stay on N 160th St. to cross Aurora Ave. N at a stoplight. At Ashworth Ave. N, jog north, east and north to continue east on N 163rd St. to Corliss Place N (mile 9.3). Ascend steps into **McCormick Park**, which has a flower garden and picnic table. Cross the meadow and exit north and west to Meridian Ave. N at N 167th St. Go west to Wallingford Ave. N, then north to **Meridian Park**, mile 9.9. At N 169th St., turn west, leave bicycle and explore meadows and wetland.

From Meridian Park, go west to Meridian Ave., and proceed north to N 175th St. and **Ronald Bog Park**, a wetland and pond with plantings of native and exotic species. Find many waterbirds here at some seasons. **Shoreline Library** is east on NE 175th St. at 5th Ave. NE. From Ronald Bog, mile 11, go north on Meridian Ave. N, left (west) on 177th St., and north on Wallingford Ave. N. At N 192nd St., turn west to Ashworth Ave. N, then continue north to **Echo Lake Park** on the west side of the street (restrooms, picnic table, wetland, pond). On leaving Echo Lake Park, go south to N 199th St., then turn east to Wallingford Ave. N. Go south to N 190th St., then east through a street end park to emerge on 1st Ave. NE at **Shoreline Park and Center**. Turn right to NE 185th St. Visit the **Shoreline Senior Center** at the northeast corner of the intersection.

Go east on NE 185th St. to 10th Ave. NE, then turn north, staying on 10th Ave. NE where Perkins Way NE bends east. Enter **North City Park** at mile 15.5. Look for the following native plants at numbered posts: (3) Western hemlock, Douglas fir, (7) Elderberry, Oregon grape, (10) Madrone, (11) Raspberry, (13) Huckleberry, and (14) Hazel.

From North City Park, go south on 10th Ave. NE to the beginning of NE Perkins Way at NE 190th St. Follow NE Perkins Way northeast and east to 15th Ave. NE, staying on the path behind the barrier on the north side of the narrow street until the street begins to descend. Turn north on 15th Ave. NE, then go northeast on NE 196th St. to cross McAleer Creek. At the first intersection after crossing McAleer Creek, bend southeast on Forest Park Drive NE to the next corner, then follow 25th Ave. NE across Ballinger Road NE (stoplight) to **Bruggers Bog Park** (mile 17) just east of Ballinger Road (meadows, play equipment). Look for red cedar, madrone, and exotic pines.

Return south on 25th Ave. NE, northwest on Forest Park Drive NE, and southwest on NE 196th St. across McAleer Creek. Go east on NE 195th St. into Lago Place NE and exit into Perkins Way NE. Turn left (east) and descend along McAleer Creek in shady forest. The street becomes NE 180th St. before crossing NE 178th St. at **Eagle Scout Park** (exercise equipment, picnic table) into Brookside Blvd. NE. Continue south on Brookside Blvd. to Bothell Way to find Metro 340, 307, 372 buses (mile 20) or cross Bothell Way to the Burke-Gilman trail on the southeast side and proceed northeast to parking at Tracy Owen Station (mile 21).

EDMONDS–MUKILTEO, 11 miles, no gain (Maps: USGS Edmonds West, Mukilteo). **Hike-2**. This beach walk is recommended only at the lowest tides, -1' or lower. Begin the beach walk two hours before low tide (see tide tables in US West Seattle Yellow Pages). From Aurora Transit Center (parking), take Community Transit 670 to Edmonds at the ferry terminal. Begin at **Brackett's Landing** (restrooms) north of the ferry terminal. For most of the way to Mukilteo, the route is pebble or sandy beach and crosses many creeks, none difficult.

Walk north on the beach, passing through an area of rocks fallen from the railroad embankment at the north end of the Marine Park. After two miles, pass the first bluff, where rocks spread out from the railroad embankment to the water line. North of this bluff, Brown's Bay begins, with the Meadowdale Marina standing on pilings. Find the underpass to **Meadowdale Park** at mile 4 (restrooms, picnic tables). After leaving Meadowdale Park, pass the Norma Beach Boat House and a decaying boat hull stranded on the beach just south of the boat house. **Picnic Point Park** is the next pedestrian railroad overpass, about half of the distance from Edmonds to Mukilteo. North of Picnic Point, pass several wooden hulls stranded on the beach, left from a ship breaking operation at the end of World War II.

Round the next headland to Naketa Beach, with a cluster of houses west of the railroad tracks. Beyond Naketa Beach, at mile 10, pass the last bluff. Look back to see Edmonds in the distance, best identified when a ferry is approaching or leaving the dock. At **Mukilteo State Park** (restrooms), find CT 170 stop on Mukilteo Drive (SR-525) south of Front Street and return to the Lynnwood Park & Ride. Transfer to CT 620 or 630 for Aurora Transit Center.

Parks:

RICHMOND BEACH PARK, high point 200' (Maps: USGS Edmonds West). **Walk.** This park lies on Puget Sound at the north end of King County. Take Metro 315 to 20th Ave. NW in Richmond Beach. Walk south on 20th Ave. NW to the park. Trails, steps and a bridge over the railroad track provide access to the beach. Facilities: picnicking, beach combing, play areas, restrooms open all year. For group picnic reservations, call 206-296-2977.

CARKEEK PARK, high point 250', 3+ miles, 500' gain (Maps: USGS Seattle North). **Hike-1.** Take Metro 15 to the end of the line at 14th Ave. NW and NW 105th St. Walk north on 14th Ave. NW and Woodbine Way to Carkeek Park. Descend on a trail to the valley of Piper's Creek. Turn west past a picnic area to the beach across a bridge over railroad tracks.

After walking loops in the park, return to the Metro Treatment Plant on Piper's Creek. Find a trail on the east side of Piper's Creek and turn south, ascending along the creek. Exit from the park at NW 100th Place. Walk south past stores to Holman Road NW and a Metro stop.

TRACY OWEN STATION, 20' (Maps: USGS Edmonds East). **Walk.** Look for this park off SR-522 on the shore near the north end of Lake Washington. Take Metro 307, 340, or 372 to the stop at Bothell Way NE and NE 61st St. Walk south from Bothell Way NE and west on an extension of NE 175th St. to the park. Facilities: fishing pier, restrooms, play area, and swimming beach where the water temperature exceeds 70° by July.

KENMORE PARK, 30' (Maps: USGS Bothell). **Walk.** Find this park on the south bank of the Sammamish River on 68th Ave. NE in Kenmore near the north end of Lake Washington. Take Metro 234 to the corner of 68th Ave. NE and NE 170th St., or Metro 307, 340, 372 to 68th Ave. NE on Bothell Way NE. Walk south 0.4 miles on 68th Ave. NE to NE 170th St. Facilities: picnicking, restrooms in summer, trails, shelter, wetlands, rhododendron garden, playfields. For group picnic reservations and date of rhododendron tour (May), call: 206-296-2977.

BLYTH COMMUNITY PARK, high point 480', 2 miles of trails, 460' possible gain (Maps: USGS Bothell). **Hike-1.** The city of Bothell maintains this park on the east bank of the Sammamish River. Take

Metro 307 or 340 to NE 180th St. on Bothell Way in Bothell. Walk south on Bothell Way (SR-522) to the stoplight at the corner of Waynita Drive. Turn east and descend a ramp to a bridge over the Sammamish River. Cross the river and turn southeast to the park. If driving, go south on 102nd Ave. NE from Main Street in Bothell. Cross SR-522 and the Sammamish River, then turn right at Riverside Drive to the park. Facilities: playground, access to the Sammamish River, restrooms, picnic tables, shelter, trails on the forested hillside with access to the Tolt Pipeline and Norway Hill.

SNOHOMISH MARINE PARKS, high point 546', 11 miles, 1300' gain (Maps: USGS Edmonds East, Mukilteo). **Bicycle or Walk parts.** Ride Community Transit 621 to 200th St. SW and 64th Ave. W in Lynnwood.

Ride north on 64th Ave. W past **Daleway Park**: playground, horseshoe court, tables, public art and restrooms (open summer weekends). Continue north to 176th St. SW, then jog left (west) to Olympic View Drive. Continue north briefly, then turn left (northwest) on Meadowdale Beach Road at 174th St. SW to 76th Ave. W. Now go north into **Meadowdale Beach Park** (service and handicapped motor vehicles only). Facilities: volleyball, toilets, tables, beach access through a tunnel under railroad tracks.

From the beach access area (mile 4.5), ascend east near Lund's Gulch Creek, leaving the park at mile 5.6 (parking) into 156th St. SW. At 56th Ave. W, jog north to 152nd St. SW, before continuing east to 52nd Ave. W. Turn north to Picnic Point Road and descend northwest to **Picnic Point Park** (mile 9). Facilities: parking, toilets, tables on beach side of railroad tracks, accessible overpass to beach.

On leaving the park, ascend southeast on Picnic Point Road, bending east at the junction with 140th St. SW to Beverly Park Road. Find CT-170 stops north or south on Beverly Park Road.

East of Lake Washington.

FINN HILL–DENNY CREEK–ST. EDWARD LOOP, high point 400', 9 miles, 1200' gain (Maps: USGS Kirkland, Seattle North). **Hike-2.** Take Metro 234 to the corner of 84th Ave. NE and NE 138th St. Walk west on NE 138th St. or drive to the parking area in **Big Finn Hill Park** east off Juanita Drive NE and south of NE 1348th Place.

From the parking area, walk south on the west side of the playfield to find a trail going west. Follow this trail to Juanita Drive NE. Cross Juanita Drive west to a trail. Take the first branch left and go south, parallel to Juanita Drive, keeping at junctions. At NE 132nd St. (power line), turn right (west) to 72nd Ave. NE. Go left (south) 350'. Find a trail on the right (no sign, no bicycles). Descend southwest in mixed forest.

Where the trail levels and the ridge to the south ends (elev. 100'), turn left (southeast) on a well-travelled trail that crosses into the main creek channel. Ascend along the creek, crossing the creek as necessary, and passing a dead tree that was one of the largest fir trees in the area. Find a pump house on the northwest side of the stream near a bridge across the creek, but stay on the northwest side. Eventually cross the creek to the east side and ascend steeply (steps) to a junction. Take the right (south) fork to emerge at the intersection of 76th Ave. NE and NE 124th St. Go south on 76th Ave. NE to NE 120th St., then turn right (west). After a brief rise, descend to an intersection with 72nd Ave. NE. Turn right (north) to reenter **O. O. Denny Park**. Find a trail and descend west across Holmes Point Drive NE. Find restrooms, picnic tables, beach access, and shelter.

To continue the loop, go east across Holmes Point Drive NE into a parking area to a trail. Ascend northwest, keeping left at trail junctions into the west branch canyon to emerge on 72nd Ave. NE. Turn right on 72nd Ave. NE and go south to the street end. Descend on the utility track that continues south to a viewpoint southeast into the canyon. Return north to 72nd Ave. NE and continue to NE 132nd St. Go right (east) on a gravel road. Where the pavement begins, find a trail north into the forest parallel to 72nd Ave. NE. Avoid trails that go to the right (east) away from 72nd Ave. NE or trails that end at 72nd Ave. NE. Where 72nd Ave. NE bends right (east) and becomes NE 138th Place, cross the paved road and continue north. Do not take any of the paths that descend west, but round to the east on the plateau to Holmes Point Drive near Juanita Drive. Cross Holmes Point Drive and continue north on a path parallel to Juanita Drive (see alternate below).

Cross the **St. Edward State Park** driveway, going on to the north end of St. Edward State Park where a trail exits to Juanita Drive NE. Now descend west, keeping to the right at trail junctions to emerge on the shore of Lake Washington. Turn left (south) along the shore, passing trail junctions. Near the south boundary of the park, ascend east until the forest ends near buildings. Go left (north) to the buildings of St. Edward State Park and a road that goes east. Turn right (east) on the road or trail to Juanita Drive NE, then go south on a path.

Alternate Loop. Immediately after crossing Holmes Point Drive, find a trail and go west. This trail ascends steeply to emerge near the buildings of Bastyr College. Continue west past the water tower into the South Boundary Trail. Descend to the shore of Lake Washington. Hike north along the shore, passing trails east. Ascend on the North Boundary trail to the buildings of the State Park, then continue east on trails to the northeast corner of the park. Turn south on the path along Juanita Drive.

After crossing Holmes Point Drive, continue south. Cross NE 138th Place where this street turns south and becomes 72nd Ave. NE, then turn east to return toward Juanita Drive NE. Go south parallel to Juanita Drive NE to a trail that goes left to Juanita Drive. Cross Juanita Drive NE to **Big Finn Hill Park** and the starting point.

KINGSGATE PARKS, high point 260', 7 miles RT, 300' gain (Maps: USGS Kirkland). **Hike-1.** Ride a Metro Bus (340, etc.) to the Kingsgate Park & Ride on I-405. From the west side of I-405 at the intersection of 116th Way NE and NE 132nd St., walk west on NE 132nd St. (Metro buses 255, 931). Turn north on 108th Ave. NE (mile 0.5) to **Edith Moulton Park** at mile 0.7. Go east into the park (parking, shelters). Trails explore the park on both sides of a branch of Juanita Creek. Find many large red cedar trees as well as a variety of other native plants: hazel, western hemlock, big leaf maple. The Meadow Entrance has accessible paths and descriptive information.

From Edith Moulton Park, return south on 108th Ave. NE to NE 132nd St. and turn left (east) to pass under I-405 before turning north on 116th Ave. NE. Reach **Kingsgate Park** at NE 140th St. Hike trails clockwise around the park. A north extension of a trail on the west side of the park enters Juanita Creek valley (private land north of the creek) before turning south to follow the east boundary to the NE 140th St. NE entrance. Return south on 116th Ave. NE and west on NE 132nd St. to Kingsgate Park & Ride.

SAMMAMISH RIVER TO SNOQUALMIE VIEW, high point 570', 17.5 miles RT, 1200' gain (Maps: USGS Redmond, Kirkland). **Mt. Bicycle or Hike-1.** For bicycle trip, begin at the intersection of the Sammamish River Trail and the Tolt Pipeline on the east side of the Sammamish River and 0.3 mile north of the parking lot off SR-202 at the Sammamish River. Reach this pipeline-trail intersection by riding the Burke–Gilman Trail and the Sammamish River Trail from Seattle (four miles from 102nd Ave. NE in Bothell) or by taking Metro 307 to the first Metro stop on NE 175th St. in Woodinville. Ride west to the Sammamish River Trail, then turn south for 1.7 miles. Restrooms are 0.2 mile south of the intersection of the Sammamish River Trail and the Tolt Pipeline. If driving, park on 148th Ave. NE at the Tolt Pipeline crossing 0.3 mile north of NE 145th St.

For hike, park as above on 148th Ave. NE (13 miles RT), or park at the pipeline crossing on Bear Creek Road off Avondale Road (6 miles RT).

From the Sammamish River Trail, mile 0.0, elevation 40', ride east on the Tolt Pipeline to 148th Ave. NE. Go south 0.3 mile for a view of Hollywood School (1912). Return to the Tolt Pipeline and ascend steeply east on the pipeline right-of-way to cross a ridge, 350'. Where the route makes a sharp descent to cross paved 155th Ave. NE, elevation 260', minimize further damage by walking bicycles down this now deeply eroded path. Continue east on the pipeline, crossing two paved roads and another ridge, 545', before reaching Avondale Road NE at mile 3.5. Cottage Lake Creek is immediately east of Avondale Road NE and Bear Creek Road NE is the next road, 0.1 mile east of Avondale Road NE. Cross Bear Creek at mile 4.1, 180', and begin climbing to a plateau. The route descends briefly at mile 4.5 to cross Struve Creek where the pipeline is exposed. At mile 6.3, leave the pipeline right-of-way from the north side, and continue east on gravelled NE 145th St. over the high point, 570', to a viewpoint northeast over the Snoqualmie River Valley to Duval and the Cascade Mountains. From the viewpoint go south to the pipeline, mile 7.3. Turn west on the pipeline across Struve Creek and Bear Creek to the second paved cross road with a centerline (Bear Creek Road), mile 11 and 0.5 mile west Bear Creek.

Turn right (northwest) to Avondale Road NE, mile 11.1. Go north on Avondale Road NE to NE 165th St., mile 11.8. Turn left (west), crossing Cottage Lake Creek at mile 12.5. Continue into 174th Ave. NE and 172nd Place NE. Cross 154th Ave. NE and ascend. The street, now NE 175th St., passes a gazebo with seats at the corner of 155th Place NE, mile 14.7. Continue west on NE 173rd St. At the next intersection, go right, staying on NE 173rd St., which becomes NE 171st St. before entering 140th Ave. NE at mile 16.

To return to parking on 148th Ave. NE at the Tolt Pipeline, turn left (south) on 140th Ave. NE, which bends east as 140th Place NE into 148th Ave. NE. At the intersection of 140th Place NE and 148th Ave. NE, **Gold Creek Park** is 0.4 miles north on 140th Ave. NE, and the Tolt Pipeline is 0.2 miles south on 148th Ave. NE.

To proceed into Woodinville, on reaching the intersection of 140th Ave. NE and NE 171st St., turn right to the main street of Woodinville, NE 175th St. Go left (west) past **DeYoung Park** (gazebo, benches) to the **Woodinville Pioneer Cemetery** at Woodinville-Snohomish Road. Find a Metro 307 stop on NE 175th St., mile 17.5, or go west to the Burke–Gilman Trail where NE 175th St. crosses a bridge over the Sammamish River.

BRIDLE TRAILS TO MARYMOOR PARK, high point 520', 5

miles minimum, 200' gain (Maps: USGS Redmond, Kirkland). **Hike-2**. Take any Metro bus that goes to the Houghton Park & Ride, or take Metro 340 to I-405 and NE 70th St. If driving, park at the Houghton Park & Ride off I-405 at NE 70th St. (weekends only).

From the west side of I-405, cross I-405 on the NE 70th St. overpass and turn south on 116th Ave. NE. From the east side of I-405 at the Houghton Park & Ride, walk south on 116th Ave. NE. Go two blocks, then turn east on NE 67th St. into a playfield. Go south on a path to the southeast corner and continue south. Turn right (west) on NE 60th St. to an entrance into **Bridle Trails State Park** opposite the Transfer Station. Enter the park, going right at the first 'Y'. At the southwest corner of the park, find restrooms, water, horse corrals, information, and a viewing stand.

Go east and south on a choice of trails (28 miles of trails total, 150' of relief, compass useful) and wander freely (no bicycles). The highest point in the park is 535' and the lowest point is 380'. To leave the park, go to the north-south powerline that bisects the park and follow this power line toward the north boundary. At the parade ring, which is 0.25 miles south of NE 60th St., turn east and northeast to the northeast corner of the park and exit to 132nd Ave. NE at NE 60th St. Find **Bridle Crest Trail** at a narrow entry. Go east on the trail (can be steep, muddy, and ponded), crossing 140th Ave. NE and passing along the north boundary of the Bellevue Municipal Golf Course. After crossing SR-520 on NE 60th St. (Metro 221, 253, 266 stops), reach 156th Ave. NE. Turn right (south) on 156th Ave. NE for one block, passing NE 59th St., to a park. Turn east on the north side of the playground and descend on grass. Find a path and descend south and east in **Westside Park** to W Lake Sammamish Parkway at **Marymoor Park** (Metro 247, 249). Cross into Marymoor Park to find play areas, a variety of trails on both sides of the Sammamish River, restrooms, and picnic areas.

From Marymoor Park, walk north on the west side of the Sammamish River to the first bridge over the river. Cross into Redmond. At the first street, turn north on 159th Place NE to Redmond Way NE and a Metro stop. Metro 251 and 254 go to the Houghton Park & Ride and downtown Seattle.

KIRKLAND PARKS, high point 425', 18 mile loop, 900' gain (Maps: Kirkland Trail Map, USGS Kirkland). **Mt. Bicycle or Hike-1 part**. Take a Metro Bus (251, etc.) to the Kirkland Transit Center or park at Kirkland Park & Ride (weekends only).

From Kirkland Transit Center, go west on Park Lane to Lake St. Turn south on Lake St., then go west on Kirkland Ave. to **Kirkland Marine Park** (restrooms, shelters, picnic tables, mooring for visiting boats).

From Marine Park, go south down a ramp into a parking area and continue south along the waterfront on pathways provided by the adjacent property owners. When a shoreside pathway is not available, return to Lake St. and continue south, passing **David E. Brink Park, Marsh Park, Houghton Beach Park**, and Carillon Point. Most of these parks have public art and restrooms. From Carillon Point, continue south along the edge of a marina to rejoin Lake Washington Blvd. after passing a corner of the **Yarrow Bay Wetlands** (sight access only).

Continue south on Lake Washington Blvd., then turn southeast at NE 38th Place to the Kirkland Park & Ride. Go east through a corner of the Park & Ride to emerge on 108th Ave. NE. Go north to NE 45th St. Turn east to enter **Watershed Park** at 110th Ave. NE. In the park, go south on a wide path and descend to Watershed Creek for a wetland view. Return to a trail junction near the entrance and go east, taking the first trail to the right to an old reservoir. From the reservoir, go south to a viewpoint southeast to the tall buildings of Bellevue and south to hills. At the viewpoint, trails go west, south, and east. Take the east path and descend, passing a trail that branches north after 50' and taking the next trail north. At a junction, go right (north) to emerge from the park into 114th Ave. NE at NE 50th Place.

At NE 53rd St., go west to 112th Ave. NE. Turn north to NE 60th St., then east, crossing I-405 at a pedestrian walkway. Go north on NE 116th St. Cross back west over I-405 at NE 70th St. and descend to 6th St. S. Turn north on 6th St. S to 9th Ave. S, then go east to 8th St. S. Turn north on 8th St. S to **Everest Park** (playgrounds, playfields, picnic tables, shelter, restrooms). Leave Everest Park east to 10th St. S. Go north to Kirkland Ave., east to 116th Ave. NE, north to the end of the street, then continue north on a path along I-405 to NE 85th St. Turn west to cross a railroad track. The path steepens to steps before emerging on 10th St. at 5th Ave. Go west, leaving 5th Ave. where this street bends southwest to stay west on a paved cutoff to 6th St. Turn north to 15th Ave., then jog west one block to continue north on 5th Place. **Crestwoods Park** begins at 18th Ave. (restrooms, playground, playfields, picnic tables, paved paths). From 6th St. at 108th Ave. NE, descend steps of Crestwood Trail to Forbes Creek Drive. Find the Forbes Valley Trail after a jog east. The trail becomes a path opposite building 10818, emerging north into 112th Ave. NE. At NE 112th St., go west for one block into the grounds of the Alexander Graham Bell School. Leave the school grounds at the northwest corner to a paved path that goes to 110th Ave. NE. At NE 116th St., turn west to 104th Ave. NE, and again turn north to NE 124th St. Find the **North Kirkland Community Center** across NE 124th St. (playground, restrooms).

Go west on NE 124th St. At 100th Ave. NE, turn south and southwest into 98th Ave. NE and the shopping area of Juanita. At the intersection of Juanita Drive NE, go one block west to **Juanita Beach Park** (restrooms, picnic tables, changing rooms, protected swimming area). From the intersection of Juanita Drive NE and 98th St. NE, go south on the causeway through the Juanita Bay Wetlands (interpretive signs). After leaving the south end of the causeway, turn right in **Juanita Bay Park** (restrooms, picnic tables), taking a trail north to the waterfront. Exit west from the Juanita Bay Park to follow 10th St. W as it ascends. Turn southeast on 16th Ave. W, then go right (southeast) on 8th St. W through an unpaved street-end that goes southeast to connect with 14th Ave. W. Turn right (southwest) on 6th St. W to Waverly Way. **Waverly Beach Park** is west of the intersection down a driveway (pier, restrooms, swimming beach). Go south on Waverly Way, bending through to the open space of **Waverly Site** to Market St. Go south to **Kirkland Marine Park**. Exit east on Kirkland Ave. at Lake St. Go north one block, then east on Park Lane to reach the Kirkland Transit Center on 3rd St.

REDMOND PARKS AND STREAMS, high point 500', 16 miles one-way, 500' gain (Maps: USGS Redmond). **Mtn. Bicycle and/or Hike-1 parts**. Ride Metro 251 to Avondale Road and NE 132nd St., elevation 122'.

Ride or walk east on NE 132nd St., crossing a branch of Bear Creek. The street jogs north and becomes NE 133rd St., continuing east to cross branches of Bear Creek and Seidel Creek. Reach the **Redmond Watershed Preserve** at mile 1.8. Turn right (south) into the preserve, passing the Trillium Trail on the right (south) at mile 2. Go left (east) on the Pipeline Regional Trail (gravel) across the north end of the preserve, crossing a gas pipeline swath immediately and reaching the junction with the Collin Creek Trail at mile 2.3. From here the Tolt Pipeline Trail is two miles east and north.

From the junction with the Collin Creek Trail, go south on the Pipeline Regional Trail, entering the pipeline (gas) swath at mile 3.1 and passing the Siler's Mill Trail (no bicycles) on the left at mile 3.4. Reach a four-way junction at mile 3.8. The trail to the left goes to the east boundary. The trail south, a continuation of the Pipeline Regional Trail, goes to NE Novelty Hill Road. Turn west on the Powerline Regional Trail to another four-way junction at mile 4.2. The Trillium Trail goes right (north, no bicycles), and the Powerline Regional Trail continues west. Turn south to the parking area to find: toilet, information board, Trout Loop Trail, and Treefrog Loop Trail (see Redmond Watershed Preserve below). Take time to walk one or more of these short trails before continuing.

Return north to the junction with the Trillium Trail, mile 4.5, then turn left (west) on the Powerline Regional Trail, passing out of the Preserve at mile 4.9. The trail deteriorates to a narrow horse-trampled bog, then exits to 206th Ave. NE. Go north to NE 116th St. and west to Avondale Road (mile 6.7, Metro 251). Turn north to visit the **Classic Nursery** (mile 7.4), which has an interpretive trail along Bear Creek. Park bicycle and walk the trail. Return south on Avondale Road to a powerline crossing, mile 8.4. Turn left (east) on the Powerline Regional Trail across Bear Creek into **Farrel-McWhirter Park**, mile 8.9. Continue east to the next street for another view of horse pastures, then go right to the park entrance and reenter the park. Wander through the farm area, then go south to Redmond Road. Turn southwest, joining Avondale Road to continue south. At the junction with Union Hill Road (mile 11.8), cross to a bikeway and go west into Redmond.

Emerge from parking lots and sidewalks to Redmond Way and continue northwest to **Anderson Park**, located east of 168th Ave. NE, north of Redmond Way, and south of NE 78th St., mile 12.6. Facilities: log houses, restrooms in summer, shelter, playground, and picnic tables. From Anderson Park, continue west and north, either to the Redmond Park & Ride at NE 83rd St. and 161st Ave. NE for Metro buses or to the Sammamish River Trail, mile 14.4, to continue north and west. From the Redmond Way crossing of the Sammamish River, Woodinville is six miles, Bothell is eight miles, 61st Ave. NE in Kenmore is 11 miles and the University District in Seattle is 22 miles.

REDMOND WATERSHED PRESERVE, high point 575', 8 miles of trails, 300' gain (Maps: Redmond Watershed Preserve, USGS Redmond). **Hike-1**. Take Metro 251 to Avondale Road at 132nd St. NE. Walk east on 132nd St. NE and 133rd St. NE, reaching the Preserve at mile 1.8. If driving, find the main entrance to the park off NE Novelty Hill Road at 218th Ave. NE. Facilities: information sign board, maps, toilet, hitching rail. The longest trail loop from the parking lot is 5.4 miles.

Treefrog Trail. A paved, accessible trail (0.3 miles) to a pond with viewpoint and explanatory signs. The trail makes a loop through wetland.

Trout Trail. This dirt-surface trail (0.6 miles) goes past an inactive beaver dam on Mackey Creek, then circles though mixed forest.

Pipeline Regional Trail. Go north from the parking area to the first junction (0.1 mile), then turn east to another junction, mile 0.5. Now go north, passing the Siler's Mill Trail at mile 1.0 and the Collin Creek Trail at mile 2.0. Reach a junction with the Trillium Trail at mile 2.3 and NE 133rd St. at mile 2.5.

Trillium–Siler's Mill Loop. High point 500', 5.4 miles, 300' gain. Go north from the parking area to the first junction (0.1 mile). Continue north on the Trillium Trail on the slope east of Seidel Creek . Cross branches of Seidel Creek, then reach a junction with the Old Pond Trail. Go left on this trail to a view of a pond on Seidel Creek. Look for the beaver dam at the outlet. Return to the Trillium Trail and continue north. At two miles from the parking area, meet the Pipeline Regional Trail. The left fork trail goes to the north boundary on NE 133rd St. (0.2 miles). Turn right (east) to a junction with the Collin Creek Trail. Now continue east on the left fork for 0.4 mile, then turn south on the Siler's Mill Trail past a beaver pond. Rejoin the Pipeline Regional Trail and go south to a junction with the Powerline Regional Trail. Turn west to the next trail junction and return south to parking.

Alternate access to Trillium–Siler's Loop. From Avondale Road, drive east on NE 132nd St. and NE 133rd St. to the Preserve entrance, 1.8 miles from Avondale Road.

FARREL–McWHIRTER PARK, high point 300', 10 miles RT, 460' gain (Maps: USGS Redmond). **Hike-1**. Take a Metro bus to the Redmond Park & Ride at 161st Ave. NE and NE 83rd St. If driving, find the park on Redmond Road east of Avondale Road. This Multipurpose Trail can also be reached by riding a Metro 251 Bus to a stop near NE 116th St. on Avondale Road NE. Find the Multipurpose Trail under a power line and walk east to the park.

Walk west on NE 83th St., then turn north on 158th Ave. NE. Go across NE 85th St. into Redmond City campus (Redmond Library on the right) and continue to the Sammamish River Trail on the west side of City Hall (public art). From the Sammamish River Trail 0.8 miles north of NE 85th St. in Redmond, turn northeast on the Redmond Multipurpose Trail under a Puget Power powerline.

A clump of western red cedar trees stands at the sharp bend where the trail begins to ascend from the valley floor 0.1 mile from the Sammamish River. Cross the Woodinville-Redmond Road at mile 0.3. Continue to ascend steeply north, crossing 160th and 170th streets before bending east over 172nd Ave. NE. At the highpoint (300'), look east to a sharp notch in the Cascade Range. This is the canyon of the Tolt River. Mt. Phelps is the butte-shaped summit to the right of the low point of the Tolt River canyon. Cross Avondale Road and Bear Creek to **Farrel-McWhirter Park** 3.3 miles from the Sammamish River Trail.

In the park, go left on the perimeter trailcltravelling through dense regrown forest. Several trails into the interior of the park turn off from the perimeter trail. On returning to the parade circle at the west entrance (mile 4.8), go southeast on a paved path to find goats, sheep, cows, rabbits, chickens, and ponies in a miniature farm. The restrooms and a viewpoint are in a converted silo. Pony rides for children are available (call 425-556-2309). Return to the west entrance and walk west on the Multipurpose Trail, crossing Avondale Road NE (Metro 251). Return to Redmond Transit Center on the outgoing route.

BELLEVUE PARKS, high point 425', 22 miles RT, 800' gain (Maps: Bellevue Parks, Bellevue Nature Trails, USGS Mercer Island, Issaquah). **Mt. Bicycle or Hike-1 parts.** Ride a Metro bus to the Bellevue Transit Center. If driving, park at the South Bellevue Park & Ride (weekends only) and ride north on Bellevue Way and 112th Ave. NE to NE 4th St. Go west to 110th Ave. NE then north to the Bellevue Transit Center.

From the Bellevue Transit Center, ride east to the first north-south street, 110th Ave. NE. Turn north to the **Bellevue Library** at NE 12th St. Go west on NE 12th St. to 100th Ave. NE. Turn south to NE 8th St. then go west to 98th Ave. NE. Turn south to 98th Place NE, which begins south of NE 5th St. Go southwest on this street under Lake Washington Blvd. NE into **Meydenbauer Beach Park** (restrooms, lake access).

After visiting the shoreline, return northeast to 98th Ave. NE and go south one block to NE 4th St. Go east to 100th Ave. NE, then turn south one block from NE 4th St. to enter 20 acre **Downtown Park**. The park has an impressive 240' wide waterfall and extensive lawns. Circle the park counter-clockwise to view flower gardens and the **aero sculpture** at the northeast corner. Exit south to NE 1st St. and go east to Bellevue Way NE. Turn south to Main St. Go east on Main St. across I-405 to 116th Ave. NE. Go south one block, then turn northeast to ascend on SE 1st St., which joins Main St. at the top of the hill. Enter **Wilburton Hill Park** east of 118th Ave. SE.

Ride east and southeast through the park, stopping at the **Botanical Garden** for a tour of native and exotic plants. From the Botanical Garden, descend southeast, first on a paved path then on gravel, passing playgrounds and playfields, to exit from the southeast corner to 128th Ave. SE. Turn south to SE 7th Place, passing SE 4th Place, which goes east into **Kelsey Creek Park**. Go west toward the Lake Hills Connector. Before reaching the stoplight at Lake Hills Connector, find a paved path that goes south 50' to the Lake Hills Connector. Turn left (southeast), passing wetlands and taking the first right on Richards Road. Ride south, passing an entrance to **Bannerwood Park** (playfields). Continue south on Richards Road to SE Eastgate Way. Turn east, then ascend north on 140th Ave. NE on the west side of the Eastgate Park & Ride. Go east on SE 32nd St. to **Bellevue Community College** on Coal Creek Road. Follow the road through the campus to reach the main cluster of buildings (bookstore, student union) and a Metro Bus stop.

After touring the campus, go north on the campus road past playing fields and east on SE 24th St. into **Robinswood Community Park**. Go right (south) on a paved path past the **Robinswood House** to two log cabins built by Hans Miller in 1884, still in their original locations. A barn is used as a day camp. From the log cabins, return north, passing playfields and a wetland. At SE 22nd St., turn east through a parking lot into a forest of Douglas fir, red cedar and western hemlock. Go south on bark-covered paths (walk bicycle on paths), passing west of a tennis center.

Continue on one of several paths to the Spiritridge Trail, which crosses the south boundary of the park. Turn left (east), crossing 156th Ave. SE and continuing on a gravel path into an open space, all that remains of the Bellevue Airfield. Go left (northeast) on the second gravel path east of 156th Ave. NE. This path descends past ponds. Find a bark-covered path branching northeast and follow this path as it winds through forest to SE 24th St. Turn right on Phantom Lake Walkway along the south side of SE 24th St., then round north on 168th Ave. SE, along the border of **Weona Beach Park** (two miles of trails). For bus access to this park, take Metro 271 to the intersection of SE Eastgate Way and 161st Ave. SE. After visiting **Spiritridge Park** (playground), walk north on a forest path on the west side of 161st Ave. SE to SE 24th St. Turn east to the park (0.8 mile from Metro stop).

North of SE 24th St., find a trail that goes east to W Lake Sammamish Parkway SE in Weona Beach Park. Other trails go east from SE 19th St. and SE 16th St. to W Lake Sammamish Parkway SE. Park bicycle and walk one or more of the trails to view waterfalls (wet season) and dense forest. The unstable stream banks are glacial deposits, newly exposed by a recent increase in stream flow. Note boulders in the stream bed. From Weona Beach Park, turn west on SE 14th St., passing **Lake Hills Park** with playgrounds and playfields. At 156th Ave. SE, turn south to **Phantom Lake Park** (restrooms, fishing pier, lake access for small boats, no motors).

From Phantom Lake, return north along 156th Ave. NE to SE 16th St. Cross to the northwest corner. The Ranger Station, which has nature walks every Saturday in summer at 10:00 AM, is 200' northwest in a demonstration garden. Produce from market gardens is also sold at this corner. Continue northwest on paths in the **Lake Hills Greenbelt**, crossing Lake Hills Blvd. (water). The **Lake Hills Library** on adjoins the path. Continue north through fields of blueberries (private) to Larsen Lake. North of the lake, turn west to 148th Ave. NE. Go north to Main St., and west to 140th Ave. NE. Turn south to SE 3rd St. then west to enter **Kelsey Creek Park**. At the foot of steps, go southwest on a gravel path, then descend more steps into the valley of Kelsey Creek. After crossing the creek, turn left (south) to reach the barns and farm animal displays (cows, horses, goats, sheep). Look for the Frazier Cabin.

Circle the meadows west to observe the plantings (restrooms, picnic tables, playground). To leave the park, ride northwest and west into SE 4th Place. Turn south on 130th Ave. SE, then go west on SE 7th Place. Cross the Lake Hills Connector into SE 8th St. and continue west under **Wilburton Trestle** (1904) and I-405. West of I-405, turn south on 118th Ave. SE to enter the **Mercer Slough Nature Park** at the Educational Center. This wetland area was exposed when the level of Lake Washington was lowered by opening the Montlake Cut. Continue south in the wetland (walk bicycle) to return to 118th Ave. NE briefly before re-entering the Mercer Slough wetlands. Continue southwest on paths and wood walkways (interpretive signs) across Mercer Slough to reach Bellevue Way SE and the South Bellevue Park & Ride (Metro 226, 235, 340). The Winters House (1920s) is 0.3 mile north of the Park & Ride.

ISSAQUAH TO MARYMOOR PARK, high point 100', 14 miles, minimum gain (Maps: USGS Issaquah, Redmond). **Bicycle**. Ride Metro 215 to Issaquah Park & Ride.

Ride north on the Renton-Issaquah Road over I-90, then, at mile 0.6, turn left (west) on NW Sammamish Road. At mile 0.9, turn right (north) on a paved path into **Lake Sammamish State Park** (shelters, picnic tables, restrooms, lake access, boat launch). Circle through the State Park to the waterfront (restrooms). Continue north to the mouth of Issaquah Creek in a wetland.

Return south to exit from the State Park at mile 3.0 and go right (west) on W Lake Sammamish Parkway SE (narrow shoulder in places). At mile 5.0, turn right (northwest), continuing on West Lake Sammamish Parkway SE and passing **Vasa Park** (camping, lake access, fee) at mile 6.1. West Lake Sammamish Parkway SE has a bicycle shoulder on the west side of the street. **Idylwood Park**, at mile 11.8, has a guarded swimming beach, picnic facilities, and restrooms. After joining Bellevue-Redmond Road, enter **Marymoor Park** at mile 13.8 (Metro 249). From Marymoor Park, the Sammamish River Trail goes north on the west side of the Sammamish River, reaching Woodinville (Metro 307) in seven miles, Bothell in nine miles, and the University district in 22 miles.

ISSAQUAH TO REDMOND, high point 220', 18 miles one-way, 300' gain ((Maps: USGS Issaquah, Redmond). **Bicycle**. Take Metro 215 to Issaquah Park & Ride.

Ride north on SR-900 over I-90. Go right (mile 0.7) on 12th Ave.

NW and wander east through the mall. Find and explore Pickering Barn (1878) on 10th Ave. NW. Continue north to NW Sammamish Road. Turn right (east) to the intersection of SE 56th St. (mile 1.9). Now go north on E Lake Sammamish Parkway SE where a paved shoulder on the west side provides space for bicycles on this street with heavy though intermittent traffic. After Lake Sammamish begins to appear in breaks in the trees, find an entrance to the launch ramps and parking at **Lake Sammamish State Park** (mile 2.9). Turn left (west) and circle through the park (restrooms). Cross east over E Lake Sammamish Parkway SE into the Hans Jensen Group Youth Camping Area (no parking) and continue to the end of the developed park. A rough trail continues up the creek for one mile.

Return to the group camp entrance (mile 4.2) and continue north, crossing SE 43rd Way at mile 4.5. Here the bicycle shoulder narrows to a minimum of 3'. Pass stores at mile 5.9 and SE 24th Way at mile 6.2. E Lake Sammamish Parkway SE now ascends over the highest point of the route, 220' (mile 6.9). Pass Weber Point at mile 11.2 (no lake access). At the north end of Lake Sammamish (mile 12.2), turn right (east) on 187th Ave. NE over a rise to SR-202. Go east (wide shoulder) to mile 13.2. Turn left (north) on 196th Ave. NE. Near 55th Place NE, the red bricks of the **Old Yellowstone Road** are exposed. This road was originally paved in 1913, and connected Seattle with Boston. An signboard gives the history of this longest stretch of exposed brick paving in King County.

Cross Evans Creek at mile 13.5 in a wetland. Turn left (west) on NE Union Hill Road toward Redmond. The southwest corner of the intersection is **Arthur G. Johnson Park** (undeveloped). Cross Evans Creek again at mile 14.5 and continue west on a busy street. A sidewalk begins at mile 15.2 before passing the Bear Creek Park & Ride. Find a bakery thrift store at mile 15.6. Pass Avondale Road at mile 16.0 and continue west on Avondale Way, riding a pedestrian-bikeway. Another bakery is south of the street. Where Avondale Way bends to the north, continue west into a shopping area, following Cleveland Street (sidewalk) through central Redmond. At mile 17.0, turn southwest on Leary Way to the Sammamish River Trail. From Leary Way at the Sammamish River, Woodinville is seven miles and Bothell is nine miles. To reach the Redmond Transit Center, turn north on Brown St., west on Redmond Way, and north on 161st Ave. NE to NE 83rd St.

SNOQUALMIE TO WOODINVILLE, high point 570', 25 miles, 600' gain (Maps: USGS Snoqualmie, Carnation, Duvall, Redmond). **Mt. Bicycle**. Ride Metro 209 to the town of Snoqualmie, leaving the bus at SE King St. Visit and begin the road log at the **Snoqualmie Railroad**

Museum.

Go north on the sidewalk on the west side of Railroad Ave. N, then turn west across the railroad tracks. Pause at the historic **Log Pavilion** where an eight-foot diameter log on a carrier is displayed. At SE Northern St., cross east over tracks into a bikeway and continue north, passing old railroad equipment standing on sidings. The display includes several locomotives, of which two are gear-drive logging engines. At mile 0.8, turn right (east) to SE Snoqualmie-Fall City Road (SR-202) and cross the Snoqualmie River. At the north end of the bridge, turn right (east) on Mill Pond Road for 0.1 mile, then go left (north) on the first branch road (SE 66th St.). Ascend to the next street, Tokul Road SE, and turn right (northeast). Stop to read a sign at the site of Tokul (mile 1.8), the location of Logging Camp A of the Snoqualmie Falls Lumber Company, which later became the Weyerhaeuser Company. The location of the sign above the road provides an excellent view of Mt. Si (124°) and summits northwest of Mt. Teneriffe.

At mile 1.9, the road crosses the right-of-way of the Chicago Milwaukee St. Paul & Pacific Railroad, now the **Snoqualmie Valley Trail**. Descend south from the road to the trail. Follow the old railroad grade north. A timber trestle over Tokul Creek now has a concrete surface and well-protected guard fences. Stop in the middle of the bridge to look down at rushing Tokul Creek 200' below. Continue northwest on the gently descending railroad grade, getting a view southwest to Tiger Mt. Bend north out of the canyon of Tokul Creek, and cross a road (356th Drive SE) (mile 5.3). The trail crosses an 80' deep gully, newly bridged in 1996, then passes the location of the old Fall City Station at a road crossing, mile 6.7. A **King County Park** (wetland) is 0.8 mile west on this gravel road. Cross a bridge over an active landslide and pass a recently built retaining wall in another landslide zone. At mile 10.2, cross a long bridge over a meadow and Griffin Creek. South of the Griffin Creek Road, pass a sawmill and Don Bosco Camp (mile 10.8), then cross Langlois Road. The railroad grade has now descended to the valley floor and the land is dairy farms, gardens, and, at mile 11.9, a Christmas Tree farm. At the next overpass, mile 12.0, Remlinger Farms, with its scenic railway and other attractions, is (east). Cross the Tolt River and enter the town of Carnation.

At mile 14.1, the trail crosses the Carnation-Duvall Road (SR-203), traveling across flood plain with lush fields on both sides. This area is private property and the fields are closed to trail users. At miles 15.6 and 16.4, pass parking areas, and in the next three miles, cross several farm roads. The Snoqualmie River meanders near at mile 17 and stays alongside the trail for a mile (high bank, no access). At NE 124th St. (mile 19.5), turn left (west) across the Snoqualmie River on a narrow bridge (no bikeway). At mile 20.5, turn right (north) on the West Snoqualmie Valley Road, then go left (west, mile 21.1) to ascend on NE 133rd St. to the Tolt River Pipeline. Continue northwest on the pipeline right-of-way over the high point, 570'.

Descend to cross Struve Creek (mile 24.0), where the pipeline is exposed briefly, and Bear Creek. Reach Avondale Road NE at mile 25.0 and find a Metro 251 bus stop. To ride into Woodinville and the Sammamish River Trail, follow the route of **Pipeline: Sammamish River-Snoqualmie View**.

SOUTH HAYSTACK MOUNTAIN, 4162', 31 miles RT, 4100' gain (Maps: Weyerhaeuser Snoqualmie & White River, USGS Lake Joy, Devils Slide, Gold Bar). **Mtn. Bicycle**. Drive SR-203 to MP-8, three miles north of Carnation or seven miles south of Duvall. At the Stillwater Store, turn east on NE Stillwater Hill Road, which rounds north into Harris Creek Road NE, passing the Lake Joy Road two miles from SR-203. Stop at the pipeline crossing and gate on the east side of the road, three miles from SR-203, 340'. Park here or at a second gate and parking area 0.2 miles east on the pipeline road. The first gate is open 6am to 6pm on work days. On work days, only authorized motor vehicles are allowed on the paved road east of the second gate. Hikers, bicyclists, and horses should use the path north of the fence.

Ride east on the Tolt Pipeline, rising to a first high point (620') at mile 1.1, then dropping to a creek crossing and ponds at mile 2.6. The pavement ends 4.2 miles from the Harris Creek Road where the road begins to make several bends. Take a left fork at mile 4.5 into a forest road (W-23200), passing a Weyerhaeuser gate onto a road that goes generally northeast above the west side of the North Fork of the Tolt River (not visible). Pass a branch road on the right (east) immediately after the gate and another road to the right (east) 0.3 miles from the gate. Pass three more roads on the left (west) at mile 6, mile 7, and mile 7.6, and cross branches of Yellow Creek. Cross the main channel of Yellow Creek at mile 7.8. The road now rounds to the southeast before returning to a northeasterly course. A road fork at mile 8.6 in an open flat has an outstanding view of Mt. Index (63°). This road fork is 0.1 mile west of a bridge over the North Fork of the Tolt River. Turn northwest on W-23000, rounding first to the north, then, after a mile, take a branch west to ascend a buttress of Haystack Mountain, getting views of the nearby hills.

At mile 11.6, 2250', where branch road W-23300 curves west, take the right branch (W-23000) to go northeast across a creek. At a road junction, mile 12, 2360', take W-23400 left (north), and at mile 12.5, 2535', stay to the right (east) on W-23400. Reach the next road junction at mile 12.9, 2620'. Take the left (north) fork (W-23420) and continue generally north with some bending to the west or northwest, passing a quarry at 3400'. At a road fork, signed W-23427 and 3700', go right (east), passing a road to the right before reaching the crest of the ridge, 3900', and a view north. Go northwest on the southwest side of the ridge to end near the King County–Snohomish County line. Enjoy the view of the Olympic Mountains, Seattle, and summits south: Mt. Phelps (130°), Mt. Si (180°), and Mt. Rainier. An opening on a pile of discarded logs ascends to within 10' of the summit but ends in an impassable tangle of huckleberry, salmonberry, and young conifers.

To get a view north, return 0.2 mile south on the road. At an open, gravel and dirt slope on the east side of the road, leave the road and ascend to the crest. The next ridge north is another part of Haystack Mountain. The higher summit beyond is Ragged Ridge north of the town of Goldbar. Return to the road and descend south. Where the road down bends east at 4000', look directly along the road (90°) at Mt. Index. Below the quarry, 3500', the road points at Mt. Persis (72°).

TOLT RIVER FORKS, high point 800', 8 miles RT, 1000' gain (Maps: Weyerhaeuser Snoqualmie & White River, USGS Lake Joy). **Hike-2 or Mtn. Bicycle.** Drive SR-203 south from Duvall or north from Fall City to the Stillwater Store (MP-8). Turn northeast on NE Stillwater Hill Road toward Lake Joy. The street becomes Kelly Road NE. Pass the Lake Joy Road on the right (east) at 2.2 miles from SR-203 and the entrance to the Tolt Pipeline at 3.1 miles. At mile 3.3, where the main roads bends to the left (northwest), continue north on NE Stossel Creek Way. The pavement ends 4.7 miles from SR-203. Park near gated branch roads where the road bends north on the west side of Stossel Creek, six miles from SR-203, elevation 589'.

Ride or hike southeast past the gate on a road signed ST-1000, descending toward Stossel Creek and passing a branch road to the right (south) at 0.3 mile. Cross Stossel Creek (mile 0.4) and begin to ascend north at mile 0.6 after passing an overgrown road on the right. Enter an open valley where the road turns east. The general direction here should be east, staying on the most travelled road. Pass two roads to the right at mile 1.3 and and another to the right at mile 1.5. Pass a more travelled road to the left at mile 1.6, ST-1200, near a creek. Now the road bends south over the high point, 800', to a road junction. The road left is signed ST-5000. Go south past a Weyerhaeuser gate into road W-25720, getting a view east of Mt. Phelps. Join road W-25700, then reach the Tolt Pipeline at mile 2.8.

At the pipeline crossing, look east to Mt. Phelps (100°) and Mt. Index (73°). Cross the pipeline, going south on road W-25800 past new reservoirs. This road bends southwest, ascending briefly, then passes a road on the right (west) at mile 3.2 (W-25860) before turning south. If road W-25800 south of the pipeline is closed by construction, turn right (west) for 0.25 mile to an overgrown forest road. Go south to join W-25800. Reach the edge of the steep drop to the Tolt River at mile 3.6 where the driveable road turns west. The rocky, overgrown track down ends on a bench. Descend east over rocks to the confluence of the North and South Forks of the Tolt River. A track west passes a river-level gauging station and cableway across the river. Paths provide access to the shore.

To make a loop on the return, go left (west) on W-25860. This road turns west 0.4 mile north from the south edge of the plateau above the river. At the Tolt Pipeline, go west across Stossel Creek (ponds and wetland), then, 0.1 mile west of Stossel Creek, turn north on W-25902 .

TOLT RIVER GORGE, high point 780', 7 miles RT, 800' gain (Maps: USGS Lake Joy). **Mtn. Bicycle or Hike-1**. Drive as above for **Tolt River Forks** and park at the gate 2.7 miles from Kelly Road, elevation 589'.

Ride or hike southeast past the gate on a road signed ST-1000, descending toward Stossel Creek. At mile 0.3, take the right branch and ascend south to intersect the Tolt Pipeline at mile 0.9. Follow the Tolt Pipeline east to the bridge over the gorge, mile 3.5. The land east of the bridge is closed to public entry.

NORTH FORK CREEK, high point 1400', 23 mile loop, 2200' gain (Maps: Weyerhaeuser Snoqualmie & White River, USGS Sultan, Lake Joy). **Mtn. Bicycle**. From Duvall on SR-203 and 0.1 mile north of the junction with the Woodinville–Duvall Road, drive east on NE Cherry Valley Road. At 6.9 miles from SR-203, turn left (north) on Stossel Creek Road NE. The pavement ends 8.3 miles from SR-203. Pass gates south (road ST-1000) and northwest (road ST-2000) at mile 9.5 before the road turns north on the west side of Stossel Creek. At mile 11.7 from SR-203, park at a road fork where the left-hand road points 345° and the right-hand road points 360°. The right-hand road has a gate and is signed road ST-5000.

Ride the Stossell–Youngs Creek Truck Road to the left (north), passing roads left at miles 0.7 and 1.3. After crossing Cherry Creek at mile 1.4, look for a waterfall below on the left (west). At a sign 'End Maintained County Road', mile 1.6, pass the Cherry Valley Truck Road on the left. A spur road goes north at mile 1.8, but stay on the Stossel–Youngs Creek Road as it bends right (east). Look for a concrete slab (mill site) on the right at mile 2.0, then at mile 2.1, where the main road bends east, continue north on a branch road that descends briefly to cross a a branch of Cherry Creek, mile 2.6. After passing a fork left (west) at mile 2.7, bend left (northwest) and ascend to the crest of **Elwell Scarp**, high point 920'. Pass spurs to the left (west) at miles 3.3, 3.5, and 3.7, continuing to a viewpoint at mile 3.9. Look west across Elwell Creek to a group of forested hills near High Rock and northeast to summits: Pilchuck (6°), Three Finger (16°), Big Bear (17°), Liberty (19°), and Bald Mtn. (25°).

Return south on the road, stopping at all spurs to go west to the edge of Elwell Scarp to look down the glacier-carved precipice. Return to the Stossel–Youngs Creek Road, mile 5.7, and ride east to mile 6.1. Turn southeast on a branch road, passing a gate at mile 6.3 and ascending to a crossing of Cherry Creek below a waterfall at mile 6.9, elevation 770'. Leave bicycle and ascend southeast on a faint track that may be hidden in windfalls, staying on the south side of the creek. This track gradually curves east to **Cherry Lake** (900') one mile from the road.

Return to the road at the Cherry Creek crossing, bicycle mile 6.9, and go south to a junction, ST-5300, mile 7.4. A sign points right (west) to road ST-5000. Take the left fork, going uphill, passing a road to the left, then reaching another gate at a junction, mile 8.6, elevation 900'. Turn left (north) on road ST-5200 and continue to another junction, mile 9.6, elevation 1200'. The road left goes into a quarry. Now go right, staying on road ST-5200 and ascending a switchback to pass road ST-5240 on the right (east) (mile 9.8). At mile 10, leave bicycle and walk east into a forested area with a tattered 'No Camping' sign. Find **Drunken Charlie Lake** 100' east of the road, elevation 1400'.

Return to road ST-5200 and ride south to the junction with road ST-5300, elevation 900', mile 11.4. Turn southeast and ascend gradually to a junction, mile 11.7. Turn right (southwest) on road ST-5400, descending briefly to cross a branch of North Fork Creek. Proceed south and southeast on the east side of the valley of North Fork Creek to a high point, 1200'. Where a branch road goes right (west), mile 13.3, continue south to pass a Weyerhaeuser gate. Bend southeast, now on road W-23230, to a junction with road W-23200 at mile 14.3. This is the main road from the Tolt Pipeline into the North Fork Tolt River country. Turn right (southwest), then curve south to pass another Weyerhaeuser Gate and meet the Tolt Pipeline at mile 15.6. Go west on the pipeline, crossing North Fork Creek and ascending to a road crossing at mile 16.6. Road W-25800 goes south toward the junction of the North and South Forks of the Tolt River.

Turn north (mile 16.6) away from the pipeline on road W-25700, passing a road to the right, then, where road W-25700 goes left (west), keep north on road W-25720 to pass a gate at mile 17.4, elevation 680'. Immediately after passing the gate, turn right (east) on road ST-5000 and, after ascending briefly, pause to appreciate the most comprehensive view of the trip: Mt. Phelps (98°), the tower of Cascade Lookout (117°), Twin Peaks (123°), Bessemer Mtn. (136°), Green Mtn. (152°), Teneriffe Mtn. (156°), and Mt. Si (164°). From the viewpoint, ascend and contour north on the west side of North Fork Creek, high point 1200', then descend to a junction at mile 21.4. The road to the right connects with the outgoing route. The road on the left (north, ST-5000) returns to the start. Go left, passing a road to the left (southwest) at mile 21.7. Now road ST-5000 gradually curves west and south to the starting point, mile 23.

Parks:

ST. EDWARD STATE PARK, high point 400', 5 miles of trails, 400' gain (Map: USGS Kirkland). **Hike-1**. This park of 480 acres is located on the east side of Lake Washington near the north end of the lake. Take Metro 234 to the corner of Juanita Drive NE and NE 153rd Place and walk south on the west side of Juanita Drive NE to a trail entrance. Facilities: swimming pool, restrooms, playfields, forested trails in canyons and along the Lake Washington shoreline.

O. O. DENNY PARK, high point 400', 3 miles of trails, 400' of gain (Map: USGS Kirkland). **Hike-1**. This park is located on the east shore of Lake Washington north of Kirkland. Take Metro 234 to Juanita Drive NE and NE 132nd St. Walk south, west, and northwest on Holmes Point Drive 3 miles to the park. Facilities and activities: waterfront, picnicking, shelter, trails, restrooms. For picnic reservations, call: 206-296-2977. For trail description, see Finn Hill-Denny Creek-St. Edward Loop.

BIG FINN HILL PARK, high point 400', 4+ miles of trails, (Maps: USGS Kirkland). **Hike-1**. This park is located along Juanita Drive NE between Kirkland and Kenmore. Take Metro 234 to the corner of 84th Ave. NE and NE 138th St. Walk west on NE 138th St. If driving, go east from Juanita Drive NE on NE 138th St.

Facilities: playfields, trails in wetlands and forest, restrooms. From the parking area on the south side of NE 138th St., go south of the playfield to find a trail that goes southeast to Big Finn Hill Junior High School. Branches circle east and north through wetland to 84th Ave. NE and NE 138th St. Another track goes west across Juanita Drive and makes connections to St. Edward State Park and O. O. Denny Park on Lake Washington.

JUANITA BEACH PARK, 20' (Maps: USGS Kirkland). **Walk.** The park is located on Juanita Bay on the east shore near the north end of Lake Washington and north of Kirkland. Take Metro 234 to the park entrance west of 98th Ave. NE. Facilities: picnicking, play areas, fishing pier, protected swimming area. For group picnic reservations, call: 206-296-2977.

GOLD CREEK LODGE, high point 340', 2 miles of trails (Maps: USGS Kirkland). **Bicycle and/or Hike-1.** This park is located on 148th Ave. NE at NE 160th St. in Woodinville (limited parking). Take Metro 307 or 251 to NE 175th St. at 140th Ave. NE in Woodinville. Ride or walk south on 140th Ave. NE and 140th Place NE to 148th Ave. NE. Turn north on 148th Ave. NE to Gold Creek Lodge, two miles from the Woodinville Park & Ride. Facilities: 2+ miles of trails in forest, meeting rooms, overnight facilities for groups. For reservations, call: 206-296-2977.

COTTAGE LAKE PARK, 240' (Maps: USGS Maltby). **Bicycle.** This park is located on NE Woodinville–Duvall Road at 188th Ave. NE. Take Metro 307 to the Woodinville Park & Ride and ride east four miles on the Woodinville–Duvall Road or ride Metro 251 to the park. Facilities: swimming, picnicking, playfields, trails.

JOHN McDONALD PARK, high point 580', 2+ miles of trails, 530' gain (Maps: USGS Carnation). **Hike-1.** Drive SR-203 to Carnation. Turn west on NE 40th St. to the park, elevation 60'. Facilities: shelter in rebuilt barn, picnicing, restrooms, campground, walk-in campground across a footbridge over the Snoqualmie River, trails with views east to the Cascade Mts. From parking, walk west over the foot bridge and continue west uphill to find a rabbit warren of trails on the plateau west of the Snoqualmie River.

Tacoma–Olympia Area.

TACOMA PARKS, high point 425', 22 mile loop, 1300' gain (Maps: USGS Tacoma South, Tacoma North). **Mtn. Bicycle.** Ride Pierce Transit Seattle Express 594X to the Tacoma Dome Station. If driving, take Exit-134 from southbound I-5 (Exit-135 northbound) and park in the Tacoma Dome area.

From the Tacoma Dome Station, ride west to East D St. Turn left (south) across I-5 into McKinley Way. Immediately after crossing I-5, go left (east) on a paved path in **McKinley Park**, ascending to ride parallel to Upper Park St. Pass a pond on the left at mile 0.6 and a trail descending north into the park at mile 0.8. Exit east from the park on E 29th St. and descend east. Cross East L St. and continue to a street end, then descend around a barrier to East M St. Turn left (north) to E 28th St. and continue east to cross E Portland St. At East R St., go right (south) to E 29th St., then east to the grounds of the **Puyallup Nation** (bingo, administration building, etc.).

Continue east, then bend south around the east side of the Puyallup Nation administration building (multistory yellow bricks) and exit to E 32nd St. Go west to Roosevelt Ave. (mile 2.4) and continue south into **Swan Creek Park**. At the southeast corner of the paved streets of a former military installation, leave bicycle and descend east (trail) into the canyon of Swan Creek for a brief introduction. Return to bicycle and ride south on one of several trails to emerge on E 56th St., mile 5.

Go west on E 56th St. across E Portland Ave. to East K St. Now go left (south) along the crest with views of the Cascades and Mt. Rainier. At E 64th St., go west across Pacific Ave. (SR-7) (mile 6.4). At mile 7.2, cross W Sheridan Ave. and descend west into **Wapato Park**. At a bridge over a wetland, turn south to **Wapato Lake**, elevation 310'. For bus access, take Pierce Transit 45 to Yakima Ave. and S 68th St. Walk west to enter Wapato Park at Sheridan Ave. Facilities: shelter, picnic tables, play equipment, beach. After touring the park, including a loop to cross over the wetland bridge at the north end of the park, leave the park west to Alaska St., mile 9.3.

Go north on Alaska St. to S 56th St. Turn west (sidewalk) to Alder St., then go north to S 54th St. Jog west to enter **South Park** opposite Lawrence St. Facilities: benches, playground, and South Park Community Center. Continue northwest to S Tacoma Way at S 48th St. Go north, then cross S Tacoma Way at S 47th St. Continue west to Washington St. Turn north to rejoin S Tacoma Way at mile 11.5. Stay on the sidewalk on the west side of S Tacoma Way until S Tacoma Way begins to bend east. Where Union Ave. crosses S Tacoma Way, go north on the sidewalk on the west side of the southbound off ramp from Union Ave. and continue north along the west side of Union Ave. to Center St. Turn west to Madison St. and north into **Oakland Park**. Facilities: playground, playfield, restrooms. Exit north, then go west on S 31st St. to Tyler St. Turn north along a gravel path on the east side of Tyler St. to Snake Lake Nature Center, mile 14. Park bicycle and walk the nature paths.

From **Snake Lake Nature Center**, go north across S 19th St. and continue on Tyler St. to S 15th St. Turn east to Union Ave. Jog one block north to Melrose St., then go east to Puget Sound Ave. and **Franklin Park** (playfields, playground, shelter, restrooms in summer), mile 15. On leaving Franklin Park, go north on Puget Sound Ave., jogging west on N 8th St. to Union Ave., then turn north to enter the grounds of the University of Puget Sound at N 14th St. Tour the campus, exiting northeast into Washington Ave. Proceed north to N 31st St., then go west to enter **Puget Park** at the intersection with Proctor St. (mile 17.8). Park bicycle and descend on a trail to the floor of the canyon and go east to **Puget Gardens** (rhododendrons and azaleas) at the east end and lowest point of the park.

Return to bicycle and ride south on Proctor St. Turn east on N 21st St. and proceed into Yakima St. Pass streets paved with sandstone blocks from the Wilkeson quarry at N 10th and N 11th. Ride down one street and back up the other to appreciate the texture. Cross Division Ave. and begin **Wright Park**, mile 20.5. Facilities: ponds, paved paths, conservatory, and gardens. Tour the park, then go east to G St. and south to S 9th St. Descend east to Commerce St. Find PT 594X between 10 and 11th Sts.

SWAN CREEK PARK, high point 380', 6 miles of trails, 400' gain (Maps: USGS Tacoma South). **Hike-2**. Take Pierce Transit 594X and PT 41A to E 44th St. and Roosevelt Ave. If driving, see below. Walk east on E 44th St. into the park, then turn south on a paved road. Where the pavement turns west, descend east on a trail to Swan Creek.

For a longer hike, ride Pierce Transit Seattle Express 594X to the Tacoma Dome Station, then hike the route as described in **Tacoma Parks** to E 32nd St. south of the Puyallup Nations administration building. Go east to Grandview Ave. E, turn right (south) on Grandview Ave. E for 0.3 mile, then descend southeast on E Browning Road to Pioneer Way. Follow Pioneer Way southeast to a crossing of Swan Creek, mile 3. Find a track on the east side of the creek (may be overgrown) and go south to a flood basin. Circle left (east) around the pond, then walk east to the park entrance south of Pioneer Way.

If driving, take Exit-135 from I-5 into SR-167 going toward Puyallup. After 0.7 mile turn right (south) on Pioneer Way and go south to Swan Creek. Enter a parking area on the east side of Swan Creek and north off Pioneer Way.

From the parking area north of Pioneer Way and east of Swan Creek, cross Pioneer Way to a park entrance and walk south to a path on the east side of Swan Creek, then cross a bridge. Proceed south on a narrow trail that goes up and down to pass obstacles, sometimes on steps and sometimes on boardwalks (slippery when wet or icy). Look for the following native plants along the trail: hemlock, red cedar, Douglas fir, vine maple, bigleaf maple, elderberry, blackberry, salmonberry, yew, devils club, sword fern, and salal.

Take one or more of the trails that turn west up the slope to explore more of the park. Return to the trail along the west side of Swan Creek and continue south to a decayed bridge that crosses Swan Creek. Turn west and ascend on switchbacks, passing a street-end barrier and, after reaching the plateau, go west to a junction with E 56th St. To return to Pierce Transit 41, go west to Portland Ave. To return to parking off Pioneer Way, go north on any trail on the plateau west of Swan Creek canyon. On reaching pavement, descend east (trail) into the canyon and the outgoing route. Turn north to parking off Pioneer Way.

SNAKE LAKE NATURE CENTER, high point 423', 2 miles of trails, 150' of gain (Maps: USGS Tacoma South). **Walk**. If driving, take the Union Ave. exit from SR-16. Drive north on Union Ave. and west on S 19th St. to the park. For bus access to Snake Lake Nature Center, take Pierce Transit 594X and PT 27 to S 19th St. and Tyler St.

Facilities: programs, interpretive signs, guidebook, displays, accessible trails. One path circles Snake Lake, and another path loops over a hill east of the lake. Look for the following native plants: black cottonwood (1), cascara (4,7), bitter cherry (5), snowberry (7), Douglas fir, salal (9), hazel (9), Oregon ash, madrone, rose, dogwood, and honeysuckle.

TACOMA WATERWAYS, high point 405', 16 miles, 300' gain (Maps: USGS Tacoma North, Tacoma South, Poverty Bay). **Mtn. Bicycle**. Ride Metro 194 to the South Federal Way Park & Ride.

Ride west on S 348th St. At 0.3 mile, pass **Hylebos State Park** (toilet, picnic table, nature trail with interpretive signs). Turn south on 1st Ave. S, then west on S 356th St., ascending over the high point. At 21st Ave. SW, the street crosses into Pierce County and becomes NE 29th St. Bend left (south) on Northpoint Way NE (mile 2.6) and descend, curving to the northwest to pass sand and gravel quarries in deposits left by the Puget Glacier. Go right (northwest) on Marine View Drive (SR-509), mile 4.2, in the Tacoma industrial area. At E 11th St., mile 4.5, turn left (southwest) across the Hylebos Waterway.

At a stop light, turn left (southeast) on Alexander Ave., passing a casino before joining SR-509 (mile 7.5). Cross Port of Tacoma Road, mile 8.1. Go straight ahead (west) where a ramp ascends onto a bridge. Bend left (south) on Milwaukee Way (mile 8.9), keeping right at a junction to go under Pacific Highway. At mile 9.4, turn right on 20th St. Drive. Before going under I-5, turn right again (west) into a driveway over railroad tracks to the Puyallup River, mile 9.4. Go left (southeast) on the dike under I-5 to end at a railroad bridge, then return northwest on the dike. Pass under a railroad bridge at mile 10, under old Pacific Highway at mile 10.1, then cross railroad tracks at grade level before going under the SR-509 bridge at mile 10.4.

At mile 10.7, turn right (east) away from the river to circle the **Gog-Le-Hi-Te Wetland**, stopping to read the interpretive signs and appreciate several viewpoints. From the wetland interpretive trail, go northwest across E 21st St., finding a road that reconnects to the dike. Continue north along the Puyallup River, leaving the dike at the E 11th St. bridge. Ride northwest under the bridge, at first on a paved street, then walk a dirt path to the mouth of the Puyallup River at the shore of Puget Sound and a viewpoint northwest to the Olympic Mountains, mile 13. Summits visible include: Mt. Elinor (294°), The Brothers (309°), Mt. Constance (316°), and Mt.Townsend (326°).

Return southeast under E 11th St. on the street or the dike to E 21st St., mile 14.5. Turn right (southwest) over the Puyallop River to Portland Ave. Go right (northwest), bending left into St. Paul Ave., mile 14.9. Turn west on E 11th St. over a bridge, stopping to view the Thea Foss Waterway and the decaying Tacoma Dock below. Continue west across A St. to Pacific Ave., mile 16. Go left (south) on Pacific Ave. past 15th St. S. Find a ramp descending northeast under I-705 to a bridge, then go east across the railroad tracks. Descend steps or a ramp. Turn south on Dock St. until east of Union Station. Turn east into a paved walkway that follows north along the edge of Thea Foss Waterway. North of the 11th St. bridge, the walkway is sometimes on boardwalk viewing platforms. After visiting **Thea's Park** near the mouth of the waterway, turn west and cross the 4th St. bridge. Go left (south) on the west side of Schuster Parkway. At the first building, a former Tacoma Cityhall, ascend steps west to emerge on Commerce St. Turn south past 9th St., then ascend ramps west in the **Water Park** to Theater Square. Go south on Broadway St. past a fountain at 10th St. Descend east on 11th St. to Commerce St. Find the PT 594X on Commerce St. between 10th and 11th Sts.

POINT DEFIANCE PARK, high point 260', 10+ miles of trails and paved paths (Maps: USGS Gig Harbor). **Bicycle or Hike-1**. From Seattle, take Pierce Transit 594X to Tacoma, then ride PT-11 to the park, or take Metro 54, Vashon ferry, Metro 118, and Tahlequah ferry. For a loop trip with bicycle, take the passenger ferry from downtown Seattle to Vashon Island, Metro 118 or 119 to the town of Vashon, ride west on SW 204th ST., south on 111th Ave. SW, west on SW 220th St., south on Wax Orchard Road and Vashon Highway to Tahlequah and the ferry to Point Defiance. For the return, ride into downtown Tacoma and take PT 594X to Seattle from Commerce St. at 10th St. For walkers that come by Tahlequah ferry, take PT-11 to the Transit Center at 10th and Commerce Sts. to return to Seattle by PT-594X. If driving, take Exit-132 from I-5 into SR-16. Turn north from SR-16 into Pearl St. (SR-163) and drive three miles north to the park entrance (limited parking on weekends).

Facilities: beach access, waterfront promenade, zoo, aquarium, Fort Nisqually restoration, logging and railroad museum, train rides, nature trails, flower gardens. Ride bicycles only on paved paths, roads, or trails at least 6' wide.

Hike-3. 4 mile loop, 200' gain. Accessible only at minus tides. Ride PT 11 to the ferry landing in Point Defiance Park. Hike northwest along the beach promenade. At the northernmost point, stop at a wave-cut terrace to examine the sandstone cliffs. These exhibit a family of stress-relief faults (not the kind that cause earthquakes) with vertical displacements of up to two feet in the strata. Continue rounding the point to the west and south to Salmon Beach. Near the south end of the houses, find steps or a ramp to the boardwalk along the houses and a path or steps rising to a parking area for the houses. Follow the street east (gate) to emerge on 52nd St. Go east on the paved street to Pearl Ave. and a PT 11 stop.

FOOTHILLS TRAIL, high point 280', 8 to 27 miles, no gain (Maps: USGS Orting, Sumner). **Walk or Bicycle**. Ride Pierce Transit 594X to Tacoma, PT-400 to Puyallup and PT-403 to Orting. If driving, take SR-162 south from SR-410 in Sumner and park south of the Puyallup River bridge, four miles from SR-410.

From the bus stop in Orting at the Foothills Trail crossing, walk or ride southeast on the paved trail. At mile 1.3, cross a bridge over Voight Creek that was restored in 1997 by A Company of the 864th Engineers. Travel near the Carbon River at mile 1.8, then get the nearest view of Mt. Rainier. Find more bridges at miles 3, 3.2 and 3.8. The last bridge is over wetland. Cross the Carbon river at mile 3.9 and leave the end of the pavement (1999). Beyond mile 6, the trail is rutted and ponded and it becomes impassable at the next road crossing (mile 6.5). The Carbon River Road nearby provides an alternate route to continue to the village of South Prairie (mile 7.8).

On the return, after crossing Voight Creek, diverge right (north) on the river levee to the next road where the levee is blocked by gates, then return south to the trail. The levee road continues to the Puyallup River confluence but sections are private land. In Orting (mile 15.6, reader board), continue northwest to pass the trail parking area at the Puyallup River where the pavement ends (mile 18.3). Cross the Puyallup River into McMillan and find a PT-403 stop or continue north on SR-162 to Pioneer Ave. (mile 22.2), then go west into Puyallup to find the PT 400 off Pioneer Way at 3rd St. SW (mile 26.5).

If driving, from the parking area at the Puyallup River, walk or ride southeast and east on the trail to the end of the pavement and return as above, distance 14 miles RT.

STEILACOOM AREA PARKS, high point 400', 26 miles RT, 400' gain (Maps: USGS Tacoma South, Steilacoom). **Mtn. Bicycle and Hike-1.** Ride Pierce Transit 594X to the SR-512 Park & Ride or, if driving, park at the SR-512 Park & Ride.

From the SR-512 Park & Ride, ride west across S Tacoma Way, then turn north. Turn right (west) at the first street, Perkins Lane SW, and follow Becker Drive SW north and 101st St. SW west to the Southgate Elementary School. In front of the school, at Early Ave. SW, turn right (north) on a gated road to reach 100th St. SW. Note location of this street (signed Southgate Elementary School) for the return. Proceed west (gravel shoulder), crossing railroad tracks and Lakeview Ave. At Lakewood Drive SW, mile 1.7, after passing a Fred Meyer store, turn north on the east side of **Seeley Lake Park** to a park entrance. Leave bicycle and walk the trail (1.2 miles) through a wetland. Return to bicycle and go north to the Lakewood Community Center, bicycle mile 2.3. Exit north from the Community Center, then turn west on the first street to pass along the south side of an apartment complex and find an elevated view of Seeley Lake. Pass a motor vehicle barrier to continue west into 59th Ave. SW. Turn south across Bridgeport Way SW, then go northwest to Mt. Tacoma Drive SW. Turn west, crossing Gravelly Lake Drive SW. Bend right (north) to continue southwest on Motor Ave. SW into Mt. Tacoma Drive SW.

Follow the arterial as it bends left (south) into Interlaaken Drive SW (no shoulder) to cross **Steilacoom Lake**, mile 4.2. Cross Lake Steilacoom Drive SW into Short Lane SW, going south to 104th St. SW. Turn right (west), and right again (north) on Hipkins Road SW for two blocks. Bend left (northwest) into Angle Lane SW past a motor vehicle barrier, mile 5.2, and enter **Fort Steilacoom Park**. Turn left (west) on a wide gravel path toward forest. At mile 5.4, park bicycle and hike up a steep, wide trail to the high point near a water tank (no distant view). Return to bicycle on another trail and continue west.

At a 'T' junction, bicycle mile 5.7, turn right (northwest) to **Waughop Lake**. Circle the lake, then return to the main access road and go northeast to the barn area. These buildings were formerly used by the farm that was part of Western State Hospital. Ride around the barns and visit the cemetery east of the barns that has dates from 1876 to 1953, then return to Waughop Lake. Turn west, taking a trail that goes right to the crest of the hill to view abandoned Western State Hospital buildings. At the northwest corner of the lake, find a paved path and go southwest into the grounds of Pierce College. Exit west from the College to Farwest Drive SW, mile 8.5. Turn left (south) to Lakes High School. At the north boundary of the school, turn right (west) and ride a paved road through the grounds, exiting to 107th Ave. SW. Go left (south) to Military Road SW. Turn right (northwest) to enter the town of Steilacoom (mile 9.6). At mile 9.8, turn left (south) on Briston Lane to Oak Drive. Now go west, passing Randolph Ave., into a street that ends at a trail entrance into **Farrels Marsh Park**.

Explore the park, either on foot or by bicycle. A main trail goes south to the boundary of Fort Lewis and another trail goes along the west side of the marsh from near the north entrance. Explore trails to the edge of the marsh. Exit north from the park to the intersection of Beech Ave. and Chambers St. (mile 10.5). Ride north and northwest on Chambers St., jogging southwest for a block to continue northwest on Frederick St. At Union Ave., continue northwest to the ferry dock where ferries go to Anderson Island and McNeil Island. From the ferry dock, go northeast on Commercial St., passing the Steilacoom Railroad Station to **Pioneer Memorial Park**, which has a bandstand, lawn swing, and view finders (see below for list). Go southeast on Wilkes St. past a monument to the first Protestant church north of the Columbia River, established 1853.

Turn left (northeast) on Lafayette St., descending on a busy highway with bike lane. At mile 12, cross railroad tracks into **Sunnyside Beach Park**. Facilities: shelter, beach access, restrooms, showers, playfield. An interpretive sign shows many of the following points of interest: Mt. Elinor (307°), Mt. Washington (309°), Mt. Pershing, Mt. Stone, The Brothers (322°), Mt. Mystery, Mt. Constance (330°), Mt. Jupiter (331°) Iron Mtn., Mt. Deception, Mt. Townsend, Ketron Island (240°), Anderson Island (260°), McNeil Island (290°), and Fox Island (345°).

From Sunnyside Beach Park, proceed north on Chambers Creek Road (part bike lane), going along the shore of Chambers Bay and passing a wood products factory. At the bridge over Chambers Creek, mile 13, park bicycle and hike northeast into **Chambers Creek Park** on a gravelled utility corridor (bicycles allowed). Several muddy or marshy tracks provide access to the creek and a wide trail goes south up the steep slope but all branches end in private land. The utility corridor ends on the plateau one mile from Chambers Creek Road at the intersection of

70th St. SW and 91st Ave. Court (no parking). Return to bicycle and proceed south on Chambers Creek Road and Lafayette St. On reentering the town of Steilacoom, mile 16.5, turn left (southeast) on Balch St., left (northeast) on Rainier St., and right (southeast) on Puyallup St. to Steilacoom Blvd.

Ascend the hill. East of Farwest Drive SW, enter the grounds of Western State Hospital, mile 18. Proceed east on driveways in the hospital grounds. At the east end of the main cluster of buildings, turn north on a paved street to greenhouses. At a low point, find a dirt road that goes west to a gate. Leave bicycle and walk down the road to **Garrison Springs** and a fish hatchery. The main group of springs discharges from a pipe in the middle of a pond. Other springs drain the north-facing slope. Return to the paved road and continue northeast, passing several buildings and exiting north to Golf Course Road. Turn west to the golf course. Park bicycle and hike north and west on a trail on the north side of the golf course. This trail descends for 0.5 mile in a forested canyon to end at a fence. Return to bicycle and go east to 87th Ave. SW. Turn south to Steilacoom Blvd. SW, then go east, staying on gravel paths or sidewalks on the north side of Steilacoom Blvd. SW. At Phillips Road SW, mile 20, turn left (north) to the **South Puget Sound Wildlife Area and Fish Hatchery** where some of the grounds are open to visitors (no dogs). Return south on Phillips Road to Steilacoom Blvd. SW (mile 20.7) and cross to the south side of the street. Ride east past the end of Steilacoom Lake to Edgewater Drive SW. Turn south on this street to **Steilacoom Lake Park** (fishing access, boat ramp).

From Steilacoom Lake Park, go south into Waverly Drive SW. Turn east on Mt. Tacoma Drive SW, jogging briefly northeast on Motor Drive SW to continue east on Mt. Tacoma Drive SW. At Bridgeport Way SW, cross north and go southeast to 100th St. SW. Now ride east in parking lots or on gravel sidewalk. At Lakeview Ave. SW, cross to continue east. After crossing the railroad tracks, look for the outgoing route turning south from 100th St. SW and return past the Southgate School to the SR-512 Park & Ride.

SPANAWAY PARKS, high point 350', 16 mile loop, minimum gain (Maps: USGS Tacoma South, Spanaway). **Bicycle**. Ride Pierce Transit 594X to the SR-512 Park & Ride.

Ride south on S Tacoma Way. At mile 0.3, turn east on 112th St. S, crossing McChord Air Force Base. Look south along runways where Globemasters take off and land. Pass wetland on both sides of the street at mile 1.4. Turn right (south) on 10th Ave. S (mile 2.0), then go east on Wheeler St. S into the campus of Pacific Lutheran University. Tour the campus, including the Scandinavian Cultural Center with its artistic suggestion of a Viking ship. Best time: May and June when the rhododendrons are in bloom. Leave the campus by going south on Yakima Ave. S. Turn right (west) on Tule Lake Road S and left (south) on 10th Ave. S to **Gonyea Park**, mile 6. Facilities: playground, playfields, restrooms.

Continue south on 10th Ave. S, jogging left (east) on 142nd St. S to 8th Ave. S. Turn right (south) into 8th Court S to enter **Bresemann Forest** in **Spanaway Park** where trails are open to bicycles. Ride, or preferably walk, one or more loop trails in the park, one of which follows Spanaway Creek briefly. Leave Bresemann Forest at the southeast corner (climbing rocks). Turn west on Military Road, then go south on Bresemann Blvd. into the rest of Spanaway Park (mile 8.7). Explore the various facilities in the park: swimming beaches, restrooms, changing rooms, shelters, picnic areas, play areas, and ponds.

Return to Military Road (mile 11.5) and go west past the Bresemann Homestead (established 1873, not public) to Spanaway Loop Road (mile 12.1). Now go north, passing Gonyea House (not public). At mile 14, turn right (east) on 116th St. S to Alaska Street S, left (north) to 112th St. S, left (west) to S Tacoma Way, and right (north) to the SR-512 Park & Ride.

NISQUALLY NATIONAL WILDLIFE REFUGE, 10', 8 miles of trails, no gain (Maps: Refuge map, USGS Nisqually). **Hike-1**. Take Exit-114 from I-5. Drive west 0.5 mile to parking at the refuge (fee). No bicycles or jogging.

Facilities: observation platforms, displays, 5.5 mile perimeter loop trail, 1 mile accessible trail. Trails follow the Nisqually River, McAllister Creek, and a dike at the edge of tidelands.

OLYMPIA PARKS, high point 200', 22 mile loop, 700' gain (Maps: USGS Tumwater). **Bicycle or Walk parts**. From Seattle, take Pierce Transit 594X to Tacoma and transfer to Olympia Express 620X or 603X. Leave bus at Olympia Transit Center.

For access only to the State Capitol (one mile), walk west to Columbia St., then go south past 7th Ave. SW. Where Columbia St. begins to rise, find a path south off a driveway on the west side of the street.

From the Transit Center, ride east on State Ave., then go north on East Bay Drive, passing a shoreline interpretive viewpoint in **Eastbay Park**. Reach **Priest Point Park** at mile 1.8. Facilities: interpretive signs, trails in forest, beach access, viewpoints, restrooms, tables, kitchens with wood stoves. Park bicycle and walk the trail to the beach for a view of the state capitol across Budd Inlet. Return to East Bay Drive and go south, turning west on State Ave., mile 4.2. At the west end of State Ave., enter **Percival Landing Park**. Facilities: restrooms, interpretive signs, historical pictures, tables, benches, viewpoints. Walk to the north end for the view of Budd Inlet, then return south to 4th Ave. Turn right (west) for one block, passing public art by Richard S. Beyer, then reenter another section of Percival Landing Park to find more historical pictures, a restroom, a public boat landing, and viewpoints over Budd Inlet.

Return to 4th Ave. and go west over the end of Budd Inlet. At the west end of the bridge bend right (northwest) up the hill into Harrison St. Continue west to Cooper Point Road, mile 7.2. Turn left (south) and enter **Yaugher Park** through a gate (mile 7.5). Facilities: two miles of trails, interpretive signs, shelter, restooms, picnic tables, playfields. Park bicycle and walk a wetland trail. Return to bicycle and ride south to emerge on Capitol Mall Drive SW. Turn left (east) to cross Cooper Point Road, mile 8.9. Continue east, bending into Percival St. SW. Go right (east) on 5th Ave. W, bending north to 4th Ave.

From the west end of the bridge, bend right (south) to **Capitol Lake**, then follow the west shore of the lake south along Deschutes Parkway, passing **Marathon Park** (picnic tables, lake access). At mile 12, turn left (southeast) into **Capitol Lake Interpretive Center**. Find interpretive signs and viewpoints over the lake (restrooms in summer). Continue southeast and south on the path under I-5 to **Tumwater Historical Park**, mile 13. Facilities: restrooms, interpretive signs, playground, picnic tables. From the park, take the exit road south, stopping on the way up the hill and walk down toward the river for a view of **Tumwater Falls** from downstream. Exit to Deschutes Parkway SW and continue south, passing a bridge over the river to the Olympia Brewery (Boston St.). Enter **Tumwater Falls Park** at mile 13.5. Park bicycle and walk the trails and bridges for the complete view. Return to the park entrance, go north to take the bridge east toward the Olympia Brewery. At Custer Way, where a bridge crosses west over the river and I-5, go east past the brewery (tours) to Capitol Blvd., mile 14. Turn left (north) to begin the **State Capitol** campus at Maple Park Drive, mile 15.4. Find information and maps at the junction of Capitol Way and 14th Ave.

On the Capitol Campus, look for the following points of interest: Lady Dancing, totem pole, sunken garden, war memorials, Governor's Mansion (tours by reservation on Wednesday's), Winged Victory Monument, and Tivoli Fountain. The predominant stone in the Capitol Building is Wilkeson sandstone.

After touring the State Capitol campus, return to Maple Park Drive at Capitol Way, mile 16.4. Go east on Maple Park Drive, which becomes

16th Ave. At the east end of the street, bend left (north) into Cherry St. Cross the freeway ramp (14th Ave.), then turn right (east) to enter a bikeway (marked by yellow markers) on the north side of the ramp. Descend over railroad tracks and Plum St., then go left at a bikeway junction to Plum St. Turn left (south) along Plum St., crossing to the west side of Plum St. to go southeast under I-5 (northbound vehicles on Plum St. tend to invade the bikeway). Go southeast into Henderson Blvd. Reach **Olympia Watershed Park** at mile 18. Leave bicycle for a loop walk on two miles of trails (no bicycles or jogging in the park), crossing Moxlie Creek twice. Look for: ancient nurse log, nurse stump, giant stump, giant ancient red cedar and hemlock trees, and devil's club thickets.

If driving, reach **Olympia Watershed Park** from southbound I-5 by taking Exit-105B. Turn south on Plum St. under I-5 into Henderson Blvd., reaching the park one mile from I-5. If northbound on I-5, take Exit-105, curving right to Henderson Blvd. Turn left (southeast) to the park entrance.

From Olympia Watershed Park (mile 18), return northwest on Henderson Blvd. under I-5, staying on the southwest side of the street until the street bends into Plum St. Proceed north on the east side of Plum St. to the **Japanese Gardens** at mile 19.4, north of Union Ave. Tour the gardens, then continue north on Plum St. Turn left (west) on Legion Way through downtown Olympia to **Capitol Lake Park**. Facilities: picnic tables, restrooms, lake access, paved paths and road south to **Marathon Park**. From Capitol Lake Park, go north on Water St., bending right (east) into State Ave. to the Transit Center at Washington St., mile 22.

EVERGREEN STATE COLLEGE, high point 180', 4 miles of trails, 400' gain (Maps: USGS Olympia). **Hike-2**. Take Pierce Transit 594X, Olympia Express 620X, and IT-41 to the campus. If driving, leave I-5 at Exit-104 and drive northeast on SR-101. At the The Evergreen State College exit, go north on Evergreen Parkway to the college (parking fee).

From the bus stop, walk northwest to the library and get a map of the campus. After exploring the campus, including visits to the Organic Farm and the Longhouse Cultural Center, go northeast on the north side of the College Activities Building through the residence area. Find the trail to Geoduck Beach on Eld Inlet at the northwest corner of Parking Lot 'F', north of Driftwood Road. Hike the trail to the beach (one mile). Near the beach, the trail to the right (north) reaches the beach in 300'. The trail to the left (south) descends to the beach, then makes a loop east to return to the main trail. Another trail goes south from the main trail 0.5 mile from Lot 'F', passing a fire circle, to make another loop to

Eld Inlet.

MILLERSYLVANIA STATE PARK, high point 260', 8 miles of trails and roads, minimum gain (Maps: USGS Maytown). **Bicycle or Hike-1**. From I-5, take Exit-95. Drive east two miles to a 'T'. Turn north 0.8 mile to the entrance.

Facilities: paved roads and gravel paths (open to bicycles), nature trail, exercise course, swimming beach on Deep Lake, interpretive signs, kitchens, shelters, camping with hookups.

MIMA MOUNDS, 240', 2 miles of trails, minimum gain (Maps: USGS Littlerock). **Walk**. A strange area of mounds up to 10' tall that have not been satisfactorily explained. The 445 acre area was originally purchased by the Nature Conservancy and the Isaac Walton League. Operation is now a joint project of the Washington State Interagency Committee for Outdoor Recreation and the US Heritage Conservation and Recreation Service.

From I-5, take Exit-95. Drive west through the town of Littlerock (mile 3), continuing one mile west to a 'T'. Turn right (north) for 0.8 mile to the Mima Mounds entrance on the left (west) side the the road. Drive west to parking five miles from I-5.

Facilities: paved accessible trails, viewpoints, restrooms, explanatory displays, nature trail. Look for the following native plants: strawberry, violets, camas (Camassia), shootingstar (Dodecatheon), buttercup (Ranunculus), kinnikinick, ocean spray, Indian plum, service berry, hazel, cascara, white oak, Oregon grape, and salal.

MIMA FALLS, high point 640', 8 mile loop, 600' gain (Maps: Capitol Forest, USGS Littlerock). **Mtn. Bicycle or Hike-2**. Horses are allowed on these trails from April 1 to November 1. Expect muddy trails. Call 1-800-527-3305 (Central Area Office) for trail closures.

From I-5, take Exit-95. Drive west through the town of Littlerock (mile 3), continuing one mile west to a 'T'. Turn left (south) for 1.3 miles to Bordeaux Road. Turn right (west) 0.7 mile to Marksman Road. Go right (north). After one mile on Marksman Road SW, where Marksman Road SW bends northeast, continue north 0.2 mile to Mima Falls Campground and a trailhead at the north end of the campground, seven miles from I-5 at Exit-95. This loop trail is also accessible from Margaret McKenney Campground. Drive as above toward **Mima Mounds**. From the entrance to Mima Mounds, continue northwest and north for two miles to Margaret McKenny Campground, seven miles from I-5 at Exit-95. Find the trail on the south side of the road near the campground entrance, elevation 240'.

From the trailhead (Greenline Trail #6) at Mima Falls Campground, hike 0.5 miles north to a junction. Take the right fork, which continues north across a clearcut to descend into a shallow valley and another junction. The right fork goes to Waddell Creek and Margaret McKenney Campground. Take the left fork, crossing the low point of the valley (no visible creek in October) and ascending briefly in forest to a junction. The trail to the right goes to Waddell Creek. Follow the west side of a creek that shows mostly as small ponds and flows southeast to Waddell Creek. After bending west, cross two roads. At mile 2, a trail goes right (north) to Margaret McKenny Campground (one mile). Continue west to a junction at mile 3 with Greenline Trail #10. This trail goes north to Falls Creek Campground.

Go south on Greenline Trail #10, crossing an overgrown road. The trail passes the high point, then contours the west side of a ridge above a branch of Mima Creek. Continue south to a junction with Porter Trail #8, four miles from Mima Falls Trailhead. Turn right over a branch of Mima Creek. Continue 0.5 miles to Mima Falls. After viewing the falls, return north to the junction with Trail #8. Take the right fork and hike east across roads to the outgoing route. Turn right (south) to the trailhead.

Alternate entrance: From the trailhead at the Margaret McKenny Campground entrance, hike west across Waddell Creek. Now go southwest to intersect the trail coming from Mima Falls Campground.

CAPITOL PEAK, 2659', 10 miles RT, 2100' gain (Maps: Capitol Forest, USGS Capitol Peak). **Mtn. Bicycle or Hike-2**. Horses are allowed on these trails from April 1 to November 1. Call 1-800-527-3305 (Central Area Office) for trail closures.

From I-5, take Exit-95. Drive west on SR-121 through the town of Littlerock (mile 3), continuing one mile west to a 'T'. Turn south 1.3 miles, then go west on Bordeaux Road SW. At mile 8.7 from I-5, turn northwest on a paved road to ascend over a ridge. At mile 11, reach Sherman Creek and a four-way junction. Sherman Valley Campground is 0.1 mile west. Turn north on a gravel road in Sherman Creek valley to the Fall Creek Trailhead (mile 14.6 from I-5) or Fall Creek Campground (mile 15).

From the trailhead, hike north around the west side of Falls Creek Campground, descending to cross Falls Creek at the north end of the campground, 640'. Continue north, entering a regrowing clearcut, then crossing a gravel road at elevation 700' to enter standing forest. Exit the forest into another clearcut, ascending on a trail or logging spur to a main road, 1200', where the trail jogs right (east). Contour west above the road, crossing a bridge over a branch of Falls Creek at 1250'. A trail goes left to the road west of the bridge. Join an old railroad grade at 1400' to continue west. The railroad grade ends abruptly at 1550' near another branch trail. At this junction, turn right (north) to ascend in switchbacks to a road below the west ridge of Capitol Peak, 1900'. Contour east on the trail, which crosses or follows the road. The trail leaves the road to ascend switchbacks north to the west ridge of Capitol Peak and a main road, 2300'. Go east to the summit, which has several communication towers. Look northeast to the State Capitol building (66°) and embayments of Puget Sound.

Puget Sound Area.

VASHON ISLAND LOOP, high point 400', 36 mile loop, 1600' gain (Maps: USGS Vashon, Poverty Bay, Tacoma North, Gig Harbor, Olalla, Duwamish Head). **Bicycle**. Take Metro 174, 194, etc., to the South Federal Way Park & Ride. Ride west on S 348th St., passing (mile 0.3) **West Hylebos State Park** (toilet). Continue into SW Campus Drive, passing the **Weyerhaeuser Washington State Aquatic Center** (mile 1.2) and a Federal Way Park (mile 2.0). At mile 2.2, turn north on 21st Ave. SW to **Lakota Park** (mile 3.6, toilet) at Dash Point Road (SR-509).

From Lakota Park, go west on Dash Point Road, descending toward Puget Sound. At mile 4.6, cross a bridge over a deep ravine with a view of Puget Sound. Reach **Dash Point State Park** at mile 7.0 (picnic tables, restrooms, camping, beach access). To visit **Dash Point County Park** (restrooms, beach access, shelter, picnic tables), go west on Markham Ave. NE. To return to SR-509, follow Soundview Drive NE south. At mile 7.7 diverge right (west) on Hyada Blvd. NW to **Brown's Point Lighthouse**. Go south and east on Tok-A-Lou and Le-Lou-Wah Streets to SR-509.

Two miles beyond the turnoff to Brown's Point Lighthouse, SR-509 rises to the top of a bluff with a view west over Commencement Bay. SR-509 now goes south along the shoreline, passing industrial and water related activities. At mile 12.0, turn right (west) on E 11th St. across bridges over the waterways in the Tacoma Waterfront Industrial Area. Sidewalks and bikeways make bicycle travel possible in this active area (watch for trains). After passing over the Tacoma ship landing, reach the first intersection in Tacoma at mile 15. Turn right (north) on 'A' Ave. into **Fireman's Park** to go along the east side of the buildings of Old Tacoma. The park is a viewpoint over the waterfront to Mt. Rainier. View a display of pictures of old Tacoma and admire a restored totem pole. Exit to Pacific Ave. past the **Fawcett Memorial Water Fountain** at S 7th St. The former Northern Pacific Railroad Administration building nearby has interesting roof detail.

Go north on the sidewalk on the west side of Pacific Ave., which becomes Schuster Parkway, descending along the east edge of a park. Where the street levels, a trail diverges left (west) to impressive **Stadium High School** on the bluff above (no bicycles on trails). At mile 17 enter a district of stores and restaurants. Turn right (east) on McCarver St. to cross railroad tracks into Schuster Parkway (restrooms). After passing the site of the Asarco smelter, continue north through a narrow tunnel into Ruston. In Ruston, ride left (west) on Bennett St. to Pearl St. Turn right (north) to the ferry landing in **Point Defiance Park**, 21 miles from the starting point.

Ride the ferry to Tahlequah on Vashon Island and continue north on Westside Highway SW. At two miles, go straight ahead on Wax Orchard Road SW, then, after bending east into SW 220th St., turn left (north) again four miles from the ferry dock on another segment of the Westside Highway. This road becomes Cedarhurst Road SW before going east to join Vashon Island Blvd. SW. Turn north for two miles to the ferry dock. Take the passenger ferry to downtown Seattle or the ferry to Fauntleroy and a Metro 54 stop.

FORT WARD LOOP, high point 300', 20 miles, 1400' gain (Maps: USGS Suquamish, Bremerton East, Shilshole Bay, Duwamish Head). **Bicycle**. Take a Metro Bus to the International District Station. Go west on Jackson St. and north on Alaskan Way to the ferry dock. Ride the Bainbridge ferry to Winslow. Road log begins at the ferry dock.

Ride north to the first cross street, Harborview Drive, and turn left (west) for 50'. Begin a paved path on the right into **Eagle Harbor Waterfront Park**. Explore the viewpoints, shoreline, and playground areas, then exit west and north to Bjune Drive. Turn west to Madison Ave., south to Parfitt Way, and wander west and north to exit from Grow Ave. to W Wyatt St. Go west and south, keeping right at the first two intersections after turning south and left at the third and fourth, to Lynwood Center at the north end of an inlet off Rich Passage, mile 4.4. At mile 5.1, bend right (southeast) into Pleasant Beach Drive to **Fort Ward State Park** at mile 6 (map, informative signs, tables, toilets, bird-watching blinds).

Proceed south along the beach drive to Vinton Battery. Along the way, look west to summits in the Olympic Mountains: Mt. Washington (262°), The Brothers (279°), Jupiter (287°), Constance (294°), and Mt. Townsend (308°). After visiting the fortification, ascend a paved path to the upper picnic area. Continue north through the picnic area to a trail and descend west (walk bicycle), exploring another battery of four gun emplacements before reaching the beach area. Now go south along the beach to exit from the park at mile 9. Pause at a fortification to look across Rich Passage to Manchester State Park, the site of Middle Point Fort. At mile 10, turn north on Toe Jam Hill Road to go over the high point. Descend to Country Club Road and go west, passing Fort Ward Hill Road. At a junction, turn right, keeping right at the first intersection to follow a loop road through the Port Blakely Mill site (readerboard).

Return to Blakely Ave. Now ascend east on Hall Hill Road, which becomes Rockaway Beach Road and Eagle Harbor Drive. Pause frequently for the view east to Seattle and the Cascade summits: Mt. Baker, Whitehorse, Three Fingers, and Mt. Rainier. At the west end of Eagle Harbor, find another readerboard that describes the former culture of strawberries in this area. Rejoin the outgoing route and follow W Wyatt St. to the top of the hill. Find Grow St. and go south and east through a shopping area to return to the ferry dock.

KINGSTON TO WINSLOW, high point 350', 35 miles, 1200' gain (Maps: USGS Edmonds West, Port Gamble, Suquamish). **Bicycle**. Take a Metro bus to the Aurora Village Transit Center. Ride northwest through parking to exit at the northwest corner. Ride north on the east side of Aurora Ave. N across the on-ramp to Edmonds Way, rounding west, then ride northwest downhill on Edmonds Way (SR-104) to the ferry dock in Edmonds (mile 4.5).

Take the ferry to Kingston. Ride north to NE Kingston Road W. Turn left (west), and again left at mile 5.4 into S Kingston Road NE to cross an arm of Appletree Cove. Pass **Arness Park** (beach access) and begin a gradual ascent. Near the high point, where the road turns south at a viewpoint (mile 8.0), look west at Mt. Constance and The Brothers.

At the junction with Indianola Road NE, continue south on Kingston St. NE. In the community of Indianola (mile 10.2), turn right (west) on NE Shore Drive. Where NE Shore Drive continues into an area with no outlet, jog right (north) on Wildwood St. NE for one block, then continue west on NE Seaview Ave. with occasional views of Miller Inlet, Mt. Jupiter, and The Brothers. At mile 10.9, turn right (north) on Gerald Cliff Road NE, reaching Indianola Ave. NE at mile 11.2. Turn left (west) reaching a junction with Miller Bay Road NE (mile 13.2) at a salmon hatchery operated by the Suquamish Tribe (open to the public).

Continue south on Miller Bay Road NE, entering the Port Madison Indian Reservation at mile 15.6 and reaching the community of Suquamish at mile 16.7 (stores, beach access, fishing pier, launch ramp). To find the grave of **Chief Sealth**, go west on NE South St. for one block to the St. Peters Catholic Mission.

Return to Suquamish Way (mile 17.0) and go southwest to NE

McKinstry St. (mile 17.5). Turn left to the **Old Man House** on the beach, a partial reconstruction of the Indian Longhouse where Chief Sealth lived (water, toilets). Return and continue west and south on Suquamish Way, turning left (east) on SR-305 (mile 19.5) to cross the bridge over Agate Passage (narrow walkway) onto Bainbridge Island. Go south on the east side of SR-305, then east on Hidden Cove Road (mile 21.6) to join Phelps Road. Turn northeast to the community of Port Madison. Go right on East Euclid Ave. NE, following the signs to **Fay Bainbridge State Park**, mile 24.7: view, beach access, camping, water, tables, restrooms.

From the State Park, go south on Sunrise Drive NE, turning left (east) on N Valley Road at the community of Rolling Bay (stores) to pass Skiff Point and ride along the shoreline of Manitou Beach for 0.5 mile. Turn left (south) on Moran Road NE, bending east on NE Lofgren Road at mile 29.9, then rounding south into Ferncliff Drive NE, which becomes Ferncliff Ave. NE. At mile 30.7, turn southeast on Grand Ave. NE, continuing into NE Park Ave. On reaching Wing Point Ave., turn right (west), passing a golf course before returning to Ferncliff Ave. Go south to the **Winslow** ferry (mile 34). From the Seattle Ferry terminal, go right on Alaskan Way, and left on S Jackson St. to the Metro International District station.

KINGSTON TO BREMERTON, high point 380', 38 miles, 1800' gain (Maps: USGS Edmonds West, Poulsbo, Port Gamble, Suquamish, Bremerton East). **Bicycle**. Take Metro 317, 340, 358 to the Aurora Village Transit Center. Cross northwest to Aurora Ave. N. Go north, then curve into Edmonds Way. Ride northwest downhill on Edmonds Way (SR-104) to the ferry, mile 4.5. Ride the ferry to Kingston.

From the ferry (mile 0.0), ride north, then go west on NE Kingston Road. Continue west past the Kingston Junior High School, mile 2.2. Turn south on Miller Bay Road, passing Indianola Road at mile 5.0, the location of a salmon hatchery. Reach Gunderson Road at mile 5.2. Go west to Port Gamble Road NE, then turn south to Lincoln Road. Circle west and southwest around the basin of a creek that drains north to Port Gamble Bay. Cross SR-305 at mile 11 into the town of **Poulsbo**, passing an old church and cemetery. Continue west to stores (bakery) and **Liberty Bay Park** on the waterfront (restrooms, water, picnic tables, shelter, fire pit).

From Liberty Bay Park, go north on the wooden causeway along the shore into paved and gravel pathways of **Legionnaire Park**. Exit to Front St. NE at the **Poulsbo Community Center**. Continue north and west, crossing the northern tip of the bay. At Viking Ave. NW, turn south along the west shore of Liberty Bay. At mile 17.2, go west on SR-308 to the community of Keyport, home of the submarine fleet in Puget Sound. After passing the road to Brownsville, continue east, taking a right to the **Naval Undersea Museum**. On display in the grounds is the Trieste II, used by Jacque Cousteau in deep diving explorations. The building has displays of undersea equipment.

From Keyport, return to Brownsville Highway NE and go south on SR-303. At Brownsville, mile 23.7, turn south on Illahee Road NE, which becomes Trenton Ave. NE, to the intersection with NE Sylvan Way (SR-306). Go left (east) to **Illahee State Park** at mile 29.3 (camping, restrooms). From Illahee State Park, go south on Ridgeview Drive NE and west on NE 30th St. to return to Trenton Ave. and continue south. Turn west on E 11th St. across the Manette Bridge. Go south on Washington Ave. to the Bremerton ferry (public art), mile 33.

SOUTHWORTH TO BREMERTON, high point 120', 25 miles, 400' gain (Maps: USGS Duwamish Head, Bremerton East). **Bicycle**. Ride the person ferry from downtown Seattle to Vashon, then transfer to the Southworth ferry or take the ferry from Fauntleroy (Metro 54) to Southworth.

From the ferry dock ride west on the old highway, SE Southworth Drive, toward Bremerton, passing MP-11 where SR-160 turns left (south). At one mile, turn right (north) toward Port Orchard to go along the shoreline. Look east to Blake Island and northwest to Mt. Baker showing between Blake Island and Bainbridge Island. Where the road turns west again, leaving the shoreline at the Harper public fishing pier, look east to butte-shaped Mt. Phelps. After another mile, the street returns to a shoreline where many birds congregate. Here the street has only a two to four foot shoulder, but minimum traffic.

At three miles, turn right on Yukon Harbor Drive SE to continue along the shoreline, with occasional access paths to the beach and views of downtown Seattle and the Cascade Mountains. Emerge on Colchester Drive SE and continue north, turning right on Miracle Mile Road SE (mile 4.8) away from the busy highway. Return to Colchester Drive E to pass stores in the community of Manchester. Jog west on Main St. to pass the **Manchester Library**, then turn right on Beach Drive E and continue north toward **Manchester State Park**. Pass a lake cut off from Little Clam Bay and take a right turn at the intersection with Nevada Ave. to stay on Beach Drive E to the turnoff to Manchester State Park. Turn northeast 0.3 mile to the park. Facilities: restrooms, camping (summer), beach access, wetland, picnic shelter in a brick building that was torpedo and mine storage for Middle Point Fort. An interpretive trail has the following stops (guide available): (1) Rhododendron. (2) Bigleaf maple burls. (3) Bigleaf maple. (4) Fallen Douglas fir. (5)

Red alder. (6) Hazel. (7) Douglas fir. (8) Nurse log. (9) Western hemlock. (10) Sword fern. (11) Springboard notch. (12) Madrone. (13) Huckleberry. (14) Red cedar. (15) Oregon grape. (16) Indian plum. Return to Beach Drive E, mile 9.

Beach Drive E now passes north through a densely forested ravine with creek before turning west to rejoin the shoreline opposite Rich Passage. Look north over Port Orchard Inlet toward the SR-305 bridge at Agate Pass. The beach along this shoreline is private property and not open to the public. Beginning at mile 10, note steeply-dipping sedimentary beds exposed at low tide. Pass a public fishing pier at the Port of Waterman, mile 11.1. At the entrance to the fishing pier, look west to the Olympic Mountains, extending from Mt. Washington (267°) in the south to Mt. Townsend (315°) in the north, with Mt. Duckabush (278°), The Brothers (284°), Mt. Jupiter (294°), and Mt. Constance (300°) in between. Shortly after passing the fishing pier at Port Waterman, enter a narrow bikeway on the north side of the highway. Look for the Retsil Veterans Home on the hill to the south, mile 13.7. Cross Blackjack Creek into **Port Orchard**. Enter north into Port Orchard Marina parking at mile 15. A **Park** has the Port Orchard Library, restrooms, elevated viewpoint, shelter, picnic tables, and walkway along the waterfront. Find winter restrooms at the west end of the marina parking area. A passenger-only ferry leaves for Bremerton every half-hour (bicycles allowed).

From Port Orchard, ride a wide shoulder on the north side of the highway west around Sinclair Inlet with a view of the ships across the inlet in the Puget Sound Naval Shipyard. The highway from Port Orchard (SR-166) merges with SR-16 (mile 18), then passes Elandan Bonsai Gardens (mile 18.5). Pause at a wildlife viewing area before joining SR-3 (mile 19) near the community of Gorst at the west end of Sinclair Inlet. From SR-3, turn right on SR-304 into Bremerton. Stop along the way to look at the warships in storage or under repair in the shipyard. In places, the bikeway shoulder along this busy highway narrows or disappears. Turn east on Farragut St. toward an entrance to the Naval Shipyard, then go left (north) either on Callow Ave. (sidewalk) or Montgomery Ave. Turn right (east) on Burwell St. into Bremerton, then go right on Washington St. to the ferry. Wander the Bremerton Marina to view displays of public art until the ferry leaves.

EDMONDS–PORT TOWNSEND–MUKILTEO, high point 500', 100 miles, 3900' gain (Maps: USGS Edmonds East, Port Gamble, Lofall, Port Ludlow, Port Townsend South, Gardiner, Port Townsend North, Nordland, Coupeville, Camano, Freeland, Langley, Maxwellton, Mukilteo). **Bicycle**. Public transit buses along the route have bicycle racks. Plan to stay overnight at Hostelling International hostels at Fort

Flagler and Fort Worden (reservations often necessary). Take Metro 340, 358, etc., to the Aurora Village Transit Center.

From the Transit Center, ride northwest to Aurora Ave. N (SR-99). Go north, then follow the on-ramp east, south, and west to SR-104 (Edmonds Way). Descend northwest 4.5 miles to the Edmonds Ferry Terminal. Ride the ferry to Kingston. Begin mileage log at the ferry terminal.

Kingston to Port Gamble, high point 168', 8.2 miles, 300' gain. Ride west and northwest on SR-104. Get a good view of the Olympic Mountains at mile 1.8. Here, the highway points between Mount Constance (on the left) and Mount Townsend. Mount Townsend directly along the highway at mile 3.7. At mile 4.1, turn north toward Port Gamble on SR-107, passing near an inlet with a view north at mile 4.9. Reach Port Gamble at mile 8.0. A house here is the oldest continuously occupied house in Washington State, built in 1859. The church was built in 1870. Where the highway turns left (west) to the Hood Canal Bridge, continue north to a viewpoint and flagpole. Take time to tour Port Gamble, a former company town devoted to lumber production. See also: picnic area, cemetery, and a postoffice established in 1853.

Port Gamble to Fort Flagler, high point 280', 26 miles, 1300' gain. Continue west from Port Gamble (mile 8.3), passing a county park at mile 9.0 and reaching the east end of the Hood Canal Bridge at mile 9.4. Cross the floating bridge (no bike lane). From the west end of the Hood Canal Bridge (mile 11.2), turn right (north) on Paradise Bay Road. Pass the entrance to a State Park at mile 12, and enter the community of Paradise Bay at mile 13.5, with a view of Mt. Baker. Reach Port Ludlow Village at mile 17.1 (store, food). Turn right on Oak Bay Road to pass the Inn at Ludlow Bay (food). Watch for another view of Mt. Baker at mile 19. Pass the Mats Mats General Store at mile 19.3. At Mats Mats, ride straight ahead on Oak Bay Road. At mile 24.0, stay on Old Oak Bay Road for a brief diversion from the highway, then, at mile 26.0, turn east on Flagler Road toward Indian Island and Fort Flagler, signed SR-116 after the turn. Find a park with shelter and picnic tables after crossing the bridge over Indian Inlet. Jefferson County provides access to the beach at several places on the north end of Indian Island.

At mile 28.7, cross a low point to Marrowstone Island. Take the left fork to go north, passing a store in Nordland at mile 31.2, and **Mystery Bay State Park** at mile 31.9 (shelter, beach access, dock). Enter **Fort Flagler State Park** at mile 34.0 (HI hostel). Take time to walk around the various fortifications at Fort Flagler, which include two examples of the type of 3" guns that were in use at the fort.

Fort Flagler to Fort Worden, high point 500', 27 miles, 1200' gain.

After leaving Fort Flagler (mile 34.7), return south and west to Oak Bay Road, mile 42.6, and go right (north) to Port Hadlock (mile 44.4, services). At the first main intersection in Port Hadlock, turn right (north) on Chimacum Road, which bends west and becomes Irondale Road, passing through the community of Irondale (no services). Turn north briefly on SR-19 at mile 46.4, then, where SR-19 bends to the right, continue north (mile 46.6) on a highway signed 'To Port Angeles and Highway 101'. Cross SR-20 at mile 47.9 into S Discovery Bay Road and continue west to the shore of Discovery Bay, with occasional views of the Olympic Mountains extending from Mount Townsend to Mount Angeles. At mile 49.2, turn left on Cape George Road to continue north and find more views to the west, especially at mile 51.3. Turn right (east) on Beckett Point Road at mile 53.0. Go to the left at mile 55.0, Cape George Wye, to join Hastings Ave. and continue northeast and east. At Discovery Road in Port Townsend, go northwest to San Juan Ave., then go left (north) to Admiralty Ave. Turn right to enter **Fort Worden State Park**, mile 60.6, on Eisenhower Ave. The HI hostel is north on Battery Way, mile 62.

Tour the extensive fortifications of Fort Worden. At low tide, walk the beach west from the lighthouse to the west end of the State Park, then return on a path over the hill that goes past the main fortifications. Look for the 160' pedestrian tunnel.

Fort Worden to Clinton, high point 420', 33 miles, 1100' gain. From Fort Worden, mile 62, go south on Cherry Ave., east on 'F' St., southeast on Tyler St., northeast on Jefferson St., southeast on Quincy St., and southeast on Water St. to the ferry dock, mile 65.7. Ride the Keystone Ferry to Whidby Island. From the ferry dock go left (north) to explore **Fort Casey State Park**, which has two examples of the type of 10" disappearing guns that were originally mounted in the fort. After leaving the fort (mile 68.3), go east on SR-20 to join SR-525. Turn south on SR-525 (mile 72.2), riding an off-and-on bikelane for the first six miles then continuous bikelane into Clinton, mile 95. Take the ferry to Mukilteo. Ride Community Transit 170 to Lynnwood Transit Center for connecting buses.

I–90 Region

Mercer Island.

ISLAND CREST PARK, 332', 8 miles RT, 300' gain (Maps: USGS Mercer Island). **Bicycle and/or Hike-1**. Take Metro 215, 226, etc., to the North Mercer Island Park & Ride or on weekends, drive to the same Park & Ride. Metro 202 serves this park (limited parking).

Ride or walk south on 80th Ave. SE over I-90, crossing SE 27th St. and continuing south on 80th Ave. SE. Jog right at SE 32nd St. and continue south on 80th Ave. SE. At mile 1.0, reach SE 40th St. at the corner of Homestead Field. Continue south on a paved path on the west side of the field, rounding east along the south side of the field to restrooms and a playground. Return north to SE 40th St., then turn right (east) to Island Crest Way (mile 1.5). Ride south on a mostly paved path along Island Crest Way. Island Crest Park begins at mile 3.1. Turn into the park and walk or ride west past a childrens playground to a trailhead.

Facilities: picnicking, playfields, restrooms, two miles of trails (not suitable for bicycles), fire circle.

PIONEER PARK, 300', 10 miles RT, 500' gain (Maps: USGS Mercer Island). **Bicycle and/or Hike-1**. Take Metro 215, 226, etc., to the North Mercer Island Park & Ride or, on weekends, drive to the same Park & Ride. Metro 202 serves this park. No vehicle parking.

Ride or walk south as described above for **Island Crest Park**. Continue south on Island Crest Way for 0.5 mile to Pioneer Park.

Facilities: nature trail, two miles of trails (not suitable for bicycles). Native plants commonly found in the park: Douglas fir, western hemlock, Oregon grape, salmonberry, Indian plum, madrone, and elderberry.

MERCER ISLAND LOOP, high point 250', 14 miles, 500' gain (Maps: USGS Mercer Island). **Bicycle**. Take Metro 215, 226, etc., to North Mercer Island Park & Ride, or park at the North Mercer Island Park & Ride on weekends.

Ride west on N Mercer Way parallel to I-90 and continue on N Mercer Way after it curves away from I-90. Where the street turns southwest, it becomes W Mercer Way. Cross over I-90 at mile 1.2 (restrooms, water) and continue south, passing, at mile 4.8, a street that drops right (west) to Groveland Park Beach (no parking). After the street becomes E Mercer Way at the south end of the island, reach a junction with SE 70th Place at mile 8.5. Pioneer Park is 0.7 mile west at Island Crest Way (200' gain). Continue north on E Mercer Way to reach I-90 at SE 36th St. (mile 12.3). Turn left (west) on SE 36th St. for 0.3 mile, then go right (north) on N Mercer Way across I-90. Follow N Mercer Way west to return to the Park & Ride.

LUTHER BURBANK PARK, high point 120', 1 mile of trails, (Maps: USGS Mercer Island). **Hike-1**. The site was originally a school for truant boys (1903). Take Metro 215, 226, etc., to the North Mercer Island Park & Ride and walk east 0.5 mile to the park on SE 26th St., or drive to the park north and east from I-90 at Exit-7.

Facilities: playground, playfields, shelter, picnicking, beach access, one mile of trails, restrooms.

Bellevue to Snoqualmie Falls Area.

COUGAR MOUNTAIN: COAL CREEK TO ISSAQUAH, high point 1425', 8 miles one-way, 1500' gain (Maps: Cougar Mtn., USGS Mercer Island, Issaquah). **Hike-2**. Ride Metro 240, 340, etc. to Coal Creek Parkway near I-405, elevation 75'. If driving, leave I-405 at Exit 10 and park off Coal Creek Parkway SE at the crossing of Coal Creek, elevation 160'.

From the Metro stop, hike southeast on Coal Creek Parkway SE to the crossing of Coal Creek and a trail entrance to Coal Creek Park. Ascend east along Coal Creek. At mile 1.1, go left on the Primrose Trail to pass near Sandstone Falls. The trail crosses to the south side of Coal Creek near the falls, before ascending on the tailings of the Scalzo Mine (ore cart wheels). Rejoin Coal Creek Trail at mile 1.9. Enter the meadow of the cinder mine area, then, where the gravel road turns up to Newcastle-Coal Creek Road, find a trail that contours above Coal Creek to pass North Fork Falls and a nearly filled mine entrance. Cross Lakemont Blvd. to the Red Town Trailhead (maps, toilets, information).

Ascend east on Red Town Trail for 0.2 mile, then go northeast and southeast on Cave Hole Trail for a mile to a junction. Go east on the Bypass Trail to cross Clay Pit Road into Klondike Swamp Trail. Follow this trail for another mile, then turn east on the Lost Beagle Trail, crossing a ridge just south of Anti-Aircraft Peak. After a bend to the south, continue east to Tibbets Marsh Trail. Now go north to join Shangri La Trail, a wide break in the forest. Descend southeast for one mile, then, where the Shangri La trail bends north (950'), continue southeast on the Bear Ridge Trail. After crossing the West Fork of Tibbets Creek,

1000', descend to a trail fork, 630'. Go right (southeast) and continue down to Renton-Issaquah Road (SR-900). Turn left (north) one mile to the Metro 215 stop.

COUGAR MOUNTAIN: DE LEO WALL TO REDTOWN LOOP, high point 1200', 8 miles RT bicycle and/or 8 miles RT hike, 1600' gain (Maps: Cougar Mtn., USGS Mercer Island, Issaquah). **Bicycle and/or Hike-1**. This trip makes a loop on the southwest side of Cougar Mountain. If driving, begin the hike at Redtown trailhead (see below), reached from I-90 at Exit-13 by going south on Lakemont Blvd. for four miles to the trailhead, elevation 620'. From I-405, take the Coal Creek exit (Exit-10) and drive southeast on Coal Creek Parkway SE. At mile 2.5 from I-405, turn east on SE 72nd Place, then go left on SE Newcastle–Coal Creek Road to the trailhead 4.8 miles from I-405.

Take Metro 106, 340, etc. to I-405 at the Kennydale Exit, Exit-5, at 30th St., elevation 170'. Ride east on NE 30th St., which becomes successively Kennewick St. and NE 27th St. Where NE 27th St. turns south into Edmonds Ave. NE at the Kennydale Hall, continue east past a gate into **May Creek Park** (one mile of trails) on an extension of NE 27th St., crossing a branch of May Creek (trailhead) before ascending to exit from the park at 122nd Ave. SE and SE 95th Way. Continue east on SE 95th Way to emerge on Coal Creek Parkway SE. Turn left (north) on Coal Creek Parkway SE across May Creek then leave Coal Creek Parkway SE to ascend right (north) on 136th Ave. SE (Thomas Rouse Road). Stay right on 136th Ave. SE at the junction of 134th Ave. SE, then go right on SE 79th Drive. Turn right on 144th Ave. SE to a junction marked 144th Ave. SE, SE 84th Court, and SE 84th St. Go north downhill one block on SE 84th St. to a gated road, the entrance to Water Department property. Go east past the gate, at first on gravel, then on paved Watertank Road to a second gate at the entrance to the Cougar Mountain Regional Wildland Park. Park bicycle here, four miles from I-405. Bicycles are not allowed on most trails in the park.

Walk east on the paved road 500' to find trails going north and south. Leave the paved road and hike south on the De Leo Wall Trail, passing immediately a trail descending southwest. Follow the trail as it goes east along the crest of the cliffs and steep slopes of De Leo Wall. Take side trails out to promontories for a look down the wall. Pass a high point of 1200', Marshall's Hill, and continue east, dropping to cross a creek. Reach a junction with the Wildside Trail, 1.1 mile from Watertank Road. Continue east across a creek then turn southeast on the Indian Trail for 0.3 mile to the junction with the Far Country Trail. The park boundary is 0.3 mile southeast on the Indian Trail through a forest of young alder trees. Turn northeast on the Far Country Trail over Far Country Lookout, with a view to the southwest, and passing a junction with the Deceiver Trail, which goes south and east to Longview Peak. At a junction with Fred's Railroad Trail, turn north over a ridge to Clay Pit Road. Just east of the road, turn west on a bypass trail parallel to the Clay Pit Road to cross a branch of Coal Creek. After the creek crossing, turn right at a junction with Cave Hole Trail to the Clay Pit Road then go west on the road to **Nike Park**. Wander the meadow and examine the artifacts, then return east on Clay Pit Road for 0.1 mile, turning south and west on Cave Hole Trail, passing a trail south to Coal Creek Falls and a trail north to Red Town Creek before descending to Red Town trailhead. Facilities: toilets, informative signs, map, and parking.

From **Red Town trailhead**, hike southwest on the China Creek Trail for 300' to a 'T' junction. Turn left to go over China Summit, passing the Rainbow Town Trail, the Lazy Porcupine Trail, the China Summit Trail, and the Almost Nowhere Trail. The Marshall's Hill Trail joins from the left 0.2 miles before reaching Watertank Road. Turn right on the road to the entrance.

Find the following native plants along the way: salal, Douglas fir, western hemlock, alder, salmonberry, devils club, elderberry, madrone, red cedar, indian plum, Oregon grape, and huckleberry.

COUGAR MOUNTAIN: LEWIS CREEK TO ISSAQUAH, high point 1459', 8 miles one-way, 1600' gain (Maps: Cougar Mtn., USGS Issaquah). **Hike-2**. Ride Metro 215 to SE Newport Way and 180th St. SE, the last stop before the bus turns north under I-90 at Exit-13, elevation 200'. No parking.

Walk south on the sidewalk of Lakemont Blvd. on the west side of Lewis Creek into Lakemont Gorge. One-fourth mile after the street returns to ground level, look for the beginning of the Lewis Creek Trail on the east side of the street and just south of the end of the vehicle guard rail. On reaching Lewis Creek, turn upstream in forest containing many cedar trees, some 18" in diameter. After the trail bends to the west (mile 0.75), meet a junction with Peggy's Trail, which crosses the creek and goes up the steep slope in switchbacks. The trail on the northwest side of the creek now becomes a wide path. Note an exposed bank of cinders left from coal mining on the south side of the creek. The trail crosses the creek, ascends west, then passes several trail branches (nature trail) before reaching **Lakemont Park** (restrooms, playground). The deep canyons here have all been incised since the end of the glaciers 15,000 years ago.

Turn southeast past stormwater retention ponds to find a paved trail that ascends east on the north side of houses and crosses bridges over branches of Lewis Canyon. Cross 175th Place SE near SE 55th St. and continue on the paved path to cross 176th Place SE. Exit to 178th Ave. SE at 179th Ave. SE. Continue southeast on 178th Ave. SE to Village Park Drive SE at a junction with 179th Ave. SE. Peggy's Trail goes north here from 178th Ave. SE to descend into Lewis Canyon, a return route to the starting point. Go south on 179th Ave. SE for one block to find a wide sewer easement that contours and ascends southeast to exit at SE 60th St. Turn right (west) and ascend to a junction with SE Cougar Mountain Drive. Turn southeast for 0.5 mile. Find Coyote Creek Trail on the south side of the street and go southeast 200' into the Shangri La Trail. Follow this trail as it contours east to another trail junction at 0.6 mile. Leave the Shangri La Trail and go southwest and south to **Radar Park**. Facilities: picnic tables, restrooms, parking. A point at the north edge of the meadow gives a view of Mt. Baker (10°) and Mt. Shuksan (16°).

After circling around Radar Park, including visits to an information signboard and the communication tower on the highest point of AA Peak, return east to the parking lot at the end of the street. Walk east to another viewpoint that provides a view of Lake Sammamish and of the Cascade Range from Mt. Si north, then return to the parking lot and continue southeast on the Shangri La Trail. After going 300' on the Shangri La Trail, turn south on the Tibbets Marsh Trail, passing immediately a junction with the AA Ridge Trail, which goes right (west). In another 0.5 mile, note the Protector Trail turning off to the northeast. A 4' exotic boulder sits next to the trail south of the Protector Trail. Continue south on the Tibbets Marsh Trail, passing a junction with the Cougar Pass Trail to the right (west). Emerge on Clay Pit Road. Turn left (east) on the road to the clay pit, then follow the south edge of the clay pit past a junction with the East Fork Trail, which goes south and west toward Wilderness Peak. Using care to avoid stepping in wet clay, reach one of the best viewpoints in the park on the north shoulder of **Clay Pit Peak**. Depending on the state of excavation of the clay pit, seams of coal are sometimes exposed near this viewpoint. Summits visible include: Mt. Baker (8°), Persis (50°), Index (54°), Mt. Phelps (66°), and Mt. Si (94°). From here a trail continues south over the east shoulder of Clay Pit Peak to Wilderness Peak.

Return north across the West Fork of Tibbets Creek on the Tibbets Marsh Trail to find a connector trail east to the Bear Ridge trail. Follow the Bear Ridge trail southeast as it descends to SR-900. Go left to the Issaquah Park & Ride and a Metro 215 bus stop.

EAST COUGAR MOUNTAIN, high point 1440', 8 mile loop (Maps: Cougar Mtn., USGS Issaquah). **Hike-3**. Ride Metro 215 to the Issaquah Park & Ride or park at Tibbets Park nearby, off I-90 at Exit-15, elevation 75'.

Walk to the intersection of SR-900 with Newport Way. Go northwest on Newport way for 0.5 mile to Oakcrest Drive. Turn left (west) and walk Oakcrest Drive to the end. Go up the grass slope to enter the forest where the trail is obvious. Ascend northwest, then turn south, descending into a gully. Turn west and ascend, passing a giant log before contouring north across a steep slope on a minimum trail. Pass a trail that goes north to Kline Hill Road, then go west up a ridge. At 400', contour southeast on the Precipice Trail. After crossing AA Creek (steep and muddy), ascend Harvey's Mud Slide (handline). At 500', turn up a ridge southwest, passing a signboard 'Big Tree Ridge' at 700'. Continue south to a powerline clearing, then ascend west under the powerline until the powerline bends north, 1150'.

Now go south, ascending more gradually on a wide trail, emerging on the Shangri La Trail. Turn west and ascend to Radar Park (restrooms, picnic tables, viewpoint, parking). After exploring the summit area, return to the parking area and descend on the Shangri La Trail to 900'. Turn southwest on the Bear Ridge Trail and contour across the West Fork of Tibbetts Creek, passing unmarked trails that turn up and down the slope. Shortly after crossing the West Fork of Tibbetts Creek, begin to descend southeast, passing fern covered **Fantastic Erratic** at 800'. Continue to descend east, going left at 600' to cross the West Fork of Tibbetts Creek twice before turning southeast away from the creek to SR-900. Go north to the Issaquah Park & Ride.

SOUTHEAST COUGAR MOUNTAIN, high point 1400', 8 miles RT, 1500' gain (Maps: Cougar Mtn., USGS Issaquah). **Bicycle and/or Hike-2**. Take Metro 215 to Issaquah Park & Ride. Ride or hike south on SR-900 for 1.2 miles to the trailhead on the west side of the street. If driving, leave I-90 at Exit-15. Drive 1.7 miles south and west on SR-900 to limited trailhead parking on the west side of the road, elevation 150'.

Hike west, keeping to the right at a trail junction immediately after leaving the parking area. Cross the West Fork of Tibbets Creek or branches at 250', 325', and 450'. Go right (northwest) at a trail junction (600') to meet the Bear Ridge Trail at 1020'. Go right to the Shangri La Trail. Turn left and ascend to **Radar Park**. Explore the park including viewpoints north and northeast.

Descend east on the Shangri La Trail, then go south on the Tibbets Marsh Trail. After joining the Protector Ridge Trail, and 200' north of the West Fork of Tibbets Creek, turn east on a connector to descend to the Bear Ridge Trail. Now go southeast, crossing the West Fork of Tibbets Creek. Keep right at a junction, 600', and exit to SR-900 at the starting point.

COUGAR MOUNTAIN: WILDERNESS PEAK, 1595', 6 miles RT hike + 6 miles RT bicycle, 1300' gain (Maps: Cougar Mtn., USGS Issaquah). **Bicycle and/or Hike-2**. Take Metro 215 to Issaquah Park & Ride. Ride south and west on SR-900 for 2.9 miles to the trailhead on the north side of the street. If driving, leave I-90 at Exit-15. Drive 3.4 miles south and west on SR-900 to trailhead parking on the north side of the road, signed King County Park, elevation 360'.

Hike northwest up the gorge of Wilderness Creek on the Wilderness Creek Trail, going right on the Wilderness Cliffs Trail at 0.3 mile. At 1.0 mile, turn east on the Wilderness Peak Trail. The summit lies in deep forest (register). On the return, go west for 0.5 mile to Shy Bear Pass. Continue west at a junction on the Longview Peak Trail to reach Longview Peak, with a keyhole view into May Valley. From Longview Peak, return at first on the outgoing route, avoiding a trail to the right that connects with a private road, then go right (south) on Wilderness Creek Trail to descend in the canyon of Wilderness Creek to the trailhead.

SQUAK MOUNTAIN, 2000', 5 miles RT hike + 5 miles RT bicycle, 2000' gain (Maps: USGS Issaquah). **Bicycle and/or Hike-2**. Take Metro 215 to Issaquah Park & Ride. Ride 2.3 miles south on SR-900 to the trailhead at a gated road (sign behind gate) on the left (east) side of the highway. If driving, leave I-90 at Exit 15 and drive 2.8 miles south on SR-900 to find limited parking near an inconspicuous gated branch road, elevation 400'.

Leave bicycle and ascend northeast on the road, passing another gate at 0.3 miles. At mile 0.8, pass a junction with a trail on the left that descends to the Mountainside Drive entrance. The Chybinski trail goes to the right at 1250'. This trail rejoins at 1650'. Another trail descends to Mountainside Drive at mile 1. The Central Peak trail turns left at mile 1.3 (1500'). Meet the West Peak trail on the crest of the ridge. Go right to the West Peak or left to the Bullit Fireplace (mile 2.0). Continue southeast to the Central Peak, mile 2.2.

SQUAK MOUNTAIN, 2000', 6 miles RT, 1800' gain (Maps: USGS Issaquah). **Hike-2**. Leave I-90 at Exit 15 or I-405 at Exit 5 and drive the Renton Issaquah Road for 5 miles. Go east on the May Valley Road for 4 miles to Squak Mtn. State Park on the north side of the road (parking, toilets), elevation 340'.

Find the trail entrance on the west side of parking area and go north to a road. Follow the road northeast and north, turning west from the road on a narrow trail (possibly not signed) at 1000'. After curving north, take a trail west and descend to a viewpoint over Maple Valley, 1750'. Look for Echo Mtn. (210°). Return east, then go north and east on the West Peak Trail to reach the West Peak (1900') and a decaying communications building.

Continuing east, pass a trail to the north entrance, then walk an old road to the Bullitt Fireplace near the high point of Squak Mtn. Now go southeast, either on the main trail or a logging grade, to the southeast summit, which has communication towers. Descend on the South Access Road, soon turning left (east) on the summit trail (steep), which joins the Phils Creek Trail and passes the East Ridge Trail (on left) before joining the Equestrian Loop Trail. Follow this trail south to return to the South Access Road, 600'. Turn left to find a connecting trail to parking.

SQUAK MOUNTAIN, 2000', 6 miles RT, 1500' gain (Maps: USGS Issaquah). **Hike-2**. Take Exit-17 from I-90. Drive south on Front St. in Issaquah. Turn right (west) on Sunset Way and proceed into Mountain Park Blvd. Go left on Mountainside Drive. Park off pavement beyond the Timbercrest sign where the street turns sharply left uphill, two miles from Front St. S in Issaquah, elevation 500'.

A trailhead interpretive sign with map is behind the street end barrier. The area has seven miles of maintained trails. Hike west on an old road that continues behind the barrier. At two miles, go left to ascend to the summit. Wander a variety of trails on the return.

WEST TIGER–1, 2948', 10 miles RT, 3200' gain (Maps: Tiger Mtn., USGS Fall City, Maple Valley, Hobart, Issaquah). **Hike-2**. Take Metro 215 and 209 to Issaquah. In Issaquah, leave Metro 209 on SE Bush St. at 2nd Ave. SE, elevation 100'. If driving, leave I-90 at Exit-17. Drive south on Front St. At a signal, turn east on Sunset Way, then go south on 2nd Ave. SE, and east on SE Evans St., one block north of Issaquah High School. Park 0.25 mile east of 2nd Ave. SE on SE Evans St. at an old railroad grade, marked by a gate, elevation 180'.

From the Metro 209 bus stop, hike south on 2nd Ave. SE and go four blocks to SE Evans St. Turn left (east) on SE Evans St. for 0.25 mile, passing Clark School, to an old railroad grade immediately east of a clump of fir trees on the south side of the road and east of the school grounds.

From SE Evans St., walk south on the railroad grade for three-eighths of a mile, along the east side of Issaquah High School. When opposite the stadium and tennis courts, turn east on a wide trail to pass a gate. Continue ascending east on the road, passing a junction with the Adventure Trail. Bend south at a crossing of Round Creek to a multiple trail junction near a power line, 0.5 mile from Issaquah High School, elevation 500'.

Turn north to the first power line tower, then go right (east) to cross a north-south pipeline clearcut where the Section Line trail continues east. Turn southeast into the trail to Poo Poo Point and ascend gradually. The trail levels at 1200' to cross three bridges over branches of creeks in Many Creek Valley then turns east to ascend more sharply in short switchbacks to a junction with the **West Tiger Railroad Grade**, 2000'. From this point, the Poo Poo Point trail diverges south. Cross the West Tiger Railroad Grade and continue ascending east in dense forest over several minor summits to the Tiger Mountain Trail (TMT), four miles from Issaquah High School. Turn right (southeast) on the TMT for one-fourth mile to a trail junction in a saddle. Turn left (northeast) and ascend, at first steeply, to the Tiger Mountain Road. Cross the road and find a steep trail ascending east and northeast up a ridge. After passing through tall forest, reach the summit of West Tiger–1 with its many transmitter towers. The best views are south and west.

This trail is not obvious from the summit platform. If arriving from the north or east, look for the trail descending southwest from the summit east of the western group of buildings.

POO POO POINT, 1800', 10 miles RT, 2000' gain (Maps: Tiger Mtn., USGS Issaquah, Fall City, Maple Valley, Hobart). **Hike-2**. Drive or ride the Metro bus and hike as above for **West Tiger–1**.

Hike from Issaquah by way of SE Evans St. to the junction with the West Tiger Railroad Grade, 2000'. From this junction, turn right, at first contouring southwest then descending west 200' to the West Side Road. On reaching the road, continue south to Poo Poo Point, an open viewpoint. The view extends from Mt. Rainier to Issaquah. During some part of the Puget glaciation, the canyon below carried much of the flow of the Cascade rivers.

WEST TIGER–3, 2522', 8 miles RT, 2500' gain (Maps: Tiger Mtn., USGS Issaquah). **Hike-2**. Ride Metro 209 to E Sunset Way at 6th Ave. SE in Issaquah, elevation 100'. If driving, leave I-90 at Exit-17. Drive south on Front St. in Issaquah. At a signal, turn east on Sunset Way. Park at the trailhead off E Sunset Way east of 6th Ave. SE, elevation 100'.

From the Metro 209 stop, walk east on E Sunset Way one block to the Tiger Mtn. trailhead on the south side of the street. Ascend south on the trail to a powerline at the west edge of the Tradition Lake plateau. Turn east on the road under the powerline for 0.5 mile to a trail junction west of a substation. Now go south on the Round Lake Wetland Trail to pass on the west side of Round Lake. Emerge to a powerline clearing at the south end of Round Lake. Turn east into a trail that crosses a pipeline clearing, then enters forest as the Bus Trail. Proceed east for 0.5 mile, passing trails north to Tradition Lake, to the Nook Trail. Ascend south to **Talus Caves**, a jumble of large block talus with viewpoints into the gaps between the rocks, 1100'.

From the highest talus viewpoint, turn west to contour across the north slope of West Tiger–3 to the Section Line Trail, 1150'. Turn left (south), ascending more steeply across the West Tiger Railroad Grade Trail at 2000' to the summit of West Tiger–3.

WEST TIGER–3, 2522', 8 miles RT, 2500' gain (Maps: Tiger Mtn., USGS Issaquah). **Hike-2**. Drive or ride transit and hike as above for **West Tiger–1**, to the powerline and pipeline crossing, elevation 500'.

Continue east on the Section Line trail, which begins to the left after the trail goes over a rock outcrop, ascending gradually at first, then more steeply, passing two trails joining from the north. After the second trail joins, the trail ascends south in switchbacks near a section line to the West Tiger Railroad Grade at 2000'. Cross the Railroad Grade and continue up to join a trail from the left just before reaching the summit. This Section Line trail is obscure from the summit. Hikers coming from the east should look for this trail 200' northwest of the rock that marks the summit of West Tiger–3 at the point where the trail descending from the summit flattens after an abrupt drop.

WEST TIGER–2, 2757', 8 miles RT, 2300' gain (Maps: Tiger Mtn., USGS Fall City). **Hike-2**. Take Metro 209 to High Point, east of the city of Issaquah, or drive I-90 to Exit-20 and park south of I-90, elevation 470'.

Walk south on 270th Ave. SE, the continuation of the road under the I-90 underpass, to a power line. Turn left (east) on the trail under the power line to cross High Point Creek on a log bridge. Ascend east halfway up the slope to a junction, which may be obscure. Turn right (south) on the High Point Trail, passing Dwight's Way going east before joining the Tiger Mountain Trail (TMT) at 1350'. Turn left (east) on the TMT. Pass a trail joining from the left, then round to the south. Continue ascending and contouring south to rejoin the High Point Trail. Cross a branch of High Point Creek that drains from a nearby marsh before joining the West Tiger Railroad Grade at 2000'.

Turn right, contouring west on the West Tiger Railroad Grade and crossing branches of High Point Creek. After bending north, reach another trail junction. Leave the West Tiger Railroad Grade and ascend, at first west, then southwest on switchbacks to the summit of West Tiger–2. Mt. Baker and Glacier Peak are often visible north and Mt. Rainier stands to the south. Return to High Point by the outgoing route or descend northwest on the trail to West Tiger–3 and return to High Point or Issaquah on one of the West Tiger–3 routes.

WEST TIGER–1, 2948', 9 miles RT, 2600' gain (Maps: Tiger Mtn., USGS Fall City). **Hike-2**. Take Metro 209 to High Point, the first stop on I-90 east of Issaquah, or drive to High Point (Exit-20) and exit to the south side of I-90, elevation 470'.

Hike as above for **West Tiger–2** on the High Point Trail to the West Tiger Railroad Grade at 2000'. Turn left on the railroad grade and ascend southeast for one-fourth mile, turning right (southwest) at a trail junction (2250') and ascending on the north ridge of West Tiger–1 to the summit. Return the same way or descend southwest and west to Issaquah (see West Tiger–1).

HIGH POINT TRAILHEAD, 470' (Maps: Tiger Mtn., USGS Fall City). **Walk**. Take Metro 209 to High Point or drive I-90 to Exit-20 and park south of I-90.

When the gate is closed, walk 0.4 mile west to the interpretive center. Facilities: parking, toilets, interpretive center, shelter, maps, displays, ranger talks. Trails: Swamp, Tradition Lake, Round Lake, Brink, Nook, and West Tiger–3.

WEST TIGER–3, 2522', 8 miles RT, 2100' gain (Maps: Tiger Mtn., USGS Fall City). **Hike-2**. Take Metro 209 to High Point or drive I-90 to Exit-20 and park south of I-90, elevation 470'.

Walk west to a multiple trailhead. Continue south 600', then turn left (east) and ascend on the Tradition Lake trail, an old logging road. Go left at a junction with the Caves Trail. Stay left on the more travelled branch at two more trail junctions. The trail ascends the north ridge of West Tiger in switchbacks near a fall-line track. Cross the West Tiger Railroad Grade at 2000' and continue south to the summit with views north, south, and west.

PRESTON TO ISSAQUAH, high point 1600' or 2522', 8 or 10 miles one-way, 1200' or 2200' gain (Maps: Tiger Mtn., USGS Fall City,

Issaquah). **Hike-2**. Take Metro 209 to Preston. Leave bus on SE 82nd St. at the first stop, elevation 540'.

Walk south on SE 82nd St. across I-90 to SE Preston Way. Turn right (west) on SE Preston Way to the power lines, 0.2 mile. Turn left (south) under the power lines on the power line service road and ascend for one mile to the crest of a ridge. Find a trail that goes south away from the power line clearcut into dense forest. At mile 0.5, cross Dwight's Way, which goes east, then join the new TMT, 1350'. For the low elevation option, turn west on the TMT, cross High Point Creek, and descend toward Tradition Lake. From Tradition Lake, go west on any of various trails to Issaquah and bus stops on Front Street, eight miles from Preston.

For the high elevation option (10 miles total), continue south, contouring into the canyon of High Point Creek. Ascend near the creek to the West Tiger Railroad Grade, 2000'. Turn right (west) and contour across branches of High Point Creek (bridges). After the West Tiger Railroad Grade curves north, find a junction and turn left on the TMT to ascend west on switchbacks toward the summit of West Tiger Mountain. When the towers on West Tiger–2 appear, look carefully for a trail fork. Turn right on the TMT, descending briefly, then contour in dense forest across the north aspect of West Tiger–2. Turn right on the trail coming down the northwest ridge from West Tiger–2 to reach the summit of West Tiger–3, 2522'. To go on to Issaquah, descend northwest on the trail for 200'. Where the trail levels after a sharp descent, look left to find a trail dropping northwest. Follow this trail to Issaquah.

PRESTON TO BELLEVUE, high point 540', 20 miles one-way, 200' gain (Maps: USGS Fall City, Issaquah, Mercer Island). **Mtn. Bicycle**. Ride Metro 209 to Preston-Fall City Road at SE 84th St. in Preston (stores), the second stop after leaving I-90 at Exit-22, elevation 540'.

Find a bikeway on the north side of the street, and ride west parallel to SE High Point Way. Join SE High Point Way at mile 0.6. Pass Greenbank Farms Cheese Factory at mile 0.8. Where High Point Way intersects I-90 (mile 2.6), turn right (west) on a rail bikeway on the north side of I-90 across a bridge over the east branch of Issaquah Creek. At mile 4.8, descend south on a branch over Issaquah Creek on a decaying bridge, then pass under I-90 to E Sunset Way. Ride into Issaquah. At mile 6, turn left (south) on SE 2nd St. to SE Andrews St. Now go west to **Gilman Town Hall**.

If the bridge over Issaquah Creek at mile 4.8 is not passable, return to High Point, mile 7.0, cross under I-90, then go west on the frontage road to enter the Tiger Mountain State Forest and follow a route to Issaquah through the State Forest that is open to bicycles. Reach the

Tiger Mountain Interpretive Center and High Point Trailhead at mile 7.8. Continue west from the Interpretive Center on the road under the powerline, passing a viewpoint over Tradition Lake before reaching a powerline and pipeline junction at mile 8.5. Turn left (south) on the powerline road. At mile 8.8, the Round Lake Wetland Trail joins from the west. Continue south on the road under the powerline to the Section Line Trail at mile 9.2. Now turn right (west) and descend on a road to reach, at the east boundary of Issaquah High School, the continuation of the railroad grade coming from High Point. Turn north on this railroad grade along the high school boundary, then, at the west edge of the high school grounds, turn left to SE 2nd St. Go right (north), then left (west) on SE Andrews St. to **Gilman Town Hall** (mile 11) to join the route coming from High Point by way of Issaquah Creek. The route past Tradition Lake adds 5 miles to the total distance.

At **Gilman Town Hall,** (1898, open Saturdays 11 to 3) find the concrete jail (1914) south of the building. Continue west on Andrews St. to Rainier Ave. and **Railroad Park**. Cross southwest to the Stationmasters House, now the Issaquah Trails Center, and a collection of artifacts left from logging: tools and a steam donkey engine. Go north in Railroad Park across Sunset St. to the **Issaquah Depot** (1889), now a museum (open Saturdays 11-3), to view railroad cars and other artifacts. Return to Sunset St. and turn west across Front St. to visit the **Fish Hatchery**, which has been in operation since 1898. Return to Front St.

Turn left (north) on Front St., then go left (northwest) on NW Gilman Blvd. At the junction with Renton-Issaquah Road (SR-900), turn right to cross north over I-90. Go west on NW Sammamish Road on an intermittent bikeway or wide shoulder, passing **Lake Sammamish State Park** (restrooms) and **Timberlake Park** (1 mile of trails, tables, Lake Sammamish access).

At W Lake Sammamish Parkway SE, mile 14, cross to the Sunset Elementary School. Find the bikeway on the north side of the school and go west, ascending to the level of I-90. Pass a pedestrian overpass and two neighborhood connecting trails. The trail ends at an extension of SE Eastgate Way, mile 15.6. At SE 35th Place, turn left (southwest) through the tunnel to emerge on SE 37th St. At 150th Ave. SE, jog north to find a pedestrian bridge over an I-90 off ramp to SE 36th St. Ride west on the street or on the sidewalk to 128th Ave. SE. Cross to the southwest corner and continue west on a bikeway on the south side of the I-90 off-ramps to go under I-405. At the next street, Lake Washington Blvd. SE, cross the street to find a bikeway on the west side of the street. Proceed north under I-90, then turn west on a pedestrian causeway through **Mercer Slough Park**. After crossing the last bridge in Mercer Slough Park reach a trail junction. The left branch goes southwest under I-90 to continue across the Mercer Island Bridge to Seattle. The right branch goes north to the South Bellevue Park & Ride (Metro 240, 340, etc.).

PRESTON–SNOQUALMIE VIEW, high point 540', 10 miles RT, 500' gain (Maps: USGS Fall City, Snoqualmie). **Bicycle or Hike-1**. Ride Metro 209 to the first stop on the Preston–Fall City Road at SE 84th St. (stores) after leaving I-90 at Exit-22, elevation 540'. If driving, leave I-90 at Exit-22, enter Preston and park on the north side of Preston–Fall City Road at SE 84th St., 0.3 mile from I-90. Access also from Lake Alice Road off Preston–Fall City Road, 0.7 miles south of the Snoqualmie River Bridge.

Walk or ride east and northeast on a paved Rail Trail. Steps and a paved path descend to the Preston Community Center at mile 1 (usually not open). The Preston Mill site (1892) is east. Follow the paved trail and path to an overlook where a former trestle crossed the Raging River. Return south to a paved path that descends and crosses the Preston-Fall City Road. Now go southwest along the highway to the Luten bridge (1915). Turn northeast and ride or walk the old highway and the sidewalk to the continuation of the trail. Ascend in switchbacks to continue east for views north over the valley of the Snoqualmie River. Pass parking (toilet) at the Lake Alice road, mile 3, then reach the end of the trail at a deep gully for a distant look at the upper part of Snoqualmie Falls.

Return west to the Lake Alice Road. Descend north, passing the Fall City Cemetery where many pioneers and members of the Snoqualmie Tribe are buried. At the Preston–Fall City Road, either look for a Metro Stop or continue north to Fall City. Cross the Snoqualmie River and turn west on SR-203 to **Fall City Park**. In the park, visit a hop shed that was built in 1889 and moved to the present site in 1904. Return to Fall City and a Metro stop.

RATTLESNAKE MOUNTAIN NORTH, 3262', 16 miles RT, 2400' gain (Maps: USGS Fall City, North Bend). **Mtn. Bicycle**. Take Exit-25 south from I-90 into SR-18. Drive 0.1 mile south and turn left (east) on SE 104th St. to park in a large parking area at the entrance to a gated road that goes east into Weyerhaeuser property, elevation 900'.

Pass the gate and ride east and south on road W-35000, passing a substation and another gate at one mile. At mile 1.4, the road bends east above Canyon Creek, heard in the canyon below but only occasionally seen. Cross Canyon Creek at mile 2.7, then pass a junction on the right with road W-35090. At mile 3.0, look directly up the road at the towers on North Rattlesnake Ridge. At mile 4, the road to the right, W-35300, goes to the site of **Kerriston**, near the Raging River. This former sawmill town has disappeared completely. To explore the Kerriston site, go right on W-35300 for 0.4 mile, turn right on W-35310 and keep to the right where W-35311 turns left at 0.5 mile from W-35000. Now W-35310 curves to the west, descending. At 0.8 mile from W-35000, again turn right (north) before bending west above a creek to reach the Kerriston site, 1.5 miles from W-35000, 1300'.

From the Kerriston turnoff, mile 4.0, continue southeast on road W-35000. At mile 4.9, pass road W-35400 going left (northeast) uphill. A branch of this road also goes to North Rattlesnake Mountain. Now road W-35000 bends east, reaching a quarry at mile 5.8 and the junction with road W-35500, mile 6.0, 2200'. Take the left, uphill, fork, W-35500. Now the way begins to climb more steeply, bending north above a branch of the Raging River. After a road fork goes east at mile 7.6, 3000', bend northwest to the summit, a forest of communication towers. Keyhole views include Mt. Index (31°), the towers on Tiger Mtn. (284°) with The Brothers in the Olympic Mountains directly behind, and, on the return trip as the road bends from east to south, look for Kaleetan Peak (92°), McClellan Butte (124°), and Mt. Rainier.

EAST TIGER MOUNTAIN, 3004', 8 miles RT, 1700' gain (Maps: Tiger Mtn., USGS Hobart). **Mtn. Bicycle or Hike-1**. This is the highest summit of the Tiger Mountain complex. Take Exit-25 from I-90 and drive south on SR-18 for 4.5 miles. South of milepost 24, turn west and park at the East Tiger parking lot, elevation 1370'.

Take the right hand road (north) past a gate and ascend, passing, at 0.2 miles, the Northwest Timber Trail on the right (east) side of the road and the Connector Trail on the left (south) side of the road. Cross a stream (mile 0.7) and begin to get views to the south. Pass an information signboard (mile 1.4) on the use of biosolids in forestry at a viewpoint west toward the Olympic Mountains. Reach a junction (mile 2.7). Take the right (east) fork to reach another junction at a saddle between Tiger Mountain and a lower summit southeast. Now go left (northwest) past a gate and ascend to the summit platform, a former lookout site with communication towers and a view southwest.

WEST TAYLOR MOUNTAIN, high point 2500', 8 miles RT, 1800' gain (Maps: USGS Hobart). **Mtn. Bicycle and/or Hike-2**. Take Exit-25 from I-90 and drive south on SR-18 for 4.5 miles. South of milepost 24, turn west and park at the East Tiger parking lot, elevation 1370'.

Cross east over SR-18 and go north along the road to find a gated gravel road going southwest under a power line. Ride or hike this road, passing a spur road on the left at 0.1 mile and turning left (south, 160°) at the next road, 0.25 mile from SR-18. At the next junction, 0.6 miles from SR-18, where a road contours northeast, take the right branch road and ascend southeast. Now stay on the most traveled road, bending toward the north and rising to 2100' before descending to a road junction at 1800'. Continue northeast and east to reach a view point on the north shoulder of Taylor Mtn. Summits visible include: Mt. Baker (2°), Three Fingers Mtn. (10°), Mt. Persis. (32°), Mt. Index (36°), Glacier Peak (37°), Little Phelps Mtn. and Mt. Phelps (46°), and Mt. Si (68°). The best viewpoint changes as logging extends the road.

TAYLOR MOUNTAIN, high point 2500', 10 miles RT, 1400' gain (Maps: USGS Hobart). **Mtn. Bicycle and/or Hike-2**. Drive and begin trip as above for **West Taylor Mtn.**

From SR-18, ride or hike south on a gravel road, passing branch roads left at 0.1 mile and 0.2 mile. Continue south on the road for 1.4 miles from SR-18 to a four-way intersection. Stay on the road south for another 0.5 mile to pass a pond and reach a viewpoint toward Mt. Rainier. Return to the four-way intersection. Turn east and ascend on this road, passing a road to the right at 1700'. Stay on the main road, ascending on the west side of Taylor Mtn. At 2400', the road deteriorates to an open track that eventually reaches the Seattle Watershed fence. Follow this fence north to a viewpoint west.

SNOQUALMIE LOOKOUT, high point 1691', 27 miles, 1600' gain (Maps: Weyerhaeuser Snoqualmie & White River, USGS Snoqualmie, Lake Joy, Fall City). **Mtn. Bicycle**. Ride Metro 209 to the stop at Snoqualmie Falls, elevation 460'. If driving, leave I-90 at Exit-27. Follow signs to Snoqualmie Falls. East of Snoqualmie Falls, drive northeast on Tokul Road SE for 0.7 mile and park on the roadside where the road crosses above the Snoqualmie Valley Trail (may not be marked), elevation 500'.

From the Metro stop, ride south on SR-203, then turn east (mile 0.1) on Tokul Road SE, passing a viewpoint and informative sign at mile 0.7. Cross the Snoqualmie Valley Rail Trail, mile 0.8. Bend southeast into SE 53rd Way at mile 1.5 and continue on to join the Mainline Truck Road at mile 2.2. Turn left (north), going through a Weyerhaeuser gate at mile 3.1. The pavement ends at mile 3.3. Pass minor roads east and west, then turn left (northwest) on the J-Line road (mile 4.8, 908'). Cross Ten Creek at mile 5.5, then enter the Tokul Creek valley with its dense and tangled wetland. Where road W-31500 goes north, turn left (northwest) and cross Tokul Creek into road W-26000, mile 9.0. Look for bits of an old railroad trestle south of the creek crossing. Immediately west of the Tokul Creek bridge, turn north on road W-27000 to ascend on the west side of Tokul Creek. Pass roads W-27100 (mile 9.8) and W-27200 (mile 9.9) on the left. At mile 10.7, go right on road W-27300, then at mile 11, take the left fork where the road to the right begins to descend. Begin to get views of the Olympic Mountains at mile 12.4. Stay north on the main road to mile 12.6, 1320', then go right (east), ascending more steeply on road W-27340. At the first road fork, 1500', park bicycle and go left (north) across a landslide that has removed the road, bending south to the lookout site, a thicket of broom. Look for the following summits: Persis (41°), Index (50°), Cascade Lookout (76°), Phelps (78°), Lennox (86°), Twin Peaks (112°), Green (152°), Teneriffe (158°), Fuller Mtn. (161°), and Mt. Si (169°).

Return to road W-26000 at the crossing of Tokul Creek (mile 16.8), then proceed northwest. Cross the east fork of Griffin Creek at mile 19.6, and after passing a junction with road W-26700 going north, go left (west) across Griffin Creek, mile 21.1. After passing several road branches to the right (west), turn right (northwest) at mile 22.6 on road W-26400 to visit Loop Lake, a wetland with little open water. Return to road W-26000 and continue south, getting views of the wetland along Griffin Creek. Stay on road (W-26000) which bends southwest and west, to a Weyerhaeuser gate at mile 30.

Continue west on the Griffin Creek Road, meeting the Snoqualmie Valley Rail Trail at mile 30.5. Turn left (south) on the Trail, crossing Griffin Creek immediately and another bridge over a landslide at mile 33. Pass the location of the former Fall City siding at mile 33.9 before crossing a high bridge. Reach a paved road, 356th Drive SE, at mile 35.3. Turn right (west) and descend to highway SR-203 and a Metro 209 stop, mile 35.7.

To return to a car parked on Tokul Road, continue east on the Snoqualmie Valley Trail across 356th Drive SE, ascending gradually and crossing the Tokul Creek bridge. After going through an underpass under Tokul Road, leave the Snoqualmie Valley Trail and ascend to the road, mile 39.

SNOQUALMIE FALLS, high point 470', 1 mile of trails, 300' gain (Maps: USGS Snoqualmie). **Hike-1**. Take Metro 209 to the bus stop at Snoqualmie Falls, elevation 460'. If driving, leave I-90 at Exit-27 and follow signs to Snoqualmie Falls.

Facilities: restrooms, viewpoints at top and base of falls. If visiting the falls during times of high river flow, travel by Metro bus.

SNOQUALMIE FALLS TO NORTHBEND, high point 1060', 20 miles, 700' gain (Maps: USGS Snoqualmie, North Bend, Chester Morse Lake). **Mtn. Bicycle.** Ride Metro 209 to the first stop in Snoqualmie at Snoqualmie Falls.

After exploring the various viewpoints, ride southeast on the west side of SR-202 across the Snoqualmie River bridge. Continue on a paved path, passing stored equipment of the Snoqualmie Valley Railroad, the historic Log Pavilion, and the Snoqualmie Museum in the former Snoqualmie Depot (1890). At SE River St., mile 2, turn left (northeast), then go east near the Snoqualmie River on Park Ave. SE and SE Park St. At Meadowbrook Way SE, turn left (north) over the Snoqualmie River and continue east on SE Reinig Road, entering the **Sycamore Corridor** (planted 1929). Reach **Three Forks Park** at mile 4.8 (reader board). Leave bicycle and explore the short trail to the Snoqualmie River at the junction of the North and Middle Forks. Return to bicycle to go east on Reinig Road and south on 486th Ave. SE, the North Fork Snoqualmie River Road. Cross the North Fork bridge at mile 5.2 and reach the Middle Fork bridge at mile 5.5. Pause at the reader board, which describes the nearby Norman Bridge, a timber and steel bridge that is part of **Three Forks Park**.

Return north on 486th Ave. NE and west on Reinig Road to Park St., mile 8.5, passing the Snoqualmie Valley Trail at a bridge over the river (future access to trail). Turn south on Park St., entering **Meadowbrook Farm Park**. At mile 8.9, go east on a service road (gravel) to the Snoqualmie Valley Trail. Return north to the bridge for the view, then proceed south past a golf course. Meadowbrook Farm Park (undeveloped) lies on both sides of the trail. At the bridge over the South Fork of the Snoqualmie River, mile 11.7, leave the rail trail to go south on the east bank of the river. Cross under the North Bend–Snoqualmie Highway and over the Preston–North Bend Highway. At SE North Bend Blvd., the Mt. Si Senior Center is left (north) near the Mt. Si Museum. Follow the levee southeast along the river to **Si View Park** (picnic tables, field house, swimming pool), mile 12.7 The river bank beyond is closed to public access.

Go east on SE Orchard Drive until Orchard Drive bends north toward SE North Bend Way. Turn right (east) past a barrier to find a paved path on the right. Follow this paved path south to the South Fork Snoqualmie River dike (picnic tables, playground). Explore downstream (west) to a gate, then return along the river, passing under I-90 at mile 14.8. Reach the end of the dike at Cedar Falls Road, mile 16. Return to 424th Ave. SE. Leave the dike and go north under I-90 to SE Cedar Falls Way. Turn left (northwest) and proceed into North Bend. After joining SE North Bend Way, turn left on E Park St. to the Metro 209 stop on Main St. The Mt. Si Senior Center is west of the bus stop.

North Fork Snoqualmie River Area. From I-90 at Exit-31, drive north into North Bend. In North Bend at the stop signal, drive east on North Bend Way for two blocks. Turn north on Ballarat Ave. into the North Fork Snoqualmie River Road. Cross the Middle Fork of the Snoqualmie River 2.2 miles from North Bend Way, and the North Fork of the Snoqualmie River 2.6 miles and 15 miles from North Bend. The Weyerhaeuser logging roads in this area are open free to foot and bicycle travel except during logging. Map: Weyerhaeuser Snoqualmie & White River.

GREEN MOUNTAIN, 4824', 20 miles RT, 3900' gain (Maps: USGS Mt. Si, GT Mt. Si). **Mtn. Bicycle and Hike-3**. Drive eight miles north from North Bend on the North Fork County Road. Park at Gate 10, elevation 1000'.

Ride east through Gate 10 on the Weyerhaeuser logging road, passing roads right and left, then curving north before crossing a bridge over the North Fork of the Snoqualmie River. After crossing the river (mile 1.4), the road divides into three branches. Take the right (south) fork and ride through a recent clearcut with a view south of the steep western scarp of the Mt. Si–Teneriffe uplift. Cross Hancock Creek at mile 2.1. After a spur road goes right at 2.8 miles, the road ascends more steeply in dense forest, passing two cascades on the left (mile 3.4). The first is nearly hidden in vegetation but the second is worth a pause. At mile 4.4, a pipeline in a clearcut slash descends the steep slope to a small generating station. Look for Fuller Mountain and Klaus Lake from this opening. Pass a pipeline access structure at mile 4.6 where the grade eases and the road enters a hanging valley (2100'). Note a stream cut terminal moraine on the slope south.

At a road fork (mile 4.8, 2200'), go left and continue ascending southeast. After passing a branch road south at mile 5.9 (2800'), the road makes a reverse turn and ascends north. Take the right fork at 7.1 miles (3150') and go up a ridge, passing logging spurs to a road fork at 4000', mile 8.5. Both roads have gates. The road to the left has been covered by mounds of debris. Take the right fork as it descends briefly and deteriorates, crossing the west slope of the ridge to a saddle, 4350', mile 9. Look east into the valley of the Middle Fork of the Snoqualmie River. The road continues up, at first on the east side of the ridge, then crosses to the west side to pass two minor bumps. After the second bump, the road goes back to the east side to pass through colorful rocks. Look down the steep canyon wall where only stumps remain.

After crossing the ridge south of a 4760' point, the road descends 100' before rising to 4600'. Where the road begins to descend, park bicycle, and ascend east, at first on rubble and talus, then through huckleberry brush and logging slash to the summit, occupied by ancient mountain hemlock trees.

FULLER MOUNTAIN, 1880', 4 miles RT, 900' gain (Maps: USGS Mount Si, Snoqualmie, GT Mt. Si). **Hike-2**. At eight miles from North Bend, turn west from the North Fork Snoqualmie River Road and park at Gate 10, an entrance to the Mainline Truck Road, elevation 1000'.

Pass Gate 10 and walk west across the Mainline Truck Road to find a sometimes overgrown trail. Go northwest on this trail to Ten Creek. Turn right (north) for 100' to a foot log. Cross to continue northwest on an overgrown trail to a road (W-31120). Turn left (west) on this road for 0.3 miles to a 4-way junction with roads W-31100 and W-31130, one mile from Gate 10. Turn right (northeast) on W-31130 for 100' then take the first road to the left (north). This road goes to a quarry on the southeast slope of Fuller Mtn. Look carefully on the left (west) side of this road to find a trail beginning 200' from W-31130. This trail, built by students from Green River College, begins in small alder trees and Douglas fir, and is sometimes hidden by sword fern. After leaving the clearcut into more open terrain, the trail is obvious, but may have fallen trees. The trail goes across the forested or talus west slope of Fuller Mtn. almost to the north ridge, then turns southeast to ascend in switchbacks to the summit plateau.

Wander open forest with a dense under-story of sword fern for keyhole views west and north. For the best views south and east, go north 200' from the highest point, then turn east to a mossy bald rock promontory at the top of cliffs to view the following summits: Twin Peaks (74°), Bessemer Mtn. (105°), Green Mtn. (144°), Mt. Teneriffe (156°), Mt. Si (177°), and Little Si (183°).

KLAUS AND BOYLE LAKES, high point 1090', 5 miles RT, 200' gain (Maps: USGS Mt. Si, Snoqualmie, GT Mt. Si). **Hike-1**. Drive, park, and hike as above toward Fuller Mtn. to the junction of roads W-31100 and W-31120, one mile from Gate 10.

Turn left (west) on road W-31100, passing a stub road (W-31119) on the right immediately and turning right (north) 0.1 mile from W-31120 on the next road to reach a grass opening on the shore of Klaus Lake. Return to W-31100, turn left (east) to the junction of W-31100 and W-31120. Turn north on W-31100, rising to cross a broad ridge on the west flank of Fuller Mtn. Where the road descends to a low point, take a stub road left (northwest) to the end of the road to find a trail to Boyle Lake. Cross the stream and follow a trail on an old logging track near the west shore of Boyle Lake until the route is blocked by fallen trees and brush. The easiest approach to the lakeshore is at the outlet.

KLAUS, BOYLE, BRIDGES LAKES, high point 1100', 20 miles RT, 800' gain (Maps: USGS Mount Si, Snoqualmie, GT Mt. Si). **Mtn. Bicycle and Hike-1**. Drive as above for **Fuller Mtn.** and park at Gate 10 on the North Fork Snoqualmie River Road.

Ride left (southwest) on the Mainline Truck Road of the Weyerhaeuser Company for 0.6 miles to the junction with road W-31000. Go right (north) on this road, crossing Ten Creek at mile 0.9. At mile 1.1, turn right (northeast) on road W-31100, passing a four-way intersection at mile 1.3. At mile 1.5, take a road left (north) for 0.1 mile to the south end of Klaus Lake. Return to road W-31100, then continue east to a 4-way junction with roads W-31120 and W-31130, mile 1.8. Turn left (north), staying on W-31100, and ascend across the west flank of Fuller Mtn. A stub road on the left at the first road high point goes west to a viewpoint over Klaus Lake. Descend to a low point. Where road W-31100 turns to the east, mile 2.8, go northwest on a branch road to find a trail. Leave bicycle and walk the trail to the outlet of Boyle Lake. This trail continues on an old logging grade along the west side of Boyle Lake, but is partially blocked by fallen trees and brush. Return to road W-31100, mile 3.4, and go north on the road to viewpoints over Boyle Lake and Bridges Lake, the next lake north. A high point, mile 4.4, on the east side of the road gives views northeast.

Return south on road W-31100 to the junction with roads W-31120 and W-31130, mile 6.4, and turn right (southwest), staying on W-31100. At a 4-way road junction, mile 6.7, bend right (west) to join road W-31000 at mile 6.9. Now ride northwest. Pass road W-31190 on the right (north) at mile 7.0 and road W-31200 going left (west) at mile 7.8. Cross the outlet from Klaus Lake at mile 8.0, then at mile 8.3, take road W-31300 to the right (east) to a Klaus Lake overlook and a view east. Return to road W-31000, mile 9.1, and continue north. Pass road W-31500 on the left (west) at mile 10.1, road W-31610 on the right (east) at mile 10.3, then go to the right (east) on road W-31620 at mile 10.4. Keep left (northeast) at mile 10.7 where the road right goes steeply uphill. At a high point marked by a 2' Douglas fir tree and a clump of smaller cedar trees, mile 11.0, find a trail that descends east to Bridges Lake at a makeshift causeway of logs (slippery) that crosses the wetland to the shore. Look east to the multiple summits of Twin Peaks beyond Lake Phillipa.

Return to road W-31000, mile 11.6, and continue north, at first in a tunnel in dense alder forest that overhangs the road, then in more open country. Reach a junction with road W-31720 at mile 13.3, which goes west to connect with the Tokul Creek Road. Turn right (east), staying on road W-31000. Beaver Creek flows west to Tokul Creek in the valley to the north. After passing branch roads right and left, reach the Mainline Truck Road at mile 15.6. Turn south on this wide, smooth road to pass on the east side of Fuller Mtn., reaching the starting point at mile 19.4.

CASCADE LOOKOUT, 3702', 14 miles RT, 2600' gain (Maps: USGS Devils Slide, GT Mt. Si). **Mtn. Bicycle**. From North Bend Way in North Bend, drive north on the North Fork Snoqualmie River Road, crossing a bridge over Deep Creek at mile 13.8. Park at an intersection with gated logging roads, mile 14, elevation 1298'.

Ride north and northwest on Weyerhaeuser Road W-29000, passing through a recent clearcut. Pass a stub road right (east) at 0.3 miles and another stub road left at 0.5 miles. At a four-way intersection, mile 1.3, continue ascending north on the middle road, W-29600, crossing a creek at mile 1.4. Go right at a 'Y', bending east. Top a grade at mile 2.2, 1800', then, at 2000', pass a branch road right (east). At mile 3.0 a spur road, W-29617 goes left. Reach a viewpoint west at mile 3.3, 2300'. The road now rounds east on the north side of the ridge under cliffs with a steep drop below. Pass a road and cross Deep Creek at mile 3.8, 2500'. Road W-29630 goes left (north) at mile 4.0. At 2900', mile 4.4, the road levels briefly, travelling on the south side of a ridge. After passing minor roads, reach a major intersection with road W-29660 at mile 5.6, 3200'.

Turn left on W-29660 and ascend north, passing minor roads left and right, then taking the left (west) branch at mile 5.8, 3545', where W-29660 goes right (north). Now continue west (W-29663) on the crest of the ridge, passing minor roads, staying west (uphill) on W-29666 where road W-29663 turns southwest from the ridge. Reach the lookout tower at mile 7. Ascend several flights of steps to a 360° viewpoint above the trees. Look west to the buildings of Seattle (260°), northeast to Mt. Index (40°), directly east to Mt. Phelps, and south to summits near Mt. Si.

LITTLE PHELPS MOUNTAIN, high point 4950', 22 miles RT, 4000' gain (Maps: USGS Devils Slide, Mt. Phelps, GT Mt. Si). **Mtn. Bicycle and Hike-3**. On maps, this summit is designated as Mt. Phelps. Drive and ride as above toward **Cascade Lookout** to the intersection of roads W-29600 and W-29660 at mile 5.6, elevation 3200'.

Continue riding east on road W-29600, crossing creeks to a viewpoint on a promontory that looks south across the North Fork of the Snoqualmie River into the Sunday Lake canyon. Note the roads on the steep slopes west of Sunday Creek. At mile 6.5, 3400', road W-29670 goes right (southeast) and descends toward the North Fork. Stay on road W-29600, gradually ascending to a saddle at mile 7.5, 3660'. The Tolt Reservoir is visible in the canyon north. Road W-29660 (see above) reconnects here. From mile 7.5 on, find fallen rocks on the road. Reach the ridge again at mile 8.6, 3750', where the Tolt Reservoir is again visible. Look for Mt. Persis (8°) and Mt. Index (18°). After dropping to 3800', the road rises in switchbacks, passing several rock fangs. Reach the road end at mile 10.7, 4700'. Leave bicycle and hike northeast across the clearcut into ancient forest. From the ridge crest, look northeast at the cliffs of Mt. Phelps (65°). Note the logging roads on the slopes north of the Tolt River canyon. Hike up the ridge in mountain hemlock to reach the high point at the beginning of the cliffs leading to the summit of Little Phelps. The cliffs are climbing country.

SUNDAY LAKE, 1850', 6 miles RT, 350' gain (Maps: USGS Mt. Phelps, GT Mt. Si). **Hike-2. Alpine Lakes Wilderness.** From North Bend, drive 18 miles on the North Fork Snoqualmie River Road, three miles past a Snoqualmie River bridge and 0.5 mile past the Sunday Creek bridge, to park at a gated road on the right (south), elevation 1500'.

Hike southeast past the gate. Ponds in the road can usually be bypassed on the east. At mile 0.5, pass a road going steeply uphill on the left (east) and, where the road turns right (west) (mile 0.8), turn left (southeast) into an opening that looks like a dry watercourse. Cross Sunday Creek, a torrent in the spring but often dry in the fall. Enter ancient forest at the Alpine Lakes Wilderness boundary. Several trail branches provide access to the lake. The main trail, almost impassable beyond the lake, continues two miles up the canyon to the site of an old miner cabin.

MOUNT PHELPS, 5535', 8 miles RT, 3500' gain (Maps: USGS Mt. Phelps, GT Mt. Si). **Hike-3**. Climbers give the name Mt. Phelps to the highest point of the ridge between the Tolt River and the North Fork of the Snoqualmie River where the North Fork is joined by Lennox Creek. This summit is marked McClain Peaks on the USGS 7-1/2' map and the National Forest map. Mount Phelps is the prominent butte-shaped summit seen directly east from NE 85th St. in Seattle.

Drive the North Fork Snoqualmie River Road for 20 miles to a junction 0.2 mile east of the west boundary of the Mt. Baker–Snoqualmie National Forest (sign) where the road becomes FS-57. Turn left (northeast), crossing Lennox Creek, then, where FS-57 turns southeast to follow Lennox Creek, continue northeast on road FS-5730 across the North Fork of the Snoqualmie River. Drive 2.5 miles from the Lennox Creek Bridge on road FS-5730 to a road junction, elevation 2240', passing a first road left 1.5 miles from the Lennox Creek Bridge.

Drive or hike southwest on road FS-5736 for 1.1 miles. Before reaching the end of the road, park where the road bends west into a gully (2480'). Ascend right (northwest) on a steep, rough vehicle track to an old mine at the southwest corner of a clearcut. East of the collapsed adit, ascend north through a clump of trees to find a boot track continuing up in the clearcut. This track generally follows the line between the south-facing slope and the southwest-facing slope dropping into a gully.

Enter ancient forest at 3800' to find a faint and intermittent track traversing the slope northwest to a 4200' saddle. In preparation for the return trip, pay close attention to the route on this traverse to be able to find the way back from the 4200' saddle to the boot track in the clearcut. On the return, don't be tempted to descend in the attractive gully that drops southeast from the 4200' saddle. The gully soon becomes too steep, and, east of the gully below 3800', an avalanche slope of nearly impenetrable small yellow cedar trees bars the way to the clearcut.

To continue up from the 4200' saddle, turn northeast and ascend, passing a rock point on the left (north), then stay on or near the crest of the ridge. Pass another rocky protuberance (4500') also on the left. At 5100', pass the first set of slabs on the left. At 5200', pass the second set of slabs on the right by ascending in a dry water course. At the top of the second set of slabs, 5250', contour left below cliffs and steeper rocks to an open ramp that ascends northeast to the summit block. Use care to return by the same route. The other three sides of the summit pyramid of Mt. Phelps are nearly vertical.

LENNOX MOUNTAIN, 5894', 10 miles RT, 3000' gain (Maps: USGS Mt. Phelps, Grotto, GT Mt. Si, Skykomish). **Hike-3, Snow. Alpine Lakes Wilderness.** Drive on the North Fork Snoqualmie River Road, turning left to cross Lennox Creek at 20 miles from North Bend. Continue northeast across the North Fork of the Snoqualmie River, going east for five miles to the end of road FS-5730 at elevation 2600' in a clearcut south of a creek that descends steeply southwest from the ridge north of Lennox Mountain. This creek doesn't show on the USGS map.

From parking at the end of the road, descend on a rough track to the creek. Contour across all branches of the creek then turn southeast and ascend a steep, brushy, water-cut slope to the top of the bank above the creek. Continue up the fall-line on this re-growing slope, entering ancient forest at 2900'. Turn left (north) and contour to the top of the steep bank that descends to the stream. The crown of this bank on the southeast side of the creek gully has been the least brushy route of several trips. Ascend along the line above the gully to a talus slope that descends from the north ridge of Lennox Mountain. Continue up to the ridge, then turn southeast to the summit. The central position of Lennox Mtn. provides a magnificent view of Fernow (62°), Daniel (116°), Hinman (119°), Big Snow Mtn. (152°), Garfield (188°), Phelps (287°), and Index (326°).

BARE MOUNTAIN, 5353', 7 miles RT, 2500' gain (Maps: USGS Mt. Phelps, Grotto, GT Mt. Si, Skykomish). **Hike-1. Alpine Lakes Wilderness.** Drive the North Fork Snoqualmie River Road to the Lennox Creek crossing, 20 miles from North Bend. Immediately after crossing Lennox Creek, turn right (south) and continue three miles on FS-57 to the Bear Creek trail, elevation 2050'.

Park and hike east on the Bear Creek trail (FS-1037) for two miles to a trail junction, 3500'. Turn left (north) and ascend on switchbacks to the lookout site, which overlooks Paradise Lake. Look for Lennox (47°) and Phelps (315°).

BEAR CREEK MINES, high point 3900', 6 miles RT, 1800' gain (Maps: USGS Mt. Phelps, Grotto, GT Mt. Si, Skykomish). **Hike-1. Alpine Lakes Wilderness.** Drive and begin hike as above for Bare Mtn.

Hike east two miles to a trail junction. Continue east in the valley to a nearly level basin and cabin site. Look for scattered mining artifacts, and consider the difficulty of transporting these large objects over the existing trail.

ANDERSON LAKE, high point 4620', 10 miles RT, 2500' gain (Maps: USGS Lake Philippa, Snoqualmie Lake, GT Mt. Si, Skykomish). **Hike-2. Alpine Lakes Wilderness.** Drive as above for **Bare Mtn.** on road FS-57 two miles past the Bear Creek trailhead and 26 miles from North Bend to the end of the road at the Anderson Lake trailhead, elevation 2700'.

The trail begins up a rocky track that was originally a mine road, and then ascends the steep north-facing slope in switchbacks in ancient forest. The route has been altered many times to avoid windfallen trees. Note a 6' diameter yellow cedar tree that has fallen near the trail at 3200'. This tree is possibly more than 500 years old. In some places above this elevation, yellow cedar is predominant. To the south, many standing yellow cedar snags remain from a fire. At 4300', reach the end of the switchbacks and begin to contour southeast on the south slope of the Lennox Creek basin toward Anderson Gap. As the trail turns to the east to reach Anderson Gap, it leaves the forest and crosses heather-huckleberry meadow where granite slabs are exposed. After passing Anderson Gap, 4600', descend to Anderson Lake, 4200'.

DOG MOUNTAIN, 5408', 8 miles RT, 2500' gain (Maps: USGS Mt. Phelps, Snoqualmie Lake, GT Mt. Si, Skykomish). **Hike-3. Alpine Lakes Wilderness.** Drive, park, and hike as above for **Anderson Lake** toward Anderson Gap.

At 4400', where the trail crosses gently sloping granite slabs and the notch of Anderson Gap is directly east, leave the trail and hike west, ascending at first on granite slabs or on the slope nearby (low heather-huckleberry), then on talus toward cliffs. At 5000', below the cliffs, contour right and ascend to a ridge. Go southwest on this ridge to an open slope and continue to the summit, which has an impressive view of the north faces of Garfield Mtn. (174°) and Treen Peak (154°).

Middle Fork Snoqualmie River Area.

Leave I-90 at Exit-32 or Exit-34. Drive north 0.5 miles to North Bend Way. The Middle Fork road beyond the Taylor River bridge is often rough, canted, or washed out, but is always open to bicycles.

LITTLE SI, 1576', 4 miles RT hiking, 1100' gain (Maps: USGS North Bend, Mt. Si, GT Mt. Si). **Bicycle and/or Hike-2**. Take Metro 209 to North Bend. Leave the bus on North Bend Blvd. south of North Bend Way. Return north, then ride southeast on SE North Bend Way for 1.4 miles, passing the North Bend Ranger Station at mile 0.8. Turn left (north) on Mt. Si Road. After crossing the Middle Fork Snoqualmie River bridge (mile 1.8), turn left (northwest) to the trailhead, mile 2.0. Leave bicycle at the trailhead. If driving, leave I-90 at Exit-32. Go north 0.5 miles to the intersection with North Bend Way, then go west 0.2 miles to the Mt. Si road. Turn north, cross the Middle Fork of the Snoqualmie River and park west of the road near the north end of the bridge.

From parking, walk west for 0.2 mile on the paved road to a sign at the trailhead, elevation 480'. Hike north, at first on an old logging road. Go left (west) at a road junction, 880', where the road narrows to a trail, then cross a creek. Continue north up the valley on the trail, passing between Little Si and Mt. Si to reach the north ridge of Little Si. Ascend south on this ridge to the summit, a cluster of bald knobs with open views.

LITTLE SI, 1576', 3 miles RT hiking, 1100' gain (Maps: USGS North Bend, Mt. Si, GT Mt. Si). **Bicycle and/or Hike-4†**. The 'scramble' route. Take Metro 209 to North Bend and ride bicycle to the trailhead, or drive, park, and hike as above toward Little Si.

After crossing the creek, 880', bend north in the valley between Little Si and Mt. Si. The rock route to Little Si begins one mile from the trailhead where a talus finger descends from Little Si almost to the trail, 950'. With care, find a route on rock that does not exceed **Hike-4†** difficulty. Return by the Little Si trail.

MOUNT SI OLD TRAIL, high point 4000', 8 miles RT hiking, 3500' gain, (Maps: USGS North Bend, Chester Morse Lake, Mt. Si, GT Mt. Si, Bandera). **Bicycle and/or Hike-2**. Take Metro 209 to North Bend and ride to the trailhead, or drive, park, and begin hike as above for **Little Si**.

After the road narrows to a trail 0.6 mile from the trailhead and bends to the left (west), descending, watch for a narrow trail branching right. Follow this trail north through a thicket of alder trees, then begin a switchback ascent of the Mt. Si carp. At 1400', pass through a narrow cleft in the rocks (landslide?), then continue up the south side of Mt. Si. Cross an old logging road at 1800' and reach a junction with the new Mt. Si trail at 3000'. Turn left and ascend either on the new Mt. Si trail or on the steeper ridgeline trail. The trail ends at 4000'. The summit pyramid, 4167', is classification **Hike-4†**.

MOUNT SI MIDDLE TRAIL, high point 4000', 8 miles RT hiking, 3500' gain (Maps: USGS North Bend, Chester Morse Lake, GT Mt. Si, Bandera). **Bicycle and/or Hike-2**. Ride bicycle or drive and park as above for **Little Si**.

Hike 0.4 mile north on an old logging road to the junction with another road, 880'. Turn right on this road, contouring east, and rising to a saddle, 1250'. The road passes near several moss-covered rock viewpoints. After the saddle, the road descends to 1100' before rising to a road fork (1250'). Now go left (north) and ascend on the road, passing a cliff. At 1600', where the road is going east, look for a steeper trail turning left. Ascend northwest on this trail, which joins the Old Mt. Si trail at 1700'. Now turn right to follow the Old Mt. Si trail.

MOUNT SI NEW TRAIL, high point 4000', 8 miles RT hiking, 3500' or 3700' gain (Maps: USGS Chester Morse Lake, Mt. Si, GT Mt. Si, Bandera). **Bicycle and/or Hike-1**. Take Metro 209 to North Bend at North Bend Way. Ride north on North Bend Way to Mt. Si Road. Turn left (north) to the trailhead two miles northeast of the Snoqualmie River Bridge. If driving, leave I-90 at Exit-32. Drive north 0.5 miles to North Bend Way, then go west 0.2 miles to Mt. Si road. Turn north on Mt. Si road and drive two miles from the bridge to a parking lot on the north side of the road (toilets), elevation 600'.

Hike the trail north to the summit area. The summit pyramid, 4167', is the upper limit of difficulty for classification **Hike-4†**.

MOUNT TENERIFFE, 4788', 12 miles RT hiking, 4000' gain (Maps: USGS Chester Morse Lake, Mt. Si, GT Mt. Si, Bandera). **Bicycle and/or Hike-3**. Take Metro 209 and ride bicycle or drive as above for **Mt. Si New Trail**. Continue on the Mt. Si road to the school bus turnaround, three miles from the Snoqualmie River Bridge, elevation 900'.

Ascend west (300°) past a gate on a road, avoiding a left fork at 0.6 miles. Keep to the left at a narrow branch road east, 1400' and 0.8 mile. Reach older forest at 1800' where the road steepens. At the ridge crest, 4400', leave the road and ascend southeast on or near the ridge to the open summit.

GROUSE RIDGE, 4841', 8 miles RT hiking, 4100' gain (Maps: USGS Chester Morse Lake, GT Bandera). **Bicycle and/or Hike-3**. This summit is also known as **Mailbox Peak** and is the western summit of the Mt. Defiance ridge. Take Metro 209 to North Bend at North Bend Way, elevation 440'. Ride east on SE North Bend Way for 2.7 miles, then turn left on SE 140th St. Go left again into the Middle Fork Road at mile 3.8. Reach the trailhead 6.5 miles from the bus stop in North Bend (pavement ends). If driving, leave I-90 at Exit-34. Drive north 0.7 mile, then turn east on the Middle Fork Road, keeping to the right at mile 1.7 from I-90 (signed SE Lake Dorothy Road), rejoining the SE Middle Fork Road. Park 3.2 miles from I-90 at a branch road right (east), elevation 800'.

Walk this gated road, first to the east, then bending south, passing a left fork to the east at 0.1 miles. Where the road bends sharply right (west) 0.4 miles from the Middle Fork Road and crosses a small creek, find a trail east hidden in the brush beside the road. Look for an arrow board marked 4841 nailed to a tree on the right (south) side of the trail. Ascend east on switchbacks in open forest to 3000'. Now contour southeast through a narrow brushy zone to an open fern and heather slope. Ascend east, crossing talus at 4000'. A mailbox on the summit contains a register.

UPPER GRANITE LAKE, 2900', 3100', 12 miles RT, 2200' gain (Maps: USGS Chester Morse Lake, Bandera, GT Bandera). **Mtn. Bicycle and/or Hike-3**. Take Metro 209 to North Bend and ride as above to the Grouse Ridge Trailhead (adds 13 miles RT bicycling). If driving, leave I-90 at Exit-34. Go north 0.7 miles, then turn east on the Middle Fork road for 3.2 miles from I-90 to park at the **Grouse Ridge** parking area (see above), elevation 800'.

Ride east on the Middle Fork Road for 0.3 miles, then turn right into a gated road that ascends east. At 1.3 miles, the former road that passed above cliffs has been replaced by a switchback. Enter the Granite Creek basin at mile 3.0, 1900', then travel above cascades of Granite Creek before crossing the creek at mile 3.3, 2000'. At 2600', mile 4.5, pass an overgrown road on the right that crosses the creek and ascends west toward the crest of Grouse Ridge. At 3100', mile 5.2, contour right (south) on a branch road. At mile 5.7, where this branch road descends southwest toward Granite Creek, look for a footpath that wanders south through brush to a grass opening on the shore of the lake under a large hemlock tree.

THOMPSON LAKE, 3650', high point 4300', 14 miles RT, 4400' gain (Maps: USGS Bandera, GT Bandera). **Mtn. Bicycle and/or Hike-1. Alpine Lakes Wilderness.** Ride or drive and park as for **Upper Granite Lake** above.

Ride or hike to the road fork leading to Upper Granite Lake, 3100'. Keep left and continue ascending on the road, which now curves north. At 3200', turn right (east) and ascend on a steeper and rougher road, bending south. After passing an overgrown track on the right (south) at 3500', the road curves north and makes several switchbacks. At the southeast end of a switchback, 3950', look for a narrow track that contours southeast. Follow this track into ancient forest (signed 'Thompson Lake Trail 1009A'). After descending briefly across a creek, the trail ascends southeast to the crest of the ridge, 4300', then descends 700' to the lake. On the descent, stop at a switchback at the edge of talus to look at Kaleetan Peak (85°). Where the trail reaches the shore, Preacher Mtn. (53°) is the only summit clearly visible and bits of Caroline Mtn. (66°) can be seen through forest.

THOMPSON POINT 5124, 5124', 16 miles RT, 4400' gain (Maps: USGS Bandera, GT Bandera). **Mtn. Bicycle and/or Hike-2**. Approach as for **Thompson Lake** above.

From the fork to Thompson Lake, 3950', continue ascending north and east on the road to the ridge, 4800'. Go northeast on the road to a landing at a pile of logging debris. Leave the road and ascend east to the first summit, which looks down on Thompson Lake.

THOMPSON POINT 5454, 5454', 18 miles RT, 4700' gain (Maps: USGS Bandera, GT Bandera). **Hike-3**. Approach as for Thompson Point 5124 above.

Hike north along the ridge, descending to 5000'. The ridge is now forested. At the summit, look down on Russian Butte, still two miles away and 300' lower.

RUSSIAN BUTTE, 5123', 22 miles RT, 4800' gain (Maps: USGS Bandera, GT Bandera). **Mtn. Bicycle and/or Hike-3. Snow**. Begin as for **Thompson Point 5454** above. June, with firm snow, is the best time.

From 5454, hike north along the ridge, dropping on the east side of the ridge where the ridge crest is more difficult. At the saddle between a rock fang and the final summit, look for an easy ramp that ascends north on the west side. Few people have signed the register in recent years.

BESSEMER MOUNTAIN, 5028', 10 miles RT, 4000' gain (Maps: USGS Lake Phillipa, GT Mt. Si). **Mtn. Bicycle and/or Hike-2**. Leave I-90 at Exit-34. Drive north 0.7 miles to the Middle Fork Road, then go east. After crossing the Snoqualmie River, 5.9 miles from I-90, drive northeast two miles to a branch road, 7.9 miles from I-90, elevation 930'.

Ride or hike this branch road north, meeting the old CCC road at mile 1.1, 1300', east of a large creek. Turn right (east) on the CCC road, crossing minor creeks. At mile 1.3, before crossing a larger creek, turn left (north), ascending in switchbacks. After passing below waterfalls on a northeast leg at 2000', go left (west) at a road junction to cross the creek again. Just before another switchback, 2200', an overgrown branch road goes west to the south side of Green Mtn. Now the road ascends northeast to 2900' and another switchback. Look for dikes of granitic rock in the bedrock exposed at the turn. Reach another road junction at 3200'. Take the right fork and ascend north in short switchbacks to a junction near the crest of the ridge, 4000'. Diverge north at this junction to the crest of the ridge and a view north into the upper basin of Hancock Creek.

Now go east on the road to ascend more gradually to the southeast ridge of Bessemer Mtn. Turn west on the crest of the ridge to a junction. The right fork goes to a quarry on the east aspect of the summit. Continue west across south facing slopes to the west ridge, then turn northeast to the end of the road below the summit. Look east and south to these summits: Hinman (86°), Daniel (87°), Garfield (88°), Stuart (100°), Chikamin (109°), Huckleberry (113°), Thompson (115°), Granite Mtn. (146°) up the valley of the Pratt River, and Russian Butte (162°).

MIDDLE FORK TRAIL, high point 1400', 12 miles RT, 1000' gain (USGS Lake Philippa, Snoqualmie Lake, GT Mt. Si, Skykomish). **Mtn. Bicycle and/or Hike-1**. Drive as above for Bessemer Mtn., continuing on the Middle Fork road to the Middle Fork Trailhead, 12.5 miles from I-90, elevation 1000'. For a loop trip, park bicycle at the the Dingford Creek trailhead (see Hester Lake) or arrange a bicycle exchange.

Cross the Middle Fork bridge and hike east (no bicycles), passing impressive cliffs at mile 1 and getting occasional views of the spires of Mt. Garfield (north). After mile 1.5 the trail sometimes follows the route of an old railroad grade (look for tie marks). Cross the cascade of Cripple Creek one mile before reaching the bridge at Dingford Creek (mile 6).

TAYLOR RIVER, high point 1865', 14 miles RT, 800' gain (Maps: USGS Lake Philippa, Snoqualmie Lake, GT Mt. Si, Skykomish). **Mtn. Bicycle and/or Hike-1** . The Taylor River area has only two official trails that go beyond the Taylor River Road–to Snoqualmie Lake and Nordrum Lake–but the area has an enormous potential for trails to lakes and summits. This former logging road is occasionally rough or covered with flood debris, and often overgrown by salmonberry. Rewarding destinations include: Lipsy Lake and Otter Falls (9 miles RT), the bridge over Big Creek (10 miles RT), Snoqualmie Lake (see below), and Nordrum Lake (see below). Leave I-90 at Exit-34. Drive north 0.5 mile to the Middle Fork Snoqualmie River Road. Turn east on FS-56, crossing the Taylor River Bridge at mile 13 from I-90. Turn north, passing the Middle Fork Snoqualmie River Road on the right. Park near the gate that blocks the road, elevation 1160' and 13.5 miles from I-90.

Pass the gate, cross the Taylor River bridge and ride or hike north. At 0.4 mile on a driveable road, go right (east) on a bouldery track, passing several places with access to the river. The first creek, at mile 1.1, is not named. Next, at mile 3.0, cross a timber and plank bridge over Marten Creek, coming from Marten Lake. The track to **Marten Lake** begins 100' west of the bridge. At mile 3.3, a boulder pile from floods obscures the road for 100'. The next creek, mile 3.6, where the road is a stream course for 200', descends from Anderson Lake. A way through the debris of an avalanche gully at mile 4.0 has been cleared. At mile 4.3, where the apparent summit of Treen Peak reads 190°, look for the trail to **Lipsy Lake** 300' east of a creek in a 5' diameter culvert. **Otter Falls** skips down 200' of granite cliffs into the lake.

At mile 5.0, 1700', cross a concrete bridge over Big Creek, coming from Dream Lake. The view of water cascading over bedrock is spectacular during high water. Reach the beginning of the Snoqualmie Lake Trail, FS-1002, on the left (east) at mile 6.6. Continue on to the end of the road on the bank of the Taylor River at the beginning of the Nordrum Lake trail, FS-1004, mile 6.8. The trails to Snoqualmie Lake and Nordrum Lake enter Wilderness and bicycles are prohibited.

NORDRUM LAKE, 3670', 18 miles RT, 2600' gain (Maps: USGS Snoqualmie Lake, GT Mt. Si, Skykomish). **Mtn. Bicycle and/or Hike-3. Alpine Lakes Wilderness.** Drive and ride or hike as above to the **Taylor River** crossing 6.8 miles from the Taylor River bridge.

From the end of the Taylor River road, 1865', hike south on trail FS-1004, crossing the Taylor River (easy in late summer), then ascend on a sometimes rough trail into giant ancient forest. Pass an enormous double cedar tree at 1900' and shortly thereafter a fallen giant red cedar. The trail now ascends southeast on a minor ridge, giving partial views into the upper Taylor River valley. At 2800', the trail crosses a creek on exposed slabs, a crossing that would not be easy during high water. At 3400', enter yellow cedar country, crossing the slope southwest. In talus below cliffs, 3600', cairns point the way to exit from the upper west edge. At 3700', turn southeast to ascend through a notch to the dumbbell-shaped lake. At the lake, go southeast to find a campsite. A nearby underwater rock provides a swim step.

On returning from the lake, pause on the brink of the descent for the view of complex Cascade Mtn. north across the valley of the Taylor River.

SNOQUALMIE LAKE, 3147', 16 miles RT, 2000' gain (Maps: USGS Snoqualmie Lake, GT Mt. Si, Skykomish). **Mtn. Bicycle and/or Hike-2. Alpine Lakes Wilderness.** Approach as above for Nordrum Lake to the trailhead near the end of the Taylor River Road, 1860'.

Hike east on trail FS-1002, ascending in a regrowing clearcut and crossing an avalanche track. Below 2100', pass several giant trees that have fallen across the trail. At 2350', view cascades as the trail passes close to the river, then go north across a rocky avalanche track to the lake. In late summer, a sandy beach is exposed. The trail continues to Deer, Bear, and Dorothy Lakes, eventually reaching the road on the Miller River.

HESTER LAKE, 3886', 11 miles RT, 2500' gain (Maps: USGS Snoqualmie Lake, GT Skykomish). **Mtn. Bicycle and/or Hike-2. Alpine Lakes Wilderness.** Leave I-90 at Exit-34. Drive north 0.5 mile to the Middle Fork Snoqualmie River Road. Turn east and drive on the Middle Fork Snoqualmie River Road, FS-56, across the Taylor River Bridge. Ride or drive east (rough, 5mph) for six miles to the Dingford Creek trailhead, elevation 1400' and 19 miles from I-90.

Hike northeast on trail FS-1005. At mile 3.0, turn right (east and south) on trail FS-1005.1, which often is a muddy mess, to the lake, lying in a steep-walled basin under Mt. Price.

LITTLE MYRTLE LAKE, high point 4300', 13 miles RT, 3000' gain (Maps: USGS Snoqualmie Lake, GT Skykomish). **Mountain Bicycle and/or Hike-1**. Drive or ride and hike as above for Hester Lake to the trail fork three miles from the trailhead.

Take the left fork and ascend to **Myrtle Lake** and a view of Big Snow Mtn. (southeast). Cross the outlet and follow the trail (recently brushcut) around the east side of the lake, ascending through cliffs (giant yellow cedars) to Little Myrtle Lake, lying in a talus-rimmed basin. The trail disappears into dense growth at the north end of the lake.

HARDSCRABBLE CREEK, high point 2960', 24 miles RT, 2000' gain (Maps: USGS Big Snow Mtn., GT Skykomish, Snoqualmie Pass) **Mtn. Bicycle**. Drive the Middle Fork Snoqualmie River Road for 13 miles from I-90 to the bridge over the Taylor River, elevation 1100'.

Ride east on the Middle Fork Snoqualmie River Road, passing the Dingford Creek trail at mile 6 and the crossing to Goldmeier Hot Springs at mile 10. Pause frequently for views of river and summits.

DUTCH MILLER GAP, 5000', 16 miles RT, 2000' gain (Maps: USGS Big Snow Mt., Mt. Daniel, GT Skykomish, Stevens Pass). **Mtn. Bicycle and/or Hike-1. Alpine Lakes Wilderness.** Leave I-90 at Exit-34. Drive north 0.5 mile to the Middle Fork Snoqualmie River Road. Turn east and drive across the Taylor River Bridge. East of the bridge, take the right fork and continue to the end of the road at Hardscrabble Creek, elevation 2960'. If the road becomes too rough for driving, ride a mountain bicycle to the end of the road (12 miles from the Taylor River). No bicycles beyond Hardscrabble Creek.

Hike east on trail FS-1030, passing a trail left (north) to Williams Lake at seven miles. Summit Chief Mountain can be ascended as a day trip from Dutch Miller Gap (see below).

SUMMIT CHIEF MOUNTAIN, 7464', 6 miles RT, 3000' gain (Maps: USGS Big Snow Mtn., Mt. Daniel, GT Skykomish, Stevens Pass). **Hike-4†. Alpine Lakes Wilderness.** The distance and elevation gain given for this trip are from Dutch Miller Gap. If approaching from the Cooper Lake trailhead by way of the Pacific Crest Trail and trail FS-44 west of Waptus Lake, leave trail at 4200', southwest of Lake Ivanhoe, and ascend west, passing north of the unnamed lake shown at 5200' on the USGS Big Snow Mtn. map to meet the route coming from Dutch Miller Gap at 5600'.

From Dutch Miller Gap, contour south near or below 5600' until south of and below the ridge that descends east from Little Big Chief, the summit shown at 7200' on the USGS map. Once past this sharp ridge, turn west and ascend in broken terrain to the south ridge of Summit Chief Mtn., 7000'. Cross the ridge to the southwest slope of the mountain and ascend northeast in talus and scree.

WILLIAMS LAKE, 4600', 16 miles RT, 1600' gain (Maps: USGS Big Snow Mt., Mt. Daniel, GT Skykomish, Stevens Pass). **Hike-1. Alpine Lakes Wilderness.** Drive and/or ride and hike as above toward **Dutch Miller Gap**.

Turn north at seven miles, 4400', on trail FS-1030 to the lake, center of former mining. Few artifacts remain from this activity.

LA BOHN PEAK, 6585', 20 miles RT, 3700' gain (Maps: USGS Mt. Daniel, GT Stevens Pass). **Hike-3. Alpine Lakes Wilderness.** Drive and/or ride and hike as above to **Williams Lake**.

From Williams Lake, ascend the slope northeast, east of the creek that enters Williams Lake. At 5300', turn north to pass through the Chain Lakes basin and continue to **La Bohn Gap**, 5900', the saddle between the Middle Fork Snoqualmie River and Necklace Valley.. La Bohn Gap is incorrectly marked on the USGS map. Turn west and ascend broken rocks to the summit for a view of Iron Cap (252°) and Summit Chief Mtn. (200°). Bears Breast Mountain is southeast (144°).

MOUNT HINMAN, 7492', 24 miles RT, 4700' gain (Maps: USGS Mt. Daniel, GT Stevens Pass). **Hike-3, Snow. Alpine Lakes Wilderness.** Drive and/or ride and hike as above to **Williams Lake**.

From Williams Lake, hike to **La Bohn Gap** (see **La Bohn Peak above**). From the high point of La Bohn Gap, turn east and northeast to ascend the broad, gentle slope on the north side of the west ridge of Mount Hinman. The Hinman Glacier is below. Most of this slope is snow, but the highest parts of the west ridge become snow-free in late summer.

After crossing over the broad north ridge of Mount Hinman, 7300', turn southeast to the summit.

South Fork Snoqualmie River Area. The I-90 corridor east of North Bend to Exit-47.

CEDAR BUTTE, 1880', 8 miles (hike) RT or 23 miles (bicycle & hike) RT, 1500' gain bicycling, 1000' gain hiking (Maps: USGS North Bend, Chester Morse Lake). **Mtn. Bicycle and/or Hike-2.** Take Metro 209 to North Bend at North Bend Way, elevation 440'. If driving, find on-street parking in North Bend. For **Hike-2** only, leave I-90 at Exit-32. Drive south on Cedar Falls Way for three miles. Park at Rattlesnake Lake, elevation 900'.

Bicycle. Ride east on North Bend Way, bending right into Tanner Ave. at mile 1.7 to continue east. At mile 2.3, where Tanner Ave. rejoins North Bend Way, turn southeast on the Snoqualmie Valley Rail Trail, passing under I-90 and crossing the South Fork of the Snoqualmie River. At mile 3.8, look down on the South Fork. Cross a branch of Boxley Creek on a high trestle that was rebuilt in 1997, mile 4.9. Near mile 5.7, cross several roads (no parking), then reach Seattle Water Department Property at mile 7.0. Jog right to Cedar Falls Road and continue south to Rattlesnake Lake (mile 7.4).

Pass the Rattlesnake Ledge Trail at the north end of the lake. Explore the facilities at the lake, then continue south on the east side of the lake on a paved path (daylight hours only). Where the paved path meets Cedar Falls Way, mile 8.6, go right (south) for 0.5 mile to Cedar Falls and explore the facilities: outdoor museum with log cabin, informative displays, and 6' log. Turn back north on Cedar Falls Road. At mile 10.0, turn northeast past a gate on the Rail Trail, getting views west to Rattlesnake Ledge and east to Cedar Butte. Cross Boxley Creek at mile 11 (loose gravel). Find the trail to Cedar Butte at mile 11.1. Park bicycle and ascend southeast, entering dense forest. Find a benchmark and a view south over the Cedar River valley. Return to North Bend on the outgoing route or on Cedar Falls Road.

Hike. From parking at Rattlesnake Lake, follow the bicycle route as described above.

RATTLESNAKE LEDGE, 2079', 3 miles RT, 1200' gain (Maps: USGS North Bend). **Hike-2.** Leave I-90 at Exit-32. Drive south for three miles from I-90 on Cedar Falls Road and park at Rattlesnake Lake (toilets), elevation 910'. For transit access, take Metro 209 to North Bend and ride as above for Cedar Butte to Rattlesnake Lake.

Walk around the north end of the lake on a wide trail to a picnic area on the west side of the lake. Find the Rattlesnake Ledge trail at a signboard. Ascend west on this trail to the top of the rock cliff that overlooks Rattlesnake Lake and Chester Morse Lake. Follow the trail west to two more ledges, 2300' and 2500'.

RATTLESNAKE MOUNTAIN, 3517', 6 miles RT, 2700' gain (Maps: USGS North Bend). **Hike-2**. Hike as above to the highest **Rattlesnake Ledge**, 2500'.

Continue northwest up the ridge on a trail. This trail crosses an overgrown road at 2900' and joins another, more recent road, at 3050' at the north boundary of the Seattle Watershed. Follow a road north, passing a quarry and rounding west to another road. Go right (north) on this road near the crest of the ridge. At 3340', take the left (northwest) branch (280°) to the summit. At 3340', the road that continues north (344°) on the east side of the ridge descends briefly then rises to the ridge (3400') north of the highest point. From this point, a track returns south to the summit.

IRON HORSE STATE PARK. This Rail Trail uses the Milwaukee St. Paul and Pacific Railroad grade. Guide available from WA Parks and Recreation, PO Box 42650, Olympia WA 98504-2650.

Exit-32. Drive south on Cedar Falls Road for three miles to parking at Rattlesnake Lake, elevation 910' (toilets, picnic tables, trails). The Rail Trail begins 0.5 mile south on the road to Cedar Falls. For transit access, see Rattlesnake Ledge.

Exit-38. At the west end of the frontage road on the south side of I-90, turn west into a parking area, 0.5 miles from the eastbound I-90 off-ramp, 1200'. A wide ramp and a trail ascend west. The trail to Mt. Washington begins 0.1 mile west, the trail to Twin Falls is 0.5 mile west, and the trail to Cedar Butte is 3.5 miles west. Rattlesnake Lake is 5 miles west. Going east, find the Hall Creek bridge at mile 1.7 and road FS-9020 at mile 3.6.

Road FS-9020. At the east end of the Exit-38 frontage road on the south side of I-90 (two miles from eastbound Exit-38), ascend southeast for one mile to the Iron Horse State Park, elevation 1250'. The Hall Creek bridge is 1.9 miles west. Going east, find the McClellan Butte trail (mile 2), Hansen Creek bridge (mile 6), Annette Lake trail (mile 9), and the Snoqualmie Tunnel (mile 11).

Exit-42. Drive south from I-90 to the McLellan Butte trailhead, 1.5 miles from I-90, elevation 1450'. Access in one mile to the Rail Trail for all users. No bicycles or horses on trails south of the Rail Trail.

Exit-47. From I-90, drive south to a 'T', then turn east to the Annette Lake trailhead, 1920'. Access in one mile to the Rail Trail for all users. No bicycles or horses on the Annette Lake Trail south of the Rail Trail. The Snoqualmie Tunnel is two miles east.

Exit-54. Drive west, then turn southeast on the west side of I-90. At the DMV facility, turn right (southwest) to the Lake Keechelus trailhead on the west side of the road (toilets), 1.2 miles from I-90, elevation 2500'. The Snoqualmie Tunnel is one mile northwest and the Stampede Pass Road is eight miles south.

Exit-62. Drive west one mile from I-90 on the Stampede Pass Road to the Rail Trail crossing, 2480'. Easton is ten miles south.

Exit-71. From I-90, drive west into Easton, then turn south on the west side of the railroad tracks to the trailhead 0.5 miles from I-90, 2150' (tables, toilets). Cle Elum is 14 miles south.

Exit-84. From I-90, drive southwest through South Cle Elum to the trailhead, 1900'. Thorp is 20 miles south.

Exit-101. From I-90, go north for 0.5 mile. Turn left (west) on West Depot Road across the Rail Trail to parking, 1700'.

IRON HORSE LOOP, high point 1360', 24 miles, 900' gain (Maps: USGS North Bend, Chester Morse Lake, GT Bandera). **Mtn. Bicycle**. Ride Metro 209 to SE North Bend Way in North Bend or, if driving, find on-street parking in North Bend, elevation 450'.

Ride as above for Cedar Butte to the beginning of the Cedar Butte Trail, mile 11.1. Continue east on the Rail Trail, passing exposures of the underlying volcanic rocks at mile 12.1. Cross Boetze Creek at mile 13.2 (waterfall). Pass a substation at mile 14.5, the trail to Twin Falls at mile 14.7, and the trail to Mt. Washington at mile 15.1. At mile 15.2, descend left on a road to parking (toilets) and the frontage road, mile 15.6. Turn left (north) under I-90 and take the on-ramp west. Ride the freeway to Exit-34. Turn north on 468th Ave. SE (mile 19), then go west on SE North Bend Way. Stop at the Tanner viewpoint and readerboard (mile 21) before proceeding into North Bend, either on North Bend Way or on the Rail Trail (gravel). If on North Bend Way, turn left on E Park St. at mile 22 to the Metro Stop on Main Ave. S, mile 23.6. If on the Rail Trail, cross the Mt. Si road at mile 22 and Ballarat Ave. at mile 23. At the next street, Main Ave. N, turn left (south) and proceed across North Bend Way to the Metro 209 stop east of Park St., mile 24.

TWIN FALLS, high point 900', 3 miles RT, 600' gain (Maps: USGS Chester Morse Lake, GT Bandera). **Bicycle and/or Hike-1**. Leave I-90 at Exit-34. Drive south on the paved road for 0.6 miles. Before crossing the river, turn left (east) to a parking area, 1.2 miles from I-90 and elevation 600'. For transit access, take Metro 209 to North Bend, then ride east on SE North Bend Way to 468th Ave. SE (mile 4). Turn south under I-90 and follow the road as above to the parking area (mile 5.5). No bicycles in the park.

Hike the trail east as it ascends in the forest near the river. Reach the first view of the falls at 0.8 mile, a giant ancient Douglas fir tree at 0.9 mile, a turnoff to another viewpoint at 1.1 miles, and the bridge over the South Fork of the Snoqualmie River at mile 1.2, elevation 900'. Cross the river to the grade of the former Milwaukie Railroad at mile 2.1, now the Iron Horse State Park Rail Trail, elevation 1300'. The trail to Mt. Washington begins 0.3 miles east.

MOUNT WASHINGTON, 4400', 10 miles RT, 3000' gain (Maps: USGS Chester Morse Lake, GT Bandera). **Hike-2**. From I-90, take Exit-38. From the west end of the frontage road on the south side of I-90, turn west into a parking area, elevation 1200'.

Find a trail at the west end of the parking area and ascend to the Iron Horse State Park. At the railroad grade, go 300' west to a trail that goes south, ascending the slope in switchbacks. Pass a spring emerging from a cliff at 2400'. The trail crosses a creek (2800') in a valley that descends north. At this crossing, the summit is southwest. After crossing the creek, follow an old logging road to ascend south on the west side of the creek, recrossing the creek in 0.25 mile.

Route 1. At a 'T' road intersection near an intermittent pond (3400'), turn left and follow the road, going at first east, then circling to the north, east, and south, gradually rising to pass east of the 4320' summit that stands north from the main ridge. Cross the narrow crest southwest of the 4320' summit to the ridge south of Mt. Washington. Turn northwest and ascend a road and track to the summit and a view of Chester Morse Lake.

Route 2. Hike-3. For a shorter, more direct route, turn right at the 'T' intersection (3400') and contour northwest on the road to the north ridge of Mt. Washington. Leave the road (3500') and ascend south on the ridge through a clearcut (about 1970), climbing over logs and leaving the ridge as necessary to pass obstacles. Climb over a tangle of logs and other debris left from logging to a road, 4100'. Ascend southwest on the road until east of the summit. Leave the road and follow a track west. Return by the same route or on the road that goes at first south, then circles east and north (Route 1).

OLALLIE NATURE TRAIL, 1200', 1 mile RT, 100' gain (Maps: USGS Chester Morse Lake, GT Bandera). **Walk**. From either end of Exit-38, drive on the frontage road to Olallie State Park, one mile from I-90.

Find a sample of ancient forest, waterfalls, and a mini-generating station (restrooms).

WEST DEFIANCE MOUNTAIN, 4680', 8 miles RT, 3500' gain (USGS Chester Morse Lake, Bandera, GT Bandera). **Hike-3**. Take Exit-38 from I-90 and drive to the northeast end of the frontage road on the north side of I-90. Park at the gate to the Fire Training Center, elevation 1360'.

Walk the road north past the gate for 0.3 miles to find an overgrown and eroded logging road. Turn northeast on this road and ascend to a landing, 2540'. The route to this point is usually snow-free. A nearby point, 2613', provides a view south. From the landing, continue northwest on the overgrown and rocky road until the road turns west and begins to contour, 4000'. Leave the road and continue north in open forest to the summit.

McCLELLAN BUTTE, 5162', 10 miles RT, 3800' gain (Maps: USGS Bandera, GT Bandera). **Hike-1, Hike-4†**. Leave I-90 at Exit-42 and drive south across the river to the parking area 1.5 miles from I-90, elevation 1450'.

Hike the trail southeast to the Iron Horse State Park Rail Trail. Go west to find the continuation of the McClellan Butte trail west of the gully of Alice Creek. Ascend south, crossing a logging road to enter ancient forest at 2600'. Several avalanche gullies are dangerous when snow-filled. At the saddle south of the summit, turn north on the west side of the ridge. The final summit pyramid is classification **Hike-4†**. The west side of the ridge has many huckleberries in late summer.

TALAPUS LAKE, 3300', 4 miles RT, 800' gain (Maps: USGS Bandera, GT Bandera). **Hike-1. Alpine Lakes Wilderness.** Take Exit-45 from I-90 and drive west one mile to a fork. Turn right (northeast) and park at the trailhead four miles from I-90, elevation 2600'.

Hike northeast on the trail to the lake, which lies in ancient forest.

OLALLIE LAKE, 3800', 6 miles RT, 1200' gain (Maps: USGS Bandera, GT Bandera). **Hike-1. Alpine Lakes Wilderness.** Drive and hike as above to **Talapus Lake**.

Continue on the trail past Talapus Lake, going left at a trail junction, 3600', to Olallie Lake.

PRATT MOUNTAIN, 5099', 12 miles, 2500' gain (Maps: USGS Bandera, GT Bandera). **Hike-3. Alpine Lakes Wilderness.** Drive and hike as above past **Talapus Lake.**

Turn right (east) at a trail junction one-fourth mile past Talapus Lake, 3600', to join the Pratt Lake Trail, FS-1007. Head north to the saddle above Olallie Lake, 4160'. At a trail junction in the saddle, go left (west) and ascend to the south shoulder of Pratt Mtn. (4500'). Leave the trail and ascend, partly on talus, to the summit.

MASON LAKE, 4160', 6 miles RT, 2200' gain (Maps: USGS Bandera, GT Bandera). **Hike-3. Alpine Lakes Wilderness.** Take Exit-45 from I-90 and drive west one mile on road FS-9030 to a fork. Go left (west) on FS-9031 to the trailhead five miles from I-90, elevation 2200'.

Follow an old logging road, at first northwest, then turn southeast on a gentle grade. At one mile, cross the outlet creek from Mason Lake, which drops over rocks. Go 0.1 mile past the stream and look for a trail ascending steeply east from the old road at 2500', near the edge between a regrowing clearcut (south) and ancient forest in a deep canyon (north). At a first high point, 3600', on the edge of talus, either contour east across talus (cairns), or descend north on one of several tracks to the bottom of the canyon. Turn east up the canyon, avoiding much of the talus. Both routes rejoin at the east edge of the talus field to continue through a brush zone into ancient forest to emerge at the outlet of Mason Lake. Please use the designated campsites.

MOUNT DEFIANCE, 5584', 10 miles, 3600' gain (Maps: USGS Bandera, GT Bandera). **Hike-3. Alpine Lakes Wilderness.** Drive and hike as above to **Mason Lake.**

Pass the north side of the lake to a junction with the trail (FS-1009) that comes from Olallie Lake. Turn left (west) and ascend to the southeast shoulder of Mt. Defiance, 5200'. Where the trail turns west to contour across the final pyramid, leave the trail and ascend northwest in open forest to the summit. The view extends from Mt. Baker to Mt. Rainier.

BANDERA MOUNTAIN, 5157', 8 miles RT, 3000' gain (Maps: USGS Bandera, GT Bandera). **Hike-2.** Drive as above for **Mason Lake** on road FS-9030 and FS-9031 to the trailhead, elevation 2200'.

From the end of the driveable road, hike at first northwest then go southeast on an old logging road. After passing the Mason Lake trail junction at one mile, continue southeast on the old logging road for 0.5 mile. Leave the road at 3000' on an old logging spur and ascend east, beginning a steeper boot track at 3400'. At the crest of the ridge, 5000', turn northeast and continue up the ridge in open forest and low huckleberry brush to the western summit of Bandera Mtn.

MASON LAKE–BANDERA MOUNTAIN LOOP, high point 5157', 10 miles RT, 3100' gain (Maps: USGS Bandera, GT Bandera). **Hike-3. Alpine Lakes Wilderness.** Drive and hike as above to **Mason Lake**.

Hike past the north side of the lake to trail FS-1009. Turn right (southeast) toward Olallie Lake and ascend to the trail high point, 4480'. Where the trail begins to descend, leave the trail and ascend south in moderate brush. On the crest of the ridge, the route can be nearly brush-free. Pass a 10' deep prospect hole at 4600', a small pond at 4700' and begin a talus slope at 4900'. Reach the summit after passing through a fringe of mountain hemlock trees.

Find the trail at the summit and descend west and south to return to the starting point.

HUMPBACK MOUNTAIN, 5174', 6 miles RT, 2500' gain (Maps: USGS Bandera, Findlay Lake, Snoqualmie Pass, Lost Lake, GT Bandera, Snoqualmie Pass). **Hike-3.** Leave I-90 at Exit-47. Drive south to a 'T' intersection, then go west on road FS-55 for 1.4 miles toward Hansen Creek. Turn south on the Hansen Creek Road (FS-5510), passing a logging road left (east) and park at the second road left, four miles from I-90, elevation 2800'.

Hike this branch road north until the road bends east around the northwest ridge of Humpback Mtn. Leave the road at 3200' and ascend southeast in a growing forest, entering ancient forest at 4000'.

LAKE ANNETTE, 4100', 6 miles RT, 2400' gain (Maps: USGS Snoqualmie Pass, Lost Lake, GT Snoqualmie Pass). **Hike-1.** Drive south from I-90 at Exit-47 to a 'T', then go left (east) to the trailhead 0.8 mile from I-90, elevation 1920'.

Hike the trail south, crossing the Iron Horse State Park at one mile. After crossing the railroad grade, the trail enters ancient forest. The lake is walled on the east and south by Silver and Abiel Peaks.

SILVER PEAK, 5605', 9 miles RT, 3900' gain (Maps: USGS Snoqualmie Pass, Lost Lake, GT Snoqualmie Pass). **Hike-3.** Drive and hike as above to **Lake Annette**.

From the east side of the lake, ascend east on one of several boot tracks and on talus to the ridge south of the summit. Turn north on the ridge to the summit.

Alternate Route: Leave the Lake Annette Trail near the high point, 4300', before the trail begins to descend to the lake. Ascend east to the north ridge of Silver Peak. Turn south to the summit.

SNOQUALMIE TUNNEL LOOP, high point 3000', 16 miles RT, 1100' gain (Maps: USGS Snoqualmie Pass, GT Snoqualmie Pass). **Mtn. Bicycle or Hike-1 part**. The tunnel is closed November 1 to May 1. Drive south from I-90 at Exit-47 to a 'T', then go left (east) to the **Annette Lake** trailhead, 0.8 mile from I-90 and elevation 1920'. For bicycle on transit access, follow the route to Cedar Butte (above) and continue on the rail trail (75 miles RT and 2600' gain from North Bend).

Ride or walk bicycle southeast one mile up the Lake Annette trail to the railroad grade, 2360'. Turn left on the Rail Trail and ascend gradually. Beyond mile 1.3, get views north to Granite Mtn. Pass an old signal tower, mile 2.1, and enter the Snoqualmie Tunnel, mile 2.6, elevation 2520'.

Suggestion: allow 15-30 minutes inside the tunnel for dark adaptation before beginning ride. Look ahead to the visible tunnel exit 2.3 miles away. Although most of the surface is firm gravel, watch for occasional loose patches and ruts where water falls from the roof. The worst water leaks are near the east end. Ride or hike through the tunnel (good light necessary) to the exit, 2580', just east of the Hyak Ski Area parking lot, mile 4.9. The adjoining land along the grade near the tunnel exit is private land. Continue on the railroad grade, rounding east to the Lake Keechelus Trailhead (restrooms), mile 5.8.

Turn left (north) on the paved road, going near the shore of Lake Keechelus to a junction near the highway maintenance station, mile 6.5. Turn left past the Hyak parking lot. Continue north on the road, crossing Coal Creek, mile 7.5. Pass an entrance to Ski Acres at mile 7.6 and a road that goes to I-90 at Exit-53. Reach Travellers Rest at mile 9.2 (store, restrooms). Pass under I-90 (mile 9.6), then turn west on the second road (old Snoqualmie Pass Highway) to descend along the South Fork of the Snoqualmie River, going under I-90 again. At mile 11.2, pause to explore a trail to **Franklin Falls** and a short section of the **Snoqualmie Pass Wagon Road**. Pass a road (mile 12.4) on the right (north), which goes to the beginning of another trail to Franklin Falls. At this road intersection, find another short section of the Snoqualmie Pass Wagon Road on the southeast side of the paved road. The Denny Creek Campground extends south from this road intersection. Pass the road to the Asahiel Curtis Picnic Ground at mile 14.9 and the road to the Pratt Lake trailhead at mile 15.3. Cross over I-90. Go south to a

'T' then turn left to the Lake Annette trailhead. If returning to North Bend, turn right at the 'T' on FS-55 to return to I-90 at Exit-42. Take the frontage road again at Exit-38, then leave I-90 at Exit-32 to go into North Bend.

GRANITE MOUNTAIN, 5629', 8 miles RT, 3700' gain (Maps: USGS Snoqualmie Pass, GT Snoqualmie Pass). **Hike-1. Alpine Lakes Wilderness.** From the north side of I-90 at Exit-47, drive west 0.3 mile to the Pratt Lake trailhead, elevation 1880'.

Hike northeast and northwest one mile on trail FS-1007, then, at 2600', take the right (northeast) fork and ascend on trail FS-1016, first in forest, then on switchbacks in an avalanche track. After leaving the avalanche track, the trail ascends more gently northeast across the open south slope where huckleberries are plentiful in late summer. At 4600', the trail turns back northwest near a watercourse to pass through a hanging valley to reach the lookout tower on the summit. The summit panorama includes the following: Kaleetan (2°), Tooth (56°), Chikamin Peak (61°), Mt. Stuart (82°), and Hibox (88°).

PRATT LAKE, 3400', 12 miles RT, 2500' gain (Maps: USGS Snoqualmie Pass, Bandera, GT Snoqualmie Pass, Bandera). **Hike-1. Alpine Lakes Wilderness.** From the north side of I-90 at Exit-47, drive west 0.3 mile to the Pratt Lake trailhead, elevation 1880'.

Hike northeast and northwest for one mile on trail FS-1007. At 2600', where a trail goes right (east) to Granite Mtn., take the left (northwest) fork and continue on trail FS-1007, ascending northwest and north to pass a lookout cabin site with stream (3400'). At 3700', a trail goes left to Olallie and Talapus Lakes and at 4200' (saddle) another trail goes left (west) to Pratt Mountain and Mason Lake. From this saddle north of Olallie Lake, descend north to Pratt Lake.

GRANITE MOUNTAIN WEST SIDE, 5629', 8 miles RT, 3700' gain (Maps: USGS Snoqualmie Pass, GT Snoqualmie Pass). **Hike-3. Alpine Lakes Wilderness.** Drive and hike as above toward **Pratt Lake**.

After passing the trail fork to Granite Mtn. at 2600', continue on the trail toward Pratt Lake across the gully that descends south from Granite Mtn. After crossing the gully, the trail makes two switchbacks. Where the trail turns west the second time at 2880', leave the trail and ascend north along the line formed by the junction of the south-facing slope and the southeast facing slope that descends steeply into the gully. A faint track can be followed in places along this line. Where the forest is no longer continuous and the steepness of the slope diminishes (4500'), turn northeast and ascend or contour across mostly open slopes to the densely forested saddle (5200') northwest of the summit of Granite Mtn. At the saddle, turn southeast and ascend, either on the crest of the ridge, or near the crest on the southwest side to the summit. Return to the starting point on the Granite Mtn. trail.

NORTH GRANITE LOOP, high point 5566', 10 miles RT, 4400' gain (Maps: USGS Snoqualmie Pass, Bandera, GT Bandera, Snoqualmie Pass). **Hike-3. Alpine Lakes Wilderness.** Drive and park at the Pratt Lake trailhead, elevation 1880'.

Hike as above for **Granite Mtn. West Side** to the rocky and open slope west of the summit of Granite Mtn., elevation 4500'. Continue north to a rocky ridge and ascend over an intermediate summit (5160') to the 5566' point northwest of Granite Mtn. for a spectacular view of Kaleetan Peak (12°).

From the summit, follow the ridge northwest (330°) to 5400'. Turn toward the west (290°) and descend to the beginning of a subsidiary ridge that isn't visible from the main ridge at 5400'. Follow a faint track near or on the crest of this ridge (290°) down to 4500'. Leave the ridge, turning southwest (220°) in mostly brush-free forest to meet the Pratt Lake Trail between 4000' and 4100'. Turn left (south) to the starting point.

The ridge that descends north toward Lake Tuscohatchie from Point 5566' is easy and interesting travel at first, but then becomes steep and covered with nearly impenetrable devil's club, huckleberry, and salmonberry before reaching the south end of the lake. Find the Pratt Lake–Melakwa Lake Trail north of the lake through dense salmonberry and huckleberry.

DENNY CREEK TRAIL, high point 4600', 8 miles RT, 2400' gain (Maps: USGS Snoqualmie Pass, GT Snoqualmie Pass). **Hike-1. Alpine Lakes Wilderness.** Leave I-90 at Exit-47. From the north side of I-90, drive east and north on road FS-58 to the trailhead at the north end of the Denny Creek campground, elevation 2280' and two miles from I-90.

After leaving the trailhead, the trail first passes under I-90 then crosses Denny Creek where the creek makes a display as it runs over slabs. Several cataracts of Denny Creek are also visible from the trail. Reach the high point at Hemlock Pass.

MELAKWA LAKE, 4500', 10 miles RT, 2500' gain (Maps: USGS Snoqualmie Pass, GT Snoqualmie Pass). **Hike-1. Alpine Lakes Wilderness.** Drive and park at the Denny Creek trailhead.

Hike the **Denny Creek Trail** (see above) north over Hemlock Pass to the lake, lying in a basin west of Bryant and Chair Peaks. Please camp at least 100' from the lake. No fires.

BRYANT PEAK, 5801', 10 miles RT, 3700' gain (Maps: USGS Snoqualmie Pass, GT Snoqualmie Pass). **Hike-3. Alpine Lakes Wilderness.** Drive and hike as above on the Denny Creek Trail toward **Melakwa Lake** to Hemlock Pass, elevation 4600'.

From Hemlock Pass, leave trail and hike northeast on the crest of, or on the south side of the ridge that goes from Hemlock Pass to join the main northwest-southeast ridge. Bryant Peak is at the junction of the ridges.

HEMLOCK PEAK, 5560', 10 miles RT, 3500' gain (Maps: USGS Snoqualmie Pass, GT Snoqualmie Pass). **Hike-3. Alpine Lakes Wilderness.** Drive and hike as above toward **Bryant Peak**.

Where the subsidiary ridge that goes northeast from Hemlock Pass begins to steepen toward Bryant Peak at 5200', contour southeast into the saddle, 5320', between Bryant Peak and Hemlock Peak, then ascend south to the summit.

KALEETAN PEAK, 6259', 13 miles RT, 3800' gain (Maps: USGS Snoqualmie Pass, GT Snoqualmie Pass). **Hike-4†. Alpine Lakes Wilderness.** Drive and hike as above to **Melakwa Lake**.

Continue around the west side of the lake and ascend in the valley toward Melakwa Pass. After passing the buttress of the 5700' summit of the ridge that encloses Melakwa Lake on the west, turn west at 4800' and ascend the loose scree slopes toward the saddle between the 5700' summit and Kaleetan Peak. A steep, rock slope leads to the saddle, 5520'. Turn right (north) and ascend scree between rock outcrops to the summit, using caution to prevent rockfall.

Snoqualmie Pass Area.

I-90: Exit-52 to Exit-62. Find a Visitor Information Center (maps, permits, and information) 0.2 mile south of I-90 from Exit-52 and restrooms in Travelers Rest 0.5 mile south of I-90 from Exit-52.

DENNY MOUNTAIN, 5520', 5 miles RT, 2500' gain (Maps: USGS Snoqualmie Peak, GT Snoqualmie Pass. **Hike-3, Snow.** Take Exit-52 from I-90 and drive north to the end of the road at the Alpental parking area, elevation 3080'. Denny Mtn. makes an excellent snow ascent anytime in spring after the ski lifts close except during periods of avalanche danger.

Hike west across the bridge over the South Fork of the Snoqualmie River and ascend southwest on the ski slopes east of Denny Mountain. At 4400', where a ski lift ends, turn northwest and continue ascending in a valley on the west side of the next ski lift. The rock summit is north of the highest ski lift terminal.

SNOW LAKE, 4016', 8 miles RT, 1800' gain (Maps: USGS Snoqualmie Pass, GT Snoqualmie Pass). **Hike-1. Alpine Lakes Wilderness.** From Exit-52, drive as above for **Denny Mtn.** to the Alpental parking area, elevation 3080'.

Hike the Snow Lake trail (FS-1013) north over a saddle (4400') in the west ridge of Snoqualmie Mtn. to the lake, which lies under Chair Peak. From the footlog bridge over the outlet, look for Chair Peak (230°) and Mt. Roosevelt (274°). Please camp only in designated sites. No fires.

GEM LAKE, 4857', 10 miles RT, 2700' gain (Maps: USGS Snoqualmie Pass, GT Snoqualmie Pass). **Hike-1. Alpine Lakes Wilderness.** Drive to the Alpental Parking area, north from I-90 at Exit-52, elevation 3080'.

Hike as above for **Snow Lake**, then ascend on trail FS-1013 one mile past Snow Lake to Gem Lake in a basin south of Wright Mtn. Mt. Roosevelt is southwest.

MOUNT ROOSEVELT, 5880', 14 miles RT, 3700' gain (Maps: USGS Snoqualmie Pass, GT Snoqualmie Pass). **Hike-4†. Alpine Lakes Wilderness.** Drive and hike as above to **Gem Lake**.

Where the trail descends to Gem Lake, follow a track west on the south side of the lake. Cross the outlet of Gem Lake, then ascend west to the northeast ridge of Mt. Roosevelt. Find a track and continue southwest near or on the crest of this ridge. At 5350' where the track disappears in talus, turn left (south) to contour and descend 100' below cliffs. At a second talus field below a gully, ascend west in the steep gully (trees), bending left (southwest) across a heather meadow, then ascending over a rock step to reach a basin (5500'), which usually has snow patches even in late summer. A scree saddle in the northeast ridge of Mt. Roosevelt is north. Now ascend a rock and heather ramp diagonally southwest to the south shoulder of Mt. Roosevelt. Turn northwest and ascend rocks to the summit. A final 6' pitch is nearly vertical.

GUYE PEAK, 5168', 6 miles RT, 2500' gain (Maps: USGS Snoqualmie Pass, GT Snoqualmie Pass). **Hike-4†. Alpine Lakes Wilderness.** From I-90 at Exit-52, drive north to the end of the road at the Alpental parking area, elevation 3080'.

Cross the road east to a trail south of the creek. After going through a brushy clearing, the trail becomes steep and rough, ascending east. Look for varicolored boulders of limestone along the trail above 4000'. Cross the creek north at 4400' on a narrow ledge between an upper and a lower waterfall. Where the trail leaves the forest on the south ridge of Snoqualmie Mtn., 4750', turn south and descend to a flat and open valley, 4700', where a creek meanders. Cross the valley at the west end and ascend south on a faint track over the southwest end of Cave Ridge, 4800'. Descend to a saddle, 4600', then ascend south on the north ridge of Guye Peak.

SNOQUALMIE PEAK, 6278', 8 miles, 3300' gain (Maps: USGS Snoqualmie Pass, GT Snoqualmie Pass). **Hike-4†. Alpine Lakes Wilderness.** Drive and hike as above for **Guye Peak** until the trail leaves the forest at 4750'.

Turn left and ascend north on an intermittent track near or on the ridge. At the summit, Lundin Peak is northeast.

CAVE RIDGE, 5270', 5 miles RT, 2200' gain (Maps: USGS Snoqualmie Pass, GT Snoqualmie Pass). **Hike-4†. Alpine Lakes Wilderness.** Drive and ascend as above for **Guye Peak** to the open valley south of Snoqualmie Mtn., elevation 4700'.

Continue northeast on an intermittent track in the valley between Snoqualmie Mtn. (north) and Cave Ridge (south). At 4900', the valley narrows briefly then opens into an almost level basin. Turn southeast and ascend, using care to avoid depressions if on snow. Much of this area is limestone and some of these depressions overlie deep holes eroded in the limestone. On reaching the crest of the ridge, turn south to the highest point for the view of Mt. Rainier and other summits. No fires, please.

PACIFIC CREST TRAILHEAD NORTH, (Maps: USGS Snoqualmie Pass, Chikamin Peak, Polallie Ridge, Mt. Daniel, The Cradle, Scenic, Stevens Pass, GT Snoqualmie Pass, Kachess Lake, Stevens Pass). **Hike-1. Alpine Lakes Wilderness.** Leave eastbound I-90 at Exit 52. Drive north from I-90 toward Alpental, then go right (east) on the first road after leaving I-90 to reach the PCT trailhead, elevation 3000' and 0.5 miles from I-90 (toilets).

Destinations on the Pacific Crest Trail going north from Snoqualmie Pass: Red Mtn. trail junction, 2.5 miles; Ridge Lake, 7.3 miles; Park Lakes trail junction, 15 miles; Pete Lake trail junction, 21 miles; Waptus River crossing, 33 miles; Deep Lake, 41 miles; Deception Lakes, 53 miles; Hope Lake, 62 miles; Stevens Pass, 71 miles.

RED MOUNTAIN, 5890', 10 miles RT, 3000' gain (Maps: USGS Snoqualmie Pass, GT Snoqualmie Pass). **Hike-3. Alpine Lakes Wilderness.** Drive as above to the PCT trailhead north of I-90 at Exit-52.

Hike north on the PCT for 2.5 miles. At a trail junction, 3800', turn left on the Commonwealth Basin trail. At 4800' on the west side of Red Mtn., leave the trail and ascend a steep, open slope east.

KENDALL PEAK, 5784', 10 miles RT, 3000' gain (Maps: USGS Snoqualmie Pass, GT Snoqualmie Pass). **Hike-2. Alpine Lakes Wilderness.** Drive to the Pacific Crest Trail trailhead north of I-90 at Exit-52 (see above).

Hike the PCT north. Where the trail levels near the summit of Kendall Peak at 5400', leave the trail and hike southeast on one of several tracks to the summit.

CHIKAMIN PEAK, 7000', 2 miles RT from PCT , 1200' gain from PCT (Maps: USGS Chikamin Peak, GT Snoqualmie Pass). **Hike-4†. Alpine Lakes Wilderness.** For those who are hiking the Pacific Crest Trail north from Snoqualmie Pass, Chikamin Peak makes a rewarding diversion.

At mile 11 (from Snoqualmie Pass) on the Pacific Crest Trail, one mile after the PCT turns south from Huckleberry Mtn., leave the PCT and ascend east and northeast to the ridge south of Chikamin Peak. Turn north on the ridge and continue to the rock summit.

PACIFIC CREST TRAILHEAD SOUTH, 3000' (Maps: USGS Snoqualmie Pass). **Hike-1.** From Exit-52 on I-90, go south on the frontage road on the west side of I-90. Immediately after leaving I-90, turn west and northwest around the north edge of the Snoqualmie Summit Ski Area to the road end, elevation 3000'.

Destinations on the Pacific Crest Trail south from Snoqualmie Pass: Lodge Lake, 2 miles; Mirror Lake, 9 miles; Stirrup Lake, 14 miles; Stampede Pass, 18 miles; Tacoma Pass, 29 miles; Blowout Mtn., 36 miles; Government Meadow, 46 miles; Big Crow Basin, 58 miles; SR-410, 70 miles; US-12, 99 miles.

LODGE LAKE, 3125', 4 miles RT, 900' gain (Maps: USGS Snoqualmie Pass, GT Snoqualmie Pass). **Hike-1**. From I-90 at Exit-52, drive west at the north edge of the Snoqualmie Summit Ski Area to the Pacific Crest Trail trailhead, elevation 3000'.

Ascend south for one mile under ski lifts to the high point (3500') near Beaver Lake. Enter ancient forest and descend on the west facing slope to the lake, named for a Seattle Mountaineer Lodge that formerly stood near the lake.

TWIN LAKES, 3100', 2 miles RT, 300' gain (Maps: USGS Lost Lake, GT Snoqualmie Pass). **Hike-1**. Take Exit 54 from I-90. At the first intersection on the west side of I-90, drive south on paved Hyak Drive E, which becomes road FS-9070, turning right past the north and west sides of the sewage disposal area. The Cold Creek trailhead, FS-1303, Trail is 3.7 miles from I-90, elevation 3320'.

Hike the trail southwest to the lakes.

MOUNT CATHARINE, 5052', 4 miles RT, 1400' gain (Maps: USGS Lost Lake, GT Snoqualmie Pass). **Hike-1, Snow**. Drive as above for **Twin Lakes** on road FS-9070 for 5.5 miles from I-90 to the trailhead, elevation 3700'.

The trail (FS-1348) ascends east, first on an old logging road, then in ancient forest to the summit and a view of Keechelus Lake and the summits of the Snoqualmie Pass area. If ascending on snow, expect a summit cornice.

SILVER PEAK, 5605', 6 miles RT, 2000' gain (Maps: USGS Lost Lake, GT Snoqualmie Pass). **Hike-3**. Drive as above for **Twin Lakes**, continuing to the saddle, elevation 3800', and a crossing of the Pacific Crest Trail (may not be signed) in a clearcut, 5.8 miles from I-90.

Hike south on the PCT, ascending gradually in ancient forest for two miles to a junction (unmarked) in a meadow, 4300'. This meadow is located north of the cliffs of Tinkham Peak. The PCT turns sharply east here to contour below these cliffs. At the meadow, go west on a faint track or find a more obvious track that leaves the PCT 100' north of the meadow. Ascend west to the saddle between Silver Peak and Tinkham Peak, 4720'. Turn north, still on a trail, and ascend toward the south side of Silver Peak, passing a faint track to Abiel Peak. Follow a rough track north up a talus slope.

ABIEL PEAK, 5365', 6 miles RT, 1800' gain (Maps: USGS Lost Lake, GT Snoqualmie Pass). **Hike-3**. Drive and hike as above to the south shoulder of **Silver Peak**, elevation 4925'.

Continue west on a faint track along the southwest ridge of Silver Peak to Abiel Peak, passing through a saddle above Annette Lake. The land south of the crest of the ridge is Seattle Watershed (no public entry).

SILVER–ABIEL LOOP, high point 5605', 9 miles RT (Maps: USGS Snoqualmie Pass, Lost Lake, GT Snoqualmie Pass). **Hike-3**. Drive as above for **Silver Peak** on road FS-9070 to the saddle and park at the Pacific Crest Trail crossing, 5.8 miles from I-90 and elevation 3800'.

Hike northwest on the road in the clearcut, going left (west) at the first branch road. Pass a branch road (4000') that contours south, then go left (southwest) at the next road fork toward the western edge of the clearcut. At 4150', take a stub road left (south), then continue through an edge of open brush into ancient forest. Turn west and ascend to a subsidiary ridge that leads to the north ridge of Silver Peak. Now go south on the ridge or below the crest on the west side to the summit, 5605'.

From the summit of Silver Peak, descend the track on the south slope to 4900'. Turn west on a faint track along the ridge south of Lake Annette to Abiel Peak, 5365'. Return east on the ridge to the south shoulder of Silver Peak, passing north of the 5040' hump on the ridge that connects Abiel with Silver Peak. Turn southeast on the trail and descend to the Pacific Crest Trail, 4300'. Go northeast on the PCT to the starting point.

MOUNT MARGARET, 5560', 5 miles RT, 2000' gain (Maps: USGS Chikamin Peak, Stampede Pass, GT Snoqualmie Pass). **Hike-2**. Leave I-90 at Exit-54. Go east, then south on the paved frontage road, FS-4832, which turns away from I-90 and becomes gravel at mile 2.6. Go left at mile 4.1 on road FS-4834 and park at the trailhead, mile 4.6, elevation 3600'.

Hike east on the road for 0.1 mile, then turn left from the gray gravel road on a red gravel road and pass a gate. Follow signs to go generally northeast on roads or trails in a clearcut (route changes). Enter ancient forest at 4800' and go north on the west side of the ridge. After passing the trail east to Lake Margaret, 5150', ascend northeast on one of many tracks to the summit, going over or bypassing an intermediate point, 5480'. The summit is forested, but openings provide a view of Mt. Stuart.

LAKE LILLIAN, 4800', 8 miles, 2000' gain (Maps: USGS Chikamin

Peak, Stampede Pass, GT Snoqualmie Pass). **Hike-1. Alpine Lakes Wilderness.** Drive and hike as above toward **Mt. Margaret.**

After passing the trail to Lake Margaret, continue north on the trail, ascending over the shoulder of Mt. Margaret, 5300', before descending to pass the ponds of Twin Lakes and contouring above the canyon of Rocky Run to the lake.

RAMPART RIDGE, 5870', 11 miles RT, 3100' gain (Maps: USGS Chikamin Peak, Stampede Pass, GT Snoqualmie Pass). **Hike-3. Alpine Lakes Wilderness.** Drive and hike as above to **Lake Lillian.**

From the south end of the lake, go north on a track around the east side. This track continues to Rampart Lakes. Leave the track at its high point and go northwest in open terrain to the crest of Rampart Ridge. The highest point of the ridge is near the south end.

STAMPEDE CREEK–CABIN CREEK LOOP, high point 4000' or 4520', 25 miles, 2000' to 4100' gain (Maps: USGS Stampede Pass, Blowout Mtn., Easton, GT Easton, Snoqualmie Pass, Kachess Lake). **Mtn. Bicycle.** This trip is only possible when Cabin Creek is low, from mid-July through September. From Exit-62 on I-90, drive 1.4 miles west on the Stampede Pass Road, FS-54. Park at a crossing of the Iron Horse State Park, elevation 2480'.

Ride south on the railroad grade, crossing a bridge over Stampede Creek at mile 0.4, then going through a long cut. After crossing other creeks and passing under power lines, traverse a short tunnel at mile 2.2. A road crosses at mile 2.5. Old signal tower foundations remain at mile 4.0. A road parallels from mile 5.9 to the end of the State Park at mile 6.2. Continue south on the railroad grade, now a road, then, after travelling near existing tracks of the Burlington-Northern Railroad and crossing a bridge over Cabin Creek, turn west from the railroad grade to the Cabin Creek Road, FS-41, at mile 6.9. Go right (west) on the paved road, which turns to gravel at mile 7.3. Reach Cole Creek at mile 8.9, where the bridges over Cole Creek and Cabin Creek and portions of the road were flood damaged in 1990 and have not been replaced. Cross Cole Creek and continue in the flood track on the south side of Cabin Creek to the remains of the Cabin Creek bridge, mile 9.2. Cross the stream below the bridge.

Continue west, passing a huge and recent landslide scar at mile 9.8, to the junction with road FS-4110 at mile 11.7. Continue west on FS-41, passing the road to Tacoma Pass (FS-4112) on the left (south) at mile 14. Other roads (FS-4111 and FS-4113) go left (west) at miles 15.1 and 15.8 before road FS-41 crosses a saddle at mile 17.2 (4000') to leave the

Cabin Creek basin. At mile 18.5, two roads, FS-122 and FS-126, go west. For a diversion, ride northwest on road FS-126, to the cluster of buildings and antennas on a summit, 4520', for a 360° view. Return to FS-41 and continue north to the Stampede Pass Road, FS-54, at mile 22.1. Turn right and descend on FS-54 to the starting point.

PACIFIC CREST TRAIL: STAMPEDE PASS TO SNOQUALMIE PASS, high point 4500', 23 to 31 miles, 3700' gain (Maps: USGS Snoqualmie Pass, Lost Lake, Stampede Pass, GT Snoqualmie Pass). **Hike-1, Bicycle**. Ride the Greyhound Bus to Exit 62 on I-90, elevation 2400'. If driving, leave a bicycle at Forest Service information, Snoqualmie Pass. Park at the Iron Horse Trail 1.4 miles west from I-90 at Exit-62, elevation 2480'.

From the bus, hike west on the Stampede Pass road (FS-54) for five miles from I-90 (3.6 miles from the Iron Horse Trail) to the Pacific Crest Trail crossing at Stampede Pass. Hike north on the PCT (no bicycles), passing the branch trail west to Stirrup Lake (camping) at five miles and Mirror Lake (camping) at 10 miles from Stampede Pass. Olallie Meadow, now surrounded by clearcuts, is 14 miles. Reach Lodge Lake (camping) at 16 miles, then pass little Beaver Lake at the edge of the Snoqualmie Pass ski area. The PCT now descends under ski lifts to the trailhead at the north end of the ski complex 18 miles from Stampede Pass. Find the bus stop across the highway from Travelers Rest. If driving, find bicycle and return to vehicle by riding south on the frontage road to the Kachess Lake Trailhead on the Iron Horse State Park, then ride the Rail Trail 8 miles east.

MIRROR LAKE, 4195', 4 miles RT, 800' gain (Maps: USGS Lost Lake, GT Snoqualmie Pass). **Hike-1**. From I-90, take Exit-62 and drive west on the Stampede Pass Road. Turn north toward Lost Lake (road FS-5480) at one mile from I-90. At three miles from I-90, take the right fork. Pass east of Lost Lake to a road block, eight miles from I-90, elevation 3400'.

Hike the road north, then follow the trail northwest and west past Cottonwood Lake to the Pacific Crest Trail. Turn south to Mirror Lake and a well-used campsite, overshadowed by Tinkham Peak.

TINKHAM PEAK, 5395', 6 miles RT, 2000' gain (Maps: USGS Lost Lake, GT Snoqualmie Pass). **Hike-3**. Drive and hike as above to **Mirror Lake**.

Find a track at the south end of the lake and ascend west to the crest of the ridge. Turn right (northwest) to the open summit.

STIRRUP LAKE, 3550', 3 miles RT, 400' gain (Maps: USGS Stampede Pass, GT Snoqualmie Pass). **Hike-2**. From I-90, take Exit-62 and drive west on the Stampede Pass Road. Turn north toward Lost Lake (road FS-5480) at one mile from I-90. At three miles from I-90, turn left (west) on road FS-5483. At mile 5.7, go left for 0.1 mile to the trailhead on the south side of Stirrup Creek, 3200'.

Hike west on this little used trail to the lake at the edge of ancient forest. This route avoids creek crossings.

MEADOW MOUNTAIN, 5440', 23 miles RT bicycling, 11 miles RT hiking, 3100' gain bicycle & hike, 2500' gain hike only (Maps: USGS Stampede Pass, Lost Lake, GT Snoqualmie Pass). **Mtn. Bicycle and/or Hike-3**. This route enters the Tacoma Watershed. From Exit-62 on I-90 drive northwest 0.6 mile on the Stampede Pass Road, FS-54, to parking (bicycle tour) at Crystal Springs Campground, elevation 2420'. If hiking, drive west from Exit-62 on road FS-54 for 1.4 miles and north on road FS-5480 toward Lost Lake. At mile 3.1, bend southwest on the Meadow Creek Road, FS-5483, passing road FS-5484 on the left at mile 6.0. At mile 6.8, 3150', turn left (south) on road FS-5483-117, crossing Meadow Creek immediately. Park here, elevation 3000', for trip distance of 11 miles or drive on until the road is blocked by fallen trees. Follow directions as described below from the Meadow Creek crossing.

Bicycling. From Crystal Springs campground, ride west on road FS-54. At mile 0.8, turn northwest toward Lost Lake on road FS-5480. Cross the Iron Horse State Park Rail Trail at mile 2.3. Near the south end of Keechelus Lake, mile 2.5, turn southwest on the Meadow Creek Road, FS-5483 to ascend along Meadow Creek. At mile 5.4, pass road FS-5484 going to the left (southwest). At 3150', mile 6.2, turn south on the Meadow Pass Road, FS-5483-117, crossing Meadow Creek immediately and the Pacific Crest Trail at mile 7.0, 3600'. West of the Pacific Crest Trail crossing, Stirrup Lake is southwest of the road, hidden at the edge of ancient forest. Continue ascending to Meadow Pass, mile 8.1 and 3640'.

Go right (north), then at mile 8.8, 3840', take a branch left (west). After the road rounds again to the north, look below on the left to a **waterfall** (early season). Pass a spur road left (west) at mile 9.6. Continue on the road as it switchbacks up the south side of Meadow Mountain to the end of the road near the south ridge. Leave bicycle and find a way southeast through the clearcut to the south ridge. Ascend north on the ridge in ancient forest to the summit. The high point and lookout site is at the north end. The Seattle Watershed (west) is closed to public entry.

To visit Stirrup Lake on the return, when 0.8 miles east of Meadow

Pass, go right (south) at 3660' on a logging spur, then head southeast in the clearcut to the lake at the outlet. An abandoned trail also goes to the lake from Meadow Pass.

STIRRUP LAKE, 3550', 11 miles RT, 1300' gain (Maps: USGS Stampede Pass, Lost Lake, GT Snoqualmie Pass). **Hike-1**. From I-90 at Exit-62, drive west five miles on road FS-54 to Stampede Pass, elevation 3700'.

From Stampede Pass, hike north on the Pacific Crest Trail for five miles to the Stirrup Lake trail junction, 3400', south of Stirrup Creek. Turn southwest 0.5 mile to reach the lake and campsites.

SNOWSHOE BUTTE, 5135', 12 miles RT, 2500' gain (Maps: USGS Stampede Pass, Blowout Mountain, GT Snoqualmie Pass, Lester). **Hike-1**. From I-90 at Exit-62, drive west five miles on road FS-54 to the Pacific Crest Trail at Stampede Pass, elevation 3700'.

Hike south on the Pacific Crest Trail past the Stampede Pass weather Station (lookout site) to the open summit with a 360° view (lookout site).

STAMPEDE RAILROAD GRADE, high point 4000', 2 miles RT, minimum gain (Maps: USGS Stampede Pass, GT Snoqualmie Pass). **Hike-1**. This switchback railroad grade served for only one year prior to the opening of the Stampede Tunnel in 1888. Much of the grade has been superceded by logging roads but the marks left from the railroad ties are still visible in several places. Visit the Washington State Museum in Tacoma to see a pictorial history of this railroad grade.

From Exit-62, drive west on road FS-54, passing the Iron Horse State Park at mile 1.4. Park under power lines where a road ascends steeply left (south), 2.9 miles from I-90. Hike this branch road, passing a powerline tower. Southwest of the tower, find the old railroad grade. Turn right (north) on the grade, which shows many tie marks. The grade ends where a former trestle crossed a gully. Hike south on the grade (mostly road) for 0.5 miles toward the Stampede Tunnel. Near the tunnel, find more tie marks.

Return to vehicle and drive west toward Stampede Pass. At mile 3.4, where the road bends south, the grade crosses the road (3046'), then bends west into a switchback up Mosquito Creek (no evidence). The return route from Mosquito Creek crossed the present road at 3257', then made a curve south before turning west toward the pass. Park 4.5 miles from I-90 at recent logging (1998). Ascend south to a road on the grade. Walk west until the grade disappears in a cliff with road FS-54 immediately below.

Return to vehicle and drive to Stampede Pass, mile 4.8. Walk east from the pass to find a bit of the old railroad grade on the south side of road FS-54. Return to the pass to find the Pacific Crest Trail on the north side of the road. Hike west on the PCT. The trail lies on the railroad grade for 50', then the railroad grade continues west into dense growth. No obvious tie marks. Now drive west to mile 6. Park 200' east of a power line tower that stands on a flat area beside the road. Walk west to the tower. Turn south and go 50' to find a section of railroad grade with tie marks. Explore east into dense vegetation, then return west on the grade to a trestle abutment (steep drop west). The trestle made a curve north to connect with the grade coming from Stampede Pass.

RACHEL LAKE, 4640', 8 miles RT, 1600' gain (Maps: USGS Chikamin Peak, GT Snoqualmie Pass). **Hike-1. Alpine Lakes Wilderness.** From I-90 at Exit-62, drive northeast on FS-49 and FS-4930 to the trailhead, 10 miles from I-90, elevation 2760'.

Hike trail FS-1313 to the lake, lying in a basin east of Rampart Ridge.

RAMPART LAKES, 5120', 10 miles RT, 2100' gain (Maps: USGS Chikamin Peak, GT Snoqualmie Pass). **Hike-1. Alpine Lakes Wilderness.** Drive and hike as above to **Rachel Lake**.

Hike the trail west from the north side of Rachel Lake to a saddle and trail junction, then go south on a trail to the lakes on a gently sloping bench below Rampart Ridge.

RAMPART RIDGE, 5870', 11 miles RT, 2900' gain (Maps: USGS Chikamin Peak, GT Snoqualmie Pass). **Hike-3. Alpine Lakes Wilderness.** Drive and hike as above to **Rampart Lakes**.

Ascend west to the ridge. Find the highest point at the south end.

ALTA MOUNTAIN, 6265', 12 miles RT, 3200' gain (Maps: USGS Chikamin Peak, GT Snoqualmie Pass). **Hike-2. Alpine Lakes Wilderness.** Drive and hike as above to **Rachel Lake**.

Hike west on trail FS-1313 toward Rampart Lakes to the saddle above Rachel Lake. Take the right (north) fork and continue up the gentle ridge to the highest point.

Easton Area. Exit-70 to Exit-78.

EASTON RIDGE, 4517', 8 miles RT, 2100' gain (Maps: USGS Kachess Lake, Easton, Ronald, GT Kachess Lake, Easton). **Hike-2.** From the east side of I-90 at Exit-70, drive northwest on the frontage road for 0.7 mile. Turn right (north) on the Lake Kachess road to the power line crossing, one mile from I-90. Turn east under the power line. At 1.7 miles from I-90, just before the power line bends south, go left (northeast) on a narrow dirt road to minimum parking (one car) two miles from I-90, elevation 2350'. The trailhead may not be marked.

Hike east to Silver Creek. Cross the creek and ascend northeast and east, crossing a road at a switchback in the road, 2720'. Where the trail levels near the crest of the ridge, 3500', find a junction. Turn southeast on a trail that ascends near or on the ridge. After another mile, leave the trail at 4400' to the highest point, getting views ranging from Mt. Stuart (37°) in the east to Mt. Rainier in the southwest.

MOUNT BALDY, 5107', 8 miles RT, 2800' gain (Maps: USGS Kachess Lake, GT Kachess Lake). **Hike-2.** Drive and hike toward **Easton Ridge** as described above.

At the trail junction near the crest of the ridge, 3500', continue north, skirting the west boundary of a watershed (closed). The trail follows the edge of the deep canyon of Silver Creek. At a junction with the Thomas Mtn. Trail, FS-1308, 4942', turn south to the first open summit.

DOMERIE PEAK, 4771', 10 miles RT, 3200' gain (Maps: USGS Kachess Lake, GT Kachess Lake). **Hike-2.** Drive and hike as above to **Mt. Baldy**.

From Mt. Baldy, continue south on trail FS-1308 for one mile.

THOMAS MOUNTAIN, 5269', 8 miles, 3000' gain (Maps: USGS Kachess Lake, GT Kachess Lake). **Hike-2.** Drive and hike as above toward **Mt. Baldy** to the junction with trail FS-1308 at 4942'.

Turn north for one mile on trail FS-1308 to the forested summit. Look in this area for quartz crystals that were deposited in vugs.

To make a loop (**Hike-3**), descend north from the summit to the first low point (4600'), then leave the trail, turning west to descend to Silver Creek Trail, elevation 3800'. Return south (see below).

SILVER CREEK MEADOWS, high point 5000', 12 miles RT, 2700' gain (Maps: USGS Kachess Lake, GT Kachess Lake). **Hike-2.**

From the east side of I-90 at Exit-70, drive northwest on the frontage road for 0.7 mile. Turn right (north) on the Lake Kachess road to the power line crossing, one mile from I-90. Turn east under the power line. At 1.7 miles from I-90, just before the power line bends south, go left (northeast) on a narrow dirt road to a parking area at the end of the road, 2.3 miles from I-90, elevation 2350'.

Hike north on trail FS-1315, climbing past the narrow canyon cut by Silver Creek in colorful volcanic rocks and reaching the lip of a hanging valley at two miles. The trail now ascends more gently, crossing the creek several times, to pass a junction with the Thomas Mtn. trail, FS-1308, five miles from the road and 4840'. After passing trail FS-1308, FS-1315 leaves the forest and enters an open valley with many fine campsites. The meadows at the head of the valley are especially colorful in the fall. Huckleberries and mushrooms are also plentiful at this time. Distance and elevation gain are to the ridge that closes the Silver Creek valley. An eroded volcano core stands west of the saddle. Please avoid camping in meadows and use existing fire rings.

FRENCH CABIN MOUNTAIN, WEST PEAK, 5724', 12 miles RT, 3500' gain (Maps: USGS Kachess Lake, GT Kachess Lake). **Hike-3.** Drive and hike as above for **Silver Creek Meadows**, ascending along Silver Creek.

After passing the junction with the Thomas Mtn. trail, FS-1308, five miles from the trailhead, continue to the creek crossing, 4680'. Leave the trail and ascend east over meadow to the summit.

KACHESS RIDGE POINT 5525, 5525', 14 miles RT, 3200' gain (Maps: USGS Kachess Lake, GT Kachess Lake). **Hike-3.** Drive and hike as above to **Silver Creek Meadows.**

Stay on the trail to 4800'. The meadows tend to be wet in early summer but they are delightful in September. Leave the trail, cross the meadows northwest and ascend in open forest to a high point on the north-south ridge for a view of summits: Silver (284°), Mt. Margaret (300°), and Hibox (330°).

KACHESS RIDGE POINT 5194, 5194', 8 miles RT, 3000' gain (Maps: USGS Kachess Lake, GT Kachess Lake). **Hike-3, Snow.** Begin hike as above for **Silver Creek Meadows.**

Ascend northeast for 600' of gain until the trail begins to round north into the canyon of Silver Creek. Leave the trail at 2900' and ascend northwest in open forest to the crest of a north-south ridge. Continue on this ridge, passing minor points on the ridge at 4615' and

4884', and descending sharply after passing the 4884' summit. Point 5194', an open viewpoint, is 0.5 mile beyond the 4884' summit. Do this trip on snow in April or May when avalanche danger is high elsewhere.

GOAT PEAK, 5040', 12 miles bicycle + 4 miles hiking or 10 miles RT hike only, 3000' gain (Maps: USGS Easton, USGS 30' Easton, GT Easton). **Mtn. Bicycle and/or Hike-3**. Take Exit-71 west into Easton. Cross the railroad tracks and continue northwest into the Cabin Creek Road, FS-41. Pavement ends 2.8 miles from Easton. Park near a branch road, 3.3 miles from Easton, 2300'.

Ride or hike southeast on this branch road, passing a gate. Cross Tucker Creek at mile 2.4, then pass a road on the left (north) at mile 2.7 that descends toward Easton. If hiking, turn right (south) at mile 2.9 (the first road to the right after crossing Tucker Creek) on a road that leads into the Goat Peak Trail. If riding, pass a road east at mile 3.1. At mile 4.7, where a fork goes south, bend back north to the end of the road at mile 5.6, 3900'. Leave bicycle and ascend south in a clearcut into ancient forest. Contour west at 4000' to a ridge. Follow the ridge northwest on a track, bypassing west of or going over a rise to a broad, brush-free saddle, 3840'. The USGS 30'(1961) shows a trail in this saddle. Either look north for the trail here or ascend the fall line in open forest to find the trail at a switchback, 4100'. Now follow the trail northwest and west through rock outcrops to the site of the old lookout. The rock pinnacle (climbing) at the south end of the summit plateau is slightly lower than the lookout site. Summits: Mt. Stuart (36°), Hicks Butte (124°), and Mt. Clifty (165°).

Find the following plants blossoming in July: lupine, beargrass, scarlet gilia, yarrow, daisy, azalea, tiger lily. Look also for: white pine, lodgepole pine, spruce, mountain hemlock, grand fir, and subalpine fir.

HICKS BUTTE, 5517', 8 miles RT, 2800' gain (Maps: USGS Easton, Ronald, GT Easton). **Hike-3**. Leave I-90 at Golf Course Road, Exit-78. Drive south, passing Nelson Siding Road on the right at 0.3 miles from I-90 and the West Side Road at 0.8 miles. Bend left (west), crossing a canal. At mile 1.7, keep to the right into Fowler Creek Road. At mile 2.5, bend right into road FS-4517 and drive west to a powerline, mile 3.5. Turn south under the powerline. This road bends west, passing a road right (north) at mile 4.2. Cross Granite Creek and park 4.5 miles from I-90, elevation 2800'.

Hike an overgrown road southwest into trail FS-1326, ascending near, and crossing Granite Creek twice. The trail is subject to washouts, especially at the upper creek crossing. At a trail junction, 4600', where a road is 100' south and a branch of trail FS-1326 goes east, turn southwest on the trail briefly. Leave the trail and ascend west in open ancient forest, entering a recent clearcut at 4900'. Continue ascending west to the summit. For the descent, find an old trail that descends south from the summit but is hard to follow in the clearcut below 5000'. Reach trail FS-1326 at 4800'. Turn northeast on the trail, crossing the outlets of two springs that are just above the trail. Descend left at 4600'.

Look for the following native plants along the trail: grand fir, Douglas fir, Oregon grape, kinnikinnik, willow, soap berry, service berry, falsebox (Paxistima myrsinites is the dominant ground cover in some areas), hazel, devils club, and huckleberry.

NORTH RIDGE LOOKOUT, high point 5960', 14 miles RT, 3500' gain (Maps: USGS Easton, GT Easton). **Hike-2**. Leave I-90 at Golf Course Road, Exit-78. Drive south, passing Nelson Siding Road on the right at 0.3 miles from I-90 and the West Side Road at 0.8 miles. Bend left (west), crossing a canal. At mile 1.7, keep to the right into Fowler Creek Road. At mile 2.5, bend right into road FS-4517 and follow this road west to a powerline, mile 3.5. Continue northwest, turning southwest in a switchback at mile five where a road goes right (north). Park at the trailhead, seven miles from I-90, elevation 3160'.

Hike the trail west for 0.3 miles, crossing a logging road, to a trail junction. Turn left (southwest) and ascend on trail FS-1321, high above Big Creek (north). On the way, look north to the rocky pinnacles of Goat Peak across the valley of Big Creek. Turn south to ascend near or on the ridge, going over a minor summit at 5268'. Pass a trail junction (FS-1334) at 4960', then reach another high point (5140') before descending to a saddle, 4980'. Now ascend southwest on the trail across the north flank of North Ridge. Turn east at a trail junction to the broad, open summit. Those who leave the circuitous trail after passing the 4980' saddle and ascend directly south to the summit, should either stay on the trail on the return or use care (compass) to follow the outgoing route back to the 4980' saddle. The attractive open east slope of North Ridge descends toward Little Creek and does not intersect trail FS-1321.

Cabin Creek Area.

The bridges on road FS-41 west of Easton over Cole Creek and Cabin Creek have not been repaired as of 1998. Until these bridges are replaced, gain access to this area by driving road FS-54, the Stampede Pass Road, west from I-90 at Exit-62 for 3.7 miles, then go south on road FS-41. Reach the junction with road FS-4110 on Cabin Creek 14 miles from I-90. If the bridges are replaced, this intersection is eight miles from I-90 at Exit-71 on road FS-41 by way of Easton.

BLOWOUT MOUNTAIN, 5750', 9 miles RT, 2900' gain (Maps: USGS Blowout Mtn., GT Lester). **Hike-2**. From road FS-41 drive south on road FS-4110 for five miles to the saddle between Log Creek (north) and Big Creek (south). Turn right (west) on road FS-119 (marked FS-116 on Wenatchee Forest map), passing road FS-113 on the right (west) at 0.3 miles, roads FS-129 (north) and FS-130 (west) on the right at 1.4 miles from FS-4110, and a road to the left (south) at 1.8 miles from road FS-4110. Reach the Blowout Mtn. trailhead on the left (south) side of the road two miles from road FS-4110 and 21 miles from I-90, elevation 4800'. The last 0.5 mile is rough and steep.

Ascend southwest on a wide stony track, trail FS-1318, entering ancient forest at 5000'. The trail goes over 5495' before dropping to 5040'. Continue southwest to a saddle and trail junction at 5240', then turn west (250°) and contour 500' on a less travelled and possibly overgrown trail (no vehicles) to a junction with the Pacific Crest Trail. Turn left (south) and ascend the PCT on or near the crest of the ridge. Take time more than once to step to the edge of the cliffs that form the east wall of Blowout Mtn. for the view of the meadows at the head of Big Creek. At the trail high point, 5500', signed **Blowout Mtn.**, leave the trail and ascend east to the summit. In July, the north ridge of Blowout Mtn. is a colorful display of yellow and lavender daisies, lupin, azalea, and an especially brilliant paintbrush.

Alternate Route. To make a loop across Big Creek Basin, at the trail junction in the saddle, 5240', go at first southeast, then turn south on a trail, descending in meadows to a low point, 5000'. Pass ponds on the east slope of Blowout Mtn. before ascending to a trail junction on the crest of the ridge that separates Big Creek (north) from Blowout Creek (south). Turn west and ascend a narrow, deeply eroded track (from wheels) to the summit. For more views down the cliffs that form the east slope of Blowout Mtn., descend south from the summit along the edge to the Granite Creek Trail, FS-1388, at 5620'. Contour west on the Granite Creek Trail to the PCT coming from the south. Turn north on the PCT, pass the **Blowout Mtn.** sign, then descend to 5200'. Find, at a low point in the ridge, a trail that goes east to the outgoing route, trail FS-1318.

COLE BUTTE, 5504', 7 miles RT, 1500' gain (Maps: USGS Easton, Blowout Mtn., GT Easton, Lester). **Hike-1**. From road FS-41 drive south on road FS-4110 for five miles to the saddle between Log Creek (north) and Big Creek (south). Turn left on road FS-4110-118 to the trailhead, two miles from FS-4110 and 20 miles from I-90 at Exit-62, elevation 4000'.

Hike east on trail FS-1304, ascending to the open crest and going over high points of 5382' and 5362' before reaching the summit of Cole Butte.

GOAT PEAK, 5040', 12 miles RT, 2700' gain (Maps: USGS Easton, Blowout Mtn., GT Easton, Lester). **Hike-1**. Drive and hike as above to **Cole Butte**.

Hike east on trail FS-1304 past Cole Butte to the open lookout site. A rock promontory, which is not the highest point, stands on the east shoulder.

MOUNT CLIFTY, 6245', 9 miles RT, 2700' gain (Maps: USGS Easton Mt. Clifty, GT Easton). **Hike-2**. From road FS-41, drive south on road FS-4110, passing the road to the Blowout Mtn. trailhead at five miles from road FS-41. Continue on road FS-4110 to the Blazed Ridge trailhead on the east side of the road, 10 miles from road FS-41, elevation 4040', and 24 miles from I-90 at Exit-62.

Hike generally south on the Blazed Ridge Trail, FS-1333, soon passing along the east edge of a clearcut at 4300'. In places, especially on switchbacks, the trail has been deeply eroded by motorcycles. On reaching the crest of Blazed Ridge at 5300', diverge north to the top of a rock knob for the view down the cliff. After going over a summit, 5413', the trail drops below 5300' before rising to a junction with the Granite Creek Trail, FS-1388, on the ridge above Bear Creek. FS-1388 goes west to Blowout Mtn. and the trail east, FS-1321.2, drops to cross Greek Creek, then continues to North Ridge. Go south, now on trail FS-1388, ascending to 5700'. Where the trail begins to descend across the west side of Mt. Clifty, leave the trail and contour east through gaps in the forest to a track that ascends directly up a steep, open, sand and gravel slope. Turn left (northeast) and ascend this track, meeting a trail, FS-1321.3, on the ridge, then continue northeast on the trail to the summit, a rock prominence.

BEARPAW BUTTE, 4800', 6 miles RT, 2000' gain (Maps: USGS Blowout Mtn., GT Lester). **Hike-3**. From Exit-62, drive west for 3.7 miles on road FS-54 and south on FS-41 to the junction with road FS-4112, 11.5 miles from I-90. Turn southwest on road FS-4112 for one mile to Tacoma Pass and a crossing of the Pacific Crest Trail, 12.5 miles from I-90, elevation 3460'.

Hike north on the PCT, going almost over a 4059' point on the ridge before descending to Sheets Pass, 3700'. Leave the Pacific Crest

Trail at 3900', where the PCT bends west, and ascend northwest on the east ridge to the summit.

Cle Elum River Area.

From I-90 at Exit-80, drive four miles north and northeast to Roslyn and continue north to Cle Elum Lake and the Cle Elum River basin. If coming west on I-90, turn north at Exit-85 through Cle Elum to reach Roslyn and continue north to Cle Elum Lake and the Cle Elum River area.

HEX MOUNTAIN, 5034', 4 miles RT, 1500' gain (Maps: USGS Cle Elum Lake, GT Kachess Lake). **Hike-1**. Six miles north of Roslyn on SR-903, before reaching Wish Poosh Campground, turn right (east) on Corral Creek Road, FS-4305. Keep left where branch roads go south, 0.4 mile and 1.2 miles from the paved road. Turn left off FS-4305 at 2.4 miles from SR-903, and drive north one mile on a rough, rutted dirt road and park, elevation 3600'.

Hike north on a broad track (FS-1340) to the summit. The trail enters and stays in dense forest.

SASSE MOUNTAIN, 5730', 10 miles RT, 2500' gain (Maps: USGS Cle Elum Lake, GT Kachess Lake). **Hike-1**. Drive, park, and hike as above to **Hex Mtn**.

From Hex Mtn., continue on trail FS-1340 in dense forest, circling the basin of Hex Creek to the east and following the ridge between Howson Creek (west) and Tumble Creek (east). The trail goes over minor summits of 4692', 5159', and 5350'.

THORPE MOUNTAIN, 5854', 6 miles RT, 2300' gain (Maps: USGS Kachess Lake, GT Kachess Lake). **Hike-1**. Drive to the north end of Cle Elum Lake, 12.6 miles north of Roslyn. Turn west on French Cabin Creek Road, FS-4308, keeping right at a road fork 0.6 miles from paved CR-903. At 3.3 miles from CR-903, turn right (northeast) on the Thorpe Creek Road, FS-4312, for 1.5 miles to a fork. Go north on FS-4312/121 across Thorpe Creek for 0.1 mile to another junction. Turn west 0.1 mile and park at a dirt barrier, elevation 3500'.

Ascend west for 0.5 mile to the Thorp Mountain Trail, FS-1316, on the right side of the road. Ascend west on the trail to the crest of Kachess Ridge then turn north to reach the summit, which still has a lookout house.

THORPE MOUNTAIN, 5854', 10 miles RT, 2500' gain (Maps:

USGS Kachess Lake, GT Kachess Lake). **Hike-1**. Much of this route follows a ridge in open, ancient forest.

From the north end of Cle Elum Lake, 12.6 miles from Roslyn, drive west on French Cabin Creek Road, FS-4308, for seven miles to park at a road fork in French Cabin Basin, elevation 4100'. The beginning of the French Cabin Basin trail, FS-1305, is 0.4 mile west up the right fork, a rough road that may not be driveable.

Ascend west on trail FS-1305 for one mile to a junction with trail FS-1315. Turn north and ascend in ancient forest, passing over or near Points 5766', 5841', and 5545' of Kachess Ridge to the summit of Thorpe Mountain.

FRENCH CABIN MOUNTAIN LOOP, 5498', 5569', 5724', 12 miles RT, 3600' gain (Maps: USGS Kachess Lake, GT Kachess Lake). **Hike-3**. From the north end of Cle Elum Lake, 12.6 miles from Roslyn, drive west on the French Cabin Creek Road, FS-4308 for seven miles, passing the Thorp Creek Road, FS-4312, at three miles, and the Knox Creek Road at five miles from CR-903. At seven miles from paved CR-903, park at a road junction, elevation 4100'. From here FS-4308 turns southeast and a branch road goes to the west uphill to the beginning of the French Cabin Basin Trail, FS-1305.

Hike southeast on road FS-4308 (gate), crossing immediately the West Fork of French Cabin Creek. Continue on the road to cross the South Fork of French Cabin Creek, where the road bends north, then returns south across the west face of the North Peak of French Cabin Mountain. After passing a talus slope at 4600' that descends west from the North Peak, and when directly west of the starting point, leave the road and ascend east in or near a clearcut to the ridge of French Cabin Mountain. Turn north to the summit of the North Peak, 5498'. Limestone is exposed here. From the north summit, return south in open forest on the ridge to the trail, FS-1308, at a low point. Continue south to the south summit, 5569', east off the trail in dense forest.

From the summit of the South Peak, continue south on the trail to a junction. Turn west, staying on trail FS-1308 and going south of a 5563' summit to pass through meadows and forest above a branch of Silver Creek. One mile after turning west from the South Peak, where the West Peak is almost directly west and the trail is beginning to descend, leave the trail at 5400' and ascend west to the summit of the West Peak, 5724', the highest of the three summits. From the summit of the West Peak, descend west on a moderately steep, open slope to the Silver Creek Trail, FS-1315, near a crossing of Silver Creek. Turn right (north) on the trail and ascend into the meadows of upper Silver Creek. Continue on the trail over the saddle past a row of volcanic knobs and descend into the basin of French Cabin Creek. Near the low point of the trail, 4900', turn right (east) on trail FS-1305 to return to road FS-4308 and parking.

RED MOUNTAIN, 5722', 6 miles RT, 3000' gain (Maps: USGS Davis Peak, Polallie Ridge, GT Kachess Lake). **Hike-3**. Drive the Cle Elum River Road for 15 miles from Roslyn and 19 miles from I-90 at Exit-80. Turn left on the Cooper Lake Road, FS-46, for 1.7 miles to the trail where it crosses the road. Find limited parking 0.1 mile north of the trail, elevation 2600'. This trail begins in Salmon la Sac campground.

Hike west on the trail past a mine at 5200', then go south to the summit.

PARK LAKES, 4700', 10 miles RT, 2400' gain (Maps: USGS Polallie Ridge, Chikamin Peak, GT Kachess Lake, Snoqualmie Pass). **Hike-1. Alpine Lakes Wilderness.** Drive the Cle Elum River Road for 15 miles from Roslyn. Turn left on the Cooper Lake Road, FS-46, for 9.7 miles, driving over Cooper Pass, 3000', to the Mineral Creek trailhead, FS-1331, elevation 2400'.

Hike northwest on trail FS-1331, ascending along Mineral Creek to the lakes and a junction with the Pacific Crest Trail, 4900'. Find campsites nearby on the PCT.

GLACIER LAKE, 4750', 14 miles RT, 3600' gain (Maps: USGS Chikamin Peak, Polallie Ridge, GT Snoqualmie Pass, Kachess Lake). **Hike-2. Alpine Lakes Wilderness.** Drive and hike as above to **Park Lakes**.

Continue north across the Pacific Crest Trail into the abandoned Chikamin Lake trail, which may be hard to find, crossing a 5360' saddle before descending to Glacier Lake, lying in an open, rocky basin above Spectacle Lake and surrounded by summits: Lemah Mountain (north), Chikamin Peak (northwest), Three Queens (southwest), and many others.

CHIKAMIN LAKE, 5800', 18 miles RT, 4800' gain (Maps: USGS Polallie Ridge, Chikamin Peak, GT Kachess Lake, Snoqualmie Pass). **Hike-2. Alpine Lakes Wilderness.** Drive and hike as above to **Park Lakes**.

Continue north across the Pacific Crest Trail into the Chikamin Lake Trail (FS-1360), ascending past Glacier Lake (4750') into a bare, rocky, glacial cirque enclosed by Chikamin Peak (west) and Lemah Mountain (north).

CHIKAMIN PEAK, 7000', 20 miles RT, 5000' gain (Maps: USGS Chikamin Peak, GT Snoqualmie Pass, Kachess Lake). **Hike-4†. Alpine Lakes Wilderness.** Drive and hike as above for **Park Lakes** on the Mineral Creek Trail, FS-1331, to the junction with the Pacific Crest Trail.

Turn west on the PCT over Park Saddle, then go north on the west side of the Four Brothers Ridge. At 5600', where the trail begins to descend, leave the trail and ascend northeast to the crest of the Chikamin-Four Brothers Ridge. Turn north to the rock summit. The summit can also be reached from Glacier Lake (see above) by ascending northwest from the lake.

PETE LAKE, 2980', 8 miles RT, 200' gain (Maps: USGS Polallie Ridge, GT Kachess Lake). **Hike-1. Alpine Lakes Wilderness.** Drive the Cle Elum River Road for 15 miles from Roslyn. Turn left (west) on the Cooper Pass Road (FS-46) for 4.8 miles. Turn right (north), passing **Cooper Lake** (walk-in campground) to the trailhead, 22 miles from Roslyn, elevation 2800'.

Hike trail FS-1323 northwest to Pete Lake, lying in a densely forested basin north of Island Mountain.

SPECTACLE LAKE, 4300', 18 miles RT, 1500' gain (Maps: USGS Polallie Ridge, Chikamin Peak, GT Kachess Lake, Snoqualmie Pass). **Hike-1. Alpine Lakes Wilderness.** Hike as above for **Pete Lake** from the Cooper Lake trailhead.

Continue on a trail west and southwest to join the Pacific Crest Trail and reach Spectacle Lake. The area has spectacular views north to the Lemah Mountain range. A track continues north from Spectacle Lake into the Chikamin Lake basin.

JOLLY MOUNTAIN, 6443', 12 miles RT, 4100' gain (Maps: USGS Davis Peak, GT Kachess Lake). **Hike-1.** Drive the Cle Elum River Road for 15.9 miles from Roslyn to Cayuse Campground, 0.1 mile south of the Salmon la Sac Forest Service Station, elevation 2400'.

The Jolly Mountain Trail, FS-1307, begins at the east end of Cayuse Campground and ascends near Salmon la Sac Creek. Pass a trail left (north) to Paris Creek at three miles, and a trail to Sasse Mountain, FS-1340, to the right (south) at four miles. For the last two miles, the trail follows the crest of a sparsely forested ridge, allowing views east.

DAVIS PEAK, 6490', 12 miles RT, 4000' gain (Maps: USGS Davis Peak, GT Kachess Lake). **Hike-1. Alpine Lakes Wilderness.** Drive the Cle Elum River Road for 16 miles from Roslyn to the Salmon la Sac

Forest Service Station. Continue north for 1.7 miles on road FS-4330, which branches to the right (north) near the Forest Service Station. After crossing Paris Creek, turn left (west) to a parking area off road FS-4330, elevation 2600', or descend 0.3 mile toward the trailhead to additional parking.

The trail crosses a high bridge over the river, then ascends north in open forest to the site of the lookout. The highest point of the summit area is at the west end. Summits in view include: Hawkins (90°), Three Queens (270°), Hinman (324°), Daniel (331°), and Cathedral Rock (342°).

PADDY-GO-EASY PASS, 6100', 6 miles RT, 2800' gain (Maps: USGS The Cradle, GT Stevens Pass). **Hike-1. Alpine Lakes Wilderness.** Drive the Cle Elum River Road for 16 miles from Roslyn to the Salmon la Sac Forest Service Station. Take the right fork and continue on the Cle Elum River Road (FS-4330) for 12 miles. Park at the trailhead north of Tucquala Lake, elevation 3350'.

Ascend southeast and north on trail FS-1595 to the pass. Much of the bedrock exposed along the trail and at the pass is serpentine. Note cliffs and steep slopes of unweathered serpentine (green) south of the trail where the trail turns north at 4700'. Summits visible from the pass or from the ridges north or south: Bull's Tooth (5°), The Cradle (53°), Jack Ridge 7828' (102°), Harding (108°), Stuart (122°), Hawkins (154°), Hibox (232°), Three Queens (235°), Chikamin (248°), Lemah (252°), Chimney Rock (256°), Overcoat Peak (258°), Summit Chief (262°), Bears Breast (267°), Cathedral Rock (282°), Hinman (283°), Daniel (284°), and Glacier Peak (356°).

PADDY POINT 6573, high point 6440', 7 miles RT, 3100' gain (Maps: USGS The Cradle, GT Stevens Pass). **Hike-3. Alpine Lakes Wilderness.** Drive and hike as above to **Paddy-Go-Easy Pass.**

Hike northwest up the ridge toward the summit, finding a ramp on the west side that goes to a high viewpoint. The final summit block is beyond the hiking classifications of this book.

PADDY POINT 6360, 6360', 6.5 miles RT, 3000' gain (Maps: USGS The Cradle, GT Stevens Pass). **Hike-2. Alpine Lakes Wilderness.** Drive and hike as above to **Paddy-Go-Easy Pass.**

Ascend south and southwest on an intermittent track to the first summit above the pass for the view of Mt. Stuart. **Sprite Lake** is just below.

PEGGYS POND, 5560', 11 miles RT, 2200' gain (Maps: USGS The Cradle, Mt. Daniel, GT Stevens Pass). **Hike-1. Alpine Lakes Wilderness.** Drive the Cle Elum River Road for 16 miles from Roslyn to the Salmon la Sac Forest Service Station. Continue past the Forest Service Station, taking a right fork on the Cle Elum River Road (FS-4330) for 14 miles to the trailhead at the end of the road, elevation 3400'.

Hike southwest on trail FS-1345 to a junction with trail FS-1322, then turn northwest, staying on trail FS-1345 to meet the Pacific Crest Trail. Jog west briefly on the PCT before going northwest on trail FS-1375 to the lake.

MOUNT DANIEL, 7986', 18 miles RT, 5400' gain (Maps: USGS Mt. Daniel, The Cradle, GT Stevens Pass). **Hike-4†, Snow. Alpine Lakes Wilderness.** Drive and hike as above to **Peggys Pond**.

From Peggys Pond, ascend west, then, at 6800', continue west, staying on the south side of the east ridge of Mt. Daniel to avoid glacier. At 7200', turn northwest, passing east of the first summit of Mt. Daniel, 7662'. Continue northwest on the broad summit past the middle summit, 7899', to the highest point, the westernmost of the pair of summits that overlook the Lynch Glacier (north).

TUCK AND ROBIN LAKES, 5268', 6178', 14 miles RT, 2000' or 3000' gain (Maps: USGS The Cradle, GT Stevens Pass). **Hike-2. Alpine Lakes Wilderness.** From the Salmon la Sac Forest Service Station, 16 miles from Roslyn, drive north 14 miles on the Cle Elum River Road, FS-4330, to the trailhead at the end of the road, elevation 3400'.

Hike northwest on trail FS-1376 past Hyas Lake and Little Hyas Lake toward Deception Pass. At mile 4.5, 4200', turn east and ascend on a steeper trail, FS-1376A, to benches containing the lakes. Robin Lake, the upper lake, is one mile beyond Tuck Lake.

TRICO MOUNTAIN, 6700', 18 miles RT, 3600' gain (Maps: USGS The Cradle, GT Stevens Pass). **Hike-3. Alpine Lakes Wilderness.** Hike as above to Robin Lake.

From Robin Lake, find a track that leads north up the open ridge to the summit, passing the Granite Mountain Potholes, which are just east of the crest. The summit is at the intersection of King, Chelan, and Kittitas counties.

Teanaway River Area.

Leave I-90 at Exit-85. Drive seven miles east on SR-970, then turn north on the Teanaway Road. The pavement ends 21 miles from I-90.

YELLOW HILL, 5527', 8 miles RT, 3000' gain (Maps: USGS Teanaway Butte, GT Mt. Stuart). **Hike-1**. Drive the Teanaway River road for 7.5 miles from SR-970 to a road junction after crossing the North Fork of the Teanaway River. Turn left (west) on the Middle Fork Road. At 0.8 mile, turn right (northwest) to stay on the Middle Fork Road. Reach the trailhead six miles from the North Fork Teanaway Road, elevation 3100'.

Hike northwest on trail FS-1222 to the open summit and a view over the rolling hills of the Teanaway country.

RED TOP MOUNTAIN, 5361', 14 miles RT, 3000' gain (Maps: USGS Red Top Mountain, GT Mt. Stuart). **Hike-2**. Hike an abandoned trail in open, regrowing clearcuts. Drive the Teanaway Road for 7.5 miles from SR-970 over the bridge to the east side of the North Fork of the Teanaway River. Park 0.5 miles north of the bridge, elevation 2400'.

Hike east 100' to a track. The area between Dickey Creek (south) and Middle Creek (north) consists of two ridges with a minor valley between. Either ascend east on a wide track on the northern ridge or go south to find narrower tracks on the southern ridge. These ridges come together at 2800'. Stay on this ridge, travelling on roads or tracks and crossing roads at 4100' and 4500'. Meet the Dickey Creek road five miles from the Teanaway Road, elevation 4800'. Turn left (north) along the road (or a track nearby) on or near the crest of the ridge to the summit. Along the way, look for geodes and agates. This area is part of the **Red Top Agate Beds**.

EARL PEAK, 7036', 10 miles RT, 4000' gain (Maps: USGS Red Top Mountain, Enchantment Lakes, GT Mt. Stuart). **Hike-2**. Drive the Teanaway Road north to the end of the pavement. Continue north one mile to a 'Y'. Go right (northeast) for one mile along Stafford Creek. Turn left (north) on Standup Creek for one mile to the trailhead, elevation 3100'.

Hike the trail, FS-1369, north along Standup Creek. Where the trail turns east at a junction, 5700', go left on trail FS-1391A to 6000' and the southwest ridge of Earl Peak. Leave the trail and ascend northeast to the open summit. The summits visible to the north and east include: Ingalls Peak, 312°; Mt. Stuart, 328°; Colchuck Peak, 357°; Little Annapurna, 18°; and Navajo Peak, 64°.

STAFFORD LOOKOUT, 3784', 2 miles RT, 800' gain (Maps: USGS Red Top Mountain, GT Mt. Stuart). **Hike-1**. Drive as above for Earl Peak to the end of the road on Standup Creek, elevation 3100'.

Ascend the road southwest to the lookout site.

NAVAJO PEAK, 7223', 12 miles RT, 4200' gain (Maps: USGS Red Top Mountain, Enchantment Lakes, GT Mt. Stuart). **Hike-2. Alpine Lakes Wilderness.** Drive the Teanaway Road to the end of the pavement. Continue north one mile to a 'Y'. Go right (northeast) for three miles along Stafford Creek to the junction of Bear and Stafford Creeks, elevation 3100'.

Park and hike north on the Stafford Creek Trail, FS-1359, passing a junction with the Standup Creek Trail, FS-1369, at 4.8 miles, 5100', and reaching the saddle between Stafford Creek and Ingalls Creek at six miles, 6000'. Turn right (east) on the County Line Trail, FS-1226, and ascend to 6400'. Where the trail turns to contour across the south slope, leave the trail and ascend northeast on the ridge to the summit.

THREE BROTHERS, 7303', 7200', 7169', 20 miles RT, 5000' gain (Maps: USGS Enchantment Lakes, Red Top Mtn., GT Mt. Stuart). **Hike-2**. Drive and hike as above toward Navajo Peak to the west shoulder, 6400'.

Continue east on the trail, rounding southeast under Navajo Peak across the south ridge, turning northeast to the saddle between Negro Creek (south) and Falls Creek (north), 6000'. Leave the trail and ascend east and northeast to the first summit of Three Brothers, 7303'. Continue along the ridge over the middle summit, 7200', to the lookout site, 7169'. This last summit is also reached by a trail from Negro Creek.

MILLER PEAK, 6402', 10 miles RT, 3300' gain (Maps: USGS Red Top Mountain, Enchantment Lakes, Blewett, GT Mt. Stuart, Liberty). **Hike-1**. Drive the Teanaway River to the end of the pavement. Continue north one mile to a 'Y'. Go right (northeast) on road FS-9703 for four miles to the junction of Miller and Bear Creeks, elevation 3200'.

Park and hike northeast on the Miller Peak Trail, FS-1379. After leaving Miller Creek at 4300', the trail passes below Point 5349' before ascending to the west ridge of Miller Peak and a junction with trail FS-1226. Turn north on FS-1226 to follow the ridge to the open summit, which has views east over the Peshastin Creek valley.

JOHNSON CREEK POINT 5220, 5220', 9 miles RT, 2200' gain (Maps: USGS Mt. Stuart, Teanaway Butte, GT Mt. Stuart). **Hike-2**. The upper part of Johnson Creek points directly (210°) at this summit, which is not named on the USGS or National Forest maps. Drive the Teanaway Road to the end of the pavement. Continue north one mile to a 'Y'. Go left (northwest) for four miles on road FS-9737 to Beverly Campground, elevation 3100'. At the north end of the campground, find the trailhead at a bridge.

Hike west on trail FS-1383, keeping left (southwest) at 0.5 mile on trail FS-1383A where trail FS-1383 goes northwest. At a trail junction in the first saddle, turn right on trail FS-1235 to contour west across the north side of Johnson Point. On reaching the next saddle, 4800', leave the trail and hike southeast on the forested ridge to the summit.

MALCOLM MOUNTAIN, 5480', 12 miles RT, 2600' gain (Maps: USGS Mt. Stuart, Teanaway Butte, GT Mt. Stuart). **Hike-3**. Drive and park as above for Johnson Creek Point 5220.

Hike to the 4800' saddle northwest of Johnson Point 5220 and a trail junction. Leave trail FS-1383 and go north on trail FS-1225, following the ridge between Malcolm Creek (west) and Johnson Creek (east). Malcolm Mountain is now visible (296°). One mile after turning north on trail FS-1225, where the trail reaches the northeast ridge of Malcolm Mountain, 5000', leave the trail and turn southwest up the ridge to the summit.

KOPPEN MOUNTAIN, 6031', 8 miles RT, 2400' gain (Maps: USGS Mt. Stuart, GT Mt. Stuart). **Hike-2**. Drive the Teanaway Road to the end of the pavement. Continue north one mile to a 'Y'. Go left (northwest) for seven miles on road FS-9737 to the De Roux Campground and trailhead, elevation 3760'.

Hike northwest on the De Roux Creek trail, FS-1392. At mile 1.5, turn left on trail FS-1392.1 and ascend south and southwest to the crest and a trail junction, 5040'. Turn left (southeast) and follow the trail up the ridge. Where the trail contours across the west side of the summit, leave the trail and ascend on a track to the summit. Serpentine is exposed in the summit area.

DEROUX CREEK POINT 6260, 6260', 8 miles RT, 2600' gain (Maps: USGS Mt. Stuart, GT Mt. Stuart). **Hike-3**. Drive as above for Koppen Mtn. to the De Roux trailhead.

Hike northwest and west on the De Roux Creek Trail, FS-1392, crossing the North Fork of the Teanaway River. Cross DeRoux Creek at one mile and, at 1.5 miles, 4100', turn left on trail FS-1392.1, ascending southwest to the ridge crest, 5040'. At a trail junction in the saddle, go right, descending northwest. Before reaching the first switchback, leave the trail after crossing a serpentine (greenish rock) talus slope and contour northwest on a track around the west side of the first hump on the ridge to the crest of the ridge. Now ascend northwest and west, near or on the open or sparsely forested ridge to the highest point, which gives a view north to Esmeralda Peaks and Hawkins Mountain, both less than two miles away, and west to many summits near the Cascade Crest.

GALLAGHER HEAD LAKE, 5600', 8 miles RT, 2000' gain (Maps: USGS Mt. Stuart, GT Mt. Stuart). **Hike-1**. Drive as above for **Koppen Mountain** to the De Roux trailhead.

Hike west, northwest, and north on the De Roux Creek trail, FS-1392, taking the right fork at trail junctions and joining an old mining road shortly before reaching the lake. This small, shallow, spring-fed lake lies near the saddle between De Roux Creek and the South Fork of Fortune Creek. Hawkins Mtn. stands to the northwest and complex Esmeralda Peaks are east.

ESMERALDA WEST PEAK, 6765', 10 miles RT, 3000' gain (Maps: USGS Mt. Stuart, GT Mt. Stuart). **Hike-3**. This is the highest summit of the Esmeralda Peaks, a complex mountain with many summits. Drive as above for **Koppen Mountain** to the De Roux Campground and trailhead.

Hike as above toward **Gallagher Head Lake**. From south of the lake, 5560', ascend east on the south side of the ridge that descends west from the summit. The west end of the ridge has two summits. The USGS map marks the eastern point at 6765' but the western point is possibly higher.

HAWKINS MOUNTAIN, 7160', 12 miles RT, 3600' gain (Maps: USGS Mt. Stuart, GT Mt. Stuart). **Hike-3**. Drive and hike as above toward **Gallagher Head Lake**.

Where the trail, FS-1392, from De Roux Creek Campground meets a road 0.2 mile southwest of the lake, 5500', ascend west on a 4-wheel track into the basin of Big Boulder Creek on the south side of Hawkins Mountain. At 6000', leave the track and ascend north in an alpine basin to a saddle, 6800'. Follow the ridge west and north to the summit.

IRON PEAK, 6510', 8 miles RT, 2600' gain (Maps: USGS Mt. Stuart, GT Mt. Stuart). **Hike-2**. Drive the Teanaway Road to the end of the pavement. Continue north one mile to a 'Y'. Go left (northwest) on road FS-9737 for eight miles to the trailhead, elevation 3900'.

Ascend east on trail FS-1399 to the saddle, then go south to the summit, an exposure of serpentine. For a loop trip, park one mile south of the De Roux Campground. Ascend northeast near the creek that descends southwest from the ridge of Iron Peak. Return by trail FS-1399 and the road.

Alternate Route: From **Beverly Basin** hike northwest on trail FS-1391 to the junction with trail FS-1399, 5200'. Ascend west on trail FS-1399 to the saddle, 6100'. Leave the trail and go south to the summit. Round trip distance from Beverly Basin: 4 miles.

TEANAWAY POINT 6779, 6779', 8 miles RT, 3000' gain (Maps: USGS Mt. Stuart, GT Mt. Stuart). **Hike-3.** This unnamed summit is one mile north of Iron Peak. Drive as above to the trailhead for **Iron Peak**.

Hike east on trail FS-1399 to the saddle north of Iron Peak, 6100'. Turn left (north) and ascend through steep but broken rocks.

For a gentler route, continue east on the trail from the saddle north of Iron Peak to trail FS-1391 at 5200'. This trail comes from the Beverly Creek trailhead (see Beverly Basin). Turn left (north) and ascend to the saddle, 5800', between Turnpike Creek (north) and Beverly Creek. At the saddle, leave the trail and ascend west on the ridge (track) to the summit for a spectacular view of Mt. Stuart.

LONG'S PASS, 6200', 4 miles RT, 2200' gain (Maps: USGS Mt. Stuart, GT Mt. Stuart). **Hike-2.** This pass gives an unimpeded view of Mt. Stuart. Drive the Teanaway Road to the end of the pavement. Continue north one mile to a 'Y'. Go left (northwest) on road FS-9737 for nine miles to the trailhead at the end of the road, elevation 4200'.

Hike trail FS-1394 north for 0.5 mile, then go right (east) on trail FS-1390. At a trail junction, mile 1.0, turn east on a minimum trail up a talus slope to the crest of the ridge and a view of Mt. Stuart from two miles away.

INGALLS PASS, 6500', 6 miles RT, 2400' gain (Maps: USGS Mt. Stuart, GT Mt. Stuart). **Hike-2.** Drive the Teanaway Road as above for Long's Pass.

Hike trail FS-1394 north for 0.5 mile, then go east on trail FS-1390. At a trail junction, mile 1.0, continue north to Ingalls Pass. An airy campsite south of the pass is made possible by a spring coming out of the cliffs near the trail. A 6878' viewpoint is nearby.

LAKE INGALLS, 6463', 10 miles RT, 2500' gain (Maps: USGS Mt. Stuart, GT Mt. Stuart). **Hike-3. Alpine Lakes Wilderness.** Drive the Teanaway Road and hike as above to Ingalls Pass.

Follow one of several tracks through a forest of western larch to the lake, surrounded by slabs and broken boulders of serpentine, a part of the earth's mantle that was carried to the surface by the intrusion of the Mt. Stuart batholith.

FORTUNE POINT 7382, 7382', 10 miles RT, 3400' gain (Maps: USGS Mt. Stuart, GT Mt. Stuart). **Hike-3**. This summit stands at the head of the Fortune Creek Basin and southeast of Lake Ann. Drive the Teanaway Road and hike as above to Ingalls Pass.

From the pass, turn left (northwest) and hike up the ridge to the summit.

INGALLS SOUTH PEAK, 7640', 12 miles RT, 3800' gain (Maps: USGS Mt. Stuart, GT Mt. Stuart). **Hike-3. Alpine Lakes Wilderness.** Drive and hike as above to **Lake Ingalls**.

Near the lake, turn left (west) and ascend in the gully toward the saddle between Ingalls Peak and Ingalls South Peak. At 7200', before reaching the saddle, turn southwest and ascend through broken rocks to the summit. From the summit, continue south on or near the ridge to **Fortune Point 7382**. Turn left (east) and descend near or on the ridge to Ingalls Pass and the trail. Turn right (south) to the starting point.

BEVERLY BASIN, 5400', 7 miles RT, 2000' gain (Maps: USGS Mt. Stuart, Enchantment Lakes, GT Mt. Stuart). **Hike-1**. Drive the Teanaway Road to the end of the pavement. Continue north one mile to a 'Y'. Go left (northwest) on road FS-9737 for three miles to the Beverly Creek road. Turn north one mile to the trailhead, elevation 3400'.

Cross Beverly Creek and hike north on the east side of Beverly Creek for one mile to the junction of Beverly and Bean Creeks. At a trail junction, go left (northwest), crossing Bean Creek and continue to ascend along Beverly Creek to find campsites above 5200'. Many summit and trail hikes are possible from this basin: Volcanic Point (below), Navajo Peak (below), Iron Peak, Teanaway Point 6779, and Fourth Creek Point 6917 (below). The old County Line Trail, which runs east near the ridge that forms the boundary between Kittitas and Chelan counties, begins at the saddle between Beverly and Turnpike Creeks.

VOLCANIC POINT 6600, 6600', 5 miles RT, 1600' gain (Maps: USGS Mt. Stuart, Enchantment Lakes, GT Mt. Stuart). **Hike-4†**. **Alpine Lakes Wilderness.** The round-trip distance and elevation gain given for this hike are from **Beverly Basin** (see above).

From Beverly Basin, hike north on the Fourth Creek trail, FS-1218, to the saddle between Fourth Creek and Beverly Creek Basin. Turn right (east) on the County Line Trail for two miles to a saddle, 6400', south of the eroded remains of an old volcanic vent. From the east side, a narrow ramp ascends around the south side to the summit.

NAVAJO PEAK, 7223', 12 miles RT, 2500' gain (Maps: USGS Mt. Stuart, Enchantment Lakes, GT Mt. Stuart). **Hike-2**. The round-trip distance and elevation gain given for this hike on the **County Line Trail** are from Beverly Basin.

From Beverly Basin, hike north on the Fourth Creek trail, FS-1218, to the saddle between Fourth Creek and Beverly Creek Basin. Turn right (east) on the County Line Trail on the north side of the ridge-line boundary between Kittitas and Chelan counties, passing the Hardscrabble Creek Trail, FS-1218, going to the north at two miles and the Cascade Creek Trail going north at four miles. Where the trail leaves the ridge-line to contour the south slope of Navajo Peak, leave the trail and ascend northeast to the summit of Navajo Peak, the highest summit along this ridge.

FOURTH CREEK POINT 6917, 6917', 10 miles RT, 3600' gain (Maps: USGS Mt. Stuart, GT Mt. Stuart). **Hike-4†, Snow. Alpine Lakes Wilderness.** This rock summit, also known as Bill's Peak, is northwest of the saddle between Beverly Creek and Fourth Creek. Drive and hike as above to Beverly Basin.

At the beginning of Beverly Basin, 5200', turn right (north) on trail FS-1219 toward Fourth Creek. Reach a saddle at 5560', where the County Line Trail, FS-1226, goes to the east, and the Fourth Creek trail descends northeast to Icicle Creek. The summit is the high point exactly northwest (315°) from the pass.

Alternate Route 1. If snow is gone, leave the trail and ascend northwest on a steep, sandy, talus slope to a sloping forested bench, 6100'. Continue up in open forest to a gully that points northwest to the right (north) of the apparent high point. Ascend on dirt and talus to a bench. Angle left to the highest rock point. Summits visible include: Sherpa Peak (3°), Little Annapurna (52°), Navajo (96°), Earl (120°), Hibox (270°), Three Queens (273°), Davis (278°), Chikamin (280°), Lemah (282°), Esmerelda (284°), Hawkins (286°), Summit Chief (291°), Hinman (303°), Daniel (305°), Cathedral Rock (308°), Ingalls (320°), and Stuart (352°).

Alternate Route 2. If snow patches remain at the saddle between Fourth Creek and Beverly Creek, contour north (20°), going below a steeper rock outcrop (5700'). After crossing a watercourse, angle up into an opening in the brush and small trees. Now go directly up the slope (northwest) on snow. On this route at 6000' Volcanic Point 6600' is directly east (90°). Ascend in a shallow valley to a nearly level basin at 6500'. Continue northwest toward the rocky points on the skyline, which are north of the summit. At 6800', ascend left (west) to the summit.

BEAN CREEK POINT 6743, 6743', 10 miles RT, 3500' gain (Maps: USGS Enchantment Lakes, GT Mt. Stuart). **Hike-3.** Drive as above to the trailhead for Beverly Basin.

Hike north along Beverly Creek on trail FS-1391 for one mile to the junction of Beverly and Bean Creeks. Turn right (northeast) on a trail along Bean Creek, crossing avalanche gullies that are filled with snow until early summer, and continue into the Bean Creek basin. In the basin at 5800', leave the trail and continue north, at first over alpine meadow, then ascending on talus and through broken rocks to the summit, on the boundary between Chelan and Kittitas counties.

EARL PEAK, 7036', 10 miles RT, 3900' gain (Maps: USGS Enchantment Lakes, GT Mt. Stuart). **Hike-3.** Drive as above to the trailhead for Beverly Basin.

Hike north along Beverly Creek on trail FS-1391 for one mile to the junction of Beverly and Bean Creeks. Leave the trail and ascend east up the ridge south of Bean Creek. Near a point on the ridge, 5693', turn northeast to stay on the ridge to the summit of Earl Peak. This route may be nearly snow free by June.

Taneum Creek Area. Visit a working forest on the drier east side of the Cascade Mountains. This area is heavily used by motor vehicles on weekends. If eastbound on I-90, take Exit-93, cross east over I-90 and drive southeast on Thorp Prairie Road for four miles. Cross west over I-90, then turn northwest on West Taneum Road. Begin road FS-33 when six miles from I-90 at Exit-93. If westbound on I-90, take Exit-101, cross west over I-90 and drive northwest on Thorp Cemetery Road to begin West Taneum Road at four miles, then drive as above on the Taneum Creek Road, FS-33.

QUARTZ MOUNTAIN, 6290', 25 miles RT, 2000' gain (Maps: USGS Frost Mtn., Quartz Mtn., GT Cle Elum, Easton). **Mtn. Bicycle.** Drive northwest on the Taneum Creek Road, FS-33, passing Taneum Campground. After passing Icewater Campground eight miles from I-

90, turn left (south) on road FS-3330 and drive seven miles from FS-33 to an unofficial camping place signed Gnat Flat, elevation 4600'. This area is named Grasshopper Flat on the USGS map. Park here, 19 miles from I-90 at Exit-93.

Ride south on road FS-3330 in dense forest, then through several open sagebrush meadows with scattered yellow pine trees, a plant association characteristic of this area. Pause at a signboard with map and other information, mile 1.5. At mile 1.9, join road FS-3120 and turn west. Tamarack Spring is two miles east on road FS-3120. At mile 2.3, road FS-3111 goes south to Buck Meadows and Ellensburg. Now the road wanders west near the crest of ridges, offering a view of Mt. Stuart at mile 4.9. When going uphill, spend at least half the time walking in order to enjoy the views through this open forest, which has almost no shrub understory in many places. Where the road bends southwest, look southeast over the hills of Manastash Ridge rolling into the distance.

After dropping 100' to mile 6.5, join road FS-31, continuing northwest to pass Frost Meadows at mile 7.3, elevation 4800' (campsite). Expect only a trickle of water in a branch of the South Fork of Manastash Creek in late August. The Frost Mtn. Trail, FS-1366, begins here, ascending east to the summit of Frost Mtn. At mile 8.7, 5600'a trail, FS-1380, goes to Taneum Lake in one mile. Now road FS-31 bends the south, returning to a northwest direction after ascending to the crest of a subsidiary of Manastash Ridge at the beginning of a habitat conservation area (no wood cutting or gathering). At mile 9.9, walk east 50' to look north at the Stuart Range. Note nearby cliffs on the east side of this offshoot of Manastash Ridge.

After passing a pond on the right (east) side of the road, mile 10.5, roads go left to Wells Meadow and Hereford Meadow. Spruce trees begin to be common at this elevation, 5800'. Pass a reservoir on the left (west) at mile 11.5 that stores water from a spring at the head of the South Fork of Manastash Creek. A generous meadow fills the valley north of the reservoir. The road bends west to the crest of Manastash Ridge and a campground with tables and fire circles, mile 12.0 and 6200'. Ascend more steeply, passing a junction with trail FS-1388, which goes northwest to pass near Mt. Clifty and meet the Pacific Crest Trail on Blowout Mtn. After the junction, the road bends south and east to a large parking area on the north shoulder of the summit. The actual summit, where several communication towers stand, is covered by view-obscuring forest. The best views are from the edges of the north shoulder: Fife's Peaks (238°), Clifty (300°), Lookout Mtn. (317°), Hibox (338°), Hinman (350°), Daniel (353°), Cathedral Rock (355°), and Stuart (18°),

FROST MOUNTAIN, 5740', 12 miles RT, 2300' gain (Maps: USGS Frost Mtn., Quartz Mtn., GT Cle Elum, Easton). **Hike-1**. Drive the Taneum Creek Road, FS-33, from Exit-93 or Exit-101 on I-90. At 2800', 14 miles from I-90 at Exit-93, keep left on the South Fork Taneum Creek Road, FS-3300. At 18 miles, turn left (west) to the South Fork Meadow trailhead, elevation 3500'.

Hike west on trail FS-1367, ascending the South Fork of Taneum Creek to 3600'. Turn left (southeast) and ascend the Frost Mountain Trail, FS-1366 and FS-1366.2, to the lookout site.

LOOKOUT MOUNTAIN, 6188', 8 miles RT, 2300' gain (Maps: USGS Quartz Mtn., Mt. Clifty, GT Easton). **Hike-2**. Drive the Taneum Creek Road (FS-33) to MP-19.5, 26 miles from I-90 at MP-93 or MP-101. Park in the limited space at a gate, elevation 4000'. The last 0.5 mile of the road is narrow and steep.

Hike southwest on the road past the gate, passing a branch road right at 0.2 mile that crosses a bridge over the North Fork of Taneum Creek and eventually reaches Cle Elum. At mile 1.8, and 4350', after bending south, take the blocked branch road to the right and cross a minor creek. Go 0.25 mile west on the logging road to a trail that descends right (north) to North Fork Taneum Creek, passing a trail, FS-4350, on the south side of the creek. Cross the creek and go west and northwest, entering ancient forest in which some of the trees are white pine. Reach Taneum Shelter, an old miner cabin, at mile 3.3, 4580'.

Beyond the shelter, the trail ascends more steeply in switchbacks to Windy Pass, mile 4.5 and 5380', at a junction with the Granite Creek Trail, FS-1326. This trail goes northwest past the North Ridge Trail (0.5 mile) and joins the Pacific Crest Trail (13 miles). Turn east and ascend on trail FS-1326, crossing steep meadow to the north shoulder of Lookout Mtn., 5760'. Where the main trail turns northeast, leave the trail and follow one of several tracks southeast along the ridge. Note the contrast between the forest on the northeast side of the ridge and meadows on the southwest side. Find whitebark pine, subalpine fir, and mountain hemlock. The summit is an outcrop of schist, colored orange in places by lichen. Summits visible include: Davis (5°), Ingalls (18°), Stuart (23°), Navajo (36°), Miller (42°), Quartz Mtn. (138°), Adams (195°), Curtis Gilbert (198°), Goat Peak (American River) (209°), Fife's Peaks (224°), and Mt. Clifty (258°).

South Cascades Region

SR-410 Area

SR-410 Area. Drive east on SR-410 from Enumclaw. MP-25 is 0.2 miles east of the junction of SR-164 with SR-410.

PINNACLE PEAK, 1801', 2 miles RT hiking + 4 miles RT bicycling, 1000' gain (Maps: USGS Enumclaw. GT Enumclaw). **Bicycle and Hike-1**. Take Metro 912 or 915 to Enumclaw at the intersection of Griffin Ave. and SR-410. Ride south and east to the intersection of 276th Ave. SE and SE 472nd St. If driving, from SR-410 go south on 284th Ave. for 1.4 miles, passing west of the King County Fairgrounds, then go west on SE 472nd St. for 0.6 miles to the trailhead at 276th Ave. SE, two miles from SR-410, elevation 800'.

Ascend southeast on a heavily used trail in dense regrowing forest. The trail, which crosses steep slopes, is narrow in places. Join a service road at 1400'. Where the road makes a sharp turn southwest at 1600' on the north side of the peak, nearly horizontal columns of basalt are exposed at the edges of the road. Then, after the road rounds to the south side, the exposed columns of basalt are vertical. At the summit, only the foundation blocks of the former lookout tower remain, but segments of columnar basalt look like pieces of an ancient ruin. The distant view is mostly obscured by vegetation.

GRASS MOUNTAIN, 4382', 21 miles RT, 3000' gain (Maps: USGS Enumclaw, Cyclone Creek, GT Enumclaw). **Mtn. Bicycle**. From Enumclaw, drive east on SR-410 for 5 miles and park 0.3 miles east of MP-30 on the north side of the highway at the junction with the Grass Mtn. Road, FS-7110, Weyerhaueser Road 5200, elevation 1494'. This road is open to foot and bicycle travel except during logging and on weekends is open to motor vehicles by permit.

As FS-7110 leaves SR-410, look north and northeast for two groups of communication towers. These stand on Radio Peak (left) and Grass Mtn. (right). Ride generally northeast on a meandering logging road and for the first eight miles, the road gradient averages less than 5%. Where FS-7110 bends right (east) at one mile, pass a gated, grass overgrown road that goes straight ahead (north). At mile 2.4, keep right again where the road to Radio Peak goes left (north). Pass another road contouring right (southeast) at mile 2.9. Cross Scatter Creek at mile 3.8, 2200', and pass a road to the left at mile 4.0. Go under a powerline at mile 5.2, 2650'. As the road makes a sharp U-bend at mile 5.6, look up to the towers on Grass Mtn., then go back under the powerline at mile 6.6, 2940'.

At mile 8.1, the road gradient increases to 10% and the surface deteriorates in places to coarse rocks and loose gravel. At mile 9.5, 4000', reach a gate at a saddle on the ridge between the White River (south) and the Green River. Turn west and ascend near or on the ridge, going under the powerline one last time, to the summit for a 360° view. Summits visible include: Mt. Baker (2°), Chimney Rock–Mt. Daniel group (46°), and Mt. Stuart (66°). Look down to Eagle Gorge Reservoir on the Green River.

FEDERATION FOREST STATE PARK, 1650', 2 miles of trails. (Maps: USGS Greenwater, GT Greenwater). **Hike-1**. Drive SR-410 east from Enumclaw for 16 miles (MP-41).

Facilities and activities: fishing, hiking, nature trails in ancient forest that have interpretive signs for five different forest communities, and the Catherine Montgomery Interpretive Center with displays of the seven life zones of Washington State. A guide to the nature trails is available. The route of the Naches Pass pioneer wagon road follows the east bank of the White River.

Look for the following native plants along the nature trails: Douglas fir, western hemlock, red cedar, yellow cedar, white pine, lodgepole pine, grand fir, bigleaf maple, silver fir, cottonwood, red alder, Sitka spruce, aspen, mountain ash, salal, vine maple, rose, huckleberry, devils club, salmonberry, elderberry, red-osier dogwood, thimbleberry, gooseberry, yew, Oregon grape, honeysuckle, ocean spray, rhododendron, currant, cascara, juniper, false box, raspberry, willow, service berry, mock orange, manzanita, hardhack, goatsbeard, and spirea.

HUCKLEBERRY MOUNTAIN, 4764', 7 miles RT, 2700' gain (Maps: USGS Greenwater, Nagrom, GT Greenwater). **Hike-1**. Drive 17 miles east of Enumclaw on SR-410. East of MP-42, before crossing a bridge over the Greenwater River, turn north, then go east on road FS-7125 for 0.2 miles. At a junction, go right (east) 0.3 mile and park near a gate, elevation 2100'.

Hike southeast on the road past the gate, descending to cross a creek 0.3 mile from the gate. Now begin to ascend, finding the beginning of the Christoff Trail, FS-1171, 0.1 mile beyond the creek. Go northeast on the trail to the ridge crest, then turn east to the first summit, which is marked Christoff on the USGS map.

NACHES PASS EMIGRANT TRAIL, high point 3100' or 4960', 2 to 11 miles RT, 700' or 2600' gain (Maps: USGS Noble Knob, GT

Lester). **Hike-2**. Explore an old wagon route to Puget Sound that went west from the Naches River to the Greenwater River. Near MP-45 east of Greenwater and 19 miles east of Enumclaw, turn east on road FS-70 to follow the Greenwater River. Immediately after crossing the Greenwater River, eight miles from SR-410, turn right (south) across Pyramid Creek to a large parking area, 2440' (toilets).

Find the trail between the parking area and road FS-70 (signboard). Ascend steeply east (no wheels or horses), at first on the ridge, then going southeast across the slope. At 2900', find a concrete and steel shelf and a tree with rope marks. Cross road FS-70 at 3000' and road FS-7065 at 3100'. East of road FS-7065, the Emigrant Trail is open to motor vehicles and the route is deeply eroded. Reach Government Meadows and Naches Pass (4960') 5.5 miles from the trailhead. For the return, a bypass trail begins west of road FS-70 and ends below the steepest parts of the Emigrant Trail.

KELLY BUTTE, 5409', 18 miles RT, 3600' gain (Maps: USGS Sun Top, Lester, Noble Knob, GT Greenwater, Lester). **Mtn. Bicycle and Hike-1**. Near MP-45 on SR-410 east of Greenwater, turn east on road FS-70 to follow the Greenwater River. Park 7 miles from SR-410 near the junction with road FS-7030 where the paved road descends after bypassing a landslide that destroyed the former location of FS-70, elevation 2400'.

Ride north on the Whistler Creek Road (FS-7030), ascending to a 4-way junction in a saddle, mile 4, elevation 4166'. Continue north on Road FS-7030, passing a road to the right at mile 4.8 and going right (north) at mile 5.3 to stay on road FS-7030. After the road turns west, leave the road at mile 7.3, elevation 4500', and ascend a trail north to the lookout site for a view into the upper canyon of the Green River, once occupied by the logging and railroad community of Lester.

COLQUHOUN PEAK, 5173', 11 miles RT, 2800' gain (Maps: USGS Sun Top, Noble Knob, Lester, GT Greenwater, Lester). **Mtn. Bicycle and Hike-1**. Drive and ride as above for **Kelly Butte** to the 4-way junction in the saddle at 4166', mile 4.

Ascend east on the right fork (road FS-7036) for 0.4 mile, then turn southwest for 0.3 mile on a branch road (110) to the end of the road. Now follow a trail to the rocky summit, a former lookout. Yellow cedar and subalpine fir obscure most of the view.

PYRAMID PEAK, 5715', 16 miles RT, 3900' gain (Maps: USGS Sun Top, Noble Knob, Lester, GT Greenwater, Lester). **Mtn. Bicycle and**

Hike-1. Drive and ride as above for **Kelly Butte** to the 4-way junction in the saddle at 4166', mile 4.

Turn right (east) on road FS-3060 and ascend to a saddle on the east flank of Colquhoun Peak, mile 5.3, 4700'. Contour and ascend southeast, then descend briefly to another road junction, mile 6.5, elevation 4700'. Take the right fork and ascend a 'Z', reaching Windy Pass and the Pacific Crest Trail at mile 7.6, elevation 5200'. Leave bicycle and ascend south to the summit. The PCT is closed to bicycles.

CLEAR WEST PEAK, 5644', 5697', 3 or 22 miles RT, 1400' or 3000' gain (Maps: USGS Clear West Peak, GT Greenwater). **Mtn. Bicycle and/or Hike-1**. Drive SR-410 for 22 miles east of Enumclaw. South of MP-47, turn right (southwest) across the White River and drive along the West Fork of the White River on road FS-74, keeping right at a junction six miles from SR-410 and crossing the river 6.5 miles from SR-410. If bicycling, park here, elevation 2400'. For hike only, drive on, taking a left fork on road FS-7430 at mile 8 from SR-410 and park at the trailhead, 14 miles from SR-410, 4700'.

Ride west on road FS-74, going left on road FS-7430 at mile 1.4. Cross Viola Creek at mile 3.7, then ascend on the north side of Clear West Peak. At the end of the road, mile 9, leave bicycle and continue on the trail to the west summit (5644') for an overall view of the south side of Mt. Rainier National Park. Look for the following summits: Redstone Peak (180°), First Mother (228°), Castle Peak (234°), Bearhead Mtn. (280°), Kaleetan Peak (22°), and Mt. Stuart (50°). To reach the rocky east summit, 5697', descend east on the trail until the trail turns south. Follow an intermittent track northeast.

LAKE JAMES, 4400', 10 miles RT, 1700' gain (Maps: Rainier: Wilderness Trip Planner, USGS Sunrise, GT Mt. Rainier East). **Hike-1**. Drive SR-410 for 22 miles east of Enumclaw. At MP-47, turn right (southwest) across the White River and drive along the West Fork of the White River on road FS-74, keeping to the right at a junction six miles from SR-410 and crossing the river 6.5 miles from SR-410. At mile 6.8, go left (south) on road FS-7410. Park at the Pigeon Creek bridge, three miles from road FS-74, elevation 2750'.

Hike one mile south on the road to the end, then go east to the river and cross, either on logs, or by wading. In late summer, the river is ankle deep in places. Find a trail and hike south two miles to a junction. Turn right toward Windy Gap and ascend to the lake (camping by permit only). Lake Ethel is 800' northwest.

REDSTONE PEAK, 5680', 13 miles RT, 3000' gain (Maps: Rainier: Wilderness Trip Planner, USGS Sunrise, GT Mt. Rainier East). **Hike-4†**. Drive and hike as above to **Lake James**.

Continue on the trail toward Windy Pass, taking the left (south) fork at 4700' to the Lake James Patrol Cabin on Van Horn Creek. Leave the trail at the Patrol Cabin and ascend the fall line east in open forest on the north edge of a talus slope. After the talus ends, continue southeast, going left (east) around cliffs to a notch on the north ridge of Redstone Peak. Use great care at the notch to avoid loose rock. Cross the notch south and descend 30'. Turn right (west) and ascend to the summit.

SLUISKIN SQUAW, 6960', 14 miles RT, 4300' gain (Maps: Rainier: Wilderness Trip Planner, USGS Sunrise, GT Mt. Rainier East). **Hike-3**. Drive and hike as above for **Lake James**.

Continue on the trail toward Windy Gap. Leave the trail at 5500' before reaching Windy Gap and ascend south to the saddle between Sluiskin Chief on the left (east) and Sluiskin Squaw on the right (west). Turn west and ascend in an open gully to the summit.

From the summit, look south over Vernal Park to Old Desolate, a talus summit.

NATURAL BRIDGE, high point 5800', 14 miles RT, 3600' gain (Maps: Rainier: Wilderness Trip Planner, USGS Sunrise, GT Mt. Rainier East). **Hike-1**. Hike as above to **Lake James**.

Continue on the trail toward Windy Gap, taking the trail north to Natural Bridge at the trail junction near the east edge of Windy Gap, 5760'. At 0.5 mile from Windy Gap, descend northeast on a branch trail to a viewpoint overlooking the Natural Bridge.

TYEE PEAK, 6000', 17 miles RT, 4200' gain (Maps: Rainier: Wilderness Trip Planner, USGS Sunrise, Mowich Lake, GT Mt. Rainier East, Mt. Rainier West). **Hike-3**. Drive and hike as above to **Lake James**.

Continue on the Northern Loop Trail over Windy Gap and descend past a pond to a trail junction at 5750', six miles from the Mt. Rainier National Park boundary at the West Fork of the White River. This trail junction can also be reached in seven miles from the Ipsut Creek trailhead on the Carbon River.

Turn north past ponds to the meadow at the high point of **Chenuis Mountain**, 6150'. Continue west in the meadow, then descend the ridge to the base of Tyee Peak, a rock point protruding from the ridge. Ascend west.

CRESCENT MOUNTAIN, 6715', 17 miles RT, 4200' (Maps: Rainier: Wilderness Trip Planner, USGS Sunrise, Mowich Lake, GT Mt. Rainier East, Mt. Rainier West). **Hike-3**. Drive and hike as above to **Lake James**.

Continue on the Northern Loop Trail over Windy Gap and descend west from the Gap to the first pond on the south side of the trail, 5775'. This pond can also be reached in 6.5 miles from the Ipsut Creek trailhead on the Carbon River.

Leave the trail at the pond and ascend south on talus to the ridge of Crescent Mountain. Turn southwest to the summit, which is barely above much of the ridge, but it has a marvelous view of the Carbon Glacier and other glaciers on the north side of Mt. Rainier.

SKOOKUM FLATS TRAIL, high point 2440', 7 miles hike + 6 miles bicycle, 600' gain (Maps: USGS Sun Top, GT Greenwater). **Bicycle and/or Hike-1**. Hike near the west bank of the White River in grove after grove of giant ancient forest. The north end of trail FS-1194 begins from road FS-73 on the west side of the White River, elevation 1880'. To reach road FS-73, drive 24 miles east of Enumclaw on SR-410 (MP-49). Turn right (west) and drive 0.3 miles to parking on the west side of the bridge over the White River. To make a one-way hike without a car shuttle, leave a bicycle near the junction of trail FS-1194 with road FS-7160, on the west side of the White River off SR-410 south of MP-54.

From road FS-73, hike south on trail FS-1194. At the start of the trail, note the tangle of trees that have fallen into the river from the bank. The giant ancient forest here consists mostly of western hemlock and Douglas fir, and the youngest trees are almost entirely hemlock, with an occasional yew or red cedar. Later, giant red cedar trees are more common. At forks in the trail, stay on the trail nearest the river. Use care in passing near undercut river banks that may collapse.

Pass the waterfalls of Skookum Creek (May) on the right (west) at mile 2. Get occasional views of the Snoquera Palisades east across the White River. Look for the narrow ribbon of Explorer Falls at the east end of the Palisades. At the best view of these falls, the compass reads 45°. Near the crossing of Buck Creek, a branch trail goes north to a footbridge over the White River. This trail continues north for 0.25 mile to SR-410 near MP-53 and Camp Sheppard. South of the bridge over Buck Creek, watch for Little Ranger Peak (33°), the last high point of the Palisades, and the rock outcrop of Ranger Viewpoint (73°) in the midst of a sea of forest. At a junction, 2.5 miles from the Mt. Rainier National Park boundary, where a connector to Buck Creek Trail (FS-1169) goes west, take the left branch (northeast) down toward the river. The trail now stays on a flat beside the White River. At the road FS-7160 bridge over the White River, the trail divides, one branch goes left under the bridge, while the branch to the right connects with road FS-7160.

Find bicycle and ride 0.1 mile east to SR-410, five miles north to road FS-73, and 0.3 miles west across the White River to the starting point.

SUN TOP, 5271', 12 miles RT, 3200' gain (Maps: USGS Sun Top, GT Greenwater). **Mtn. Bicycle**. Drive 24 miles east of Enumclaw on SR-410. South of MP-49, turn west on road FS-73 across the White River and park at the Snopark, 1.4 miles from SR-410, elevation 2100'. Road FS-7315 goes south from FS-73 here.

Ascend on road FS-7315 to the summit and lookout building, passing through a saddle and road/trail junction at mile 5.

SUN TOP, 5271' (Maps: USGS Sun Top, GT Greenwater). Drive to the summit for the sunset view (no camping).

LAKE ELEANOR, 4985', 3 miles RT, 500' gain (Maps: Mount Rainier: Wilderness Trip Planner, USGS Sunrise, GT Mt. Rainier East). **Hike-1**. Drive 24 miles east of Enumclaw on SR-410. South of MP-49, turn west on road FS-73 across the White River. Cross to the east side of Eleanor Creek at mile 6 and park at the next crossing of Eleanor Creek, mile 10, elevation 4500'.

Find the trail on the east side of Eleanor Creek and hike south to the lake.

GRAND PARK, high point 5700', 9 miles RT, 1500' gain (Maps: Mount Rainier: Wilderness Trip Planner, USGS Sunrise, GT Mt. Rainier East). **Hike-1**. Drive and hike as above to Lake Eleanor.

From the lake, continue south, crossing a branch of Huckleberry Creek at 4880', then follow the west edge of the huge meadow of Grand Park to a junction with the Northern Loop Trail and the high point, 3.3 miles from Lake Eleanor.

THE DALLES NATURE TRAIL, 2165', 1 miles RT, no gain (Maps: USGS Sun Top, GT Greenwater). **Hike-1**. Drive 25 miles east of Enumclaw on SR-410, MP-50. Park in the picnic area at The Dalles Campground.

Walk north in the campground in ancient forest. A 9.5' diameter Douglas fir tree that is more than 700 years old has an explanatory sign. This tree survived a fire 300 years ago. Several other giant trees of similar age are near the trail that goes north near the White River to road FS-73.

SNOQUERA PALISADES VIEWPOINT, high point 3300', 5 miles RT, 1300' gain (Maps: USGS Sun Top, GT Greenwater). **Hike-3**. Drive 28 miles east on SR-410 from Enumclaw. East of MP-53, park at Camp Sheppard on the east side of SR-410, elevation 2420' (toilets).

Hike northeast through Camp Sheppard to the White River Trail, FS-1199, in the edge of the forest east of the camp buildings. Turn northwest, passing a branch to Snoquera Falls at one mile and reaching the junction with the Palisades Trail, FS-1198, at mile 1.5. Turn east and ascend, crossing The Dalles Creek at 0.25 miles. Continue up in switchbacks, passing under cliffs of the Snoquera Palisades when the trail returns near The Dalles Creek, which has minor cascades visible from the trail. Near 3200', before the trail crosses the creek to the south side, the trail ascends steeply on a loose dirt and gravel slope where the switchbacks in the trail have collapsed.

After crossing the creek, the trail contours south to an airy viewpoint over the valley of the White River.

CAMP SHEPPARD NATURE TRAIL, high point 2440', 2 miles RT, 100' gain (Maps: USGS Sun Top, GT Greenwater). **Hike-1**. Drive 28 miles (east) on SR-410 from Enumclaw. East of MP-53, park at Camp Sheppard on the east side of SR-410, elevation 2420'.

Find a trail at the south edge of the parking area and walk southeast into the nature area of giant red cedar trees. Other plants in the area include: spruce, hemlock, and vine maple.

Cross SR-410 to the west near the entrance to Camp Sheppard and find a faint trail descending toward the river to a junction with a disused trail on the east bank of the White River. Walk the trail south to view a tangle of fallen trees in a bit of ancient forest.

SNOQUERA FALLS, high point 3200', 4 miles RT, 1000' gain (Maps: USGS Sun Top, GT Greenwater). **Hike-1** to **Hike-4**†. The falls are best in May. Drive 28 miles from Enumclaw. East of MP-53, park at Camp Sheppard, elevation 2420' (toilet). Depending on the state of repair, the trail to the falls from the west can be up to grade **Hike-4**†. The trail from the east to the creek crossing just below the falls is usually grade **Hike-1**.

Hike-1. From Camp Sheppard parking, hike northeast through the camp, passing under the overhead power line, to the White River Trail,

FS-1199, in the edge of the forest east of the camp. Turn southeast for 0.25 mile to a multiple trail junction. Take the uphill trail east for 0.25 mile to another trail junction. Now go left (east) on the Snoquera Falls Trail (FS-1167), and ascend in switchbacks to the creek crossing below the falls. Return on the same trail.

Hike-3. From the trail at the creek crossing below the falls, ascend one of several loose, rocky tracks to the cliffs at the base of the falls for the view directly upward to watch the play of wind on the water. On windy days, the water breaks up into clouds of spray that spread over much of the cliff.

Loop (possibly **Hike-4**†). From Camp Sheppard, hike northwest on the White River Trail, FS-1199, for 0.5 mile. Turn northeast on the Snoquera Falls Trail, FS-1167, and ascend, bending southeast. Above 2900', this trail crosses several avalanche/slide gullies that can be steep, loose, and hazardous. Where the trail disappears at a gully, look horizontally across the gully for the continuation. After crossing several gullies, the trail makes a switchback in the middle of a large talus field. Go northwest on the trail until it crosses a 2' diameter fallen log that has a saw cut at the level of the trail. If the trail to the west disappears in a tumble of fallen rocks, leave the trail and ascend directly up the slope near the log with the saw cuts. Rejoin the trail going southeast above the upper end of the log. Now ascend in several short zig-zags to a creek crossing below the falls. From here, after taking one of the rough tracks to view the falls from directly below, descend southeast on the trail to the first junction, then turn northwest to return to Camp Sheppard. This loop is harder to follow and more hazardous in the reverse direction.

DALLES RIDGE, high point 5781', 14 miles RT, 3400' gain (Maps: USGS Sun Top, GT Greenwater). **Hike-3**. Drive 29 miles east from Enumclaw on SR-410. At the next intersection after passing Camp Sheppard and 0.3 miles south of MP-54, turn right (west) on road FS-7160 over the White River and park in a parking area on the south side of the road near the White River, elevation 2450'.

Walk east to SR-410, then go north on the highway for 0.1 mile. Find a short connecting trail to the White River Trail, FS-1199, on the east side of SR-410. Go south 0.3 miles on trail FS-1199 to the junction with trail FS-1197. Turn left in ancient forest and ascend northeast on trail FS-1197 near Ranger Creek. Get the only close view of Ranger Creek where the trail makes a switchback two miles from trail FS-1199, 3000'. At mile 2.6, 3700', a spur trail goes left (south) to Ranger Viewpoint, a rock outcrop in a sea of forest. At mile 4.8, 5000', the Palisades Trail, FS-1198 joins from the left. This trail passes near

Little Ranger Peak one mile from FS-1197. Nearby is a shelter built by the Boy Scouts. Continue north on trail FS-1197 to the Dalles Ridge trail, FS-1173, at mile 5.8 and 5300'. Turn east on the Dalles Ridge trail for 0.3 miles, then leave the trail at an opening in the brush and ascend in open forest or alpine meadow to the crest of the ridge, 5700'. Turn north to the first high point, 5781'. Nearby summits: Noble Knob (88°), and Sun Top (266°).

SUN TOP, 5271', 11 miles RT, 2500' gain (Maps: USGS Sun Top, GT Greenwater). **Hike-1**. Drive 29 miles east from Enumclaw on SR-410. South of MP-54, turn west on road FS-7160 over the White River. Follow road FS-7160, passing a road to an airstrip at mile 0.5 and another road before reaching the Sun Top trail (FS-1183) beyond MP-7, elevation 4300'.

Hike southwest on the trail, rounding the head of Buck Creek to go north on the east side of the ridge, contouring across steep slopes. Cross flowery exposures of basalt below Point 5590', then reach a viewpoint and lookout site, elevation 5440'. The trail now descends north in dense forest to a road crossing, 4761', then ascends in switchbacks, crossing the road twice to the summit and lookout building (for rent).

MUTTON MOUNTAIN, 6142', 9 miles RT, 3800' gain (Maps: USGS Sun Top, Noble Knob, GT Greenwater, Lester). **Hike-1**. Drive 31 miles east from Enumclaw on SR-410 (0.1 mile south of MP-56). Turn east on the Corral Pass Road, FS-7174, and drive 0.8 mile from SR-410 to park at a trailhead, elevation 2974'.

Hike north on trail FS-1199 for 0.5 mile, entering ancient forest at 0.25 mile, to a bridge over Deep Creek. On the north side of the creek, 2840', find a trail junction and ascend east on the Deep Creek Trail, FS-1196. Viewpoints at 3100' and 3200' look into the valley of the White River. The trail travels in open ancient forest with almost no brush, giving cathedral-like vistas. At the crest, 4800', where the trail wanders through windrows of fallen trees. Above 5000' many of the trees are yellow cedar, festooned with moss. At 5500', the trail crosses a rocky area with a view south. At 5900', a trail goes left (north) to Noble Knob. Take the trail right (east) toward Corral Pass, descending briefly across a saddle, then ascend toward the southwest shoulder of Mutton Mountain. Leave the trail where it bends away from the west ridge and ascend east in open terrain on one of several tracks to the highest point. The summit has a view northeast over the headwaters of the Greenwater River. Mt. Rainier fills the skyline to the west. The obvious butte southeast (118°), is Fife's Peaks.

NOBLE KNOB, 6011', 9 or 17 miles RT, 600' or 3300' gain (Maps: USGS Sun Top, Noble Knob, GT Greenwater, Lester). **Mtn. Bicycle and/or Hike-1**. Drive 29 miles east from Enumclaw on SR-410 (0.1 mile south of MP-56). Turn left (east) on the Corral Pass Road, FS-7174 and park at the Corral Pass trailhead, five miles from SR-410 (camping). This road is sometimes closed at one mile from SR-410, elevation 2974'. If the road is closed, ride a bicycle from the gate to Corral Pass, adding eight miles and 2700' gain to the roundtrip distance.

From Corral Pass, hike northwest on trail FS-1184 past trail FS-1196. Continue on trail FS-1184 along the ridge. Where trail FS-1184 goes left (northwest) at a junction with trail FS-1185, continue north up the ridge to the summit.

NORSE PEAK, 6856', 9 miles RT, 2900' gain (Maps: USGS Norse Peak, GT Bumping Lake). **Hike-1. Norse Peak Wilderness**. Drive 32 miles east and south from Enumclaw on SR-410 (MP-57). Turn left (east) on road FS-7190 toward the Crystal Mtn. Ski Area for four miles to the Norse Peak trail, FS-1191, elevation 4000'. Park on a wide shoulder or turn right into Sand Flat, a horse facility, where trail FS-1191 ascends east. From the parking area on road FS-7190, hike 500' southeast on a branch road on the east side of road FS-7190 to Trail FS-1191.

Ascend east for four miles, getting views of Mt. Rainier and the Crystal Mtn. ski area at several places, then turn south to the summit. Trail FS-1191 goes on to connect with the Pacific Crest Trail in the Norse Peak Wilderness at 5.2 miles from road FS-7190. Peaks visible from the summit include: Chimney Rock group (12°), Daniel (20°), Stuart (38°), Fife's Peaks (80°), Aix (140°), Goat Rocks (180°) with Adams directly behind, Crystal Mtn. (230°), and Kaleetan (358°),

CRYSTAL MOUNTAIN, 6776', 6840', 10 miles RT, 2600' gain (Maps: USGS Norse Peak, GT Bumping Lake). **Hike-3**. Drive 32 miles east from Enumclaw on SR-410 (MP-57). Turn left (east) on road FS-7190 for six miles and park at the Crystal Mountain Ski Area, elevation 4400'.

Begin by going south around the west side of the ski buildings. Keep to the right, following a road and bending west and north. Immediately after passing under a ski lift, turn left (northwest) and ascend a 4-wheel track, at first in dense forest, then making one bend in a talus field below cliffs. At 5900', where the road turns south to a ski lift station, leave the road and ascend northwest, following a creek and valley to a small lake (tracks). Continue up in steep meadow to the ridge and a road. Turn south on the road to a saddle at the upper station of a ski lift. Turn left (north) and ascend to Point 6776'. After going south to the ski terminal and restaurant on Point 6840' for the view, return north to the low point, then descend east in meadow to the road at a ski lift terminal. Return on the road to the starting point.

CRYSTAL EAST LOOP, high point 6856', 14 miles RT, 4000' gain (Maps: USGS Norse Peak, GT Bumping Lake). **Hike-3**. Drive as above to the Crystal Mountain Ski Area parking lot.

Hike south from the parking lot, passing left (east) of the church. Find a trail and ascend, at first southeast for 100' of gain, then turning northeast into a 4-wheel track. Begin the Bullion Basin Trail (FS-1156) at 4800' and ascend east on switchbacks to a junction (5800'). Take the left fork twice to join the Pacific Crest Trail, 6100'. Now go north to Scout Pass, 6560', where the PCT crosses to the east side of the ridge. Leave the PCT and ascend north to the summit of **Norse Peak**, 6856'. For summits, see above.

Return south from the summit, crossing the PCT and continue south on the ridge, going over Points 6760', 6654', and 6720' (cairn and cross). Look for Mt. St. Helens (214°). Follow the ridge south to a 6430' knob. Go south on the ridge (rocks) or drop west (brush) to the PCT and go south to Blue Bell Pass and a junction. Hike the PCT as it bends west around the next point to another junction. The trail right (northwest) descends to Bullion Basin. Turn left (northeast) and ascend a trail to Point 6479', passing a prospect with mining artifacts. Go south on the ridge, rejoining the PCT briefly, then ascend to **Crown Point**, 6480'. Descend south from Crown Point to the PCT. Now follow the PCT east and southwest through Pickhandle Gap, 5920'. After passing the Gap, leave the trail and ascend southwest to the summit of Pickhandle Point, 6361'. Follow the ridge southwest to Bear Gap, 5882'. Turn north to the starting point.

CRYSTAL LAKE, 5830', 7 miles RT, 2400' gain (Maps: Rainier: Wilderness Trip Planner, USGS White River Park, GT Mt. Rainier East). **Hike-1**. Drive 36 miles (MP-61) east from Enumclaw on SR-410 to the trailhead near Crystal Creek, elevation 3500'. Park near the maintenance sheds.

Hike southeast on the Crystal Lake trail, passing the trail to Crystal Peak at mile 1.3.

CRYSTAL PEAK, 6595', 8 miles RT, 3200' gain (Maps: Rainier: Wilderness Trip Planner, USGS White River Park, GT Mt. Rainier East). **Hike-2**. Drive as above to the trailhead for **Crystal Lake**.

Hike southeast toward Crystal Lake for 1.3 mile. Turn right at 4600' and ascend at first south, then go northeast on a rocky trail to an old lookout site.

TAMANOS MOUNTAIN, 6790', 12 miles RT, 3100' gain (Maps: Rainier: Wilderness Trip Planner, USGS White River Park, Chinook Pass, GT Mt. Rainier East). **Hike-3. Snow**. Drive 37 miles east (MP-62) from Enumclaw on SR-410. Turn right (west) through the White River entrance to Mt. Rainier National Park and park 3.7 miles from SR-410, elevation 3720'.

Hike south on the Owyhigh Lakes Trail. At 5400' in the Owyhigh Lakes basin near the saddle between Shaw Creek and Kotsuck Creek, leave the trail and ascend northwest to the ridge, then turn north to the summit for an impressive view of Governors Ridge (east). Tamanos Mtn. makes an ideal snow trip in May or June.

SUMMERLAND, 6000', 9 miles RT, 2200' gain (Maps: Rainier: Wilderness Trip Planner, USGS White River Park, Chinook Pass, Mt. Rainier East, GT Mt. Rainier West). **Hike-2**. Drive 37 miles east (MP-62) from Enumclaw on SR-410. Turn right (west) through the White River entrance to Mt. Rainier National Park and park 4.5 miles from SR-410 on the north side of the Fryingpan Creek bridge, elevation 3800'.

Hike south and west in the valley of Fryingpan Creek. At 4200', pass waterfalls that are more heard than seen. Find avalanche debris near the crossing of Fryingpan Creek (5200') where the trail is subject to frequent change and may cross snow even in September (may collapse). Reach the meadows of **Summerland** at 5950' (shelter, camping, toilet).

PANHANDLE GAP, 6760', 12 miles RT, 3000' gain (Maps: Rainier: Wilderness Trip Planner, USGS White River Park, Chinook Pass, Mt. Rainier East, GT Mt. Rainier West). **Hike-2**. This trip is most impressive during a fall storm. Pick a day when the freezing level is below 6000'. Drive and hike as above to **Summerland**, elevation 6000'.

Turn south from the shelter and ascend, at first in meadows, then passing near snow patches in bleak, forbidding country, crossing below the Fryingpan Glacier and viewing many cascades in branches of Fryingpan Creek. The trail crosses one of these branches on a footlog (intimidating if snow covered). Pass a tarn at 6350'. Before reaching Panhandle Gap some of the route above the tarn may be snow covered at any time of year. Find a viewpoint toward Ohanapecosh Park at the south edge of the gap.

MOUNT RUTH, 8690', 9 miles RT, 4600' gain (Maps: Rainier: Wilderness Trip Planner, USGS Sunrise, GT Mt. Rainier East). **Hike-3. Snow**. Drive 37 miles east (MP-62) from Enumclaw on SR-410. Turn right (west) through the White River entrance to Mt. Rainier National Park and, at five miles from SR-410, where the road turns northeast to ascend to Sunrise, go left for one mile to parking. Find the trailhead at the west end of the White River campground, elevation 4300'.

Hike west on the trail along the Inter Fork of the White River into Glacier Basin, passing a trail north to Burrough Mtn. at 2.4 miles. From Glacier Basin ascend south to the ridge, 7000', then turn southwest to a broad platform on the ridge between the Emmons Glacier and the Inter Glacier. The ascent of Mt. Ruth is best done in June when loose talus is covered by snow.

BURROUGHS MOUNTAIN, 7828', 10 miles RT, 2500' gain (Maps: Rainier: Wilderness Trip Planner, USGS Sunrise, GT Mt. Rainier East). **Hike-2**. Drive 37 miles east (MP-62) from Enumclaw on SR-410. Turn right (west) through the White River entrance to Mt. Rainier National Park and continue on the road to parking at the end of the road in Sunrise, 14 miles from SR-410, elevation 6300'.

Hike southwest over two intermediate summits (7200', 7402') to the highest point of Burroughs Mtn. and an awe-inspiring view over the Winthrop Glacier to Mt. Rainier.

BURROUGHS MOUNTAIN LOOP, high point 7828', 12 miles RT, 3600' gain (Maps: Rainier: Wilderness Trip Planner, USGS Sunrise, GT Mt. Rainier East). **Hike-2**. Drive as above for **Mt. Ruth** to parking at the trailhead near the west edge of the White River Campground, elevation 4300'.

Hike west along the Inter Fork of the White River for 2.4 miles. Turn north and ascend toward Burroughs Mtn. Where the trail turns northeast on the plateau of Burroughs Mtn., leave the trail and hike west to the highest point of Burroughs Mtn., overlooking the Winthrop Glacier. Return to the trail and proceed northwest to Sunrise. Find the trail returning to the White River Campground west and south of the Visitor Center and descend on switchbacks.

SHRINER PEAK, 5846', 9 miles RT, 3500' gain (Maps: Rainier: Wilderness Trip Planner, USGS Chinook Pass, GT Mt. Rainier East). **Hike-1**. Drive 41 miles east from Enumclaw on SR-410 to the junction at Cayuse Pass. Turn south on SR-123 for eight miles. Park at the Shriner Peak trailhead, elevation 2500'.

Ascend east and north on the trail to the summit. Elk often range in this area. Peaks visible from the summit include: Mt. Aix (95°), and, to the south, the Goat Rocks peaks north of Mt. Adams.

GROVE OF THE PATRIARCHS, 2200', 1 mile RT, no gain (Maps: Mt. Rainier National Park, USGS Chinook Pass, GT Mt. Rainier East). **Walk.** From SR-410 at Cayuse Pass, drive 11 miles south on SR-123 to the Stevens Canyon Entrance to Mt. Rainier National Park. Turn west 0.2 mile to parking.

Wander a grove of giant red cedar and Douglas fir trees, some over 8' in diameter.

FRYINGPAN MOUNTAIN, 5723', 12 miles RT, 2600' gain (Maps: USGS White Pass, GT White Pass). **Hike-3.** From Cayuse Pass on SR-410, drive 16 miles south on SR-123 to US-12. Turn east two miles, then go northeast and east on roads FS-45 and FS-4510 for five miles to the end of the road at Soda Springs Campground near an old coal mine, elevation 3200'. Cross Summit Creek (campground) at mile 2.5 from US-12.

Hike east on trail FS-44, passing a connecting trail left (northwest) to the Cowlitz trailhead at 0.5 miles. Take the left fork (northeast) at mile 2.2 on trail FS-43 to another trail junction (4400') at mile 3.1 near Jug Lake (to the north). Now go east, then turn left (northeast) staying on trail FS-43 where trail FS-41 goes east to Penoyer Lake. Pass Fryingpan Lake, then go left (west) at 4800' on a trail to the summit of Fryingpan Mtn.

TIPSOO LAKE, 5276', 1 mile RT, minimum gain (Maps: Mt. Rainier, USGS Chinook Pass, GT Mt. Rainier East). **Hike-1.** Drive 43 miles east from Enumclaw on SR-410 or 65 miles west from I-90 near Yakima on US-12 and SR-410. Park at Tipsoo Lake.

Walk trails in the meadows surrounding the lake.

NACHES PEAK LOOP, high point 5900', 4 miles RT, 700' gain (Maps: Mt. Rainier, USGS Chinook Pass, Cougar Lake, GT Bumping Lake, Mt. Rainier East). **Hike-2.** Drive as above and park at **Tipsoo Lake**, elevation 5200'.

From north of the lake, ascend on the trail east to Chinook Pass. Cross the pedestrian bridge over SR-410, then follow the Pacific Crest Trail east and southeast to a high point on the southeast shoulder of Naches Peak. Bend south and southwest, finding a trail junction 400' after passing the high point. Take the right (west) branch to cross the south side of Naches Peak. Continue on the trail as it rounds to the north, then descends to cross SR-410 and reach the starting point.

YAKIMA PEAK, 6226', 2 miles RT, 900' gain (Maps: USGS Chinook Pass, GT Mt. Rainier East). **Hike-3**. Drive 44 miles east from Enumclaw on SR-410 or 64 miles west from I-90 near Yakima on US-12 and SR-410. Park on the northwest side of the highway just east of Chinook Pass, elevation 5400'.

Leave the road and ascend west and northwest on a track to the summit.

NACHES PEAK, 6452', 4 miles RT, 1100' gain (Maps: USGS Chinook Pass, Cougar Lake, GT Mt. Rainier East, Bumping Lake). **Hike-4†**. Drive 44 miles east from Enumclaw on SR-410 or 64 miles west from I-90 near Yakima on US-12 and SR-410. Park on the east side of the highway at Chinook Pass, elevation 5400'.

Hike south to the Pacific Crest Trail. Cross the PCT and ascend southeast on a track, following the northwest ridge. Diverge on the west side to pass steeper rocks, then ascend east from 6400' to the narrow ridge crest. A final exposed 6' step down leads to the summit.

DEWEY LAKES, 5100', 6 miles RT, 1400' gain (Maps: USGS Chinook Pass, GT Mt. Rainier East). **Hike-1**. Drive 44 miles east from Enumclaw on SR-410 or 64 miles west from I-90 near Yakima on US-12 and SR-410. Park on the south side of highway SR-410 at Chinook Pass, elevation 5400'.

Hike southeast on the Pacific Crest Trail, ascending to 5900' south of a tarn before descending into the Dewey Lakes basin.

SEYMOUR PEAK, 6337', 8 miles RT, 2600' gain (Maps: USGS Chinook Pass, GT Mt. Rainier East). **Hike-3 or Hike-4†**. Drive, park, and hike as above to the **Dewey Lakes** basin.

Where the trail turns south to go between the upper and lower lakes, find a track that turns southwest along the west shore of the upper lake. After passing the south end of the upper lake, continue south on a track, ascending briefly, then contouring southwest at 5400' into an open basin that drains to the north and west. For a steeper route (**Hike-4†**), continue south on one of many tracks to the low point (5900') in the ridge between Seymour Peak and Dewey Peak to the east. Turn west and ascend on the ridge and on the south side of the ridge (steep meadow) to the summit.

For an easier route (**Hike-3**), continue southwest from the meadow at

5400' into an open valley, following a track part of the way. This valley heads into a talus slope. At 6000', turn south and ascend on snow, talus, or meadow to the east ridge. Turn right (west) to the summit. The rock fang north is lower.

FIFE'S WEST PEAK, high point 6880', 12 miles RT, 4100' gain (Maps: USGS Goose Prairie, GT Bumping Lake). **Hike-3. Norse Peak Wilderness.** East of MP-81 on SR-410, 12 miles east of Chinook Pass or 52 miles west of I-90 near Yakima, park at the Fife's Peak Viewpoint and Crow Lake trailhead, elevation 3400'.

Hike northwest on trail FS-953 above the valley of Miner Creek (north). At Grassy Saddle, 5800', leave FS-953 to contour northeast (track) across two streams, the beginnings of Miner Creek. After crossing the second stream (track disappears), ascend northeast in meadow through scattered trees to the crest at a low point, 6440'. Follow the ridge northeast to the summit cliffs (various tracks). Look down to a patch of green with a visible trail in the middle of cliffs below. Descend (50') near the base of the first buttress to a break in the cliff, then, at a shelf, contour east past a clump of dead trees through the green patch. Ascend a 10' step. Turn north in scree and broken rocks.

FIFE'S RIDGE EAST POINT, 6386', 11 miles RT, 3100' gain (Maps: USGS Goose Prairie, GT Bumping Lake). **Hike-2. Norse Peak Wilderness.** East of MP-82 on SR-410, 13 miles east of Chinook Pass or 51 miles west of I-90 near Yakima, park at the Fife's Ridge trailhead, elevation 3300'.

Hike northwest on trail FS-953 in the valley of Wash Creek, getting views of the spectacular summits of Fife's Peaks. Reach a saddle (5200') north of Fife's Peaks, then turn northeast to ascend in forest on Fife's Ridge. At 6300', before reaching the trail high point (6480'), turn right (south) to the edge of the cliffs above the American River. Look across to Goat Peak (166°).

GOAT PEAK, 6473', 8 miles RT, 3300' gain (Maps: USGS Goose Prairie, GT Bumping Lake). **Hike-1. Douglas Wilderness.** East of MP-83 on SR-410, 14 miles east of Chinook Pass or 50 miles from I-90 near Yakima, park east of a bridge over the American River. Find the trailhead across from Hell's Crossing Campground, elevation 3300'.

Hike south on the Goat Creek Trail, FS-958C, to the crest of American Ridge, meeting trail FS-958 on the ridge, 5800'. Turn southwest and ascend to the summit, an old lookout site.

OLD SCAB MOUNTAIN, 6608', 10 miles RT, 3700' gain (Maps: USGS Old Scab Mtn., GT Old Scab Mtn.) **Hike-3. Douglas Wilderness.** East of MP-88 on SR-410, 19 miles east of Chinook Pass or 45 miles from I-90 near Yakima, turn south on road FS-18 for 5.4 miles to the Soda Springs Campground. Turn left (east) into the campground and drive 0.2 miles to the trailhead at the footbridge over the Bumping River, elevation 3000'. Find the mineral springs on the east side of the river.

Cross the footbridge and turn right (upstream) for 0.1 mile. At a trail junction, turn left (east) and ascend on trail FS-975, meeting an older version of the trail at mile 0.8, 3600'. Stay on the trail as it ascends south, sometimes steeply, toward the east shoulder of Old Scab Mtn. At 5600', where the trail turns to the southeast in an open forest of small lodgepole pine trees (note depression west of the trail), leave the trail and go southwest, rising gradually but staying below a tumble of talus blocks. After passing the last of the talus blocks and emerging from forest, turn north to the southeast ridge of Old Scab Mtn., avoiding steeper terrain. Ascend the open sandy slope northwest. Pass over or around rocky false summits to the final peak. On the return, look for a pond in the saddle (5700') southeast of Old Scab Mtn.

MOUNT AIX, 7779', 12 miles RT, 4200' gain (Maps: USGS Bumping Lake, GT Bumping Lake). **Hike-1. Douglas Wilderness.** East of MP-88 on SR-410, 19 miles east of Chinook Pass or 45 miles from I-90 near Yakima, turn south on roads FS-18/395 past Bumping Lake. Find the trailhead 15 miles from SR-410 where FS-18 crosses Copper Creek, elevation 3660'.

Hike southeast on trail FS-982. The last two miles are above 7000', along an airy ridge, especially impressive if a storm is on the way.

TWIN SISTERS LAKES, 5200', 6 miles RT, 1000' gain (Maps: USGS Bumping Lake, Spiral Butte, GT Bumping Lake, White Pass). **Hike-1. Douglas Wilderness.** East of MP-88 on SR-410, 19 miles east of Chinook Pass or 45 miles from I-90 near Yakima, turn south on roads FS-18/395 past Bumping Lake to the end of the road at Deep Creek Campground, elevation 4200' and 20 miles from SR-410.

Hike south on trail FS-980 to the first of the Twin Sisters Lakes Turn west to the second and larger lake.

BLANKENSHIP MEADOW, 5200', 6 miles RT, 1000' gain (Maps: USGS Bumping Lake, Spiral Butte, GT Bumping Lake, White Pass). **Hike-1. Douglas Wilderness.** Camp here on the edge of the meadows to explore this region of many lakes and summits. East of MP-88 on

SR-410, 19 miles east of Chinook Pass or 45 miles from I-90 near Yakima, turn south on roads FS-18/395 past Bumping Lake to the trailhead 29 miles from SR-410, elevation 4040'.

Hike south on trail FS-1105 to the first trail junction in well-named Mosquito Valley. Many campsites and elk.

TUMAC MOUNTAIN, 6339', 8 miles RT, 2200' gain (Maps: USGS Spiral Butte, GT White Pass). **Hike-1. Douglas Wilderness.** Hike as above to the first **Twin Sister Lake.**

From the trail junction east of the lake, continue south on trail FS-44 to the summit. If camping in Blankenship Meadow, go to the trail intersection at the north end of the meadows, then turn west for 1.4 miles to trail FS-44. Turn south to the summit.

PEAR BUTTE, 6372', 8 miles RT, 1500' gain (Maps: USGS Spiral Butte, GT White Pass). **Hike-3. Douglas Wilderness.** Hike as above to **Blankenship Meadows.**

Continue southeast on trail FS-1105 for less than a mile to a trail junction near Blankenship Lakes. Turn east on the same trail to another trail junction near Indian Meadows. Now go north on trail FS-1148 to a junction near Apple Lake. From here, Pear Lake is 0.5 mile east on trail FS-1148. Continue north on trail FS-979 for one mile to the west shoulder of Pear Butte, 5800'. Leave the trail and ascend northeast.

Carbon River Area. From SR-167 or SR-512 east of Tacoma, exit east to SR-410. At 12 miles, turn south on SR-165 through Wilkeson and Carbonado, old coal-mining settlements. Cross a spectacular bridge over the Carbon River five miles south of Wilkeson, then turn left (east) to reach the Carbon River entrance into Mt. Rainier National Park, 20 miles from SR-410. This paved road is usually open by the first of May. Forest road FS-7810 going north across the Carbon River from near the entrance to Mt. Rainier Park has been closed for several years. Reopening is planned. The road to Ipsut Campground has also been closed. Call Park Information 206-470-4060.

WILKESON, 800', minimum gain (USGS Wilkeson). **Walk.** This area is noted for coal mining and a sandstone quarry. Park in the center of the town for a stroll along the main street and on side streets to the turn of the century church with green onion dome. The City Hall and Library on the west side of the street and the schoolhouse on Railroad St. at the south end of town are built of Wilkeson sandstone.

Drive or walk east on Railroad St. for 0.2 miles to the double row of coke ovens on the south side of the street. Some of these date from before 1900 and range from nearly intact to completely collapsed. At least one is still filled with material that was never fired. The tree-covered hill to the west is mostly spent material from the coke ovens.

The entrance to the Wilkeson Sandstone Quarry is 0.3 miles east of the coke ovens at the next intersection. The quarry (private) is nearly hidden in the trees to the north of the road.

OLD BALDY MOUNTAIN, 5796', 6 miles RT, 2600' gain (Maps: USGS Bearhead Mtn., Old Baldy Mtn., GT Enumclaw). **Hike-3**. From SR-165 near the Carbon River entrance to Mt. Rainier National Park, turn north across the Carbon River on road SR-7810 for three miles. Park where a rough branch road goes north, elevation 3268'.

Hike this branch road north and west, crossing Kennedy Creek. At 3900', where the road bends east, leave the road and ascend west.

BEARHEAD MOUNTAIN, 6089', 6 miles RT, 1800' gain (Maps: USGS Bearhead Mtn., GT Enumclaw). **Hike-1. Clearwater Wilderness.** From SR-165 near the Carbon River entrance to Mt. Rainier National Park, drive north across the Carbon River on road SR-7810 for seven miles to the trailhead above Conley Lake, elevation 4400'.

Hike trail FS-1179 to a junction, 5200', then go north to the summit, a lookout site. Peaks visible from the summit include: Frog Mtn. (56°), Redstone Peak (138°), Florence Peak (230°), and Tolmie Peak (24°).

EAST BEARHEAD MOUNTAIN, 6041', 8 miles RT, 2000' gain (Maps: USGS Bearhead Mtn., GT Enumclaw). **Hike-2. Clearwater Wilderness.** Drive as above to the trailhead for **Bearhead Mtn**.

Hike trail FS-1179 south and south east past the junction of the trail going to Bearhead Mtn. Continue southeast on trail FS-1179 until the trail turns east at the southwest ridge of East Bearhead Mtn. Leave the trail and ascend northeast to the summit.

FLORENCE PEAK, 5501', 9 miles RT, 3800' gain (Maps: USGS Golden Lakes, GT Mt. Rainier West). **Hike-3. Snow.** Drive to the Carbon River entrance to Mt. Rainier National Park, elevation 1760'.

Find the West Boundary Trail by hiking south on either branch of the interpretive trail, which begins on the south side of the road near the entrance. At a high point, 4500', before the trail begins to descend to Tolmie Creek, leave the trail and ascend southeast, at first in forest, then on an open ridge, to the summit. This trip can be done in May or

June when some of the travel will be on snow.

TOLMIE PEAK, 5939', 12 or 21 miles RT, 3800' gain (Maps: Rainier: Wilderness Trip Planner, USGS Golden Lakes, Mowich Lake, GT Mt. Rainier West). **Mtn. Bicycle and/or Hike-2**. From the Carbon River entrance to Mt. Rainier National Park, ride or drive east into the park for five miles to the Ipsut Creek trailhead, elevation 2300'.

Ascend southwest in the Ipsut Creek Valley to Ipsut Pass, 5150'. Turn right (north) on the trail past Eunice Lake to the lookout site then go east to the summit, an excellent overlook to summits: Mother Mountain (120°), Fay Peak (142°), and Observation Rock southeast of Spray Park (139°).

CARBON GLACIER, high point 3600', 17 miles RT, 2000' gain (Maps: Mt. Rainier: Wilderness Trip Planner, USGS Mowich Lake, GT Mt. Rainier West). **Mtn. Bicycle and Hike-1**. From the Carbon River entrance to Mt. Rainier National Park, elevation 1760', ride or drive east and southeast for five miles to the Ipsut Creek trailhead, elevation 2300'.

Park or leave bicycle and hike southeast along the Carbon River, passing the trail to Ipsut Pass, the Northern Loop Trail (mile 2.0), and joining the Wonderland Trail at mile 3. Cross the Carbon River on a high, unstable suspension bridge. Turn right and ascend to a view of the ice at the end of the glacier. The upper surface is covered by rocks. Plan to have lunch at this viewpoint. In 30 minutes, expect to see rock fall several times. On the return, make a loop by descending on the northeast side of the Carbon River to the Northern Loop trail. This trail crosses the Carbon River on log bridges (handrails) that may not be accessible during high water.

Mowich Lake Area

Drive as above toward the **Carbon River** entrance to Mt. Rainier National Park. South of the bridge over the Carbon River, turn right on the Mowich Lake road and drive 11 miles to the park entrance, 3500'. Reach the parking area at Mowich Lake, 5000', at 19 miles from the Carbon River Road. The road to Mowich Lake east of the park boundary is usually closed until at least the first of July. Call Park Information, 206-470-4060.

MARTIN, VIRGINIA, AUGUST, BERRY PEAKS, 4880', 4880', 4680', 5120', 8 miles RT, 3000' gain (Maps: USGS Golden Lakes, GT Mt. Rainier West). **Hike-3CMA**. These are summits only green belt summit baggers or forest elves will love, but almost all of the off trail travel is in delightful, open, ancient forest on gentle gradient.

Drive the Mowich Lake road to the east boundary of Mt. Rainier National Park. Park near the Boundary Trail 0.1 mile east of the park boundary sign, elevation 3600'.

This trail is no longer maintained and may be hard to find. Look for the trail at the north edge of the road in a clump of trees at the first place east of the boundary sign that is not a steep bank. Hike north on the Boundary Trail, finding a 'Trail Not Maintained' sign. Where the trail levels on the east side of Martin Peak, 4500', leave the trail and ascend west to the summit. Continue north from Martin Peak to join the trail on the ridge leading to Virginia Peak. Where the trail crosses the west ridge of Virginia Peak, 4700', leave the trail and ascend east to the summit. Return west to the trail and continue north and northwest on the south side of August Peak to cross the park boundary and meet a road in the saddle between Evans Creek and Tolmie Creek. From this saddle, hike the ridge east to August Peak. Contrast the appearance of the terrain outside the park with that inside the park. Give thanks for National Parks and be happy to pay user fees.

On the return, leave the trail at 4400' where the trail turns south after crossing under August Peak. Ascend east to the Berry Peak ridge and follow the ridge to Berry Peak. Return west to the trail and follow the trail south to the Mowich Lake road and the starting point.

PAUL PEAK, 4800', 5 miles RT, 1700' gain (Maps: Mount Rainier, USGS Golden Lakes, GT Mt. Rainier West). **Hike-3CMA**. The rewards: views of many different aspects of open ancient forest and, to the south, the tantalizing blue depths of the Mowich River valley, plus the challenge of not getting lost in this confusing terrain. Drive the Mowich Lake road 0.7 miles east of the boundary of Mt. Rainier National Park to parking for the Paul Peak Trail, elevation 3700'.

Hike the trail south in ancient forest, descending to a crossing of Meadow Creek, then contouring near 3500' across the west and south sides of Paul Peak. Where the trail begins to descend in switchbacks into the valley of the Mowich River, leave the trail and ascend northwest in open forest, passing west of cliffs at 4400'. This rock buttress makes a good landmark for the return. Reach the west ridge above the buttress and turn east to the summit (cairn). On the return, use care to return to the trail somewhere on the south side of Paul Peak. Do not follow the ridge that descends west from the summit as it bends to the northwest. With luck, find a curious forested flat above the trail and east of the southwest ridge of Paul Peak.

TOLMIE PEAK, 5939', 7 miles RT, 1000' gain (Maps: Rainier: Wilderness Trip Planner, USGS Golden Lakes, Mowich Lake, GT Mt. Rainier West). **Hike-1**. Drive to parking at the north end of Mowich Lake, elevation 5000'.

From Mowich Lake, hike the Ipsut Pass trail north around the west side of the lake. At Ipsut Pass, take the left fork (northwest) to go around Eunice Lake and ascend to the lookout. Go on to the east summit for the view into the Ipsut Creek canyon.

GOVE PEAK, 5310', 8 miles RT, 1500' gain (Maps: Mount Rainier, USGS Mowich Lake, GT Mt. Rainier West). **Hike-3CMA**. An orienteering challenge. Drive as above to parking at the north end of Mowich Lake.

From Mowich Lake, hike north around the lake to Ipsut Pass. Take the left (northwest) fork toward Eunice Lake, then leave the trail west of the pass and ascend north to 5650'. Continue north, descending to the northwest side of the Gove Peak ridge. Turn northeast and follow the crest of the ridge or the northwest side (some brush) over an intermediate 5500' point to forested Gove Peak. Beyond, the ridge drops sharply.

CASTLE SOUTH PEAK, 6120', 4 miles RT, 1800' gain (Maps: Mount Rainier, USGS Mowich Lake, GT Mt. Rainier West). **Hike-3CMA**. Drive as above to parking at the south end of Mowich Lake. The South Peak of Castle is slightly higher than the point marked on the USGS map as the summit of Castle Peak.

From Mowich Lake, hike north around the west side of the lake on the trail toward Ipsut Pass. Where the trail begins to descend (5050') and 0.25 mile from Mowich Lake, leave the trail and ascend northeast in dense forest on a faint track. As the slope becomes steeper, bend east to follow along the break in the slope. At 5300', pass through meadows. At 5400', where a contour line on the slope points southeast, turn north and ascend to the west ridge of Castle Peak, 5560'. The north side of this ridge is open and brush free, providing a view into the canyon of Ipsut Creek.

Continue east up this ridge to cliffs. Pass these rocks on the right (south) side into a talus slope. Ascend east to pass through a notch and reach the crest of the southwest ridge. At the crest of the ridge, continue east to the highest point, 6120'. From the high point, descend south, finding a track in the dense growth of mountain hemlock on the west side of the ridge. Emerge to an open saddle, 6000'. A track goes north from this saddle around the east side of the south peak to the named summit (USGS map) of Castle Peak. Now go south and southeast on an open, meadow ridge, ascending over another minor point, 6320'. Continue southeast on this open ridge to the pinnacles that are the beginning of Mother Mountain. Now turn southwest and descend in trees or steep meadows (cliffs) into the canyon that drops west from Knapsack Pass, meeting the Knapsack Pass trail in meadows near 5700'. Turn west and descend on the trail, passing the Mowich Lake Ranger Cabin.

MOTHER MOUNTAIN POINT 6480, 6480', 4 miles RT, 1600' gain (Maps: Mount Rainier, USGS Mowich Lake, GT Mt. Rainier West). **Hike-2**. Drive as above to parking at the south end of Mowich Lake.

From Mowich Lake, hike around the south and east side of the lake to the beginning of the trail to Knapsack Pass, located at the Mowich Lake Ranger Station. This trail ascends near the creek that descends west from Knapsack Pass, crossing several branches. From the pass, turn north and ascend a track to the ridge of Mother Mtn. Go east, passing north of the first pinnacle to Point 6480'.

FAY PEAK, 6492', 4 miles RT, 1600' gain (Maps: Mount Rainier, USGS Mowich Lake, GT Mt. Rainier West). **Hike-3**. Drive as above to parking at the south end of Mowich Lake.

From Mowich Lake, hike as above for Mother Mountain Point 6480 toward Knapsack Pass. At 5400', where the trail bends northeast near a stream, cross the stream to follow a track south, ascending to the west ridge of Fay Peak. At the crest of the ridge, turn east up the ridge (track) to the summit.

SPRAY PARK, high point 6400', 8 miles RT, 2300' gain (Maps: Rainier: Wilderness Trip Planner, USGS Mowich Lake, GT Mt. Rainier West). **Hike-1**. Drive as above to parking near the south end of Mowich Lake.

From Mowich Lake, hike south on the Wonderland Trail, leaving the Wonderland Trail at mile 0.2 to contour south and southeast, crossing Lee Creek. At mile 1.5 a spur trail descends 50' to a viewpoint over Eagle Cliff, and at mile 2.0 a trail goes southeast to Spray Creek and a view of **Spray Falls**. Reach the beginning of the meadows of Spray Park at mile 2.5, 5700'. No camping and no fires in these fragile meadows.

MOUNT PLEASANT, 6454', 7 miles RT, 2400' gain (Maps: Mount Rainier, USGS Mowich Lake, GT Mt. Rainier West). **Hike-3**. Drive as above to parking at the south end of Mowich Lake.

Hike as above to the beginning of Spray Park, 5700'. At the west end of a pond, find a well-used track that crosses the outlet from the pond. Hike north on this track, ascending to the saddle between Mt. Pleasant and Hessong Rock, 6200'. Turn right (east) at the saddle and ascend on a track that continues to the rock summit.

HESSONG ROCK, 6385', 8 miles RT, 2400' gain (Maps: Mount Rainier, USGS Mowich Lake, GT Mt. Rainier West). **Hike-3**. Drive as above to parking near the south end of Mowich Lake.

From Mowich Lake, hike as above for Mt. Pleasant to the saddle (6200') between Mt. Pleasant and Hessong Rock. At the saddle, turn left (west) and descend briefly on the north side of the east ridge of Hessong Rock, then ascend on a talus field or snow toward the west ridge. On nearing the west ridge, find a track that ascends east to the summit.

ECHO ROCK, 7870', 14 miles RT, 3700' gain (Maps: Mount Rainier, USGS Mowich Lake, GT Mt. Rainier West). **Hike-4†, Snow**. From parking at Mowich Lake, hike as above to **Spray Park**.

At a high point, 6400', where the trail begins to descend toward the Carbon River, leave the Wonderland Trail and go southeast on a track, ascending toward Echo Rock. At 7200', near the base of Echo Rock, turn south and continue up along the west side of Echo Rock. The remnant ice of Flett Glacier is immediately west and some of the surface is often exposed by August or September. Near the crest of the ridge that connects Echo Rock to Mt. Rainier, 7640', turn north and find the well-traveled route to the top of Echo Rock.

OBSERVATION ROCK, 8364', 15 miles RT, 4300' gain (Maps: Mount Rainier, USGS Mowich Lake, GT Mt. Rainier West). **Hike-4†, Snow**. Hike as above to the crest of the ridge that connects **Echo Rock** with Observation Rock, 7640'.

Turn south to 7800', then go southeast and ascend on snow or loose talus to the slope south of Observation Rock. At 8100', turn northwest to the summit. Above 7200', much of this route is almost always snow-covered.

Nisqually River Area

From I-5 at Tacoma, drive south on SR-7, or from SR-512 near Puyallup, drive south on SR-161, meeting SR-7 south of Eatonville. Where SR-7 turns south, continue east on SR-706.

NORTHWEST TREK WILDLIFE PARK, 700', 5 miles of trails,

100' gain (Map: USGS Tanwax Lake). **Hike-1**. A Division of the Metropolitan Park District of Tacoma, the park is located south of MP-9 on SR-161 between Puyallup and Eatonville.

Facilities and activities: tram tour of animals of the northwest, accessible trails, self-guided nature tours, hands-on education center, picnic pavilion, theater. Fee.

PACK FOREST, high point 2080', 10 miles RT, 1300' gain (Maps: USGS Eatonville). **Hike-1**. The facility is located between Tacoma and La Grande on SR-7 south of MP-27 and the junction with SR-161, elevation 800'. The University of Washington operates the Charles L. Pack Experimental Forest for research. Visitors are encouraged and the forest is open to pedestrians and bicyclists during daylight hours except during logging. Find maps of the area at the information building located on SR-7. On week days, some roads are open to motor vehicles.

HUGO PEAK, 1780', 4 miles RT, 1000' gain (Maps: Pack Forest, USGS Eatonville). **Hike-1**. Drive as above to parking at the entrance to **Pack Forest**, elevation 800'.

The trail begins on the south side of the entrance, crossing road 1600 at 1000' and road 1000 at 1040'. After leaving road 1000, the trail bends northwest before turning east to cross road 1400, elevation 1300'. At road 1081, turn left (north) to road 1080, then continue left (north) to the summit. North of the intersection of roads 1080 and 1081, the trail continues on the west side of the gravel road. From the summit, trees block the view to the east, but Mt. Baker (10°) and the Olympic Mountains are visible.

Return to the junction of roads 1080 and 1081, then turn southeast on road 1080, descending to Kirkland Pass. At Kirkland Pass, find and follow the Trail of the Giants, descending southwest in giant ancient forest. Along the way, this trail follows the top of a fallen log for 50' and passes through a cut in a 5' diameter cedar tree. Below the ancient forest, the trail ascends east in a regrowing clearcut to road 2000. Return northeast on the road to Kirkland Pass. Now follow road 1000 west, crossing or taking the Hugo Peak Trail to the starting point.

This trip can also begin from the visitor parking area north of the administration building and 0.3 mile from the entrance on SR-7. Hike 0.5 mile south on road 1000 to the crossing of the Hugo Peak Trail south of the junction with road 1600.

PACK LOOKOUT, 2040', 9 miles RT, 1200' gain (Maps: Pack Forest, USGS Eatonville). **Mtn. Bicycle or Hike-1**. From the entrance to the Pack Forest on SR-7, drive 0.3 mile northeast to park in the Visitor Parking Area north of the administration building, elevation 900'.

Immediately east of the parking area, ride or hike northeast on North Lathrop Drive (road 1000), passing a gate that is closed at 4:30pm. Roads 1010, 1020, 1200, 1040, 1050, and 1060, turn off right or left at miles 0.6, 1.1, 1.2, and 1.4. Reach storage tanks at mile 1.8, elevation 1150'. The road to the left, 1070, goes to the Falls Trail. Keep right on road 1000, which bends south, then turn left (south) at mile 2.0 on road 1300 where road 1000 bends southeast. At mile 2.9, 1660', road 1330 turn left (northeast) to the Eatonville-Alder Road. Stay right on road 1300 to join road 2500 at mile 3.2, 1780'. At mile 3.6, go right on road 2080, a narrow, rough, grass track, meeting road 2000 near the summit. Across from the junction with road 2000, find a trail going west into the forest to the foundations for the former lookout tower. The forest obscures the view.

Continue west on the trail to rejoin road 2000 at mile 3.9. Descend briefly west, then turn north on road 2070 to a viewpoint north and west. Return south to road 2000 and continue southwest to road 2500 at mile 4.2, a viewpoint south and southeast. Road 2300 goes southeast at mile 4.8. At mile 5.6, near a junction with road 2010, 1700', find the Windy Ridge Trail at the north edge of a recent clearcut (1996). Hike this trail east along the edge of ancient forest to another summit (2020') and viewpoint. Return to road 2000 and continue north to Kirkland Pass, mile 7.0 and elevation 1580'. From Kirkland Pass, the Trail of the Giants goes southwest into giant ancient forest, road 1080 goes north to Hugo Peak, road 2000 goes southeast to Pack Lookout, road 1000 goes east to a junction with road 1300 before continuing to the parking area. Turn west and descend on road 1000, rounding south before turning west, northwest and north, to return to the start.

LITTLE MASHEL FALLS, high point 1170', 6 miles RT, 700' gain (Maps: Pack Forest, USGS Eatonville). **Hike-2**. From the entrance to the Pack Forest on SR-7, drive 0.3 mile northeast to park in the Visitor Parking Area north of the administration building, elevation 900'.

Immediately east of the parking area, hike north on North Lathrop Drive (road 1000), passing a gate and reaching storage tanks at mile 1.8, 1150'. Go left (east) on road 1070 to the beginning of the Falls Trail, mile 2.1. Descend north on the trail to a junction, mile 2.4. Go right (east), keeping right to the highest falls. Return on the trail, taking two more right forks to other waterfalls before returning to the main trail.

Descend for 0.1 mile, going over a rough, bouldery washout, to another branch. Turn east on a rough, steep trail to the pool at the base of the multiple falls. Return to the main trail and descend to the grade of the Tacoma Eastern Railroad at mile 3.4, elevation 800'. Turn left (east) to road 1010 at mile 5. Go left (northeast) and ascend past a gate to road 1000. Turn right (southwest) to the start.

ELBE, 1800', 0.5 mile RT, no gain. **Walk**. Drive SR-7 for 40 miles south from Tacoma.

Points of interest: Evangelische Kirche (Lutheran) with 46' steeple dates from 1906. The Railroad Museum, with two gear drive logging locomotives (one still operating), has a restaurant and motel that uses old railroad cars. Steam train excursions in summer.

OSBORNE MOUNTAIN, 5116', 9 miles RT, 3400' gain (Maps: USGS Sawtooth Ridge, GT Randle). **Hike-3**. Near MP-10, two miles east of Ashford on SR-706, turn south on road FS-52, crossing the Nisqually River. Stay on road FS-52 as it bends east. Park at the trailhead in Big Creek Campground, elevation 1800', two miles from SR-706.

Hike south on trail FS-250, turning left (east) three miles from road FS-52 on the west ridge, 3900'. At the first clearcut, 4200', Mt. St. Helens is visible. Where the trail meets a road in a saddle, 4650', look south to the fangs of Sawtooth Ridge. Turn left (north) on the road as it bends west to the west ridge, 4900'. Leave the road and ascend the ridge east to the highest mossy bald viewpoint: Rainier, Adams, and High Rock Lookout. Continue along the ridge to an opening where the road is immediately below and pointing south (158°) at the 4650' saddle. Descend to road and return to the trailhead by the outgoing route.

HIGH ROCK LOOKOUT, 5685', 3.2 miles RT, 1400' gain (Maps: USGS Sawtooth Ridge, GT Randle). **Hike-2**. Near MP-10, two miles east of Ashford on SR-706, turn south on road FS-52, crossing the Nisqually River. Stay on road FS-52 as it bends east. East of MP-4, turn south on road FS-84, passing road FS-8410 on the right at mile 9.3 from SR-706, road FS-8420 at mile 10 and road FS-8430 at mile 11.6. At mile 12, go right on road FS-8440, ascending in the valley of Berry Creek. At mile 13, get a first view of the lookout on the top of its cliff. The road then bends west to the ridge crest and the trailhead, 15 miles from SR-706, elevation 4300'.

Hike northwest on the crest of a narrow ridge. A bench at 4800' provides a view of the lookout building. At 5400', the trail travels on the summit rock. This is definitely not a place to wander around in a fog. Some of the cracks in the summit block drop 500'. The building stands exactly on the edge of the cliff and provides a 360° view: Camp

Muir (36°), Cowlitz Chimney (45°), Pinnacle Peak (60°), Unicorn (66°), Goat Rocks (120°), St. Helens (203°), and Beljica (346°). Look down the face of the cliff from the protection of the cables that anchor the building.

In July, the following flowers were in blossom: tiger lily, honeysuckle, beargrass, lupine, penstemon, and arnica.

LOOKOUT MOUNTAIN, 5475', 2 miles RT, 1000' gain (Maps: USGS Wahpenayo, GT Randle). **Hike-3**. Drive as above for High Rock Lookout to the junction of roads FS-52 with FS-84. Stay on road FS-52. East of MP-9, where road FS-52 bends south, continue east on road FS-5230. Drive 5.9 miles from road FS-52 and park at a landing and log pile, elevation 4700'.

Hike the road southwest until near the crest of the ridge. Leave the road, ascend to the ridge crest, then go east on intermittent tracks on or near the ridge to the high point. Summits in view: Chutla (2°), Wahpenayo (12°), Denman (30°), Plummer (35°), Pinnacle (38°), Tatoosh Lookout (96°), Wow (304°). Iron (336°), and Eagle (358°).

LAKE CHRISTINE, 4802', 6 miles RT, 1100' gain (Maps: USGS Mt. Wow, GT Mt. Rainier West). **Hike-1. Glacier View Wilderness.** Near MP-10, and three miles east of Ashford on SR-706, turn north on road FS-59. At 4.5 miles from road SR-706, go right on a branch road for a mile to the trailhead, 4400'.

Hike the trail, which ascends first on the south side of the ridge, then contours and ascends in giant ancient forest to the lake. Find several campsites beyond the north end of the lake (no fires).

MOUNT BELJICA, 5475', 8 miles RT, 1800' gain (Maps: USGS Mt. Wow, GT Mt. Rainier West). **Hike-1. Glacier View Wilderness.**

Drive and hike as above to Lake Christine, 4802'. Continue north past the lake to a junction at 5000' on the southwest shoulder of Mt. Beljica. Take the left (northwest) fork and ascend to the summit for a spectacular viewpoint toward Mt. Rainier. Other summits: High Rock Lookout (166°), Mt. Adams (152°), Mt. St. Helens (195°), and Mt. Wow (110°). In the trees southwest of the summit, look for pieces of the tool shed formerly used by the lookout .

The trail that branches to the right at 5000' goes on to Goat Lake, then enters Mt. Rainier National Park near Gobblers Knob.

South Mount Rainier Area. Maps: Mount Rainier.

WESTSIDE ROAD, high point 4100', 25 miles RT, 3000' gain (Maps: Rainier: Wilderness Trip Planner, USGS Mount Wow, Mt. Rainier West, GT Mt. Rainier West). **Mt. Bicycle**. One mile east of the entrance to Mt. Rainier National Park, turn north and park at the gate, elevation 2000'.

Ride northeast and north, getting a view of Tahoma Creek at mile 1.7, then travelling just above the tangle of flood-carried trees along the creek at mile 2.3. At mile 2.9, pass a forest of dead trees, killed by past floods. Note the dense new growth of young alder trees in the dead forest. At mile 3.2, reach the Fish Creek gate (information), elevation 2900'. After crossing Fish Creek at mile 3.5, the road deteriorates briefly as a result of outburst floods from Tahoma Creek. Reach Tahoma Vista at mile 5.4, 3500'. Note the well-fitted boulder retaining walls and other constructions at the vista. Trails go east to a viewpoint and north to restrooms, now closed. Look southwest to the summit of Mount Wow. The road now makes a switchback southwest to Round Pass, mile 7 and elevation 3900'. Pause at the monument commemorating a Marine airplane crash in 1946. The trail to Gobblers Knob Lookout (2.4 miles) and Lake George (0.9 miles) begins here.

After Round Pass, the road descends to cross the South Fork of the Puyallup River, 3500' and mile 8.3, where the South Puyallup Trail goes east. Beyond a low point, 3250', the road rises to cross St. Andrews Creek, 11.2 miles, 3800'. Trails on each side of the bridge over St. Andrews Creek descend to a view of **Denman Falls**. Near the bridge over the creek, look southwest (206°) to Mount Beljica. The St. Andrews Ranger Station is 0.1 mile upstream from the north side of the bridge and a trail also connects to the Wonderland Trail. Continue to Klapatche Point, mile 12.1 and 4100', the end of the bicycle route. From here, the old road, now a trail, descends 2.8 miles to the North Fork of the Puyallup River and a junction with the Wonderland Trail, 3600'.

LAKE GEORGE, 4292', 14 miles RT bicycling and 2 miles RT hiking, 2400' gain (Maps: Rainier: Wilderness Trip Planner, USGS Mount Wow, GT Mt. Rainier West). **Mtn. Bicycle and Hike-1**. One mile east of the entrance to Mt. Rainier National Park, turn north and park at the now closed Westside Road, elevation 2000'.

Ride north on the Westside Road for seven miles to Round Pass, 3900'. Leave bicycle and hike west and south for one mile on the trail to Lake George.

GOBBLERS KNOB, 5485', 14 miles RT bicycling and 5 miles RT hiking, 2600' gain (Maps: Rainier: Wilderness Trip Planner, USGS Mount Wow, GT Mt. Rainier West). **Bicycle and Hike-1**. Drive, ride, and hike as above to **Lake George**.

Continue on the trail past the lake and ascend west, meeting a trail from Goat Lake 1.2 miles west of Lake George. At the trail junction, turn right (north) to the rock summit, part of an ancient volcanic eruption.

INDIAN HENRYS HUNTING GROUND, high point 5600', 12 miles RT, 3500' gain (Maps: Rainier: Wilderness Trip Planner, USGS Mt. Rainier West, Wahpenayo Peak, GT Mt. Rainier West, Randle). **Hike-1**. Three miles east of the Nisqually Entrance to Mt. Rainier National Park, park at the Kautz Creek trailhead, elevation 2400'.

Hike north on the trail for six miles, passing over the east shoulder of Mt. Ararat, to join the Wonderland Trail in Indian Henrys Hunting Ground, 5500'.

Alternate approach: from the trailhead at Longmire, 2800', hike north over Rampart Ridge, then cross Ranger and Kautz Creeks to Indian Henrys Hunting Ground in the same distance and 3000' gain.

MOUNT ARARAT, 6010', 9 miles RT, 3700' gain (Maps: Mount Rainier, USGS Mt. Rainier West, Wahpenayo Peak, GT Mt. Rainier West, Randle). **Hike-3. Snow**. Park and hike as above from the Kautz Creek trailhead toward **Indian Henrys Hunting Ground**.

Leave the trail where it turns northeast at 5400' and continue north in open forest to the summit. This summit makes an excellent snow trip in May or June.

COPPER MOUNTAIN, 6300', 14 miles RT, 4600' gain (Maps: Mount Rainier, USGS Mt. Rainier West, Wahpenayo Peak, GT Mt. Rainier West, Randle). **Hike-3**. Drive, park, and hike as above to the Wonderland Trail junction in **Indian Henrys Hunting Ground**, or camp at one of the designated campsites.

From the junction of the Kautz Creek Trail with the Wonderland Trail, 5300', continue north on the Wonderland Trail until the Wonderland Trail begins to descend to Tahoma Creek, 5300'. Go right (northeast) on the trail toward the Mirror Lakes area. Leave the trail at 5400' and ascend southeast to the south ridge of Copper Mtn. Turn north up the ridge to the summit.

IRON MOUNTAIN, 6283', 14 miles RT, 4600' gain (Maps: Mount

Rainier, USGS Mt. Rainier West, Wahpenayo Peak, GT Mt. Rainier West, Randle). **Hike-3**. Drive, park, and hike as above for **Copper Mtn.**

From the saddle south of Copper Mtn., ascend southeast to the summit of Iron Mtn.

PYRAMID PEAK, 6937', 16 miles RT, 5200' gain (Maps: Mount Rainier, USGS Mt. Rainier West, Wahpenayo Peak, GT Mt. Rainier West, Randle). **Hike-3**. Hike as above for **Copper Mountain** to Mirror Lakes, 5400'.

Continue northeast on a track that ascends on the south ridge of Pyramid Peak to the summit and a view over the Tahoma Glacier (north). Look up to the summit of Mt. Rainier more than 7000' higher.

LONGMIRE, 2700' (Maps: Rainier: Wilderness Trip Planner, USGS Mt. Rainier West, Wahpenayo Peak, GT Mt. Rainier West, Randle). Drive five miles east of the Nisqually Entrance to Mt. Rainier National Park. Facilities and activities: one mile nature trail, store, Visitor Center, information, hotel, schedule of activities, trail access, back country permits.

EAGLE PEAK, 5958', 8 miles RT, 3300' gain (Maps: Rainier: Wilderness Trip Planner, USGS Mt. Rainier West, Wahpenayo Peak, GT Mt. Rainier West, Randle). **Hike-4†**. Drive five miles east from the Nisqually Entrance to Longmire, elevation 2700'.

Hike east on the Eagle Peak Trail to the saddle between Eagle Peak and Chutla Peak. Leave the trail and ascend north, crossing an airy ledge to the summit of Eagle Peak.

CHUTLA PEAK, 6000', 8 miles RT, 3400' gain (Maps: Rainier: Wilderness Trip Planner, USGS Mt. Rainier West, Wahpenayo Peak, GT Mt. Rainier West, Randle). **Hike-3**. Drive, park, and hike as above for **Eagle Peak** to the saddle between Eagle Peak and Chutla Peak.

Leave the trail at the saddle and ascend south to the summit.

WAHPENAYO PEAK, 6231', 9 miles RT, 3600' gain (Maps: Rainier: Wilderness Trip Planner, USGS Mt. Rainier West, Wahpenayo Peak, GT Mt. Rainier West, Randle). **Hike-3**. Drive, park, and hike as above to **Chutla Peak**.

Descend east to the saddle between Chutla Peak and Wahpenayo Peak. Ascend east and southeast to the west ridge of Wahpenayo Peak, then continue east and southeast on or near the crest of the ridge on the north side to the summit.

COMET FALLS, high point 5000', 4 miles RT, 1500' gain (Maps: Rainier: Wilderness Trip Planner, USGS Mt. Rainier West, GT Mt. Rainier West). **Hike-1**. Drive 6 miles northeast of Longmire in the Nisqually River valley. Park at the Comet Falls trailhead near Christine Falls, elevation 3600'. View **Christine Falls** best from the road.

Hike north, crossing a bridge above Christine Falls, then ascending above the east side of Van Trump Creek. The trail crosses a branch of the creek (bridge) at 4700' before reaching the first view of **Comet Falls**. Continue to ascend on the trail to the level of the base of the falls for a variety of views. Several tracks contour from the high point to the pool below the falls for the best view of the falling comets.

VAN TRUMP PARK, high point 5800', 5 miles RT, 2300' gain (Maps: Rainier: Wilderness Trip Planner, USGS Mt. Rainier West, GT Mt. Rainier West). **Hike-1**. Drive, park, and hike as above to **Comet Falls.**

From Comet Falls, continue on the trail up to Van Trump Park, passing the trail to **Mildred Point** at 5500'. The best viewpoint toward Mt. Rainier is 100' north of the end of the trail (5800'). The trail is often partly covered by snow until late July.

MILDRED POINT, 5935', 7 miles RT, 2700' gain (Maps: Rainier: Wilderness Trip Planner, USGS Mt. Rainier West, GT Mt. Rainier West). **Hike-2**. Drive, park, and hike as above toward **Van Trump Park**.

From the trail junction at 5500' near the beginning of Van Trump Park, go left (west), descending to cross Van Trump Creek above Comet Falls. After crossing the creek, continue southwest on the trail to a junction with the Rampart Ridge trail, 5400'. Turn right (west) and ascend to the ridge crest, then go north through or near the flowery meadows of Van Trump Park to a high point for a view of cliffs and glaciers. The Kautz Glacier is directly north. Look down 1000' to Kautz Creek directly below. The Kautz Creek lahar originated in this area.

NISQUALLY GLACIER, high point 4600', 4 miles RT, 1000' gain (Maps: USGS Mt. Rainier West, Mt. Rainier East, GT Mt. Rainier West, Mt. Rainier East). **Hike-3**. Drive 12 miles northeast of the Nisqually Entrance to the Nisqually River bridge. Park west of the bridge, elevation 3900'.

Walk north across the west end of the bridge. Find a track and descend to the grass and brush bank near the river. Ascend northeast along the upper, northwestern edge of the tumbled rocks along the Nisqually River. Some of these boulders were left by the receding glacier and some have been brought here by outburst floods. In case of such an event, ascend directly away from the stream.

On a warm summer day, the glacier gives the impression of rapid movement. Water and rocks are falling down the face of the ice and the pile of debris below looks as if a giant bulldozer was at work.

PARADISE, 5400' (Maps: Rainier: Wilderness Trip Planner, USGS Mt. Rainier East, GT Mt. Rainier East). Drive 18 miles east of the Nisqually Entrance to parking at Paradise.

Facilities and activities: Visitor Center, restaurant, hiking, back country permits, activity program (schedule available at Visitor Center). In many years, the ground at Paradise does not appear from snow until August.

NISQUALLY VISTA, high point 5900', 2 miles RT, 300' gain (Maps: Mount Rainier, USGS Mt. Rainier East, GT Mt. Rainier East). **Hike-1**. From parking in the upper Paradise parking lot, hike northwest to a viewpoint over the Nisqually Glacier (interpretive signs). Please stay on the paths or on snow.

NISQUALLY MORAINE, high point 5900', 4 miles RT, 800' gain (Maps: Mount Rainier, USGS Mt. Rainier East, GT Mt. Rainier East). **Hike-3**. The moraine is only exposed from snow late in summer.

From parking in the upper parking lot at Paradise, hike north on the Skyline Trail for one mile, then turn west on the Moraine Trail into the valley carved by the Nisqually Glacier. Approaching the glacier is reasonably safe, but going on the glacier is only safe for those using appropriate glacier-travel techniques.

PANORAMA POINT, 6900', 5 miles RT, 1600' gain (Maps: Mount Rainier, USGS Mt. Rainier East, GT Mt. Rainier East). **Hike-1**. From parking at Paradise Visitor Center, ascend north on the Skyline Trail in view of the Nisqually Glacier. At 6600', turn right (south) and circle around a promontory to a viewpoint. Summits visible include: Pinnacle Peak (182°), Wahpenayo (206°), and Unicorn (160°). Above Panorama Point, a branch trail returns to Paradise by way of Golden Gate.

CAMP MUIR, 10188', 11 miles RT, 5000' gain (Maps: Mount Rainier, USGS Mt. Rainier East, GT Mt. Rainier East). **Hike-3. Snow.** Those inexperienced in glacier travel should not attempt this trip in stormy weather or without good visibility.

From parking in the upper parking lot at Paradise, hike north on the Skyline Trail, which begins behind the Ranger Station. Pass the trail to Panorama Point at 6600', cross Pebble Creek at 7200', and pass McClure Rock (east) at 7400'. Above McClure Rock, the Muir Snowfield, an inactive glacier between the Paradise Glacier and the Nisqually Glacier, begins at 8200'. This snowfield is free of crevasses and is considered safe for unroped travel. By June, the rocks of the ridge between the Muir Snowfield and the Paradise Glacier (east) are often exposed from snow.

ANVIL ROCK, 9584', 10 miles RT, 4300' gain (Maps: Mount Rainier, USGS Mt. Rainier East, GT Mt. Rainier East). **Hike-3. Snow.** Drive, park, and hike as above toward Camp Muir.

At 9200', head northeast to rocks for an awesome view east to the bergschrund and crevasses of the Cowlitz Glacier. Look for remnants of the foundation of a lookout building that formerly stood here, but proved useless under the prevailing weather conditions. Much of the time this area is either in or above a sea of clouds. Those with no acrophobia can look down from the lookout site into the gaping mouth of the Cowlitz Glacier bergschrund immediately below.

PINNACLE PEAK, 6562', 6 miles RT, 1800' gain (Maps: Mount Rainier, USGS Mt. Rainier East, GT Mt. Rainier East). **Hike-4†.** Drive 15 miles east of the Nisqually Entrance to Mount Rainier National Park. Where the road branches left (north) to Paradise, turn right (east) toward the east entrance and park at the Reflection Lakes trailhead, 17 miles from the Nisqually Entrance, elevation 4867'.

Hike south on the trail to the saddle between Pinnacle Peak and Plummer Peak. If the trail is covered by snow, leave the parking area at the east end and ascend in a shallow valley for 100' of elevation gain. Contour southwest below steeper terrain into the basin west of Pinnacle Peak. Now turn south and ascend to the saddle between Pinnacle and Plummer Peak. Turn northeast and ascend, either on the southwest ridge of Pinnacle Peak or on the east slope of the ridge. If on snow (June), contour east until directly south of the summit pyramid, then ascend on snow until talus begins. Stay near or on the southwest ridge until the slope gets steeper below a buttress, 6400', then bend right to ascend into a shallow gully. At the ridge crest, turn right (northeast) to the summit.

PLUMMER PEAK, 6370', 6 miles RT, 1600' gain (Maps: Mount Rainier, USGS Mt. Rainier East, GT Mt. Rainier East). **Hike-3**. Drive, park, and hike as above on the trail to the saddle between Pinnacle Peak and Plummer Peak.

Continue southwest on the trail to reach the summit, the last bit in yellow cedar trees.

MOUNT DENMAN, 6006', 4 miles RT, 1300' gain (Maps: USGS Mt. Rainier East, GT Mt. Rainier East). **Hike-3. Snow**. Drive, park, and hike as above to Plummer Peak.

From Plummer Peak, descend northwest to the ridge that connects Plummer Peak to Mount Denman. Continue to the summit.

COWLITZ DIVIDE, high point 5648', 10 miles RT, 2800' gain (Maps: Mount Rainier, USGS Mt. Rainier East, Chinook Pass, GT Mt. Rainier East). **Hike-1**. Drive east from the Nisqually entrance, going right where the road to Paradise turns left 16 miles from the park entrance. Park east of the bridge over Box Canyon, 25 miles from the Nisqually entrance or 11 miles from the Stevens Canyon entrance, elevation 3000'.

Hike north across the highway for 100' from the parking area (restrooms) to a junction with the Wonderland Trail, then go east, ascending in dense forest across Nickel Creek (camping). The trail now passes through open ancient forest of Douglas fir, hemlock, and yellow cedar trees that gradually increase in size until, at 4200', many of the trees are 3-4' in diameter. At the ridge crest, go north to the Olallie Creek Trail, 4800'. From here the Olallie Creek Camp is 1.4 miles east at an elevation of 3900'.

Continue north on the trail to 5500'. Where the trail begins to descend, leave the trail and follow a ridge up and down northeast to the high point, 5648', and a broad view over the Ohanepecosh River basin. Summits visible: Cowlitz Chimney (350°), Double Peak (20°), Goat Rocks (160°), and Mt. Adams (174°).

US-12 Area. Drive east from I-5 at Exit-68.

TONGUE MOUNTAIN, 4838', 5 miles RT, 2000' gain (Maps: USGS Tower Rock, GT McCoy Peak). **Hike-4†**. From Randle on US-12, drive south one mile on road FS-25 then go southeast on road FS-23. At mile 9 from US-12, turn south on road FS-28 for one mile, then go southeast on road FS-29 across the Cispus River for 4 miles. Turn east on road FS-2904 for 4 miles from road FS-29 and park at a saddle, elevation 3600' and 18 miles from US-12.

Ascend north on trail FS-294, then go northwest to the saddle south of the summit. Ascend northwest on an exposed rubbly slope to the lookout site.

SUNRISE PEAK, 5892', 14 miles RT, 2600' gain (Maps: USGS Tower Rock, McCoy Peak, GT McCoy Peak). **Hike-1**. Drive as above to the trailhead for **Tongue Mountain** on the saddle between Lambert Creek on the west and the Cispus River valley to the east, elevation 3600'.

Hike south from the saddle, going over **Point 5227'**, **Juniper Peak (5611')**, and **Point 5526'** along the way.

JUMBO PEAK, 5801', 10 miles RT, 2100' gain (Maps: USGS McCoy Peak, GT McCoy Peak). **Hike-2**. From Randle on US-12, drive south one mile on road FS-25 then go southeast on road FS-23. At mile 9 from US-12, turn south on road FS-28 for one mile, then go southeast on road FS-29 for 20 miles. Park at the Boundary Trail (FS-1), elevation 3900'.

Hike east to Dark Meadow, passing north of Dark Mtn., then turn north on trail FS-261, mile 2.2. At mile 3.0, trail FS-263 goes east. Hike over **Point 5244'**, then leave the trail at 5400' on the west side of Jumbo Peak. Ascend southeast through a gap in basalt cliffs to the summit.

BADGER LAKE, 4900', 6.5 miles RT, 1000' gain (Maps: USGS French Butte, GT McCoy Peak). **Hike-1**. From Randle on US-12, drive south on road FS-25. South of MP-21, turn east on road FS-28 for 2.8 miles to the Mosquito Meadow trailhead (FS-292), elevation 4000'.

Hike south on trail FS-292 for one mile to join the Boundary Trail, FS-1. Turn east, ascending gradually to **Badger Lake** near a junction with trail FS-257. Find many campsites near the lake or hidden in the forest nearby. The water temperature of the lake exceeds 70°F by August.

BADGER PEAK, 5664', 8.5 miles RT, 1800' gain (Maps: USGS French Butte, GT McCoy Peak). **Hike-2**. Drive, park, and hike as above for Badger Lake to the junction with trail FS-257 immediately northwest of the Badger Lake meadow.

Turn northeast on trail FS-257 for 0.5 miles, then go southeast on an unmaintained branch trail and ascend more steeply (possible fallen trees) to an old lookout site. Look for McCoy Peak (46°), Sunrise Peak (62°), Jumbo Peak (73°), which is nearly surrounded by a skirt of basalt cliffs, Dark Mtn. (93°), and Mt. Adams (105°).

CRAGGY PEAK, high point 5720', 12 miles RT, 1800' gain (Maps: USGS French Butte, McCoy Peak, GT McCoy Peak). **Hike-3**. Drive, park, and hike as above to **Badger Lake**. The distance and elevation gain given are from Badger Lake.

From Badger Lake, hike southeast on the Boundary Trail, FS-1, passing north and east of impressive Kirk Rock, then ascend over the north shoulder of Shark Rock, 5200'. From the east side of Shark Rock, descend to a saddle, 5000'. Follow trail FS-1 as it bends around the west side of Craggy Peak before turning east to the crest. Leave the trail and ascend north on a faint and intermittent track to a high point a few feet below the actual summit, a rock pinnacle beyond the scope of this book.

PURCELL MOUNTAIN, 5442', 6 miles RT, 2700' gain (Maps: USGS Purcell Mtn., GT Randle). **Hike-3**. At MP-121 on US-12, go left on the Davis Creek Road (old highway) for one mile. West of the Davis Creek bridge, drive north on road FS-63 for 4.8 miles. Park at the junction with road FS-6310, 2900'.

Hike west on road FS-6310, crossing a deep washout and reaching the beginning of trail FS-285 at mile 0.5, 2800'. The route follows an old road for another 0.5 mile (to 3200'), then the trail ascends north in a clearcut, beginning ancient forest at 3800'. The trail enters mountain beaver meadows (dangerous for horses) at 4500' where the trail becomes hard to find except in clumps of forest. Hint: at 4500', the trail traverses left (west) across a steep, narrow gully, then begins switchbacks, which ascend generally west. Join trail FS-284 on the ridge and continue north to the lookout site. Look for the following peaks: Unicorn (34°), Tatoosh LO (49°), Aix (64°), Adams (150°), Sunrise Peak (168°), Hood (177°), St. Helens (210°), High Rock (338°), and Wow (350°).

DRY CREEK LOOKOUT, 3815', 6 miles RT, 2800' gain (Maps: USGS Packwood, GT Packwood. **Hike-1**. East of MP-127 on US-12, go right (south) on road FS-20 and park at the trailhead, 0.2 miles from US-12, elevation 1000'.

Hike south on trail FS-125 to the lookout site and a view into the valley of the Cowlitz River and to the towers of Smith Ridge (east).

SOUTH POINT, 5980', 8 miles RT, 3400' gain (Maps: USGS Packwood, GT Packwood). **Hike-1**. East of MP-127, drive south on road FS-20 for 5 miles and park at the trailhead, elevation 2700'.

Ascend east on trail FS-123, which is an old road to 4500'. Find a tiny spring near the trail at 4600'. Enter dream forest (if in clouds) at

5200', then, on reaching the ridge, go south to the summit and lookout site.

ANGRY MOUNTAIN, 6045', 10 miles RT, 4300' gain (Maps: USGS Packwood Lake, GT Packwood). **Hike-2. Goat Rocks Wilderness.** East of MP-128, three miles west of Packwood, drive southeast on road FS-21 for seven miles. Turn east on road FS-2120 to the trailhead, 0.3 miles from FS-21, elevation 2700'.

Hike east on trail FS-90, entering a cathedral of ancient forest at 3150'. Look west at the layered rocks of South Point and south to Mt. Adams. The trail turns south at 4700' over a trickling spring, then crests on a ridge, 4900'. The Angry Mtn. lookout site, 5245', is 0.2 miles north on this ridge. Pass a high point (5050'), then descend to 4600' before ascending on the west ridge of Angry Mtn. Where the trail tops a ridge, 5750', leave the trail and ascend southeast in open forest and meadow to look south down cliffs. Find the highest point in a clump of yellow cedar. Of the Goat Rocks summits, only Johnson Mtn. is visible (68°).

TATOOSH LOOKOUT, 6310', 12 miles RT, 4300' gain (Maps: USGS Tatoosh Lakes, GT Packwood). **Hike-1. Tatoosh Wilderness.** From Packwood on US-12, drive northwest on the Skate Creek road (FS-52) over the Cowlitz River. Turn right at the second intersection after crossing the river and go north and northeast on Cannon Road (FS-5290). At a 4-way intersection (mile 6), turn left (north) to the trailhead, 9.5 miles from US-12, elevation 2400'.

Hike west, then go north, passing Hinkle Tinkle shelter at 3100'. The trail enters meadows at 5000'. After the trail crosses to the west side of the ridge, 5800', mile 5, go right at a junction and ascend to the summit. Summits in view: Shriner (42°), Aix (74°), Goat Rocks (143°), Adams (166°), Hood (182°), St. Helens (216°), Lookout Mtn. (278°), Wow (293°), Unicorn (328°), and Stevens (348°).

MOUNT ADAMS, 12276', 14 miles RT, 6700' gain (Maps: USGS Mt. Adams East, GT Mt. Adams). **Hike-4†, Snow. Mt. Adams Wilderness.** Carry crampons. From Randle on US-12, drive south and southeast on road FS-25 for one mile, then continue east and southeast on road FS-23. This road is paved except for 10 miles. Reach the town of Trout Lake at 56 miles from Randle. Get Wilderness Permit and sign in for the summit hike at the Mt. Adams Ranger Station 0.5 mile west on road SR-141 from the road FS-23 intersection. From the Mt. Adams Ranger Station, return east to road FS-23, go north one mile, then continue north on road FS-80 to enter the Mt. Adams Wilderness, reaching Morrison Creek

Campground at 11 miles from road FS-23. Turn northeast to continue for three miles on a rough gravel and rock road to the end of the road and parking near Cold Springs, elevation 5600'. Best time: July to mid-September.

Hike north on an old road, now trail, ascending on McDonald Ridge in open forest. Expect snow over much of this trail above 6500' into August. Follow the route of the trail (tracks in snow and cairns) to 7300' in a flat area below the Crescent Glacier. The trail now turns west and ascends to the crest of the ridge that encloses the Crescent Glacier on the west. This route then continues to the Lunch Counter at 9200'. If the trail above 7300' is under snow (nearly vertical headwall), turn east below the Crescent Glacier and ascend across snow and talus to the ridge (7600') that forms the east boundary of the valley that contains the Crescent Glacier. Much of this ridge east of the Coleman Glacier is snowfree up to 9300' by the end of July. Find campsites on this broad ridge that leads north on Suksdorf Ridge to the Lunch Counter. These campsites will be near scattered whitebark pine trees below 7800' (no fires). Get water from snow patches.

From the Lunch Counter, ascend north on steeper snow (step ladders) to the false summit, 11657', often clear of snow by the end of July. Continue north and west of north, at first across a gentle slope, then on steeper snow (ice patches may require crampons) to the summit. The summit building is often under snow until August. Look for the following summits: Goat Rocks (9°), Mt. Stuart (17°), Mt. Hood (190°), Mt. St. Helens (268°), and Mt. Rainier (344°).

Goat Rocks Wilderness.

East of MP-128 on US-12, turn southeast on road FS-21 for 13 miles. Turn left on road FS-2150 to parking at Berry Patch (camping). Permits required.

GOAT ROCKS LOOP, high point 6785', 14 miles RT, 2800' gain (Maps: Goat Rocks Wilderness, USGS Hamilton Buttes, Old Snowy Mtn., Packwood Lake, Walupt Lake, GT Packwood Lake, Blue Lake, Walupt Lake, White Pass). **Hike-1**. Camp only in designated sites.

From the parking area at Berry Patch, 4600', hike northeast on trail FS-96, crossing Goat Creek at two miles, to **Snowgrass Flat**, 5800', four miles from the parking area and near the Pacific Crest Trail. From Snowgrass Flat, take day trips to Old Snowy Mtn. or Ives Peak, and hike the PCT to Elk Pass (north) and Cispus Pass (south).

From Snowgrass Flat, hike north on the Lily Basin Trail, FS-86, for four miles, passing **Goat Lake** in a barren cirque, to the Goat Ridge Trail, FS-95. Find a view campsite at 6600' near a spring on a bench south of

Hawkeye Point and west of Goat Lake near the junction with the Goat Ridge Trail. From this campsite, Hawkeye Point is a late afternoon stroll. Johnson Mtn. is a day trip.

From the junction of the Goat Ridge Trail, FS-95, with the Lily Basin Trail, FS-86, hike south on the Goat Ridge Trail. South of the junction of trails FS-95 and FS-86, leave the trail near a saddle, 6600', and ascend south on the ridge to the high point of **Goat Ridge**, 6785', for the view. Return to the trail, then at 5900', take the left branch of trail FS-95 to go over the former **Goat Ridge Lookout** site, 6240'. The trail ends at Berry Patch.

OLD SNOWY MOUNTAIN, 7930', 5 miles RT, 2000' gain (Maps: Goat Rocks Wilderness, USGS Walupt Lake, Old Snowy Mtn., GT White Pass, Walupt Lake). **Hike-3. Snow**. The gentle slope and far-reaching view makes this summit an ideal diversion for those hiking the Pacific Crest Trail. The distance and elevation gain given for this trip are from camping at Snowgrass Flat, eight miles RT and 1600' gain from parking at Berry Patch.

From Snow Grass Flat, hike north on the PCT, passing the Dana Yelverton shelter. Just before the PCT reaches the crest of the ridge, leave the trail at 7200' and ascend southeast on gently sloping talus to the summit. Be prepared to cross snow patches.

OLD SNOWY NORTH RIDGE, high point 7200', 8 miles RT, 2400' gain (Maps: Goat Rocks Wilderness, USGS Old Snowy Mtn., Walupt Lake, GT White Pass, Walupt Lake). **Hike-2**. The distance and elevation gain for this trip are from camping in Snowgrass Flat.

From Snowgrass Flat, hike north on the Pacific Crest Trail, ascending over the ridge just north of Old Snowy Mountain, then descending on or near the ridge crest until the PCT turns east at Elk Pass. The PCT in this area often has steep snow patches that last all summer.

IVES PEAK, 7932', 8 miles RT, 2300' gain (Maps: Goat Rocks Wilderness, USGS Old Snowy Mtn., Walupt Lake, GT White Pass, Walupt Lake). **Hike-3**. The distance and elevation gain given for this trip are from camping in Snowgrass Flat.

From Snowgrass Flat, hike south and east on the Pacific Crest Trail into the basin of the Cispus River. Leave the trail where it turns south toward Cispus Pass and ascend north in a flower meadow to the saddle southeast of Ives Peak, then follow the ridge northwest to the talus summit.

WARM LAKE, 6350', 20 miles RT, 4700' gain (Maps: Goat Rocks Wilderness, USGS Hamilton Buttes, Walupt Lake, GT Blue Lake, Walupt Lake). **Hike-3**. This trip is best combined with a longer exploration of Goat Rocks Wilderness. The lake makes a good base for hiking to the summits of Curtis Gilbert Peak and Tieton Peak.

From the parking area at Berry Patch, 4600', hike northeast on trail FS-96, crossing Goat Creek at two miles, and taking the bypass trail to the right (east) after crossing Snowgrass Creek, 5600'. This trail contours to meet the Pacific Crest Trail south of Snowgrass Flat at 6000'. Continue east on the Pacific Crest Trail to find tent sites on a bench above the Pacific Crest Trail where the trail crosses a creek that descends south from Ives Peak to join the Cispus River. This campsite is near the beginning of the off-trail route to Ives Peak.

From the campsite in the Cispus Basin, continue east and south on the Pacific Crest Trail to Cispus Pass, 6450'. Leave the Pacific Crest Trail at Cispus Pass and descend east in the head basin of the Klickitat River on an old, faint trail that contours east and southeast around the beginnings of the Klickitat River. Drop to 5800' before ascending to the crest of the southeast ridge of Curtis Gilbert Peak at 6700' near Warm Lake. Where the trail disappears in the meadows of the Klickitat River basin, look for it in forested areas. From the southeast ridge of Curtis Gilbert, descend a talus slope to Warm Lake.

Warm Lake can also be reached from US-12 near Rimrock Lake by driving the South Fork Tieton River Road to the trailhead. Hike six miles on the South Fork Tieton Trail, FS-1120, to Surprise Lake then continue west and north on the Goat Rocks Trail, FS-1132, for three miles. Leave the Goat Rocks Trail at 5600' where the trail bends east and ascend northwest to the lake basin.

CURTIS GILBERT PEAK, 8201', 5 miles RT, 2000' gain (Maps: Goat Rocks Wilderness, USGS Hamilton Buttes, Walupt Lake, GT Blue Lake, Walupt Lake). **Hike-4†**. Distance and elevation gain are from **Warm Lake**.

From camping at Warm Lake, ascend the talus slope west to the southeast ridge of Curtis Gilbert Peak, 6700'. Turn northwest on the crest of the ridge and follow the ridge to the summit area, then ascend on the southwest side to the peak.

TIETON PEAK, 7768', 8 miles RT, 2800' gain (Maps: Goat Rocks Wilderness, USGS Old Snowy Mtn., Walupt Lake, GT White Pass, Walupt Lake). **Hike-4†**. The distance and elevation gain given for this trip are from **Warm Lake** (see above).

From Warm Lake, hike north, contouring at 6000' around the east side of Curtis Gilbert Peak and crossing branches of Conrad Creek. Look southwest at the colorful cliffs of Curtis Gilbert Peak. After crossing the last branch of Conrad Creek coming from the Conrad Glacier on the north side of Curtis Gilbert Peak, near a beautiful campsite at the edge of the forest, ascend north to the ridge that descends southwest from Tieton Peak. On reaching the crest of the ridge, continue northeast to the summit. Admire the Devils Horns to the east.

HAWKEYE POINT, 7431', 2 miles RT, 900' gain (Maps: Goat Rocks Wilderness, USGS Old Snowy Mtn., GT White Pass). **Hike-3.** The distance and elevation gain given for this trip are from the campsite near the junction of the Lily Basin Trail (FS-86) and the Goat Ridge Trail (FS-95), 6600'. This campsite is 11 miles RT and 2000' gain from the trailhead at Berry Patch.

From the campsite near the junction of trails FS-86 and FS-95, hike north up the ridge to the summit.

JOHNSON PEAK, 7487', 8 miles RT, 1600' gain (Maps: Goat Rocks Wilderness, USGS Old Snowy Mtn., Packwood Lake, GT White Pass, Packwood). **Hike-3.** The distance and elevation gain given for this trip are from the campsite near the junction of the Lily Basin Trail (FS-86) and the Goat Ridge Trail (FS-95), 6600'. This campsite is 11 miles RT and 2000' gain from the trailhead at Berry Patch.

Hike the Lily Basin Trail, FS-86, north and northwest, descending to 6000'. Where the trail turns west, descending toward Heart Lake, leave the trail and ascend a steep meadow to the ridge that descends southwest from Johnson Peak. On the crest of the ridge, turn northeast to the summit. On the descent, continue down the ridge to intersect trail FS-86. Turn east and follow the trail back to the starting point.

Mount Saint Helens Area

Between MP-52 and MP-49 on I-5, note the piles of debris west of the highway that were dredged from the Toutle River after the eruption of Mt. St. Helens.

MOUNT SAINT HELENS VISITOR CENTER, 500' (Maps: USGS Silver Lake). From I-5 at Exit-49, drive east for six miles on SR-504 to the Visitor Center at Silver Lake.

Facilities and activities: hourly multi-media shows, exhibits, information, maps, Silver Lake wetlands nature trail. Fee.

SEDIMENT RETENTION STRUCTURE, 950', 2 miles RT, 200' gain (Maps: USGS Toutle Mtn.). **Walk**. From I-5 at Exit-49, drive 21 miles east on SR-504. Turn left (south) one mile to the visitor parking area. Alternate route: Leave I-5 at Exit-63 and drive southeast and east on SR-505 for 15 miles to meet SR-504. Turn east for six miles then proceed as above.

A Visitor Center has informative displays. Go 300' north of the parking area to a viewpoint over the facility. Another trail from the parking area goes 0.5 mile to the Sediment Retention Structure. Walk west to a ramp that descends north to the level of the retained lake near the outlet and overflow channel. Note the wood debris that accumulates during high water runoff and examine the nature of the sediment. A road descends west to the base of the dam for a close view of the outlet. Five levels of outlet gates will gradually be covered by sediment during the life of the structure, estimated to be 45 years. The water will then flow over the outlet channel on the west side of the dam.

HOFFSTADT BLUFFS VISITOR CENTER, 1400' (Maps: Mt. St. Helens National Volcanic Monument, USGS Hoffstadt Mtn.). **Hike-1**. From I-5 at Exit-49, drive 27 miles east on SR-504 (MP-26). Alternative route: Leave I-5 at Exit-63 and drive SR-505 through Toledo to meet SR-504.

This Visitor Center outside the eruption damage area and provided by Cowlitz County, has information on the debris flow that devastated this valley. A model of the area is most useful for seeing the relationships of the various damage areas after a visit to the region. A viewpoint overlooks Hoffstadt Creek immediately below and the Toutle River at the south edge of the valley. Note the braided channels that the river has cut into the flood deposits. Activities: elk viewing tours (weekends only in winter) and helicopter rides. Elk are most often seen in the spring. Elk tracks and a trail descend from here to the valley bottom, 1050'.

HOFFSTADT BRIDGE VIEWPOINT, 1700' (Maps: USGS Hoffstadt Mtn.). From I-5 at Exit-49, drive 30 miles east (MP-29) on SR-504. Alternative route: Leave I-5 at Exit-63 and drive SR-505 through Toledo to meet SR-504.

The viewpoint is located at the western edge of the eruption damage zone, 14.8 miles from Mt. St. Helens crater. Stop here on the return from visits to Coldwater Ridge and Johnston Ridge. Contrast the growing forest to the east, which was planted, with the area inside the Monument that has been left to regenerate naturally.

FOREST LEARNING VISITOR CENTER, 2600' (Maps: Mt. St. Helens National Volcanic Monument, USGS Hoffstadt Mtn.). From I-5 at Exit-49, drive 33 miles east on SR-504. Alternative route: Leave I-5 at Exit-63 and drive SR-505 through Toledo to meet SR-504.

This Visitor Center at the North Fork Ridge Viewpoint, near the western edge of the blast zone and provided by the Weyerhaeuser Company, has information on the blast area and the efforts being made to replace the forests lost during the eruption.

ELK ROCK, 4360', 1 mile RT, 600' gain (Maps: Mt. St. Helens National Volcanic Monument, USGS Elk Rock). **Hike-3**. From I-5 at Exit-49, drive 37 miles east on SR-504. Alternative route: Leave I-5 at Exit-63 and drive SR-505 through Toledo to meet SR-504. Park at Elk Rock Viewpoint.

Walk north on the highway until the highway begins to descend, 3800'. Leave the highway at a creek crossing and ascend west to a logging track. In growing trees, follow zig-zag logging tracks or elk paths west to the summit for views of Mt. Rainier, Mt. Adams, Mt. St. Helens, and a general panorama of the eruption damage area. Look for bricks and an old stove near one of the summits (lookout site?).

COLDWATER RIDGE VISITOR CENTER, 3100' (Maps: Mt. St. Helens National Volcanic Monument, USGS Elk Rock). **Walk**. From I-5 at Exit-49, drive 43 miles east on SR-504. Alternative route: Leave I-5 at Exit-63 and drive SR-505 through Toledo to meet SR-504.

Facilities and activities: nature walks in the eruption damage area, displays, multi-media shows, fee.

Winds of Change Trail: A paved, barrier-free, 0.25 mile trail with informative signs displays the changes occurring in the vegetation with time. This area had been logged before 1980 and doesn't have the windrows of fallen trees that are visible on the east and north sides of the mountain. Guided walk in summer season.

Elk Bench Trail: 2 miles RT, 700' gain. A steep trail descends east to **Coldwater Lake** below the Visitor Center. Notable sights: Recent deep erosion of gullies from storm runoff after the loss of vegetation cover at the time of the eruption. The shoreline at the lake is nearly vertical in places as a result of wave action in this recently filled lake. Several 6" or larger cottonwood trees are survivors that have regrown from roots since the eruption.

COLDWATER LAKE, 2490' (Maps: Mt. St. Helens National Volcanic Monument, USGS Elk Rock, Spirit Lake West). **Walk**. From the Coldwater Ridge Visitor Center, drive two miles east on SR-504 to the parking area and boat launch at the lake.

Facilities and activities: **Birth of a Lake Trail**, 0.25 mile, no gain, barrier-free. The trail follows a paved or board walkway along the edge of the lake and through hummocks of landslide debris. Note the wide area of sediment across the outlet to the east. New trees are now covering this area.

HUMMOCKS TRAIL, high point 2550', 2 mile loop, 200' gain (Maps: Mt. St. Helens National Volcanic Monument, USGS Elk Rock). **Hike-1**. From the Coldwater Ridge Visitor Center, drive two miles east on SR-504 to parking on the south side of the highway (MP-45).

Hike in an area of tumbled landslide debris and along S Coldwater Creek.

COLDWATER MOUNTAIN, 5720', 12 miles hiking, 6 miles bicycling, 4000' gain (Maps: St. Helens National Monument, USGS Spirit Lake West, GT Spirit Lake). **Hike-1, Bicycle**. Drive 52 miles east from I-5 at MP-49 to **Johnston Observatory**. Leave bicycle at the Observatory and return west to park at the S Coldwater trailhead (FS-230A) near MP-46, elevation 2500'.

Hike northeast on the trail, ascending the ridge between Coldwater Lake and South Coldwater Creek. Pass eruption damaged logging machinery at 3500' (mile 2) and also at mile 3.1, 4000', where the route joins and turns east on trail FS-230. Pass Ridge Camp at mile 3.5 (toilets, no water). Now ascend generally east in blowdown forest (some standing dead trees) to a junction with trail FS-1 at mile 5.4, 5000'. Turn left, contour north for 0.5 mile, then ascend west to the summit on trail FS-1G. Look for Mt. Hood (160°) and hills south of the Columbia River (254°).

Return on the trail to the junction of trails FS-1 and FS-230. Go south on trail FS-1, passing through a hole in the ridge before going along the west side of Harry's Ridge into the the spillover zone where the landslide at the beginning of the eruption overtopped the ridge. Note the variously colored jumble of debris that was originally deep inside the cone of Mt. St. Helens.

At a junction with trail FS-207, go west to Johnston Ridge Observatory. Along the way get views south toward Mt. St. Helens over the the former North Fork Toutle River channel. Find bicycle and descend west to the starting point. The tunnel that drains Spirit Lake exits under the South Coldwater Creek bridge.

JOHNSTON RIDGE OBSERVATORY, 4200' (Maps: Mt. St. Helens National Volcanic Monument, USGS Spirit Lake West). **Walk**. From I-5 at Exit-49, drive 52 miles east on SR-504. Alternative route: Leave I-5 at Exit-63 and drive SR-505 through Toledo to meet SR-504.

Facilities and activities: displays, multi-media presentation, and ranger walks. Best general view of the landslide that preceded the eruption and of the Pumice Plain, which was deposited on top of the landslide by the subsequent pyroclastic flow. The landslide from Mt. St. Helens stopped a few feet below the site of the present observatory. Look east for darker gray deposits of this landslide where it overtopped the crest of the ridge. Note standing dead trees within the blowdown zone in a protected area near Coldwater Peak .

MOUNT SAINT HELENS, 8363', 9 miles RT, 4600' gain (Maps: Mt. St. Helens National Volcanic Monument, USGS Mt. St. Helens, GT Mt. St. Helens). **Hike-3**. The summit provides the best view of the growing dome in the crater. From Exit-21 on I-5, drive east on SR-503 for 23 miles to Jack's Store in Yale to register and pay the climbers fee. To pre-register for a given date, write Mt. St. Helens National Volcanic Monument, 42218 NE Yale Bridge Road, Amboy, WA 98601. Get applications for pre-registration from the Outdoor Recreation Information Center located in the REI store (222 Yale Ave. N) in Seattle. From Jack's Store continue east on road SR-503 and FS-90 for 12 miles. Turn north on road FS-83 for three miles, then go left (northwest) on road FS-81 for two miles, following signs to the Climbers Bivouac. Turn east on road FS-81-830 for three miles to the trailhead, 3800', 43 miles from I-5 at MP-21. Best time: August to mid-September when the route is snow-free.

From the Climbers Bivouac (camping, toilets, no water), hike north on the Ptarmigan Trail (FS-216A) for two miles, crossing the Loowit Trail (FS-216) at one mile. The maintained trail ends at 4800', near timberline. From this point, the route, which ascends for 2000' through lava boulders near or on Monitor Ridge, is marked by posts. Above 7000', the surface is loose pumice with several obvious tracks. The crater rim gives the best view of the post-1980 lava dome.

APE CAVE, 2080', up to 4 miles RT, 500' gain (Maps: Mt. St. Helens National Volcanic Monument, USGS Mt. Mitchell, GT Mt. St. Helens). **Hike-3**. From Exit-21 on I-5, drive east on SR-503 to Cougar. Continue east on road FS-90. At MP-3, turn north on road FS-83 for two miles, then go west on road FS-8330 for one mile to parking.

Visit the longest known lava tube in the United States, formed

1,900 years ago.

META LAKE, 3600', 0.5 miles RT, no gain (Maps: Mt. St. Helens National Volcanic Monument, USGS Spirit Lake West, GT Spirit Lake). **Hike-1**. From US-12 at Randle, drive south on road FS-25 or from I-5 at Woodland (MP-21), drive east on roads SR-503 and FS-90, then turn north on road FS-25 when 47 miles from I-5. Near MP-19 on road FS-25, turn west on road FS-99 for nine miles.

Facilities and activities: water, interpretive trail, wetland, and the Miner's Car, a relic of the eruption.

SPIRIT LAKE, 3408', 2 miles RT, 700' gain (Maps: Mt. St. Helens National Volcanic Monument, USGS Spirit Lake East, GT Spirit Lake). **Hike-1**. Drive as above to **Meta Lake**, then continue on road FS-99 for 4.5 miles to the Harmony Trailhead, elevation 4100'.

Hike west downhill to the lake, passing Harmony Falls. Examine forest debris stranded above the lake shore and view floating trees. Look across the lake to the line of blowdown that rises to the north. The forest material below this line was washed into the lake by the wave generated by the landslide that initiated the eruption. Mt. Margaret is directly north.

WINDY RIDGE VIEWPOINT, 4246', 0.5 miles RT, 100' gain (Maps: Mt. St. Helens National Volcanic Monument, USGS Spirit Lake West, GT Spirit Lake). **Hike-1**. Drive as above to **Meta Lake** and continue southwest on road FS-99 to parking at Windy Ridge, 4140'.

Facilities and activities: toilets, information. Ascend steps to the viewpoint for a view of the 0.73 cubic mile landslide from Mt. St. Helens that raised the level of Spirit Lake and filled the North Fork Toutle River channel west of Spirit Lake for 13 miles.

NORWAY PASS, 4500', 4.5 miles RT, 600' gain (Maps: Mt. St. Helens National Volcanic Monument, USGS Spirit Lake East, GT Spirit Lake). **Hike-1**. From US-12 at Randle, drive south on road FS-25 or from I-5 at Woodland (MP-21), drive east on roads SR-503 and FS-90, then turn north on road FS-25 when 47 miles from I-5. Near MP-19 on road FS-25, turn west on road FS-99 for nine miles. East of Meta Lake, turn north on road FS-26 for one mile to the Norway Pass trailhead (water, toilets).

Hike west on the Norway Pass Trail in the Mt. St. Helens eruption blowdown area, passing the Independence Pass trail at one mile, then contouring northwest to Norway Pass and a viewpoint overlooking the north end of Spirit Lake.

'GRIZZLY SADDLE', 5120', 7.5 miles RT, 1300' gain (Maps: Mt. St. Helens National Volcanic Monument, USGS Spirit Lake East, GT Spirit Lake). **Hike-1**. Drive and hike as above to Norway Pass.

Continue north on the trail beyond Norway Pass for a better view into the crater of Mt. St. Helens. One mile from Norway Pass, a trail (FS-211) goes north to Bear Pass and Grizzly Lake. Reach the saddle directly south above Grizzly Lake at 1.5 miles from Norway Pass. Look down on the lake, which is still nearly filled with floating trees (1997). All of the summits of Goat Mtn. are visible from this saddle (350°, 6°, and 22°).

MOUNT MARGARET, 5840', 12 miles RT, 2500' gain (Maps: Mt. St. Helens National Volcanic Monument, USGS Spirit Lake West, Spirit Lake East, GT Spirit Lake). **Hike-1**. Drive and hike as above to 'Grizzly Saddle'.

Continue west on the trail, passing a trail north to Mt. Whittier east of the rock pinnacle that stands east of Mt. Margaret. From this junction, the trail descends southwest briefly to round the rock pinnacle before ascending west to the south shoulder of Mt. Margaret. Bend right (north) at a junction on the south shoulder to the summit.

RYAN LAKE, 3300', 1 mile RT, 200' gain (Maps: Mt. St. Helens National Volcanic Monument, USGS Spirit Lake East, GT Spirit Lake). **Hike-1**. Drive as above past the entrance to the **Norway Pass Trailhead**. Continue north on road FS-26 for five miles from road FS-99 to parking at Ryan Lake.

Facilities and activities: interpretive trail, toilets. The immediate surroundings of Ryan Lake have been left to regenerate naturally, but nearby forest areas have been planted. The interpretive trail travels through replanted forest.

GOAT MOUNTAIN, 5106', 5400', 5407', 9 miles RT, 2600' gain (Maps: Mt. St. Helens National Volcanic Monument, USGS Spirit Lake East, GT Spirit Lake). **Hike-3**. The summits of Goat Mtn. provide excellent places from which to observe the vagaries of the limits of the pyroclastic flow from Mt. St. Helens. Drive as above to the entrance to Ryan Lake. Continue north on road FS-26 for 0.1 mile. Turn west on road FS-2612 to the trailhead, 0.6 miles from the Ryan Lake entrance, elevation 3300'.

Hike north on trail FS-217, at first in an area from which trees that were damaged by the Mt. St. Helens eruption have been removed. Pass through a tongue of remaining ancient forest at 3700', and enter ancient forest at 3800', going northeast. Turn west at 4500' to the crest of Goat Mtn. Turn east on or near an old trail to a first summit, 5106'.

For the middle summit, 5400', leave the main trail at 4900' where it crosses the southeast ridge of the middle summit and ascend northwest on a faint track to rock outcrops and a view north into a basin with ponds and several visible trails. A faint track also goes east on the ridge to the middle summit from the main trail where this trail touches the crest of the ridge between the middle and west peaks. Note the lobes of forest damage north of the ridge of Goat Mtn.

To ascend the west peak of Goat Mtn., 5407', leave the main trail at 5000' where this trail turns northwest from the main ridge. Follow a faint track up the ridge through scattered eruption killed but still standing trees to the highest rock point.

DEADMAN LAKE, 4352', 10 miles RT, 2500' gain (Maps: Mt. St. Helens National Volcanic Monument, USGS Spirit Lake East, Vanson Peak, Cowlitz Falls, GT Spirit Lake). **Hike-1**. Drive and hike as above to **Goat Mtn.**

Continue on the trail as it contours across the east face of the west summit of Goat Mtn., then descend to a trail junction at 4300'. Turn west to the lake to find many campsites. The east edge of the lake is shallow and water temperature exceeds 70° by August.

VANSON PEAK, 4948', 7 miles RT, 1600' gain (Maps: Mt. St. Helens National Volcanic Monument, USGS Vanson Peak, GT Spirit Lake). **Hike-1**. Drive and hike as above to Deadman Lake. The distance and elevation given for this trip are from Deadman Lake.

From Deadman Lake, hike north on trail FS-217, passing immediately trail FS-218, which goes northeast to Tumwater Mtn. Trail FS-217 goes near or over two high points, 4842' and 4884', and drops to one low point, 4600', before ascending to a trail junction, 2.5 miles from Deadman Lake and 4700'. The trail to the left descends to go northwest above Vanson Lake. Take the trail to the right (north), going to the old lookout site on Vanson Peak, passing two branch trails on the left (west). From the summit, the view includes Mt. Rainier, Mt. Adams, Mt. St. Helens, Gilbert Peak at the south end of the Goat Rocks group (80°), and Mt. Hood (163°) through a notch in the ridge east of Mt. Margaret.

From the summit of Vanson Peak, return south on the trail, then turn right on either of the branch trails that go west from the ridge. The first trail is an older version and is steeper and brushier. The two trails connect below 4600'. Descend to 4100' to rejoin trail FS-217. Turn left (southeast), passing a branch to Vanson Meadow (FS-213A) that connects with the Green River Trail. Continue southeast, then take a branch to the right (south) at 4200' to Vanson Lake (campsites but no beach). Find a track along the east side of the lake that goes to an inlet stream and the best campsite. From here, a trail ascends east to trail FS-217 and a junction with the trail that goes north to the lookout site. Go right (south) to return to Deadman Lake.

DEEP LAKE, 3986', 1 mile RT, 500' gain (Maps: Mt. St. Helens National Volcanic Monument, USGS Cowlitz Falls, Vanson Peak, GT Spirit Lake). **Hike-2**. For those who want an isolated campsite. The distance and elevation gain given are from Deadman Lake.

From Deadman Lake, return east to trail FS-217, taking the right branch immediately after leaving the lake. Cross trail FS-217 and continue east, passing branch trails that turn north or south. Stay on the north side of the stream course (campsite south of the stream), then descend more steeply to Deep Lake. The lake is shallow and accessible along the east shore.

US–2 Region

Everett Area.

LYNNWOOD–EVERETT, high point 508', 20 miles one-way, 200' gain (Maps: USGS Edmonds East, Everett, Bothell). **Bicycle**. Begin at the Lynnwood Park & Ride, reached by many Community Transit buses. From Aurora Transit Center (parking, Metro 340, 358, etc.) take CT 620, 621, or 630 to Lynnwood Transit Center. If driving, take Exit-181 from I-5 and park at Lynnwood Park & Ride (200th St. SW and 48th Ave. W) weekends only.

From the Lynnwood Park & Ride, ride north to 200th St. SW, then go east to 40th Ave. W (mile 0.5) to begin a short section of the Interurban Bikeway. Ride the bikeway NE, emerging on 37th Ave. W at mile 0.7. Proceed north on 37th Ave. W, going to the west side of this street to cross 196th St. SW. Continue north one block to the next stoplight, then turn northeast on Alderwood Mall Blvd., which rounds north. The bikeway resumes on the east side of Alderwood Mall Blvd. at 33rd Ave. SW, mile 1.2. Pass under a street at mile 1.7 and join a street at mile 1.9. The bikeway reappears briefly before joining 26th Ave. W. Turn east on Maple Road, going under SR-525 and over I-5 before bending south on Butternut Road at mile 3.0. Round west to resume the bikeway north on the east side of I-5.

Exit to Meadow Road, crossing Martha Lake Road (164th St. SW) at mile 4.5. Resume the bikeway at mile 4.8. Pass a bit of forest at mile 6.5, emerging to 3rd Ave. SE at a drive-in theater, also a swap meet, mile 6.9. Join 128th St. SE at mile 7.3. Turn right on 128th St. SE to visit **McCollum Park** (restrooms, picnic tables, shelter, trails). If driving, reach McCollum Park from I-5 by taking Exit-186 and driving east to the first stoplight. Turn south around the Park & Ride to the park.

From McCollum Park, return west on 128th St. SE across I-5. Find the bikeway beyond the southbound freeway off ramp, mile 9.5. The bikeway crosses under 112th St. SW at mile 11. Exit to 112th St. SE, turn right (east) and cross I-5 to **Silver Lake Park** on the east side of I-5. Facilities: swimming, restrooms, shelter, picnic tables, one mile nature trail. If driving, reach Silver Lake Park from I-5 at Exit-186. Go east on SR-96 to 19th Ave. SE, 1.7 miles from I-5. Turn left (north) 0.6 mile to Silver Lake Road. Turn left (west) on Silver Lake Road one mile to parking for Silver Lake Park, 3.3 miles from I-5.

From Silver Lake Park, return west across I-5 and go north on the bikeway (mile 13), which now veers away from I-5, ascending a gentle grade to emerge on West Mall Drive. Cross Everett Mall Way, mile 14.1. Continue north on West Mall Drive, resuming the bikeway at mile 14.4. The bikeway ends at 84th St. SE, mile 14.9. Go left (west). At 7th Ave. SE, jog right then turn right on E Casino Road, mile 15.3, to go under SR-526 and continue northeast. Join Beverly Blvd. at mile 16 to go north into Colby Ave. At mile 19.3, jog left (west) one block on Wall St. to Hoyt Ave. Turn north to the CT stop south of Hewitt St., mile 19.5. For the return, take CT 610 to Aurora Transit Center or take CT 620, 621 to Lynnwood Park & Ride.

EVERETT PARKS AND WATERFRONT, high point 380', 14 miles one-way, 350' gain (Maps: USGS Everett). **Bicycle**. Ride Community Transit bus 610, which begins at the Aurora Transit Center in Seattle (parking), to 41st St. at Evergreen Way in Everett.

Ride west on 41st St., which becomes Mukilteo Blvd. At mile 0.3, the intersection with Elk Hill Drive, turn left (southwest) into a paved path that ascends into **Forest Park**. Cross a paved path, which is an extension of Federal Ave., and descend west on a dirt path to a paved street. Turn left (south) and ascend to the park center: Floral Hall, Swim Center, playgrounds, trails, shelters, Recreation Office. Take time to walk one or more of the trails in the dense forest, but ride bicycles only on paved paths and streets. Visit the animal farm, which is down the slope west of the parking area.

When ready to leave the park, return to the Recreation Office opposite Floral Hall and go northeast and east on the incoming route to the extension of Federal Ave. east of the park entrance road. Turn left (north) and cross a walkway over Mukilteo Blvd. (mile 1.7) into Federal Ave. and continue north. Beginning at 40th St. and continuing north to Charles St. (on left), where Federal Ave. begins to descend, look east in gaps to mountains: Mt. Baker (18°), Whitehorse (56°), Three Fingers (60°), Pilchuck (72°), Big Four (81°), Bald Mtn. (86°), Stickney (98°), Baring (110°), Persis (113°), Index (114°), and Phelps (122°).

Turn left on 35th St. Stop at the first street, Kromer Ave., for a view of the Everett waterfront, then continue west on 35th St. Turn right (north) on Snohomish Ave., descending to 34th St. Turn left into Laurel Drive and continue down to pass **Rucker Hill Park** at the corner of Niles Ave. (descriptive sign). Go north on Laurel Drive to Warren St. Turn left (west) to a viewpoint southwest toward the Olympic Mountains. Return east on Warren St. to Kromer Ave. Turn left (north) and descend to Pacific Ave. Go left on Pacific Ave. At the intersection with Wall St. and Bond St., go left (west), passing under one railroad track and crossing another railroad track to Terminal Ave. (mile 3.8). Turn right (northeast) to pass a log storage and sorting area near a

Kimberley-Clark mill. Turn right (east) on California St. and ascend across railroad tracks to W Marine View Drive.

Turn north on W Marine View Drive to 25th St. Bend left (northwest) into Lower Norton St., crossing four railroad tracks. Continue north, then go right under a viaduct into an on-ramp to return to W Marine View Drive. Turn left (west) at 18th St. toward Marina Village, passing the **Everett Chamber of Commerce** in a restored Weyerhaeuser building (information, maps). Go west, jogging right past gates into the Naval Station, and ride on a paved path that continues west to **Everett Marina Village**. Tour the waterfront, bending north, then return east along the edge of the marina to W Marine View Drive (mile 6.5). Turn north, and again go west to circle the marina and reach the Everett Yacht Club. Walk up steps to a viewpoint at the north edge of the parking area, then go east on 14th St. on the north side of parking, passing **Firefighters Museum**, which has displays visible through windows: 1907 Ahrens steam power fire fighting pump, 1924 Seagrave Fire Truck, and a 1937 Ahrens Fox Fire Truck.

Go north on W Marine View Drive to 10th St., then go west to the **Everett Public Marina**, passing a decaying wooden boat hull under a roof. The marina has multiple boat ramps, fishing pier, restrooms, views to the Olympic Mountains, information displays, and free ferry to Jetty Island in summer. Exit east to W Marine View Drive. Turn north on a bumpy paved path past viewpoints over **Port Gardner Bay** and ascend a sidewalk on the west side of the W Marine View Drive viaduct. At the south end of the viaduct, turn right (northwest) on Alverson Blvd. to **Legion Memorial Park** (shelter, picnic area, arboretum, restrooms, golf course).

From Legion Memorial Park (mile 11.4), go southwest on Alverson Blvd. At mile 11.8, bend left (south) into Colby Ave., passing Everett High School. At Hewitt Ave., mile 14., turn right one block to Hoyt Ave. and the CT 610 stop for the return to Aurora Transit Center.

FOREST PARK, high point 360', 2 miles of trails, 100' gain (Maps: USGS Everett). **Walk**. From I-5, take Exit-192, then drive west on 41st St. into Mukilteo Blvd. At 1.2 miles from I-5, turn south into Forest Park and park at the top of the hill. For bus access, ride Community Transit 610 from Aurora Village Transit Center to 41st St. Walk west on 41st St. and Mukilteo Blvd. to the park.

Facilities: Floral Hall, swimming pool, playground, trails in forest, and animal farm with cows, sheep, horses, llamas, chickens, and goats. Opportunity to feed and touch the animals.

JETTY ISLAND, 10', 2 miles long, no gain (Maps: USGS Everett). **Walk**. From northbound I-5, take Exit-192 into Broadway Ave. Proceed north to Pacific St., then go west to Marine View Drive. Turn north to 10th St. Turn left (west) to parking at the waterfront and free ferry to the island (July and August, telephone 425-259-0300 for times). From southbound I-5, take Exit-194 into Everett. Go west to Marine View Drive. Turn north to 10th St., then drive west to parking at the waterfront. For bus access, ride Community Transit 610 to Everett. Walk west to Marine View Drive and north to 10th St. Distance: two miles.

Facilities: beach, nature walks and programs, picnic tables, restrooms. The water temperature exceeds 70° in summer. For warmest water, visit during incoming tide (see US West Yellow Pages).

EVERETT–SNOHOMISH, high point 220', 11 miles one-way, no gain (Maps: USGS Everett, Snohomish). **Bicycle**. Ride Community Transit 610 from Aurora Transit Center to 41st St. and Evergreen Way in Everett.

Ride east on 41st St., crossing I-5 at mile 0.5, then turn right (south) into S Third Ave., signed Broadway-Lowell. Pass **Lowell Park**, which begins at 46th St. (mile 1.1). Facilities: restrooms, shelter, playground, picnic tables, perimeter paved path with view of wetlands. Continue south on S 3rd Ave. into S 2nd Ave. Stop briefly at mile 1.8, a parking area with river and wetland overlook. At mile 2, turn left on Lowell River Road and at mile 2.2, go left (north) into Lowell Riverfront Trail and ride north downstream along the Snohomish River on a paved path that wanders through wetlands and sandy flood plain near the riverbank. Pass the remains (pilings) of a former bridge at mile 2.6. The paved path ends near a railroad track at mile 3.5.

Return south to the park entrance (mile 4.9) and continue east on Lowell River Road or a paved riverfront path, passing wetlands. Pass flood control gates at mile 5.5. Look across the Snohomish River to dairy barns and meadows in the flood plain of Ebey Island. A dairy barn at mile 9.2 on the south side of the river provides a near view of the chief activity of this area. Go under SR-9 at mile 10.2. Many of the houses here have been raised to cope with frequent floods. Reach Airport Way at mile 10.8. Turn left (north) across the Snohomish River into the town of Snohomish. North of the river, find the historic district beginning to the right (east) on First St. For the return to Everett, find Community Transit 720 stops on 2nd St., another block north.

MARYSVILLE–SNOHOMISH RIVER, high point 140', 17 miles

one-way, 180' gain (Maps: USGS Everett, Marysville). **Bicycle and/or Hike parts**. See at close hand the flood plains east of Everett that are visible from I-5. Ride Community Transit 610 from Aurora Transit Center to Everett, then take Community Transit 210 to Marysville. Leave bus at State Ave. and Grove St. If driving, take Exit-198.

Ride east on Grove St. (72nd St.) to 51st St. (Arlington-Marysville Road). Turn right (south) to **Jennings Park** on Allen Creek (restrooms, ponds, wetlands, shelter, picnic tables, paths). On leaving the park, ride south on Arlington-Marysville Road (Armar Road), which bends right and becomes Liberty Ave. Turn right (west) on 3rd St. to State Ave., then go south into SR-529, staying on the east side of the street to cross the bridge over Ebey Slough. Now SR-529 divides. Continue south on the east side of south-bound SR-529 over Steamboat Slough. Between these bridges the highway crosses wetlands. After crossing Steamboat Slough, go to the west side of south-bound SR-529 to exit from SR-529 into a frontage road, mile 2.8. Continue south, passing a return to SR-529, then bend left (east). Go under SR-529, then turn right into Smith Island Road past boat storage facilities. At mile 4.6, turn right to follow the shore of the Snohomish River. Reach **Langus Riverfront Park** at mile 5. Ride south on the paved path along the riverfront (shelter, boat launch, picnic tables, restrooms, river viewpoints, fishing piers).

Pass under I-5, then bend southeast before turning north to follow the bank of Union Slough away from the Snohomish River. Reach a bridge to Spencer Island at mile 7.3. The paved path ends at mile 7.8. Return to the bridge and cross south to **Spencer Island Park**, mile 8.4. Leave bicycle and explore the island. This area was previously a farm and storage area for wood waste that covered former wetland. The wetland has been restored by removal of the wood waste and one of the barns that was used for hay storage still remains. Many informative signs explain features of this tidal wetland. Cross the wetland on a causeway for a close view of the ponds and vegetation. A four mile perimeter trail follows the banks of the Snohomish River and Steamboat Slough. Find many Sitka spruce trees in the riparian woodland near the waterways.

On leaving Spencer Island (mile 8.5), return west on the paved path under I-5 and on the road past the boat storage facilities. At a junction, mile 12.1, take the left fork toward Everett to pass under SR-529. Go south at mile 12.6 into SR-529, crossing the Snohomish River. Escape west from SR-529 into 8th St., then follow Legion Drive and Waverly Ave. west and south. Go west to Colby Ave. and south to Hewitt Ave. Jog west one block to Hoyt Ave. and the CT 610 stop to return to Seattle.

MARYSVILLE–KAYAK POINT–SMOKEY POINT, high point 490', 36 mile loop, 1900' gain. (Maps: USGS Marysville, Tulalip, Stanwood, Arlington West). **Bicycle.** Ride Community Transit-610 from Aurora Transit Center to Everett, then take CT-210 to Marysville.

Leave bus at 5th Street on State Ave. Cross into **Comeford Park**. Facilities: restrooms in summer, tables, Senior Center, totem pole. Ride west on 5th St. to Delta Ave., then go south to 4th St. Turn right (west) across tracks. Find Chamber of Commerce information and maps at the caboose south of 4th St. on Cedar Ave. Continue west on 4th St. into Tulalip Road, entering the Tulalip Indian Reservation. Cross wetland at miles 0.9 and 1.2. Begin a narrow gravel shoulder at mile 1.8 and a wide paved shoulder at mile 3.8.

At mile 5.3, turn left (west) on 64th St. toward Mission Beach, then go right (northwest) on Totem Beach Road, passing Mission Bay. At mile 5.9, enter the grounds of the Tulalip Tribal Headquarters to see long boats and visit a viewpoint over Mission Bay. Return to Totem Beach Road and continue north. Pass the Tulalip Senior Center at mile 6.5 and reach **St. Anne's Catholic Church** (built 1904) at mile 6.8. After visiting the church grounds to read the signboard, turn left toward the marina to follow the shoreline past a gate and barrier to emerge on Waterworks Road. Turn right on the paved road past **The Silos** and another sign. This area was part of the Mission Indian School farm.

At mile 7.5, turn left on 36th Ave. NW to return to Marine Drive. Now go north. The wide paved shoulder soon ends but the traffic is light. Reach **Kayak Park**, a facility of Snohomish County, at mile 14.5 (restrooms, shelters, camping, fishing pier, boat launch ramp, beach access). Return to Marine Drive (mile 15.7) and continue north, passing 180th St. NW at mile 17.6 to the end of the street at mile 18. Return to 180th St NW. Go east to Marine Drive (mile 18.5), then turn north to the intersection with Lakewood Drive (mile 19). Turn left (west) on 188th St. NW into Warm Beach. Go south on Soundview Drive NW to a beach level viewpoint (no beach access), then return north on Soundview Drive, passing a high bank viewpoint to rejoin Marine Drive at mile 21. Go south for a mile to Lakewood Drive.

Turn east, passing **Myrtle Lake** (boating access east on 84th Drive NW). At mile 24, turn south on W Lake Goodwin Road to circle Lake Goodwin, passing Lake Shoecraft and a junction with 46th Ave. NW on the right before reaching **Wenberg State Park** at mile 28. Facilities: camping, restrooms, **Lake Goodwin** access, boat launch ramp, trails. Continue north on E Lake Goodwin Road to return to Lakewood Drive, mile 30. Turn right (east), now on SR-531, passing along the shore of Lake Ki. Take the left (east) fork at mile 33. Begin a bikeway at Lakewood High School (mile 34), cross railroad tracks, then go over I-5 into the community of Smokey Point. Turn left (north) on the first street to the CT 210 station, mile 36.

CAMANO ISLAND, high point 250', 22 miles RT, 1300' gain (Maps: USGS Stanwood, Camano Island, Juniper Beach, Utsalady, Crescent Harbor). **Bicycle**. From Aurora Transit Center, ride Community Transit 610 to Everett, CT-210 to Smokey Point, and CT-240 to Stanwood. Leave bus at Camano St. and 270th St. NW. If driving, park on 270th St. in Stanwood.

Ride west on 270th St. NW, then go south to SR-532. Turn west, crossing bridges over the Stillaguamish River and Davis Slough. Continue west to Good Road (mile 2.4). Turn north, curving west into Utsalady Road. Look north over Skagit Bay to Mt. Baker, south to Mt. Rainier, and east to Whitehorse (94°), Three Fingers (98°), and Mt. Pilchuck (113°). Join N Camano Drive at mile 6.5 and continue west. After N Camano Drive bends south, turn southwest on Sunset Drive. Pass street end beach viewpoints at miles 11 and 11.5. The beaches are private and not open to the public.

At mile 11.7, turn left on Madrona Beach Road and ascend east, meeting West Camano Drive at mile 12.2. Turn north to Dynes Road (mile 13.3), then go right (east) over the central ridge of Camano Island. The mountain directly east is Whitehorse. Bend northeast into Cross Island Drive and descend to meet East Camano Road. Turn northeast to join North Camano Drive and continue east to close the loop at Good Road (mile 19). Ride east on the outgoing route into Stanwood. Find bus stops for the return to Smokey Point on Camano St., 271st St. NW, south of 271st St. NW on 88th Ave. NW, and public restrooms in the Police Station at the intersection of 271st St. NW and 88th Ave. NW.

Snohomish–Monroe Area.

CENTENNIAL TRAIL, high point 240', 9 miles one-way, 200' gain (Maps: USGS Snohomish, Lake Stevens). **Bicycle or Walk**. A one-way trip using Community Transit buses, or, if driving, return to the starting point on the outgoing route. The paved Centennial Trail follows the route of the Seattle Lakeshore & Eastern Railroad, which began operation in 1889. The track was used until 1987.

Ride Community Transit 720 from Everett to 2nd St. and Maple Ave. in Snohomish. From Seattle, take Community Transit 610 from Aurora Transit Center (parking) to connect with the CT 720 in Everett. If driving, take US-2 five miles east from I-5 to SR-9. Turn north on SR-9 to the first cross street, then east on Bunk Foss Road to Machias Road.

The street becomes Ritchey Road after crossing Old Machias Road. Go south on Machias Road under US-2 to a parking area adjacent to the Centennial Trail, two miles from US-2.

Leave the CT Bus at Maple Ave. in Snohomish, then walk or ride east on 2nd St. to Cypress Ave. Turn south into **Pilchuck Recreation Area** (restrooms, picnic tables, shelter). From the park, return to Maple Ave. and 2nd St. Begin mileage log at 2nd St. and Maple Ave. Go north and northeast on Maple Ave. to the Centennial Trail at the junction of Pine Ave. and Maple Ave., 0.6 mile from 2nd St.

Pass a parking area with picnic tables near the Pilchuck River at mile 2.0. Cross Division Street in the village of Machias (parking, restrooms, information) at mile 5. North of Machias the trail crosses **Little Pilchuck Creek** into a nature observation area. Reach the Lake Stevens area at 16th St., mile 8.0 (play field, toilet). Turn west on 20th St. NE where the paved trail ends. North of 20th St. NE the railroad grade is either overgrown or it disappears under buildings. Extension north to Arlington is planned.

Turn left (west) on 20th St. NE to 124th Ave. NE. Go left (southwest) to Lake Stevens City Hall (restrooms, picnic table, information), library, Senior Center, and **North Cove Park** (tables, waterfront access) on the shore. To return to Everett, find the CT 280 stop on 20th St. NE and west of 124th Ave. NE.

LORD HILL PARK, high point 620', 8 miles loop, 10 miles of trails, 800' gain (Maps: Lord Hill Park, USGS Maltby). **Hike-1**. From the town of Snohomish, drive south on Lincoln Ave. into Old Snohomish-Monroe Road and go two miles. Turn south on Lord Hill Road (127th Ave. NE) and drive 1.5 miles to the park entrance on the left (toilets, information, map). From Seattle, take SR-522 north. Leave SR-522 at MP-23 to 164th St., then go west on Old Snohomish-Monroe Road for four miles. Turn south on Lord Hill Road (127th Ave. NE). The following is a sampler tour of the park.

Hike or ride east on a trail (boardwalks) to a 'T'. Turn right (southwest), ascending to a service gate at a house (no exit). Bend left (southeast) and proceed in dense forest of hemlock, fir, alder, and big leaf maple with a impenetrable understory of salmonberry and devils club. At mile 0.8, take a branch road that bends west. Continue west to an Olympic Mtns. viewpoint on Devils Butte, 580'. At the north edge of the viewpoint, find a trail returning east. Follow this trail along the edge of the bluff until it joins a road. Turn right (south) on the road to the outgoing route. Go left (east) to the main road. Turn south over minor ups and downs, passing a beaver dam on the east edge of the road. At a junction where the glacier-rounded underlying volcanic rock is exposed, turn right (southwest) and descend to the Snohomish River, elevation 20'. Look for mussel shells along the shore and beaver marked trees higher on the bank. East of the point where the track meets the river a bluff blocks the view up the river, but an overgrown track contours east to a view of the SR-522 bridge and beyond.

Return north from the river to a trail going east up a valley at elevation 200'. Follow this trail as it turns north to rejoin the outgoing route at the junction where the rounded underlying rocks are exposed. Go east from this junction to meet the pipeline trail. Jog north 100' on the pipeline to find a trail branching northeast. Take this trail east to Temple Pond, also the result of beaver activity. Return the same way to the pipeline, then go north on the pipeline over the high point to a road crossing. East of the crossing, hike up a glacier rounded rock prominence, 620', for a partial view. The road and trail east goes to Temple Pond. Return to the pipeline and continue north, passing another trail east that makes a loop to Temple Pond. Descend on the pipeline to Beaver Lake, the largest beaver pond in the park. The dam is on the east side of the trail. From the northwest corner of this pond, hike west to a junction with the outgoing route. Turn northwest to the start.

ECHO LAKE, high point 1800', 8 miles RT, 1400' gain (Maps: USGS Lake Chaplain). **Hike-3CMA**. A confusion of old railroad grades and roads makes this trip an adventure. If the trail seems to disappear, look carefully for a change in direction.

From US-2 in Monroe, turn north immediately east of the Red Barn, east of the stoplight at Chain Lake Road and west of the stoplight at Main Street. Drive north on Woods Creek Road. Two miles from US-2 where Kellogg Road goes to the left, continue straight ahead on Woods Creek Road. Yeager Road enters from the right (east) three miles from US-2. Turn right (north) on Lake Roesiger Road at a junction 11 miles from US-2, keeping right at mile 11.1 to drive through **Lake Roesiger Park** (restrooms, camping in summer, swimming). At Lake Roesiger Store, 13.4 miles from US-2, turn right on gravelled Camp Monroe Road and drive 3.3 miles, passing the Camp Brinkley entrance 1.2 miles from the paved road. Park near a gate, 16.7 miles from US-2, 750'.

Walk north past the gate for 0.3 mile to another creek crossing. This north-south valley is a meltwater channel cut during the retreat of the Puget Glacier. Turn east from the road and walk a wide path to the creek. **Explorer Falls** above is partially hidden by vegetation. Cross to the south side of the creek and ascend east in short switchbacks on a steep, narrow trail. Above the falls, the trail drops to cross the creek, then continues to ascend east, crossing an old railroad grade at 1200'.

The trail rises to the crest of a narrow ridge and continues east, passing a shelter camp at a small stream before reaching the plateau, 1700'.

On the plateau, follow a wide corridor east for 0.4 mile, then turn back northwest and north to follow another logging grade. Keep right at a fork to pass a pond partially filled with decaying logs. The pond was formed when the grade obstructed a creek. Continue north, then join another grade. Turn east on this grade, beginning a gentle descent near a creek for 0.5 mile. Where this grade bends to the southeast, watch for a branch that goes northwest, passing another pair of ponds on either side of the trail. The lower pond on the east side of the trail is an old beaver pond. Continue generally north 0.4 mile from the beaver pond on this trail, crossing gullies that drain east and passing the high point, 1800'. Where the grade crosses a wide gully and the center of the grade at this crossing has collapsed in a 20 feet wide hole with a creek at the bottom, look down on the east side to see the remains of two logs, each two feet in diameter protruding east from the bottom of the fill. North of this point, the grade has many more fallen trees. Leave the grade on the north side of the creek and go east on a narrow trail to the lake. A wood causeway leads to the shore of the lake. A sharp point of Bald Mountain is directly east.

WEST HAYSTACK MOUNTAIN, 4118', 22 miles RT, 4000' gain (Maps: USGS Sultan, Gold Bar). **Mtn. Bicycle.** From Seattle, drive north on SR-522, leaving I-5 at Exit-171. Go right (east) from SR-522 at MP-23 on 164th St., which becomes Main St. in Monroe. At 1.8 miles from SR-522, bend right into W Fremont St., then, at the second stop sign, go south on Lewis St. (SR-203), crossing the Skykomish River 2.4 miles from SR-522. Turn left on Ben Howard Road at 2.7 miles from SR-522 and drive east 7.7 miles from SR-203 and 10.6 miles from SR-522 to roadside parking at a gated road near McCoy Creek, elevation 178'. Alternate approach: From US-2 in Monroe (Lewis St.), drive south on SR-203 until 0.3 miles past the Skykomish River. Turn east on Ben Howard Road and drive as above to the parking area.

Ride east past a gate on a road marked W-22000, ascending briefly, then more gently, passing a minor road to the right at mile 0.6 and a bridge over McCoy Creek at mile 0.8. At mile 0.9, begin to get a view east of Haystack Mtn. Pass logging spurs to the right or left at miles 1.0, 1.1, 1.4, 2.2, a lake at mile 2.5, and more roads at mile 2.9. A branch road at mile 3.4 goes left (north) to a beaver pond. Beginning at mile 3.6, the main road passes south of a tree-studded double hill, then rounds to the north after passing a road to the right that crosses a bridge. Pass a viewpoint north to Mt. Pilchuck and Mt. Stickney at mile 4.2. More stub roads go right and left and at mile 5, 900', the grade steepens, starting up the scarp of Haystack Mtn. At mile 6.9, 2200', pass road W-22600 turning left (east). Reach a road junction with a view (mile 7.2, 2400'): Pilchuck (350°), Three Fingers (5°), Stickney (48°), and Ragged Ridge (68°).

Go left (southeast). The road deteriorates, going generally south and passing a branch road to the left (east) at mile 7.4. Reach Airplane Lake at mile 8.0, 3100'. A road over the outlet has been washed out. Cross and continue west on the road, now more overgrown and, in places, little more than a stream course on bedrock. The road passes above talus on the right (north) with a birds view of Monroe, Sultan, the valley of the Skykomish River, and many summits. Reach the crest at a junction (mile 8.7, 3560', lookout site). Turn east on road W-21980 and ascend on the south side of the ridge, passing a road descending right (southeast) at mile 9.2, 3600'. Keep left to enter a quarry at mile 9.8. Ascend the rubble at the west edge to find an old road. Proceed west until 100 feet east of the road end. Now ascend north (cairn) and continue up in young trees, then in thick but low salmonberry and thorny currant to a talus slope that leads to a rock summit surrounded by snags of ancient forest. The nearly 360° view includes: Three Fingers (4°), Stickney (39°), Sloan (48°), Glacier Peak (54°), Gunn (86°), Index (117°), Lennox (128°), Phelps (138°), and South Haystack immediately to the south.

HAYSTACK MOUNTAIN, 4384', 19 miles RT, 3800' gain (Maps: USGS Sultan, Gold Bar). **Mtn. Bicycle**. Drive as above for West Haystack Mtn. into Ben Howard Road. On Ben Howard Road, drive east 6.5 miles from SR-203 and 9.4 miles from SR-522 to Cedar Ponds Road. Turn south on Cedar Ponds Road, going right when 1.4 miles from Ben Howard Road. Cross Youngs Creek at 1.9 miles, then turn left (east) 0.5 mile from the Youngs Creek bridge to continue on Cedar Ponds Road, crossing Youngs Creek again. Pass Cedar Ponds Lake (private) to park at a gate 1.8 miles from Youngs Creek and 14 miles from SR-522, elevation 722'.

Pass the gate and ride northeast on road W-21000. At mile 1.9, curve south across the head of a glacial melt water channel and ascend a scarp carved by glaciers. Pass a view northwest of Dagger and Tomtit Lakes at mile 3.0. A road curves north (mile 3.1) and another road (mile 3.8) descends right (southeast). At mile 3.9, 1804', bend northeast, then turn south, getting a view of the buildings of Seattle. The canyon of Youngs Creek is below. At mile 5.3, 2280', road W-21700 branches south. Go east to a 4-way junction, mile 5.4 and 2350', then continue east on road W-21820 to another intersection at mile 5.9, 2590', where road W-21820 turns southeast downhill. Now go east on road W-21810, contouring to cross a creek, mile 6.1 and 2600'. After crossing the creek, road W-21810 curves north, ascending, and logging spurs go east: road W-21812 at 2600' (mile 6.1) and road W-21814 at 2720' (mile 6.2). Beyond the junction with road W-21812, from elevation 2600' to 2800', for 0.3 mile, road W-21810 is deeply eroded and rocky but improves after bending northeast to pass an unmarked and overgrown track not shown on the USGS map on the left at mile 6.4, 2800'. At mile 6.8, 3000', where another stub goes east, stay on road W-21810 as it bends southwest before resuming a northwest direction to pass another branch road east at mile 7.1, 3200'. Now road W-21810 curves north and east to meet road W-21900 at mile 7.9, 3540'. Turn left to join the ridge road at mile 8.0, 3620'. Now go right, passing a stub road right at mile 8.5, 3860', and a stub into a quarry at mile 8.7, 3940', the route to West Haystack Mtn. Continue to the end of the road, mile 9.2 and 4100'. Leave the road and continue east through the clearcut to the summit, which is barely inside the Mt. Baker Snoqualmie National Forest and still ancient forest.

ELWELL SCARP, 920', 3 miles RT, 300' gain (Maps: USGS Sultan). **Hike-1**. Drive as above for Haystack Mtn. to the crossing of Youngs Creek, 12 miles from SR-522 at MP-23. Continue south on the Youngs Creek Road, keeping right at a junction 4.7 miles from Ben Howard Road. Turn right (west) where a road (gated) goes south to Cherry Creek. Park at a junction, 6.4 miles from Ben Howard Road, and 15 miles from SR-522, elevation 620'.

Hike north on the branch road, descending briefly to a crossing of a branch of Elwell Creek, then, after passing a road left (west), bend left (northwest) to the plateau of Elwell Scarp, 920'. Follow the road to a viewpoint at the north end of the plateau, then, on the return, take all the branches that go west to the edge for the view down the glacier-carved wall.

Sultan Area.

The watershed around Spada Lake north of Sultan on the Sultan Basin Road is the source of water for Everett and South Snohomish County. The entire basin east of Olney Pass is designated for day use only except for camping at Greider and Boulder Lakes (closed to camping October 15 to June 15).

SULTAN TO SNOQUALMIE, high point 2600', 40 miles one way, 2900' gain (Maps: USGS Sultan, Gold Bar, Devils Slide, Mt. Si, Lake Joy, Snoqualmie, GT Index, Mt. Si). **Mtn. Bicycle**. Ride Community Transit 610 to Everett from Aurora Transit Center in Seattle, then take

CT-720 from Everett to Sultan. Leave bus in Sultan at the first stop after crossing the Sultan River bridge, elevation 140'.

From US-2, ride south on 311th Ave. SE (Mann Road), crossing the Skykomish River and Shinglebolt Slough (public fishing access parking). At mile 0.9, go west on Ben Howard Road, crossing McCoy Creek at mile 1.4. At mile 1.8, begin to get views of the Skykomish River on the right (north). Pass the gated road that leads to West Haystack Mtn. at mile 1.9. Enter Elwell Creek Valley at mile 2.5, then turn south on Cedar Ponds Road at mile 3.0, marked Dead End. The pavement ends at mile 4.1. Bend right at mile 4.3, then pass a gated road at mile 5.1. Pass another gated road going left at mile 5.3, elevation 506'. Descend briefly to cross a bridge over Youngs Creek, then continue south, leaving Cedar Ponds Road at mile 6.3 where this road turns left (east). Another road goes right at mile 6.8, elevation 574'. Pass a road to the left at 7.4 and a gravel pit parking area on the left at mile 7.6.

The road now bends to a little west of south, reaching a junction. Take the left (south) branch and begin to climb, passing a gate (Hancock Timber Resource Group) at mile 8.3, 1120'. The road is open to horses, bicycles, and hikers. Just beyond the gate, pass a road left and continue ascending south. Reach a high point at mile 8.6, 1300', then turn east, descending briefly to cross a glacial melt water channel before ascending across a north-facing slope.

The general direction through this confusing country of multiple logging spurs is south. If in doubt about which road to take at junctions, take the road to the right since, if wrong, these will end quickly. Reach another high point at mile 9.0, elevation 1650'. Take the road to the right at mile 9.4 and go southeast (120°), passing another road to the right at mile 9.7. The road curves north and descends briefly before turning back east. Take a branch right at mile 9.9 and cross another gully at mile 10.1. Now the road (W-21100) bends south and passes a Weyerhaeuser gate to a junction with road W-23359 at mile 10.5, which branches left (northeast), 1850'. Continue south on road W-23359, passing a viewpoint north at mile 11. Reach a critical junction at mile 11.2 of roads W-23359, W-23350, and W-31100, 2000'. The road south (W-31100) contours the west side of the scarp of Drunken Charlie Mtn. with little gain to join a main road (W-23200) on the north side of the North Fork of the Tolt River near a crossing of Yellow Creek (see South Haystack Mtn.)

Turn left (northeast) on road W-23350 and ascend around the north end of Drunken Charlie Mountain. Pass road W-23356 at mile 12.8 and road W-23352 at mile 13.2. Road W-23357 goes right (west) at mile 13.3, 2300'. The highest point of this ridge, 2800', is southwest from the 2300' intersection. Ascend right (north) on W-23357 and left (west) on road W-23358 to views of South Haystack Mtn. (74°) at 2400' and Haystack Mtn. (50°) at 2500'. Return to road W-23350, 2300', and continue south, joining road W-23300 near mile 14, 2400', and passing road W-23330 going right (west) at mile 14.5. Pass a gravel pit on the left (east) and a view of South Haystack Mtn. (24°) at mile 15.3. Cross the depression that becomes Yellow Creek at mile 16 and join road W-23000.

Turn right and descend south on road W-23000, then curve east to the broad valley of the North Fork of the Tolt River. Cross the North Fork Tolt River bridge at mile 19.0, 1200', now on road W-25000, and continue south across the ridge between the North and South Forks of the Tolt River. At mile 20.7, join the Tolt Pipeline and turn to the east for views up the South Fork Tolt River valley toward Mt. Phelps. The pipeline is exposed where the road crosses Lynch and Crazy Creeks. Join the Mainline Truck Road before crossing the South Fork of the Tolt River at mile 23. Now the road goes south, descending imperceptibly along the steep wall of the Cascade Mountains. Pass close on the east side of Fuller Mountain at mile 32, and reach the Gate 10 connection to the North Fork Snoqualmie River Road at mile 33. Continue southwest on the Mainline Truck Road, beginning pavement and passing a Weyerhaeuser Gate at mile 37. Stay on the main paved road through another gate, descending toward the Weyerhaeuser sawmill. Turn right near the sawmill, and follow the paved road west. At a junction with Millpond Road, turn right to SR-202, then go right again on SR-202 to the Metro 209 stop at Salish Lodge.

BLUE MOUNTAIN LOOP, high point 3080', 20 miles, 2700' gain (Maps: USGS Lake Chaplain, Wallace Lake). **Mtn. Bicycle**. The Blue Mountain Range stands in a bend of the Sultan River. Drive one mile east on US-2 from the Sultan River bridge in Sultan, then turn north on the Sultan Basin Road. Park near a gate, signed Sultan Watershed, after the paved road turns east, 5.3 miles from US-2 and 740'.

Ride north past the gate on a level gravel road, crossing a creek and the Sultan Pipeline at 0.4 miles. At one mile, the road bends west and descends before turning back north to cross a creek. At mile 2.0, the wide logging road narrows to a forest road. A branch road left (west) at mile 2.2 descends to the Sultan River. Turn left (northwest) on a more travelled road at mile 3.3. Take the right branch at mile 4.0, 1240', to cross a bridge over a cascade, then again go right (southeast) at mile 4.2, 1320'. Keep to the right again at mile 5.0, 1630', continuing generally east. Note many giant stumps. At 1800', the road bends north, becoming steeper and more eroded for the next mile and 500' of gain.

At mile 7.0 the road tops out on the crest of Blue Mountain at a lookout site, 2842', but growing trees hide the view. The road now drops to 2709' before rising to junctions, the first at mile 8 and 2811' with a road that goes northwest, and the second at mile 8.3 and 2849' with a road that goes south. Continue northeast and east to the high point at a communication tower, 3080'. For visible landmarks, see Blue Mtn. below. Going east, the road passes a gate at mile 9.7, 3000', to another viewpoint south. After passing a road left at mile 10.1, begin a steady descent to the Sultan Basin Road at mile 11.7, 2034'. Turn right (west) on the road, passing the Olney Creek Road, which goes to the left (east) at mile 13.2, and crossing to the west side of Olney Creek at mile 13.5. The road now descends more steeply with loose gravel and sharp curves, reaching pavement at mile 15.1. Cross west over Olney Creek again at mile 17.4 and reach the starting point at mile 20.

BLUE MOUNTAIN, 3080', 6 miles RT, 1200' gain (Maps: USGS Wallace Lake, GT Index). **Hike-1**. The Blue Mountain Range, which fills the area south and east of the Sultan River, ends at Olney Pass. One mile east of Sultan, turn north on the Sultan Basin Road. Drive the Sultan Basin road north and east for 12.8 miles and park at a junction with a road north, 2034'.

Hike north on the branch road, passing immediately a road right (northeast), then go west. Pass a stub road northwest, mile 1.6, 2955', and reach the crest at 3000'. A wide platform east of a gate (mile 2, 3064') provides views both south and north. Mt. Stickney is southeast (124°). Spada Lake is north. A log pile at mile 2.5 gives the best view west. Continue to the communication tower on the highest point, 3080', reached at mile 3.0 from the Sultan Basin Road. The north edge of the clearing stands above a steep bedrock slope that should be free of view-obscuring vegetation for many years. Look north to Mt. Pilchuck (340°), Bald Mtn. (59°), and Big Four Mtn. (60°). The west edge of Spada Lake reads 65°.

MOUNT STICKNEY, 5280', 10 miles RT, up to 3600' gain (USGS Wallace Lake, Mt. Stickney, GT Index). **Hike-4†, Snow**. While travelling east on US-2, look northeast from the Gold Bar area to see Mt. Stickney on the west side of the Wallace River, the deep notch in the skyline west of Wallace Falls. The summit stands on a narrow ridge, the culmination of the steep wall that rises northwest from the Wallace River. This summit should only be done when snow fills the gully to the final ridge (May or early June). Later, when the rocks are bare, the technical difficulty of this gully is probably beyond **Hike-4†**.

One mile east of Sultan, drive north and northwest on the Sultan Basin Road, crossing to the east side of Olney Creek at mile 7 and crossing back to the north side of Olney Creek at mile 11. After the second crossing of Olney Creek, and 11.3 miles from US-2, turn right (east) at a side road, 1679'. Depending on the state of logging activity in the area, this branch road is sometimes driveable. If not driveable, hike or ride a bicycle east and southeast, gradually rising above Olney Creek. Jog back to the north at a junction, 2090', before continuing southeast. At 3400' the road turns north briefly to the saddle between Olney Creek and the South Fork of the Sultan River and then goes southeast on the east side of the ridge. Park where the road levels southeast of the saddle near a 15' wall of exposed schist on the west side of the road, 3800'.

Walk southeast from the parking area for 220' beyond the point where the road becomes level. Find a faint trail on the right (west) side of the road that ascends southwest toward ancient forest. Follow this trail south and southwest, joining a trail coming from the north near the crest. Turn south on the joined trail, ascending in ancient forest. At 4300', where the trail is hard to follow, leave the crest of the ridge and descend south on open benches to One Acre Lake, 4107'. On the open benches leading to One Acre Lake, look for Mt. Stickney at 150° directly over the lake.

Pass the lake and ascend southeast (150°) in open forest or meadows. On the talus slopes that descend north from Stickney Ridge, ascend southeast (easy when snow covered), to a steep gully that heads into a notch in the ridge immediately west of the summit. The proper gully is the first gully west of the cliffs that drop north from the summit of Stickney. Ascend in this gully to the ridge, then turn east on the narrow, exposed ridge to the summit.

MIDDLE FORK SULTAN RIVER, high point 2400', 9 miles RT, 400' gain (USGS Wallace Lake, Mt. Stickney, GT Index). **Mtn./ Bicycle and/or Hike-2**. A Ragged Ridge Roadless Area view sampler (see Goldbar Area). One mile east of Sultan, turn north on the Sultan Basin Road. Drive the Sultan Basin road north and east to the Sultan Watershed entry near Olney Pass, 13.2 miles from US-2 and 2000'. Park at the information and registration kiosk (toilets).

Three roads continue from Olney Pass. The left hand road goes to Culmback Dam on Spada Lake. The middle road descends to the east shore of Spada Lake. Ride or hike the road to the right (southeast), passing a gate and contouring and ascending from the pass, travelling high above the Middle Fork of the Sultan River. Take the left fork at mile 0.3 and, at mile 0.6, begin to get views of Greider Mtn. (east) and Spada Lake (northeast). Cross a repaired road washout at mile 1.2 and a bedrock wall at mile 2.3 just before crossing a bridge over a branch of the Sultan River. Beyond the bridge, take the left fork to round a buttress to a viewpoint that looks east up another branch of the Sultan River to a saw-tooth ridge (part of Ragged Ridge).

Where the road travels almost directly south, it points at Mt. Stickney. Continue to the collapsed bridge over the Middle Fork of the Sultan River. The cliffs to the southeast are part of Prospect Peak, above the Kromona Mine across the Middle Fork. The Wallace River lies south of the ridge.

GREIDER LAKES, high point 3500', 6 miles RT, 2000' gain (USGS Mt. Stickney, GT Index). **Hike-1**. Drive the Sultan Basin road past Spada Reservoir to the trailhead, 21 miles from US-2, 1560'. The lake is closed to camping October 15 to June 15.

Ascend south on the trail, passing a burned out cedar snag at 0.5 mile. The trail varies in difficulty, depending on when it was last rebuilt, as it goes over, under, and through cliffs to Little Greider Lake, 2900'. Find several campsites near the outlet. Cross the outlet on a long bridge and continue to a junction, 3000'. The trail left goes to Big Greider Lake, 2932' (campsites). The trail right (southwest) ascends a rocky track to an airy viewpoint perched on the top of a cliff overlooking Big Greider Lake. Look south to an impressive headwall and southwest to Greider Mountain, 4880'. Don't expect to go on to Greider Mountain without great difficulty (brush and cliffs).

On the return to the starting point, take the loop trail that begins one-fourth mile from the parking area and go east through a wetland to the road.

BOULDER LAKE, 3706', 8 miles RT, 2300' gain (USGS Mt. Stickney, GT Index). **Hike-2**. Drive the Sultan Basin road past Spada Reservoir to the trailhead, 22 miles from US-2, 1840'. The campsites at the lake are closed from October 15 to June 15.

Ascend east on an old road to cross a bridge built in 1986 by the Washington Conservation Corps. The road deteriorates in places to little more than a rocky watercourse, then, at 0.8 mile turns into a narrow, rocky track, sometimes overgrown. At two miles, near the beginning of ancient forest, a detour has been built around a landslide, then, at 2.5 miles, where the trail begins to make switchbacks up the slope, get views southwest over an avalanche track toward a nearly vertical headwall across the valley. At three miles, cross a flowery meadow on a wood walkway. Beyond the meadow, in area where many of the standing trees are yellow cedar, pass through a cut in a 3' diameter fallen yellow cedar.

At the trail end, find several campsites above the northwest shore of the lake (toilet).

Goldbar Area.

From Goldbar to Index Junction. The Ragged Ridge Roadless Area north of Goldbar could be part of an intensive use trail recreation area that would be within an hour of both Seattle and Everett. The area contains more than 50 square miles of ancient forest, many lakes, including Lake Isabel and the Ragged Ridge Lakes, and at least 15 summits worthy of trails. User density could rival that of Mt. Si or Tiger Mtn. For the best general view of the area, visit Jumpoff Ridge. Persis also overlooks Ragged Ridge. The high country of Ragged Ridge is National Forest and the approaches are State Land.

WALLACE LAKE, 1800', 13 miles RT, 1500' gain (Maps: USGS Wallace Lake, Gold Bar). **Mtn. Bicycle or Hike-1**. In Goldbar, drive north on First St. for 0.4 mile. Turn east on McKenzie Road, then where May Creek Road goes east, continue north on Ley Road to **Wallace Falls State Park**, 320' and two miles from US-2 (camping, picnicking, restrooms, trails).

Ride or hike northeast on a trail under power lines (mile 0.3), passing the Woody Trail (mile 0.4), and an interesting old stump (mile 0.6). Turn a switchback (mile 0.9), cross a creek and come to a sign with map of the park (mile 1.5). Go left, leaving the Old Railroad Grade Trail, into a narrower trail with boulders and roots partially blocking the way. Turn another sharp switchback at mile 1.7, then pass under fallen trees in a marvelous moss-festooned forest. Join a DNR road at mile 2.4, going right (uphill). Pass a cliff on the right at mile 2.8 and a viewpoint south over the Skykomish River basin at mile 4.3. Reenter the State Park at mile 5.9 with the Wallace River below on the right (north) side of the road. Before crossing the Wallace River, turn left (west) on a narrow forest road to Wallace Lake, mile 6.6 (interpretive sign, foot bridge). Roads go left (west) around Wallace Lake to Jay Lake (1.6 miles) and right (east) to Wallace Falls (2.5 miles).

WALLACE FALLS, high point 1700', 7 miles RT, 1400' gain (Maps: USGS Gold Bar, Wallace Lake, GT Index). **Hike-1**. In Goldbar on US-2, drive north on First St. for 0.4 mile. Turn east on McKenzie Road, then where May Creek Road goes to the east, continue north on Ley Road to Wallace Falls State Park, 320' and two miles from US-2.

From parking at the State Park, hike the trail north, taking a right (east) fork at 0.4 miles on the Woody Trail. This trail ascends along the west side of the Wallace River and reaches the North Fork Wallace River bridge at mile 2. Detour briefly on the **Small Falls Logging Interpretive Trail** to read the explanatory signs and view stumps of 500-year-old trees. After visiting the waterfall viewpoints, return on the trail to the North Fork Wallace River bridge. South of the bridge, take a right fork to the Old Railroad Grade to complete the return to the parking area on a trail that passes through dense forest.

WALLACE RIVER BASIN, high point 1900', 12 miles RT, 1700' gain (Maps: USGS Gold Bar, GT Index). **Hike-2**. Drive and hike as above for **Wallace Falls** to the end of the trail at the highest viewpoint.

Leave the trail and ascend on one of several tracks for 0.1 mile in dense forest to a railroad grade. Go east on the railroad grade to the Wallace River above Wallace Falls and look northeast at the steep wall of the Ragged Ridge Roadless Area. Go west on the railroad grade, keeping right (north) at a 'Y' and ascend gradually into the upper Wallace River Basin, which lies between Mt. Stickney and Ragged Ridge. The railroad grade becomes steeper and more overgrown as it enters the basin. The view of Mt. Stickney is worth the trip.

WALLACE LAKE, 1844', 14 miles RT, 1500' gain (Maps: USGS Gold Bar, Wallace Lake, GT Index). **Hike-2**. Hike as above to Wallace Falls and continue toward **Wallace River Basin**. Take a left fork above Wallace Falls to reach Wallace Lake in 2.5 miles from the top of the falls.

LAKE ISABEL, 2847', 8 miles RT, 2400' gain (Maps: USGS Gold Bar, Index, GT Index). **Hike-3**. This lake, more than one mile long, lies in the Ragged Ridge Roadless Area (see Goldbar Area). Around 1900, it was a popular destination for the people of Everett. Now, to get to Lake Isabel is an adventure.

At MP-30 on US-2, two miles east of Goldbar, drive north on Reiter Road. At 0.8 mile, continue northeast (straight ahead) where May Creek Road goes left (north). At two miles from US-2, where Reiter Road bends east, turn left (northwest) into forest on a ponded road. Drive 0.3 miles from Reiter Road and park near power lines, 500'.

Find a road in the forest 100' north of the power lines and go northeast on this road parallel to the power lines. Pass two roads that descend to the east and get occasional views of towering Mt. Index (southeast). At 1.3 miles, stay on the main road as it turns west. Pass a road on the right that turns east and a road left that contours west. Round a bend (east) to the remains of the Copperbell Mine (1200') two miles from parking. Look for the partially collapsed mine adit at the eastern edge of the level area.

From the mine adit return west 160'. Ascend a track north past a stump wrapped with 1" steel cable to find a trail that ascends gradually northwest across the slope. This trail follows the route of a conduit that carried water from May Creek to the mine. At 1700', find a construction of heavy timbers on the left (west) side of the trail, the remains of the water line intake. Look west of the trail for a segment of old wooden pipe with several steel hoops. From the water line intake, continue north on the trail, which may become hard to follow depending on the number of fallen trees that have not been cleared. The route here varies, but this confusing area is brief. Join a stony road near 2000'. To the left (west) on this road is a bridge that crosses May Creek.

Ascend north, then follow the road as it bends in a sharp U-turn east and south away from May Creek. Leave the road 100' southeast of the turn and ascend east for 50' on what looks initially like a stream bed. Bend north from this rocky track into a well-defined trail that leads to an area of ancient trees with little underbrush near May Creek. Stay on the most travelled track north to the shore of May Creek, climbing over tree roots. Now follow the zig-zag route of the century-old road up the steep slope, finding fragments of wood decking. Detour on tracks around tangles of fallen trees, passing a mine adit part way up the slope. At the lake, go west to a log jam at an outlet. A second outlet, farther west along a shoreline track, provides a better view of the lake and a summit of Ragged Ridge (see cover).

RAGGED RIDGE LAKES, high point 4638', 8 miles RT, 2000' gain (Maps: USGS Index, Mt. Stickney, GT Index). **Hike-3**. These lakes could be part of a Ragged Ridge Recreation Area (see Goldbar Area) but now, reaching them is a challenging route finding problem. At milepost-30 on US-2, two miles east of Goldbar, turn north on Reiter Road. At 0.8 mile, where May Creek Road turns left (north), go straight ahead (east) on a paved road (becomes gravel at mile 2.6). Pass a paved road right at mile 2.4. At 3.8 miles from US-2, elevation 850', go left (east). The road on (south) goes to the town of Index. Drive a rough road southeast, east and northeast, passing minor side roads. Park 9.5 miles from US-2 at a fork, 2800'. The left road goes west up a minor summit and the right fork contours north.

Hike the narrow, brushy road north toward North Star Creek, crossing above a cliff that faces east and getting views of Jumpoff Ridge and Gunn Peak across the North Fork of the Skykomish River. At 0.5 mile, the road is closed by dense vegetation. Look for a track that wanders west through dense regrowth. Ascend this rough track into ancient forest. The track continues to ascend northwest across the slope toward North Star Creek, then disappears. Leave the track where the brush is least dense, sooner is probably better than later, and ascend the fall line west to the crest of a ridge that runs east-west above a talus slope that descends northeast to North Star Creek. On reaching the crest of this ridge, 4200', a single track is again obvious. Follow this track as it curves around toward the north on the crest of the ridge until the track disappears in level, open forest. At the north end of this open forest, 4300', turn northeast and ascend a talus slope of giant boulders to go over a minor summit, 4638', where the track again reappears. Follow this track to a basin with several lakes (no fires). More lakes (fish) lie on the west side of the ridge.

RAGGED RIDGE POINT 5150, 5150', 10 miles RT, 2600' gain (Maps: USGS Mt. Stickney, Index, GT Index). **Hike-3**. Ride and hike as above to the largest of the **Ragged Ridge Lakes**, which drains east, 4400'.

Circle around the eastern side of the lake, crossing the outlet, then ascend northwest across a ridge into an open basin with a small pond. Continue ascending northwest on the east side of a north-south ridge, then reach the highest point of the north-south ridge near the junction with an east-west ridge. This summit overlooks the north end of Lake Isabel, which is almost directly west (280°). For a look into the wild upper Wallace River basin, continue northwest in open forest and alpine meadows to Point 4937' where the main ridge turns west.

MOUNT PERSIS, 5464', 8 miles RT, 2700' gain (Maps: USGS Gold Bar, Index, GT Index). **Hike-3**. East of milepost-33 on US-2, turn south on a gravel road, FS-62. Where the main road bends southwest, mile 3.7, 1623', turn left (south) on a branch road. After this road bends east, park five miles from US-2 at the second of two roads branching left (north), 2800'.

Hike north up the second road for 0.5 mile to a landing and road fork. Turn up the west fork. From the point where the road begins to descend, continue 800' west to a well-defined track (2900') ascending steeply north in a clearcut. This track enters ancient forest at 3100' and crosses a talus slope at 4200'. Ascend in the talus slope to find the track continuing east up the ridge in a clump of vine maple. West of the first minor summit, 5017', descend southeast along the base of a talus slope, then contour east on a track across a low point, 4900'. Pass ponds at 5200' on the south slope of the Persis ridge and continue northeast to the open summit. The group of summits immediately north across the Skykomish River is the Ragged Ridge Roadless Area that surrounds the Skykomish River is the Ragged Ridge Roadless Area that surrounds Lake Isabel. The peak of Mt. Index fills the view southeast. Watch for trains on the curving tracks of the Burlington Northern Railroad in the valley below.

MOUNT INDEX, 5997', 12 miles bicycling + 12 miles hiking, 5200' gain (Maps: USGS Gold Bar, Index, GT Index). **Mtn. Bicycle, Hike-4†, Snow**. This trip is best done in June when snow is firm and no avalanche danger. East of milepost-33 on US-2, turn south on a gravel road, FS-62. Bend southwest on the main road at 3.7 miles from US-2, 1623'. Park at a gate, six miles from US-2 and 1600'.

Ride south, descending two miles to a junction near a bridge over the Tolt River, 1400'. Turn left (east) on the north side of the Tolt River, passing a road left (north) at one mile. Another road goes right (southeast) at 1889'. Continue to another junction, six miles from the gate and 2000'. Turn left (north), passing immediately a road that goes right (east) to a quarry. Park bicycle here where the road deteriorates briefly, or continue with bicycle.

Ascend northwest on the road in a regrowing clearcut, bending northeast at a switchback (2440') to pass a road on the right, 2840', which contours east. Leave bicycle here where the road deteriorates to boulders and continue ascending more steeply northeast, crossing a creek at 3000'. From shortly beyond the creek, the road has been covered with dirt and rocks. Continue to the end of the road, 4000'. Descend west to cross the creek (two branches), then ascend northwest through a tangle of 2' to 3' diameter blowdown at the edge of the clearcut for 200' of gain. Turn north on the east-facing slope near the crest of a north-south ridge. Enter ancient forest at 4300'.

Reach the main Persis-Index ridge at 5040'. Turn east and follow the crest of the ridge, bypassing a 5212' point on the north (steep snow). Descend to a low point (4900'). Now ascend east and northeast, staying near the crest of the ridge on open snow slopes.

BRIDAL VEIL FALLS, 1600', 4 miles RT, 1000' gain (Maps: USGS Index, GT Index). **Hike-1**. Drive 0.2 miles east of MP-35. South of the US-2 bridge over the Skykomish River, drive east on the Mt. Index Road. At a junction 0.25 mile east of US-2, turn right (south) and park in a large parking area, 600'.

Hike south on the branch road, passing a gate. Pass a road to the left 500' south of the gate, then cross a creek. Follow a rough track where the road has been eroded, then at 900', round east. Turn south at 1200', passing a branch road east (blocked), to a landing at 1250'.

Now follow a new trail (1998) that contours east across the slope. Before crossing Veil Creek, go right (uphill) at a branch, passing a collapsed cabin at 1500'.

LAKE SERENE, 2521', 6 miles RT, 2000' gain (Maps: USGS Index, GT Index). **Hike-1**. Drive and hike as above toward Bridal Veil Falls.

At a trail junction, 1200', continue east, crossing Veil Creek before ascending in switchbacks to the lake. Look up 2000' of cliffs rising to Mt. Index. On the return, pause before descending for the view of Ragged Ridge, Mt. Stickney (348°), and the Monte Cristo group (38° – 40°).

PHILADELPHIA MOUNTAIN, 4258', 9 miles RT, 3600' (Maps: USGS Index). **Hike-3. Snow**. Drive and hike as above to **Lake Serene**.

From the Lake Serene outlet, turn southeast and hike up the ridge to the forested summit. This trip is best done on snow in May or June after avalanche danger is past.

North Fork Skykomish River Area.

At Index Junction, 0.6 miles east of MP-35, turn north on the North Fork Skykomish River Road, FS-63.

JUMPOFF RIDGE, high point 2800', 8 miles RT, 2000' gain (Maps: USGS Index, Baring, GT Index, Monte Cristo). **Hike-2**. A logging road provides one of the best overall views of the Ragged Ridge Roadless Area. Park four miles from US-2 at a branch road blocked by a gate, 800'.

Hike an overgrown road south as it climbs up the canyon wall, then turn northeast, eventually crossing Bitter Creek, elevation 2300'. Continue to the road end. Look west to the ridges and summits of Ragged Ridge (see Goldbar Area).

IRON MOUNTAIN, 5241', 10 miles RT, 4300' gain (Maps: USGS Baring, GT Monte Cristo). **Hike-3**. After crossing Trout Creek, park six miles from US-2 at a branch road, 840'.

Hike this road, at first northeast, passing a branch south 150' from the paved road. The road bends southeast to travel on the north side of Trout Creek for one mile to a road fork, 1300'. Turn left at the fork and ascend northeast and east, rising above the valley of Trout Creek. Along the way, look south to the cliffs of Jumpoff Ridge and Gunn Peak. Where the road ends at 4300', leave the road and ascend an open slope to the ridge crest. Turn west along or near the forested crest of the ridge to reach the rock summit.

MINERAL CITY SITE, high point 2200', 10 miles RT, 1300' gain (Maps: USGS Monte Cristo, GT Monte Cristo). **Hike-3 to Hike-4†**. View a tumbling creek, many cascades, and visit the site of Mineral City, an old mining town. Nine miles north of US-2, turn left (west) over the Galena bridge and park 0.1 mile west of road FS-63 where a road turns north, 1100'.

Hike north on the Silver Creek road, FS-6335. At one mile, the road disappears in an active landslide and the route, for a short distance, becomes at times classification **Hike-4†**. Along the way to the Mineral City site, look for the following: one cabin (new), one bus (old), one adit, several clearcuts on nearly vertical slopes, and tumbling cascades in Silver Creek and branches. At Mineral City site, where the track is overgrown and bends northeast, any remaining evidence of past human habitation is hard to find.

TROUBLESOME CREEK NATURE TRAIL, 1250', 1 mile RT, 100' gain (Maps: USGS Monte Cristo, GT Monte Cristo). **Hike-1**. Drive 11 miles north of US-2 to the Troublesome Creek Campground, 1200'.

The nature trail begins in the campground and goes north along the creek under the FS-63 bridge, then crosses the creek (bridge) and returns to the campground on the east side of the creek. Look for water-carved rocks in the stream bed and the following plants in giant ancient forest: Douglas fir, red cedar, western hemlock, yew, salmonberry, devil's club, salal, service berry, and huckleberry. Branch trails go to benches in hidden corners.

BLANCA LAKE, 3972', 7 miles RT, 3300' gain (Maps: USGS Blanca Lake, GT Monte Cristo). **Hike-1. Henry M. Jackson Wilderness.** Visit a nearly one-mile-long lake in a cliff-rimmed glacial cirque beneath Kyes Peak, a spectacular setting. Drive 15 miles north and east of US-2 on road FS-63 to the junction with the Jack Pass Road. Turn northeast on the continuation of the North Fork Skykomish River road, FS-63, to the trailhead, 17 miles from US-2, 1900'.

Hike the trail north over the ridge (high point 4600') to the lake. Kyes Peak encloses the lake on the northeast.

KYES PEAK, 7280', 16 miles RT, 6100' gain (Maps: USGS Blanca Lake, GT Monte Cristo). **Hike-4†, Snow. Henry M. Jackson Wilderness.** Drive and hike as above toward Blanca Lake.

At Troublesome Ridge Pass, 4600', leave the trail and ascend north, on or near the crest of the ridge. At 5400', contour on the west side of a 5845' point on the ridge, then ascend north across the slope or on the ridge to a survey station, 7025', marked Monte Cristo on the USGS map. Continue north on the ridge and up ledges to the summit for a view toward the peaks of the Monte Cristo range. To make a loop on the return, descend on snow to Blanca Lake.

BALD EAGLE MOUNTAIN, 5680', 12 miles RT, 3200' gain (Maps: USGS Blanca Lake, GT Monte Cristo). **Hike-2. Henry M. Jackson Wilderness.** Drive 19 miles from US-2 to the trailhead, 2500'.

Hike north on a former mine trail, FS-1050, until just below Curry Gap, near an old miner camp, 3900'. Turn east on a trail that ascends to the ridge then continue southeast to the saddle east of the summit, 5200'. Leave the trail and ascend southwest to the summit.

BENCHMARK MOUNTAIN LOOP, high point 5816', 18 miles RT, 3600' gain (Maps: USGS Blanca Lake, Benchmark Mountain, GT Monte Cristo, Benchmark Mountain). **Hike-1. Henry M. Jackson Wilderness.** Drive 21 miles from US-2 to the end of the North Fork Skykomish River road, elevation 2800'.

Hike northeast on trail FS-1051 for two miles. Turn east on trail FS-1053 up Pass Creek to a junction with the Pacific Crest Trail. Trail FS-1053, as it begins across the valley of the North Fork of the Skykomish River, is subject to washouts and may be hard to follow in early summer. Where trail FS-1053 joins the PCT, Cady Pass is to the left (north) 0.5 mile. Go south on the PCT past the junction with trail FS-1054 to **Saddle Gap** to find a campsite south of the Gap, 5000'. This campsite near Saddle Gap makes a good base from which to explore south to Fortune Mountain and Peach and Pear Lakes.

To complete the loop, from Saddle Gap return north on the PCT for 0.5 mile to the junction with trail FS-1054. Turn left and ascend west to the south shoulder of **Benchmark Mountain**. Take a branch trail north 0.3 mile to the open grass-covered summit of Benchmark Mountain for a wide view from a summit that stands west of the Cascade Crest. From the summit, return south to trail FS-1054 and descend west on West Cady Ridge (huckleberries in season) to road FS-63. Hike road FS-63 northeast for two miles to the start.

BENCHMARK MOUNTAIN, 5816', 14 miles RT, 3500' gain (Maps: USGS Blanca Lake, Benchmark Mountain, GT Monte Cristo, Benchmark Mountain). **Hike-1. Henry M. Jackson Wilderness.** Benchmark

Mtn. can be hiked as a one-day trip from the Cady Ridge trailhead (2400') on the North Fork of the Skykomish River 19 miles from US-2.

Hike trail FS-1054 south and east up West Cady Ridge, going over the shoulder of Excelsior Mtn. Where the trail crosses the south shoulder of Benchmark Mountain, 5600', turn left (north) over the open plateau to the summit, an old lookout site.

FORTUNE MOUNTAIN, 5903', 10 miles RT, 2400' gain (Maps: USGS Benchmark Mountain, GT Benchmark Mountain). **Hike-3. Henry M. Jackson Wilderness.** Roundtrip distance is the distance from camping south of Saddle Gap.

From camping at Saddle Gap (see Benchmark Mountain Loop above), hike 2.5 miles south on the Pacific Crest Trail past the junction with trail FS-1057 at Fortune Ponds. Follow the PCT south above Fortune Ponds for 0.3 mile. Where the trail ascends east out of an open gully (5100') to cross a ridge to Pear Lake, leave the trail and continue south in the gully to the east ridge of Fortune Mountain. After leaving the PCT, the route is open and free of brush. At the ridge, turn west to the summit. Look for garnets in exposures of mica schist.

PEACH AND PEAR LAKES, 4807', 4809', 12 miles RT, 4200' gain (Maps: USGS Benchmark Mtn., Captain Point, GT Benchmark Mtn.). **Hike-3. Henry M. Jackson Wilderness.** The roundtrip distance and elevation gain given for this trip are from the camp site at Saddle Gap (see Benchmark Mountain Loop).

Hike as above to **Fortune Mountain**. From the east end of the summit plateau, descend southeast to Peach Lake at the head of the North Fork of the Rapid River. From the south end of the lake at the outlet, contour northeast above Grass Lake to the Pacific Crest Trail south of Pear Lake. Turn north on the PCT to the campsite at Saddle Gap.

PEAR LAKE, 4809', 8 miles RT, 1200' gain (Maps: USGS Benchmark Mountain, GT Benchmark Mountain). **Hike-1. Henry M. Jackson Wilderness.** From camping south of Saddle Gap (see Benchmark Mountain Loop), hike south on the Pacific Crest Trail past Fortune Ponds to Pear Lake. Pear Lake can also be reached from **Top Lake**.

South Fork Skykomish River Area.

From Index Junction to the Foss River Road, east of MP-50.

EAGLE FALLS, 700' (Maps: USGS Index, GT Index). **Hike-2.** Near MP-39, park at the falls.

Hike trails to the shore to view the falls, tumbling over water-carved bedrock.

HEYBROOK LOOKOUT, 1824', 3 miles RT, 1000' gain (Maps: USGS Index, GT Index). **Hike-1.** East of MP-37 on US-2, park on the north side of the highway at the sign marking the Mt. Baker-Snoqualmie National Forest boundary, 800'.

Find trail FS-1070 ascending northeast in the forest. The lookout tower stands on a spur of Heybrook Ridge. Summits visible include: Mt. Persis (252°), Mt. Index (228°), and Palmer Mtn. (163°).

HEYBROOK RIDGE, high point 5842', 6 miles RT, 3800' gain (Maps: USGS Index, Baring, GT Index, Monte Cristo). **Hike-4†.** In the village of Baring, east of MP-41 on US-2, turn north on Barclay Creek Road, FS-6024. Park 4.3 miles from US-2 at an overgrown branch logging road that goes north, 2200'.

Go north on this logging road, crossing Barclay Creek. Ascend north on an overgrown road or track (serious brush) for 700', at first in a regrowing clearcut, then in ancient forest where the travel improves. Stay west of the stream that forms the waterfall.

At 3400', where the cliffs begin, the track contours right (east), dropping steeply at one point to cross a gully. After crossing the gully, the route turns northeast and ascends a devious but passable route through dense brush. If in doubt about the return route, leave marking along the way. At 4200', the track leaves the brush and continues in open terrain to the crest of Heybrook Ridge. Turn northwest up one of several ramps to a high point. Merchant Peak is east. Look for Gunn Peak (38°).

BARCLAY LAKE, 2422', 4 miles RT, 300' gain (Maps: USGS Baring, GT Monte Cristo). **Hike-1.** From the village of Baring (MP-41), drive north on the Barclay Creek road, FS-6024, to the trailhead, 4.4 miles from US-2, 2200'.

Hike east, crossing Barclay Creek once (footlog with rail) to the lake, lying in an impressive setting under the north face of Baring Mountain.

BARING MOUNTAIN, 6125', 8 miles RT, 4000' gain. (USGS Baring, GT Monte Cristo). **Hike-4†, Snow.** This is the summit with the vertical north face seen from US-2 when looking east between Sultan and Goldbar. Drive as above to the trailhead for Barclay Lake, 2200'.

Ascend south in a tangle of dog-hair alder trees and salmonberry (tracks) to the crest of a subsidiary north-south ridge that ascends to the west ridge of Baring Mtn. The crest of the north-south ridge is less brushy than the sides. At the east-west ridge, 4200', turn east, leaving the ridge at 4400' to contour in forest at the base of the cliffs on the south side. After passing the cliffs, cross to the north slope into a boulder field (easiest when snow-covered). Ascend east across this boulder field, passing north of another summit, 6000', to the next saddle, 5600'. Turn northeast at the saddle and ascend on the exposed west side of the ridge to the summit.

DOROTHY LAKE, 3059', 4 miles RT, 1000' gain (Maps: USGS Snoqualmie Lake, GT Skykomish). **Hike-1. Alpine Lakes Wilderness.** At MP-46, turn south from US-2 on the old Cascade Highway, then, one mile from US-2, go right (south) on the Miller River road, FS-6410. The trailhead is 10 miles from US-2, elevation 2100'.

Hike trail FS-1072 to the lake, one of the largest lakes in the Alpine Lakes Wilderness. The trail continues around the east side of the lake to reach Bear, Deer, and Snoqualmie Lakes, all within six miles of the road.

RED MOUNTAIN, 5576', 5 miles RT, 3200' gain (Maps: USGS Mt. Phelps, Grotto, GT Mt. Si, Skykomish). **Hike-3**. At MP-46, west of the tunnel, turn south off US-2 on the old Cascade Highway for one mile. Go right (south) on the Miller River Road, then turn right (west) on the Money Creek Road, FS-6420. Continue west on the Money Creek Road for six miles, going beyond the upper end of a switchback to park at 2600' on the west side of a creek gully.

Leave the road and ascend north through dense regrowing forest, entering ancient forest at 3000' with an understory of huckleberry. Follow a relatively brush-free minor ridge on the west side of the gully to 4000', then bend northwest below steeper rocks to the east ridge of Red Mountain. Turn west on the ridge to the open summit. Crosby Mountain is east and Lennox Mountain is south.

TEMPLE MOUNTAIN, 3407', 8 miles RT, 2500' gain (Maps: USGS Grotto, GT Skykomish). **Hike-3. Snow**. This mountain is probably only of interest to confirmed summit baggers or connoisseurs of ancient forests. It is best done in the early spring when snow is firm and the snow depth is sufficient to cover the logging debris. At MP-46, go southeast from US-2 on the old Cascade Highway. After turning right (south) at the beginning of the Miller River road one mile from US-2, again turn right (west) on the Money Creek road, FS-6420, and park at the bridge, 1.7 miles from US-2, elevation 1000'.

Hike an old logging road (FS-6422) southwest on the south side of Money Creek, turning left (east) at one mile and ascending away from the creek in switchbacks. From the end of the road at 3300', continue north in ancient forest to the summit.

CLEVELAND MOUNTAIN, 5287', 10 miles RT, 4300' gain (Maps: USGS Grotto). **Hike-3. Snow. Alpine Lakes Wilderness.** Drive and park as above for **Temple Mtn.**

Follow the route as above for **Temple Mtn.** to the end of the old logging road at 3300'. Ascend east to the crest of the ridge, turn right and continue southwest, south and southeast up the ridge to the summit. This trip is best done in spring when snow covers logging debris.

EAGLE ROCK, 6515', 9 miles RT, 3500' gain (Maps: Mt. Baker Snoqualmie National Forest, USGS Evergreen Mtn., GT Monte Cristo). **Hike-4†. Snow.** One mile east of the town of Skykomish, turn north on the Beckler River Road, FS-65, for 0.7 mile. Turn left (west) on road FS-6510 and ascend north, taking a left fork on road FS-6514 at 1.1 miles from the Beckler River road. The road ascends into the canyon of Eagle Creek, passing a road left at 4.9 miles from the Beckler River Road. Park at a road junction, 6.2 miles from the Beckler River Road, 3300'. This trip is best done in the late spring (mid-May to mid-June) when snow covers brush in the avalanche track but when the danger of avalanches is past.

Hike the right branch road (northwest), descending 0.25 mile on a narrow road with no turning space to cross a bridge over Eagle Creek (gate). Hike east on the road for one-half mile. After passing the canyon that ascends north to the notch between Eagle Rock and Flapjack Point, leave the road and ascend northeast, at first in a brushy avalanche track, then in steep, open forest to the rock summit.

TOWNSEND MOUNTAIN, 5936', 9 miles RT, 3900' gain (Maps: USGS Baring, Evergreen Mtn., GT Monte Cristo). **Hike-3.** Drive and hike as above for Eagle Rock to the bridge over Eagle Creek.

After crossing the bridge, leave the road and ascend northwest on the north side of Eagle Creek, at first in a dense regrowing clearcut for a distance of 400', then in ancient forest with an understory of open huckleberry brush. Where the ancient forest ends at a talus slope, leave the creek and ascend northwest on open slopes of talus or low heather-huckleberry to the summit. Eagle Lake is south. The nearby summits include: Gunn (294°), Merchant (270°), Spire (353°), and Baring (235°).

SCORPION MOUNTAIN, 5540', 8 miles RT, 3600' gain (Maps: USGS Evergreen Mtn., Captain Point, GT Monte Cristo, Benchmark Mtn.). **Mtn. Bicycle and/or Hike-1**. East of Skykomish, turn north on the Beckler River Road, FS-65, for seven miles to a road junction just south of a bridge over the Rapid River, elevation 1400'. Turn right on the Johnson Ridge Road, FS-6520, for five miles to the trailhead, 2100'. In future, if road FS-6520 is closed to motor vehicles, ride a Mtn. Bicycle to the trailhead.

Hike east on trail FS-1067 over **Sunrise Mountain**, 5056', to the open summit. Peaks visible from the summit include: Labyrinth (60°), Lichtenberg (94°), Captain Point (175°), and Fernow (210°).

EVERGREEN MOUNTAIN, 5587', 4 miles RT, 2100' gain (Maps: USGS Evergreen Mtn., GT Monte Cristo). **Mtn. Bicycle and/or Hike-1**. North of the town of Skykomish on US-2, drive north on the Beckler River Road, FS-65, for 13 miles to Jack Pass and a multiple road junction, 2589'. Turn east and south on road FS-6550 for 0.9 mile, then take the left fork (southeast, road FS-6554) and ride or drive to the trailhead, nine miles from road FS-65 and elevation 3500'. This road is now open for motor vehicles but in future may not be maintained.

Hike northeast two miles to the summit. Find huckleberries in the fall.

Foss River Area. East of MP-50 on US-2, drive south on the Foss River Road, FS-68.

MOUNT SAWYER, 5501', 6 miles RT, 1500' gain (Maps: USGS Skykomish, Scenic, GT Skykomish, Stevens Pass). **Hike-1**. **Alpine Lakes Wilderness.** At 3.5 miles from US-2 on the Foss River Road, turn left on road FS-6830. At 10 miles from US-2, turn right, staying on FS-6830, and drive 1.3 miles south to the trailhead, 4300'.

Hike southeast along Tonga Ridge on trail FS-1058. At two miles from the trailhead, after going across a shallow valley that descends south, turn left (northeast) on a branch trail and ascend to the summit (huckleberries in season). Look for the following peaks: Glacier Peak (10°), Captain Point (12°), Windy Ridge (32°), Labyrinth Mtn. (34°), Jim Hill Mtn. (62°), Big Chiwaukum (80°), Bulls Tooth (85°), Surprise (111°), Trico (131°), Stuart (132°), Hinman (156°), Terrace Mtn. (158°), Daniel (162°), Rainier (204°), Malachite Peak (242°), Index (296°), Baring (308°), Monte Cristo Peak (346°), Sloan (349°), and Fernow (358°),

FISHER LAKE, 4763', 10 miles RT, 1400' gain (Maps: USGS Skykomish, Scenic, GT Skykomish, Stevens Pass). **Hike-2. Alpine Lakes Wilderness.** Drive and hike as above toward **Mt. Sawyer**.

After passing the fork to **Mount Sawyer** two miles from the trailhead, continue east to the broad saddle east of Mt. Sawyer where the trail begins to descend into the Deception Creek valley. Turn south in the saddle to find two well-defined tracks continuing south. One track goes southeast, descending slightly before turning south. The other begins 100' west of an isolated clump of trees: two mountain hemlocks , 30" and 12" in diameter, and three yellow cedars . This trail goes directly south. Ascend south on one of these trails, which rejoin before passing over a ridge to the lake.

NECKLACE VALLEY LAKES, 4600', 12 miles RT, 3000' gain (Maps: USGS Skykomish, Mt. Daniel, GT Skykomish, Stevens Pass). **Hike-1. Alpine Lakes Wilderness.** East of MP-50 on US-2, drive south on the Foss River road, FS-68. At four miles from US-2, park at the beginning of the East Fork Foss River Trail, elevation 1600'.

Hike southeast on the trail, FS-1062, turning southwest at four miles to ascend into Necklace Valley and reach Ilswoot Lake, the first of the lakes, six miles from the road.

COPPER LAKE, 4600', 12 miles RT, 3000' gain (Maps: USGS Skykomish, Big Snow Mountain, GT Skykomish). **Hike-1. Alpine Lakes Wilderness.** East of MP-50 on US-2, drive south on the Foss River road, FS-68, passing a road left to Tonga Ridge at 3.5 miles. Take the left fork at 4.7 miles from US-2, staying on road FS-68. The trailhead is 6.7 miles from US-2, elevation 1700'.

Hike south on trail FS-1064, passing Trout Lake in two miles, then ascending more steeply west to pass 0.25 mile east of Malachite Lake. Reach Copper Lake six miles from road FS-68. Camp only in the designated campsites at any of the lakes in this area.

BIG HEART LAKE, 4545', 14 miles RT, 3000' gain (Maps: USGS Skykomish, Big Snow Mountain, GT Skykomish). **Hike-1. Alpine Lakes Wilderness.** Hike as above to **Copper Lake**.

Follow the trail around the east side of Copper Lake to pass **Little Heart Lake**, 4204', and reach Big Heart Lake, seven miles from the road. Climb the rocky ridge, 5359', east of Heart Lake to look down on

Angeline Lake, surrounded by cliffs.

EVANS LAKE, 3700', 1 mile RT, 100' gain (Maps: Mt. Baker Snoqualmie National Forest, USGS Skykomish, GT Skykomish). **Hike-1. Alpine Lakes Wilderness.** East of MP-50 on US-2, drive south on the Foss River road, FS-68, passing the road to Tonga Ridge at 3.5 miles. Pass the road going left to the Foss Lakes trailhead at 4.7 miles from US-2 and continue on road FS-6840, which bends north after crossing a bridge over the Foss River. At 8.3 miles from US-2, turn left (south) on a branch road and park at the trailhead, 11 miles from US-2 and 3600'.

Hike west on the trail to **Evans Lake**. Find a generous campsite in ancient forest at the west end of the lake.

ROCK LAKE, 4546', high point 5280', 6 miles RT, 2500' gain (Maps: USGS Skykomish, GT Skykomish). **Hike-3. Alpine Lakes Wilderness.** Drive as above for Evans Lake to the end of the road and park in a large flat area, 3700' and 11.5 miles from US-2.

Return north down the road 100' to find a narrow grass track going west into a brush overgrown clearcut. Note culvert at the proper point to leave the road. The trail ascends near the crest of a minor ridge and enters ancient forest (4160'). After dropping briefly to a dumbbell-shaped pond, 4700', ascend west, going over a rock rib (5280') to north-south Maloney Ridge. Turn south for 0.5 mile, descending to 5100', then, at a fork in the trail, go left (east) to descend to Rock Lake, crossing heather-huckleberry meadows and a talus field.

MALONEY RIDGE POINT 6000, 6000', 8 miles RT, 2500' gain (Maps: USGS Skykomish, GT Skykomish). **Hike-3. Alpine Lakes Wilderness.** Hike as above toward **Rock Lake**.

At 5100' on Maloney Ridge, where the trail turns down to **Rock Lake**, continue south on a faint track on the ridge. Where the ridge steepens, 5700', turn southwest and drop to an open slope and continue south. Ascend until the ridge begins to descend. Turn west to reach the open summit. View the cliffs of Malachite Peak (170°) and the multiple summits of Cascade Mountain across the valley of the Miller River.

Tye River Area. From Foss River Road (MP-50) to Tunnel Creek Road (MP-60).

BECKLER PEAK, 5062', 8 miles RT, 2200' gain (Maps: USGS Skykomish, GT Skykomish). **Hike-3.** East of MP-52, turn north on the

Beckler Peak Road, FS-66. Turn left at a road fork, 3000', 7.0 miles from US-2 and drive to a road block, 7.5 miles from US-2 and 3100'. In future, the road beyond the road fork (mile 7) will not be maintained.

Hike the road northeast past a landslide and washout to a landing, 3200', where an overgrown road continues northeast. Turn west on an old logging road, going over a dirt barrier on the east side of a stream bed. This road was eradicated by the Forest Service and planted in 1996. After rounding the first bend, look directly west to a growing clearcut area above the route of the road, which can be seen as a light green line crossing the slope at the lower edge of the clearcut. The checkpoint to locate is the east edge of this cleacut. Cross two deep gullies, passing ancient forest above the road after the first gully. The clearcut above the road begins after the second gully.

Leave the road at 3200' and ascend the east edge of the clearcut along a border of ancient forest with a gully to the right (east). The obvious track here is apparently maintained by animals. At the upper edge of the clearcut, continue up in ancient forest to find a faint trail at 4200' that goes from the west summit of Beckler Peak to Alpine Baldy. Turn west on the trail, which may be hard to follow in places, passing below a cliff system that descends south from the lower east peak of Beckler. After passing the low point of the cliffs (4400'), ascend northwest, staying where possible on the trail west of cliffs. Where the trail levels near the summit, turn north and ascend a rocky knob. The highest of these involves technical climbing. The lookout was on a lower site farther west.

ALPINE BALDY, 5200', 10 miles RT, 3400' gain (Maps: USGS Skykomish, Scenic, GT Skykomish, Stevens Pass). **Hike-3**. Drive and hike as above toward Beckler Peak to the old trail at 4200'.

Turn east and follow the old trail as it ascends to the crest of the ridge east of Beckler Peak, then descends to the saddle between Beckler Peak and Alpine Baldy. Continue east, ascending on or near the ridge to pass the meadow area from which the peak received its name. Find the summit surrounded by forest.

JAKES LAKE, 5060', 14 miles RT, 4100' gain (Maps: USGS Skykomish, Scenic, Captain Point, GT Skykomish, Stevens Pass, Benchmark Mountain). **Hike-4†**. Drive and hike as above to Alpine Baldy.

From the summit of Alpine Baldy, go north on a track on the ridge that separates Harlan Creek (west) and the creek that drains from Jakes Lake. Drop briefly east or west from the ridge where steeper rocks bar the way, passing over or near a 5403' point on the ridge. Where the slope begins to rise into the ridge leading to Mt. Fernow at 5100', descend east to Jakes Lake.

MOUNT FERNOW, 6190', 16 miles RT, 5200' gain (Maps: USGS Skykomish, Scenic, Captain Point, GT Skykomish, Stevens Pass, Benchmark Mountain). **Hike-4**†. Drive and hike as above to Jakes Lake.

Pass the lake on the left (west) and ascend north to the summit. This trip is best done in June while snow still covers the brush above Jakes Lake.

IRON GOAT TRAIL WEST, high point 2800', up to 12 miles RT, 400' gain (Maps: USGS Scenic, GT Stevens Pass). **Hike-1**. This trail follows the railroad grade that preceded the present Burlington Northern track. This grade took nine miles to go from the location of Scenic to the Old Cascade Tunnel. The route passes the site where an avalanche destroyed trains in 1910. *Iron Goat Trail Guidebook*, which describes the history of the railroad in this area, is available from **The Mountaineers**.

East of MP-55, turn northeast from eastbound US-2 on road FS-67, the old Cascade Highway. Turn left (north) on road FS-6710 at 2 miles and park at the Martin Creek Trailhead, 4 miles from US-2 and elevation 2400' (toilet, maps, information).

The barrier-free trail goes downhill toward Scenic from the Martin Creek Trailhead for more than one mile. Two connecting trails provide access to the upper railroad grade, which goes around Windy Point to the old Cascade Tunnel. Near concrete avalanche roofs over the grade and one mile west of the old Cascade Tunnel, the route reaches the area of the 1910 avalanche. Pieces of the two trains that were caught by this avalanche still remain below the grade. Continue on the old railroad grade to the entrance to the tunnel under Stevens Pass. Look for tunnels and old timbers that were either part of snow sheds or rock-filled cribbing used as retaining walls. Please leave any artifacts in place and refrain from entering tunnels or constructions.

SCORPION MOUNTAIN, 5540', 10 miles RT, 2900' gain (Maps: USGS Captain Point, Scenic, GT Stevens Pass, Benchmark Mtn.). **Hike-2**. East of MP-55, turn northeast from eastbound US-2 on road FS-67 (US-2 bypass). Turn left (north) on road FS-6710 at 2 miles from US-2. At 5.5 miles from US-2, turn left to a bridge (Martin Creek) and park, 2900'.

Contour west for one mile on an overgrown (alder, cottonwood, willow) but passable (in 1998) logging track, then continue west on a trail in ancient forest to a junction with the Kelly Creek Trail on the east side of Kelly Creek. Turn right (north) and ascend high above the creek, passing west of Captain Point on a trail that was reopened about 1985. At a saddle north of Captain Point, 5000', where a faint trail branches east, continue north on a trail along the ridge between Johnson Creek (west) and the Rapid River (east) to the summit.

CAPTAIN POINT, 5724', 8 miles RT, 3000' gain (Maps: USGS Captain Point, GT Benchmark Mountain). **Hike-3**. Drive as above for Scorpion Mtn. and park near the bridge over Martin Creek, 2900'.

Cross the bridge over Martin Creek and hike north on a road that ascends in the clearcut on the south slopes of Captain Point. Where the road ends on the south shoulder, leave the road and follow a track north to the summit. The mountains visible include: Labyrinth (50°), Lichtenberg (73°), Fernow (244°), and Spire (304°).

EMBRO LAKE, 4152', 4 miles RT, 1000' gain (Maps: USGS Scenic, GT Stevens Pass). **Hike-2**. Drive as above for Scorpion Mtn. When 5 miles from US-2, turn right on a branch road and park at the crossing of Embro Lake Creek, 6 miles from US-2, elevation 3200'.

Look for a track 100' east of the creek. Ascend this track east and south, staying on the east side of the creek to reach the lake.

WINDY MOUNTAIN, 5386', 6 miles RT, 2400' gain (Maps: USGS Scenic, GT Stevens Pass). **Hike-3**. Drive as above for Embro Lake to the crossing of Embro Lake Creek.

West of the creek, ascend southwest in open forest to a ridge. Follow the ridge south to a 5073' point. Turn east (brush) to the summit and a limited view. The descent to Embro Lake is possible but not easy (brush and steep terrain).

SURPRISE LAKE, 4508', 8 miles RT, 2400' gain (Maps: USGS Scenic, GT Stevens Pass). **Hike-1**. **Alpine Lakes Wilderness**. Drive 0.7 miles east of MP-58, then turn southeast from US-2 into the site of Scenic, a former railroad station. Cross the railroad track and turn west 0.3 miles to park at the trailhead, 2200'.

Hike south on trail FS-1060 to the lake, ascending near Surprise Creek. Please do not camp within 100' of the lake. Trail FS-1060 continues south to meet the Pacific Crest Trail at 4900' between Surprise Lake and Glacier Lake, 4.7 miles from the trailhead. Trail FS-1060A branches east from the north end of Surprise Lake to meet the Pacific Crest Trail in 0.6 mile.

LITTLE PLUG, 6016', 10 miles RT, 3900' gain (Maps: USGS Scenic, GT Stevens Pass). **Hike-3. Alpine Lakes Wilderness.** Hike as above to the outlet of Surprise Lake.

Cross the outlet and go west, ascending granite boulders and slabs to **Little Plug Lake**. From the lake, go west up a forested slope to the summit.

GLACIER LAKE, 4806', 10 miles RT, 2700' gain (Maps: USGS Scenic, GT Stevens Pass). **Hike-1. Alpine Lakes Wilderness.** Hike as above to Surprise Lake and continue past the east side of Surprise Lake to Glacier Lake. No camping within 100' of the lake.

SURPRISE MOUNTAIN, 6330', 14 miles RT, 4300' gain (Maps: USGS Scenic, GT Stevens Pass). **Hike-2. Alpine Lakes Wilderness.** Drive and hike as above to Surprise Lake.

Hike trail FS-1060 south past Surprise Lake and Glacier Lake. South of Glacier Lake, leave the Pacific Crest Trail where it turns west to cross the ridge of Sparkplug Mountain and hike south up valley on an old version of the Pacific Crest Trail to Surprise Gap. On the east side of the Gap, find a trail that ascends west to the summit.

DECEPTION LAKES, 5053', 17 miles RT, 4700' gain (Maps: USGS Scenic, GT Stevens Pass). **Hike-1. Alpine Lakes Wilderness.** Drive as above for Surprise Lake.

After passing Surprise Lake, join the Pacific Crest Trail. Continue past Glacier Lake and Surprise Mtn. on the PCT to reach the lakes, an excellent location for hiking the nearby summits of the Cascade Crest. No camping within 100 feet of the lakes.

SURPRISE CREEK–STEVENS PASS LOOP, high point 5800', 17 miles one-way, 5300' gain (Maps: USGS Scenic, Stevens Pass, GT Stevens Pass). **Hike-1. Alpine Lakes Wilderness.** Ride the Greyhound Bus to Scenic at MP-58, elevation 2200'.

Hike trail FS-1060 to **Surprise Lake**. Turn east and ascend 0.6 mile to meet the Pacific Crest Trail, then follow the PCT east and north to reach Stevens Pass and a Greyhound Bus flag stop, passing above Trap Lake and near Hope and Mig Lakes. This loop can be extended to include Deception Lakes and Deception Pass, adding eight miles and 2000' of elevation gain for the round trip.

MAC PEAK, 6859', 4 mile RT, 2000' gain (Maps: USGS Scenic,

Stevens Pass, GT Stevens Pass). **Hike-3. Alpine Lakes Wilderness.** The distance and elevation gain given for this trip are from camping near **Deception Lakes** (see above).

From Deception Lakes, hike southeast through curiously grooved (glacial?) open forest for 0.5 mile, then over meadows in a valley. From the head of the valley, ascend southeast to the summit.

DECEPTION PASS, 4500', 7 miles RT, 1000' gain (Maps: USGS Scenic, Mt. Daniel, GT Stevens Pass). **Hike-1. Alpine Lakes Wilderness.** Drive and hike as above to **Deception Lakes**. The distance and elevation gain given for this trip are from camping near **Deception Lakes**.

From Deception Lakes, hike south on the nearly level Pacific Crest Trail to the pass. Openings in the forest along the way provide views of Terrace Mtn. (west) and Daniel and Hinman (southwest).

TRICO MOUNTAIN, 6640', 11 miles RT, 2800' gain (Maps: USGS Scenic, Mt. Daniel, The Cradle, GT Stevens Pass). **Hike-3. Alpine Lakes Wilderness.** Drive and hike as above to **Deception Lakes**. The distance and elevation gain given for this trip are from camping near Deception Lakes.

From Deception Lakes, hike the Pacific Crest Trail south to Deception Pass. Leave the trail at the pass and hike east up the ridge to the summit. This summit is at the corner of King, Kittitas, and Chelan counties and provides a view of many of the summits of the central Washington Cascades: Highchair Mtn. (110°), The Cradle (124°), Stuart (130°), Daniel (228°), Hinman (246°), and Terrace Mtn. (294°).

OLD CASCADE HIGHWAY, high point 4000', 12 mile loop, 1800' gain (Maps: USGS Scenic, Labyrinth Mtn., Captain Point, Stevens Pass, GT Stevens Pass, Benchmark Mtn.) **Mtn. Bicycle.** East of MP-58 and west of the bridge over the Burlington Northern Railroad tracks, park at the beginning of a branch road that goes northeast, the Old Cascade Highway, elevation 2200'.

Ride this paved road, passing the entrance to the new Cascade Railroad Tunnel at 0.4 mile. Cross a foot bridge over the Tye River at mile 1.6 and pass a gated road that descends northwest to the old railroad grade at mile 3.1. A powerline crosses the old Cascade Highway near this branch road. Continue ascending on the old Cascade Highway (gravel in places) to US-2 near Stevens Pass, mile 6.6. Turn west and descend on US-2 (Wheee!) to return to the starting point.

SCENIC HOT SPRINGS, 3500', 4 miles RT, 1200' gain (Maps:

USGS Scenic, GT Stevens Pass). **Hike-2.** Park 0.3 miles east of MP-59 (east of bridge over railroad track at Scenic) on the north side of US-2, 2300'.

Walk west on US-2 for 0.1 mile, cross the highway into a steep, rough road that ascends 0.3 mile south to a power line clearcut, 2700' (two power lines). Ascend southeast on the road or on rough trail short cuts under the power lines to the road high point, 3100'. The road ends 200' east at a steep drop to a creek. Turn right on a wide trail at the road high point and ascend south. The first creek comes from an undeveloped warm spring (84°F) a short distance above the trail. Continue on the trail to the main Scenic Hot Spring (elevation 3500'), which has several fiberglass pools and wood decks (clothing optional). In July 1997, the flow at the main discharge was about 10 gallons per minute at 115°F.

HOPE LAKE, 4400', 4 miles RT, 1400' gain (Maps: USGS Stevens Pass, GT Stevens Pass). **Hike-1. Alpine Lakes Wilderness.** East of MP-60, turn east from US-2 on the Tunnel Creek Road, FS-6095, to the trailhead, 1.3 miles from US-2, elevation 3000'.

Hike trail FS-1061 southeast to Hope Lake on the Pacific Crest Trail. **Mig Lake** (4661'), more open, is 0.5 mile north on the PCT.

SWIMMING DEER POINT 5520, 5520', 8 miles RT, 2800' gain (Maps: USGS Stevens Pass, GT Stevens Pass). **Hike-3. Alpine Lakes Wilderness.** Drive and hike as above to **Hope Lake**.

Hike north on the Pacific Crest Trail to the saddle (5200') next after passing Mig Lake. Look down on Swimming Deer Lake (east). Turn south and ascend open ramps and shelves on the east side of the ridge to the first rock summit and viewpoint: Jim Hill Mtn. (53°), Big Chiwaukum Mtn. (96°), Mt. Stuart (156°), and Cowboy Mtn. (316°).

Stevens Pass Area.

PACIFIC CREST TRAIL SOUTH TO SNOQUALMIE PASS, high point 6000', 71 miles, 14,000' gain (Maps: USGS Stevens Pass, Scenic, Mt. Daniel, Chikamin Peak, Snoqualmie Pass, GT Stevens Pass, Kachess Lake, Snoqualmie Pass). **Hike-1. Alpine Lakes Wilderness.** If travelling to the trailhead by bus, hike the PCT from Stevens Pass to Snoqualmie Pass. The Greyhound Bus has a scheduled stop at Snoqualmie Pass and only a flag stop at Stevens Pass.

Destinations on the PCT south from Stevens Pass: Hope Lake, 8 miles; Glacier Lake, 14 miles; Deception Pass, 21 miles; Deep Lake, 29 miles; Waptus River, 37 miles; Lemah Creek, 50 miles; Park Lakes, 56 miles; Ridge Lake, 64 miles; Snoqualmie Pass, 71 miles. Do not camp within one-fourth mile of lakes.

COWBOY MOUNTAIN, 5853', 4 miles RT, 2000' gain (Maps: USGS Stevens Pass, GT Stevens Pass). **Hike-2.** Park at Stevens Pass ski area, elevation 4000'.

Hike southwest under the ski lifts toward Grace Lakes and Summit Lake. At the southernmost of the lakes, ascend south to the notch in the ridge, then continue east to the summit and a view over the ski area to the surrounding mountains.

BIG CHIEF MOUNTAIN, 5858', 8 miles RT, 2000' gain (Maps: USGS Stevens Pass, GT Stevens Pass). **Hike-2.** Park in the area reserved for Pacific Crest Trail hikers on the east side of Stevens Pass (toilet).

Hike south on the PCT for two miles to the saddle at the edge of the ski area, 5200'. Where the PCT turns southwest and begins to descend toward Mill Creek, leave the trail and go northeast, ascending the open southeast side of the ridge to the summit.

LAKE JOSEPHINE, 4681', 11 miles RT, 2000' gain (Maps: USGS Stevens Pass, GT Stevens Pass). **Hike-1. Alpine Lakes Wilderness.** Park in the area reserved for Pacific Crest Trail hikers on the east edge of Stevens Pass and the south side of US-2.

Hike south on the PCT, leaving the ski area at a saddle, 5200', and then crossing under several power lines at the head of Mill Creek. The trail passes Lake Susan Jane before ascending to another minor saddle and a junction with the Icicle Creek Trail where the PCT branches south. Turn left (north) to descend to Lake Josephine.

LAKE VALHALLA, 4830', 10 miles RT, 1300' gain (Maps: USGS Labyrinth Mtn., GT Benchmark Mtn.). **Hike-1. Henry M. Jackson Wilderness.** Park in the area reserved for Pacific Crest Trail hikers on the east edge of Stevens Pass and the north side of US-2 (toilet). The trail begins east of the substation.

Hike north on the PCT, crossing slopes that avalanche frequently in the winter.

LICHTENBERG MOUNTAIN, 5844', 12 miles RT, 2500' gain (Maps: USGS Stevens Pass, Labyrinth Mtn., GT Stevens Pass, Benchmark Mtn.). **Hike-3. Henry M. Jackson Wilderness.** Drive and hike as above to Lake Valhalla.

Leave the trail at the south end of the lake and contour east to the open slopes of the south side of the mountain, then ascend north to the summit plateau. The rocks protruding at the west end of the summit plateau are the highest point. Be careful to return by the same route. The west slopes are much steeper.

Icicle Ridge Area

ICICLE RIDGE: STEVENS PASS TO LEAVENWORTH, high point 7100', 40 miles, 12,000' gain (Maps: USGS Stevens Pass, Chiwaukum Mountains, Big Jim Mountain, Cashmere Mountain, Leavenworth, GT Stevens Pass, Chiwaukum Mountains, Leavenworth). **Hike-2. Alpine Lakes Wilderness.** Ride the Greyhound bus to Stevens Pass, 4000'. Find the entrance to the Pacific Crest Trail on the east edge of the pass area on the south side of US-2 (parking area, toilets).

Hike south on the PCT, ascending through the Stevens Pass ski area to a saddle, 5200', that gives a view east down the valley of Mill Creek. A ski lift terminal is nearby. Descend south across the head of Mill Creek, passing under power lines and crossing roads. Pass Lake Susan Jane and ascend over a minor pass to reach a junction at 5000' and 4.5 miles from Stevens Pass where the PCT turns south. At this junction, turn left (north) to curve around the east side of Josephine Lake. From the lake, descend southeast 0.5 mile on trail FS-1551 along Icicle Creek to pass a junction with the Whitepine Creek Trail. Continue south down Icicle Creek another two miles to the junction with the Chain Lakes Trail, 3800' and 7.5 miles from Stevens Pass (camping). This trail junction can also be reached in 8.5 miles from the end of the Icicle Road (FS-76), 19 miles from US-2 in Leavenworth.

Leave the Icicle Creek Trail and ascend east to **Chain Lakes**, 5600', three miles from Icicle Creek, and lying in a basin below **Bull's Tooth Mountain**. Several impressive granitic monoliths dominate the skyline to the east, but the highest summit of this group is one of the less distinguished points southeast of Chain Lakes (see Bull's Tooth Mtn.). Continue east past Chain Lakes to hike over a saddle (6200') between two of the granitic monoliths, then descend into the basin of **Doelle Lakes** to find several picturesque campsites (toilet) on the benches near the upper and lower lakes.

After passing the lakes, cross to the south side of the outlet stream from the lower lake and descend on the old, sometimes overgrown Doughgod Creek Trail. At 5450', 500 feet before reaching a meadow that fills an old lake bed, the trail escapes from the brush to cross to the east side of the creek and continue southeast, disappearing in meadow. Look for the trail as it ascends southeast in a 20' wide corridor in the forest to go south under cliffs before descending. Where the trail levels (5400') and turns east near a pile of six foot boulders, look for a talus slope fallen from the cliffs above. The Doughgod Creek trail that formerly went to Icicle Creek disappears completely at this point, thus getting off the route here is difficult.

The trail continues east across the base of this talus slope and then contours across a bouldery slope. After entering forest, ascend on switchbacks to a saddle, 5600'. At the west edge of the saddle, turn right (south) at the junction with a fainter trail that goes east to Wildhorse Creek. The trail now ascends steeply, then crosses to the east side of the ridge. Continue south, descending to 5700'. Look for 0.25" garnets in blocks of schist scattered in a meadow.

While travelling, watch ahead for the location of the trail. The trail sometimes is hard to find in meadows and the location is often more apparent from a distance. At least one of the meadows that the trail crosses has a stream, making camping possible (no fires). Where the trail bends east around the head of the valley of Wildhorse Creek, find an established camp on a knoll. A stream crosses the trail 400' east of the campsite. Reach **Frosty Pass**, four miles from Doelle Lakes, 15 miles from Stevens Pass and 5800'. The pass area has room for many tents (no fires). Find water 0.25 mile south in the canyon or 0.5 mile west on the trail to Doelle Lake.

From Frosty Pass, continue east on trail FS-1570, passing a trail (FS-1592) left (north) that descends in the valley of Wildhorse Creek, then goes northeast near Whitepine Creek to a road (nine miles). **Big Chiwaukum**, the highest point in the Chiwaukum Mountains is accessible from this trail (see Big Chiwaukum). Ascend southeast to **Lake Mary**, 6450'. Several designated campsites have been established near this lake among the granitic domes of a pluton that invaded the surrounding schist and solidified around 40 million years ago (please camp only in established sites, no fires). A non-glaciated remnant surface high on **Snowgrass Mountain** is easily accessible from Lake Mary (see Snowgrass Ridge).

From Lake Mary, continue east and south on trail FS-1570 to cross, at 6800', the ridge south of **Ladies Mountain**. Ladies Mountain, 7708', is less than a mile northeast from this saddle (see below). Now follow trail FS-1570 as it contours east above Upper Florence Lake to Ladies Pass, 6800', and a junction with the South Fork Chiwaukum Creek Trail (FS-1571). Continue east on trail FS-1570 across the north face of **Cape Horn**, which may have steep snow fingers until late August. Cape Horn (below) makes a brief diversion. Reach **Lake Edna** at 6650', lying in a bare, rock-strewn cirque and not a comfortable place to camp. At the junction with the Chatter Creek Trail, FS-1580, find a magnificent view campsite (can be windy). **Grindstone Mtn.** is south.

From the junction of trails FS-1570 and FS-1580, descend east on trail FS-1570 near a creek to Index Creek at a junction with trail FS-1572, 4900'. Cross Index Creek and continue east on trail FS-1570 over a ridge, 6700', into the valley of Painter Creek to find little **Carter Lake**, 6150', and the junction with trail FS-1575. From Carter Lake, contour east on trail FS-1570 into the valley of the next stream, which drains north into Painter Creek (camping). From here, hike up **Lake Ida Point 7763** (below), the twin of Big Jim across Lake Augusta.

Cross the branch of Painter Creek and ascend east on trail FS-1570 to **Lake Augusta**, 6854', where level campsites abound. From here, **Big Jim Mountain**, 7763', a non-glaciated remnant surface, is a short hike (below). From Lake Augusta, continue east on trail FS-1570, passing trail FS-1577, coming from Hatchery Creek Road. Trail FS-1570 continues southeast along the ridge, then descends south to cross Cabin Creek, 5000' (camping). After crossing Cabin Creek, trail FS-1570 returns to the crest of Icicle Ridge and turns southeast, remaining at 6000' to 7000' and passing near the easily ascended rock prominence that was the site of **Icicle Ridge Lookout**, 7029', near the junction with the Fourth of July Creek trail, FS-1579, nine miles from Lake Augusta.

From the junction with the Fourth of July Creek Trail, continue east, still on trail FS-1570, on or near the broad crest of Icicle Ridge, gradually descending. Below 5200', the trail descends more rapidly in switchbacks to a campsite at 4200', which has a broad view to the east over rolling hills. Get water from Steep Creek, 200 feet north on a path. From the camp site, descend in more switchbacks to the Icicle Road in Leavenworth. Go north one mile on the road to Leavenworth and the Greyhound bus stop.

BULL'S TOOTH MOUNTAIN, 6807', 6840', 2 miles RT, 1000' gain (Maps: USGS Stevens Pass, GT Stevens Pass). **Hike-3. Alpine Lakes Wilderness.** The roundtrip distance and elevation gain given for this trip are from the trail above the highest of the Chain Lakes. This point is 11 miles one-way and 3200' of elevation gain from Stevens Pass (see Icicle Ridge).

Go south from 5800' in the valley toward the two points on the southern skyline. Near the notch between these two points, ascend the summits through big blocks of granitic rock. The western point is marked as the summit on the USGS map but the eastern point is slightly higher.

BIG CHIWAUKUM MOUNTAIN, 8040', 6 miles RT, 3000' gain (Maps: USGS Chiwaukum Mountains). **Hike-4†. Alpine Lakes Wilderness.** The roundtrip distance and elevation gain given for this summit are from Frosty Pass.

From Frosty Pass, ascend east toward Lake Mary for 0.1 mile then descend north on the Wildhorse Creek Trail, FS-1592, for one mile. At 5400', where the trail begins to descend again after crossing meadows, leave the trail and ascend northeast on open slopes to the west end of Lake Grace, passing rock outcrops. Cross the outlet stream and ascend north to the crest of the subsidiary ridge that drops west from Chiwaukum ridge. On the crest of this subsidiary ridge, turn east and ascend, staying on or near the ridge crest. Where this subsidiary ridge disappears into the broad slope of Big Chiwaukum, continue up to the crest of the north-south ridge. Turn north, staying on the ridge or on the west side, and ascend on broken rocks to a notch. From the notch, a narrow ramp leads around the west side of the summit block to the highest point.

The ascent of Big Chiwaukum can also be made from the end of the Whitepine Creek Road, FS-2800, three miles on road FS-6950 from US-2 near Milepost-78, by following the White Pine Creek Trail (FS-1582) west for 2.5 miles and the Wildhorse Creek Trail (FS-1592). At five miles south on the Wildhorse Creek Trail, 5200', turn left (east) near the outlet stream from Lake Grace (waterfall) and ascend on a track to Lake Grace. Continue to the summit from Lake Grace as described above. Roundtrip distance for the ascent from the Whitepine Creek Road is 19 miles and the elevation gain is 5300'.

SNOWGRASS RIDGE, high point 7800', 5 miles RT, 1800' gain (Maps: USGS Chiwaukum Mountains, GT Chiwaukum Mountains). **Hike-3. Alpine Lakes Wilderness.** This point on Snowgrass Mountain provides a marvelous view. The roundtrip distance and elevation gain are from Lake Mary, which is 1.5 miles from and 650' above Frosty Pass.

From camping at Lake Mary, return to trail FS-1570 and cross to the northwest side of Frosty Creek. Leave the trail and ascend the open slope near the creek. At 6300', turn right (east) above trees and go diagonally upward, staying on the north side of the stream. Continue east, either near the stream or on benches above the stream, into the basin under the cliffs of Ladies Mountain. Note swirly blocks of schist that have fallen from the cliffs of Ladies Mtn. Turn north, following the stream as it ascends into the valley between the 7161' point northeast of Lake Mary and the ridge of Snowgrass Mountain. Where this valley ends on the saddle east of the 7161' point, turn northeast and ascend the grass slope to the the ridge south of Snowgrass Mountain,

7300'. This relatively flat area is a non-glaciated remnant surface. Turn north and ascend the gentle, nivated slope to a notch with vertical walls. Summits visible from this point include: Cashmere Mtn. (154°), Stuart (172°), Highchair (198°), The Cradle (214°), Rainier (220°), Daniel (242°), Phelps (274°), Baring (294°), and Glacier Peak (345°).

CAPE HORN, 7316', 1 mile RT, 200' gain (Maps: USGS Chiwaukum Mountains, GT Chiwaukum Mountains). **Hike-3. Alpine Lakes Wilderness.** From trail FS-1570, one-half mile east of Ladies Pass where the trail begins to descend toward Lake Edna, leave the trail and ascend south to the narrow rock summit (marmots).

GRINDSTONE MOUNTAIN, 7533', 4 miles RT, 1500' gain (Maps: USGS Chiwaukum Mountains, GT Chiwaukum Mountains). **Hike-3. Alpine Lakes Wilderness.** The distance and elevation gain given for this trip are from the junction of trails FS-1570 and FS-1580 on Icicle Ridge. The summit is also accessible from Icicle Creek (below).

From the junction of trails FS-1570 and FS-1580, one mile southeast of Lake Edna, hike southwest on trail FS-1580 until the trail turns south. Leave the trail and ascend west over the low point in the ridge north of Grindstone Mountain. Turn south, contouring and ascending to the summit, composed of big blocks of granite.

LAKE IDA POINT 7763, 7763', 4 miles RT, 1800' gain (Maps: USGS Big Jim Mountain, GT Chiwaukum Mountains). **Hike-3. Alpine Lakes Wilderness.** The upper part of this mountain, which has the same summit elevation as Big Jim Mtn., is a non-glaciated remnant surface. The distance and elevation gain are given from trail FS-1570 in the valley of a branch of Painter Creek, one-half mile east of Carter Lake.

Ascend south in the valley from trail FS-1570 toward **Lake Ida**. On reaching the saddle above Lake Ida, 7100', turn east and ascend the broad, gentle slopes.

BIG JIM MOUNTAIN, 7763', 2 miles RT, 1000' gain (Maps: USGS Big Jim Mountain, GT Chiwaukum Mountains). **Hike-2. Alpine Lakes Wilderness.** The distance and elevation gain for this trip are from Lake Augusta. The upper part of this mountain is a non-glaciated remnant surface.

From trail FS-1570 at the south end of Lake Augusta, hike around the east side of the lake, then go north up the gentle slope to the summit.

From US-2, make the ascent of Big Jim Mountain from the Hatchery Creek Road, FS-7905, which begins near MP-90 across from Tumwater Campground. Drive two miles to the trailhead, 2800'. Hike southwest on trail FS-1577 for 3.0 miles to a junction with trail FS-1576, then 3.5 miles on trail FS-1577 to a junction with trail FS-1570. Go west for two miles on trail FS-1570 to Lake Augusta and continue as above. The roundtrip hiking distance from the Hatchery Creek Road is 20 miles (5400' gain). Additional map: GT Leavenworth.

Nason Creek Area. Smithbrook Road, MP-68, to Coles Corner, MP-84.

UNION PEAK, 5696', 4 miles RT, 1500' gain (Maps: USGS Labyrinth Mtn., GT Benchmark Mtn.). **Hike-2. Henry M. Jackson Wilderness.** East of MP-68 on US-2, turn north on Smithbrook Road and park 3.3 miles from US-2 at 4200', after the road bends sharply east.

Hike west on the Smithbrook Trail. At Union Gap, where the Smithbrook Trail, FS-1590, meets the Pacific Crest Trail 0.6 miles from the road, leave the trail and ascend on a track up the southwest ridge of Union Peak to the summit.

JOVE PEAK, 6007', 6 miles RT, 2800' gain (Maps: USGS Labyrinth Mtn., GT Benchmark Mtn.). **Hike-2. Henry M. Jackson Wilderness.** Drive and hike as above to the summit of Union Peak.

From the summit of Union Peak, continue on a track along the ridge to Jove Peak, passing a low point of 5200'.

LAKE JANUS, 4146', 6 miles RT, 600' gain (Maps: USGS Labyrinth Mtn., GT Benchmark Mtn.). **Hike-1. Henry M. Jackson Wilderness.** Near MP-68 on US-2, turn north on Smithbrook Road. At 3.3 miles from US-2, park at the trailhead, 4200', after the road bends sharply east.

Hike west on the Smithbrook Trail. At Union Gap, where the Smithbrook Trail, FS-1590, meets the Pacific Crest Trail 0.6 miles from the road, turn north on the PCT to the lake. Lake Janus is one of the few lakes of the Cascade Crest where the water temperature rises above 70°F in the summer.

GRIZZLY PEAK, 5597', 16 miles RT, 2000' gain (Maps: USGS Labyrinth Mtn., Captain Point, GT Benchmark Mtn.). **Hike-1. Henry M. Jackson Wilderness.** This destination makes a goal for a hike north along the Pacific Crest Trail, starting from the Smithbrook Road.

From the parking area on the Smithbrook Road, 3.3 miles from

US-2 at MP-68, hike as above to **Lake Janus**. Continue north and west, leaving the PCT at 5520' where the PCT turns north to contour across the west side of Grizzly Peak.

NASON RIDGE, high point 5300', 6 miles one-way hiking and 5 miles bicycling, 2000' gain (Maps: USGS Labyrinth Mtn., Mt. Howard, GT Benchmark Mtn., Wenatchee Lake). **Mtn. Bicycle, Hike-3CMA**. This trail, which shows on the 1975 GT map, has been abandoned and is hard to follow in places, but is open except for occasional blowdowns and low brush. East of MP-68 on US-2, turn north on Smithbrook Road, FS-6700, passing the trailhead to Union Gap and the Pacific Crest Trail at mile 3.3 from US-2. Leave a bicycle at **Rainy Pass**, four miles from US-2, and continue driving, descending north and east to a junction five miles from US-2. Take the right fork and drive east to the Snowy Creek trailhead, nine miles from US-2, 3600'.

Hike the trail south up Snowy Creek for one mile. After crossing, at 3850', the west branch of Snowy Creek, which drops over cliffs on the right (west) side of the trail, continue on the trail for 600', passing a sawed 24" log on the east side of the trail 300' after crossing the west branch of Snowy Creek. Find and follow a faint trace that ascends northwest on the right (west) side of the trail. Where this trace turns southwest at 4000', note a tall cedar tree in which steps have been ax cut (why?). Follow the trail southwest near the west branch of Snowy Creek, crossing northwest over a branch of the creek near 4100' (several blazes). The route of the old trail is hard to follow here. Go southwest between two water courses, at first in brush and small trees, then in open forest. Cross to the north side of the valley and continue southwest to west near the floor of the canyon (note talus slope to the south across the canyon), finding occasional blazes and traces of the trail. Ascend north above the creek the minimum necessary to find a way through rocks and dense brush in avalanche tracks, then continue southwest or west. Near 4700', the trail is more distinct where it turns northwest (330°) to ascend in switchbacks. The trail then goes west to the ridge (5120'). West from this ridge crest the trail is well-defined.

Contour west across the north slope of a high point (5480') on the main east-west ridge to the low point (5150') of a subsidiary north–south ridge. The trail now turns southwest to go below cliffs across the north slope of another point (5406') to the saddle (5120') west of this high point. Continue west on the trail, often hidden by vegetation, across the south slope of a final 5576' point. When south of the 5576' point, the trail makes one switchback (not obvious) toward the summit, before continuing west to turn the corner of the ridge at 5300'. The trail now descends northwest in switchbacks to Rainy Pass and the road, 4600'.

Avoid brush and marsh by exiting in a meadow east of a pond. On reaching the road, find bicycle and ride downhill to vehicle.

NASON RIDGE POINT 5576, 5576', 3 miles RT, 1100' gain (Maps: USGS Labyrinth Mtn., GT Benchmark Mtn.). **Hike-3**. Drive as above for Nason Ridge to Rainy Pass, elevation 4600'.

Hike southeast in the meadow 100' east of the pond, then go south on a track into the valley southeast of the pond. The trail becomes obvious on the slope above the brush surrounding the pond. Follow the trail (switchbacks 4800'-5050') until it bends east on the south-facing slope, then leave the trail and ascend east to the summit.

NASON RIDGE POINT 5406, 5406', 4 miles RT, 1600' gain (Maps: USGS Labyrinth Mtn., GT Benchmark Mtn.) **Hike-3**. Drive and hike as above to Nason Ridge Point 5576.

From the summit of Point 5576', descend southeast on the ridge to the old Nason Ridge trail, 5100'. Turn east across the saddle between Point 5576 and the next summit of Nason Ridge, Point 5406. Leave the trail at the east end of the saddle and ascend east on the crest of the ridge or on the south side of the ridge to pass cliffs.

NASON RIDGE POINT 5480, 5480', 6 miles RT, 1700' gain (Maps: USGS Labyrinth, GT Benchmark Mtn.) **Hike-3**. Drive and hike as above to the saddle between Points 5576 and 5406.

Continue east and northeast on the trail across the base of the cliffs of Point 5406 to the next saddle, then stay on the trail across the north side of Point 5480. Leave the trail at the saddle, 5120', and ascend a faint track southwest up the ridge to the summit. Walk south to a viewpoint.

NASON RIDGE POINT 5550, 5550', 6 miles RT, 1800' gain (Maps: USGS Labyrinth, GT Benchmark Mtn.) **Hike-3**. Drive and hike as above to the saddle (5120') northeast of Point 5480'.

From the saddle, hike northeast (intermittent track) on or near the ridge to the open summit. Summits in view: Rock Mtn. (90°), Arrowhead (142°), Chiwaukum Mts. (150°), Jim Hill (174°), Daniel (204°), Hinman (210°), Lichtenberg (258°), Gunn Peak (272°), Union (286°), Jove (300°), Labyrinth (342°), and Glacier Peak (348°).

ROCK MOUNTAIN, 6852', 10 miles RT, 3400' gain (Maps: USGS Mount Howard, GT Wenatchee Lake). **Hike-1**. Near MP-68 on US-2 east of Stevens Pass, turn north on Smithbrook Road, FS-6700. Drive north and east past Rainy Pass to a junction five miles from US-2. Take the right fork and drive east for four miles to the Snowy Creek Trailhead, 3600'.

Hike the trail south up Snowy Creek into the meadow basin west of Rock Mtn. Follow the trail east in the basin and ascend the west slope of Rock Mtn. to the crest of the south ridge. Turn north on the ridge and ascend to the summit.

MINOTAUR LAKE, 5550', 6 miles RT, 2000' gain (Maps: USGS Labyrinth Mtn., GT Benchmark Mtn.). **Hike-1. Henry M. Jackson Wilderness.** Near MP-68 on US-2 east of Stevens Pass, turn north on Smithbrook Road, FS-6700. After crossing Rainy Pass, take the left fork five miles from US-2 and again go left seven miles from US-2. The trailhead is 7.6 miles from US-2.

Hike trail FS-1517 to the lake. Theseus Lake is on the next bench below.

LABYRINTH MOUNTAIN, 6376', 8 miles RT, 2800' gain (Maps: USGS Labyrinth Mtn., GT Benchmark Mtn.). **Hike-3. Henry M. Jackson Wilderness.** Take an easy hike to rewarding views of summits and peaks. Best time: in the fall for the color of huckleberry foliage.

Drive and hike as above to Minotaur Lake. Continue around the east side of the lake and ascend north on a path to the summit.

LANHAM LAKE, 4200', 4 miles RT, 1200' gain (Maps: USGS Labyrinth Mtn., GT Benchmark Mtn.). **Hike-1.** East of MP-70 on US-2, turn south into Mill Creek Road, FS-6960 and park at the trailhead on the south side of the road, 0.2 miles from US-2 and 3000'.

Hike south to the lake, lying in a cirque under Jim Hill Mtn. The temperature of the water reaches 70° by the middle of August.

JIM HILL MOUNTAIN, 6757', 9 miles RT, 3800' gain (Maps: USGS Labyrinth Mtn., Stevens Pass, GT Benchmark Mtn., Stevens Pass). **Hike-4†.** Drive and hike as above to Lanham Lake.

At the south end of the lake, turn east (bearing 100°) and ascend to the low point in the ridge, 5300'. Follow the open heather ridge south to the summit. Ascend the final block from the east.

BYGONE BYWAYS, 3100', 1 mile RT, no gain (Maps: USGS Labyrinth Mtn.) **Walk.** West of MP-70 westbound on US-2, park by the roadside.

Follow trails to view traces of a pioneer road and an old railroad grade. Facilities: toilets, information.

ARROWHEAD MOUNTAIN, 6030', 7 miles RT, 3100' gain (Maps: USGS Mount Howard, GT Wenatchee Lake). **Hike-3. Snow.** Best time: late spring (April or May) when snow covers the clearcut above the end of the road. Leave US-2 east of MP-71 and park at a gated side road on the south side of US-2, elevation 2900'.

Hike the side road east, crossing Henry Creek, then after a short switchback, turn west to a junction. Take the left fork (east). Where the road reaches a tumbling cascade, turn back west for 0.1 mile, then again ascend east at a fork. Where the road crests at the lower edge of a clearcut, 4100', leave the road and ascend south in the clearcut. At the top of the clearcut, enter ancient forest at the northwest edge of a nearly level area, 4640'. Turn east across the level area and ascend to the north ridge. On the ridge, turn south to the summit.

The southwest ridge is also feasible. In the flat area, 4640', continue southeast to the southwest ridge of Arrowhead Mtn. On reaching the crest of the ridge, turn northeast to the summit. Peaks visible from the summit include: Rock Mtn. (350°), Mt. Howard (6°), Mt. Mastiff (18°), and Big Chiwaukum Mtn. (160°).

ARROWHEAD MOUNTAIN WEST PEAK, 5909', 7 miles RT, 3000' gain (Maps: USGS Mt. Howard, GT Wenatchee Lake). **Hike-3. Snow.** Hike this summit in spring (late April or May) when snow covers the clearcut above the end of the road. Drive and hike as above for **Arrowhead Mtn.** to the flat above the clearcut, 4600'.

Turn southwest and ascend on a minor ridge. Bypass a step in the ridge on the southeast side. On the crest of the north ridge of the west peak, turn south to the summit.

ROCK MOUNTAIN, 6852', 10 miles RT, 4300' gain (Maps: USGS Mt. Howard, GT Wenatchee Lake). **Hike-1 or Hike-3 (Snow).** This trip is an unforgetable experience on a stormy day in April or May. In late spring, ticks are plentiful on the lower slopes. Leave US-2 at MP-73 and park at the trailhead on the north side of US-2, 2600'.

Hike a road east for 0.2 mile, then ascend northwest on a branch under the power lines to another road that goes northeast on the north side of the power lines. The trail leaves this road near a tower and ascends northwest, staying below the crest of a ridge on the east side. At three miles from US-2, 6100', a branch goes right (east) to Rock

Lake. After passing the junction with the Rock Lake Trail, continue west to reach the crest of the ridge, passing a point, 6640', on the north side. After passing 6640', turn north on the ridge. Summits in view: Howard (44°), Big Chiwaukum (164°), Bull's Tooth (191°), Jim Hill (202°), Labyrinth (318°), Poe (334°), and Glacier Peak (344°).

If hiking to this summit as a snow trip, on the final approach after passing the 6640' summit, stay on the west side of the ridge below the line of protruding trees. The snow on this ridge is often deeply undercut on the east side by the rising sun and 20' or larger blocks of cornice can collapse unexpectedly. The author was on one of these blocks when it collapsed, but fortunately, the block only dropped 20' and didn't roll down the slope (see below).

ROCK LAKE, 5900', 9 miles RT, 3500' gain (Maps: USGS Mt. Howard, GT Wenatchee Lake). **Hike-1**. Drive and hike as above toward Rock Mtn.

At three miles on the trail, 6100', turn right (east) and descend to the the lake, lying in an open basin. In July, find house size blocks of snow that have fallen from the cornice that forms in winter on the south ridge of Rock Mtn.

DEADHORSE PASS, 7200', 12 miles RT, 4400' gain (Maps: USGS Chiwaukum Mountains, GT Chiwaukum Mountains). **Hike-2. Alpine Lakes Wilderness.** East of MP-78, drive west from US-2 on the Whitepine Creek Road, FS-6950, to the trailhead, three miles from US-2, 2800'.

Hike southeast on trail FS-1582 for 2.2 miles, then go south on the Wildhorse Creek Trail, FS-1592, as it ascends high on the slope east of Wildhorse Creek. At two miles on the Wildhorse Creek Trail, 4900', turn left (east) on a faint trail and ascend in open meadows to the pass and a view down to Cup Lake.

DEADHORSE POINT 7534, 7534', 13 miles RT, 4800' gain (Maps: USGS Chiwaukum Mts., GT Chiwaukum Mts.) **Hike-3. Alpine Lakes Wilderness.** Drive and hike as above to **Deadhorse Pass**.

Hike north up the ridge from the pass to the summit and a rewarding view of summits.

LAKE GRACE, 6242', 17 miles RT, 3500' gain (Maps: USGS Mt. Howard, Chiwaukum Mts., GT Chiwaukum Mts.) **Hike-2. Alpine Lakes Wilderness.** East of MP-78, drive west from US-2 on the Whitepine Creek Road, FS-6950, to the trailhead, three miles from US-2, 2800'.

Hike southeast on trail FS-1582 for 2.2 miles, then go south on the Wildhorse Creek Trail, FS-1592. At 7.2 miles from the trailhead, five miles from the Whitepine Creek Trail, cross the outlet stream from Lake Grace and ascend on a track to the lake, lying in an open meadow under Big Chiwaukum Mountain.

CHIWAUKUM LAKE, 5210', 18 miles RT bicycle, 7 miles RT hiking, 5100' gain (Maps: USGS Wenatchee Lake, Big Jim Mtn., Chiwaukum Mts., GT Wenatchee Lake, Chiwaukum Mts.). **Mtn. Bicycle and/or Hike-1. Alpine Lakes Wilderness.** At MP-82 on US-2, across the highway from the rest area, turn south across the railroad tracks, then go southeast around an airstrip before again going south. Pass a road on the right (west) before parking at a gate, 0.6 miles from US-2, elevation 2350'.

Ride south on the Coulter Creek Road, ascending over a high point, 3480', before descending to a road junction at mile 3.4, 3300'. The road left goes to Chiwaukum Creek in two miles. Go right to cross a low point at the head of Coulter Creek valley and begin to ascend northwest. Pass a spring hidden in brush on the left (east) side of the road at mile 4.0 and a creek at mile 4.1. Reach a junction at mile 4.5, 3760', turning left (west) on road FS-6935. A bit of ancient forest remains on the south side of the road. Take the left branch at another road fork at mile 4.8, 3840', entering ancient forest briefly. At mile 5.3, a trace of trail comes up from below, then goes on up the slope at mile 5.4. This trail is closed to wheels and pack stock.

Leave the forest at mile 5.5 (view east), cross a creek at mile 5.7, then take a right fork, ascending, at mile 6.0, 4430'. The road turns northwest at mile 6.2. Keep left at the next fork, mile 6.6. The right fork is marked **Tranquility**. Shortly after this junction, see Mts. Mastiff and Howard (north), and peaks of the Chiwaukum Range (west). Now pass minor logging spurs on the left before crossing another creek at mile 6.9, 4700'. Reach High Camp at mile 8.5, operated by High Country Adventures for winter sports activities (telephone 800-909-9916 or 425-844-2000).

Continue north past High Camp to the beginning of the trail to Chiwaukum Lake and Lake Julius at mile 8.8, 5320'. Leave bicycle (no wheels on trails that enter the Wilderness) and hike west on the trail. Pass the junction with the trail to Lake Julius at mile 10 (5600') and, mile 11, top the crest of McCue Ridge, 5800', entering the Alpine Lakes Wilderness. The trail in the wilderness is closed to horses. After going along the nearly level flowery crest of the ridge for 0.5 mile, the trail descends on the south side of McCue Ridge to Chiwaukum Lake, entering giant ancient forest of spruce and hemlock for the last 0.5 mile.

McCUE RIDGE, high point 6248', 23 miles RT, 4300' gain (Maps: USGS Wenatchee Lake, Big Jim Mtn., Chiwaukum Mts., GT Wenatchee Lake, Chiwaukum Mts.). **Mtn. Bicycle and Hike-2. Alpine Lakes Wilderness.** Drive, ride and hike as above toward Chiwaukum Lake.

Leave the trail anywhere on McCue Ridge above 5800' and hike northwest to the high point of the ridge, hidden in a clump of whitebark pine trees. Move around the summit area to gain views of the following summits: Big Jim Mtn. (155°), Snowgrass Mtn. (220°), Big Chiwaukum (235°), Howard (329°), Mastiff (335°), and Glacier Peak (338°).

ROUND MOUNTAIN, 5699', 4 miles RT, 1800' gain (Maps: USGS Wenatchee Lake, GT Lake Wenatchee). **Hike-1.** East of MP-82 on US-2, turn north on road FS-6910, possibly unmarked. This road is 0.2 miles east of the Rest Area on US-2. Drive north, staying on FS-6910 as it wanders toward Round Mtn. Take the right fork 4.6 miles from US-2 to the trailhead 4.7 miles from US-2, 3900'.

Hike northwest on trail FS-1529 to join trail FS-1583 on the crest of the ridge. Near the summit, 5600', openings in the forest give views south, but the summit is hidden in the forest.

ALPINE LOOKOUT, 6237', 10 miles RT, 2300' gain (Maps: USGS Wenatchee Lake, GT Wenatchee Lake). **Hike-1.** Drive and hike as above toward Round Mtn., staying on trail FS-1583 as it contours west across the south side of Round Mtn.

At 3.2 miles from the road, the trail descends slightly to cross a disturbed area: depressions and holes in the ground, and sharply broken slopes. This area is a landslide in slow motion, moving toward the Wenatchee River and Wenatchee Lake. At mile 4.5, go right (north) on a branch trail to the summit.

Nason Ridge Area.

MERRITT LAKE TO STEVENS PASS, high point 6600', 30 miles one-way, 7000' gain (Maps: USGS Mt. Howard, Labyrinth Mtn., Stevens Pass, GT Wenatchee Lake, Benchmark Mtn., Stevens Pass). **Bicycle, Hike-2. Alpine Lakes Wilderness.** We did this trip by Greyhound Bus, but the reconstruction of US-2 has eliminated the possibility of a bus stop near the Merritt Lake trailhead. Suggestion: Leave a bicycle at Stevens Pass and drive east to the Merritt Lake trailhead, east of MP-76 and 1.7 mile north of US-2, 3000'.

Hike north on the trail to **Merritt Lake** for many hiking and camping possibilities: Mastiff, Alpine Lookout, and Lost Lake. From Merritt

Lake, return 0.7 mile on the trail toward US-2, then go west on trail FS-1583, crossing Royal Creek to **Crescent Lake** (camping), four miles from Merritt Lake and 5440'. Mt. Howard is one mile north of Crescent Lake (below). From Crescent Lake, trail FS-1583 bends south for 0.5 mile before turning west to go over a ridge to **Rock Lake**, in meadows below Rock Mtn.

Continue west from Rock Lake, ascending to the south ridge of Rock Mtn. to a junction, 6600'. From this junction the summit of Rock Mtn. is 0.3 mile and 300' of gain. Descend west on the Snowy Creek Trail, FS-1583, to the meadow where the east branch of Snowy Creek begins. At the west end of the meadow, bend north, descending and crossing to the west side of the East Fork of Snowy Creek. Cross the West Fork of Snowy Creek before reaching a road, then follow this road five miles to Rainy Pass. From Rainy Pass, descend west on the road for 0.7 miles to trail FS-1590. Leave the road on the north side to hike northwest one mile to Union Gap (camping). Hiking destinations from Union Gap include Union Peak, Jove Peak, Lake Janus, and Grizzly Peak. From Union Gap, hike south on the Pacific Crest Trail for seven miles to Stevens Pass, passing Lake Valhalla.

MERRITT LAKE, 5003', 6 miles RT, 2000' gain (Maps: USGS Mt. Howard, GT Wenatchee Lake). **Hike-1**. Leave US-2 east of MP-76 and drive north 1.7 miles to the trailhead, 3000'.

Hike northeast on the trail to the lake. Please do not build ground fires in this heavily used area.

LOST LAKE, 4930', 9 miles RT, 3200' gain (Maps: USGS Mt. Howard, GT Wenatchee Lake). **Hike-1**. Drive and hike as above to Merritt Lake.

From Merritt Lake, continue around the east side of the lake on the trail over a minor ridge to Lost Lake, which drains north to the Wenatchee River.

MOUNT MASTIFF, 6741', 12 miles RT, 4200' gain (Maps: USGS Mt. Howard, GT Wenatchee Lake). **Hike-3**. Drive, park and hike as above to **Merritt Lake**.

Hike past the east side of the Merritt Lake and continue north on the trail to the saddle south of Lost Lake. Leave the trail and follow the ridge southwest, west, and northwest, diverging from the ridge to benches on the east side to pass steeper sections of the ridge. Continue north on the ridge to the summit.

ALPINE LOOKOUT, 6237', 14 miles RT, 3800' gain (Maps: USGS Mt. Howard, Wenatchee Lake, GT Wenatchee Lake). **Hike-1**. Drive and hike as above toward **Merritt Lake**.

From near Merritt Lake, continue on the trail past the east side of the lake and ascend east on trail FS-1583 to the crest of the ridge. Hike the trail near or on the crest of Nason Ridge to the lookout, reached by a branch trail north from FS-1583.

CRESCENT LAKE, 5440', 10 miles RT, 3000' gain (Maps: USGS Mt. Howard, GT Wenatchee Lake). **Hike-1**. Leave US-2 at MP-76 and drive 1.7 miles to the trailhead north of US-2, 3000'.

Hike the trail northwest. At two miles, turn west from the Merritt Lake Trail and contour across Royal Creek to Crescent Lake, lying in an open basin on the south slope of Mt. Howard.

MOUNT HOWARD, 7063', 12 miles RT, 4600' gain (Maps: USGS Mt. Howard, GT Wenatchee Lake). **Hike-3**. Drive and hike as above to **Crescent Lake**.

Pass the lake on the west side and hike north and northeast on open, occasionally rocky slopes to the summit. This is the highest and most rewarding of the Nason Ridge summits. Peaks visible from the summit include: Big Chiwaukum Mtn. (172°), Mt. Daniel (210°), Mt. Hinman (215°), Labyrinth Mtn. (302°), Poe Mtn. (326°), Glacier Peak (340°), and Mt. David (352°).

Lake Wenatchee Area.

At Coles Corner, MP-84.8, drive east from US-2 on SR-207. Go left into the Lake Wenatchee Road at mile 4.5.

DIRTYFACE LOOKOUT, 5989', 9 miles RT, 4000' gain (Maps: USGS Wenatchee Lake, GT Wenatchee Lake). **Hike-1**. Find the trail near the Lake Wenatchee Ranger Station at MP-8, elevation 2000'.

Hike the trail, FS-1500, northeast and northwest to the lookout site, crossing a road at two miles.

TOP LAKE, 4600', 10 miles RT, 1000' gain (Maps: USGS Poe Mtn., Labyrinth Mtn., Benchmark Mtn., GT Benchmark Mtn.). **Hike-1. Henry M. Jackson Wilderness.** This lake provides a high, open, view campsite close to the Pacific Crest Trail within easy day-hiking distance of Peach Lake, Pear Lake, Grizzly Peak, and Fortune Mtn. From US-2 near MP-84, drive northeast on the Lake Wenatchee Road, SR-207.

After passing Lake Wenatchee at mile 10.6 from US-2, turn left on the Little Wenatchee River Road, FS-6500. At mile 16, turn left on road FS-6700 for 0.5 mile, then go right on road FS-6701. After passing Theseus Creek Campground and road FS-400 on the left, go left on road FS-500 to the trailhead, 3700' and 25 miles from US-2.

Hike west on trail FS-1506, passing across the south slopes of **Shoofly Mtn.** and going almost over the summit of **Fall Mtn.**, 5594'.

GRIZZLY PEAK, 5597', 9 miles RT, 2000' gain (Maps: USGS Bench Mark Mtn., Captain Point, GT Benchmark Mtn.) **Hike-1. Henry M. Jackson Wilderness.** Drive and hike as above to **Top Lake**. The distance and elevation gain are from Top Lake.

From Top Lake, hike west 0.5 mile to the Pacific Crest Trail. Turn south, descending to Wenatchee Pass. After travelling on the east side of the ridge, the trail bends west around a 5770' hump then returns to the ridge. Before the trail bends east and begins to descend in switchbacks, step off the trail to the summit. On the return, at a 5400' low point leave the trail and ascend the ridge northeast (**Hike-3**) to the 5770' summit, then follow the ridge north to the trail.

FORTUNE MOUNTAIN, 5903', 8 miles RT or loop, 1600' gain (Maps: USGS Benchmark Mtn., GT Benchmark Mtn.) **Hike-3. Henry M. Jackson Wilderness.** Drive and hike as above to **Top Lake**. The distance and elevation gain are from Top Lake.

From Top Lake, hike west to the Pacific Crest Trail. Turn north on the PCT, passing Pear Lake. After ascending to a saddle, 5200', leave the trail and contour southwest into a shallow valley. Ascend south in this valley to the east ridge of Fortune Mtn. Turn west to the summit. Look for garnets in the local mica schist.

To complete a loop by way of Peach Lake, descend southeast from the east end of the summit plateau to the lake. From the south end of the lake at the outlet, contour northeast above Grass Lake to the PCT at 4700' east of Pear Lake.

WENATCHEE RIDGE, high point 6500', 13 miles RT, 4000' gain (Maps: USGS Poe Mtn., Labyrinth Mtn., Benchmark Mtn., GT Benchmark Mtn.). **Hike-2. Glacier Peak Wilderness, Henry M. Jackson Wilderness.** Find many view campsites and few people on this high ridge between the Wenatchee River and the White River. Drive the Wenatchee River Road, SR-207, for 10.6 miles from US-2, then go left on the Little Wenatchee River Road, FS-6500, to the end of the road at the Little Wenatchee Ford Campground, 25 miles from US-2, 3000'.

Hike the Little Wenatchee River Trail, FS-1525, for 0.2 mile, then turn east on the Wenatchee Ridge Trail, FS-1520, and ascend. Near the crest of the ridge (mile 3), turn north on the trail and continue past Poe Mtn. and Longfellow Mtn., hiking the crest of the ridge some of the time. Find campsites just north of the branch trail to Poe Mtn. (snow patches for water), west of Longfellow Mtn. (creek), and south of Bryant Peak at a small lake, 5900', that doesn't show on the USGS map. This lake makes a good turnaround point since the trail becomes hard to follow and is cut by avalanche gullies across the west side of Bryant Peak.

POE MOUNTAIN, 6015', 6 miles RT, 3100' gain (Maps: USGS Poe Mtn., GT Benchmark Mtn.). **Hike-1. Glacier Peak Wilderness.** Drive and hike as above for **Wenatchee Ridge** to the trail junction near the crest of the ridge.

After turning left near the crest of Wenatchee Ridge, find a branch trail that goes right (east) to the open summit, which has views over the valleys of the Wenatchee and White Rivers. Summits visible include: Mt. David (48°), Rock Mtn. (154°), Fortune Mtn. (250°), and Benchmark Mtn. (278°).

LONGFELLOW MOUNTAIN, 6577', 10 miles RT, 4000' gain (Maps: USGS Poe Mtn., GT Benchmark Mtn.). **Hike-3. Henry M. Jackson Wilderness, Glacier Peak Wilderness.** Hike as above on **Wenatchee Ridge** two miles north of the Poe Mtn. junction. Leave the trail and ascend east to the summit.

MEANDER MEADOW–CADY RIDGE LOOP, high point 5800', 24 miles RT, 5000' gain (Maps: USGS Poe Mtn., Glacier Peak East, Glacier Peak West, Benchmark Mtn., GT Benchmark Mtn., Glacier Peak). **Hike-1. Henry M. Jackson Wilderness, Glacier Peak Wilderness.** Drive the Wenatchee River Road, SR-207, for 10.6 miles from US-2. Go left on the Little Wenatchee River Road, FS-6500, to the end of the road at the Little Wenatchee Ford Campground, 25 miles from US-2 and 3000'.

Hike north on the Little Wenatchee River Trail, FS-1525, for 6.5 miles and 1900' of elevation gain to Meander Meadow, 4900' (camping). Hiking possibilities from Meander Meadow include Kodak Peak and Bryant Peak.

From Meander Meadow, continue briefly west to join the Pacific Crest Trail. Turn north on the PCT, passing Kodak Peak and crossing Indian Pass to **Reflection Pond** 5.5 miles from Meander Meadow, 5600' (camping). From here, White Mtn., White Pass, Red Pass and Portal

Peak can all be hiked in a day.

From Reflection Pond, return south on the PCT, passing the trail to Meander Meadow and stopping at **Dishpan Gap** (5200', camping), six miles and 800' gain from Reflection Pond. Find trails to Johnson Mtn., June Mtn., Blue Lake, Long John Mtn., and the North Fork Skykomish River. The PCT south from Dishpan Gap reaches Cady Pass in 4.3 miles, passing Skykomish Peak and Lake Sally Ann.

To return to the trailhead at the end of the Little Wenatchee River Road (FS-6500), go south on the PCT for 1.3 miles from Dishpan Gap to Wards Pass, then descend southeast on Cady Ridge, crossing a bridge over the Little Wenatchee River to the road, 7.5 miles from Dishpan Gap.

KODAK PEAK, 6121', 3 miles RT, 1300' gain (Maps: USGS Poe Mtn., GT Benchmark Mtn.). **Hike-2. Henry M. Jackson Wilderness.** The distance and elevation gain given for this trip are from Meander Meadow.

From Meander Meadow, hike west to the Pacific Crest Trail. Turn north, then leave the trail and ascend north on a track to the summit, which heads the valley of the Little Wenatchee River.

BRYANT PEAK, 6401', 10 miles RT, 1800' gain (Maps: USGS Poe Mtn., GT Benchmark Mtn.). **Hike-2. Henry M. Jackson Wilderness, Glacier Peak Wilderness.** The distance and elevation gain given for this trip are from Meander Meadow.

From Meander Meadow, hike west briefly to the Pacific Crest Trail. Turn north and hike one mile on the PCT to the junction with the Wenatchee Ridge Trail. Follow a trail, poorly defined in places, east and southeast for four miles along a delightfully open alpine ridge to the summit, going near or over intermediate summits of 6052', 5861', 5840', and 6295', to the highest point. South of Bryant Peak, the ridge drops abruptly and the trail disappears.

PORTAL PEAK, 6999', 10 miles RT, 1400' gain (Maps: USGS Glacier Peak West, GT Glacier Peak). **Hike-2. Glacier Peak Wilderness.** The distance and elevation gain given for this trip are from Reflection Pond.

From camping at **Reflection Pond**, 5600', hike north on the Pacific Crest Trail, crossing White Pass, 5904', where a trail descends east into the valley of the White River, to Red Pass, 6460'. At Red Pass, leave the PCT and ascend north on a track for a rewarding view of Glacier Peak (35°), Black Mtn. (331°), Pugh Mtn. (308°), and Sloan Peak (266°).

WHITE MOUNTAIN, 7043', 12 miles RT, 1500'gain (Maps: USGS Glacier Peak West, GT Glacier Peak). **Hike-2. Glacier Peak Wilderness.** The distance and elevation gain given for this trip are from Reflection Pond.

From **Reflection Pond**, hike as above for **Portal Peak** to Red Pass. Leave the trail at Red Pass and hike east along the south side of the sandy ridge to the summit for an impressive view of Glacier Peak and the summits to the east and southeast: Ten Peak Mtn., Clark Mtn., and Indian Head Peak.

From the summit of White Mtn., descend south along the ridge to return to the PCT and Reflection Pond. On the way down from the summit, look for tiny garnets in the schist exposed on the ridge.

JOHNSON MOUNTAIN, 6680', 7 miles RT, 2800' gain (Maps: USGS Benchmark Mtn., GT Benchmark Mtn.). **Hike-1. Glacier Peak Wilderness, Henry M. Jackson Wilderness.** The distance and elevation gain given for this trip are from **Dishpan Gap**.

From camping at Dishpan Gap, hike northeast on trail FS-65, taking a right fork on trail FS-652 at mile 0.7 to Blue Lake, lying in a steep-walled basin south of Johnson Mtn. Pass the lake on the west side and continue on the trail north across a steep open slope to the west ridge. At a trail fork, turn east to the summit, a former lookout.

JUNE MOUNTAIN, 5946', 6 miles RT, 1000' gain (Maps: USGS Benchmark Mtn., GT Benchmark Mtn.). **Hike-1. Glacier Peak Wilderness, Henry M. Jackson Wilderness.** The distance and elevation gain given for this trip are from **Dishpan Gap**.

From Dishpan Gap, hike west on trail FS-652, which passes near the summit.

LONG JOHN MOUNTAIN, 5697', 10 miles RT, 2000' gain (Maps: USGS Benchmark Mtn., GT Benchmark Mtn.). **Hike-2. Henry M. Jackson Wilderness, Glacier Peak Wilderness.** The distance and elevation gain given for this trip are from **Dishpan Gap**.

From Dishpan Gap, hike west on trail FS-652, passing over the summit of **June Mtn.** and continuing west along the ridge. Where the trail diverges to the south to pass across the south side of Long John Mtn., find an overgrown and obscure track that continues on the ridge to the summit.

TWIN LAKES, 2822', 7 miles RT, 1000' gain (Maps: USGS Mtn. David, Schaefer Lake, GT Wenatchee Lake). **Hike-1. Glacier Peak Wilder-**

ness. Drive east from US-2 at Coles Corner, MP-84.8, on SR-207 and north on the Lake Wenatchee Road. At 10.6 miles from US-2, go north on FS-64 to the trailhead, 16 miles from US-2 and 2000'.

Hike east on trail FS-1505 above the Napeequa River. Pass through a grove of giant red cedar trees before crossing Twin Lakes Creek. Turn south to the first lake. Find a view campsite on a rock bluff above the northeast corner of the lake. The second lake is one mile south of the first lake.

MOUNT DAVID, 7420', 14 miles RT, 5200' gain (Maps: USGS Mount David, GT Wenatchee Lake). **Hike-1. Glacier Peak Wilderness.** Drive SR-207 and the White River Road, FS-64, to the end, 20 miles from US-2, 2300'.

Cross the river at the bridge and hike south, then ascend west on trail FS-1521 to the summit. The central location of this summit makes it a rewarding viewpoint. Peaks visible from the summit include: Clark Mtn. (10°), Maude (35°), Howard (172°), Poe (220°), Indianhead Peak (300°), Saul (328°), and Glacier Peak (330°).

Chiwawa River Area.

Leave US-2 to the northeast on SR-207 at Coles Corner, MP-84.8. At 4.3 miles from US-2, go east on CR-22 for 1.3 miles, then turn north on road FS-62, passing Fish Lake.

TWIN LAKES, 2825', 5 miles RT, 400' gain (Maps: USGS Schaefer Lake, GT Wenatchee Lake). **Hike-1. Glacier Peak Wilderness.** Drive the Chiwawa River road for 2.5 miles from CR-22. After passing Fish Lake, turn left (north) on FS-63 and drive 7.5 miles to a gate, 2600', 16 miles from US-2.

Hike north on a road for two miles, then on trail FS-1537 to the lake. Pass a beaver dam along the way. Look north to the White Mountains.

BASALT PEAK, 6004', 8 miles RT, 3400' gain (Maps: USGS Schaefer Lake, Chikamin Creek, GT Wenatchee Lake, Plain). **Hike-1.** Drive the Chiwawa River Road, FS-62, for 19 miles from US-2 at Coles Corner to the trailhead at Finner Creek Campground, 2474'.

Hike Trail FS-1515 northeast, ascending in ancient forest between Finner Creek (north) and a minor creek (southeast). Find stands of yellow pine and white pine in this predominantly western hemlock forest. Dogbane, *Apocynum androsaemifolium*, is found in the understory. Pause at a viewpoint northwest over the valley of the Chiwawa River, 4100'. At two miles, 4400', pass a trail on the right (east) that descends to Road FS-6210 on Minnow Ridge. Another trail branches left to a viewpoint at 4800'. After passing a viewpoint east at 5800', leave the main trail and follow a branch trail northwest past the forested summit of Basalt Peak to a viewpoint on the west shoulder. Look for the following summits: Big Chiwaukum (205°) Howard (221°), David (266°), Chiwawa Ridge 7625' (280°), Clark (297°), and Glacier Peak (300°).

ESTES BUTTE LOOKOUT, 5397', 6 miles RT, 3000' gain (Maps: USGS Schaefer Lake, GT Wenatchee Lake). **Hike-1.** Drive the Chiwawa River Road, FS-62, for 20.7 miles from US-2 at Coles Corner to the crossing at Rock Creek, 2500'.

Hike trail FS-1527 north on the northwest side of Rock Creek, ascending many switchbacks in open forest to this minor summit on the ridge between the Chiwawa River and Rock Creek. The lookout tower is gone.

ESTES BUTTE, 5942', 9 miles RT, 4700' gain (Maps: USGS Schaefer Lake, Trinity, GT Wenatchee Lake, Holden). **Hike-1.** Drive and hike as above to **Estes Butte Lookout**.

Continue on the trail north on the ridge, descending to 4800' before ascending to the bare summit (lookout site) of Estes Butte, which gives a generous view of peaks: Clark (286°), Buck (314°), Fortress (327°), Chiwawa (332°), and Old Gib (357°).

BUCK CREEK PASS, 5800', 18 miles RT, 3000' gain (Maps: USGS Trinity, Clark Mtn., Suiattle Pass, GT Holden). **Hike-1. Glacier Peak Wilderness.** Drive the Chiwawa River Road, FS-62, to the end of the road at Phelps Creek near the old mining community of Trinity, 2700', 29 miles from US-2 at Coles Corner. The last 12 miles of this road is gravel.

Hike the trail north on the east side of the Chiwawa River on trail FS-1513. The Chiwawa River Trail, FS-1550, continues north at mile 1.5. Stay on trail FS-1513, crossing the Chiwawa River (camping). The trail ascends away from Buck Creek, traversing the south facing slopes and reaching Buck Creek Pass nine miles from the road. The flat pass area has many campsites and deer.

LIBERTY CAP, 6800', 2 miles RT, 1000' gain (Maps: USGS Suiattle Pass, GT Holden). **Hike-2. Glacier Peak Wilderness.** The distance and elevation gain given are from **Buck Creek Pass**.

From Buck Creek Pass, hike south up the ridge on a track to the summit. The High Pass High Route continues south on or near the ridge, but may have steep snow slopes.

FLOWER DOME, 6332', 2 miles RT, 600' gain (Maps: USGS Suiattle Pass, GT Holden). **Hike-2. Glacier Peak Wilderness.** The distance and elevation gain given are from **Buck Creek Pass**.

From Buck Creek Pass, hike north on the trail toward Suiattle Pass for 0.5 mile until directly east of Flower Dome. Leave the trail and descend to the saddle between the trail and Flower Dome, then ascend west in a flowery meadow to the summit and a view across the head of the Suiattle River to Glacier Peak. Make this hike in the evening for the view of the sun setting behind Glacier Peak.

HELMET BUTTE, 7366', 3 miles RT, 1600' gain (Maps: USGS Suiattle Pass, GT Holden). **Hike-3. Glacier Peak Wilderness.** The distance and elevation gain given are from **Buck Creek Pass**.

From Buck Creek Pass, hike north on the trail toward Suiattle Pass for 0.5 mile. Leave the trail and ascend northeast on meadow that become steeper near the crest. Turn west and continue up in broken rocks.

FORTRESS MOUNTAIN, 8674', 6 miles RT, 3000' gain (Maps: USGS Suiattle Pass, GT Holden). **Hike-3. Glacier Peak Wilderness.** The distance and elevation gain given are from Buck Creek Pass.

From Buck Creek Pass, go northeast on the Buck Creek Trail, FS-1513, for one mile. Where trail FS-1513 turns southeast around the head of Buck Creek and begins to descend more steeply, 5600', find the faint Massie Lake High Route going north. Ascend on this track in the valley east of Helmet Butte until the track turns east. Leave the track and ascend northeast on open slopes with the notch of Pass No Pass northwest. A band of low cliffs bars the way at 7000' but wide, possibly snow-filled gullies offer routes. From the top of the cliffs, continue northeast up talus and broken rocks.

CHIWAWA MOUNTAIN, 8459', 18 miles RT, 6300' gain (Maps: USGS Trinity, Clark Mtn., Suiattle Pass, GT Holden). **Hike-4†, Snow. Glacier Peak Wilderness.** Drive the Chiwawa River Road, FS-62, for 29 miles from US-2 at Coles Corner to the trailhead at Phelps Creek near the old mining community of Trinity, 2700'. Best time: August to mid-September.

Hike the trail northeast along the Chiwawa River, passing west of the buildings of Trinity. At mile 1.5, 3200', the Buck Pass Trail turns left. The Massie Lake trail, FS-1504, possibly not marked, turns left at a wide place in the trail, mile 3.5 and 4400'. Pass the Chiwawa Meadows trail junction at mile 5, 4800'. The trail to here is usually open and cleared of fallen trees by August. Go right at this junction, entering an avalanche slope of tangled alder trees where creeks run in the trail. After this difficulty, the trail, which follows the route of an old mining road, improves, making three switchbacks in small stands of ancient forest (some fallen trees but look for alternate tracks around these trees). After the last switchback (5800'), find campsites above the road (east) on benches near a stream (no fires).

From the campsites near 5800', continue northwest on the old road, ascending to 6000', then descending briefly. At 6100', near a tailings pile from a prospect, leave the road and descend north on talus into a basin below waterfalls, 5900'. After crossing the streams, find a ramp (track) that ascends west through steeper terrain to the top of a rock buttress that faces south. Look for this ramp to the top of the buttress from the campsites near 5800'. The bare top of the buttress also identifies the location of the ramp for the return. From the top of the buttress, continue ascending west to cross the south ridge of Chiwawa at 6600'. Before leaving the campsite area at 5800', take care to identify this south ridge and the possible difficulties of trying to cross this ridge at other places.

After crossing to the west side of the south ridge, contour into a steep meadow (snow fingers), then ascend north toward the low point between Chiwawa and Fortress, 7200'. At or just below 7100', turn northeast and ascend snow or talus toward the summit. Where a band of steeper bedrock bars the way above 8000', turn left (north) below this rock band into another talus slope that leads into the gentle west ridge of Chiwawa Mtn.

Look for the following summits: Bonanza (13°), Seven Finger Jack (102°), Maude (110°), Stuart (182°), Buck (183°), Daniel (198°), Clark (200°), Hinman (200°), Rainier (206°), Sloan (248°), Glacier Peak (249°), Fortress (250°), Pugh (266°), Mt. Baker (315°), and Shuksan (323°).

CARNE MOUNTAIN, 7085', 8 miles RT, 3600' gain (Maps: USGS Trinity, GT Holden). **Hike-1**. Drive the Chiwawa River Road, FS-62, for 29 miles from US-2 at Coles Corner. Turn right and drive two miles on road FS-6211 to the trailhead, 3500'.

Hike north on the Phelps Creek Trail, FS-1511, for 0.2 mile, then ascend east on the Carne Mtn. Trail, FS-1508, entering an open and level meadow basin at mile 3, 6200' (no fires). Reach the junction with the Estes Butte Trail (Old Gib Trail), FS-1528, at mile 3.1. Turn left (northeast) to the saddle south of Carne Mtn., mile 3.4 and 6750', then leave the main trail and hike north on a track to the open summit. Summits to look for include: Stuart (186°), Daniel (204°), Fortress (308), Chiwawa (315°), Seven Finger Jack (354°), and Mt. Maude (358°).

For a diversion, on the return go south at the junction with the Estes Butte Trail (6300') and ascend to a pass, 6500'. This pass gives the best view of Old Gib, a volcanic remnant on the ridge to the south. From this pass, a track ascends west to a minor summit, 6730', and another track contours northeast to join the Carne Mtn. trail. To reach the old lookout site on Point 6991', the next summit on the ridge south of Carne Mtn., go south from the Carne Mtn. Trail at 6700' on the west side of the ridge.

LEROY BASIN, high point 6000', 10 miles, 2500' gain (Maps: USGS Trinity, Holden, GT Holden). **Hike-3. Glacier Peak Wilderness.** Drive the Chiwawa River Road, FS-62, for 29 miles from US-2 at Coles Corner. Turn right and drive two miles on road FS-6211 to the trailhead, 3500'.

Hike north on the Phelps Creek Trail, FS-1511, passing the Carne Mtn. trail, FS-1508, and crossing Box Creek and Chipmunk Creek. At Leroy Creek, 3.5 miles from the road and 4000', turn right (northeast) and ascend on a climber track to **Leroy Basin**, 6000' and 5 miles from the road. Find many campsites among scattered larch trees (no fires please). Seven-Fingered Jack and Mt. Maude are easy day trips from Leroy Basin.

SEVEN-FINGERED JACK, 9077', 4 miles RT, 3100' gain (Maps: USGS Holden, GT Holden). **Hike-3. Glacier Peak Wilderness.** The distance and elevation gain given are from **Leroy Basin**, 6000'.

From Leroy Creek meadow, ascend northeast to a bench, 7800'. Staying well away from the cliffs and snow fields under the south ridge of Seven-Fingered Jack, contour northwest on a narrow ramp around the head of a gully. Ascend north on sandy talus, crossing seasonal snow fingers. Continue northeast up broken rock and talus to the summit.

MOUNT MAUDE, 9082', 4 miles RT, 3100' gain (Maps: USGS Holden, GT Holden). **Hike-3. Glacier Peak Wilderness.** The distance and elevation gain given are from **Leroy Basin**.

From Leroy Meadow, 6000', follow a trail southeast, the Carne Mountain High Route. At or above 6500', near a valley that points east to the south ridge of Mt. Maude, leave the trail and ascend east on sandy talus to the ridge. Continue up the gentle ridge to the summit, the least difficult above 9000' in the Washington Cascades.

Leavenworth Area.

LEAVENWORTH WATERFRONT PARK, 1100', 1 mile of trails, no gain (Maps: USGS Leavenworth, GT Leavenworth). **Walk**. In Leavenworth, take Mill, Commercial, and Scholze Sts. southwest to the entrance (parking).

Facilities: trails, restrooms (summer), playgrounds, river access, tables, and information.

ICICLE RIDGE, high point 4200', 8 miles RT, 3000' gain (Maps: USGS Leavenworth, GT Leavenworth). **Hike-1**. Drive south on the Icicle Road for one mile from US-2 to the trailhead on the west side of the highway, 1170'.

Ascend west on the trail for views east over the Leavenworth valley and toward Wenatchee. A campsite at 4200' has water from the beginning of Steep Creek.

WEDGE MOUNTAIN, high point 6850', 8 miles RT, 2500' gain (Maps: USGS Leavenworth, Blewett, GT Leavenworth). **Hike-3**. From US-2 east of Leavenworth, drive south on US-97 to MP-181. Turn southwest on the old Blewett Pass road for 0.1 mile, right (west) on the Mountain Home Ranch Road, FS-73, for 2.6 miles, and left (south) on road FS-7305, staying on the most travelled road to end at a large parking area, 4500', eight miles from US-97. The road becomes steeper and narrower after a landing six miles from US-97, 3700'. Shortly after the landing at six miles, pass on the right at 3900' the only branch road that might be confusing.

From parking at 4500', ascend a 4-wheel track steeply west, following a ridge. The 4-wheel track disappears into a trail at 5000'. Reach a cleared area at 5480' before descending to a campsite, 5440'. A trail goes southwest to a cabin on Allen Creek. Continue west on a trail that soon enters an old burn where the trail becomes harder to follow. Keep ascending west to the ridge crest, 6200'. Turn south and ascend on the east side of the crest to a rock point that overlooks the Snow Creek valley and Snow Lake to the west and gives a grandstand view of summits in the Enchantments. Also in view: Glacier Peak (336°) and Clark Mtn. (353°). The next point south on the ridge, 6885', beyond a notch, is possibly beyond classification **Hike-4**†.

TIP TOP, 4800', 15 miles RT, 2800' gain (Maps: USGS Tip Top). **Mtn. Bicycle**. From US-2 east of Leavenworth, drive south on US-97. South of MP-180, turn east on the Camas Creek Road, FS-7200, for 1.5

miles and park at the junction with road FS-7201, 2000'.

Ride south on road FS-7201, ascending with views west into the Peshastin Creek valley. At mile 2.2, pass road FS-7201-215 on the left (east) and, at mile 2.8, a viewpoint up Icicle Creek. Find an outcrop of serpentine on the left at mile 3.7. A road (not obvious) goes to US-97 on the right (south) at mile 4.1, 3400'. Along the way, see mule ear, bitter cherry, service berry, ocean spray, and ceanothus. Pass two more roads on the left near mile 4.8. A spring-fed pond lies at the lower edge of a meadow on the right, mile 5.9. Pause at the crest of the ridge, mile 6.0, 4100', for views east and west. Look for a cobble conglomerate on the side of the road, mile 6.7. From the summit: Miller Peak (245°), Three Brothers (272°), and Wedge Mtn. (303°).

MILLER PEAK, 6402', 17 or 19 miles RT, 3800' gain (Maps: USGS Blewett, GT Liberty). **Mt. Bicycle and Hike-1 or Hike-3**. Drive US-97 east of MP-173. Turn southwest on a paved road signed Old Blewett Road/Scotty Creek. At 0.8 mile from US-97, turn right (west) on the Shaser Creek Road (FS-7322), crossing a bridge over Shaser Creek. Park at a road junction 1.3 miles from US-97 where a creek joins from the northwest, 2660'.

Ride past a gate, going northwest, then turning west on the North Shaser Creek Road, staying on the north side of North Shaser Creek. Where the road levels at one mile, look west to Miller Peak. At mile 1.3 pass a road on the right and, at mile 1.7, go over a rock promontory with a view down to North Shaser Creek. At miles 2.3 and 2.6, cross North Shaser Creek. After the second crossing, begin to ascend across the east slope of Miller Peak. Pass a stub road to the right (north) at mile 3.5 and go to the right (west and northwest) at mile 5.5, 4660', where the road to the left continues east to a saddle above Middle Shaser Creek. The road ends at the crest of the ridge, mile 6.6, 5020'. Leave bicycle and take the trail to the right (north), ascending on or near the ridge.

Alternate 1. Hike-1. Leave the ridge at mile 8, 5700', and contour on the trail across the east face of Miller Peak to a junction on the south ridge. Turn right (northeast) and ascend on the trail to the summit.

Alternate 2. Hike-3. Where the trail leaves the ridge to contour across the east face of Miller Peak, 5700', leave the trail and ascend south cross country on or near the ridge to the summit.

IRON MOUNTAIN, 5480', 11 miles RT, 3000' gain (Maps: USGS Blewett, GT Liberty). **Mtn. Bicycle and Hike-3**. Drive and park as for Miller Peak above.

Ride past the gate on the North Shaser Creek Road, beginning to the north, then rounding to the west. At mile 1.2, get a glimpse of Iron Mtn. on the ridge crest (315°), then turn right (north) at mile 1.3, 3050', on a gated branch road, going away from North Shaser Creek. At mile 2.3, 4180', take the left branch at a junction. Near this junction and beyond, the road crosses an exposure of serpentine (green), mostly decomposed to small pieces and sand. The mineral, which contains iron, weathers to a red color, hence the name of the mountain. At mile 4, 5150', pass an exposure of larger, shiny blocks of serpentine. Note that areas where this mineral is exposed tend to have less vegetation than areas where the soil is derived from other kinds of rock.

Reach a saddle at mile 4.5, 5200'. Leave bicycle and ascend north and northeast to the first summit for views of the summits of Three Brothers (305°), Mission Ridge (126°), Miller Peak (226°), Navajo Peak (280°) above a notch in the ridge to the west, and several more distant summits north near Lake Chelan. The road goes to Negro Creek and a trail to Three Brothers.

BLEWETT ARRASTRA SITE, 2300' (Maps: USGS Blewett, GT Liberty). **Walk**. Park on the east side of US-97 at MP-174.

Cross US-97 to the west and walk 100' northwest on a dirt road. Take the first branch to the right (north) to the site. The stone foundations and timber supports of the water-powered arrastra for grinding ore remain. The water-wheel and most of the metal are gone.

SWAUK FOREST DISCOVERY TRAIL, 4200', 3 mile loop, 100' gain (Maps: USGS Swauk Pass, GT Liberty). **Hike-1**. From Swauk Pass on US-97, drive east on road FS-9716 for 0.5 mile and park at an interpretive sign (toilets, descriptive pamphlet).

The following native plants are signed: grand fir, western larch, western white pine, ponderosa pine, dwarf mistletoe, Douglas fir, bitterbrush, snowbrush (ceanothus), willow, lodgepole pine, and Engelmann spruce. In addition, find: vine maple, service berry, bitter cherry, ocean spray, kinnikinnick, Oregon grape, and subalpine fir.

MOUNT LILLIAN LOOP, 6120', 20 miles RT bicycle, 5 miles RT hike, 2300' gain (Maps: USGS Swauk Pass, GT Liberty). **Mtn. Bicycle and Hike-3**. Park at Swauk Pass SnoPark on US-97, 4100'. For a motor-free trip, make this tour in early June before the snow has cleared completely from roads. Expect to find only occasional patches of snow on the road.

Ride east on road FS-9716, which begins at the east end of Swauk Pass, passing the Swauk Forest Discovery Trail at mile 0.5 and crossing a creek at mile 2.6. Turn left (east) at mile 3.8 on road FS-9712 and ascend across the north-facing basalt talus slopes of Table Mountain to a saddle at mile 5.4, 5615'. Leave bicycle and hike 0.5 mile north to the summit of **Diamond Head**, 5915', for the view west toward Mt. Daniel (287°), Mt. Stuart (307°), and Glacier Peak (335°).

Return to the road at the pass (5615', bicycle mile 5.4) and ride east and northeast, descending to cross a saddle (campground) that separates Tronsen Creek (north) and Naneum Creek (south). Bend south, passing the Naneum Rim Trail (FS-1234) at mile 6.7 before turning northeast to another campground at mile 7.3. The creek comes from a spring 0.2 mile north. Continue northeast on the road to Ken Wilcox Horse Camp near Haney Meadow, mile 8.7. In the vicinity, find a cabin, tables, toilets, and informative signs with map. Grass Camp Trail (FS-1219.1) goes south from the west edge of the meadow. Going north from Haney Meadow, cross the Old Ellensberg Trail, FS-1373, going southeast at mile 9.1, and the Tronsen Meadow Trail, FS-1205, going northwest at mile 9.2. Reach a road junction, mile 9.8 and 5600', at a crossing of Naneum Creek where road FS-9712-224 goes north on the east side of the creek and road FS-9712 bends south.

Loop. To make a loop over Mt. Lillian, leave bicycle at the creek crossing, 5600'. Hike north on road FS-9712-224 for 0.3 mile, then turn southeast on trail FS-1601, skirting the edge of the canyon of Devils Gulch while ascending to the summit plateau of Mt. Lillian. Take time more than once to step east to the edge to look down the abrupt drop. Only a purist will search for the highest point of Mt. Lillian: no cairn, no register, and no view. Go on to the southeast edge of the plateau for the view and explore around some of the wind carved sandstone pinnacles that protrude from the ridge. Please leave these fragile pinnacles untouched for others to enjoy.

Return to the southeast corner of the Mt. Lillian summit plateau and go south on a less used trail. When this trail begins to descend, diverge west to the open south ridge of Mt. Lillian and follow the ridge south to the low point, 5980'. From this low point, turn west cross country for 0.2 miles through dense forest (some down trees) to road FS-9712 at a saddle. Turn north to the creek crossing and bicycle. Return to the starting point on the outgoing route.

MOUNT LILLIAN, 6120', 9 miles RT, 1800' gain (Maps: USGS Swauk Pass, GT Liberty). **Hike-3**. North of Swauk Pass and south of MP-165 on US-97, drive east on road FS-7240 and park at the trailhead, 1.5 miles from US-97, elevation 4340'.

Ascend two miles east on the Tronsen Meadow Trail, FS-1205. At a trail crossing, 5500', continue 200' east to a 'T' junction. Turn south to the road (FS-9712) coming north from Haney Meadow, 0.3 mile distant. Turn north on the road for 0.6 miles to a crossing of Naneum Creek, 5600'. Now follow the route described above (see **Loop.** in **Mt. Lillian Loop** and return to this Naneum Creek crossing.

Return to the starting point on the outgoing route.

RED HILL, 3835', 11 miles RT, 2200' gain (Maps: USGS Monitor, Tiptop, GT Liberty). **Hike-1.** This hike can often be done in April. From US-2, MP-110, drive south in Cashmere on Pioneer Ave. Jog right (west) on Binder Road, then go south on the Mission Creek Road, FS-7100, for 10 miles to the Mission Creek trailhead, 1700'. The pavement ends at mile 8.

Hike south on the Devils Gulch Trail, FS-1220, for one mile. Turn west on the Red Hill Spur Trail, FS-1223, and ascend to the Red Hill Trail, then continue southwest on the ridge to the summit.

MOUNT LILLIAN, 6120', 15 miles RT, 4500' gain (Maps: USGS Monitor, Tiptop, Swauk Pass, GT Liberty). **Hike-3.** Drive and begin hike as above for **Red Hill** at the Mission Creek Trailhead.

Hike south on the Devils Gulch Trail, FS-1220 for three miles. Where the trail crosses the creek to the east side, leave the trail and ascend an open ridge west and southwest, going over a minor bump (4575') on the ridge before meeting the Tronsen Ridge Trail, FS-1204. Turn left (southeast) on this trail, which follows near or on the ridge to the summit.

DEVILS GULCH, high point 3500', 12 miles RT, 2000' gain (Maps: USGS Tiptop, Monitor, Swauk Pass, Mission Peak, GT Liberty). **Hike-1.** Drive as above for **Red Hill** to the Mission Creek Trailhead.

Hike south on the Devils Gulch Trail, FS-1220, passing sandstone cliffs and buttresses, some of which have been wind eroded to look like Swiss cheese. The trail crosses the creek several times.

Icicle Creek Area

Leave US-2 at the west end of Leavenworth and drive south and west on the Icicle Creek road. Special regulations, which change frequently, apply to the Enchantments Area. Check with the Forest Service.

COLCHUCK LAKE, 5570', 8 miles RT, 2100' gain (Maps: Alpine Lakes Wilderness, USGS Cashmere Mtn., Enchantment Lakes, GT Chiwaukum Mts., Mt. Stuart). **Hike-1. Alpine Lakes Wilderness.** Drive the Icicle Road, FS-76, for 8 miles from US-2 at Leavenworth. Turn left (south) on road FS-7601 to the trailhead, 4 miles from road FS-76, 12 miles from US-2, and 3400'. Permits required.

Hike south on the Mountaineer Creek Trail, FS-1599, for 2.5 miles to 4500', then go left (east) on trail FS-1599A to the lake, four miles from road FS-7601 (no fires).

COLCHUCK PEAK, 8705', 8 miles RT, 3300' gain (Maps: Alpine Lakes, USGS Enchantment Lakes, GT Mt. Stuart). **Hike-4†. Alpine Lakes Wilderness.** The distance and elevation gain given are from **Colchuck Lake**.

From the south end of Colchuck Lake, hike southwest up a subsidiary valley, passing through big block talus to a saddle, 6800', south of a 6991' point on the north ridge of Colchuck Peak. Cross the saddle and contour or ascend south on the west side of Colchuck Peak to the ridge at 7700' south of the summit. Turn northeast to the summit. Many of the trees on the slope west of Colchuck Peak are larch, colorful in the fall.

ENCHANTMENT LAKES, high point 8000', 16 miles RT, 4500' gain (Maps: Alpine Lakes Wilderness, USGS Cashmere Mtn., Enchantment Lakes, GT Chiwaukum Mts., Mt. Stuart). **Hike-4†. Alpine Lakes Wilderness.** Drive and hike as above to **Colchuck Lake**.

Continue around the south end of Colchuck Lake and ascend on a steep, rough track that disappears in places to Aasgard Pass near **Isolation Lake**. Camp only in designated campsites. (Permits required, no fires).

LITTLE ANNAPURNA, 8440', 3 miles RT, 600' gain (Maps: Alpine Lakes Wilderness, USGS Enchantment Lakes, GT Chiwaukum Mts.). **Hike-3. Alpine Lakes Wilderness.** Hike as above to Isolation Lake in the Enchantment Lakes.

From camping near **Isolation Lake** in the **Enchantment Lakes** basin, hike south up a gentle, decomposed granite slope to the summit and an overall view of the peaks and lakes of the Enchantments.

EIGHTMILE LAKE, 4641', 7 miles RT, 1400' gain (Maps: Alpine Lakes Wilderness, USGS Cashmere Mtn., GT Chiwaukum Mts.). **Hike-1. Alpine Lakes Wilderness.** Drive the Icicle Road, FS-76, for 8 miles from US-2 at Leavenworth. Turn left (south) on road FS-7601 to the trailhead, 3 miles from road FS-76 and 11 miles from US-2, 3280'.

Hike trail FS-7601 southwest to the lake, passing Little Eightmile Lake and the trail to Lake Caroline. A track continues around the north side of the lake but the canyon above the lake to the west is dense brush and doghair trees. Find campsites on the terminal moraine at the east end of the lake.

LITTLE LAKE CAROLINE, 6300', 13 miles RT, 3100' gain (Maps: Alpine Lakes, USGS Cashmere Mtn., GT Chiwaukum Mts.). **Hike-1. Alpine Lakes Wilderness.** Drive the Icicle Road, FS-76, for 8 miles from US-2 at Leavenworth. Turn left (south) on road FS-7601 to the trailhead, 3280', 3 miles from road FS-76 and 11 miles from US-2.

Hike southwest on trail FS-1552. After passing Little Eightmile Lake, turn northwest and ascend on trail FS-1554 to **Lake Caroline**, lying in forest. **Little Lake Caroline**, 6300', reached after another mile and surrounded by meadows, has better campsites than Lake Caroline.

CASHMERE MOUNTAIN, 8501', 7 miles RT, 2300' gain (Maps: Alpine Lakes, USGS Cashmere Mtn., GT Chiwaukum Mts.). **Hike-4†. Alpine Lakes Wilderness.** Distance and elevation gain are given from camping at **Little Lake Caroline** (see above).

From Little Lake Caroline, continue northeast on the trail until the trail turns northwest toward Windy Pass. Leave the trail and ascend northeast, at first on alpine meadows, then in rockier terrain to reach the saddle west of Cashmere Mtn. Contour to the north side of the mountain, then ascend the northeast ridge. Although the terrain is never seriously steep, use extreme caution to prevent rock fall.

WINDY PASS POINT 7380, 7380', 3 miles RT, 1200' gain (Maps: USGS Cashmere Mtn., GT Chiwaukum Mts.). **Hike-1. Alpine Lakes Wilderness.** This minor summit gives a view of the summits of Jack Ridge across Trout Creek (west) and of the cliffs of Eightmile Mountain (south). Distance and elevation gain are from camping at **Little Lake Caroline**.

From Little Lake Caroline, hike trail FS-1554 north and west to Windy Pass, 7200'. Leave the trail at the pass and hike south to the summit. Highchair Mtn. on Sixtysix Hundred Ridge is five miles west (282°), The Cradle is eight miles west (276°), and Mt. Stuart is six miles south (190°).

ICICLE RIDGE LOOKOUT, 7029', 11 miles RT, 4800' gain (Maps: USGS Cashmere Mtn., GT Chiwaukum Mts.). **Hike-2.** Drive the Icicle Road, FS-76, for 10 miles from US-2 at Leavenworth. Park at the Forth-of-July Creek trailhead on the north side of the road, 2300'.

Ascend switchbacks in and out of forest on trail FS-1579 to the junction with the Icicle Ridge Trail, FS-1570. Turn west to a rock outcrop. Leave the trail and ascend in the rocks to find remains of the lookout. Mt. Stuart dominates the view southwest.

GRINDSTONE MOUNTAIN, 7533', 12 miles RT, 5100' gain (Maps: USGS Jack Ridge, Chiwaukum Mts., GT Chiwaukum Mts.). **Hike-3. Alpine Lakes Wilderness.** Drive the Icicle Road, FS-76, for 16 miles from US-2 at Leavenworth. West of the Chatter Creek Forest Service Station, turn right (north) to the trailhead, 2700'.

Hike the Chatter Creek Trail, FS-1580, to the saddle between Chatter Creek and Index Creek. Continue north on the trail for 0.5 mile, then leave the trail at 6400', contouring north and ascending west to a low point in the ridge north of Grindstone Mtn., 6700'. On the west side of the ridge, contour south to the north slope of Grindstone Mtn., then ascend south to the summit, composed of large granite blocks.

FRENCH CREEK–BLACKJACK RIDGE LOOP, high point 6400', 23 miles RT, 5200' gain (Maps: USGS Chiwaukum Mts., Stevens Pass, The Cradle, Jack Ridge, GT Chiwaukum Mts., Stevens Pass). **Hike-2. Alpine Lakes Wilderness.** Drive the Icicle Road, FS-76, for 19 miles from US-2 at Leavenworth to the trailhead at the end of the road, 2800'.

Hike northwest and north on the Icicle Trail, FS-1551. After crossing French Creek 1.5 miles from the trailhead, turn west on the French Creek Trail, FS-1595, and ascend on the north and west side of French Creek. The area around the junction of the French Creek Trail with the Icicle Creek Trail is being restored. Please do not camp here. Find many campsites higher along French Creek.

Pass a trail west to French Ridge at 3.6 miles from Icicle Creek. The Snowall Creek Trail to Cradle Lake turns east 4.7 miles from Icicle Creek, 3300'. The junction with the **Klonaqua Lakes Trail**, FS-1563 and 3700', is seven miles from the trailhead (camping, see also Granite Mtn. below). The trail to Paddy-Go-Easy Pass, FS-1595, goes west 11 miles from the trailhead, 4900'.

Continue southeast and east to **Meadow Pass**, 5400' (camping, see The Cradle and Meadow Pass Point 6821 below). From Meadow Pass, descend along Meadow Creek (many campsites). At five miles from the the Paddy-Go-Easy Pass trail (4000'), turn north on trail FS-1560 and ascend to **Cradle Lake**, 6200', lying in an open basin below the ridge leading to Highchair Mtn. For summits, see Cradle Ridge, and Highchair Mtn.

From Cradle Lake, return east on the trail toward Meadow Creek for 0.5 mile, 6000', to find a less traveled trail, FS-1565, turning north across Pablo Creek. Follow this trail as it contours in basins across the east side of Highchair Mtn., then ascends over the north shoulder of Bootjack Mtn. before descending north on Blackjack Ridge, emerging on the Icicle Road near Blackpine Horse Camp.

GRANITE MOUNTAIN, 7144', 9 miles RT, 3500' gain (Maps: USGS The Cradle. GT Stevens Pass). **Hike-4†. Alpine Lakes Wilderness.** The distance and elevation gain given are from the junction of the French Creek Trail, FS-1595, and the Klonaqua Lakes Trail, FS-1563 (see Klonaqua Lakes Trail, French Creek–Blackjack Ridge Loop).

Ascend west on the Klonaqua Lakes trail, passing near Bob Lake, 5190'. Pass the first lake on the north. At the west end of the upper lake, ascend west to the low point in the ridge north of Klonaqua Lakes, 6200', then turn southwest and follow the ridge as it curves around to the southeast to the summit. Descend east past Bob Lake to the trail.

MEADOW PASS POINT 6821, 6821', 2 miles RT, 1600' gain (Maps: USGS The Cradle, GT Stevens Pass). **Hike-3. Alpine Lakes Wilderness.** The distance and elevation gain are from camping at **Meadow Pass**, 11 miles from the Icicle Road.

Hike southwest from the pass in open forest and alpine meadows. The summit provides an excellent view of the route to The Cradle.

THE CRADLE, 7467', 5 miles RT, 2100' gain (Maps: USGS The Cradle, GT Stevens Pass). **Hike-3. Alpine Lakes Wilderness.** The distance and elevation gain given here are from camping at **Meadow Pass** (see French Creek–Blackjack Ridge Loop), 11 miles from the Icicle Road or six miles from the Cle Elum River Road over Paddy-Go-Easy Pass.

Ascend north from Meadow Pass to cross the south ridge of The Cradle at the low point, 6600'. Traverse north on the east side of Cradle Ridge in open sandy talus, rising gradually until east of the double summit. Turn west to the summits.

CRADLE RIDGE, 6623', 6794', 6962', 5 miles RT, 1600' gain (Maps: USGS Jack Ridge, The Cradle, GT Stevens Pass, Chiwaukum Mts.). **Hike-3. Alpine Lakes Wilderness.** The distance and elevation gain are from **Cradle Lake**.

From Cradle Lake, hike southwest and west on or near the ridge toward The Cradle, getting changing views of Meadow Creek and Snowall Creek. Beyond 6962', the ridge descends to 6600' and the route to The Cradle.

HIGH CHAIR, high points 6908', 7016', 6707', 6820', 8 miles RT, 2500' gain (Maps: USGS Jack Ridge, GT Chiwaukum Mts.). **Hike-3. Alpine Lakes Wilderness.** A superb hike on Sixtysix Hundred Ridge in exposures of serpentine. The distance and elevation gain are from **Cradle Lake**. High Chair is also accessible from Blackpine Horse Camp near the end of the Icicle Road (16 miles RT, 5500' gain).

Ascend north from the lake to the first summit and continue along Sixtysix Hundred Ridge in broken rocks and open timber. The summit marked High Chair on the USGS map, 7016', is the second summit north from Cradle Lake.

FROSTY PASS, 6200', 18 miles RT, 3200' gain (Maps: USGS Jack Ridge, Chiwaukum Mts., GT Chiwaukum Mts.). **Hike-1. Alpine Lakes Wilderness.** Drive the Icicle Road, FS-76, for 19 miles from US-2 at Leavenworth to the trailhead at the west end of the Icicle Road, 2800'.

Hike northwest and north on the Icicle Creek Trail, FS-1551, for 4.7 miles to the bridge over Icicle Creek, 3200', passing the French Creek Trail, the French Ridge Trail, and the old Frosty Creek Trail (no bridge). After crossing the Icicle Creek bridge, turn east downstream and contour across Doughgod Creek before beginning to ascend into the valley of Frosty Creek, passing a junction with the abandoned Frosty Creek Trail at 3800'.

Find a large campsite with an overhanging rock where the trail touches Frosty Creek in a meadow, 4900'. Pass a branch trail to **Lake Margaret** at 5400', 8.5 miles from the trailhead and reach broad, level Frosty Pass 0.7 mile after passing Lake Margaret. Find water in the gully south and also 0.5 mile west on the trail to Doelle Lakes. Many destinations are possible from camping in the Frosty Pass area: Doelle Lakes, Lake Grace, Big Chiwaukum, Lake Mary, and Snowgrass Mtn. Frosty Pass Point 6489 (see next below) makes a good late afternoon destination for a view of the sunset.

FROSTY PASS POINT 6489, 6489', 2 miles RT, 700' gain (Maps: USGS Chiwaukum Mts., GT Chiwaukum Mts.). **Hike-2. Alpine Lakes Wilderness.** The distance and elevation gain given are from **Frosty Pass.**

Hike west on the trail along the ridge from Frosty Pass. Where the trail turns northwest and contours away from the ridge, leave the trail and ascend west on the open ridge to the summit. View the valley of Doughgod Creek below to the west and many summits of Bulls Tooth. Mt. Stuart stands south.

Entiat River Area. Leave US-2 at the north end of Wenatchee and drive north on US-97alt on the west side of the Columbia River. After crossing the Entiat River and south of the town of Entiat (services), turn west on paved Entiat River Road.

NORTH FORK ENTIAT RIVER LOOP, high point 7200', 19 miles, 3300' gain (Maps: USGS Pyramid Mtn., Saska Peak, Silver Falls, GT Lucerne). **Hike-2**. Drive the Entiat River Road, CR-371 and FS-51 for 32 miles. At Entiat Falls, near the North Fork Campground, turn right (east) on the North Fork Entiat River Road, FS-5606, and drive to the end of the road, 4 miles from the Entiat River Road, 3960'.

Hike north on the North Fork Entiat River Trail, FS-1437, for 1.3 miles, 4110', then go northeast on the South Pyramid Creek Trail, FS-1439, for two miles to **Butte Creek** and a trail junction (camping), 4820'. From here, Graham Mtn. and Crow Hill can be hiked in a day. Now go north 2.4 miles on the South Pyramid Creek Trail, FS-1439, to the Graham Mtn. Trail, FS-1433, at 5849'. Continue 1.6 miles to the Pugh Ridge Trail, FS-1438, west of Pyramid Mountain. From camping in open forest and meadows near this trail junction , 6527', Pyramid Mtn. and a high point of Pugh Ridge (7261') can both be reached the same day.

From the junction of the Graham Mtn. Trail and the Pugh Ridge Trail, follow the Graham Mtn. Trail north across Grouse Pass, 7200'. The highest point of Pugh Ridge, 7362', is immediately west of Grouse Pass. From Grouse Pass, contour around the head of Grouse Creek to the junction with the North Fork Entiat River Trail, FS-1437, 6605', 3.3 miles from the Pugh Ridge Trail junction and 11 miles from the road. Meadows with a stream provide excellent camping near this junction. Many summits are nearby: Cardinal Peak, Skidgravel Peak, Emerald Peak, and Saska Peak.

To return to the North Fork Entiat River trailhead from the junction of the Graham Mtn. Trail and the North Fork Entiat River Trail, descend eight miles and 2500' southwest on the North Fork Entiat River Trail, FS-1437.

GRAHAM MOUNTAIN, CROW HILL, 7297', 7366', 7 miles, 3700' gain (Maps: USGS Pyramid Mtn., GT Lucerne). **Hike-3**. The distance and elevation gain given for this trip are from **Butte Creek** camp (see North Fork Entiat River loop).

From the South Pyramid Creek Trail (FS-1439) junction near the crossing at Butte Creek, 4820', hike southeast on the Crow Hill Trail, FS-1440, for 0.25 mile. Leave the trail at 5160' just before crossing Butte Creek and ascend northeast up the ridge in open forest to the summit of Graham Mtn., crossing the Graham Mtn. Trail (FS-1433) at

7000'.

From the summit of Graham Mtn., return southwest to the Graham Mtn. Trail and go south, descending to a low point, 6200', before joining the Crow Hill Trail. Continue south on the Graham Mtn. Trail, ascending southeast to 6900'. Where the Graham Mtn. Trail turns south to contour across the west side of Crow Hill, leave the trail and ascend southeast to the open summit. Look for dikes of volcanic rock in the summit ridge.

From Crow Hill, return northwest to the trail and descend, taking a left fork (west) at the junction of the Crow Hill Trail and the Graham Mtn. Trail to meet the South Pyramid Creek Trail at Butte Creek.

PYRAMID MOUNTAIN, 8243', 4 miles RT, 1800' gain (Maps: USGS Pyramid Mtn., GT Lucerne). **Hike-3**. The distance and elevation gain given for this trip are from camping at the junction of the Pugh Ridge Trail and the Graham Mtn. Trail. See North Fork Entiat River Loop.

From the Graham Mtn. Trail at the junction with the Pugh Ridge Trail, 6527', ascend east cross country, following a subsidiary ridge part of the way and meeting the Pyramid Mtn. Trail at 7700'. Follow the trail to the talus summit and lookout site.

CHELAN POINT 8189, 8189', 2 miles added, 500' gain added (Maps: USGS Pyramid Mtn., GT Lucerne). **Hike-3**. The added distance and elevation gain given for this trip are from Pyramid Mtn.

From the summit of Pyramid Mtn., descend north to the saddle and continue north along the talus ridge to the summit, going over a minor hump. Return west in meadows and open forest to the junction of the Pugh Ridge Trail with the Graham Mtn. Trail.

PUGH RIDGE POINT 7261, 7261', 1 mile RT, 900' gain (Maps: USGS Pyramid Mtn., GT Lucerne). **Hike-3**. The distance and elevation gain given for this trip are from camp at the junction of the Pugh Ridge Trail and the Graham Mtn. Trail. See North Fork Entiat River Loop.

Make this trip in the late afternoon to watch the sunset. From camp, ascend west cross-country through broken rocks to the summit.

PUGH RIDGE POINT 7362, 7362', 0.5 mile RT, 200' gain (Maps: USGS Pyramid Mtn., GT Lucerne). **Hike-3**. This is the high point of Pugh Ridge. The distance and elevation gain given for this trip are from Grouse Pass on the Graham Mtn. Trail. See North Fork Entiat River Loop.

From Grouse Pass, ascend southwest to the summit. The giant blocks that compose the summit will require time in searching for an easy route.

CARDINAL PEAK, 8590', 4 miles RT, 2100' gain (Maps: USGS Saska Peak, Pyramid Mtn., GT Lucerne). **Hike-4†, Snow**. This trip is best done in late July, while snow still covers the talus slopes and the trails are mostly snow free. Distance and elevation gain are from the junction of the Graham Mtn. Trail and the North Fork Entiat River Trail, 6605'. See North Fork Entiat River Loop.

From camping at the junction of the Graham Mtn. Trail and the North Fork Entiat River Trail, hike north on the Graham Mtn. trail for 0.5 mile. Where the trail passes west of the broad slope leading up to the saddle north of the summit, leave the trail and ascend east to the saddle. Descend east from the saddle to the snow field on the north side of the summit, then ascend south in broken rocks to the east ridge of Cardinal Peak. Turn west to the summit. Descend southeast from the summit to 6800'. Turn west and descend to the trail, emerging near the junction of the North Fork Entiat River Trail and the Graham Mtn. Trail.

SKIDGRAVEL PEAK, 8339', 4 miles RT, 2000' gain (Maps: USGS Saska Peak, Pyramid Mtn., GT Lucerne). **Hike-3**. This summit can be combined with a trip to Cardinal Peak. Distance and elevation gain are from the junction of the Graham Mtn. Trail and the North Fork Entiat River Trail (see North Fork Entiat River Loop).

From the junction of the Graham Mtn. Trail and the North Fork Entiat River Trail, hike east, crossing a subsidiary ridge north of the 7901' point at the south end of the ridge. After crossing the ridge, contour and ascend across the south slope of Cardinal Peak to the summit of Skidgravel Peak.

To combine the two summits, from the summit of Cardinal Peak, descend the south ridge, staying on the ridge as it turns southeast to the summit of Skidgravel Peak, a talus summit. From the summit of Skidgravel Peak, descend west to cross a subsidiary ridge at 7800' to the junction of the North Fork Entiat River Trail and the Graham Mtn. Trail.

EMERALD PEAK, 8422', 5 miles RT, 2000' gain (Maps: USGS Saska Peak, GT Lucerne). **Hike-3**. Distance and elevation gain are from the junction of the Graham Mtn. Trail and the North Fork Entiat River Trail (see North Fork Entiat River Loop). This summit is best done after snow is gone when rockfall danger is minimized.

From the junction of the Graham Mtn. Trail and the North Fork Entiat River Trail, 6600', go north on the Graham Mtn. Trail until the trail turns west to cross above the North Fork Entiat River, 6900'. Leave the trail and continue north until near the saddle between Saska Peak and Emerald Peak, 7800'. Ascend east on a talus ramp that begins in the area of the saddle and points toward a notch on the crest north of Emerald Peak. Before this ramp ends in cliffs, cross a rocky rib southeast into the next talus gully and ascend to the notch north of the summit. Ascend south and east on talus and broken rocks to the summit.

SASKA PEAK, 8404', 5 miles RT, 2000' gain (Maps: USGS Saska Peak, GT Lucerne). **Hike-4†**. Distance and elevation gain are from the junction of the Graham Mtn. Trail and the North Fork Entiat River Trail (see North Fork Entiat River Loop). This summit is best done after snow is gone when rockfall danger is minimized.

From the junction of the Graham Mtn. Trail and the North Fork Entiat River Trail, 6600', hike north on the Graham Mtn. Trail, FS-1433, going 0.5 mile beyond the point where the trail curves southwest above the North Fork. When below the cirque on the south side of Saska Peak, leave the trail and ascend in the cirque until just below the band of cliffs that crosses west to east above 7400'. Turn east and ascend at the base of the cliffs to the south ridge of Saska Peak. Ascend on the ridge to bypass the cliff band, then descend west from the ridge to the broad, broken rock and talus slope above the cliff band. Ascend this slope to the summit, using care to avoid rock fall. Don't attempt to descend east to the saddle between Saska Peak and Emerald Peak. This descent involves roped climbing.

If coming from Snow Brushy Creek (see Anthem-Choral-Snow Brushy Loop), ascend south from Snow Brushy Creek on the Graham Mtn. Trail across Saska Pass. Leave the trail east of Saska Pass at 7300' and contour east below the band of cliffs that crosses the cirque on the south side of Saska Peak. Where these cliffs join the south ridge of Saska Peak, ascend to the south ridge of Saska Peak and continue as described above.

SHETIPO–LARCH LAKES LOOP, high point 7400', 30 miles, 7100' gain (Maps: USGS Saska Peak, Chikamin Creek, Silver Falls, Trinity, GT Lucerne, Plain). **Hike-2. Glacier Peak Wilderness**. Find many streams, flower meadows (gentian!), 12,000 year-old pumice fields from Glacier Peak, and unused campsites. Drive the Entiat River Road, CR-

371 and FS-51 for 36 miles to the trailhead across the Entiat River in Cottonwood Campground, 3070'.

Ascend southeast on trail FS-1429 in forest near Shetipo Creek, crossing the creek twice to reach, at mile 5, a junction with the Garland Peak Trail, FS-1408, 6300'. Find campsites 0.3 mile south of this trail junction with water from a spring that flows south into Three Creek. Ascend Three Creek 6569' and Chikamin Ridge 6602' from here. Continue south 3 miles on trail FS-1409.1 to find many campsites near giant Marble Meadow, 5900' (access to Klone Peak, Kelly Mtn., and the Mad River).

From camping at Marble Meadow, return north to the junction with the Shetipo Creek Trail. Where Trail FS-1429 turns east, continue north and northwest, following the Garland Peak Trail (FS-1408) on or near the ridge. At the first trail highpoint, diverge east to **Point 6543'** (fire ring) for the view down Shetipo Creek. At the next trail highpoint, ascend east to **Point 6634'** for another look down Shetipo Creek. For a final look down Shetipo Creek, go east from the next trail highpoint to a gentle talus summit (6716') in small subalpine fir trees. Look east to Duncan Hill (19°), Pyramid Mtn. (42°), and Cardinal Peak (24°). The trail now bends west to the west shoulder of **Point 6628'**. Leave the trail and ascend east to the summit (beer cans) for a close view of Garland Peak (320°). Return to trail and descend north to the next saddle (6100') and Pinto Camp, three miles from the Shetipo Trail. A trail (not obvious) drops west 0.25 mile to a spring.

From Pinto Camp, ascend northwest across the west side of Point 7224' and Garland Peak (see below), then, after passing through the saddle west of Garland Peak, continue to the junction with the Basalt Ridge Trail, FS-1515, 7348'. Leave the trail and ascend east to the high point, 7440'. Look for the following summits: Stuart (190°), Chiwaukum Mts. (202°), Alpine Lookout (204°), Rainier (212°), Mastiff (214°), Howard (216°), Clark (280°), Glacier Peak (290°), and Carne Mtn. (320°).

From the Basalt Ridge trail junction, continue north, descending briefly before ascending 100' on the south flank of Rampart Mtn. (see below) where the trail turns west and begins to descend. After again turning north, enter the Glacier Peak Wilderness to reach Ravens Roost Camp on a branch of Rock Creek, 5900' and four miles from Pinto Camp. From Raven's Roost Camp, ascend north and northeast to Fifth of July Pass. At the pass, the trail jogs northwest briefly, ascending on the south ridge of Fifth of July Mtn. (see below). After leaving the south ridge (7200'), descend northeast above Cow Creek Meadow to pass a junction with the trail to Cow Creek Meadows (6637'). At the next creek crossing, drop pack and ascend west to view the snow-filled cirque under the north aspect (note dike) of Fifth of July Mtn. Reach **Larch Lakes** in another mile (camping, 5700'). From here, Pomas Pass is three miles (see below).

From Larch Lakes, descend east on trail FS-1430 toward the Entiat River (no bridge). At 4000', look for a tie trail that goes south to join the Cow Creek Trail, FS-1404. Now descend on trail FS-1404 to pass **Myrtle Lake** and cross a bridge over the Entiat River. Turn southeast to Cottonwood Camp.

THREE CREEK POINT 6569, 6569', 2 miles RT, 500' gain (Maps: USGS Chikamin Creek, GT Plain). **Hike-2**. Hike as above on the Shetipo–Larch Lakes Loop to the meadow with south-flowing stream 0.3 miles south of the Shetipo-Garland Peak trail junction.

Near the middle of the meadow, look for the old Three Creek trail on the east side of the creek at a blazed tree. Follow this abandoned trail northeast above Three Creek valley to the first high point and keyhole views of Glacier Peak (292°) and Pyramid Peak (36°).

CHIKAMIN RIDGE, 6602', 3 miles RT, 600' gain (Maps: USGS Chikamin Creek, GT Plain). **Hike-3**. Hike as above on the Shetipo–Larch Lakes Loop to the meadow 0.3 miles south of the Shetipo-Garland Peak trail junction.

From the meadow, hike south on Trail 1409.1 for 0.5 mile to the first trail junction. Turn west on the Chikamin Creek Tie Trail, FS-1561, passing the Pond Meadow Trail, FS-1409.2 at 0.1 mile from FS-1409.1. Continue west. After crossing a stream 0.25 miles from FS-1409.1, leave the trail and ascend west on Chikamin Ridge to the high point and a view north and west (Basalt Peak 276°).

KLONE PEAK, 6820', 6 miles RT, 1200' gain (Maps: USGS Chikamin Creek, Silver Falls, GT Plain). **Hike-1**. The distance and elevation gain given are from camping in Marble Meadow (see Shetipo–Larch Lakes Loop).

From Marble Meadow, hike south on trail FS-1409.1, then go east on trail FS-1425, the North Tommy Trail, passing trail FS-1426 at mile 1.2 from FS-1409.1. Take trail FS-1425A at mile 2.4 (6500') and ascend northeast to the summit, a former lookout site. Summits in view: Bigelow (35°), Stormy Mtn. (110°), Stuart (203°), David (270°), Clark (291°), and Maude (326°).

KELLY MOUNTAIN, 6760', 2 miles, 1000' gain (Maps: USGS Silver Falls, GT Plain). **Hike-3**. The distance and elevation gain are added to Klone Peak (see above).

From Klone Peak, descend to the trail junction on the southwest ridge, 6500'. Turn east on trail FS-1425 until Kelly Mtn. reads 120°, then descend a ridge southeast (160°–110°) to a saddle, 6100'. Ascend southeast to the rock summit. Emerald Peak is almost exactly north (357°). To return to trail FS-1425, descend to the saddle, 6100', then continue west over the south flank of Klone Peak. Cross Klone Meadow (springs) and ascend west to trail FS-1425.

MAD RIVER LOOP, high point 6200', 8 miles, 1000' gain (Maps: USGS Chikamin Creek, Silver Falls, GT Plain). **Hike-1**. The distance and elevation gain are from camping in Marble Meadow (see Shetipo-Larch Lakes Loop).

From Marble Meadow, hike south on trail FS-1409.1, then go east on trail FS-1425, the North Tommy Trail, for 1.2 miles. At a junction, turn south on the Blue Creek Trail, FS-1426, crossing and travelling near Tommy Creek. Reach **Lake Louise** (cabin) at mile 1.5 from FS-1425, **Lake Ann** at mile 2, a junction with trail FS-1424 at mile 3, and the Garland Peak Trail (FS-1409.1) at the Mad River Guard Station, mile 4 (camping). Turn northwest on trail FS-1409.1 past the Alder Ridge Trail (FS-1523). At mile 2.5, go left to visit **Mad Lake** (70°F in August). Return to trail FS-1409.1 and continue north, either on the trail or in Marble Meadow, to the starting point.

GARLAND PEAK, 7525', 1 mile RT, 600' gain (Maps: USGS Saska Peak, GT Lucerne). **Hike-3**. Distance and elevation gain are from trail FS-1409.1 on the Shetipo-Larch Lakes Loop.

Two miles north of Pinto Camp, where the trail crosses meadows on the southwest side of Garland Peak, leave the trail at 6900' and ascend east in meadows and openings in the krummholz to the south ridge of Garland Peak. At 7300', contour northwest below a false summit, then continue ascending northeast to the rock summit (benchmark). Admire Devils Smoke Stack (338°) from a mile away.

RAMPART MOUNTAIN, 7693', 1 mile RT, 500' gain (Maps: USGS Saska Peak, GT Lucerne). **Hike-3**. Distance and elevation gain are from trail FS-1409.1 on the Shetipo-Larch Lakes Loop.

One mile north of the Basalt Ridge Trail junction, where trail FS-1409.1 bends sharply west and begins to descend, leave the trail and ascend northeast to the south ridge of Rampart Mtn. Turn north, staying on or near the ridge to the summit area. Pass false summits on the right (east) to a sump, then continue north to the true summit.

FIFTH OF JULY MOUNTAIN, 7696', 1 mile RT, 500' gain (Maps: USGS Saska Peak, GT Lucerne). **Hike-3. Glacier Peak Wilderness.** Distance and elevation gain are from trail FS-1409.1 on the Shetipo-Larch Lakes Loop.

Where trail FS-1409.1 goes east from Fifth of July Pass, leave the trail and ascend north on one of several tracks. Pass east of false summits to the true summit. Peaks in view: Pinnacle (43°), Cardinal (58°), Pyramid (74°), Carne Mtn. (314°),and Maude (336°).

POMAS PASS, high point 7320', 8 miles RT, 2200' gain (Maps: USGS Saska Peak, Trinity, GT Lucerne, Holden). **Hike-1/Hike-3. Glacier Peak Wilderness.** Distance and elevation gain are from Larch Lakes, 5700', on the Shetipo-Larch lakes Loop.

Find the trail between the upper and lower lakes and ascend northwest to Larch Lakes saddle, 6440'. Continue north over open slopes. At the trail high point, 6900', leave the trail and ascend northeast (**Hike-3**) to a rock summit, 7320', for the view. On the descent to Pomas Pass, look for a massive exposure of black hornblende crystals beside the trail. At Pomas Pass, continue north on the trail briefly, then diverge west on one of several tracks to visit several minor bumps on the ridge and another saddle to find several fire circles and felled trees (old lookout site?). Carne Mtn. is almost directly west (280°).

ANTHEM–CHORAL–SNOW BRUSHY LOOP, high point 6900', 23 miles RT, 4800' gain (Maps: USGS Saska Peak, GT Lucerne). **Hike-2. Glacier Peak Wilderness.** This trail loop gives access to the impressively beautiful meadows at the heads of Choral and Anthem Creeks. Drive the Entiat River Road, CR-371 and FS-51 for 36 miles to the trailhead north of Cottonwood Campground, 3144'.

Hike northwest on the Entiat River Trail, FS-1400, for two miles to a junction south of Anthem Creek (camping). Ascend east and northeast on trail FS-1435, passing the Duncan Hill Trail at 5875', two miles from the Entiat River Trail. Cross **Anthem Creek** at 6000', four miles from the Entiat River Trail. The area near the trail crossing of Anthem Creek makes an excellent campsite for exploring the meadows and summits at the heads of Anthem and Choral Creeks: Duncan Hill, Gopher Mtn., Choral Peak, and Fern Lake Point 7909'.

From the crossing of Anthem Creek, 6000', ascend north to the saddle between Anthem and Choral Creeks, entering the Glacier Peak Wilderness. After descending in ancient forest, cross Choral Creek and continue down to Snow Brushy Creek, 4.7 miles from the trail crossing of Anthem Creek. Cross the creek, turning right (northeast) on trail FS-

1230 for 2.1 miles to the next trail junction, 5831', where the Graham Mtn. Trail, FS-1433 joins from the east. The Snow Brushy–Graham Mtn. trail junction has many campsites and possibilities for day trips: Saska Peak, Emerald Peak, Pinnacle Mtn., and Borealis Ridge. Saska Pass, 7500', with a view of the Chelan Mountains, Borealis Pass, 7900' (below), and Milham Pass, 6663', which has a view of Lake Chelan after descending a short distance on the east side of the crest, make day trip destinations for those not interested in the summits.

From the campsite at the junction of the Snow Brushy Creek Trail and the Graham Mtn. Trail, descend southwest on the Snow Brushy Creek Trail to the Entiat River Trail, FS-1400. Turn left (south) to return to the trailhead at the end of the Entiat River Road, FS-51, and 8.8 miles (2700') from the Graham Mtn. Trail at Snow Brushy Creek. Camping on the Entiat River Trail is possible at Snow Brushy Creek, but the area has been severely flood damaged.

DUNCAN HILL, 7819', 8 miles RT, 2100' gain (Maps: USGS Saska Peak, GT Lucerne). **Hike-1**. The distance and elevation gain given for this trip are from camping at the crossing of Anthem Creek, 6000' (see Anthem-Choral-Snow Brushy Loop.

From the trail at Anthem Creek, return south one mile to the junction with the Duncan Hill Trail. Turn east and ascend, keeping left on trail FS-1434A at a junction, 7400', to the summit, the location of a former lookout and a viewpoint east over the North Fork of the Entiat River to summits of the Chelan Crest. The summit is 8 miles from road FS-51.

CHORAL PEAK, 7960', 4 miles RT, 2100' gain (Maps: USGS Saska Peak, GT Lucerne). **Meadows: Hike-3, Summit: Hike-4†**. Choral Peak is the summit 0.3 mile southwest of Choral Lake. The distance and elevation gain given for this trip are from camping on Anthem Creek (see Anthem-Choral-Snow Brushy Loop).

From Anthem Creek, 6000', ascend north on trail FS-1434. At 6400', where trail FS-1434 turns west, look for a track that goes northeast on benches in open forest into the meadows at the head of Anthem Creek. The beginning of this track from trail FS-1434 is obscure, but once found is easy to follow. The meadows at the head of Anthem Creek begin at 7000' and extend to 7400'. For the summit, go north from 7400' to the saddle (7520'), then ascend left (west) on rock.

FERN LAKE POINT 7909, 7909', 4 miles RT, 2000' gain (Maps: USGS Saska Peak, GT Lucerne). **Hike-3**. The distance and elevation gain given for this trip are from Anthem Creek, 6000' (see Anthem-Choral-Snow Brushy Loop).

From Anthem Creek, hike as above for Choral Peak into the meadows at the head of Anthem Creek. At 7200', ascend east (104°) to the talus summit, with a view southeast to Fern Lake, 1000' below. Add this summit to the Choral Peak hike.

GOPHER MOUNTAIN, 8001', 6 miles RT, 3200' gain (Maps: USGS Saska Peak, GT Lucerne). **Hike-3. Glacier Peak Wilderness.** The distance and elevation gain given for this trip are from Anthem Creek (see Anthem-Choral-Snow Brushy Loop).

From Anthem Creek, 6000', ascend north on trail FS-1434 to the saddle between Anthem Creek and Choral Creek, 6900'. Continue on the trail, descending toward Choral Creek to a stream crossing, 6200'. Leave the trail and contour and ascend north in forest and brush to cross Choral Creek at 6500'. Turn northeast and ascend gentle, open forest benches into the extensive meadows at the head of Choral Creek. Continue northeast up the open slope to the summit.

On the return, cross Choral Creek at 6600' and traverse southwest and south below cliffs to return to the trail near 6200', descending as necessary to pass below steeper terrain. This return route is fairly obvious for the return, but would be difficult to find going north.

BOREALIS PASS, 7700', 4 miles RT, 2000' gain (Maps: USGS Saska Peak, GT Lucerne). **Hike-2. Glacier Peak Wilderness.** The distance and elevation gain given are from camping at the junction of the Graham Mtn. Trail and the Snow Brushy Creek Trail, 5831', (see Anthem-Choral-Snow Brushy Loop).

From the Graham Mtn. Trail junction, 5831', hike northeast on the Snow Brush Creek Trail for one mile. At 6200', look for a faint trail turning north in an opening. Follow this faint trail as it ascends in forest. Where the canyon narrows, pass a large campsite. The trail leaves the bottom of the canyon here and ascends northwest to a bench on the west side of the canyon, but may be hard to follow. The trail is obvious higher in the canyon. Either on the trail or in the valley, continue north and west to broad **Borealis Pass**, 7700', on the ridge between Pinnacle Mtn. (north) and the cliffs and pinnacles of Borealis Ridge (south). Explore along the ridge and in the open meadows leading to Pinnacle Mtn.

PINNACLE MOUNTAIN, 8402', 6 miles RT, 2700' gain (Maps: USGS Saska Peak, Pinnacle Mtn., GT Lucerne). **Hike-3. Glacier Peak Wilderness.** The distance and elevation gain given are from camping on the Graham Mtn. Trail at Snow Brushy Creek (see Anthem-Choral-Snow Brushy Loop).

Hike as above to **Borealis Pass**. Turn northeast and ascend at first on the ridge then on sandy talus to the 7840' saddle between Pinnacle Mtn. and an 8040' summit southeast. From the 7840' saddle, go north through broken rocks to the summit.

BOREALIS RIDGE, high point 7659', 4 miles RT, 2000' gain (Maps: USGS Saska Peak, GT Lucerne). **Hike-3. Glacier Peak Wilderness.** The distance and elevation gain given are from camping on the Graham Mtn. Trail at Snow Brushy Creek, 5831' (see Anthem-Choral-Snow Brushy Loop).

Descend southwest on the trail to an avalanche meadow, 5500'. Leave the trail and ascend west into a broad, open valley on the south slope of Borealis Ridge. Ascend in this valley to the crest of the ridge, seeing and crossing many rhyolite dikes exposed in the slopes and ridges. At the crest of the ridge, turn left (southwest) and ascend to a high point. The slightly higher summits of Borealis Ridge north require technical rock climbing skills.

Lake Chelan Area

LYMAN LAKE, high point 5600', 19 miles RT, 2400' gain (Maps: USGS Holden, Suiattle Pass, GT Holden). **Hike-1. Glacier Peak Wilderness.** From US-2 at Wenatchee, drive north on US-97 on the west side of the Columbia River. Where the highway follows a curve of the river northeast, turn left (north) up Navarre Coulee on CR-2 to Lake Chelan. At the lake, go north to the Field's Point Landing ferry terminal (supervised parking). Take the Lady-of-the-Lake ferry (telephone: 509-682-2224) to the terminal at Lucerne. Ride the bus that meets the ferry to Holden, 3226' (for lodging, meals, and bus reservation, write to Holden Village, Chelan WA 98816). Find camping 0.5 mile northwest on Railroad Creek (mice).

From Holden, hike west up Railroad Creek on trail FS-1256, passing Hart Lake at five miles, 3982' (camping). Reach Lyman Lake, 5587' at nine miles from Holden. The lake shore has now recovered from heavy use in the past. Please do not camp near or on the lakeshore. For the best campsites, go south from a junction east of the lake, following a trail to open benches, 5900'. From here, explore south to Spider Gap, 7100'. Black tourmaline crystals can be found in the debris from mines in the cliffs on the east side of the valley.

SUIATTLE PASS, 5900', 25 miles RT, 4000' gain (Maps: USGS Holden, Suiattle Pass, GT Holden). **Hike-1. Glacier Peak Wilderness.** Hike as above to Lyman Lake.

From Lyman Lake, follow the trail west to Cloudy Pass (6438', camping). Drop west to the first junction and contour west to Suiattle Pass (5983', camping), three miles from Lyman Lake, 12 miles from Holden, and a good location for exploring north to Image Lake and Plummer Mtn. The Pacific Crest Trail crosses at Suiattle Pass.

IMAGE LAKE, 6100', 8 miles RT, 2000' gain (Maps: USGS Gamma Peak, Suiattle Pass, GT Glacier Peak, Holden). **Hike-1. Glacier Peak Wilderness.** Distance and elevation gain are from camping at Suiattle Pass.

From camping at Suiattle Pass, hike west on the Pacific Crest Trail for 0.7 mile, then, where the PCT turns south to descend into the valley of the Suiattle River, contour west on trail FS-785 for 1.6 miles. After passing evidence of past mining activity at Glacier Peak Mines and a trail that descends south to Miner's Creek, branch right (north), staying on trail FS-785 to ascend to Image Lake and its famous view of Glacier Peak.

MINERS RIDGE POINT 6758, 6758', 1 mile RT, 700' gain (Maps: USGS Gamma Peak, GT Glacier Peak). **Hike-1. Glacier Peak Wilderness.** A minor summit north of Image Lake provides marvelous views.

From Image Lake (see above), follow the trail west one-fourth mile, then go north on a track up the ridge to the summit.

MINERS RIDGE LOOKOUT, 6210', 10 miles RT, 2200' gain (Maps: USGS Gamma Peak, Suiattle Pass, GT Holden, Glacier Peak). **Hike-1. Glacier Peak Wilderness.** The distance and elevation gain given are from camping at Suiattle Pass.

From Image Lake, continue west on the trail, FS-785, to the lookout tower, which is sometimes occupied. Summits visible from the lookout, in addition to Glacier Peak (231°), include: Fortress Mtn. (125°) and Ten Peak (180°).

PLUMMER MOUNTAIN, 7870', 5 miles RT, 2200' gain (Maps: USGS Suiattle Pass, GT Holden). **Hike-3. Glacier Peak Wilderness.** The distance and elevation gain are from Suiattle Pass.

From Suiattle Pass, hike west on the Pacific Crest Trail for 0.7 mile, then go one mile west on trail FS-785 toward the junction with trail FS-

795. Leave the trail 0.5 mile east of the junction of trails FS-785 and FS-795 and hike north up mostly open slopes to the summit area. Pass east of the first rock point and continue north in steeper talus.

CLOUDY PEAK, 7915', 6 miles RT, 2400' gain (Maps: USGS Suiattle Pass, GT Holden). **Hike-4†. Glacier Peak Wilderness.** The distance and elevation gain are from Lyman Lake.

From Lyman Lake, hike west to Cloudy Pass, 6438'. From the pass, leave the trail and ascend northeast on the east side of the ridge to the summit area. Ascend the final block from the east.

PRINCE CREEK–SAWTOOTH RIDGE, high point 7600', 20 miles RT, 4000' gain (Maps: USGS Prince Creek, Martin Peak, GT Prince Creek). **Hike-1**. Find lakes, meadows, and 8000' peaks in a near timberline setting that deserves to be protected as part of the Lake Chelan-Sawtooth Wilderness.

At Wenatchee, MP-119 on US-2, stay on US-2/97, crossing the Columbia River and turning north on the east side of the river. At MP-132, leave US-2 and continue north on US-97. Near Pateros, turn left (west) on SR-153, following the Methow River. When 16 miles from US-97, turn northwest on the Gold Creek Road, FS-4340, and drive 12 miles to the trailhead, 4800'.

Hike west on trail FS-431, contouring one mile to Crater Creek, 4900'. Turn right (north) on trail FS-416 and ascend three miles along Crater Creek to Crater Lake, 6841' (camping), four miles from the road. The summit to the northwest, Sawtooth Point 8580' (see below), is the highest summit in the area and provides a general view of the Sawtooth Range and Hoodoo Peak.

Return east to trail FS-431, the Eagle Lake Trail, and go south and west to a junction six miles from the road. Ascend a branch to Upper Eagle Lakes (camping), six miles from the road and 7100'. From the Upper Eagle Lakes junction, go west, passing the trail to Lower Eagle Lake before reaching Horsehead Pass, 7600'. Horsehead Point 8202 is north of the pass (below). Descend west from Horsehead Pass, going by shallow Boiling Lake to a junction with the **Summit Trail**, FS-1259, at a large campsite on the **Middle Fork of Prince Creek**, eight miles from the road, 6560'. This campground is a good location for making trips to Cub Lake, Surprise Lake, Mt. Bigelow, and other summits.

For a campsite that has a better view but is slightly farther to water (spring), go 1.5 miles south to the high point of the **Summit Trail**, FS-1259, at the north edge of meadows at the head of the East Fork of Prince Creek, 7100'. Find the spring by going southwest in the meadow from the trail high point. This campsite is appropriate for exploring west and south: Old Maid Mtn., Sunrise Lake, and Switchback Peak (see below).

SAWTOOTH POINT 8580, 8580', 3 miles RT, 1900' gain (Maps: USGS Martin Peak, GT Prince Creek). **Hike-3**. The distance and elevation gain given for this trip are from Crater Lake.

From Crater Lake, 6841', hike northwest in talus and broken rocks to the summit, the highest in the area. Hoodoo Peak, 8464', is exactly north.

HORSEHEAD POINT 8202, 8202', 1 mile RT, 600' gain (Maps: USGS Martin Peak, GT Prince Creek). **Hike-2**. The distance and elevation gain given for this trip are from Horsehead Pass.

At Horsehead Pass, leave the trail and ascend a track north to the summit.

MOUNT BIGELOW, 8135', 4 miles RT, 1600' gain (Maps: USGS Martin Peak, GT Prince Creek). **Hike-3**. The distance and elevation gain given are from the campground where trail FS-1259 crosses the Middle Fork of Prince Creek (see Prince Creek–Sawtooth Ridge).

Hike north from the campground on trail FS-420 to Hoodoo Pass. Leave the trail at the pass and ascend east to the summit, mostly on talus. Many peaks are visible from the summit: Hoodoo Peak (15°), Pyramid Mtn. (226°), Pinnacle Mtn. (250°), and Star Peak (304°).

CHEOPS PEAK, MARTIN PEAK, 8270', 8375', 4 miles RT (Maps: USGS Martin Peak, GT Prince Creek). **Hike-3**. The distance and elevation gain given are from the campground where trail FS-1259 crosses the Middle Fork of Prince Creek (see Prince Creek–Sawtooth Ridge).

From the campground on the Middle Fork of Prince Creek, hike south 0.5 mile on trail FS-1259 to the first stream crossing. Leave the trail and ascend east in meadow at the head of the creek to the saddle north of Martin Peak. Turn north and continue to the summit of Cheops Peak, 8270'. From the summit, return to the saddle, then go south up the ridge to Martin Peak, 8375'.

CUB PASS POINT 7642, 7642', 4 miles RT, 1100' gain (Maps: USGS Prince Creek, Martin Peak, GT Prince Creek). **Hike-3**. The distance and elevation gain given are from the campground where trail

FS-1259 crosses the Middle Fork of Prince Creek (see Prince Creek–Sawtooth Ridge).

Hike west on trail FS-1259, the Summit Trail, to the saddle where the trail begins to descend to the North Fork of Prince Creek. Leave the trail and follow the ridge east to the first summit, 7642'.

SAWTOOTH RIDGE LOOP, high points 8030', 8010', and 7841', 9 miles RT, 3200' gain (Maps: USGS Prince Creek, Martin Peak, GT Prince Creek). **Hike-3. Glacier Peak Wilderness.** This ridge hike near or above 8000' overlooks broad meadows of the upper North Fork of Prince Creek. The distance and elevation gain given are from the campground where trail FS-1259 crosses the Middle Fork of Prince Creek (see Prince Creek–Sawtooth Ridge).

From the Middle Fork of Prince Creek, hike west and northwest on the Summit Trail, FS-1259, descending to 5600' near the junction with trail FS-1254 and crossing the branch of the North Fork of Prince Creek that drains Bernice Lake. Leave the trail and ascend east on or near the ridge to the first summit, 8030'. Continue southeast on the ridge over the next summit, 8010', then turn south and drop to 7700' on the way to the final summit, 784l'. From the 7841' point, descend northeast to trail FS-420, near Hoodoo Pass. Turn south to the start.

SWITCHBACK PEAK, 8321', 4 miles RT, 1400' gain (Maps: USGS Martin Peak, GT Prince Creek). **Hike-2**. The distance and elevation gain given are from camping on the Summit Trail (FS-1259), 1.5 mile south of the Middle Fork of Prince Creek and 7100' (see Prince Creek–Sawtooth Ridge).

Hike south on trail FS-1259 for 0.7 mile. Find an obscure and abandoned trail at 7000' (shown on the USGS 1969 map and the Wenatchee National Forest map) that ascends a rocky slope east. At the trail high point, before the trail turns south toward Foggy Dew Creek, leave the trail and ascend north to the summit.

SUNRISE LAKE, 7228', 8 miles RT, 2000' gain (Maps: USGS Martin Peak, GT Prince Creek). **Hike-2**. The distance and elevation gain given are from camping on the Summit Trail (FS-1259) at 7100', 1.5 mile south of the Middle Fork of Prince Creek (see Prince Creek–Sawtooth Ridge).

Hike as above over the shoulder of **Switchback Peak** to a trail junction on the SE ridge. Take the right fork (southeast) and descend in meadows to Foggy Dew Creek. From trail FS-417 at 7000', turn south on trail FS-417A and ascend to seldom visited Sunrise Lake. On the west side of the lake, find an abandoned trail (shown on the 1985 Wenatchee Forest Map and the USGS 1969 map) and ascend west to the crest of the ridge. A high point, 8002', is southeast. Continue west to join trail FS-1258 at 7300'. Turn west on trail FS-1258 for 0.5 mile to meet trail FS-1259 at the saddle between Horsethief Basin and the Middle Fork of Prince Creek, 7400'. A minor summit west of this saddle, 7524', is easily reached. From the saddle and junction with trail FS-1259, go north on trail FS-1259 to return to the starting point.

OLD MAID MOUNTAIN, 7820', 7882', 4 miles RT, 1500' gain (Maps: USGS Prince Creek, Martin Peak, GT Prince Creek). **Hike-3**. The distance and elevation gain given are from camping on the Summit Trail (FS-1259), 1.5 mile south of the Middle Fork of Prince Creek and 7100' (see Prince Creek–Sawtooth Ridge).

Hike west up the open meadow to the first summit, 7820', then follow the ridge or contour another mile on the rocky south slopes through widely spaced whitebark pine trees to the highest point.

North Cascades Region

SR-92 Area. **Granite Falls to Barlow Pass.** From I-5 at Everett, Exit-194, drive east on US-2 for two miles, then go left (northeast) on SR-204 for two miles to SR-9. Turn north on SR-9 for two miles, then turn east on SR-92 to the town of Granite Falls. Alternative Route: From I-5 at Exit-171, drive north on SR-522 for 14 miles. Turn north on SR-9 and drive north for 17 miles. Near MP-18, turn right (east) from SR-9 on SR-92 through the town of Granite Falls. SR-92 makes a left turn to the north at the east edge of Granite Falls.

GRANITE FALLS TO SMOKEY POINT, high point 400', 23 miles, 600' gain (Maps: USGS Granite Falls, Lake Stevens, Arlington East, Arlington West). **Bicycle**. From Aurora Transit Center, ride Community Transit 610 to Everett and CT 280 to Granite Falls.

After exploring Granite Falls, ride west on SR-92 to Jordan Road on the west edge of Granite Falls. Begin road log at the intersection of SR-92 and Jordan Road. Ride north on Jordan Road, passing **Perrigoue Park** (playfields) at mile 0.5 before descending to cross the South Fork of the Stillaguamish River. Pass minor wetlands along the highway and get occasional views of the river. At mile 6.0 pause at **Jordan Park**, which has a footbridge over the river and access to the river. At **River Meadows Park**, mile 9.0, descend west to the river (restrooms, picnic tables, camping in summer). Explore loops north and south along the river and in riparian woodland.

Return to the park entrance (mile 11) and proceed north on Jordan Road on bluffs near the river. Join Arlington Heights Road at mile 14. Now the highway turns west to join SR-504 at mile 15. Go left (west) on SR-504 to enter **Twin Rivers Park** on the north side of the highway at mile 15.2 (restrooms, tables). Trails provide access to both the North and South Forks of the Stillaguamish River. Note the SR-9 bridge over the Stillaguamish River just downstream (west) from the trail on the shore of the North Fork. Return to SR-530, mile 16, and go west across the South Fork of the Stillaguamish River into Arlington. Continue west to SR-9, then turn right (north) to **Haller Park** on the south bank of the Stillaguamish River (restrooms, picnic tables, river access).

Return south on SR-9 into Arlington, then go east to Olympic Ave. Ride south through the downtown area, including a stop in Legion Memorial Park (Chamber of Commerce, pedestrian way). At E Maple St., turn southwest under SR-9 into Stillaguamish Highway. Pass the

Stillaguamish Valley Pioneer Museum at mile 19, then turn right (west) on 204th St. NE at a cemetery. The street travels on the bluff above the wetland of Portage Creek before bending into 198th Place NE. Go left (south) on 47th Ave. S, which bends right (west) into 188th St. NE. Turn left (south) on 35th Ave. NE to the CT 210 bus stop at the Stillaguamish Senior Center, mile 22.

GRANITE FALLS, high point 389', 1 mile RT, 150' gain (Maps: USGS Granite Falls, GT Granite Falls). **Hike-1**. From Aurora Transit Center, ride Community Transit 610 to Everett and CT 280 to Granite Falls. If driving, park south of the highway bridge over the South Fork of the Stillaguamish River, 1.4 miles north from E Stanley St. in the town of Granite Falls.

Walk north from Granite Falls on SR-92 to a gravel road on the west side of the highway at the south end of the highway bridge. Descend on the road or on a stairway to the river level to view the falls and the fish ladder. Find access to the river west of the end of the ladder. The falls are most impressive at high water.

MONTE CRISTO RAILROAD, high point 1040', 3 miles RT, 400' gain (Maps: USGS Granite Falls, Verlot, GT Granite Falls). **Hike-1**. Park at the beginning of the **Old Robe Trail**, seven miles east on SR-92 from the town of Granite Falls, elevation 1040'.

Descend south and southwest on a rebuilt trail to an old railroad grade near the South Fork of the Stillaguamish River. Follow the trail on the railroad grade downstream along the river past two tunnels. The track was damaged by floods so often that the railroad only occasionally was in service. Look for the grooves where the railroad ties were imbedded in concrete.

GOAT FLAT, high point 5000', 10 miles RT, 2600' gain (Maps: USGS Meadow Mtn., Whitehorse, GT Granite Falls, Silverton). **Hike-3. Boulder River Wilderness**. From the town of Granite Falls, drive SR-92 east for seven miles, then, across the highway from the beginning of the Old Robe Trail, turn north on road FS-41 (paved). At the end of the pavement, two miles from SR-92, take the left branch where road FS-4110 goes right. Minor roads go right at miles six and eight, and the road crosses Canyon Creek, mile 8.5. The Meadow Mtn. Trail begins on the right (north) at mile 10 just after the road crosses Saddle Creek. Road FS-4150 goes left (west) toward Arlington at mile 13. Go right at mile 17.5 where a minor road branches left. Reach the trailhead near Tupso Pass, elevation 3000' and 18 miles from SR-92. Goat Flats lies in the Boulder River Wilderness (no dogs, horses, or bicycles).

Ascend on the trail, which is deeply eroded between roots and rocks, going generally east into giant ancient forest. The trail crosses several rocky outcrops that will require the use of hands. From a high point on the northeast shoulder of Meadow Mountain, 3760', the trail descends to 3500', crossing below cliffs and talus before contouring south to Saddle Lake, 3771', and a junction with a trail that goes to Meadow Mtn. From Saddle Lake, continue east, crossing the only significant stream above Saddle Lake at 4200'. Several small lakes are east of the trail at 4500'. The Goat Flats meadow begins at 4800' and extends to 5200' (toilet). Water is available from ponds and a tiny stream. Please refrain from washing or bathing in the water supply. No fires.

Summits visible from the Goat Flats area (not all from one place): Mt. Baker (354°), Shuksan (6°), Bullon (30°), Whitehorse (35°), Big Bear (116°), Liberty (136°), and Pilchuck (204°). The after dark view of the lowlands is especially impressive: Everett (240°), Arlington (274°), and Mount Vernon (300°). The blinking red lights on the hill northwest are the towers of the U. S. Navy's transmitting station near Jim Creek.

TIN CAN GAP, 5760', 14 miles RT, 3400' gain (Maps: USGS Meadow Mtn., Whitehorse Mtn., GT Granite Falls, Silverton). **Hike-3. Boulder River Wilderness**. Drive and hike as above to **Goat Flats**.

From Goat Flats, hike east on the trail, going up and down on the south side of the ridge that leads up to Three Fingers. The trail ends at Tin Can Gap (USGS map), which has an awesome view down to the Queest-Alb Glacier and up to Three Fingers.

THREE FINGERS SOUTH PEAK, 6850', 16 miles RT, 4700' gain (Maps: USGS Meadow Mtn., Whitehorse Mtn., GT Granite Falls, Silverton). **Hike-4†, Snow. Boulder River Wilderness**. Drive and hike as above to **Tin Can Gap**. Best time: July. Reference: *Three Fingers Lookout* by Malcolm Bates.

From Tin Can Gap, ascend east up the ridge on a faint track to cliffs with a steep, exposed, no runout snow field on the north side of the ridge. Cross the snowfield (ice ax mandatory) to another saddle and continue east on the trail, now on the south side of the ridge. After passing a high point, reach another bump on the ridge, which has a steep drop on the east and south side. Pass this bump on the north by descending another steep, exposed snowfield and continue east on the trail, again on the south side of the ridge. At 6100', the trail bends north briefly and ascends on a shelf above the Queest-Alb Glacier before again turning east, gradually rising in a long traverse across the south slope.

After ascending in switchbacks where the trail is sometimes hard to distinguish from the talus, reach the end of the trail at 6500', identified by a bivouack shelter and debris (coils of wire) near the lower edge of a snowfield.

Now turn north and ascend on the snow (gentle slope). From the upper edge of the snow field, ascend a gravel and sandy slope mixed with bedrock for 50', then contour left (west) around a corner below steeper rocks to the beginning of the ladders to the lookout building. A few of the summits visible: Pugh (98°), Sloan (120°), Stuart (143°), and Hinman with Daniel (152°).

VERLOT PUBLIC SERVICE CENTER, 979' (Maps: USGS Verlot, GT Granite Falls). **Walk.** Drive 11 miles east from the town of Granite Falls on SR-92. This station of the Mt. Baker–Snoqualmie National Forest supplies maps and forest information seven days a week in summer.

Take the self-guided tour (pamphlet available): (1) Ranger Station with museum was built by the CCC in 1937. (2) Red cedar. (3) Restroom and information display. (4) Douglas fir. (5) Cascara. (6) Pacific yew. (7) Residence built by the CCC in 1936. (8) Silver fir. (9) Hemlock. (10) Salal. (11) Sitka spruce. (12) Bigleaf maple. (13) California black oak. (14) Sequoia. (15) Ponderosa pine. (16) Alaska huckleberry. (17) Sword fern. (18) Vine maple. (19) Lady fern. (20) Bracken. (21) Thimbleberry. (22) Deer fern. (23) Thinleaf huckleberry. (24) Red huckleberry. (25) Red alder. (26) Salmonberry. (27) Gas house and pump (1938). (28) Warehouse built by the CCC. (29) Roof from CCC powerhouse, now a display. On the south side of SR-92, find an old ore cart, typical of those that were used in the nearby mines, and an 8' diameter section from a Douglas fir tree cut in 1969 that was growing at the time Columbus discovered America (700 years old).

HEATHER LAKE, 2395', 4 miles RT, 1000' gain (Maps: USGS Verlot, GT Granite Falls). **Hike-1.** Drive 12 miles east of Granite Falls on SR-92, and one mile east of the Verlot Public Service Center. Immediately after crossing a bridge over the South Fork of the Stillaguamish River, turn right (south) on road FS-42 to the trailhead, 1.6 miles from SR-92, elevation 1400'.

Hike south on the trail in an ancient forest composed of red cedar, western hemlock, Douglas fir, bigleaf maple, and Sitka spruce.

MOUNT PILCHUCK, 5340', 6 miles RT, 2300' gain (Maps: USGS Verlot, GT Granite Falls). **Hike-1.** Drive 12 miles east of Granite Falls and one mile east of the Verlot Public Service Center. Immediately after crossing the bridge over the South Fork of the Stillaguamish River, turn right (south) on road FS-42 and drive seven miles to the trailhead, 3100'.

Hike the trail south to the summit and a recently rebuilt (1989) lookout building with information displays. Peaks visible include: Whitehorse (28°), Three Fingers (33°), Glacier Peak (83°), and Dickerman (86°).

LAKE TWENTYTWO, 2413', 4 miles RT, 1400' gain (Maps: USGS Verlot, Mallardy Ridge, GT Granite Falls, Silverton). **Hike-1**. Drive 2.4 miles past the Verlot Public Service Center and 14 miles from Granite Falls to the trailhead off SR-92, elevation 1100'.

Hike south on the trail in a preserved bit of ancient forest. The lake lies in a steep-walled cirque on the east slope of Mt. Pilchuck.

ASHLAND LAKES, 2846', 7 miles RT, 500' gain (Maps: USGS Mallardy Ridge, GT Silverton). **Hike-1**. These trails are maintained by the Washington State Department of Natural Resources. Camp only in designated campsites. Drive 16 miles east of Granite Falls and five miles east of Verlot on SR-92. Turn south on road FS-4020 for 2.7 miles. Turn right on road FS-4021 for 1.5 miles, then go left for 0.2 miles to the trailhead, 4.4 miles from SR-92, elevation 2400'.

The route goes south on an old logging road for one mile before becoming a trail in ancient forest. Cross a branch of Black Creek, then pass Beaver Plant Lake, 2820', at 1.1 miles. Continue southwest to more lakes and a waterfall. Campsites at the lakes are open from June 15 to October 15.

BALD MOUNTAIN TRAIL, high point 4800', 20+ miles or less RT, 3000' gain (Maps: USGS Mallardy Ridge, Wallace Lake, GT Silverton, Index). **Hike-1**. These trails are maintained by the Washington State Department of Natural Resources. Camp only in designated campsites. Drive and hike as above on the trail for Ashland Lakes.

At a trail junction, 1.2 miles from the trailhead, take the left fork (south) past the west side of Beaver Plant Lake, ascending to cross Bald Mtn. Ridge at 3500' (huckleberries in the fall). Turn east on the south side of the ridge in ancient forest, getting views of some of the pinnacles of Bald Mtn. and eventually reaching an open high point near a summit (climbing). The trail on east connects with the Sultan Basin Road coming north from Spada Lake and the Sultan River.

BOARDMAN LAKE, 2985', 2 miles RT, 1400' gain (Maps: USGS

Mallardy Ridge, GT Silverton). **Hike-1**. These trails are maintained by the Washington State Department of Natural Resources. Camp only in designated campsites. Drive 16 miles east of Granite Falls and five miles east of Verlot on SR-92. Turn south on road FS-4020, passing, at 2.7 miles, the road going right to the Ashland Lakes trailhead. Continue south on road FS-4020, passing a road on the left immediately after the junction to Ashland Lakes. Four miles from SR-92, pause at a viewpoint. Continue south on FS-4020 to park at the trailhead after the road turns west, elevation 2740'.

Hike south past **Lake Evan**, 2762', in ancient forest with many examples of giant red cedar trees, which characteristically have lost the top. Boardman Lake stands on a shelf on the north side of Bald Mountain.

CUTTHROAT LAKES, 4200', 7 miles RT, 1700' gain (Maps: USGS Mallardy Ridge, GT Silverton). **Hike-2**. These trails are maintained by the Washington State Department of Natural Resources. Camp only in designated campsites. Drive 18.4 miles east of Granite Falls on SR-92 (7.4 miles east of the Verlot Public Service Center). Before crossing Red Bridge, turn south on road FS-4030 for 1.3 miles, then drive west on road FS-4032 for six miles, passing branch roads on the right at three and five miles, to park at a wide place in the road before reaching the trailhead, elevation 3060'. The trailhead, which has limited space for turning a vehicle, is 7.3 miles from SR-92.

Hike the trail southeast, contouring on the valley wall above Boardman Creek. After the first 0.5 mile, the trail goes up more steeply on switchbacks and crosses under a big boulder. Pass several small meadows and a high point (3700'), then descend to cross a stream on the north edge of a large meadow (no camping). The trail now contours west for a mile under cliffs before turning southwest to ascend to a bench that is dotted with tarns and the Cutthroat Lakes (camping, toilets).

BALD MOUNTAIN, high point 4800', 9 miles RT, 2500' gain (Maps: USGS Mallardy Ridge, Wallace Lake, GT Silverton, Index). **Hike-2**. Drive and hike as above to **Cutthroat Lakes**.

Where the trail crosses the outlet of the highest Cutthroat Lake at 4200', continue 50' west, then turn south and ascend on the main trail, passing designated camp sites and going over minor ridges. After passing the south end of the highest lake, the trail makes several switchbacks. At 4560', take the right (west) branch trail (not obvious) through alpine meadows toward the rocky summit of Bald Mtn., crossing the ridge to a view south over Spada Lake, then ascending the trail on the south-facing slope to an open viewpoint near the summit. The final summit is climbing country.

YOUTH–ON–AGE NATURE TRAIL, 1300', 0.5 mile loop, no gain, accessible (Maps: USGS Mallardy Ridge, GT Silverton). **Walk.** Drive 19 miles east of Granite Falls on SR-92 (8 miles east of Verlot) to a parking area on the south side of SR-92, elevation 1300'.

The site displays ancient forest in a region with more than 100" of rainfall yearly. (1) Note the many different mosses, both on the ground and on the trees. (2) Four large Sitka spruce trees stand in a group on both sides of the trail. (3) An opening in the forest canopy grows vine maple and red alder trees. (4) Two Douglas fir trees, each more than 500 years old, are near a bench. Note deeply furrowed bark. (5) Just south of the bench, find examples of western hemlock, a shade tolerant species. (6) Reach the river. Note the pavement going into thin air as the result of a change in the river. (7) Fungi grow on the cut ends of fallen trees. Such fungi are important in the decay process.

(8) Vine maple with bright green leaves and multiple thin trunks are often the first trees to invade forest openings. (9) A bigleaf maple with many large branches is festooned with moss. (10) Spiny devil's club is found in shady places below 3500'. (11) This giant Sitka spruce with the spreading base and the hemlock it surrounds started growing on a nurse log, which has now disappeared. (12) Red alder is another tree that appears quickly in openings. The alder trees add nitrogen to the soil. (13) Notice the dead stubs of branches on many trees. These stubs will eventually disappear, leaving a straight, smooth trunk. The death of lower branches allows more nutrients to reach the upper foliage, which receives more light. (14) Find sword fern, a shade tolerant plant, throughout the lowland forest. (15) Piggy-back plant or youth-on-age, grows everywhere at the edge of the trail.

MARTEN CREEK, high point 2700', 8 miles RT, 1400' gain (Maps: USGS Silverton, GT Silverton). **Hike-2. Boulder River Wilderness.** Drive 21 miles east of Granite Falls on SR-92 to parking on the north side of SR-92, elevation 1400'.

Ascend north on a sometimes gullied trail that follows the route of a former logging road, passing several ancient red cedars and Douglas firs. At one mile, 1900', go through a Douglas fir genetics research area where seeds from different regions were planted in 1916. The trail contours the west side of Long Mtn., then approaches Marten Creek briefly at 2400'. A summit of Gordon Ridge is west. Near the high point, look northwest (325°) to a pinnacle of Three Fingers Mtn. The bare slopes of Bald Mtn. are northeast. Beyond the high point, encounter dense salmonberry and deep gullies in the trail. At the creek, an overgrown track continues north on the east side of the creek.

FORGOTTEN MEADOW, high point 5396', 10 miles RT, 3300' gain (Maps: USGS Bedal, GT Sloan Peak). **Hike-1**. Drive 26 miles east of Granite Falls, then turn north one mile on the Perry Creek road to the trailhead, elevation 2100'.

The trail ascends northeast on the east side of the canyon of Perry Creek, passing **Perry Creek Falls** on the left (west) before crossing the creek. The trail now ascends north on switchbacks, then goes east just below the crest of the ridge to Forgotten Meadow and an impressive view of Glacier Peak directly east. Ascend west to a minor summit for a better view and the high point.

MOUNT FORGOTTEN, 6005', 12 miles RT, 4100' gain (Maps: USGS Bedal, GT Sloan Peak). **Hike-4†**. Drive and hike as above to **Forgotten Meadow**.

Cross the meadow north and descend on a steep track to the saddle, 5120'. Contour east on one of several tracks to the southeast ridge of Mt. Forgotten, then ascend west and northwest to a summit.

STILLAGUAMISH PEAK, 5720', 12 miles RT, 4000' gain (Maps: USGS Bedal, GT Sloan Peak). **Hike-4†**. Drive and hike as above toward Forgotten Meadow.

At 4900', near the crest of the ridge north of the crossing of Perry Creek, where the main trail goes east to Forgotten Meadow, turn west on a track that continues near or on the crest of the ridge. At 5300', on nearing the summit, contour west across the south face of the summit pyramid to the west ridge, then ascend on the west ridge in trees to the summit.

BIG FOUR ICE CAVES, high point 1720', 2 miles RT, minimum gain (Maps: USGS Bedal, GT Silverton). **Hike-1**. Drive 27 miles east of Granite Falls to the trailhead (toilets), elevation 1720'.

Hike south on a paved trail to the cave entrance in the cone of avalanche snow below the cliffs of Big Four Mtn. The roof of this cave may collapse at any time. Don't enter the caves or climb on the snow above the caves.

MOUNT DICKERMAN, 5723', 9 miles RT, 3800' gain (Maps: USGS Bedal, GT Sloan Peak). **Hike-1**. **Snow**. Drive 28 miles east of

Granite Falls to the trailhead, elevation 1950'.

The trail ascends north in ancient forest and the trip can be done in May or June when snow often begins below 4000'. Use caution on crossing the snow-filled or snow-bridged avalanche gullies near 4000'. Such bridges collapse at any time.

HEADLEE PASS, 4700', 6 miles RT, 2500' gain (Maps: USGS Bedal, Silverton, GT Sloan Peak, Silverton). **Hike-2**. Drive the Mountain Loop Highway, SR-92, for 29 miles east of Granite Falls and one mile east of the beginning of the Mt. Dickerman Trail to the Sunrise Mine Road. Turn south and drive two miles to the trailhead, elevation 2300'.

Hike south on trail FS-707, contouring above and then crossing the Stillaguamish River. The trail then ascends southwest into a magnificent rocky and steep-walled canyon east of Sperry Peak and north of Morningstar Peak. On nearing the steeper slopes of Morningstar Peak, the trail turns west and goes up a narrow canyon in short switchbacks to Headlee Pass.

VESPER PEAK, 6214', 10 miles RT, 4200' gain (Maps: USGS Bedal, Silverton, GT Sloan Peak, Silverton). **Hike-3**. Drive and hike as above to Headlee Pass.

From Headlee Pass the trail descends briefly northwest, then contours the west slopes of Sperry Peak. Cross the beginning of Vesper Creek at a pond, 4900'. Continue west on a track, ascending on granitic slabs (quartz diorite) to the ridge south of the summit. Turn north to the summit.

SPERRY PEAK, 6120', 9 miles RT, 4000' gain (Maps: USGS Bedal, Silverton, GT Silverton, Sloan Peak). **Hike-4†**. Drive and hike as above toward Vesper Peak to the creek crossing at the south end of the pond at the head of Vesper Creek canyon, elevation 4900'.

Turn north and go along the shore of the pond into the basin above the pond. Now go east and ascend through a gap in the cliffs to the summit.

BARLOW POINT, high point 3222', 3 miles RT, 1100' gain (Maps: USGS Bedal, GT Monte Cristo). **Hike-1**. Drive east from the town of Granite Falls for 31 miles on SR-92 to Barlow Pass, elevation 2361'.

Follow trail FS-709 as it contours and descends northwest to a junction. The Old Government Trail continues northwest. On the way, note the Monte Cristo Railroad grade just below. A branch trail connects with the railroad grade. Turn northeast and ascend switchbacks, first on the west side of the ridge, then on the east side to the bare rocks of the summit. South of the summit, a mossy buttress (3050') provides the best view south. At the summit, look west to Big Four Mtn. (276°), north to Pugh Mtn. (22°), southeast across the South Fork of the Sauk River to Sheep Mtn. (126°) and south to Silvertip Peak (166°).

FOGGY LAKE, 5252', 9 miles RT, 3000' gain (Maps: USGS Bedal, Monte Cristo, GT Sloan Peak, Monte Cristo). **Hike-2**. Also called Crater Lake. Drive 31 miles east of the town of Granite Falls on SR-92 to Barlow Pass, elevation 2361'.

Park and hike one mile south on the road toward Monte Cristo to the bridge over the South Fork of the Sauk River. A trail, FS-724, continues for one mile on the west bank of the river. At the point where the South Fork of the Sauk River bends from northwest to north, leave the river and follow this trail as it goes south, then west up Weden Creek to the lake.

GOTHIC PEAK, 6213', 11 miles RT, 4000' gain (Maps: USGS Bedal, Monte Cristo, GT Sloan Peak, Monte Cristo). **Hike-3**. Drive and hike as above to **Foggy Lake**.

Go west from the lake and ascend toward the south ridge of Gothic Peak. Near the crest, turn north in broken rocks to the summit.

MONTE CRISTO SITE, 2756', 10 miles RT, 400' gain (Maps: USGS Bedal, Monte Cristo, GT Sloan Peak, Monte Cristo). **Mtn. Bicycle or Hike-1**. Drive 31 miles east of the town of Granite Falls on SR-92 to Barlow Pass, elevation 2361'.

Park and ride or hike south on the road to Monte Cristo, passing over an active landslide area at 0.8 miles, and crossing the South Fork of the Sauk River on a repaired bridge at 1.1 miles. After the river crossing, the route makes a detour in the forest on a track (often muddy and ponded) where the road has been destroyed by floods. Pass the Weden House site at mile 1.7, at one time the terminus for the Monte Criste railroad. Reach Silvertip campground at mile 3, the junction with the road to the Monte Cristo campground at mile 4.1 (left), and the end of the road at mile 4.2.

Cross the river on decking over a tumble of logs and timbers, the former bridge, then pass the trail to Poodle Dog Pass and Silver Lake (FS-708). Only a few small buildings (some private) and the rusty railroad turntable remain, but the Pelton Wheel electric generator left from mining days is still in operation.

SILVER LAKE, 4260', 14 miles RT, 2400' gain (Maps: USGS Bedal, Monte Cristo, GT Sloan Peak, Monte Cristo). **Mtn. Bicycle and Hike-1. Henry M. Jackson Wilderness.** Drive and ride or hike as above to **Monte Cristo Site**, mile 4.2. Leave bicycle on the east side of the river. Find the Silver Lake trailhead on the west side of the river.

Hike south on trail FS-708 over Poodle Dog Pass, 4350', to the lake, lying in a basin east of Silvertip Peak.

COLUMBIA PEAK, 6985', 20 miles RT, 5400' gain (Maps: USGS Bedal, Blanca Lake, Monte Cristo, GT Monte Cristo). **Mtn. Bicycle and Hike-4†. Henry M. Jackson Wilderness.** Drive, ride, and hike as above over Poodle Dog Pass to **Silver Lake**.

Continue southeast on trail 708A for two miles, crossing the meadows at the source of Silver Creek. At 5400', where the trail turns south to Twin Lakes, leave the trail and ascend east to the steep western slopes of Columbia Peak. A series of ramps and ledges lead to the west ridge. Go left (north and east) to the summit.

GLACIER BASIN, 4500', 15 miles RT, 2200' gain (Maps: USGS Bedal, Monte Cristo, Blanca Lake, GT Sloan Peak, Monte Cristo). **Mtn. Bicycle and Hike-2. Henry M. Jackson Wilderness.** Drive, ride, and/or hike as above to **Monte Cristo Site**.

At the south edge of **Monte Cristo Site**, find the trail to Glacier Basin, which goes east over Seventy-Six Creek, then on south side of the South Fork of the Sauk River. Hike east and southeast into Glacier Basin, which often has snow until August. Monte Cristo Peak encloses the basin on the south and the Wilmons Peaks are west of the basin. Several mines operated in the Wilmons Peaks area. Find mine tailings and artifacts at the entrance to the basin.

CADET PEAK, 7186', 18 miles RT, 4900' gain (Maps: USGS Bedal, Monte Cristo, Blanca Lake, GT Sloan Peak, Monte Cristo). **Mtn. Bicycle and Hike-4†. Henry M. Jackson Wilderness.** Drive, ride, and hike as above into **Glacier Basin**.

In Glacier Basin, head southeast to the 20' rock, 4400'. From the rock, cross a creek and ascend northeast on talus toward the apparent summit (60°). At the upper edge of the talus field, continue ascending northeast in scrub forest to the west ridge of Cadet Peak. Reach the north ridge by crossing a gully into easier terrain, then turn south to the summit.

SR-530 Area. **Arlington to Barlow Pass.** From I-5 at MP-208, drive

east on SR-530 through Arlington and continue east and southeast near the Stillaguamish and Sauk rivers.

MOUNT HIGGINS, 4849', 9 miles RT, 3400' gain (Maps: USGS Mt. Higgins, GT Oso). **Mtn. Bicycle and/or Hike-1**. From Aurora Transit Center in Seattle, take Community Transit 610 to Everett, CT 210 to Smokey Point and CT C23 toward Darrington. Leave bus near MP-37. If driving, go east on SR-530 from Arlington. East of MP-37, turn north across the Stillaguamish River on a gravel road. Pass roads going to the right and park at the unmarked trailhead, elevation 1440', three miles from SR-530.

The beginning of the trail may not be obvious, but it gets better. Ascend east and northeast, entering National Forest and ancient forest at one mile. At 3600', pass a trail going left (north) to **Myrtle Lake**. Continue east on the trail along the ridge to the lookout site. The summits in view include: Mt. Baker (357°), Mt. Shuksan (13°), Bacon Peak (27°), and Finney Peak (25°).

BOULDER RIVER, high point 1500', 9 miles RT, 700' gain (Maps: USGS Meadow Mtn., GT Oso, Granite Falls). **Mtn. Bicycle and/or Hike-1. Boulder River Wilderness**. The waterfalls along the route are best in the winter and spring. Ride transit as above for Mount Higgins. Leave bus near MP-41. If driving, go east on SR-530 through Arlington for 24 miles from I-5. At MP-41, ride or drive south four miles on road FS-2010 to the trailhead, elevation 900'.

Hike southwest on trail FS-734, at first on an old logging road. Look for springboard notches in giant cedar stumps along the way. After one mile, the road narrows to a trail, which bends south and enters ancient forest, primarily red cedar and western hemlock. Look north from here (32°) to Mt. Higgins. Take a narrow trail west for a view down to cascades of the Boulder River. A collapsed shelter is below the trail. At two miles on the trail, two waterfalls drop into the Boulder River. Find another waterfall at mile three. The trail crosses the high point before descending to Boulder Ford, elevation 1400'.

DARRINGTON, 580' (Maps: USGS Darrington, GT Darrington). **Mtn. Bicycle or Hike-1**. A winter adventure to view snowy mountains. Ride transit as above for Mount Higgins to Darrington. Find restrooms in the park one block south of Darrington St. Maps and information are available five days a week at the Ranger Station, one mile north on SR-530.

NORTH MOUNTAIN LOOKOUT, 3824', 3 miles (hike) or 26 miles (bicycle) RT, 500' or 3300' gain (Maps: USGS Darrington, GT Darrington). **Mtn. Bicycle or Hike-1**. Take transit as above. Go north in Darrington one mile on SR-530. If driving, for bicycle trip park at road FS-2810 near the Darrington entrance sign, elevation 500'.

Drive or ride west, northwest and north on road FS-2810, passing a road left at mile 3 where the pavement ends. At mile 7, go right (southeast) staying on FS-2810. If driving, park at a gate, mile 12, 3300', and hike to the summit and lookout tower. Look for the following summits: Illabot Peaks (48°), Green Mtn. (96°), Prairie Mtn. (116°), Whitechuck (132°), Pugh (139°), Sloan (147°), Jumbo (180°), Whitehorse (202°), Higgins (268°), Sisters (326°), Mt. Baker (344°), and Shuksan (360°).

DARRINGTON TO GRANITE FALLS, high point 2361', 54 miles one-way, 2000' gain (Maps: USGS Darrington, Helena Ridge, White Chuck Mtn., Bedal, Silverton, Mallardy Ridge, Verlot, Granite Falls, GT Darrington, Sloan Peak, Silverton, Granite Falls). **Mtn. Bicycle**. From Aurora Transit Center in Seattle, take Community Transit 610 to Everett, and CT 210 to Smokey Point. Transfer to CT C23 and ride to Darrington. Leave bus at the first stop on Darrington Street, elevation 580'. A park with restrooms is one block north.

Ride south on the Mountain Loop Highway, passing the Clear Creek Road on the left at one mile. Cross Backman Creek at mile 2.0 near the boundary of the Mt. Baker Snoqualmie National Forest. Pass Clear Creek Campground at mile 2.2. Road FS-2060 goes to the right (west) here. At mile 2.5, cross Clear Creek, coming from the west. Pass the Old Sauk trailhead at mile 3, a road to the right (west) at mile 4, and a viewpoint east at mile 5.7 where the river is near. Look for forested islands in the river. Road FS-2070 goes right (southwest) at mile 6.7, north of Goodman Creek. At mile 8.2, road FS-2080 branches right to follow the west bank of the South Fork of the Sauk River to a trailhead on Falls Creek. The canyon of Falls Creek is north of Mt. Forgotten. The Mountain Loop Highway now crosses the South Fork of the Sauk River (mile 8.2). South of the bridge, a road goes right (south) to the Beaver Lake trailhead.

The pavement ends near mile 8.5 where the White Chuck River Road (FS-23) turns east. Pause at the White Chuck viewpoint, mile 9.1 (toilet). From this viewpoint, White Chuck Mtn. is northeast across the White Chuck River and Jumbo Mtn. is west. Another trail goes west to Beaver Lake at mile 11 and the road to the Pugh Mtn. trailhead turns left (east) at mile 12.2. Next, pass the North Fork Sauk road at mile 15.7, a Forest Service Guard Station at mile 15.8, and the Bedal Campground at mile 16.1. Cross the North Fork of the Sauk River at mile 16.2, where the impressive cliffs of the south side of Spring Mtn. are in view northeast. After crossing Bedal Creek (mile 17.5), which shows evidence of recent floods, the road is often near enough to the South Fork of the Sauk River to appreciate the churning of water over boulders. Along this stretch the river drops 200' per mile. The branch road to the Goat Lake trailhead, FS-4080, turns east at mile 19.4, then the main road crosses Elliott Creek, the outlet from Goat Lake, at mile 19.6. Just after this creek crossing, watch west for a cascade descending from near the crest of the ridge south of Twin Peaks. This cascade is only visible after recent storms.

The cliffs east of the bridge over the South Fork of the Sauk River are part of Sheep Mtn. After crossing the South Fork of the Sauk River, ascend to Barlow Pass (mile 23, toilet). The road south from the pass goes to Monte Cristo. A trail at the pass ascends north to Barlow Point.

Going west from Barlow Pass, the first road to the left (mile 24.9) leads to the trailhead for Headlee Pass. Pass the Mt. Dickerman trailhead at mile 26, the road to the Perry Creek Trail at mile 27.3, and parking for the Ice Caves trail at mile 27.6 (toilets). The Deer Creek road (FS-4052) turns north at mile 30.4. Visit the site of the Sperry-Iverson mine at mile 32.6. Use caution at mile 34.5 where the road is often loose gravel as it crosses an active landslide in sediments deposited in a former lake. Pass the Youth-On-Age Nature Trail at mile 35.1, then cross the Red Bridge at mile 35.7, where a road west of the bridge goes to the Mallardy Ridge and Cutthroat Lakes trail. A road branches south to trailheads for Ashland Lakes and Boardman Lakes at mile 38.2. Then in quick succession: Lake Twentytwo trailhead (mile 40.2), Lake Twentytwo Creek (mile 41.2), the road to Mt. Pilchuck and Heather Lake (mile 41.9), and the Verlot Ranger Station (mile 43, 1000').

Now for four miles the road goes up more than down until it passes the Green Mtn. road (north) and the Old Robe Trail to the Monte Cristo Railroad grade (south) at mile 47. Continue west and south, pausing at the bridge over the South Fork of the Stillaguamish River for a view of the cascades and falls. Reach the town of Granite Falls at mile 54. Proceed south on Alder St. and west on Pioneer St. to the bus stop on Granite St. where the bus waits before beginning the run to Everett.

GREEN MOUNTAIN, 6500', 8 miles RT, 3000' gain (Maps: USGS Downey Mtn., GT Cascade Pass). **Hike-1. Glacier Peak Wilderness.** From Darrington, drive north eight miles in the Sauk River valley. After crossing to the east bank of the Sauk River, turn east for 20 miles along the north side of the Suiattle River on road FS-26, then take the left fork, road FS-2680 to the trailhead, elevation 3500'.

Hike north up a ridge, leaving the forest at 4800', to the lookout.

The summits visible, going from north to south, are: Buckindy (22°), Le Conte (53°), Spire Point (78°), Dome Peak (86°), Bannock (103°), Sitting Bull Mtn. (110°), Fortress (123°), Glacier Peak (155°), Lime Mtn. (173°), and Pugh (212°).

SQUIRE CREEK PASS, high point 4000', 8 miles RT, 2500' gain (Maps: USGS Whitehorse Mtn., GT Silverton). **Hike-2. Boulder River Wilderness.** From Darrington on SR-530, 28 miles east of Arlington, drive west on Darrington St., then go west and south on the Squire Creek Road, FS-654, for five miles from Darrington to park where the road is blocked, or becomes too rough to drive (elevation 1600').

Hike south, first on the road, then on a trail that soon enters ancient forest with many giant red cedar trees. At 3000', near a shelter rock, the trail crosses open talus below foliated granitic rock. Pause for the views of the cliffs of Whitehorse Mtn. (330°) and Three Fingers (264°). At 3400', the trail turns east to ascend near cliffs before travelling on bedrock exposed in the trail by erosion. Find many campsites near the pass, which are only useful if snow patches remain.

SQUIRE PASS 4700, high point 4700', 9 miles RT, 3200' gain (Maps: USGS Whitehorse Mtn., GT Silverton). **Hike-3. Boulder River Wilderness.** Drive and hike as above to Squire Creek Pass.

For a better view of Whitehorse Mtn. and Three Fingers, leave the trail at the pass (several cairns) and hike south on a cairn-marked track that ascends on gentle bedrock and heather. At the ridge, look south into the valley of Copper Creek and across to Liberty Mtn. (218°).

MEADOW–FIRE RIDGE, high point 5500', 11 miles RT, 3200' gain (Maps: USGS Lime Mtn., GT Glacier Peak). **Hike-1. Glacier Peak Wilderness.** From Darrington, drive south on SR-530 and road FS-20 in the valley of the Sauk River to a bridge over the Sauk River, eight miles from Darrington. Cross the bridge and, at mile 8.5, turn east on road FS-23, following the White Chuck River to the end of the road, 20 miles from Darrington, elevation 2300'.

Hike east on trail FS-643, following the White Chuck River for 1.4 miles, then, after crossing Fire Creek (bridge) at 2500', take the left fork trail, FS-657, and ascend on the slope above the south side of Fire Creek to another crossing of Fire Creek at 3700' (no bridge). After this crossing of Fire Creek, the trail ascends steeply north. On nearing the crest of Meadow Ridge, 5500', the trail turns northwest on the south side of the ridge. Find campsites, which have a view to the south of Glacier Peak and other summits, a short distance after the trail turns west.

MEADOW MOUNTAIN, 6324', 10 miles RT, 2600' gain (Maps: USGS Pugh Mtn., Lime Mtn., GT Sloan Peak, Glacier Peak). **Hike-1. Glacier Peak Wilderness.** Distance and elevation gain are given from camping on **Meadow-Fire Ridge** (see above).

From the campsite at the east end of Meadow-Fire Ridge, hike west on the trail, crossing an open glacial cirque and staying near or on the crest of the ridge. The trail passes over the south shoulder (5800') of a higher intermediate summit, **Meadow Point 6421'**, which is easily reached on the return by leaving the trail at 6000' and following the ridge east. After the second descent to 5500', the trail rises to cross the south ridge of Meadow Mountain at 5800'. Leave the trail and follow the open ridge 0.6 mile to the summit.

Views to the south are superb. Look for the following peaks: Pugh Mountain (241°) at seven miles, Glacier Peak (126°) at nine miles, and Sloan Peak (198°) at 11 miles.

FIRE MOUNTAIN, 6591', 4 miles RT, 1100' gain (Maps: USGS Lime Mtn., GT Glacier Peak). **Hike-3. Glacier Peak Wilderness.** Distance and elevation gain are given from camping on **Meadow-Fire Ridge** (see above).

From a campsite on the east end of Meadow-Fire Ridge, hike east on the trail until the trail turns south and begins to descend. Find a faint track that continues east, traversing several openings in the brush, and ascending to the south ridge of Fire Mountain. Follow this track north up the ridge to the summit. Glacier Peak (138°) is only five miles away and Lime Mtn. (336°) is north across a deep, steep-walled canyon. Green Mtn. (346°) shows over the right shoulder of Lime Mtn.

PUGH MOUNTAIN, 7201', 12-16 miles RT, 5400'-6000' gain (Maps: USGS White Chuck Mtn., Pugh Mtn., GT Sloan Peak). **Hike-4†. Glacier Peak Wilderness.** From Darrington on SR-530 east of Arlington, drive south on SR-530 and FS-20 to a bridge over the Sauk River, eight miles from Darrington. Cross the bridge and continue south on road FS-20 to a left fork, 12 miles from Darrington, elevation 1200'. This road (FS-2095) is sometimes closed by a gate.

Hike or drive two miles east on road FS-2095 to the trailhead, 1900', then ascend east on trail FS-644, passing Lake Metan at 3180' and Stujack Pass at 5700'. Reach a narrow gap with a view down the north precipice at 6800'. From this point, the trail is narrow and exposed. In the past, a lookout was maintained on the summit.

BINGLEY GAP, high point 4400', 6 miles RT, 2600' gain (Maps: USGS Sloan Peak, GT Sloan Peak). **Hike-1. Glacier Peak Wilderness.** From Darrington drive south on road FS-20 to a road fork 16 miles from Darrington. Turn left on road FS-49 along the North Fork of the Sauk River for three miles to the trailhead. **Alternate route.** From Barlow Pass, 30 miles east of Granite Falls on SR-92, continue on road FS-20. At eight miles from Barlow Pass turn east on the North Fork Sauk River road (FS-49) for three miles to the Lost Creek Ridge trailhead, elevation 1849'.

Hike north on trail FS-646 in an old clearcut, entering ancient forest at 2500', where occasional Douglas fir, western hemlock and red cedar trees are near or over 3' diameter. The trail crosses several avalanche tracks, which give partial views east. Go 0.2 mile beyond the saddle (100' of gain) to the next place that the trail reaches the crest of the ridge for the best view west to the cliffs on the north face of Spring Mountain.

ROUND LAKE, 5100', 11 miles RT, 4300' gain (Maps: USGS Sloan Peak, GT Sloan Peak). **Hike-1. Glacier Peak Wilderness.** Drive and hike as above to **Bingley Gap**.

Continue northeast on the trail, ascending at first on or near the crest of the ridge, then contouring east across the south face of a 5890' summit southwest of Round Lake. At a trail fork, 5500', south of a low point in the ridge, take the left (north) branch and ascend to the crest, 5600', where Round Lake is visible below. The trail goes left (west) to begin the descent to the lake.

ROUND LAKE POINT 5850, 5850', 9 miles RT, 4100' gain (Maps: USGS Sloan Peak, GT Sloan Peak). **Hike-3. Glacier Peak Wilderness.** Drive and hike as above to the crest of the ridge above **Round Lake**, 5600'.

Leave trail and follow a track east on the ridge to the summit. Glacier Peak is east (90°), Red Mtn. is southeast (138°), and Spring Mountain is west (256°). Bedal Peak (212°), and Sloan Peak (196°) are south.

NORTH FORK SAUK FALLS, 1400', 0.5 miles RT, 100' gain (Maps: USGS Sloan Peak, GT Sloan Peak). **Hike-1.** Drive as above toward the trailhead for **Bingley Gap** for two miles on the North Fork Sauk River road (FS-49), elevation 1500'.

Descend on the trail (steps) to a viewpoint near the falls.

GOAT LAKE, 3161', 12 miles RT, 1500' gain (Maps: USGS Bedal, Sloan Peak, GT Sloan Peak). **Hike-1. Henry M. Jackson Wilderness.** From Darrington on SR-530 east of Arlington, drive south on road FS-20 in the valley of the Sauk River to a road fork 19 miles from Darrington. Turn east and drive on road FS-4080 to the trailhead, 0.7 miles from road FS-20, elevation 1700'. **Alternate Route.** From Barlow Pass, 30 miles east of Granite Falls on road SR-92, continue east on road FS-20. At 3.6 miles from Barlow Pass, turn east to the Goat Lake trailhead.

Hike east, north, and southeast on a logging road, now trail FS-647, passing a junction at 2200' on the northbound leg where an overgrown track contours northeast into the valley of Bedal Creek. Reach a high point at 2800', near a waterfall. The route now descends 200' before narrowing to continue on an old wagon road. Look for remains of cedar puncheon. Pause to view **waterfalls** at the outlet from the lake before ascending to the half-mile long lake, lying in a basin north of Foggy Peak. Please camp in the established sites, away from the shore of the lake. Look south to the high point (7197') of the ridge between Foggy Peak and Cadet Peak (see *Over Washington*, p. 8, for an aerial view of the lake).

SR-20 Area

Concrete to Winthrop. From I-5 north of Mount Vernon, take Exit-230 to Burlington and follow SR-20 (MP-60 on SR-20) east.

SAUK MOUNTAIN, 5539', 2 miles RT, 1100' gain (Maps: USGS Sauk Mtn., GT Lake Shannon). **Hike-1.** East of MP-96 on SR-20, drive north on road FS-1030, going right when seven miles from SR-20 to the trailhead, eight miles from SR-20, elevation 4500'.

Hike trail FS-613 to the lookout tower, one of the few lookouts still in use and having an exceptional view of Mt. Baker. An excellent place to watch Mt. Baker when the mountain is active.

ROCKPORT STATE PARK, high point 960', 5 miles of trails, up to 700' gain (Maps: USGS Sauk Mtn., GT Lake Shannon). **Hike-1.** Find the park east of MP-96 on SR-20, elevation 300'.

Facilities and activities: trails in lowland ancient forest open all year, camping April to November, walk-in campsites, shelters, restrooms.

MARBLEMOUNT WILDERNESS INFORMATION CENTER, 365'. In Marblemount (MP-105), turn left (north) to the National Park Service Information Center (information, maps, back country permits).

HELEN BUTTES, 4800', 10 miles RT, 4500' gain (Maps: USGS Marblemount, Sauk Mtn., GT Marblemount, Lake Shannon). **Hike-1.** Drive as above to the Wilderness Information Center. Continue north 0.3 mile on the road past the Information Center to the trailhead, marked Cow Heaven Trail, elevation 380'.

Hike northwest on the trail to a high plateau and view north.

LOOKOUT MOUNTAIN, 5719', 10 miles RT, 4500' gain (Maps: USGS Big Devil Peak, GT Marblemount). **Hike-1.** On the east edge of Marblemount, where SR-20 turns north, continue east on road FS-15 for seven miles to the trailhead on the north side of the road, elevation 1255'.

Ascend on trail FS-743 near Lookout Creek, passing a branch trail to Monogram Lake at 2.8 miles. The summit has a view of summits east and north: Big Devil (25°), Little Devil (64°), Eldorado Peak (96°), Bacon Peak (313°), and Mt. Triumph (354°).

HIDDEN LAKE LOOKOUT, 6890', 9 miles RT, 3200' gain (Maps: USGS Eldorado Peak, Sonny Boy Lakes, GT Diablo Dam). **Hike-1.** From Marblemount, drive east on road FS-15 for 9.7 miles, then turn left (east) on road FS-1540 (Sibley Creek) for 4.5 miles to the trailhead, 14 miles from Marblemount, elevation 3700'.

Ascend east, south, and west to the lookout building, on the southwest end of the Hidden Lake Peak ridge. The following summits are visible from this superb viewpoint: Eldorado Peak (50°); Boston Peak (88°); Johannesburg Mtn. (113°); Mt. Buckindy (178°); Snowking Mtn. (209°). Hidden Lake is below.

HIDDEN LAKE PEAK, 7088', 10 miles RT, 3400' gain (Maps: USGS Eldorado Peak, Sonny Boy Lakes, GT Diablo Dam). **Hike-3.** Hike as above toward Hidden Lake Lookout.

At the saddle between Sibley Creek and Hidden Lake to the east, 6600', leave the trail and ascend 0.5 mile northeast over slabs and past broken rocks to the first high point for an impressive view east to many summits (see Hidden Lake Lookout).

CASCADE PASS, 5400', 10 miles RT, 1800' gain (Maps: USGS Cascade Pass, GT Cascade Pass). **Hike-1. North Cascades National Park.** From Marblemount, drive east on road FS-15 (gravel) for 23 miles to the trailhead, elevation 3600'. This road is sometimes not open until mid-July.

Ascend south and east on the Cascade Pass Trail with the cliffs and pinnacles of Johannesburg Mtn., Cascade Peak, and the Triplets rising to the west. In the pass area, please stay on the trail. No camping.

SAHALE ARM, high point 7800', 12 miles RT, 4200' gain (Maps: USGS Cascade Pass, GT Cascade Pass). **Hike-2. North Cascades National Park.** Drive and hike as above to Cascade Pass.

From the pass, ascend north on a trail and in meadows up to the snow. Sahale Glacier begins at 7800'. Travel on the glacier requires an ice ax and roped travel.

THORNTON LAKES, 4486', 11 miles RT, 3200' gain (Maps: USGS Mt. Triumph, GT Marblemount). **Hike-1. North Cascades National Park.** From Marblemount, continue north on SR-20 to MP-117. Turn left (north) on road FS-3745 for five miles to the trailhead, elevation 2500'.

Hike the Thornton Lakes Trail to the lakes. Camping at the lakes is limited to established campsites. The required permit can be obtained at the Ranger Station in Marblemount.

TRAPPERS PEAK, 5966', 12 miles RT, 3500' gain (Maps: USGS Mt. Triumph, GT Marblemount). **Hike-3. North Cascades National Park.** Drive and hike as above toward Thornton Lakes.

At the saddle, 5000', where the trail begins to descend northwest to the lake, leave the trail and ascend north on or near the ridge to Trappers Peak. The twisted trees that impede the way to the top of the final summit rock are yellow cedar. The view of Mt. Triumph only two miles away makes the trip worthwhile.

NORTH CASCADES VISITOR CENTER, 560'. East of MP-120 in Newhalem, drive south over the Skagit River through the Newhalem Campground entrance station for one mile to the Visitor Center. Open daily.

NEWHALEM, 500' (Maps: USGS Newhalem, GT Marblemount). **Hike-1.** Enter Newhalem east of MP-120. For tours of the Skagit power system, call Seattle City Light at 206-684-3030.

Look for the following native plants along the trails of Newhalem: dogwood, Douglas fir, western hemlock, red cedar, huckleberry, willow, vine maple, alder, yew, birch, ocean spray, service berry, lodgepole pine, silver fir, salal, and Oregon grape.

Sterling Munro Trail. 0.1 mile RT. This level, accessible boardwalk goes from the North Cascades Visitor Center (see above) to a viewpoint looking north to the Picket Range (mountain finder).

To Know a Tree Trail. 0.5 mile RT. Begin at the Newhalem Campground Entrance Station. Walk west to a trail that circles north and west near the Skagit River. Many of the trees along the way are identified.

River Loop Trail. 2 miles RT. From the Newhalem Campground Entrance Station, drive south to the first cross street, then go west to park near the utility building between campground loops A and B. Hike west on the trail to the Skagit River, then return along the river and in Campground Loop A to the starting point.

Newhalem Creek Trail. 2 miles RT. Park at the Newhalem Campground Entrance Station. Walk south to the first cross street, then turn east past campground Loops C and D. Continue east across Newhalem Creek on a service road. Find the trail on the east side of Newhalem Creek and hike south to the end of the trail.

Trail of the Cedars. One mile interpretive loop. Drive south past the General Store and park at the trailhead. Cross a bridge over the Skagit River to a trail that makes a loop through ancient forest to the Newhalem Creek Powerhouse.

Ladder Creek Falls. One mile of trails. Park on the east edge of Newhalem at the Gorge Powerhouse. Cross the pedestrian bridge to a network of trails leading through gardens of exotic and native plants to a view of Ladder Creek Falls. The falls are lighted at night during the summer.

GORGE CREEK FALLS, 1095'. (Maps: USGS Diablo Dam). East of MP-123, park near the bridge over Gorge Creek for the view of the waterfall and the deep gorge under the bridge.

SOURDOUGH LOOKOUT, 5985', 10 miles RT, 5100' gain (Maps: USGS Diablo Dam, Ross Dam, GT Diablo Dam). **Hike-1. North Cascades National Park.** From Marblemount, drive northeast on road SR-20 for 21 miles (MP-126), then turn left (east) on the road into the community of Diablo. Park at the trailhead, 0.9 mile from SR-20, elevation 900'. The trail begins at the west end of a building and goes northeast behind the swimming pool.

Hike north and east on the Sourdough Lookout Trail to the lookout for an expansive view over Ross Lake and of the summits east of Ross Lake: Jack Mtn. (74°), Crater Mtn. (90°), and Spratt Mtn. (40°). Mt. Terror (284°) is northwest.

SOURDOUGH MOUNTAIN, 6107', 11 miles RT, 5300' gain (Maps: USGS Diablo Dam, Ross Dam, GT Diablo Dam). **Hike-2. North Cascades National Park.** Drive and hike as above toward Sourdough Mountain Lookout.

Where the trail reaches the crest of the ridge of Sourdough Mtn. at 5900' and turns east to the lookout, leave the trail and hike west to the high point of the ridge.

DIABLO DAM TRAIL, high point 1220', 2 miles RT, 400' gain (Maps: USGS Diablo Dam, GT Diablo Dam). **Hike-1. Ross Lake National Recreation Area.** Drive as above past the Sourdough Lookout trailhead to the end of the road in the community of Diablo, 1.4 miles from SR-20, elevation 800'.

Ascend north on the trail, which meets the tramway halfway up the slope. At the end of the trail, follow the road from the tramway top station to the dam (restrooms).

PYRAMID LAKE, 2640', 4 miles RT, 1600' gain (Maps: USGS Diablo Dam, GT Diablo Dam). **Hike-1. Ross Lake National Recreation Area.** East of MP-126 on SR-20, park at the trailhead, elevation 1100'.

Ascend south on the trail, crossing Pyramid Creek or its branches several times. For the best view of Pyramid Mountain (216°), leave the trail where the trail begins to descend to the lake and ascend northeast for 50' to a minor ridge that opens west.

THUNDER CREEK TRAIL, high point 6100', 40 miles RT, 5000' gain (Maps: North Cascades National Park, USGS Ross Dam, Mt. Logan, Forbidden Peak, GT Diablo Dam, Mt. Logan). **Hike-1. Ross Lake National Recreation Area, North Cascades National Park.** From Marblemount, drive north and east on SR-20 to the Colonial Creek Campground at MP-130. Turn south 0.4 miles to the trailhead at the south end of the campground, elevation 1200'.

Hike the Thunder Creek Trail south. Use only the following designated campgrounds: Thunder Creek, 1300', 2 miles one-way; Neve, 1300', 3 miles one-way; McAllister, 1900', 7 miles one-way (also horse camp); Tricouni, 2000', 8 miles one-way; Junction (at Fisher Creek), 3100', 10 miles one-way; Skagit Queen, 3000', 14 miles one-way; Thunder Basin, 4300', 17 miles one-way; and, on Fisher Creek, Cosho, 3700', 15 miles one-way; Fisher, 5200', 19 miles one-way.

Day trips from camps along Thunder Creek or Fisher Creek: Easy Pass, Park Pass, Red Mtn., and Soldier Boy.

THUNDER WOODS NATURE TRAIL, high point 1300', 1 mile RT, 100' gain (Maps: North Cascades National Park, USGS Ross Dam). **Hike-2. Ross Lake National Recreation Area.** Drive as above for the Thunder Creek Trail to the south end of the Colonial Creek Campground, elevation 1200'.

Hike south on the Thunder Creek Trail 0.3 miles to begin the Thunder Woods trail, which ascends to make a loop on the western slope (guide available). Look for many examples of the following native plants: Douglas fir, red cedar, hemlock, yew, Oregon grape, and vine maple. The trail crosses unstable talus near the high point of the loop.

FISHER CREEK BASIN, high point 3700', 10 miles RT, 700' gain (Maps: North Cascades National Park, USGS Forbidden Peak, Mt. Logan, GT Diablo Dam, Mt. Logan). **Hike-1. North Cascades National Park.** A hike to the vicinity of Cosho Camp. The distance and elevation gain are given from Junction Camp on the Thunder Creek Trail.

From Junction Camp, hike east on the Fisher Creek Trail, ascending in the broad, open valley of Fisher Creek. Within view along the way are the spectacular north faces of Mt. Arriva and Mt. Logan. Look north to peaks of Ragged Ridge: Cosho, Kimtah, Katsuk, and Mesahchie.

THUNDER CREEK BASIN, high point 4400', 13 miles RT, 2500' gain (Maps: North Cascades National Park, USGS Ross Dam, Forbidden Peak, Mt. Logan, GT Diablo Dam, Mt. Logan). **Hike-1. North Cascades National Park.** The distance and elevation gain given are from Junction Camp on the Thunder Creek Trail.

From Junction Camp, continue south on the Thunder Creek trail into Thunder Basin for impressive views of summits: Mt. Logan (east), Forbidden Peak (south), and Eldorado Peak (west).

RED MOUNTAIN, 7635', 6 miles RT, 4600' gain (Maps: North Cascades National Park, USGS Forbidden Peak, Mt. Logan, GT Diablo Dam, Mt. Logan). **Hike-3. North Cascades National Park.** The distance and elevation gain given are from Junction Camp on the Thunder Creek Trail, elevation 3100'.

From Junction Camp, ascend the slope northeast in open terrain to the summit. Summits visible include: Mt. Logan (158°), Boston Peak (196°), Tricouni Peak (250°), and Ruby Mtn. (340°).

SOLDIER BOY, 7034', 5 miles RT, 4000' gain (Maps: North Cascades National Park, USGS Forbidden Peak, Mt. Logan, GT Diablo Dam, Mt. Logan). **Hike-3. North Cascades National Park.** The distance and elevation gain are from Junction Camp on the Thunder Creek Trail.

From Junction Camp, ascend southeast on the ridge between Fisher Creek and Thunder Creek to this promontory on the north ridge of Mt. Logan. Summits visible include: Mt. Logan (122°), Buckner Mtn. (190°), and Forbidden Peak (230°).

GOAT PEAK LOOKOUT, 7001', 5 miles RT, 1600' gain (Maps: USGS McLeod Mtn., GT Mazama) **Hike-1**. Drive SR-20 to Mazama junction, 120 miles from I-5 at Exit-230. Turn north across the Methow River, then go east two miles to a junction. Turn north on road FS-52 for two miles then go left on road FS-5225. At three miles, turn right on road FS-5225-200 to the trailhead two miles from FS-5225 and nine miles from SR-20, elevation 5600'.

Hike the trail south to the lookout building. Look for the following summits: North Gardner Mtn. (206°), Silver Star Mtn. (236°), Robinson Mtn. (310°), and Setting Sun Mtn. (336°).

Harts Pass Area

From Marblemount, drive north and east on SR-20 over Washington Pass for 119 miles (from I-5) to the Methow River. Turn north into the community of Mazama, then go northwest on the north side of the Methow River on road FS-374 (narrow gravel road, no trailers) for 20 miles to the Harts Pass Forest Service Station at Harts Pass, elevation 6198'.

SLATE PEAK, 7440', 2 miles RT, 600' gain (Maps: Pasayten Wilderness, USGS Slate Peak, GT Washington Pass). **Hike-1**. This summit has one of the best views into the Pasayten Wilderness. From the Forest Service Station at Harts Pass, continue driving northeast on the first road to the right for one mile, rounding one switchback to a parking area below Slate Pass, 21 miles from SR-20 and 140 miles from I-5 at Burlington, elevation 6900'. For those not intimidated by driving past the steep slope below, another limited parking area is 0.5 mile north on this road.

From either parking place, hike the airy road north to the lookout platform. The following points of interest are visible: Pasayten Peak (8°), Mount Rolo (40°), Wildcat Mtn. (48°), Devils Peak (98°), Robinson Mtn. (102°), Silver Star Mtn. (160°), and Crater Mtn. (270°). Center Mtn. (312°), at the north edge of the Barron mining area has visible evidence of mining activity.

PASAYTEN RIVER–CASCADE CREST LOOP, high point 7300', 45 miles RT, 8200' gain (Maps: Pasayten Wilderness, USGS

Slate Peak, Castle Peak, Shull Mtn., Pasayten Peak, Frosty Creek, Tatoosh Buttes, GT Washington Pass, Pasayten Peak, Jack Mtn). **Hike-2. Pasayten Wilderness.** Drive as above toward Slate Peak to the parking area below Slate Pass, 21 miles from SR-20, elevation 6900'.

Hike northeast to the pass, 6960', then go north on the Buckskin Ridge Trail, FS-498. This trail is shown on the Green Trails map but not on the USGS Pasayten Peak map. The trail contours on the open east slope of Gold Ridge, staying for the most part in flowery meadows with views to the east of Robinson Mtn., Devils Peak, Wildcat Mtn., and Mount Rolo. Reach **Silver Lake**, 6256', five miles from the road. The lake area has campsites as well as the best approach to Pasayten Peak (see below). From Silver Lake, continue north on the trail, descending to cross Silver Creek, 5700', then ascending over Silver Pass, 6500'. After crossing Silver Pass, the trail descends briefly toward Threemile Creek, 6000', then ascends east in an avalanche track to 6700' before again turning north to contour the lower edge of steep meadows. After passing a spring, the trail may be hard to follow in open meadows, which have scattered clumps of trees. The route north is marked with rock cairns. Now the trail descends to 6400' before turning east to ascend over the ridge, 7300', into the Middle Fork Pasayten River drainage. Now contour north through open basins on the east side of the ridge to **Buckskin Lake** (camping).

From Buckskin Lake, the trail contours north then descends to the level of the Middle Fork of the Pasayten River, joining the Middle Fork Trail, FS-478, near the junction of the West and Forks, 4400' and 20 miles from the road near Slate Pass. Find a large campsite and bridges over the Middle Fork and West Fork. This camp is an ideal place to stop for a day trip east to Tatoosh Buttes.

To continue the loop, go north on trail FS-478 for 0.5 mile on the west side of the combined Pasayten River, then turn west on trail FS-473, ascending in the valley of Rock Creek to the Pacific Crest Trail in a basin south of **Woody Pass** (camping) and a good location from which to hike north for a day on the PCT (see Lakeview Ridge).

From the junction of trail FS-473 and the PCT, go south on the PCT, passing between Shull Mountain (west) and Holman Peak (east). Cross Holman Pass, 5060', and, three miles later, the beginning of Shaw Creek (camping) at 5800'. Skirt the east side of Jim Peak into Oregon Basin (camping), another lovely meadow with occasional trees.

South from Oregon Basin, the PCT contours to **Jim Pass**, 6400', where a trail goes north to Jim Peak, 7033'. At Jim Pass, the PCT crosses to the west slope before returning to the east slope at Foggy Pass. The trail then contours around Tamarack Peak to **Windy Pass**, 6300', where evidence of old mining activity is still visible. At this pass, find a track west to Tamarack Peak, 7290'. South of Windy Pass, the trail goes west of the crest to contour across Slate Peak to road FS-374.

PASAYTEN PEAK, 7850', 4 miles RT, 1600' gain (Maps: Pasayten Wilderness, USGS Pasayten Peak, GT Pasayten Peak). **Hike-3. Pasayten Wilderness**. The distance and elevation gain for this summit are from camping at **Silver Lake**.

From Silver Lake, ascend northwest to the crest of the ridge south of Pasayten Peak. Turn north and continue on or near the ridge in broken rocks to the summit, passing over an intermediate summit of 7588'. The central location of this summit provides a view of the following peaks: Osceola Peak (60°), Mount Rolo (74°), Wildcat Mtn. (98°), Robinson Mtn. (140°), Slate Peak (188°), Crater Mtn. (250°), and Holman Peak (330°).

TATOOSH BUTTES, 7245', 10 miles RT, 2900' gain (Maps: Pasayten Wilderness, USGS Frosty Creek, Tatoosh Buttes, GT Pasayten Peak). **Hike-2. Pasayten Wilderness**. The distance and elevation gain given for this summit are from the campsite at the junction of the West and Middle Forks of the Pasayten River.

From the campsite, hike east, crossing a bridge over the river, then ascending on trail FS-485 in the forest. Above 6500', enter meadows. Here, where the trail bends southeast around the south side of Tatoosh Buttes, leave the trail and hike east to the summit, with its steep drop to White Lakes. Look north over rolling, forested terrain to Canada seven miles away, and south over alpine meadows culminating in Ptarmigan Peak (166°) and Osceola Mtn. (194°). Ashnola Mtn. is east (78°).

LAKEVIEW RIDGE–THREE FOOLS PEAK LOOP, high point 7920', 10 miles RT, 2000' gain (Maps: Pasayten Wilderness, USGS Castle Peak, Shull Mtn., Pasayten Peak, GT Pasayten Peak, Jack Mtn.). **Hike-3. Pasayten Wilderness**. The distance and elevation gain given for this trip are from camping below Woody Pass near the Pacific Crest Trail (see Pasayten River–Cascade Crest Loop).

Hike north on the PCT for five miles. After topping a minor hump on the ridge, 7126', continue north to look down the Devils Staircase to Hopkins Pass and Hopkins Lake (east). From the 7126' point, Castle Peak is northwest (315°), and Freezeout Mtn. (305°) is the summit south of Castle Peak. Mt. Winthrop (5°) is north, more than halfway to Canada, and Canada is only five miles away.

After looking north, return south on the PCT. Where the trail leaves the ridge at 6900' to contour west of Three Fools Peak, leave the trail and stay on the ridge, continuing south on or near the ridge to the summit of **Three Fools Peak**, 7920', a superb viewpoint east over the valley of the Pasayten River. From the summit of Three Fools Peak, descend south on the ridge to the first low point, then angle southwest to the PCT to return to the campsite south of Woody Pass.

HOLMAN PEAK, 7550', 2 miles RT, 1200' gain (Maps: Pasayten Wilderness, USGS Shull Mtn., Pasayten Peak, GT Jack Mtn., Pasayten Peak). **Hike-2. Pasayten Wilderness.** The distance and elevation gain given for this trip are from the nearest point on the Pacific Crest Trail (see Pasayten River–Cascade Crest Loop).

Two miles south of the junction with the Rock Creek Trail, FS-473, where the PCT bends east around the wide valley of Canyon Creek, leave the PCT at its most easterly reach, 6400', and ascend east to the open ridge. Turn northeast and ascend to the open summit, which has a broad view to the east over the West Fork of the Pasayten River and southeast to Buckskin Ridge. Pasayten Peak (150°) is six miles away.

MIDDLE FORK PASAYTEN RIVER, 5200', 7 miles RT, 800' gain (Maps: Pasayten Wilderness, USGS Slate Peak, Pasayten Peak, Gt Pasayten Peak). **Hike-1. Pasayten Wilderness.** A campsite on the Middle Fork Pasayten River at the junction of the Robinson Pass Trail and the Slate Pass Trail makes a good location for exploring Ferguson Lake (see below) and Wildcat Mountain. From the Harts Pass Forest Service Station, continue on the road to the right (east) for one mile, rounding one switchback to park below Slate Pass, 6900'.

Ascend northeast to Slate Pass, 6960', then descend on the east side of the ridge through meadows. At one mile, turn right (east) on a branch trail and descend two miles to cross the Middle Fork of the Pasayten River at 5200'. After crossing the river, follow the trail north to camping.

FERGUSON LAKE, 6631', 6 miles RT, 1500' gain (Maps: Pasayten Wilderness, USGS Slate Peak, Pasayten Peak, Mount Lago). **Hike-1. Pasayten Wilderness.** Drive and hike as above to the campsite at 5200' on the Middle Fork of the Pasayten River. The distance and elevation gain given are from this campsite.

From the campsite on the Middle Fork of the Pasayten River, go east to the Robinson Pass trail, FS-478, up the hill 200' from the camping area. Continue north on trail FS-478 for 0.6 mile to a junction, 5100'. Go right (east) and ascend northeast around a buttress into a nearly level valley with a creek. Continue southeast on the trail to cross the creek at 6300' then ascend north to Ferguson Lake, lying in an open basin under the north face of Wildcat Mountain. Many of the trees around the lake are larch.

WILDCAT MOUNTAIN LOOP, high point 7985', 10 miles RT, 4000' gain (Maps: Pasayten Wilderness, USGS Pasayten Peak, Mount Lago). **Hike-3. Pasayten Wilderness.** The distance and elevation gain given for this trip are from the Middle Fork Pasayten River Campground, elevation 5200'.

From campsite, hike north on the Middle Fork Pasayten River trail, FS-478, for 0.6 miles then ascend east on trail FS-474 to Ferguson Lake (see above). From the west end of the lake, ascend northeast to the ridge then turn southeast on the ridge to the first summit, **Ferguson Lake Point 7985'**, east of Ferguson Lake. From this summit, descend south and southwest on or near the ridge to the saddle, 7500'. From the saddle, ascend south on the broken rocks of the east slope of Wildcat Mountain, staying at first just below the cliffs on the east side of the ridge, then ascending to the ridge at 7700' and the summit of **Wildcat Mountain**, 7958'. Summits visible from this viewpoint include: Mount Rolo (6°), Osceola Peak (22°), Monument Peak (72°), Robinson Mtn. (164°), and Pasayten Peak (278°). All of these summits are within six miles.

From the summit, continue south on the ridge, going over a 7600'+ rise before descending southwest to a 7200' saddle where an old trail crosses from Eureka Creek to the Middle Fork of the Pasayten River. From this saddle, hike west up gentle slabs and open forest to **Point 7619'** for a view west into the valley of the Middle Fork. Return to the 7200' saddle and descend northwest on the old trail. This trail diverges onto the slope on the north side of the valley in the talus field at 6700' and then becomes hard to follow. Leave the trail and descend to the valley bottom, which is mostly brush-free. On reaching the stream, cross to the south side to continue west to rejoin the Ferguson Lake Trail, FS-474, and return to the Middle Fork.

FREDS LAKE, 6507', 14 miles RT, 2400' gain (Maps: Pasayten Wilderness, USGS Pasayten Peak, Mount Lago, GT Pasayten Peak). **Hike-1. Pasayten Wilderness.** Drive and hike as above to the campsite on the Middle Fork of the Pasayten River. The distance and elevation gain given for this trip are from parking at Hart's Pass.

After crossing the Middle Fork of the Pasayten River, 5200', go north on the Middle Fork trail, FS-478, passing the turnoff to Ferguson Lake 0.6 miles north of the Middle Fork crossing. Before reaching the turnoff to Freds Lake, 4.5 miles north of the Ferguson Lake junction, pass three generous campsites. The first campsite lies between the trail and the river 1.5 miles north of the Ferguson Lake junction. The second campsite, suitable for horses, is across the river near the first campsite, and the third is east of the trail on a level knoll at the west end of an avalanche slope below Mount Rolo.

Look for the junction of the trail to Freds Lake in open forest, 5000', south of Berk Creek. The Freds Lake Trail, FS-471, ascends in many switchbacks, reaching Freds Lake after passing an abandoned trail at 6000' that goes north to a lake in the Pleasant Valley basin.

LAKE DORIS, 6975', 8.5 miles RT, 2200' gain (Maps: Pasayten Wilderness, USGS Pasayten Peak, Mount Lago, GT Pasayten Peak). **Hike-2. Pasayten Wilderness**. Drive and hike as above to the campsite on the Middle Fork of the Pasayten River. The distance and elevation gain given for this trip are from this campsite.

Hike as above to **Freds Lake**, then continue east around the north side of the lake, ascending to a saddle, 7100'. From the saddle the trail continues to ascend briefly northeast across an open promontory. Watch carefully at 7100' for a branch that drops north to Doris Lake before trail FS-474 begins to descend northeast. The area east of the lake provides many view campsites in scattered larch trees (no fires).

MOUNT ROLO, 8096', 4 miles RT, 1600' gain (Maps: Pasayten Wilderness, USGS Mount Lago, GT Pasayten Peak). **Hike-4†. Pasayten Wilderness**. The distance and elevation gain for this trip are from Freds Lake.

From Freds Lake or Doris Lake, hike the trail to the saddle, 7100', southeast of Freds Lake. From this saddle, leave the trail and ascend southwest to a 7442' summit. Descend south to a pond at 7200' in another saddle. The pond is not shown on the USGS map. Pass east of the pond and head southwest (210°) to the ridge crest. Ascend south on the ridge to a notch with a rock tooth in the middle. Pass the rock tooth on the southwest side to an enclosed platform with a 6' step. Ascend this step, then stay on the ridge, reaching a talus bench at 7700'. Ascend left or right around a rock buttress to return to the ridge crest at 7800' and follow the narrow ridge to the summit.

Eightmile Creek Area

Drive SR-20 east to the town of Winthrop, 132 miles from I-5 at Burlington or 100 miles from Wenatchee on SR-97 and SR-153. Drive north on the Chewuch River Road for nine miles, then turn left and go northwest on the Eightmile Creek Road, FS-5130 and FS-383.

BIG CRAGGY PEAK, 8470', 9 miles RT, 4700' gain (Maps: Pasayten Wilderness, USGS Billy Goat Mtn., Sweetgrass Butte, GT Billy Goat Mtn., Mazama). **Hike-3**. Drive 13 miles on Eightmile Creek Road, FS-383, and park at the Copper Glance Creek trailhead, elevation 3800'.

Hike northwest and west on trail FS-519 on the north side of Copper Glance Creek. Leave the trail at 6100' before the trail crosses the creek and ascend northwest, at first in open forest and meadows, then on talus, to the summit. The last 1500' are loose talus, of which some parts are more stable than others.

Nearby summits in view from this outstanding peak include: Eightmile Peak (322°), Billy Goat Mtn. (348°), and Sherman Peak (176°).

BILLY GOAT MOUNTAIN, 7633', 7 miles RT, 3300' gain (Maps: Pasayten Wilderness, USGS Billy Goat Mtn., GT Billy Goat Mtn.). **Hike-3. Pasayten Wilderness**. Drive 17 miles on the Eightmile Creek Road, FS-383, to the trailhead at the end of the road, elevation 4700'.

Hike north 0.25 mile to a junction, then turn left (northwest) on trail FS-477 to ascend over Eightmile Pass. From the pass, continue northwest. Where the trail turns west and begins to descend, leave the trail and ascend on open slopes to the summit. A **fault** with an open crack 10' deep runs exactly through the summit. This fault continues north through Three Fools Pass and makes a visible notch in the ridge north of Diamond Creek.

BURCH MOUNTAIN, 7782', 12 miles RT, 3100' gain (Maps: Pasayten Wilderness, USGS Billy Goat Mtn., GT Billy Goat Mtn.). **Hike-2**. Drive 17 miles on the Eightmile Creek Road, FS-383, to the trailhead at the end of the road, elevation 4700'.

Hike north on trail FS-502A until just below Billy Goat Pass. On the south side of the pass, 6600', find the little used Burch Mtn. Trail, FS-538, and hike east. Where the trail begins to descend east, leave the trail and ascend north to the summit, a lookout site.

EIGHTMILE PASS–BILLY GOAT PASS LOOP, high point 6600', 15 miles RT, 3400' gain (Maps: Pasayten Wilderness, USGS Billy Goat Mtn., GT Billy Goat Mtn.). **Hike-1. Pasayten Wilderness**. Drive 17 miles on the Eightmile Creek Road, FS-383, to the trailhead at the end of the road, elevation 4700'.

Hike north 0.25 mile to a junction, turn left (northwest) on trail FS-477 to ascend over Eightmile Pass, 5400', then descend above Jinks Creek to **Drake Creek**, 4600' and 4.5 miles from the road (camping). One day trips from this campsite include: Lost River Gorge, Nanny Goat Mountain, and Eightmile Peak.

From the campsite where trail FS-477 crosses **Drake Creek**, go west across the creek for 0.25 miles, then turn right (northeast) on a trail (FS-502) on the north side of Drake Creek to ascend to Three Fools Pass, meeting trail FS-502A at 5400', 3.1 miles from the trail junction at Drake Creek. **Three Fools Pass** has many campsites with water available from a branch of Diamond Creek 0.5 mile north on the trail or from a spring in the immediate pass area. Several day trips are possible from Three Fools Pass: Dollar Watch Mtn., Diamond Point, and an unnamed summit east, Point 8168'. A fault runs exactly through Three Fools Pass. From the campsite, look north to a notch in the ridge beyond Diamond Creek for another expression of this fault.

To return to the starting point, from Three Fools Pass go south on trail FS-502A over Billy Goat Pass.

EIGHTMILE PEAK, 7756', 7 miles RT, 3200' gain (Maps: Pasayten Wilderness, USGS Billy Goat Mtn., GT Billy Goat Mtn.). **Hike-3. Pasayten Wilderness.** Distance and elevation gain for this trip are from the campsite at Drake Creek, elevation 4600'.

From the trail FS-477 crossing at Drake Creek, ascend east 0.5 mile on trail FS-477 toward Eightmile Pass. Leave the trail at 5100', cross Jinks Creek and ascend south in a dense spruce forest (ouch) and on an open ridge to the summit.

LOST RIVER GORGE, low point 3500', 4 miles RT, 1100' gain (Maps: Pasayten Wilderness, USGS Billy Goat Mtn., Lost Peak, GT Billy Goat Mtn.). **Hike-2. Pasayten Wilderness**. The distance and elevation gain given for this trip are from the campsite where trail FS-477 crosses Drake Creek, elevation 4600'.

From trail FS-477 at Drake Creek, descend south on trail FS-459 along Drake Creek, crossing Jinks Creek and Pat Creek to the Lost River, 3500', where tent sites can be found in a tangle of brush and flood debris (no fires). Explore up and down this wild and trailless river, wading the river as necessary. Reach Three Pinnacles from this campsite (see below).

THREE PINNACLES, 8123', 8124', 8 miles RT, 5100' gain (Maps: Pasayten Wilderness, Lost Peak, GT Billy Goat Mtn.). **Hike-3. Pasayten Wilderness**. The distance and elevation gain given for this trip are from camping on the Lost River near the mouth of Drake Creek (see Lost River Gorge above).

From the campsite on the Lost River, 3500', cross the Lost River and go downstream 0.3 mile. Turn west and ascend through mixed talus, open brush, and pine trees to the east ridge of Three Pinnacles, 6600'. The cliffs that enclose this slope on the south are impressive. Near or on the ridge, go southwest, west and northwest to the two main summits, 8124' and 8123'. The third summit, 8082', is southwest. Look northeast down a 1500' cliff.

NANNY GOAT MOUNTAIN, 7700', 10 miles RT, 3200' gain (Maps: Pasayten Wilderness, USGS Billy Goat Mtn., Lost Peak, GT Billy Goat Mtn.). **Hike-3. Pasayten Wilderness**. The distance and elevation gain given for this trip are from the campsite where trail FS-477 crosses Drake Creek.

From trail FS-477 at Drake Creek, hike west on trail FS-477, crossing Drake Creek and passing the junction with trail FS-502, which goes east. Reach Lucky Pass, 5800' at 1.5 miles from Drake Creek. Leave the trail at the pass and ascend northeast, at first in open forest, then follow the southwest ridge over alpine meadows to the broad, gentle, and nivated summit. Summits visible include: Diamond Point (47°), Remmel Mtn. (54°) over Peepsight Mtn. (56°), Billy Goat Mtn. (138°), Three Pinnacles (214°), Dollar Watch Mtn. (343°), and Ashnola Mtn. (350°).

DOLLAR WATCH MOUNTAIN, 7679', 15 miles RT, 3000' gain (Maps: Pasayten Wilderness, USGS Billy Goat Mtn., Ashnola Pass, Ashnola Mtn., GT Billy Goat Mtn.). **Hike-2. Pasayten Wilderness**. The distance and elevation gain given for this trip are from the campsite at Three Fools Pass.

From Three Fools Pass, go north on trail FS-502 across Diamond Creek, then turn north along Larch Creek for one mile to a trail junction. Turn west on trail FS-451, ascending over a shoulder before crossing Tony Creek. At 7000', Dollar Watch Pass, turn west on a minor trail to the summit, an old lookout site. Ashnola Mtn., a meadow summit, is directly north.

DIAMOND POINT, 7916', 10 miles RT, 2800' gain (Maps: Pasayten Wilderness, USGS Billy Goat Mtn., Ashnola Pass, GT Billy Goat Mtn.). **Hike-2. Pasayten Wilderness**. The distance and elevation gain given for this trip are from the campsite at Three Fools Pass.

From Three Fools Pass, hike north to a trail junction on the north side of Diamond Creek, then go northeast on trail FS-514, ascending to the pass between Diamond Creek and Fox Creek (east). Leave the trail and ascend the open slope to the talus summit, a lookout site. Find moss campion, an uncommon alpine plant with a red flower that grows near 8000'. Look northeast to Remmel Mtn. (60°) and Cathedral Peak (35°).

THREE FOOLS POINT 8168, 8168', 7 miles RT, 2600' gain (Maps: Pasayten Wilderness, USGS Billy Goat Mtn., GT Billy Goat Mtn.). **Hike-3. Pasayten Wilderness.** The distance and elevation gain given for this trip are from the campsite in Three Fools Pass.

From Three Fools Pass, hike east cross country in delightful open forest and alpine meadows to a ridge at 6600'. Follow this rocky ridge east and northeast to the highest point to get a broad view east over the basin of Fool Hen Creek.

Chewuch River Area

From Winthrop, drive north on the Chewuch River Road.

NORTH TWENTYMILE LOOKOUT, 7540', 12 miles RT, 4600' gain (Maps: USGS Spur Peak, GT Doe Mtn.) **Hike-1.** Drive 18 miles north of Winthrop on the Chewuch River Road. Immediately after passing Camp 4, turn right over the river and go east and south for 0.6 miles, then turn southeast 1.6 miles to the trailhead, elevation 3000'.

Hike north, at first on an old road, then continue on a trail that ascends in open ponderosa pines and fir forest near Honeymoon Creek. At 5600', 2.5 miles from the starting point, cross a small stream, a branch of Honeymoon Creek. Shortly after crossing the stream, the trail turns away from Honeymoon Creek and begins to switchback up the south side of the ridge. Above 6500', pass through meadows that provide views south. At the crest, 6900', see the lookout tower on the summit a mile away.

Pass a junction at 7000' where a barely visible trail goes northeast to Twentymile Road. The forest now thins to widely spaced whitebark pine trees in alpine meadows. Landmarks visible from the summit include: the Chewuch River canyon directly below to the north, Remmel Mtn. (334°), Peepsight Mtn. (323°), and Big Craggy Mtn. almost directly west (274°). Of the summits near the Canadian Border east of Remmel Mtn., only Snowshoe Mtn. (32°) stands out. North Gardner Mtn. (230°) and Silver Star Mtn. (239°) are southwest.

CHEWUCH RIVER–ANDREWS CREEK LOOP, high point 7600', 45 miles RT, 6000' gain (Maps: Pasayten Wilderness, USGS Coleman Peak, Bauerman Ridge, Remmel Mtn., Mt. Barney, GT Coleman

Peak). **Hike-2. Pasayten Wilderness**. From Methow, drive north on road FS-392 along the Chewuch river for 29 miles to the trailhead at Thirty Mile Campground, elevation 3400'.

Hike north on the Chewuch Trail, FS-510, along the Chewuch River, passing **Chewuch Falls** at three miles. Find many campsites in the open valley above 4000' near junctions with the Fire Creek Trail, FS-561, and the Basin Creek Trail, FS-360. At mile 8, where trail FS-510 turns west to follow the Chewuch River, continue north on trail FS-534, the Tungsten Trail, meeting the Boundary Trail, FS-533, at **Tungsten Mine Camp**, 14.3 miles from Road FS-392 and 6800'. Near this junction, a cabin and some mining equipment remain from the 1940's when this area was mined briefly for tungsten. From campsites in this area, supplied with water from a spring, trips can be made to nearby destinations: Wolframite Mtn., Apex Mtn., Bauerman Ridge, and Teapot Dome.

Now go west on the Boundary Trail, FS-533, to Apex Pass, 7300'. From Apex Pass, the summit of **Apex Mtn.** is only a mile south. The trail now descends briefly, then contours around the head of Cathedral Creek to Cathedral Pass, 7600', the highest point of the loop. Where the trail turns south after rounding the north end of Cathedral Creek valley, an easily reached summit, **Cathedral Creek Point 8264'** only 0.25 mile from Canada, is 0.5 mile north of the trail. From this summit, look for the cleared border between the United States and Canada.

From Cathedral Pass, descend west and south to **Upper Cathedral Lake**, 7400' (camping). From here, two easily reached summits are worth visiting: Amphitheater Mtn. and the west summit of Cathedral Peak. From Cathedral Lake, continue south on the Boundary Trail, FS-533, for 1.2 miles, then go southeast on a branch for one mile. Where the trail levels after descending briefly, turn left on a trail to **Remmel Lake**, 6871', lying in an open basin east of the divide between Andrews Creek and Remmel Creek (camping).

Find the Chewuch Trail, FS-510, on the southwest side of the lake and go southeast to descend for five miles, at first along Remmel Creek, then along the Chewuch River. At 5200', turn west and ascend on Four Point Trail, FS-508, to **Four Point Lake**, 6900' and 2.5 miles from the Chewuch River (camping). From Four Point Lake, Remmel Mtn. is a half-day hike. To leave Four Point Lake, continue west and southwest on the continuation of the Four Point Trail, FS-508, crossing Four Point Creek, and bending south under the cliffs of Remmel Mtn. The trail continues south on the west side of Coleman Ridge, mostly in open meadow country and passing a spring shown on maps, which may be stock-trampled and isn't reliable as a water source. After passing the spring, the trail descends to the south end of Coleman Ridge, then turns east toward Fire Creek.

Since this is stock range country, many unsigned trails don't show on maps. At the saddle between Andrews Creek on the west and Fire Creek on the east, 6600', find a trail that goes south over a 7059' summit, then descends southeast to the north fork of **Ram Creek**, which has good camping at 6400' in a meadow near a cattle camp. Plan to be here before the cattle, which arrived the day we left (7/21). From the campsite on Ram Creek, a day trip can be made to Reed, Coleman, and Kay Peaks. Other trails also branch south from the trail that goes east from the Fire Creek–Andrews Creek saddle. At least one of these trails goes south to Meadow Lake, a marshy area that is at times saturated with insects and not recommended as a camp site.

From camping on the north fork of Ram Creek, follow the trail downstream (south) to the Coleman Ridge Trail, FS-505, then go west and southwest to Andrews Creek. Turn south on the Andrews Creek Trail, FS-504, to road FS-392 at Andrews Creek Campground and seven miles southwest of the trailhead at Thirtymile Campground.

WOLFRAMITE MOUNTAIN, 8137', 4 miles RT, 1400' gain (Maps: Pasayten Wilderness, USGS Remmel Mtn., GT Coleman Peak). **Hike-2. Pasayten Wilderness.** The distance and elevation gain given for this trip are from Tungsten Mine Camp.

From Tungsten Mine, hike northwest on the Boundary Trail, FS-533, until the trail turns southwest. Leave the trail and hike north to the saddle between Tungsten Creek (south) and Ewart Creek (north). Turn east and hike up the open ridge to the broad gentle summit for a view that encompasses Cathedral Peak (west), the cliffs of Apex Mountain (south), and many summits north across the Canadian border.

BAUERMAN RIDGE, 8044', 9 miles RT, 1500' gain (Maps: Pasayten Wilderness, USGS Remmel Mtn., Bauerman Ridge, GT Coleman Peak). **Hike-2. Pasayten Wilderness.** The distance and elevation gain given for this trip are from Tungsten Mine Camp.

From Tungsten Mine Camp, hike east on the Boundary Trail, FS-533 for one mile past Scheelite Pass. Where the trail bends southeast at 7100', leave the trail and ascend east in one of many openings in the forest to the high point of the ridge, which gives a view north down cliffs to Scheelite Lake.

TEAPOT DOME, 7608', 14 miles RT, 1800' gain (Maps: Pasayten Wilderness, USGS Remmel Mtn., Bauerman Ridge, GT Coleman Peak). **Hike-2. Pasayten Wilderness.** The distance and elevation gain given for this trip are from Tungsten Mine Camp.

From Tungsten Mine Camp, hike as above to Bauerman Ridge. From the summit of Bauerman Ridge, follow the gentle, sparsely forested ridge east to the summit of Teapot Dome, getting views north to Canada and south down the valley of the Chewuch River.

APEX MOUNTAIN, 8297', 6 miles RT, 1600' gain (Maps: Pasayten Wilderness, USGS Remmel Mtn., GT Coleman Peak). **Hike-2. Pasayten Wilderness**. The distance and elevation gain given for this trip are from Tungsten Mine Camp.

From Tungsten Mine Camp, hike northwest and south on the Boundary Trail, FS-533, to forested Apex Pass. Leave the trail at the Pass and hike south, at first in open forest, then in alpine meadows to the gentle summit. The most impressive summits visible are Cathedral Peak (314°) and Remmel Mtn. (221°).

CATHEDRAL SOUTH PEAK, 8440', 3 miles RT, 1300' gain (Maps: Pasayten Wilderness, USGS Remmel Mtn., GT Coleman Peak). **Hike-3. Pasayten Wilderness**. The main summit of Cathedral Peak is a climb, but the south summit, only a few feet lower, is a hike. The distance and elevation gain given for this trip are from camping at Upper Cathedral Lake.

From Cathedral Lake, hike north on the Boundary Trail, FS-533, until the trail turns east to Cathedral Pass. Leave the trail and ascend north to a high point on the ridge south of the main peak of Cathedral Peak. Look northwest at the cleared border between the United States and Canada.

AMPHITHEATER MOUNTAIN, 8358', 3 miles RT, 1100' gain (Maps: Pasayten Wilderness, USGS Remmel Mtn., GT Coleman Peak). **Hike-3. Pasayten Wilderness**. The distance and elevation gain given for this trip are from camping at Upper Cathedral Lake, 7400'.

From Cathedral Lake, hike south, ascending below the cliffs south of the lake. At 7600', turn northeast and ascend around the head of a valley that descends southwest then go east to the ridge of Amphitheater Mountain. Go north at first to look down at Upper Cathedral Lake, then return south to the highest point. Cathedral Peak is north and Remmel Mtn. is south.

REMMEL MOUNTAIN, 8685', 3 miles RT, 1800' gain (Maps: Pasayten Wilderness, USGS Remmel Mtn., GT Coleman Peak). **Hike-2. Pasayten Wilderness**. The distance and elevation gain given for this trip are from camping at Four Point Lake.

From Four Point Lake, hike southwest on the trail for 0.5 mile to a creek crossing. Find a faint trail that ascends northwest in meadows to a pond, then continues west, becoming obvious on a talus slope. Cathedral Peak, 8601', is north (5°) over Amphitheater Mountain.

REED PEAK–COLEMAN PEAK–KAY PEAK, 7523', 7690', 7555', 13 miles RT, 2200' gain (Maps: Pasayten Wilderness, USGS Mt. Barney, Coleman Peak, GT Coleman Peak). **Hike-3. Pasayten Wilderness.** The distance and elevation gain given are from camping on Ram Creek.

From the campsite on the north fork of Ram Creek, 6400', hike north with little elevation gain for 0.5 mile to a meadow then turn east to the Coleman Ridge Trail, FS-505, which is in the forest east of the meadow. Turn south on the trail to Meadow Lake, 6361', 1.5 miles from Ram Creek camp. Find the trail to Reed Peak continuing south from the east side of the lake. Part of this trail is now or has recently been a main stock driveway. After emerging from the forest, turn east to follow the ridge to the first summit, Reed Peak, 7523'.

From Reed Peak, descend east on the ridge, then ascend to Coleman Peak, 7690', the highest of the three peaks and overlooking the Chewuch River valley and hills east. Continue southeast and south from Coleman Peak in open forest to Kay Peak, 7555'.

Twisp River Area.

From the town of Twisp, 91 miles north of Wenatchee on US-97 and SR-153, or 140 miles east on SR-20 from I-5 at Burlington, drive northwest on road FS-349, the Twisp River Road.

TWISP PASS, high point 6064', 11 miles RT, 2400' gain (Maps: North Cascades National Park, USGS McAlester Mtn., Gilbert, GT Stehekin). **Hike-1. Lake Chelan National Recreation Area.** Park in the hiker parking area near the end of road FS-349 (campground), elevation 3700', and 26 miles from the town of Twisp.

Hike west on the Twisp River Trail, FS-426, for 2.5 miles to the junction of the **South Fork Trail**, FS-432, 4400' (camping). From camping near this junction, Copper Pass, and Copper Point 7840, can be hiked in a day. Turn west on the South Fork Trail, FS-432, crossing the North Fork of the Twisp River (bridge), then ascend across the south flank of Lincoln Butte over mostly open slopes. After crossing the North Fork, the trail passes near or over several basalt dikes.

Camping: Find a view campsite on a bench at 5900', 0.25 mile east of Twisp Pass where the trail bends sharply north. Get water from small streams that cross the trail east of the campsite or from the stream in the gully south below the campsite (brush). Both of these sources may be dry in late season. Look for other campsites along the ridge north and south of Twisp Pass near lakes that lie nearly on the crest of the ridge that divides the Twisp River drainage from the Bridge Creek drainage. The trail to the lake north of the pass begins from Twisp Pass by going directly toward Lincoln Butte. The trail to the lake south of the pass goes southwest from the flat (benchmark) in the immediate pass area, finally disappearing on bedrock exposures before reaching the cliff-girt lake near a low point in the ridge that connects Twisp Pass with Twisp Mtn. A ramp at the north end of the lake provides access to the water.

From Twisp Pass, hike to Lincoln Butte, Stilleto Falls, Stilleto Peak, and Twisp Mtn.

COPPER PASS, high point 6700', 8 miles RT, 2300' gain (Maps: North Cascades National Park, USGS McAlester Mtn., Gilbert, GT Stehekin). **Hike-2. Lake Chelan National Recreation Area.** The distance and elevation gain given for this trip are from camping on the North Fork of the Twisp River near the junction of trails FS-426 and FS-432, elevation 4400'. If hiking from the end of the Twisp River Road, add 4 miles and 700' gain to the round trip.

Hike northwest on trail FS-426 in the canyon of the North Fork of the Twisp River. After crossing to the west side of the river at 5200', watch for twin waterfalls just above the confluence of branches of the river. After passing from dense forest into meadows, the trail deteriorates to a steep muddy track but the trip to the pass is justified by the view of Early Winters Spires (north), Corteo Peak (west), Gilbert Mtn. (south), and the canyon of Copper Creek (north).

COPPER PASS POINT 7840, 7840', 10 miles RT, 3500' gain (Maps: North Cascades National Park, USGS McAlester Mtn., Gilbert, GT Stehekin). **Hike-3 or Hike-4†. Lake Chelan National Recreation Area.** The distance and elevation gain given for this trip are from camping on the North Fork of the Twisp River at the junction of trails FS-426 and FS-432, two miles from the end of the Twisp River Road, elevation 4400'.

Hike as above on the trail to Copper Pass. Leave the trail at the pass and ascend east. At 6900', a 10' step in the ridge is classification **Hike-4†**. After passing the step, the remainder of the ridge is gentle. To bypass the step, contour southeast from the pass across a talus field to a brush and heather slope that leads to the crest of the open southwest ridge then ascend a track on or near this ridge to the summit. Peaks visible include: Silver Star (28°), North Gardner (77°), Gilbert (117°), Lincoln Butte (181°), Bonanza (212°), Stilleto Peak (242°), Frisco (264°), Whistler (290°), and Early Winters Spires (310°).

LINCOLN BUTTE, 7065', 3 miles RT, 1100' gain (Maps: North Cascades National Park, USGS McAlester Mtn., GT Stehekin). **Hike-3. Lake Chelan National Recreation Area**. The distance and elevation gain given for this trip are from Twisp Pass.

On the way to Twisp Pass (trail FS-432) for the ascent of Lincoln Butte, stop at the campsite (5900') on the east side of the ridge where the trail turns sharply north just below Twisp Pass. Look northeast at the southwest side of Lincoln Butte. Note the meadow bench that contours southeast at 6200' from the lake that lies northeast of Twisp Pass. This bench goes between steeper rocks above and below and is blocked by cliffs east of an avalanche slope that leads to the summit. Contouring the bench and ascending the avalanche slope provides the easiest and simplest route to the summit.

From Twisp Pass, take the trail that begins to the northeast directly toward Lincoln Butte. Follow the trail to the lake, elevation 6140'. Continue around the lake, then contour below the talus field and rocks on the southwest side of Lincoln Butte. Go southeast on a meadow bench to an avalanche track that is not closed by steeper rocks above. Ascend this avalanche track northeast on steep dirt and scree in scattered trees, then on easy bedrock to the summit.

Look northeast at the grand curve of the west ridge of Gilbert Mtn., which is best seen from Lincoln Butte.

STILLETO FALLS, high point 6500', 3 miles RT, 600' gain (Maps: North Cascades National Park, USGS McAlester Mtn., GT Stehekin). **Hike-2. North Cascades National Park**. The distance and elevation gain given for this trip are from Twisp Pass.

From Twisp Pass, take the trail that starts northeast from the pass directly toward Lincoln Butte. After the trail descends to the level of the lake that lies on the crest of the divide between the East Fork of McAlester Creek on the west and the South Fork of the Twisp River on the east, turn west and follow the trail as it contours across nearly level alpine meadows. Pass isolated clumps of trees to the rock dotted area below the falls on the creek coming from **Stilleto Lake**, which is 0.3 miles and 300' of elevation gain north.

STILLETO MEADOWS, high point 7000', 5 miles RT, 1400' gain (Maps: North Cascades National Park, USGS McAlester Mtn., GT Stehekin). **Hike-3. North Cascades National Park**. The distance and elevation gain given for this trip are from Twisp Pass.

Hike as above to **Stilleto Falls**, 6500'. Cross the stream below the falls and ascend west in an alpine meadow to a broad saddle, 6800'. Descend into meadows on the west side of the saddle and contour or ascend gradually west at the south edge of steeper talus fields into the broad and gentle terrain west of Stilleto Peak. Some of this area may be covered with snow into August. Cross to the north edge to view the canyon of Copper Creek and see bits of highway SR-20. An old lookout site stands on a 7223' promontory one mile west.

STILLETO PEAK, 7660', 7 miles RT, 2100' gain (Maps: North Cascades National Park, USGS McAlester Mtn., GT Stehekin). **Hike-4†**. **North Cascades National Park**. The distance and elevation gain given for this trip are from Twisp Pass.

Hike as above to **Stilleto Meadows**. On reaching the edge of the basin on the west flank of Stilleto Peak, 6800', turn north and ascend in talus to pass a rock buttress. Above the rock buttress, 7000', turn southeast and ascend across a talus slope and heather finger to the southwest ridge at 7100'. Ascend the southwest ridge, detouring briefly on the south slope at 7300' to pass steeper rocks, then stay on the ridge or its northwest side to the summit. Prominent summits in view include: Hock Mtn. (180°), McGregor Mtn. (230°), and Frisco Mtn. (274°).

TWISP MOUNTAIN, 7161', 3 miles RT, 1100' gain (Maps: North Cascades National Park, USGS McAlester Mtn., GT Stehekin). **Hike-4†**. **North Cascades National Park**. The distance and elevation gain given for this trip are from Twisp Pass, 6064'.

The route to the summit follows the prominent gully that cuts the north side of the mountain to the east ridge. Take note of this gully on the return from Stilleto Falls. From Twisp Pass, follow a track southwest from the benchmark in the pass area and, after the trail disappears, continue southeast on bedrock, passing east of a small lake and descending to an open low point, 6240', northeast of Twisp Mountain. From the low point in this saddle, ascend west (250°) on loose talus to a heather slope, then ascend south in the gully that points to a notch in the east ridge of Twisp Mtn. Above a rock buttress that rises from the east side of the gully at 6600', leave the gully on the left (east) side and ascend south in small trees and krumholz to the crest of the ridge.

Turn right (west) and descend to the notch at the head of the gully, then continue west on the gentle south side of the ridge to the summit. Hock Mtn. is the summit one mile southwest.

Iron Gate Area. The high, rolling hill country of this region with its open forest and green, alpine meadows gives a special feeling of limitless open space. The summits are human scale, not precipitous points. From Tonasket on SR-20/US-97, 29 miles north on US-97 from Okanogan, go west across the Okanogan River, then turn north and west to Loomis. Two miles north of Loomis, turn west on road FS-390, taking a right fork (north) on road FS-3938 to the trailhead at Iron Gate, 5800' and 25 miles from Loomis. Road FS-3938 is sometimes closed by snow until late July.

HORSESHOE BASIN LOOP, high point 7940', 18 miles RT, 3800' gain (Maps: Pasayten Wilderness, USGS Horseshoe Basin, GT Horseshoe Basin). **Hike-2. Pasayten Wilderness**. Most of this loop is near or above 7000' and much of the area is meadow. The summits look north on green, rounded summits that roll far into Canada. A picturesque addition: sheep are still pastured here and some of the sheepherders may be Basque, directing the sheep dogs with whistles and arm signals.

From the trailhead at Iron Gate, hike north on trail FS-533, for one mile to a junction. Turn left (west) on trail FS-343, the Clutch Trail, and descend to cross the Middle Fork of Toats Coulee Creek, 5200'. After crossing the creek, the trail ascends to a junction with the Windy Creek Trail, FS-342, at Two Bear Camp (water), 6900'.

From Two Bear Camp, go north on the Windy Creek Trail, FS-342, ascending over a shoulder of Windy Peak, 7940'. From the trail, **Windy Peak**, 8384', the highest summit in the area, is a brief detour east (0.2 mile, 400' gain). Continue north, passing the Basin Creek Trail, FS-360, at 2.5 miles from the Clutch Trail junction. From the junction with the Basin Creek Trail, trail FS-342 turns east and descends toward the valley of the Middle Fork of Toats Coulee Creek. At 7100', a faint trail goes east to **Windy Lake** in a forested setting (camping), one of the few lakes in this area. **Toats Coulee Point 7203'**, northeast, provides an evening stroll for a view over the Middle Fork of Toats Coulee Creek.

Continue north through the meadows at the head of the Middle Fork of Toats Coulee Creek to the Boundary Trail, FS-533, 7200', five miles from the trail junction at Two Bear Camp. From the junction of trail FS-342 with the Boundary Trail, **Pick Peak**, 7620', a brief diversion south, gives a broad view over Horseshoe Basin. From this junction, turn north on the Boundary Trail, FS-533, to **Horseshoe Pass**, 7000'. From camping near **Horseshoe Pass**, make day trips to: Haig Mountain, Rock Mountain, Arnold Peak, Horseshoe Point 7845', Goodenough Peak, Canadian Border Monuments, and Horseshoe Mountain.

From Horseshoe Basin, hike south for seven miles on the Boundary Trail, FS-533, to the trailhead at Iron Gate.

HAIG MOUNTAIN, 7865', 10 miles RT, 1000' gain (Maps: Pasayten Wilderness, USGS Horseshoe Basin, Bauerman Ridge, GT Horseshoe Basin, Coleman Peak). **Hike-3. Pasayten Wilderness.** The distance and elevation gain given for this trip are from camping at Horseshoe Pass.

Hike west on the Boundary Trail, FS-533. Where the trail turns south to contour around the south side of Haig Mountain, leave the trail and hike west on the open, sandy slope to the summit, less than two miles from Canada.

HORSESHOE POINT 7845, 7845', 6 miles RT, 1000' gain (Maps: Pasayten Wilderness, USGS Horseshoe Basin, GT Horseshoe Basin). **Hike-3. Pasayten Wilderness.** Suggested name: Standing Stones Mountain. The distance and elevation gain given for this trip are from camping at Horseshoe Pass, 7000'.

Hike west on the Boundary Trail, FS-533 for two miles. West of Rock Mtn., turn north and ascend to this unusual summit, composed of many standing blocks of granitic rock. Look north to Canada, only a mile away. Note the boundary clearcut that extends east and west. Even the cliffs have been cleared of occasional trees.

ARNOLD PEAK, 8076', 3 miles RT, 1100' gain (Maps: Pasayten Wilderness, USGS Horseshoe Basin, GT Horseshoe Basin). **Hike-3. Pasayten Wilderness.** The distance and elevation gain given for this trip are from camping at Horseshoe Pass, 7000'.

Hike north and northeast up open, gentle, meadow slopes to the talus summit for a view north into Canada. Find moss campion, a low-growing plant with a red flower related to the garden carnation. It blossoms in July and August.

ARMSTRONG MOUNTAIN, 8137', 6 miles RT, 1500' gain (Maps: Pasayten Wilderness, USGS Horseshoe Basin, GT Horseshoe Basin). **Hike-3. Pasayten Wilderness.** The distance and elevation gain given for this trip are from camping at Horseshoe Pass, 7000'.

Hike north cross country in a valley to Snehumption Gap. From the saddle, turn northwest and ascend to the gentle plateau of Armstrong Mtn., finding two **Border Monuments**. Look east and west at the wide swath that has been cut in the forest along the border. Hike west on the plateau for a look north down Armstrong Creek into Canada, then return east, descending to 7200' to contour north and east of Arnold Peak to Long Draw Trail, FS-340. Return west to Horseshoe Basin.

ROCK MOUNTAIN, 7619', 2 miles RT, 700' gain (Maps: Pasayten Wilderness, USGS Horseshoe Basin, GT Horseshoe Basin). **Hike-3. Pasayten Wilderness.** The distance and elevation gain given for this trip are from camping near Horseshoe Pass, 7000'.

Hike west briefly on the Boundary Trail, FS-533, then leave the trail and go south of Louden Lake to the south ridge of Rock Mtn. Ascend north to the craggy summit, which provides a birds view of Horseshoe Basin.

HORSESHOE MOUNTAIN, 7954', 2 miles RT, 1000' gain (Maps: Pasayten Wilderness, USGS Horseshoe Basin, GT Horseshoe Basin). **Hike-3. Pasayten Wilderness.** The distance and elevation gain given for this trip are from camping near Horseshoe Pass, 7000'.

Ascend southwest to the meadow summit for views east over Long Draw Creek and southeast down Little Horseshoe Creek.

North Fork Nooksack River Area.

Drive east from Bellingham on SR-542 for 34 miles to the community of Glacier and the Public Service Center of the Mt. Baker–Snoqualmie National Forest (information, maps, and backcountry trip registration).

HELIOTROPE RIDGE, high point 6000', 7 miles RT, 2300' gain (Maps: USGS Groat Mtn., Mt. Baker, GT Mt. Baker). **Hike-2. Mt. Baker Wilderness.** From the community of Glacier (MP-34), drive east on SR-542 for 0.5 mile. Turn south on road FS-39 for eight miles to the trailhead, elevation 3700' (toilet).

Hike east on trail FS-677, reaching the site of Kulshan Cabin at two miles, 4800'. Leave the trail and ascend south on flowery Heliotrope Ridge for a view of Coleman Glacier. On weekends in the summer, observe climbing schools practicing ice-climbing on the seracs of the glacier.

MOUNT BAKER VIEWPOINT, 4200', 1 mile RT, 200' gain (Maps: USGS Groat Mtn., GT Mt. Baker). **Hike-1.** Drive as above past the Heliotrope Ridge trailhead. Continue one mile to parking at the viewpoint (picnic tables).

Hike southwest on a branch road to the end for more views.

CHURCH MOUNTAIN, 6315', 9 miles RT, 3600' gain (Maps: USGS Bearpaw Mtn., Glacier, GT Mt. Baker). **Hike-1 or Hike-4†. Mt. Baker Wilderness.** From the community of Glacier, drive east four miles (0.7 mile east of MP-38). Turn north on road FS-3040 for 2.5 miles to the trailhead at the road end, elevation 2315'.

Hike north and west on the trail to an abandoned lookout site for a view of Mt. Baker and Mt. Shuksan. **Hike-4†**. From the lookout site, ascend west to the summit.

EXCELSIOR MOUNTAIN, 5712', 9 miles RT, 4000' gain (Maps: USGS Bearpaw Mtn., GT Mt. Baker). **Hike-1. Mt. Baker Wilderness.** From the community of Glacier, drive east on SR-542 for eight miles (0.1 mile east of MP-41) to the trailhead on the north side of the highway, elevation 1827'.

Ascend north on trail FS-670 to Excelsior Pass. Turn right (east) on trail FS-630 to the south shoulder. Leave the trail and ascend north to the meadow summit. Summits visible include: Tomyhoi Peak (51°), Yellow Aster Butte (76°), and Mt. Shuksan (132°).

YELLOW ASTER BUTTE, 6241', 10 miles RT, 3100' gain (Maps: USGS Mt. Larrabee, GT Mt. Shuksan). **Hike-2. Mt. Baker Wilderness.** From the community of Glacier, drive 12 miles east on SR-542 (0.3 mile east of MP-46). Turn left (north) and drive two miles on road FS-3065 to the Keep Kool trailhead, elevation 3100'.

Hike north on trail FS-699, passing ponds and meadows above 5200'. Continue north to a saddle, 5500', then turn northeast to the summit, which has an impressive view of Mt. Larrabee (40°).

WINCHESTER MOUNTAIN, 6510', 8 miles RT, 3000' gain (Maps: USGS Mt. Larrabee, GT Mt. Shuksan). **Hike-1. Mt. Baker Wilderness.** Drive past the Yellow Aster Butte trailhead and park at a roadblock, elevation 3600'.

Walk the road east to the Winchester Mtn. trailhead between Twin Lakes, 5200'. Ascend north through an alpine meadow. Take the left fork north of the lakes on trail FS-685 where the Low Pass Trail goes to the right.

GOAT MOUNTAIN, 6725', 11 miles RT, 4300' gain (Maps: USGS Mt. Larrabee, GT Mt. Shuksan). **Hike-4†, Snow. Mt. Baker Wilderness.** Drive 12 miles east of the community of Glacier on SR-542 (0.6 miles east of MP-46), then, where SR-542 turns right to cross the North Fork of the Nooksack River, continue east on road FS-32. Keep left at 1.4 miles where road FS-34 turns right. Park 2.5 miles from SR-542, elevation 2500'.

Ascend north on trail FS-673, passing, at 3700', a trail right (east) that goes to the site of the former lookout cabin. Begin the south ridge of Goat Mountain at 5000'. At 5600', where the ridge steepens, a narrow and intermittent track crosses west over steep meadows to the west ridge, then ascends the west ridge. Until August, this track often has snow patches that end in cliffs below. If this track is not free of snow, leave the track before the first snow finger and ascend in the meadow (ice ax useful). Where the angle of the slope diminishes, 5900', return to the south ridge (track) and continue up to the junction of the west ridge with the south ridge, 6600', where the trail reappears. Above 6600', bypass a minor knob (cliff on the north side) on the west side (snow) to the notch between the minor knob and the summit, then ascend north on easy rocks to the summit.

If returning by the south ridge and the meadow to 5600', be certain to leave the summit area, 6600', by way of the south ridge. Don't be led astray by following the track that descends west if snow fingers cover the track that goes from the south ridge at 5600' to the west ridge.

HANNEGAN PEAK, 6187', 10 miles RT, 3100' gain (Maps: USGS Mt. Sefrit, GT Mt. Shuksan). **Hike-2. Mt. Baker Wilderness**. Drive 12 miles east of the community of Glacier on SR-542 (0.6 miles east of MP-46), then, where SR-542 turns right to cross the North Fork of the Nooksack River, continue east on road FS-32, keeping left at 1.4 miles where road FS-34 turns to the right. Park at the end of the road, 5.5 miles from SR-542, elevation 3100'.

Ascend southeast on trail FS-674 on the north side of Ruth Creek to Hannegan Pass, 5066'. Turn north, leave the main trail, and follow a track in open forest and alpine meadows to the gentle summit. Peaks visible: Copper Mtn. (44°), Whatcom Peak (108°) at the north end of the Picket Range, Mt. Ruth (184°), Mt. Shuksan (186°), Mt. Baker (240°), and Mt. Sefrit (270°).

HEATHER MEADOWS, road high point 5100' (Maps: USGS Shuksan Arm, GT Mt. Shuksan). **Hike-2**. Drive road SR-542 past MP-54.

Bagley Lakes Loop, 4200', 2 mile loop, minimum gain. At mile 54.7, turn right (west) into a parking area (4240', information and map). Descend west to cross the lower Bagley Lake dam. Hike south on the west side of the lake, passing exposures of the 100 million-year-old rocks of Mt. Herman. Cross the bridge between the lakes and return north near more recent exposures of columnar basalt.

Fire and Ice Nature Trail, 4200', 0.7 mile loop, minimum gain, interpretive signs. At mile 55.5, drive west to a parking area overlooking Bagley Lakes. View many aspects of columnar basalt, including a broad expanse of glacier-polished polygonal tops of the columns and the use of sections as stepping stones in the trails.

Lake Ann, high point 5200', 11 miles RT, 2600' gain. Park at the Lake Ann trailhead, 4743', mile 56.5. Hike southeast on trail FS-600, descending in ancient forest to cross two branches of Swift Creek, then ascending in alpine meadows to the lake, 4700'. Continue east on the trail to the first gully that descends from Fisher Chimney for a close view of the lower Curtis Glacier. Beyond this point the debris fans are unstable, requiring climbing techniques for safe travel.

Kulshan Ridge, high point 5247', 1 mile RT, 200' gain, interpretive signs. Park at the end of the road, 5100', mile 57.5. Hike southeast along the ridge to the high point, visiting many viewpoints.

Table Mountain, 5742', 2 miles RT, 700' gain. Park at the end of the road, 5100', mile 57.5. Ascend northwest on the trail for a panoramic view of the area. Mt. Herman is north. A steep, rough track descends south from the southwest corner of the plateau to the Chain lakes trail.

Chain Lakes, high point 5560', 8 miles RT, 1000' gain. Park at the end of the road, 5100', mile 57.5. Contour west on the Ptarmigan Ridge Trail, FS-683, for one mile. Turn right (north) and begin to descend. After passing an exposure of columnar basalt, find the junction with the old Table Mountain trail. Ascend east to explore a cliff-girt plateau of ponds and meadows north of Table Mountain. Return west to the Chain Lakes trail and continue north to Iceberg Lake. Camp only in designated sites.

Ptarmigan Ridge, high point 6320', 9 miles RT, 1600' gain. Superb views. Park at the end of the road, 5100', mile 57.5. Contour west on the Ptarmigan Ridge Trail for one mile. At a junction, turn south and descend into the upper basin of Wells Creek before ascending southwest on a choice of tracks to the beginning of Ptarmigan Ridge. By the end of August, a track will usually be snow-free. Continue southeast near the crest of the ridge, then turn northwest across the south side of Coleman Pinnacle.

Hike-3. For the best view, leave the trail where it bends north at 5900' and ascend northeast in meadow and krumholz to a rocky point, 6320', southwest of Coleman Pinnacle.

INDEX

For special interests, see: Art, Boating access, Colleges, Cultural and/or historic sites, Curiosities, Fishing access, Gardens, Lakes, Lookouts, Museums, Nature sites, Parks, Rail trails, Trails, Waterfalls.

Our Other Publications:

Mun (1621) **A Discourse of Trade**, $5; Barbon (1690) **A Discourse of Trade**, $5; Mandeville (1705) **Fable of the Bees**, $2. Provocative early defenses of the present maximum entropy economic paradigm, which depends on pyramid surrogates for viability. See Keynes (1936) **The General Theory of Employment Interest and Money** for a modern reiteration.

Rogers (1897, 1900) **Free Land, Inalienable Rights of Man**, $5. Background for a minimum entropy philosophy from a former governor of Washington State.

Cram (1919) **Walled Towns**, $10. A beautiful account of what minimum entropy life could be like.

Keynes (1930) **Economic Possibilities for Our Grandchildren**, $2. The master of pyramid-dependent economics hadn't convinced himself yet.

Lewin (1967) **On the Possibility and Desirability of Peace**, $5. The definitive interpretation of the importance of militarism to modern socioeconomic systems. Applies also to all entropic activities.

Dreisbach, R (2000) **Pyramid Building and Its Consequences**, $5. Includes: **A Scientist Looks at the Pyramids** (the beginning of pyramid-dependent economics), **On Thinking About the Unthinkable** (the dilemma of human self-extinction), **One Person too Many?**, **Can We Stop a Smuggler?** (of nuclear arms), **Waldsterben** (the forest death syndrome), **Energy, Ecology, Economics** (responsible energy use), **The Faustian Bargain** (nuclear energy), **The Silent Summer** (ozone), **Endless Summer: Living with the Greenhouse Effect**, **Life Without Energy is Brutal** and **Energy Policy** (the energy industry view), **Must We Relearn How to Use Surplus?** (alternatives).

Dreisbach, R (1969) **Handbook of the San Francisco Region**, $10. Brief ecosurvey of a modern maximum-entropy socio-economic system.

Dreisbach, R (1995) **Guide to Northeast Oregon**, $8.95. Hiking, bicycling, backpacking, Oregon Trail sites, dry climate, half-day from Seattle. Included free with orders of $20 or more.

Dreisbach, C (1998) **Middle Fork Guide**, $8.95. Hiking and climbing in the Middle Fork of the Snoqualmie River basin.

All publications sent postage and sales tax prepaid. Send for our annotated catalog (entrocon@yahoo.com).